DATE DUE

DE 1 8 98			

DEMCO 38-296

In the minds of most people, the home has stood apart from the world of work. By bringing the factory or office home, homework challenges this division. Employers, trade unionists, male and female reformers, and government administrators have vigorously debated the evils of homework. *Home to Work* restores the voices of homeworking women, mostly mothers of small children, to the century-long struggle over their labor.

From the 1870s, when New York cigarmakers attempted to end tenement competition, through the minimum wage campaigns of the National Consumers' League in the early twentieth century, to New Deal prohibitions in the 1930s, gender ideology shaped the battle over homework. After World War II, the white-collar home-based labor force grew; by the 1980s the white middle-class mother at the keyboard had replaced the victimized immigrant as the symbol of homework. Presented as a solution to the work and family dilemma of our time, Reaganite deregulation of homework attempted to dismantle the New Deal legacy.

While men's right to freely dispose of their labor inhibited the regulation of homework in the late nineteenth century, by the late twentieth century the government's attitude toward homework had come full circle – women's right to employment now undermined its prohibition. Economic and political justice, whether based on rights to homework or rights as workers, will depend on homeworkers becoming visible as wage earners who happen to mother.

Home to work

Figure 1. Luther Bradley, "Sacred Motherhood," lithograph, 1907. Courtesy of the Schlesinger Library, Radcliffe College. Exhibited at the Chicago Industrial Exhibit of 1907, this image symbolized sweated motherhood for a generation of women reformers who sought to end homework, organize the garment industry, and relieve working-class mothers of their double burden of wage earning and family maintenance. The women's Trade Union League used it on a postcard to raise funds to support striking workers in 1910–11.

K

Home to work
Motherhood and
the politics of industrial homework
in the United States

EILEEN BORIS

Howard University

CAMBRIDGE
UNIVERSITY PRESS

Published by the Press Syndicate of the University of Cambridge
The Pitt Building, Trumpington Street, Cambridge CB2 IRP
40 West 20th Street, New York, NY 10011–4211, USA
10 Stamford Road, Oakleigh, Melbourne 3166, Australia

© Cambridge University Press 1994
First published 1994
Printed in the United States of America

Library of Congress Cataloging-in-Publication Data
Boris, Eileen, 1948–
Home to work : motherhood and the politics of
industrial homework in the United States / Eileen Boris.
p.   cm.
Includes index.
ISBN 0–521–44370–9
1. Home labor – United States – History. 2. Working mothers – United States –
History.   I. Title.
HD2336.u5b67   1994
31.4'4'0973–dc20
93–11104
CIP
A catalog record for this book is available from the British Library.
ISBN 0–521–44370–9 hardback

For Nelson and Daniel

Contents

vii

Illustrations and tables

Figures

Tables

Acknowledgments

I could not have undertaken the archival research for this book without generous support. I relied upon funding from the Business and Professional Women's Foundation, the American Philosophical Society, the National Endowment for the Humanities, the Howard University Department of History, Howard University's Vice-President for Academic Affairs, the Schlesinger Library, a Littleton-Griswald Research Fellowship (AHA), the Woodrow Wilson International Center for Scholars, and the Museum of American History, Smithsonian Institution. Michael Laccy and the Wilson Center provided a congenial environment for drafting the early chapters of this book and the Museum of American History, for the later ones. I also want to thank my colleagues at the Department of History, Howard University, for their willingness to grant me leave to take these two residential fellowships.

Neither could I have written this book without the generosity and help of archivists and librarians. Most of all I thank Jerry Hess, Bill Creech, and Richard Boyden of the National Archives. I depended on the staffs of the Manuscript and Photographs divisions of the Library of Congress; the Schlesinger Library, Radcliffe; the Labor-Management Documentation Center, Martin P. Catherwood Library, Cornell University; the ILGWU Archives (now housed at Cornell); the New York State Archives and Library, Albany; Illinois State Historical Society; Chicago Historical Society; University Archives, Alexander Library, Rutgers University; Manuscripts, Joseph Regenstein Library, University of Chicago; Manuscripts, Wisconsin Historical Society; Tamiment Library, Elmer Holmes Bobst Library, New York University; Samuel Gompers Papers, University of Maryland; Office of the Historian and Library, U.S. Department of Labor; Library, New York Department of Labor; and Special Collections, University of Illinois, Chicago.

I thank those who gave permission for use of parts of my previously published articles. Most of Chapter 1 appeared under the same title in Ava Baron, ed., *Work Engendered: Toward a New History of American Labor* (Ithaca, N.Y.: Cornell University Press, 1991), 114–41. Some of Chapter 4 is reworked from "Tenement Homework on Army Uniforms: The Gendering of Industrial Democracy During World War I," *Labor History* 32 (Spring 1991), 231–52. Chapter 6 contains material from "Black Women and Paid Labor in the Home: Industrial Homework in Chicago During the 1920s," in Eileen Boris and Cynthia R. Daniels, *Homework: Historical and Contemporary Perspectives on Paid Labor at Home* (Urbana: University of Illinois Press, 1989), 3–52. Chapter 7 greatly expands upon "Regulating Industrial Homework: The Triumph of 'Sacred Motherhood,' " *Journal of American History* 71 (Mar. 1985), 745–63. Chapters 9 and 11 rework part of "The Regulation of Homework and the Devolution of the Postwar Labor Standards Regime: Beyond Dichotomy," in C. Tomlins and A. King, eds., *Labor Law in America: Historical and Critical Essays* (Baltimore: Johns Hopkins University Press, 1992), 260–82. Chapter 11 also reuses part of "Homework and Women's Rights: The Case of the Vermont Knitters," *Signs* 13 (Autumn 1987), 98–120, © the University of Chicago, all rights reserved. Captions under illustrations provide appropriate permissions.

In taking my story up to yesterday's headlines, I have gained from the willingness of those in the field to share documents, information, and expertise. I am indebted to the late Hugh McDaid, chief of the sweatshop division of the New York State Department of Labor, who gave me access to old files that should have been in the archives but remain in New York City. I am truly sad that he was unable to see this book. ILGWU vice-president Susan Cowell always was willing to provide me with union perspectives and, at the last minute, a photograph. I've learned much from our joint participation on panels over the years. I also must thank Joyce Durgerian, a senior labor standards investigator at the New York Department of Labor; Dennis Chamot of the AFL-CIO Professional Employee Division; and Claire White, Hank Gudza, and Justin McLaurey of the U.S. Department of Labor. I had the privilege of knowing Clara Beyer in the years before her death in 1991; she proved inspirational.

In April 1989 the Ford Foundation sent me to an international conference on home-based labor at the Ghandi Labour Institute in Ahmedabad, India. This experience enriched my assessment of the history of industrial homework in the United States. Renana Jhabvala, secretary of the Self-Employed Women's Association, introduced me to a successful model of homeworker organization; she offers an example of the engaged life that benefits us all. Lisa Prügl also has clarified my thinking on the international context of homework. I look forward to continuing the struggle along with Renana, Lisa, and other activists and researchers seeking to gain ILO protection of homeworkers.

A number of scholars over the years have read and commented on preliminary papers. Although I have not always agreed with or been able to incorporate their advice, I have benefited from it. I especially would like to thank Paula Baker, Mary Francis Berry, Kathleen Christensen, Dorothy Sue Cobble, Cynthia Costello, Cynthia Rae Daniels, Sarah Deutsch, Nancy Schrom Dye, Evelyn Nakano Glenn, Alice Kessler-Harris, Nancy Hewitt, Ann Lane, Sybil Lipschultz, Suzanne Mettler, Sonya Michel, Phyllis Palmer, Karen

Sacks, Philip Scranton, Amy Dru Stanley, Landon Storrs, Arnold Taylor, and Christopher Tomlins. Deborah Elkin, Cynthia Harrison, and Joanne Meyerowitz shared documents. Cecilia Buckley provided me with newspaper material on New Haven and Bridgeport. At the Wilson Center, Rebecca Toth and Paul Frymer proved able research assistants. Ruel Schiller checked the form of my legal citations. Leslie Rowland's pioneer research on the cigarmakers, now housed at the Gompers Papers, allowed me to write a better chapter. Martha Fineman and her Feminism and Legal Theory conferences, particularly the first one in 1985, served as midwife to my thought. So have the feminist theory reading groups I participated in during the 1980s. I owe the most to those who have carefully read the entire manuscript: Ava Baron, Vivien Hart, Wendy Sarvasy, and Kathyrn Kish Sklar. This book is better for their efforts. I would also like to thank Frank Smith, my editor, and the staff at Cambridge University Press, especially production editor Katharita Lamoza. Jeff Danziger came through with a redrawing of his Vermont Knitters cartoon.

Nelson Lichtenstein took time away from his own manuscript to read numerous drafts. His research and writing offer a model to which I can only aspire. He continued to show that parenting need not be restricted to mothers and nurturing to women. Yaz had nothing to do with this manuscript and Daniel had everything to do with it. I began my research as a nursing mother which I sometimes think made the Kathryn Budd case stick out of the mass of the NRA Homework Committee Papers. Nelson found those papers for me; so he is partially responsible. My analysis, however, came out of a desire to combine feminist theory and historical research to address the "double day" of working women, how "home" and "work" interconnect despite their ideological separation. The deregulation of homework under the Reagan administration brought the past and present together. Nelson and Daniel remind me why we must get it better, if we can't get it right.

Abbreviations

AALL	Papers of the American Association for Labor Legislation, Labor-Management Documentation Center, Martin P. Catherwood Library, Cornell University
Abbott Papers	Papers of Grace and Edith Abbott, Joseph Regenstein Library, University of Chicago
ACWA	Amalgamated Clothing Workers of America
ACWA Papers	Papers of the Amalgamated Clothing Workers of America, Labor-Management Documentation Center, Martin P. Catherwood Library, Cornell University
AFL	American Federation of labor
AGLO	Association of Governmental Labor Officials
AHR	*American Historical Review*
Baker Papers	Papers of Newton D. Baker, LC
Beyer Papers	Papers of Clara Mortenson Beyer, SL
BPWF	Business and Professional Women's Federation
Burlington Hearings	Official Report of Proceedings before the Office of Administrative Law Judges of the USDOL, Docket no. FLSA, "In the Matter of: Public Hearing to Commence Labor Department Review of 'Homeworker Rules,'" Burlington, Vt., Jan. 1, 1981, Office of Special Minimum Wage, Division of Labor Standards, DOL, Washington, D.C.
CBB	*Bulletin of the Children's Bureau*
CIO	Congress of Industrial Organizations
CLC Papers	Papers of the Consumers' League of Connecticut, SL
CLM Papers	Papers of the Consumers' League of Massachusetts, SL
CLNJ Papers	Papers of the Consumers' League of New Jersey, Alexander Library, Manuscript Collection, Rutgers University, New Brunswick, NJ
CLU	Central Labor Union
CMIU	Cigar Makers' International Union

CMOJ	Cigar Makers' Official Journal
CMPU	Cigar Makers' Progressive Union
Corcoran Papers	Papers of Thomas G. Corcoran, LC
CTLA	Chicago Trade and Labor Assembly
D.C. Hearings	U.S. DOL, "In the Matter of: A Public Hearing to Commence Labor Department Review of 'Homeworker Rules,'" Feb. 17, 1981, Washington, D.C., Office of Special Minimum Wage, DOL, Washington, D.C.
District 65 Papers	Papers of the Distributive, Processing and Office Workers of America, Tamiment Library, Elmer Holmes Bobst Library, New York University
DLS	Division of Labor Standards
DOL	Department of Labor
DOL Files	Material Relating to Homework in Knitted Outerwear, Office of Special Minimum Wage, Division of Labor Standards, DOL, Washington, D.C.
DOL Library	Library, Frances Perkins Building, DOL, Washington, D.C.
DMMCA	Direct Mail Master Contract Association
DPOWA	Distributive, Processing and Office Workers of America
Dubinsky Papers	Papers of David Dubinsky, ILGWU Archives, Labor-Management Documentation Center, Martin P. Catherwood Library, Cornell University
ERA	Equal Rights Amendment
FERA	Federal Emergency Relief Administration
FIC	Factory Investigating Commission
FLSA *Joint Hearings*	"Fair Labor Standards Act of 1937," Joint Hearings before the Committee on Education and Labor, U.S. Senate, and the Committee on Labor, House of Representatives, 75th Cong., 1937 (Washington, D.C.: GPO, 1937)
Ford Committee	House of Representatives, 50th Cong., 1st sess., *Testimony Taken by the Select Committee of the House of Representatives to Inquire into the Alleged Violating of the Laws Prohibiting the importation of Contract Laborers, Paupers, Convicts, and Other Classes* (Washington, D.C.: GPO, 1889)
FS	*Feminist Studies*
Gompers Papers	Papers of Samauel Gompers, LC
GPO	Government Printing Office

Hatch Hearings	Hearing before the Subcommittee on Labor of the Committee on Labor and Human Resources, U.S. Senate, 98th Cong., 2d sess., "Amending the Fair Labor Standards Act to Include Industrial Homework," Feb. 9, 1984 (Washington, D.C.: GPO, 1984)
HC Records	Records of the Homework Committee, NRA, RG9, NA
HH Scrapbooks	Papers of Hull House, Special Collections, University Library, University of Illinois at Chicago
HSW Papers	Papers of Helen Sumner Woodbury, State Historical Society of Wisconsin, Madison, Wis.
IAFINA	International Association of Factory Inspectors of North America
ICFTU	International Confederation of Free Trade Unions
IJWU	International Jewelry Workers Union
ILGWU	International Ladies' Garment Workers Union
ILO	International Labor [Labour] Organization
IMA Papers	Papers of the Illinois Manufacturers Alliance, Chicago Historical Society, Chicago, Ill.
JAH	*Journal of American History*
LC	Library of Congress, Washington, D.C., Manuscript Division
LHTS	Lewis Hine Tenement House Scrapbook, Prints and Photographs Collection, Library of Congress
LWV	League of Women Voters
Miller Papers	Papers of Frieda S. Miller, SL
Morgan Scrapbook	Papers of Tommy and Elizabeth Morgan, Illinois State Historical Society, Springfield, Ill.
NA	National Archives, Washington, D.C.
Nathan Scrapbook	Scrapbooks of Maud Nathan, SL
NCL	National Consumers' League
NCLC	National Child Labor Committee
NCLC Papers	Papers of the National Child Labor Committee, LC
NCL Papers	Papers of the National Consumers' League, microfilm edition, LC
NCLVF	NCL Vertical File, SL
NCMA	National Cigar Manufacturers' Association
New York Hearing	NYDOL, "Public Hearing on Industrial Homework," transcript of proceedings, Apr. 12, 1981, NYDOL, Brooklyn, N.Y.
NRA	National Recovery Administration
NYCL	Consumers' League of New York
NYCLC	New York Child Labor Committee

NYCLC Papers	Papers of the New York Child Labor Committee, NYSL
NYCL Papers	Papers of the New York Consumers' League, Labor-Management Documentation Center, Martin P. Catherwood Library, Cornell University
NYDOL	New York State Department of Labor
NYDOL Library	Files on Homework, Sweatshops and Minimum Wages, NYDOL Library, Brooklyn, N.Y.
NYSA	New York State Archives, Albany
NYSL	New York State Library, Albany
NYWTUL	New York Women's Trade Union League
"Reemergence of Sweatshops"	Committee on Education and Labor, House of Representatives, "The Reemergence of Sweatshops and the Enforcement of Wage and Hour Standards," 97th Cong., 1st and 2d sess. (Washington, D.C.: GPO, 1982).
Report on Capital and labor	U.S. Senate, Committee on Education and Labor, *Report Upon the Relations between Capital and Labor* (Washington, D.C.: GPO, 1885)
Report on Sweating	House of Representatives, 52nd. Cong., 2d. Sess., *Committee on Manufacturers Report on the Sweating System,* N.2309 Washington, D.C.: GPO, 1893)
Report on Women and Children	*Report on Condition of Women and Children Wage Earners in the United States* (Washington: GPO, 1911)
RG1	Records of the War Labor Policies Board, NA
RG9	Records of the National Recovery Administration, NA
RG46	Records of the U.S. Senate, NA
RG86	Records of the Women's Bureau, NA
RG102	Records of the Children's Bureau, NA
RG107	Records of the Office of the Secretary of War, NA
RG155	Records of the Wage and Hour Administration, NA
RG174	General Records of the Department of Labor, 1907–1942 (Chief Clerk's Files)
SEWA	Self-Employed Women's Association
Signs	*Signs: A Journal of Women in Culture and Society*
SL	Schlesinger Library, Radcliffe College, Cambridge, Mass.
Smith Papers	Papers of Hattie H. Smith, SL
TH	Transcript of Hearings, NRA, NA
TLA	Textile Labour Association
TUC	Trade Union Congress
TVA	Tennessee Valley Authority

UGWA	United Garment Workers of America
Umhey Papers	Papers of Frederick Umhey, ILGWU Archives, Labor-Management Documentation Center, Martin P. Catherwood Library, Cornell University
UOPWA	United Office and Professional Workers of America
WBB	*Bulletin of the U.S. Women's Bureau*
WHD	Wage and Hour Division
WIS	Women in Industry Service
WMC	War Manpower Commission
WPS	Wisconsin Physicians Services Insurance Corporation
WTUL	National Women's Trade Union League
WTUL Papers	Papers of the National Women's Trade Union League, microfilm edition, LC, SL

Introduction

"Home, sweat home":
Gender, the state,
and labor standards

In the late twentieth century, the term *working mother* expresses a contradiction. To a nation that still associates mothers with the home, the specter of mothers journeying to other workplaces threatens social disaster. After all, mothers care for children; nurturing has no place in the labor market. But most women cannot remain "at home." Without adequate dependent care or paid family leave, women find themselves stretched between children and jobs.

Employers have long organized the workplace without considering the parental identity of workers. They have assumed that most working fathers have a wife to perform domestic duties. Public policies have mirrored such assumptions. The labor standards regime forged in the New Deal era defined the worker as male, that is, as a breadwinner who provided for his wife and children, not a breadgiver who transformed wages into the necessities of daily life. But the working mother, long identified as a social problem, was a persistent reminder of the inability of men to earn a family wage, a wage large enough to support a wife and children. Her need to labor while caring for children encouraged employers to send manufacturing into the home and spurred reformers to protect mothers from such a practice.

This book is about wage labor in the home and persistent attempts to abolish a form of work characterized by low pay, long hours, and hazardous conditions. It is about one group of working mothers whose space of labor has differed from that of the majority of women wage earners, but whose need to earn highlights the problems faced by most women workers responsible for dependent care. The woman who earned wages at home not only illuminates the problems of the working mother but also has stood at the center of a century-long argument over state intervention in the labor contract. Could her sewing of garments, winding of coils, and typing of envelopes, often with her children, be restricted on the basis of state responsibility for social welfare? Did her labor justify legislation that restrained the workings of the market? Her history allows us to explore the relation of the home, itself a place of family labor, to the workplace and the role of the state in shaping that relation.

The 1980s debate over industrial homework occurred at a time when feminist theory and my own experience as a mother led me to question the dichotomous categories through which we characterize social life. In scholarly

I

as well as popular thought, the home has stood apart from the world of work. By virtue of bringing the factory or office home, homework challenges this dualism even though its persistence depends on it. Behind homework lies the sexual division of labor that assigns childcare and household maintenance to women and the construction of gender that considers women's subordinate position in both the family and the labor market as "natural."[1]

The ideology of separate spheres grew with the development of industrial capitalism in the northeastern United States during the first half of the nineteenth century. White women of the middle and upper classes became defined as mothers; their economic contribution to the family turned invisible as domestic labor, what we call housework, lost its value. The idealization of motherhood further split nurturing tasks and dependent care from work. Wage labor became constituted with the ideal worker as a man, or one who did not do housework, care for children, and engage in the other forms of unpaid family labor that were distinguishing mothers' lives. To whatever extent elite women experienced the home as separate from work, this division did not exist for the enslaved or the laboring poor – unable to be true women because they worked outside the home.[2]

Waged labor at home shared the invisibility of housework. Homework belonged to a larger gendered structuring of employment. Not only were occupations defined as either male or female (and either white or nonwhite), so were the processes and places of labor. Employers structured work to take advantage of sexual divisions and gender ideology. They drew upon women's position as mothers to shift the burdens of production onto the worker whose payment by the piece encouraged sweating. Employers increased profits by saving on overhead and gained flexibility through having fewer full-time workers. Without other opportunities to fulfill all their duties, some mothers turned to homework. Whereas homework could appear as an economic strategy, even a preferred one, it became a social problem in the minds of reformers and an economic threat to trade unionists. As one labor lawyer testified in 1939, "We are used to thinking of home as the man's castle, a place to live in, and I think we have a 'Home Sweet Home,' a very sentimental song," but the conditions of the "Typical Home Worker" rewrote that title to "Home Sweat Home."[3]

[1] Carole Pateman, "Feminist Critiques of the Public/Private Dichotomy," in *The Disorder of Women* (Stanford, Calif.: Stanford Univ. Press, 1989), 118–40; Linda Kerber, "Separate Spheres, Female Worlds, Woman's Place: The Rhetoric of Women's History," *JAH* 75 (June 1988), 9–39.

[2] Jeanne Boydston, *Home and Work: Housework, Wages, and the Ideology of Labor in the Early Republic* (New York: Oxford Univ. Press, 1990); Tamara K. Hareven, "The Home and the Family in Historical Perspective," *Social Research* 58 (Spring 1991), 253–85.

[3] Elias Lieberman, "Hearing on Proposed Amendments to Part 516 of Regulations with Respect to the Keeping of Special or Additional Records by Employers of Industrial Home Workers in the United States and Puerto Rico," Jan. 4–6, 1939, 386, unpublished typescript, DOL Library.

Homeworkers considered themselves both mothers who earned for their families and workers who happened to labor at home, but few of their voices were heard in public discussions about homework during the last century. Others spoke for the homeworker, interpreting her words and actions, fashioning a meaning to meet their own agendas even when occasionally recording her words. She became their symbol, providing a medium through which questions of profit and loss, authority and subordination, power and control became resolved. Homeworker turned into a category produced and limited by the discourses through which reformers and trade unionists opposed what they named exploitation: low wages, poor working conditions, and a general lack of control over the labor process. The language of motherhood provided the rhetoric through which employers, trade unionists, male and female reformers, and government administrators struggled over the persistence of industrial homework, a battle which, in turn, reinforced dominant cultural understandings of womanhood, manhood, childhood, home, and work. Others would compose the public narrative of homeworker lives.

From the late nineteenth century, descriptions of homework were "cultural productions"[4] or interpretative constructions of experience that make a rhetorical argument. They embedded assumptions about the family economy, mother care of children, women's and men's relation to the wage system, the position of women in society, and attitude toward the labor contract, free market, and state responsibility for social welfare. Contemporary accounts and government documents provide data on industrial homework but must be read for what they tell us about interpretations of homework. Bulletins of the U.S. Women's Bureau, photographic montages of the National Child Labor Committee (NCLC), or transcripts of hearings before the National Recovery Administration (NRA) demand analysis through multiple lenses, require deconstruction even as they allow re-construction of the homework system.

In the following narrative, *woman, mother, home,* and *work* appear as symbols, as social and ideological creations. But individuals whose voices and actions move through time and space also people my retelling of the history of industrial homework. By contextualizing and situating discourse, I uncover the ways that different groups have defined the relationship between a public realm of paid labor and a private domain of the home under industrial capitalism. Bifurcated notions not only obscure interconnections – between public and private, work and home, production and reproduction – but the

[4] Sonya O. Rose, *Limited Livelihoods: Gender and Class in Nineteenth-Century England* (Berkeley: Univ. of California Press, 1992), 8, defines cultural productions as "shared cultural symbols which are used to mediate between what is already widely known or understood and the articulation of ideas about something new. They are rhetorical devices meant to persuade ... These interpretations are particular constructions which cast the events within a limited and limiting perspective . . . repress, negate, or remain silent about alternative views. When these interpretations are built into public policies they directly constrain people's lives."

evolution and permeations of such thought represent a historical question to be analyzed. Industrial homework provides an ideal vehicle to explore a continuum that politics and ideology have torn apart.

This book is not a precise economic or social history. As an underground activity, often illegal, homework has been inadequately quantified in the past – and in the present. My interest and its larger significance lie elsewhere. The history of homework regulation reveals the ways that concepts of womanhood and manhood, visions of proper homelife and childhood, and the persistent ideological separation of home from work have structured state policy. Gender has provided a language through which contending political, social, and economic forces struggle. The history of industrial homework and its regulation over the last century illustrates the historical construction of gender and the gendering of state action.[5]

The insistence that culture and history rather than biology define "woman" has led historians to *gender* as an analytic category. Its use marks the movement of women's historians beyond women's history. Gender refers not only to woman but also to man. Within this construct, male and female become masculine and feminine. But too often in feminist thought, the categories of man and woman appear fixed, their meanings certain. Under the poststructuralist gaze, gender has became a process, more fluid, contingent, and unstable than dominant cultural understandings would have it, subject to historical analysis.[6]

An identity experienced by individuals, gender also constitutes a symbolic system, one with sexual difference at the center. It is a discursive system that expresses relations of power through definitions of sexual identity and practice. As a cultural force, gender goes beyond the relations between the sexes. It permeates society, modes of thought, economic life, and political praxis. Gender exists in the home and other workplaces, in the union hall and the courts, in the legal brief and social survey. Gender is not class, or a cultural and social relation to the means of production, but class is gendered and both are racialized. That is, *woman* and *man* are not universal categories; differences exist between women and between men based on other social factors, themselves subject to diverse readings, and these change over time. Women and men of the same group struggle in common even as their gendered experiences set them apart and may push them into opposition. Men and women experience their gender, class, and race or ethnicity simultaneously, although

[5] Joan Scott, "Gender: A Useful Category of Historical Analysis," in *Gender and the Politics of History* (New York: Columbia Univ. Press, 1988), 28–50.

[6] Gerda Lerner, *The Majority Finds Its Past: Placing Women in History* (New York: Oxford Univ. Press, 1979); Gayle Rubin, "The Traffic in Women," in *Toward an Anthropology of Women*, ed. Rayna Reiter [Rapp] (New York: Monthly Review Press, 1975); Judith Butler, *Gender Trouble: Feminism and the Subversion of Identity* (New York: Routledge, 1990); Jane Flax, *Thinking Fragments: Psychoanalysis, Feminism, and Postmodernism in the Contemporary West* (Berkeley: Univ. of California Press, 1990); and Scott, "Gender."

at any one moment, one aspect of their identity may come to the fore. Concrete historical settings generate the meanings of gender.[7]

Gender ideology provided a continual rationale for homework. Most participants in the homework debate agreed that mothers should remain at home with their children; they disagreed on whether industrial labor should be part of that home environment. The fight for homework regulation was a key component of the quest for protective legislation for women and children and labor standards for all workers. It suggests the importance of concepts of female difference in structuring economic life and public policy.

Analysis of homework both questions popular meanings of *home* and expands categories of *work* and *worker*, further extending the boundaries of labor history. While an extensive scholarship has developed on domestic service and housework, homework usually appears as a condition of garment production but rarely as a topic on its own. The only existing studies derive from the political struggle over its regulation.[8] But homework is a subject rich with possibilities to bring together major theoretical and historical concerns: state formation and policy discourse; the dialectic between social movements and administrative and legal systems; the complex relation between gender definitions, women's paid labor, and family labor. No longer is the home a place of rest and the worker one who leaves the home.

This history illuminates a process: the gendering of the welfare state, Although historians often mark the welfare state by New Deal social insurance and assistance programs like social security and unemployment compensation, the welfare state includes all actions that, in the words of political sociologist Ann Shola Orloff, "intervene in civil society to alter the play of social and market forces."[9] Since the mid-1980s, historians and social scientists have sought to "bring the state back" into our study of social life.[10] The richly documented history of women has helped us redefine the "political" and again analyze state activity for this project. Whereas the concept of *women's cultures* and a focus on the private, relational aspects of life have dominated much of

---

[7] Rose, *Limited Livelihoods*, 1–21; Joy Parr, *The Gender of Breadwinners: Women, Men, and Change in Two Industrial Towns, 1880–1950* (Toronto: Univ. of Toronto Press, 1990), 7–11, 231, 242–6; Nancy Hewitt, "Reflections from a Departing Editor: Recasting Issues of Marginality," *Gender and History*, 4 (Spring 1992), 3–9.

[8] Eileen Boris, "Beyond Dichotomy: North American Women's Labor History," *Journal of Women's History* 4 (Winter 1993): 162–79; Ruth Shallcross, *Industrial Homework: An Analysis of Homework Regulation Here and Abroad* (New York: Industrial Affairs, 1939) is the only full-length study and it stops before FLSA. Shallcross was a former New York State homework inspector who ended up rejecting abolition for European type regulations that monitored the conditions under which homework occurred.

[9] Ann Shola Orloff, "Gender in Early U.S. Social Policy," *Journal of Policy History* 3 (Fall 1991), 274 n.1.

[10] Peter Evans and Theda Skocpol, eds., *Bringing the State In* (Cambridge: Cambridge Univ. Press, 1985).

the historiography about women in the nineteenth century,[11] the state has emerged as a major organizing principle for the history of women in the twentieth- century United States. Recent work has begun to shift our analysis of the Progressive Era and the New Deal so that the gendered, as well as racial and class, origins of the welfare state become central to our evaluation of its continual impact on women and their children as well as on the positions of men and women by race and class within the economy and polity.[12]

Much of the new scholarship on women and the state focuses on the redistributive aspect of state policy. Such work considers social welfare history narrowly, focusing on poor relief, mothers' pensions, and Aid to Families with Dependent Children. It argues that there was a dual welfare system in which men as breadwinners earned unemployment insurance and workmen's compensation and women as care givers gained mothers' pensions. Such a two-track system divided along gender lines not only in the intent to renew men's independence and maintain women's dependence but also in the very nature of government programs: Men obtained entitlements earned through wage-based contributions; women, seen as a burden, received welfare.[13]

[11] Nancy Hewitt, "Beyond the Search for Sisterhood: American Women's History in the 1980s," *Social History* 10 (Oct. 1985): 299–322.

[12] With Peter Bardaglio, I wrote some early pieces in this vein: "The Transformation of Patriarchy: The Historic Role of the State," in *Families, Politics, and Public Policy: A Feminist Dialogue on Women and the State*, ed. Irene Diamond (New York: Longmans, 1984), 94–114; and "Gender, Race, and Class: The Impact of the State on the Family and the Economy," in *Families and Work*, ed. Naomi Gerstel and Harriet Gross (Philadelphia, Pa.: Temple Univ. Press, 1987), 132–51. For more recent historical literature, Gwendolyn Mink, "The Lady and the Tramp: Gender, Race, and the Origins of the American Welfare State," in *Women, the State, and Welfare*, ed. Linda Gordon (Madison: Univ. of Wisconsin Press, 1990), 92–122; Noralee Frankel and Nancy S. Dye, eds., *Gender, Race, Class and Reform in the Progressive Era* (Lexington: Univ. of Kentucky Press, 1991); Nancy F. Cott, *The Grounding of Modern Feminism* (New Haven, Conn.: Yale Univ. Press, 1987); Elisabeth Israels Perry, *Belle Moskowitz: Feminine Politics and the Exercise of Power in the Age of Alfred E. Smith* (New York: Oxford Univ. Press, 1987); Robyn Muncy, *Creating a Female Dominion in American Reform, 1890–1935* (New York: Oxford Univ. Press, 1991); Susan Ware, *Partner and I: Molly Dewson, Feminism, and New Deal Politics* (New Haven, Conn.: Yale Univ. Press, 1987); Linda Gordon, "Black and White Visions of Welfare: Women's Welfare Activism, 1890–1945," *JAH* 78 (Sept. 1991): 559–90; Gordon, "Social Insurance and Public Assistance: The Influence of Gender in Welfare Thought in the United States, 1890–1935," *AHR* 97 (Feb. 1992), 19–54; Molly Ladd-Taylor, *Mother-Work: Women, Child Welfare, and the State, 1890–1930* (Urbana: Univ. of Illinois Press, 1994).

[13] Linda Gordon, ed., *Women, the State, and Welfare*, particularly Gordon, "The New Feminist Scholarship on the Welfare State," 9–35, and Barbara Nelson, "The Origins of the Two-Channeled Welfare State: Workmen's Compensation and Mothers' Aid," 123–151. Diana Pearce, "Toil and Trouble: Women Workers and Unemployment Compensation," *Signs* 10 (Spring 1985), 439–59; Molly Ladd-Taylor, "Hull-House Goes to Washington: Women and the Children's Bureau," in Frankel and Dye, *Gender, Race, Class, and Reform*, 110–26; Theda Skocpol and Gretchen Ritter, "Gender and the Origins of Modern Social Policies in Britain and the United States," *Studies in American Political Development* 5 (Spring 1991): 36–93; Orloff, "Gender in Early U.S. Social Policy."

Most of this literature fails to connect the redistributive to the regulatory aspects of state policy, which makes the welfare state appear to divide into two tracks.[14] The history of intervention in the labor market, either through labor standards legislation or regulation of corporations, stands apart from the history of welfare.[15] We have the history of labor law and the history of protective labor legislation for women and children, but the gendered assumptions of the former remain unrevealed in major studies.[16] This separation of family policy from industrial relations, women's history from labor history, or even women's labor history from labor history,[17] dichotomizes scholarship in a manner reflective of the division between home and work, private and public, that the existence of industrial homework denies. The generation of women reformers who fought to end homework conceived of welfare legislation as a solution to the labor problem and part of the quest for worker rights.[18] This study of a kind of mothers' labor suggests the dependence of labor standards on factors usually thought of as belonging to family policy – the availability of childcare, the extent of charity, and assumptions about home and family life. It shifts our orientation to the working component of the working mother without moving away from her experience(s) as a mother.

Women have emerged as actors in welfare state scholarship, with contradictory consequences. The welfare state opened new possibilities for women, the meaning of which depended on social position: whether they were initiators of state action or recipients, whether they forged a career out of social programs or found support for daily survival through them. Policies, like women's labor laws and maternal health care, that improved the immediate conditions of some working-class women provided limited power to other women: those who were native-born, white, educated, and from the middle

---

[14] One exception is Skocpol and Ritter, "Gender and the Origins of Modern Social Policies in Britain and the United States," but they argue that the failure of class legislation, as seen in the *Lochner* decision of 1905, left only policies for women available for state policy. Orloff in "Gender in Early U.S. Social Policy" maintains this duality when she sees as parallel efforts scholars who consider "the *citizen's wage*" and those who consider programs for single mothers and their children.

[15] Morton Keller, *Regulating a New Economy: Public Policy and Economic Change in America, 1900–1933* (Cambridge, Mass.: Harvard Univ. Press, 1990); Martin J. Sklar, *The Corporate Reconstruction of American Capitalism, 1890–1916: The Market, the Law, and Politics* (New York: Cambridge Univ. Press, 1988).

[16] William E. Forbath, *Law and the Shaping of the American Labor Movement* (Cambridge, Mass.: Harvard Univ. Press, 1991); Christopher Tomlins, *The State and the Unions: Labor Relations, Law, and the Organized Labor Movement in America, 1880–1960* (New York: Cambridge Univ. Press, 1985).

[17] Ava Baron, "Gender and Labor History," *Work Engendered: Toward a New History of American Labor*, ed. Ava Baron (Ithaca, N.Y.: Cornell Univ. Press, 1991), 1–46.

[18] Kathryn Kish Sklar, "The Historical Foundations of Women's Power in the Creation of the American Welfare State, 1830–1930," in *Mothers of a New World: Maternalist Politics and the Origins of Welfare States*, ed. Sonya Michel and Seth Koven (New York: Routledge, 1993), 43–93.

and upper classes. Yet these same labor and social assistance policies retained dominant gender assumptions that maintained the subordinate position of women. To claim that women reformers were merely imposing their values on working people overemphasizes their power and negates the ways that "clients" sought to use for their own purposes the very state agencies and voluntary organizations created to remake their lives.[19] It also oversimplifies a complex legacy.

Women reformers were forged in the middle-class white women's culture of the late nineteenth century, complete with its celebration of female difference. This concept of difference assigned women superior moral and personal qualities, such as nurturing, cooperativeness, and selflessness, that women could project into the body politic.[20] One of the ironies of this century certainly must be that those who held these values were midwives to the bureaucratic, administrative state.[21] These women played a major part in a script they wrote but could not fully direct; they lacked funding and political power within the state apparatus. Thus they did not control the final outcome. Their cultural belief in female difference, of women as different from men, as well as the reality of the sexual division of life, shaped white women's public life, the politics of women's groups, and state policies themselves.

The women reformers had their start in Progressive Era organizations like the National Consumers' League (NCL) and the Women's Trade Union League. They went on to staff the U.S. Women's Bureau and state departments of labor in the 1920s and, during the New Deal, the U.S. Department of Labor (DOL) itself. Historians have called them "social feminists." By the late 1920s, they themselves came to deny the term *feminist* because feminist became associated with the National Women's Party, whose support of the Equal Rights Amendment promoted abstract legal rights over women's labor legislation. The second generation of these reformers dropped the feminist designation during the New Deal. While some have considered them maternalists, constructing the state on the basis of mothers' needs, their focus on industrial conditions and labor standards requires a broader framework.[22] They were, if

19 Linda Gordon critiques social control in *Heroes of Their Own Lives: The Politics and History of Family Violence* (New York: Viking, 1988).

20 Eileen Boris, "Looking at Women's Historians Looking at Difference," *Wisconsin Women's Law Journal* 3 (1987), 213–38.

21 Kathy Ferguson, *The Feminist Case Against Bureaucracy* (Philadelphia, Pa.: Temple Univ. Press, 1984).

22 Nancy Cott, "What's in a Name? The Limits of 'Social Feminism'; or, Expanding the Vocabulary of Women's History," *JAH* 76 (Dec. 1989), 809–29; Theda Skocpol, *Protecting Soldiers and Mothers: The Political Origins of Social Policy in the United States* (Cambridge, Mass.: Harvard Univ. Press, 1992); and Sonya Michel and Seth Koven, "Womanly Duties: Maternalist Politics and the Origins of the Welfare State in France, Great Britain and the United States, 1880–1920," *AHR* 95 (Oct. 1990), 1076–1108; Sybil Lipschultz, "Social Feminism and Legal Discourse, 1908–1923," *Yale Journal of Law and Feminism* 2 (Fall 1989), 131–60; for industrial feminism, Diane Kirkby, *Alice Henry: The Power of Pen and Voice, The Life of an Australian–American Labor Reformer* (New York: Cambridge Univ. Press, 1991), 2.

you will, social democrats who would use the state for social justice.[23] They viewed women workers as mothers burdened with what a later generation named "the double day." They sought equality not on the basis of what was normal for men, but in terms of what they generalized as women's life experiences, often conflating woman with mother. At various times they emphasized that the homeworker was a worker rather than a mother, but they often justified labor standards in terms of maternal improvement. I retain the term *social feminist* only for the years of the suffrage movement and its immediate aftermath.

The implications of "difference" are not so obvious. Driven by a discourse that conceived of women as both dependent and powerful by virtue of their status as mothers, the debate over industrial homework exposes its contrary meanings: on the one hand, an ability to strengthen patriarchal structures and thinking by reinforcing the existing sexual division of social life, women's place within the home, and the consequent denial of womanhood to working-class women, especially from subordinate races, who could not stay home; on the other, a critique of capitalist social relations that promises an alternative, nondichotomous, organization of home, workplace, psyche, and social life. Homeworking women also viewed women as different from men; they agreed that mothers should remain home, but that rather than destroying the family, homework served as a way to contribute to the family economy, that pooling of all resources by family members. The meaning of "difference," then, varied widely, as did the reality of homework for different groups of women.[24]

As tropes, motherhood and difference can serve more than one mistress (or master), as the following history will explore. These terms have empowered as well as subordinated, opened spaces as well as restricted, served strategic as well as ideological ends. We must consider the homework justified in their names not only as a type of production but as a historically constructed form. It is to its emergence during early industrialization, prior to prominence as a political issue, that I first turn.

The emergence of homework

Protoindustrialization, a term much bandied about by historians of early modern Europe, does not describe the transformation to capitalist economic and social relations in the United States.[25] Cottage industry, or manufacturing

[23] Wendy Sarvasy, "Beyond the Difference Versus Equality Policy Debate: Post-Suffrage Feminism, Citizenship, and the Quest for a Feminist Welfare State," *Signs* 17 (Winter 1992), 329–62.

[24] Linda Gordon, "On Difference," *Genders* 10 (Spring 1991), 91–111.

[25] This literature is vast. Franklin F. Mendels, "Proto-industrialization: The First Phase of the Industrialization Process," *Journal of Economic History* 32 (1972), 241–61; for one critique, Christopher Clark, *The Roots of Rural Capitalism: Western Massachusetts, 1780–1860* (Ithaca, N.Y.: Cornell Univ Press, 1990).

in the home, had a shorter life and was not the cause of demographic expansion. In Europe, outwork – the "putting out" by employers of materials to be manufactured by others – preceded factory production. In the United States, it developed in a symbiotic relation to the factory system; industrial homework, or outwork in the home, was integral to the industrialization process, rather than a relic of an earlier stage of development. It is not to be confused with home manufacturing for family consumption or with independent entrepreneurship located in the home, for it represents a form of waged labor. Homeworkers were "invisible threads," in the words of Karl Marx, "an outside department of the factory, the manufactory, or the warehouse."[26] Emerging with capitalism in the countryside, homework would characterize key consumer industries of nineteenth-century metropolitan industrialization.[27] Such labor was gendered from the start, relying upon the sexual division of labor within households and between the household and the larger community. Men's interests as employers and working-class men's interests as husbands reinforced each other.

Beginning in the late eighteenth-century, outwork came to the New England countryside. Farm families sought store goods or cash to participate in a developing consumer economy. Local merchants gave out bags of cotton to be picked and cleaned, which would be sent to the new spinning mills of eastern Massachusetts and Rhode Island. Textile manufacturers put out weaving from the time of the Embargo Act of 1807 until the 1840s. When power looms began replacing home weaving in the 1820s, straw and palm-leaf hatmaking emerged as outwork industries. One estimate has at least fifty-one thousand women and children producing $1.9 million worth of these hats in Massachusetts by 1837.[28]

From the start, outwork represented a strategy of rural women. Rather than

[26] Karl Marx, *Capital*, v. 1 (New York: International Publishers, 1967), 461.

[27] Jamie Faricellia Dangler, "Industrial Homework in the Modern World-Economy," *Contemporary Crises* 10 (1986), 259–64; Thomas Dublin, "Women and Outwork in a Nineteenth-Century New England Town: Fitzwilliam, New Hampshire, 1830–1850," in *The Countryside in the Age of Capitalist Transformation*, ed. Steven Hahn and Jonathan Prude (Chapel Hill: Univ. of North Carolina Press, 1985), 51–69; Christine Stansell, "The Origins of the Sweatshop: Women and Early Industrialization in New York City," in *Working-Class America: Essays on Labor, Community, and American Society*, ed. Michael H. Frisch and Daniel J. Walkowitz (Urbana: Univ. of Illinois Press, 1983), 78–103.

[28] Estimate from Thomas Dublin, "Rural Putting-Out Work in Early Nineteenth-Century New England: Women and the Transition to Capitalism in the Countryside," *New England Quarterly* 64 (1991), 534–7; Clark, *The Roots of Rural Capitalism*, 175–84; Jonathan Prude, *The Coming Industrial Order: Town and Factory Life in Rural Massachusetts, 1810–1860* (New York: Cambridge Univ. Press, 1983), 73–8; Edith Abbott, *Women in Industry: A Study in American Economic History* (New York: D. Appleton and Co., 1910), 35–47; Sandra Albrecht, "Industrial Home Work in the United States: Historical Dimensions and Contemporary Perspective," *Economic and Industrial Democracy* 3 (1982), 413–30; Gail Fowler Mohanty, "Putting Up With Putting-Out: Power-Loom Diffusion and Outwork for Rhode Island Mills, 1821–1829," *Journal of the Early Republic* 9 (Summer 1989), 192.

a cure for idleness, as publicized by some male promoters of industrialization, such labor helped women "make ends meet" despite pay below that of a farm laborer. Unlike late nineteenth-century tenement homeworkers, daughters within male-headed households predominated, with widows comprising another major group of outworkers. When both wives and daughters worked, their labor substituted for wages earned by sons or for a cash crop. Although most were not "affluent," neither were they without other resources. Not dependent on the work for survival, they took it up at intervals, as needed. Appearing not very different from household maintenance, outwork as women's work was devalued nearly from the start. But like household manufacturing, it allowed rural families to purchase consumer goods.[29]

Precisely because workers mixed family and waged labor together, merchant employers had little control over the labor process. Not only was it easy for homeworkers to siphon off material for personal use and difficult for employers to keep track of material, but employers were without a dependable and expansive labor force. Unlike Western Europe, in New England rural farmers owned their land and were not desperate for wages. Textile mills had to search a wide area to recruit enough home workers. Such problems of supply and control encouraged the bringing of textile making into central locations. Buttons and palm-leaf hats allowed greater control over production because the materials were neither common to country households nor worth enough for families to expropriate them for independent exchange purposes.[30]

Although the availability of button outwork lessened with mechanization and prices dropped in the mid 1830s, the labor pool remained large. Not until 1870 did buttonmaking fully become a factory industry. Counterparts throughout rural New England continued to braid palm-leaf hats into the 1880s. Daughters contributed to the family income and earned money for dowries; hatmaking and other forms of rural putting out kept some from the mill towns which provided higher wages. Such women stayed within the confines of the family economy. Outwork provided them with cash but little independence from familial, particularly patriarchal, authority.[31]

Outwork also grew along with the shift from a family-labor system to a wage-labor system in shoemaking, clothing, and a host of other industries that met the needs of both trade with the South and an expanded urban consumer market. In the late eighteenth century, hundreds of urban women and children took work in, setting teeth into carding combs, spinning and weaving, and making shoes. As early as the 1820s, in port cities like New York and Boston

[29] Dublin, "Rural Putting-out Work," 531–73; Prude, *The Coming Industrial Order*, 76–7; Clark, *Roots of Rural Capitalism*, 186–9.

[30] Clark, *The Roots of Rural Capitalism*, 176–9, 180–8.

[31] Ibid., 279; Dublin, "Women and Outwork," 54–65; Helen Sumner, "History of Women in Industry in the United States," *Report on Women and Children* 9 (1910), 157–9, 65; Mary Blewett, *Men, Women, and Work: Class, Gender, and Protest in the New England Shoe Industry, 1780–1910* (Urbana: Univ. of Illinois Press, 1988), 44–5.

merchant tailors expanded production by sending work to home seamstresses. One 1828 esti-mate counted between eighteen thousand and twenty thousand sewing women (the largest category of women wage earners) in Philadelphia, New York, Boston, and Baltimore. These women cared for children under crowded urban conditions and stretched the often inadequate wages that their men earned; both family labor and lack of other forms of "women's work" limited options for wage earning. By midcentury outworkers resembled the female working class as a whole, with young unmarried women lodging on their own, daughters at home, wives and widows. Some sewing women worked with their tailor husbands in family shops that depended upon the cloth of others. "Invisible threads," mothers and daughters alike stood safely behind the closed doors of their homes, ideologically apart from the perils of the marketplace despite the realities of their lives.[32]

They faced grinding immiseration. Initially, sewing women made entire shirts, but their meager average earnings of about $1.50 a week barely covered the cost of rent. Many were forced to turn to charity, the availability of which ironically lowered further the price paid by the garment contractors who knew that such women had other sources of sustenance. While their rural counterparts wove intermittently, these expert workers sewed "from sunrise till 10 or 11 o'clock at night," crusading journalist Matthew Carey charged. They had to pick up and return their work and somehow find time to care for their children. While a number of committees passed resolutions deploring these conditions and some even suggested a diversity of occupations for women as a solution, none took concrete actions to end such exploitation. What kept women from starvation was not the help of reformers but their own and community self-reliance. Sewing was seasonal and women went in and out of such labor; it was part of an arsenal of strategies – from taking in boarders and scavenging the streets to prostitution – deployed by women of the laboring poor to make ends meet.[33]

Yet the manufacturers, beset by competition, could not have paid more even if they had wanted to. From its origins in the "slop" shops of the 1820s, producing rough clothes for seamen, frontiersmen, and the enslaved, the clothing industry suffered from the very entrepreneurial conditions that promised upward mobility to immigrants and other workingmen. Hemmed by competition, low start-up costs, undercapitalization, and a highly seasonal and variable product, garment manufacturers resorted to a system of central shops and contractors, run on credit. This organization collapsed prices and led to

[32] Abbott, *Women in Industry*, 37–8, 40–1; Sumner, "History of Women in Industry," 123; Christine Stansell, *City of Women: Sex and Class in New York, 1789–1860* (New York: Alfred A. Knopf, 1986), 105–19; Frieda Miller, "Industrial Home Work in the United States," *International Labour Review* 43 (Jan. 1941): 3–4.

[33] Sumner, "History of Women in Industry," 123–33. Stansell, *City of Women*, places sewing outwork in the context of other strategies.

underpayment, withheld payment, and long hours, all of which an oversupply of contractors and workers exacerbated. The sewing machine, introduced in the 1850s, allowed better capitalized manufacturers to increase efficiency through standardization of production. As a consequence, sewing women made buttonholes or collars rather than an entire shirt. A division into those who had machines and those who lacked them further encouraged contracting and its resultant cutthroat competition.[34]

The home binding of shoes reveals how households became incorporated into wage labor. A familial division of labor, in which wives took on one process for their artisan husbands, by the 1830s had become a sexual division, in which women sewed uppers for the bosses of shoe factories, who then gave them to unrelated men to finish into shoes. With household duties, wives had been unable to bind enough uppers for their husbands; with the central shops supplying about three-quarters of the uppers for a shoemaker, men too became more enmeshed in relations of dependency. Demands for higher wages led employers to expand shoe outwork from Lynn, Massachusetts, into New Hampshire, Maine, and rural eastern Massachusetts.[35]

Technology transformed shoe manufacturing. Although used by some urban outworkers, sewing machines ushered centralized factory production. Wages for outwork dropped, as did the amount of handwork for homebound women. By 1860, binders were earning half as much as previously, a few pennies a pair for stitching and lining women's shoes. Daughters entered the shops, creating a "dual system of production" based on kinship position. The majority of women remained outworkers until 1860. The defeat of Lynn shoemakers in the Great Strike of that year marked the emergence of the factory system as the dominant form of production.[36]

The 1860 strike exposed the divisions within the working class based on family status as well as gender. Amid declining conditions, male artisans fought the centralized factory. They drew upon their positions as breadwinners to justify higher wages for men. The homeworkers, married to men in the trade, rejected an alliance with factory girls in order to fight for increases for their men and homework for women, rather than higher wages for both sexes. Male leaders desired female participation for symbolic reasons, to emphasize their defense of "traditional values" through the moral stature of New England women.[37] This

[34] Carol Lasser, "Mistress, Maid and Market: The Transformation of Domestic Service in New England, 1790–1870," (Ph.D. diss. Harvard Univ., 1981), 83; Stansell, "Origins of the Sweatshop," 88–9; Ava Baron and Susan E. Klepp, " 'If I Didn't Have My Sewing Machine . . .': Women and Sewing Machine Technology," in *A Needle, a Bobbin, a Strike: Women Needleworkers in America*, ed. Joan M. Jensen and Sue Davidson (Philadelphia, Pa.: Temple Univ. Press, 1984), 20–59.

[35] Mary Blewett, *Men, Women, and Work*, 44–67, esp. 57, 60; Sumner, "History of Women in Industry," 167–70.

[36] Blewett, *Men, Women, and Work*, 97–115; Sumner, "History of Women in Industry," 170–4.

[37] Blewett, *Men, Women, and Work*, 115–36.

struggle between capital and labor, in which homeworking mothers functioned as a central metaphor for organizing male workers, prefigures a subtext of this book.

What follows

This book divides into four parts which move the narrative through case studies that mark transformations in the politics of homework. I have focused on representative examples and major turning points in the emergence of homework as a social and political problem, contrasting definitions and perceptions of the issue and the different strategies undertaken by workers and reformers to end the practice. I explore the evolution of the role of the state in shaping labor conditions and women's position in the labor market — not just in the sense that laws or their absence defined the limits of social action, but how the language of reform shaped the homework problem and resulting state strategies.

Moral and economic arguments, promoting motherhood and efficiency, replace images of contamination to fuel the homework debate. Which set of arguments dominated depended on a given situation. Sometimes clearly or distinctly articulated, at other times merging and overlapping with other modes of thought and expression, discourses that appear in the last third of the nineteenth century reappear in new guises during the twentieth. Talk of slavery and freedom frames discussions of victimization. The language of rights and fairness becomes conceptualized in opposition to liberty of contract, but it links women's rights to opposing notions of freedom — from regulation or exploitation. Often expressed as universals, such terms obscure the gendered nature of homework. But the gender of homeworkers transforms the language of the marketplace. Reformers come to focus on the worker and the workplace after initially tapping into the fears of the consumer. Those who argued from the maternal or familial standpoint would often deploy the language of labor standards and efficiency without dropping their earlier discourse.

The first section, "Man's Freedom, Woman's Necessity: *Jacobs* and Its Legacy," explores how man's freedom to contract ignored the conditions that fueled woman's necessity to labor at home. Courts shaped the boundaries against which homework opponents fashioned their strategies. From a trade union campaign, homework prohibition turned into a reform crusade. Chapter I analyzes the judicial response to the first legislative prohibition of homework, New York's 1884 law against tenement cigarmaking lobbied for by the Cigar Makers' International Union under Samuel Gompers. *In re Jacobs* not only stymied regulation of industrial homework for the next half century but framed those discourses of disease, dirt, and exploitation through which the battle was engaged. Male trade unionists viewed the homework system as an assault on their masculinity and status as citizens. Part of that assault derived from the competitive pressure of sweated labor which undermined the ability to earn a living wage, which they expressed in the language of freedom and slavery. The cigarmakers' struggle also reveals the roads not taken: cooperatives, unionization, and community organizing stand as alternatives to the strategy of state regulation.[38]

Chapter 2 reveals how the legacy of *Jacobs* haunted early efforts by garment workers and reformers to restrict tenement-made clothing. Massachusetts's model law that regulated home workshops in the name of public health remained operative, but Illinois's attempt to link homework with limits on women's hours succumbed to "freedom of contract" in *Ritchie v. People*. The last chapter in this section evaluates the efforts of the NCL and the NCLC to restrict homework in the first years of the century. Middle- and upper-class women reformers become more prominent than working-class trade unionists of either sex. These reformers focused on homework as an impediment toward improving the lives of working-class women and their children. In the context of the national debate over "the mother who must earn," this chapter traces a shift from moral suasion to legislative and judicial action under the leadership of Florence Kelley and from licensing tenements to reliance on the minimum wage to bypass *Jacobs*. Regulating homework would end its attractiveness and force employers to drop its use.

Part 2, "Visions and Voices," charts the conversations among reformers, business, and homeworkers themselves from World War I to the New Deal, a period that witnessed changes in the nature and rationale for homework and introduced new voices into the homework debate. The promise of federal regulation during World War I faded, leaving the problem to the states and allowing homework to continue. But the Board of Control of Labor Standards for Army Clothing, the subject of Chapter 4, foreshadowed government regulation of homework – and indeed the industrial relations system – of the New Deal. Wartime regulation suggests the gendered nature of both the concept of industrial democracy and labor standards as a whole. Discourses of patriotism and citizenship enter the homework debate; connected to concerns with wartime efficiency, they will reappear during World War II. Chapter 5 returns to state departments of labor during the 1920s, when "states' rights" again guided federal policy and considers how underfunding and lack of commitment hampered local efforts to curb a national problem.

Chapter 6 compares the experiences and self-perceptions of Italian immigrants and their children in the Northeast with African Americans in Chicago and Mexicans in Texas. Homework was never confined to any one ethnic or racial group, but regional ethnic and racial segmentation of the labor market

[38] Sheila Rowbotham, "Strategies Against Sweated Work in Britain, France, and the United States, 1820–1920," in *Dignity and Daily Bread: New Forms of Economic Organizing Among Poor Women in the Third World and the First*, ed. Swasti Mitter and Sheila Rowbotham (London: Routledge, forthcoming).

would determine who would take work into the home. This chapter describes the homeworkers, their feelings about employers and contractors, working conditions, consumption patterns, and relations to each other. Homeworkers fashioned their own discourse of economic survival, family obligation, and community support. While some conceived of themselves as mothers who needed to work at home, many looked at themselves as workers who fulfilled familial duties through home-based labor. Depression conditions drew new workers into the homework system but failed to alter substantively the nature of the work or homeworker attitudes.

Part 3, "(En)gendering the New Deal," traces the development of a labor standards regime that was profoundly gendered, embodying the dichotomy between home and work. Chapter 7 analyzes the NRA code experience on the mainland and in Puerto Rico. The patchwork quality of homework regulation under the NRA stemmed from the very nature of the NRA itself. While this era saw the triumph of "sacred motherhood," a competing discourse of rights and fairness, grounded in economic rather than familial terms, dominated the arguments of women reformers and their trade union allies. Chapter 8 suggests how New Deal success at the federal level grew in a symbiotic manner with state initiatives, analyzing the fate of a model homework bill. Gendered understandings of homeworkers and the home remained constitutive elements of state laws and their implementation. The final chapter in this section, on the Fair Labor Standards Act (FLSA), examines the judicial struggle over homework that helped to redefine the employment relationship. The commerce clause replaced the police power as the legal justification for state intervention in the labor contract. This chapter considers the silences in FLSA as well as its articulations. It also discusses, in the context of World War II, the framing of administrative bans against homework in garment-related trades that would become the subject of controversy in the 1980s. FLSA provided a mechanism to restrict the homework system but embodied assumptions about the separation of home from work that undermined its position as the linchpin of the postwar labor standards regime.

The final section, "Home/Work Redux," begins with Chapter 10 on white-collar home-based labor from the late 1940s, when proponents of homework linked mothers working in the home with fighting the Cold War, to the 1980s, when new technologies promised to transform work more than they actually did by the 1990s. What some have promoted as a work-at-home revolution has varied by the sex, race, and class of the worker, as much as by the nature of the work. Chapter 11 considers the Reaganite deregulation of homework in the 1980s, with its call for homework as "a woman's right." Homework appeared as a solution to the work and family dilemma of our time, but one that ultimately reflected an agenda that attempted to dismantle the New Deal's regulatory legacy. After the revival of feminism, homework defenders were apt to speak of women's rights in terms not very different from those expressed by the Supreme Court in the early 1920s which viewed the Nineteenth Amendment as breaking down any barriers to women's freedom of contract. Where once men's right to contract precluded regulation of homework, now women's right to employment undermined prohibition.

This history suggests how dichotomous thought became embedded in social and labor policy. It is precisely because homework regulation replicated the division between home and workplace that we need to go beyond dichotomy, beyond thinking of the home and workplace as separate and begin to develop a public policy that would relate family policy and labor standards to improve the conditions of all working women. Homework is exploitative not because the location of labor necessarily oppresses, but rather because the labor contract reflects the overall social positions of working women, some of whom earn more precisely because others earn less.[39]

Like many academics, I write at home. But I do so under conditions of relative freedom. The quality and quantity of my output has only a remote influence on my earnings, especially in this era of reduced university budgets. I am not on piece rate, am not exposed to hazardous substances (although subject to repetitive motion injury) or rarely subject to anything but self-imposed deadlines. In short, I have the autonomy of the salaried professional. Most homeworkers in the past and the present work under less favorable circumstances; they lack control over their labor, having chosen homework as the best of a bad set of options as they attempt to earn wages and care for dependents. The International Ladies' Garment Workers Union rightly argues that unionized shops should replace homework. But rather than merely condemn the practice, I seek to understand when and under what circumstances homework may be called exploitative and how and in what ways it has served some women. Homework has been a problem; it has undercut the labor standards of factory and office workers and has undermined unionized employers. Its low pay is scandalous. For most of the past, sweated labor led to sweated motherhood, to overworked women sustaining a double day, working for their family as well as for wages. But solutions to homework have failed to confront the underlying reasons why women are homeworkers. Focusing more on "home" than on "work," policymakers often forgot that homeworkers were working mothers who needed social support and sought empowerment. We need to shift that emphasis.

[39] Evelyn Nakano Glenn, "From Servitude to Service Work: Historical Continuities in the Racial Division of Paid Reproductive Labor," *Signs* 18 (Autumn 1992), 34–37.

PART I

Man's freedom, woman's necessity: Jacobs and its legacy

Figure 2. Tenement house cigar factory in East Seventy-First Street, New York City, ca. 1895. New York State, Bureau of Labor Statistics, *Thirteenth Annual Report for the Year 1895* (Albany, N.Y.: Wynkeop Hallenbeck Crawford Co., 1896). Although *In re Jacobs* (98 N.Y. 98) struck down New York's first law prohibiting tenement homework in 1885, later licensing laws permitted factory inspectors to enter immigrant homes to monitor their adherence to sanitary provisions, breaking down the division of public and private in an attempt to save the home from industrial production.

1

"A man's dwelling house is his castle": Tenement house cigarmaking and the judicial imperative

In January 1885, New York's highest court struck down a statute that prohibited cigarmaking in New York City and Brooklyn tenement houses where cooking, sleeping, and the daily activities of life took place. Unconvinced that the measure was passed to promote the public health, the court of appeals relied upon the emerging judicial understanding of "free labor" to argue that a man's property and personal liberty could not be taken away without due process of law. "This law was not intended to protect the health of those engaged in cigarmaking, as they are allowed to manufacture cigars everywhere except in the forbidden tenement-houses," declared the New York court. Writing before the era of "sociological jurisprudence," the court never considered the actual conditions in tenement houses or their impact on the larger society. By claiming that "if the legislature has the power under the Constitution to prohibit the prosecution of one lawful trade in a tenement-house, then it may prevent the prosecution of all trades therein.' " *In re Jacobs* became a hurdle that stymied regulation of industrial homework for the next half century.[1]

This interpretation of privacy and contract displayed the gendered subtext of the law. The judges who sought to save the cigarmaker from the paternalism of the state affirmed his paternalism within the family: "It cannot be perceived how the cigarmaker is to be improved in his health or his morals by forcing him from his home and its hallowed associations and beneficent influences, to ply his trade elsewhere." Individual (male) freedom to engage in work "by which he earns a livelihood for himself and family," individual (male) choice "to do his work where he can have the supervision of his family and their help" could not succumb to what the judges labeled an arbitrary law. The

---

[1] *In re Jacobs*, 98 N.Y. 98 (1885) 113–14, 105–6; 83 U.S. (16 Wall.) 36 (1873), 83–130 (1873) (dissenting opinions). William E. Forbath, "The Ambiguities of Free Labor: Labor and the Law in the Gilded Age," *Wisconsin Law Review*, no.4 (1985), 795–6; Amy Dru Stanley, *The Bonds of Contract: Wage Labor and Marriage in the Age of Slave Emancipation* (New York: Cambridge Univ. Press, forthcoming).

justices failed to notice that wives and children were not merely "help" for the male cigarmaker but central to the production of cigars by the largely Bohemian immigrant group that worked in the tenements. Nor did they consider that the cigarmaker no longer was an independent artisan but an employee working under a divided labor process and hardly the independent citizen of Republican ideology.

In its tone and reasoning, *Jacobs* set the legal boundaries for the regulation of homework. It framed the discourses of disease, dirt, and exploitation under which the battle over industrial homework occurred during the last decades of the nineteenth century. This decision expressed a set of assumptions that illuminate the interplay of gender, ethnicity, and class in law and public policy. An early negation of labor standards, *Jacobs* reveals understandings about gender that stood at the center of both the contest between capital and labor and the conflicts within a working class divided by sex, ethnicity, and skill in Gilded Age America.

Jacobs exemplified an emerging judicial understanding of "free labor" that emphasized the right to contract and rights of property. As a product of Reconstruction politics, the Fourteenth Amendment – on which late-nineteenth-century judges relied – had sought to curb Southern discrimination against African Americans "without altering radically the structure of the federal system or increasing markedly the powers of the federal government." This understanding predisposed courts to protect fundamental rights from infringement by the states despite a tendency to defer to state legislatures. The right to property, which would be protected from arbitrary laws, fell under this rubric because Gilded Age judges interpreted rights from the vantage point of a political economy that associated the marketplace with social good, the "free" marketplace with "free labor." That workers and employers did not bring equal resources to their contract negotiations was of no concern because both maintained individual ownership of their assets; they were free to contract.[2]

Women as cigarmakers and the wives and daughters of cigarmakers actively fought to better the conditions of their craft in the 1870s and 1880s. Yet *woman* was not an actual agent but the most powerful of symbols under the social conditions that generated *Jacobs*. The degraded opposite of the craftsworker, she was both the object and the beneficiary of working-class masculinity. White, "Teutonic" male workers drew more narrowly the bonds of mutuality, excluding large numbers of women workers, as they fought for their right to a family wage. Homework, they argued, undermined American values and the homelife behind those values, to which the family role of women was central. Tenement production was as alien as the immigrants who engaged in it.

---

[2] William E. Nelson, *The Fourteenth Amendment: From Political Principle to Judicial Doctrine* (Cambridge, Mass.: Harvard Univ. Press, 1988), esp. 197; Herbert Hovenkamp, "The Political Economy of Substantive Due Process," *Stanford Law Review* 40 (Jan. 1988), 379–447; Charles W. McCurdy, "The Roots of 'Liberty of Contract' Reconsidered: Major Premises in the Law of Employment, 1867–1937," *Supreme Court Yearbook 1984*, 20–33.

Homework also represented a new form of slavery. "The manufacturers say that they have inaugurated the tenement system for our benefit and at our request," Samuel Gompers told a crowd of strikers in 1877. "Yes, as the slave kneels and holds up his hands for the shackles."[3] Associating slavery with weakness, dependency, and loss of masculinity, Gompers and his supporters combined nativism with racism and male supremacy to defend a restricted vision of the working class. Tenement house manufacturing joined competition from "coolie" or Chinese labor and less skilled women as an assault on white manhood, on their freeborn rights. This working-class version of Republicanism championed the rights of man and linked the notion of a virtuous citizenry with economic equality. It had emerged out of the cauldron of Reconstruction politics as the dominant political philosophy among organizing workers, but Republicanism had its roots in the emergence of artisan self-activity earlier in the century. Laboring women had attempted to assert themselves into the Republican equation of natural rights with the superiority of the producing classes. But their quest after "self-rule" ran aground upon the competing conception of a specifically female virtue that substituted domesticity for citizenship. Free labor doctrines, embodied in the Fourteenth Amendment, embedded a gendered dichotomy: Free labor contrasted with slave labor; to be a slave was to be unmanly, a dependent, and like a woman. Such a set of interpretations shaped the terrain upon which workers resisted home labor.[4]

Ultimately the battle against tenement house cigarmaking, both in the workshop and through the law, was crucial in shaping the racialist, masculinist voluntarism of the American Federation of Labor (AFL). The lessons learned by Gompers and the Cigar Makers' International Union (CMIU) developed out of their prior understandings of gender, race, and class. Fought for the most part by groups of men against each other, this contest attempted to resolve the relation between home and workplace and what activities properly belonged to whom in which arena. The voices and needs of the mainly female and immigrant homeworkers were mute.

---

3 "A Translation of an Article in the *Social-Demokrat*," Oct. 24, 1875, in *The Samuel Gompers Papers*, 1, ed. Stuart B. Kaufman et al. (Urbana: Univ. of Illinois Press, 1986), 66–7; "Report on the Trade Union Activities of the United Cigarmakers of N[orth] A[merica] in 1874," trans. from the *Social-Demokrat*, Jan. 24, 1875, in ibid., 58. For examples of the slavery image, Demos, "Correspondence from New York," *Workingman's Advocate*, Nov. 11, 1874; Jacob Riis, *How the Other Half Lives* (New York: C. Scribner's Sons, 1890), 136; "Cigar Makers Speaking," *New York Sun*, Oct. 31, 1877.

4 Gwendolyn Mink, "The Lady and the Tramp: Gender, Race, and the Origins of the American Welfare State," in *Women, the State and Welfare*, ed. Linda Gordon (Madison: Univ. of Wisconsin Press, 1990), 92–122; Sean Wilentz, *Chants Democratic: New York City and the Rise of the American Working Class, 1788–1850* (New York: Oxford Univ. Press, 1984), 61–103; Christine Stansell, *City of Women: Sex and Class in New York, 1789–1860* (New York: Alfred A. Knopf, 1986), 146–53.

State policy and the transformation of cigarmaking

The rise of tenement house cigarmaking in the 1870s – and its demise thirty years later – demonstrates the distinction between industrial homework and household manufacturing. During the early decades of the nineteenth century, northern farm women (and often their children) rolled some of their husband's homegrown tobacco into cigars for local consumption. While a few workshop factories existed as early as the 1830s, cigarmaking grew as an artisan craft with the immigration of English, Dutch, and German craftsmen in the years before the Civil War.[5]

But state action, technological innovation, and new sources of immigration soon would transform the craft and its industry. Higher tobacco tariffs in the early 1860s encouraged native industry. The internal revenue law in 1862 taxed cigars produced in the United States, while later revenue laws required the manufacturer of cigars to file a bond on his factory. Other regulations made it more difficult for cigarmakers to purchase limited amounts of tobacco for small batch production. Reflecting on the impact of these regulations in 1877, the Ohio Bureau of Labor Statistics charged the federal government with "devising a system of taxation that drove the business into large manufactories, and compelled the cigar maker to become an employee working for wages, or a mere retailer without the privilege of making his own stock."[6]

Before the tightening of the internal revenue laws, "turn-in-jobs" dominated the trade in New York. The artisan craftsman would receive tobacco from the employer, for which he had to furnish "a deposit of almost double the value." Making the cigars at home, he would return them to the employer's storehouse, where "more often than not fault would be found with the work whether justifiably or not and the manufacturers would refuse to take the cigars which would be left upon the hands of the cigarmaker who would have to dispose of them as best he could." Employers would lock their warehouses when their supply of stock was greater than consumer demand, again denying payment for the cigarmaker's labor and forcing him

[5] Patricia A. Cooper, *Once a Cigar Maker: Men, Women, and Work Culture in American Cigar Factories, 1900–1919* (Urbana: Univ. of Illinois Press, 1987), 10–40; Dorothee Schneider, "The New York Cigarmakers Strike of 1877," *Labor History* 26 (Summer 1985), 325–52, supplemented by original materials in the Leslie Rowland files, Samuel Gompers Papers; Edith Abbott, *Women in Industry* (New York: D. Appleton and Co., 1910), 190–1; Bureau of the Census, "Special Report on Selected Industries," *Twelfth Census, 1900*, v. 9, pt. 3, (Washington, D.C.: GPO, 1902), 669–71; J. R. Dodge, "Statistics of Manufactures of Tobacco," in *Tenth Census, 1880: Report on the Production of Agriculture* (Washington, D.C.: GPO, 1883), 881–950.

[6] Dodge, "Statistics of Manufacturers," 24–30; "Special Report on Selected Industries," 671; Ohio Bureau of Labor Statistics, "Cigarmaking in Ohio," reprinted in *CMOJ*, May 10, 1878; New York State Cigar Makers Union, "Memorial to Congress at Convention," *Workingman's Advocate*, July 31, 1875.

to sell or barter cigars at less than their value to the neighborhood saloon-keeper.[7]

The new tax system was only one factor that pushed employers to organize factories. Employers took advantage of newly arrived skilled immigrants who lacked capital to be on their own. During the late sixties, the introduction of the mold by Germans further encouraged factory production. This device allowed less skilled workers to make cigars by separating bunch-making from rolling. When the men of the fledgling CMIU struck against its deployment, some employers replaced them with women, particularly recent immigrants from Bohemia who began arriving in 1869.[8]

The new technology was not very expensive and, by itself, does not account for both the growth of factories, with between twenty and fifty workers, and the birth of the tenement system during the same decade. "Concentration of capital and skill and . . . a thorough organization and division of labor" diminished cost of production. Meanwhile, the economic depression of 1873–77 forced employers to reduce costs further and quickened their output of cheap five-cent cigars. Many factories discharged employees or cut hours, further depressing wages and lowering working-class consumption. Some manufacturers responded by turning to the tenements.[9]

The tenement house system and early efforts to abolish it

Tenement house cigarmaking developed as an employer reaction to the economic depression of the 1870s. From only a few manufacturers in 1872, at least fifty deployed the system, often in multiple houses, as late as 1888. The size of the tenement-making population also varied. It accounted for about four-fifths of the entire New York product in 1877, the year of the Great Strike of the cigarmakers, when at least 1,000 families (5,000 people) worked in the tenements, and between a seventh and an eighth of the entire trade in 1885. After the licensing of homework in tenements as a regulatory measure, 775 families (4,075 people) were still known to have been making cigars in 1901; others were doubtless doing so without licenses. While such

---

[7] Samuel Gompers, *Seventy Years of Life and Labor: An Autobiography* (New York: Dutton, 1925), 1:107.

[8] Cooper, *Once a Cigar Maker*, 12–19; Gompers, *Seventy Years*, 1:108; Abbott, *Women at Work*, 196; "Samuel Gompers and Early Cigarmakers' Unions in New York City," *The Samuel Gompers Papers*, 1:45–7. For the importation of Bohemians, Daniel Harris, Ford Committee, 366–7; U.S. House of Representatives, 57th Cong., 1st sess., "Effect of the Foreign Born on Cigar-Making Trade," *Reports of the Industrial Commission on Immigration*, v. 15, pt. 3 (Washington, D.C.: GPO, 1901), 385–8.

[9] Dodge, "Statistics of Manufacturers," 21, notes that while cigar manufacturing doubled between 1870 and 1880, it stagnated during 1873–77, the panic years. See also "Falling Off in Demand for Cigars Since the Panic," *New York Times*, Nov. 3, 1873; "Workingmen as They Are. How the Panic Affects the Laboring Classes," *New York Daily Tribune*, Jan. 31, 1874.

figures represented approximations at best, most observers agreed that the introduction of new technologies, along with the union label (begun in 1880 for higher-priced cigars), had limited the system by the first decade of the new century.[10]

To recoup the internal revenue tax, a manufacturer would buy or lease a tenement house, capable of holding up to twenty families, and list it as a single factory. Often he would maintain a block of tenements, called a "nicotine hive," linking their outside gates. He would keep one apartment for storage, office, and packing purposes and rent the ground floor to a grocer or saloon-keeper. He then would compel employees to rent apartments of two or three rooms for more than the going rate as a condition of employment, withholding the rent from wages. These apartments were typical of New York's tenement districts – twelve or fifteen by twenty feet for the living/work room, with smaller and darker bedrooms; they lacked proper ventilation or sanitation.[11]

If a worker had earned less than the month's rent the first week, often the employer would provide credit in the tenement store. This procedure further enmeshed the cigarmaker in relations of "dependency" much as the owner of a company town tied workers to their jobs through debt and the threat of eviction. Employers still required deposits for tobacco. A correspondent to the *Workingman's Advocate* complained, "The independent spirit necessary to a good citizen, is endangered by the experiment of stringent rules, allowing the boss and his tools to enter the rooms at any time to watch and control the working, thus making a penitentiary of a place where the tender, sacred family ties should rule supreme." As one German cigarmaker protested, in words that resonate with the masculinist Republicanism central to the labor movement, they "were ruled over with a sway like that of a despot."[12]

Not only did the tenement house employer save factory rent and utilities by forcing workers to use their homes as his place of production, but he profited from rearranging the labor process. Stripping and casing became incorporated into the cigarmaker's job; the cigarmaker's children prepared the tobacco, as it

10 "The Cigar Makers' Strike," *New York Herald*, Oct. 17, 1877, reported Sutro and Newmark as the first to introduce the system. [Adolph Strasser,] "Appendix: Cigar-Makers' International Union," in *The Labor Movement: The Problem of Today*, ed. George E. McNeill (Boston: A. M. Bridgman & Co.,1887), 603; Strasser testimony, *Report on Capital and Labor*, 1:451; "President's Biennial Report," *CMOJ*, Sept. 1883; "The Tenement-House Cigar Law," *New York Tribune*, Sept. 30, 1883 (which gives twenty-five firms having tenements with about five thousand workers); State of New York, *Thirteenth Annual Report of the Bureau of Labor Statistics for the Year 1895* (Albany, N.Y.: Wynkeop Hallenbeck Crawford Co., 1896), 552. Robert W. De Forest and Lawrence Veiller, *The Tenement House Problem: Including the Report of the New York State Tenement House Commission of 1900* (New York: 1903), 1:53.

11 Gompers Testimony, Ford Committee, 394–6; "Pestilence in the Cigar," *New York Sun*, Sept. 26, 1874; "The Wonderful Strike," *New York Sun*, Nov. 27, 1877.

12 Vinvenzia Veprer testimony, Ford Committee, 373–7; letter from P. to *Workingman's Advocate*, Aug. 22, 29, 1874; "Perils of Tenement Workshops," *New York Tribune*, Sept. 28, 1874.

were, for nothing. The employer's greatest advantage came from low piece rates. One reporter calculated that "a man who could earn in a factory a little over \$2 a day, would net only about \$5 a week" in a tenement. Tenement house workers, however, did not work for the same hours as factory cigarmakers nor did they labor alone. Given the meagerness of the piece rate, which continuously fell during the 1870s, fourteen-hour days were common; some even made cigars on Sunday.[13]

The B family typified such family labor groups. No one spoke English in this family whose children never went to school. A baby played in the stored tobacco leaves and with old cups of paste, while its six- or seven-year-old sister minded him and, with her stunted twelve-year-old brother, stripped tobacco. Their consumptive sixteen-year-old sister joined parents and a boarder in bunching and rolling tobacco into cigars. "The light room serves as reception room, parlor, drawing room, kitchen, playground. . . . In this room the wrappers, binders and fillers are stripped and prepared, here the fillers are spread out on the floor to dry by the heat of the stove on which the bread dumpling soup. . . is simmering," reported a visitor. The dark bedrooms stored between 150 and 200 pounds of wet tobacco, as well as the family's private effects. With six persons working, they earned \$18.80 a week at \$4.00 per 1,000 cigars. With rent \$10.00 a month, food \$15.00 a week, the Bs had \$1.57 to spend on clothing, recreation, and medicine for four children and three adults.[14]

Among such workers, Bohemians predominated, with women reportedly the more proficient. Cigarmakers composed more than half of the nearly thirteen thousand Bohemians in New York City.[15] Most were from rural regions where women had rolled cigars in manufactories, while men continued to farm or practice other crafts. Unable to find work upon immigration, Bohemian men either learned bunch-making or rolling from their women, some of whom became employed in cigar workshops soon after their arrival, so that together they could form a cigarmaking team. One Czech worker defended the resulting tenement system: "Women could make better cigars than men, and it was therefore necessary that the wives should help their husbands."[16]

---

[13] "Pestilence in the Cigar." This article provides the most astute analysis of the profits to be gained: about \$2,500 on rents, \$650 savings on stripping, and close to \$500 for casing, for each house. "The Cigar Trade," *New York Times*, Sept. 28, 1874.

[14] "A Scrap of Truth," *Progress*, June 23, 1885.

[15] The precise numbers of Bohemians in the city are difficult to determine because they are first counted in "Austria-Hungry (including Bohemia)." In 1880, this figure numbered 16,937, up to 47,514 in 1890, when a separate table lists the number of Bohemians as 12,322. "The Foreign Immigrant in New York City," *Reports of the Industrial Commission on Immigration*, 467 (table 8), 469 (table 14). One 1874 report listed Bohemian cigarmakers as 4,000 women and between 2,000 and 3,000 men, nearly half of all cigarmakers. "Pestilence in the Cigar," *New York Sun*, Sept. 26, 1874.

[16] Abbott, *Women in Industry*, 196–201; "Foreign Life in New York," *New York Tribune*, Nov. 7, 1877; "The Tenement Horrors," *New York Herald*, Oct. 5, 1874; "A Tenement Trade," *New York Daily Tribune*, Sept. 23, 1874.

Despite women's skill, manufacturers considered their husbands to be the head of the cigarmaking team. Sharing a belief in male dominance, the women themselves attempted to maintain the Old World patriarchal family structure. Journalist Jacob Riis reported one woman as saying, while she continued her household duties, "'Aye . . . it would be nice for sure to have father work at his trade.' Then what a home she could make for them, and how happy they would be." Newspapers suggested that the wage-earning Bohemian women offered a model for women's rights advocates, but these immigrants accepted an inherited gender system that elevated the father as the leader within the family unit of labor.[17]

Unionized cigarmakers also celebrated such a gender division of power. From the beginning, the organized cigarmakers' campaign against the tenement house system combined a discourse of horror and disease with an ideology of gender that resembled Victorian notions of womanhood, manhood, and homelife but was rooted in artisanal culture. Skilled workers believed in respectability, hard work, masculinity, and protection of the weak. Like those organized into the Knights of Labor, they felt women's wage labor compatible with domesticity, although wage labor under exploitative conditions sullied womanhood and destroyed childlife.[18] Masculinity was central to the work culture of cigarmakers, whether they were native-born, English, or German. They associated the deskilling of their craft with its feminization. Anglo-Saxon maleness certainly defined the CMIU which, in the late 1870s, reacted to defeats by the tenement house manufacturers by turning to an exclusiveness that would characterize the AFL well into the next century.[19] But they connected their assault against tenement cigarmaking as a destroyer of the home with an attack on the economic exploitation inherent in the system. Later campaigns waged by middle-class reformers against industrial homework would mute this outrage at the bosses and capitalists.

The first significant attack against tenement manufacturing set a pattern that would continue throughout the century. Charging that contagious diseases within the tenements threatened "the neighborhood and the city," along with the consumer of cigars, trade unionists appealed to the health of the public to rid themselves of the tenement menace to their economic well-being. They

[17] Of course, Riis could be projecting his notions of woman's place onto the speaker. Jacob Riis, *How the Other Half Lives*, 142; Jane E. Robbins, "The Bohemian Women in New York," *Charities*, Dec. 3, 1904, 194–6.

[18] Susan Levine, *Labor's True Woman: Carpet Weavers, Industrialization, and Labor Reform in the Gilded Age* (Philadelphia, Pa.: Temple Univ. Press, 1984); David Montgomery, "Workers Control of Machine Production in the Nineteenth Century," *Labor History* 17 (1976), 485–509; Sherri Broder, "Informing the 'Cruelty': The Monitoring of Respectability in Philadelphia's Working-Class Neighborhoods in the Late Nineteenth Century," *Radical America* 21 (July-Aug. 1987), 34–47.

[19] Cooper, *Once a Cigar Maker*, 41–122; Gompers, *Seventy Years*, 1:183–91.

demanded in September 1874 that the New York City Board of Health strictly enforce tenement house laws. John Swinton, the labor journalist elected chair of a multiethnic meeting, contrasted the harms of the system with the humanity of the crowd, who became noble (male) citizens of the republic, fighting for the welfare of the entire community, rich and poor alike. These ordinary citizens were trying "to guard your families, to protect your health, to elevate your lives and your manhood."[20]

Fifty "turn-in-jobbers," as tenement house workmen still were called, protested this meeting a few days later and attempted to hold a mass meeting the following Sunday. Chaired by their foreman, David Reiss, these meetings suggested the divisions within cigarmaking ranks by place of employment. (They also revealed the power over tenement workers of the manufacturers – who sent letters of support to one meeting.) Reiss argued, in terms that the court of appeals would return to a decade later, "If any kind of cigar making is injurious, every kind is." Taking the line that the Board of Health would sustain, he claimed that working in a factory was more injurious because there were more workmen. He exhorted "his fellow workmen simply to stand up manfully for their right to pursue their self-supporting occupation in the way that best suited them."[21]

When it came to gendered understandings of masculinity, foreman Reiss and the tenement house men shared with John Swinton and the journeyman cigarmakers, as the factory workers were called, a discourse that associated manhood with freedom. But while both groups saw women and children as under the power of men, they had different conceptions of what was best for these subordinates. The tenement workers held a more traditional idea of family economy to which their foreman appealed. "It was better for men to work in their own homes, because they could work when they pleased and by the help of their wives and children, who could not work in outside factories, they could make much more money," Reiss argued. Then he charged, as the manufacturers' association later would, that the CMIU "opposed the tenement system . . . because they wished to prevent women from working and earning money." Rather than making a plea for women's freedom, Reiss interpreted women's right to work as a right to earn money within the confines of both domestic ideology and the actual restraints of family labor.[22]

Bohemian tenement workers themselves looked at the matter from a practical rather than an ideological viewpoint. They explained the necessity of having their more proficient wives working alongside them and highlighted the economic need that lay beneath their language of health, family, and

---

[20] "Death in the Tenements," *New York Sun*, Sept. 28, 1874; "Perils of Tenement Workshops."

[21] "The Cigar Men's Quarrel," *New York Sun*, Sept. 29, 1874; "The Tenement Horrors;" "Home News," *New York Tribune*, Oct. 5, 1875; "Tenement Cigar-Making," *New York Sun*, Oct. 5, 1874.

[22] "Tenement Cigar-Making"; "The Tenement Horrors."

freedom: "It is well for the authorities to do away with the evils of the system, as it is detrimental to health, but if they abolish it they should provide shops where workmen may earn enough to support their families. Working at home a family can make $25 a week if they work fourteen or fifteen hours a day, but that cannot be done in the shops."[23]

Against such a position, shop workmen argued "that a union of all the cigar makers would fix uniform good wages for all the men, and would release the women to attend to household duties and the children to go to school." While some men in both groups embraced the more modern concept of the family wage, its tenets were central to the definition of masculinity set forth by union workers. In addition, trade unionists defended working-class women's rights to motherhood, as they attacked the conditions that led "mothers [who] while nursing their babes made cigars, so that the infants inhaled the deadly nicotinous odor."[24]

In a series of powerful articles for the German-language *New York Volkszeitung*, written a few years later during the campaign to legislate tenement cigarmaking out of existence, Samuel Gompers most forcefully articulated this understanding of womanhood and homelife that would come to dominate organized labor under the AFL. This social construction of the home divided it from work. Respectability and sentimentality clothed his vision of the family and woman's place within it. He indicted the poison of the tenements for not only sapping the health of workers but for destroying the moral fiber of the home. Dust, scraps, stems, and filth made it difficult for the housekeeper "to keep her apartment somewhat clean" in these places without water, where disease and excrement mixed with the making of cigars. The pressures of piecework, he charged, robbed families of homelife. The housewife served smoked sausage instead of cooking, and the parents sat on the only chairs to eat it while their children crouched like animals. Not only was the work of such small children criminal (they should have been in school), but Gompers implied that homework destroyed the very basis of life, the mother-child bond. "In one room we saw a mother who had just begun to nurse her child but had not interrupted her work of making wrappers." Other mothers, he reported, rolled cigars while their dying babies seemed to cry, " 'How can I stay alive in such a place?!' " Intent upon exposing the evils of tenement house work, he was unable to see the heroic struggles of whole families or the resourcefulness of such mothers.[25]

The Board of Health – which conducted investigations and official visits with due notice to employers, who then set about cleaning up – rejected such

[23] "The Tenement Horrors"; "Tenement Cigar Making."
[24] "Home News."
[25] "A Translation of a Series of Articles by Samuel Gompers on Tenement-House Cigar Manufacture in New York City," in Kaufman, ed., *The Samuel Gompers Papers*, 1:172–3, 180–7.

an interpretation. Its assumptions matched those of tenement manufacturers. Individual factory workers earned more but, with all family members working in the tenements (including children, the old, and the disabled), "many earn money who would otherwise be idle, and the aggregate income is greatly increased, enabling the purchase of many comforts not within reach of the factory worker." A citizens' committee rebutted all the report's points and focused on the three dollars a week wages earned for sixteen-hour days by an entire family. Its own investigation showed that the factories were superior on all counts; it reminded the public that "the factories are but working places for adults for a stay of nine hours a day, whereas the tenements is [sic] the home of the whole family, and their exclusive residence." The cigarmakers called for the removal of the Board but in their weak state lacked political clout. Later tenement house inspections refuted the Board of Health study.[26]

The year 1874 would not be the last time that the CMIU turned to the state to eradicate tenement competitors. On the local level, it continued to argue for prohibition as a sanitary measure,[27] but it pushed for federal regulation through taxation. During the Great Strike of 1877, the CMIU demanded that Internal Revenue Commissioner Green B. Raum abolish the system by enforcing a rule that essentially turned every apartment into a factory needing its own bond. Raum "was not disposed to disturb existing arrangements." But the United States Court for the District of Columbia defined a factory as "an entire room separated from other parts of the building by actual and permanent partition," making the practice of bonding entire tenement blocks as a single factory illegal. Charging that the government lost two hundred and fifty thousand dollars a year, the union demanded enforcement of existing rules. Raum, regarded as "agent of the manufacturers," merely promised "a careful examination."[28]

When the commissioner acted, he applied the ruling on partitions only to small manufacturers. The CMIU called upon these manufacturers, many of whom resembled the independent artisan cigarmakers of a decade before, to join the protest.[29] The Senate amended its proposal to prohibit cigar manufac-

---

[26] "Cigar Making," *Workingman's Advocate*, Feb. 15, 1875; "The Cigar-Makers' Protest," *The New York Times*, Dec. 28, 1874; "Fighting the Health Board," *New York Sun*, Dec. 28, 1874; "Cigar-Making in Tenement-Houses: Report of the Sanitary Inspectors to the Board of Health," *Tobacco Leaf*, Nov. 11, 1874; "Tenement-House Reform," *New York Times*, Aug. 3, 1879; "Tenement House Cigar Factories Endanger the Public Health," *CMOJ*, Jan. 10, 1880; "Homes of Poor People," *New York Tribune*, Jan. 8, 1882.

[27] "Pest-Holes," *CMOJ*, July 10, 1879.

[28] "Tenement Cigar-Making. Commissioner Raum Threatening to Root Up the Whole System," *World* (N.Y.), Jan. 9, 1878; "Tenement-House Cigar Factories," *CMOJ*, Feb. 10, 1878; "Cigar Makers Again in Trouble," *New York Tribune*, Nov. 5, 1878; letter from President A. Strasser to Friend McDonnell, *Paterson Labor Standard*, Nov. 23, 1878; "What Constitutes a Lawful Cigar Factory," *CMOJ*, Apr. 10, 1878; letter to Mr. A. Strasser from Green B. Raum, Nov. 20, 1878, reprinted in *CMOJ*, Dec. 10, 1878.

[29] "The Commissioners' Duty," *CMOJ*, Dec. 10, 1878.

turing in rooms used for dwelling or domestic purposes to include the small manufacturer, a change that led to its defeat. Arnold Strasser retorted in terms that tied the defense of an unsullied domestic sphere to increasingly nativist rhetoric: "There can be no doubt that the law, if rigidly enforced, would effect [sic] small manufacturers to a certain degree, especially those who are living and working with their families in *Chinese Bunks*." [30]

The CMIU responded to legislative failure by urging renewed effort. Locals around the country held protest meetings. Relying upon the image of the independent citizen-father, one in Boston resolved "if we are to be compelled to live in small compartments, the same as our co-laborers in New York, we cannot be responsible for the moral or mental condition of our offspring." Detroit's local protested the impact of the system on their wages. Class rhetoric entered these meetings. Strasser spoke of the interests of the people as opposed to those of property which the Internal Revenue Commissioner desired to protect. [31]

Under CMIU pressure, Commissioner Raum finally investigated the New York tenements in 1879. He concluded that however objectionable the system, there existed no direct evidence of fraud in internal revenue collection and thus he could not act without congressional mandate. Frustration with the federal government would send the economically weak CMIU to lobby before the New York State legislature. [32]

The great strike of 1877

This turn to legislative lobbying – with its virulent, nearly hysterical on-slaughts against tenement house "pest holes" – was a reaction to the failure of the trade's general strike in 1877. As one employer later reflected: "At the time of the great strike, the factory hands were idle and the workers in the tenement houses were busy. The tenement-house system thus broke the strike and the labor unions have worked ever since to break up the tenement-house system." [33] His memory was more self-serving than accurate, for the relation-ship of tenement to shop proved less problematic in 1877 than it would become afterward.

Inspired by the railway rebellion of the summer, nearly fifteen thousand New York cigarmakers, about three-quarters of the trade, walked out in mid-October demanding higher wages. "The Factories Now Following the Lead of the Tenements. Cigar Making Generally Suspended Throughout the City,"

[30] "Legislation Against Tenement House Factories," *CMOJ*, Mar. 10, 1879; "Read and Judge," *CMOJ*, May 10, 1879; "The Tax on Tobacco," *New York Tribune*, Feb. 13, 1879.
[31] "Legislation Against Tenement House Factories"; "Read and Judge"; "International President's Annual Report," *CMOJ*, Oct. 10, 1880.
[32] "Read and Judge."
[33] Louis Hass in "Cigar-Making in Tenement-Houses," *New York Tribune*, March 14, 1883.

announced the *New York Sun*. Many in the shops earned four dollars per thousand cigars, but were asking for five dollars, while those in the tenements were paid two or three dollars per thousand. Some employers treated factory and tenement house workers differently, only reducing the wage rates of the factory labor force and ending these men's customary right to smoke at work, but others saw an opportunity in the strike to slash the wages of all. Generally, tenement workers asked for a dollar raise, sometimes with a dollar reduction in rent. Some insisted that their employer landlords provide gas and light "on the floors." By mid-November, they further demanded that homes "be cleaned and whitewashed" and "that only union men should be employed." Shop workers asked for varied rates, depending on whether they were strippers, bunchers, or rollers.[34]

CMIU Local 144, led by Gompers, organized the strikers into the Cigar Makers Central Organization, with Strasser as president and Marie Hausler, a Bohemian factory worker, as vice-president. Each shop, factory, and tenement sent delegates to this central committee, which collected and allocated strike funds (including the entire treasury of Local 144), ran commissary stores, and coordinated strategy. In December, the strikers would operate a cooperative factory to generate funds for the cause. In its organization and mutual aid practices, including assessments for strike relief, the central body resembled the CMIU.[35]

From the start, tenement house workers, no matter their sex, had equal representation. When the Central Organization polled workers on whether to strike a given employer, those in the tenements counted just as much as those in the shops and often forced the inside workers out. Women factory workers also were fully enfranchised. Both groups were extremely militant. Employers accused Bohemian women strikers of "having molested other girls" scabbing in one major factory. Rollers at Mendel Bros. struck for a dollar more, but the tenement house workers asked for two dollars. When a number of the shop men reported to work a few days later, the tenement workers, "partly by persuasion, partly by intimidation, prevented the shop-workers from going in, and induced them to join in the strike." When Benjamin Lichtenstein of Lichtenstein Bros., one of the largest employers of tenement labor, early on "induced" the

---

[34] "The Cigar Makers' Strike," *New York Sun*, Oct. 16, 1877; "Dissatisfied Cigar-Makers," *New York Tribune*, Aug. 6, 1877; "Strike of Cigar-Makers," *New York Times*, Aug. 29, 1877; *New York Times*, Oct. 18, 1877; "The Striking Cigar-Makers," *New York Sun*, Nov. 11, 1877; "The Cigar-Maker's Fair," *World* (N.Y.) Dec. 28, 1877, reports fifteen thousand went out, but only three to four hundred went back even at their old wages. "Strike of the Cigar-Makers," *New York Tribune*, Sept. 6, 1877; "The Cigar Makers' Strike;" "Discontent with Wages," *New York Tribune*, Oct. 16, 1877; "The Great Cigar Strike," *New York Sun*, Oct. 17, 1877; "The Cigarmakers' Strike," *New York Herald*, Oct. 17, 1877; "The Cigar Makers' Strike," *New York Times*, Oct. 18, 1877.

[35] "The Wonderful Strike;" "Changed Aspect of the Strike," *New York Times*, Dec. 9, 1877; Gompers, *Seventy Years*, 1:140–55; Schneider, "The New York Cigarmakers' Strike of 1877."

actual owner of a tenement to evict several families in his employ, tenants "hustled him out of the house together with foreman Mr. Schmidt and threw many packages of tobacco belonging to Lichtenstein on the sidewalk." Though previously unorganized, the tenement workers joined the union, sometimes en masse as with five hundred employees of Straiton & Storm, the largest manufacturer in the nation.[36]

Yet the CMIU-dominated leadership ignored the behavior of female factory and tenement workers. Their construction of the worker as male led Gompers and Strasser to separate women from the realm of worker and homes from workplaces. They condemned tenement laborers as the source of CMIU's woes. Determined to put an end to the tenement system by ending its profitability through higher wages, they demanded that all be allowed to work in factories. In 1877 they blamed the system, not the individuals caught within its web. But when the strike was lost, Gompers disingenuously recalled that the tenement house workers "all went out on strike without organization or discipline. We union men saw our hard-earned achievements likely to vanish because of this reckless precipitate action without consultation with our union." Such an account justified opposition to tenement house competition as it upheld the superiority of the craft union.[37]

The more desperate plight of the tenement workers, who had no savings, certainly drained the strike fund. By late October many of these Bohemian families had pawned or sold their household furniture.[38] The series of evictions that began in November, for rent to employers remained unpaid during the strike, created another battleground that absorbed limited resources and energy. Each eviction required a search for a new apartment to rehouse the family. While some individuals provided free housing and lawyers volunteered services, resettlement proved costly. Employers went to extremes to force people into the streets: One small manufacturer "removed the doors and windows from the rooms of a family of strikers;" another larger firm "started a sweatroom on the first floor." In less than two months employers secured 1,980 warrants, but evicted only 680. They claimed that new workers refilled the tenements.[39]

---

[36] "The Cigarmakers' Struggle;" "Ordering Men to Strike," *New York Sun*, Oct. 23, 1877; "Demands on Employers," *New York Tribune*, Oct. 17, 1877; "Striking Cigar Makers Winning," *New York Sun*, Oct. 11, 1877; "Great Uprising of Cigar-Makers in New York," *CMOJ*, Oct. 15, 1877; "The Offer to Cigarmakers," *New York Sun*, Nov. 17, 1877.

[37] "Increasing the Great Strike," *New York Sun*, Oct. 18, 1877; [Strasser], "To the Cigarmakers of the U.S. and Canada," *CMOJ*, Dec. 10, 1877; Gompers, *Seventy Years*, 1:147.

[38] See report in *World* (N.Y.), Oct. 24, 1877.

[39] "Strikers Getting Excited," *World* (N.Y.), Nov. 8, 1877; "The Cigarmakers' Strike," *New York Sun*, Nov. 3, 1877; "Ejecting Striking Cigar-Makers," *New York Tribune*, Nov. 8, 1877; "The Long Strike Waning," *New York Times*, Nov. 8, 1877; "Seventy-Three Families Ejected," *New York Tribune*, Dec. 5, 1877; "Dissension Among the Cigar-Makers," *New York Tribune*, Dec. 15, 1877; "Dispossessing Cigar-Makers," *New York Tribune*, Nov. 21, 1877.

Yet the evictions also provided some of the strike's finest moments. Workers organized to support each other and publicize the manufacturers' heartless tactics. With music playing and flags waving, the cigarmakers ushered families with their household goods onto wagons and a new life. The display of American and German, but not Bohemian, flags reflected the leadership's combination of patriotism with insensitivity to Bohemian nationalism at a time when the fight for an independent Czechoslovakia still engaged Bohemians abroad. An even more colorful procession opened the cooperative factory; shops held their own banners, declaring "No more tenement houses for cigarmakers," "A fair day's pay for a fair day's work," and "Heaven frowns upon those who grind the faces of the poor." Tenements along the parade route also displayed mottoes that counteracted images of exploitation with a universal language of fairness. Such parades built community support, which was evident in neighbors', shopkeepers', other unions', and even landlords' offers of housing and rent money. The city's nineteen Bohemian benefit societies pledged all their funds to the strikers.[40]

Gender provided the most powerful of all symbols in this struggle between "labor" and "capital." The Faborsky incident demonstrated how assumptions about domesticity, motherhood, and gender traits could create sympathy for the strikers. Levy & Uhlman evicted strike leader Faborsky as a warning to the nearly hundred other residents of its tenement. His wife "lay writhing [in childbirth] and groaning on a rude pallet" as city marshals removed the furniture to the street. While the employers claimed the woman to be "shamming," the papers emphasized her condition, reporting how the bed, when placed back in the tenement, injured her by caving in. In contrast to the employers' cruelty stood the kindhearted saloonkeeper who offered to pay the rent. "They treated her most shamefully and unmanly," the *Cigar Makers' Official Journal* reported. Outrage erupted again when a pregnant woman on a picket line was "seized with premature labor" after being pushed down by policemen. Employers appeared to have bought off the police and the courts, who had no respect for working-class motherhood.[41]

Women workers also gained symbolic value by virtue of being "women." The papers reported male strikers "abusing" working girls as they left the cigar factories.[42] The employers promoted the hiring of "American" girls to take the place of foreign strikers. In a defense of their manhood, the National Cigar

[40] "The Cigar-Makers' Strike," *New York Times*, Nov. 4, 1877; "Cigar Strike Notes," *New York Herald*, Nov. 9, 1877; "Persistency of the Cigar-Makers," *New York Tribune*, Nov. 24, 1877; "The Striking Cigar-Makers," *World* (N.Y.), Nov. 22, 1877; "The Strike of the Cigar-Makers," *New York Tribune*, Nov. 14, 1877; "The Cigarmakers' Struggle," *New York Sun*, Nov. 16, 1877.

[41] "Stripping a Home," *New York Sun*, Nov. 8, 1877; "Ejecting Striking Cigar-Makers," *New York Tribune*, Nov. 8, 1877; "Strikers Getting Excited," *World* (N.Y.), Nov. 8, 1877; "Brooklyn Joining the Strike"; news notes, *CMOJ*, Nov. 10, 1877; "The Cigar-Makers' Strike. Indignation Getting Hot Over Another Reported Outrage," *World* (N.Y.), Nov. 10, 1877.

[42] "The Cigarmakers," *New York Sun*, Nov. 15, 1877.

Manufacturers' Association (NCMA) resolved "that females more readily learn the trade than males." These employers defended tenement manufacturing by arguing that the union was trying "to throw out of business many women who could not or would not work in shops." Yet they readily admitted that shop women were "workers whose services may be depended upon at low wages." And women did not demand "smokes." By late November they had hired about four thousand girls. The union claimed that this gendered shift in work force was "anything but a success"; one firm actually had dismissed "young girl apprentices" and taken back its sixty to eighty tenement families. When the strike collapsed in early January, the *World* intensified the ideological battle over women's place in the trade by proclaiming, "American Girls Bringing Victory to the Manufacturers."[43]

In the public debate during the course of the strike the concept of *rights* became associated with working-class masculinity. The district courts may have defended the rights of girl strikebreakers to work; they certainly supported such tenement women as Emma Giess. When charging another woman with assault, she justified home cigarmaking as allowing the earning of "enough money to live on . . . and I would rather do that than live on charity."[44] But these rights interfered with the right claimed by CMIU men to defend their families. Those unable to provide "bread and shoes for their children" and send them to school were like slaves; cigarmakers should be able to maintain "the American standard of living." Gompers most powerfully linked manhood with protection of women and a living, family wage. He rallied the strikers at a mass meeting in Brooklyn: "We are now called upon as men and fathers of families to make one grand effort to better our miserable condition, which has been thrust upon us for the past five years, and, if required, we must force a different condition of affairs." With manhood rights threatened, he warned manufacturers that if they "imported" any Chinese, "they would be responsible for any violent action that might be taken to protect their wives and children, and provide them with bread. (Applause)."[45]

The concept of rights was too powerful to be confined to Gompers' working-class cult of masculinity. Union men also held a high opinion of their women, who were comrades in the struggle for workers' rights. After all, female members of the CMIU made up nearly half the audience at many rallies. As one unionist from Cincinnati declared: "I would to Heaven,

---

43 "The Cigar-Makers' Strike," *New York Times*, Nov. 12, 1877; "The Cigar-Makers' Strike Extending," *New York Daily Tribune*, Oct. 24, 1877; "Girls Making Good Cigars," *New York Sun*, Nov. 26, 1877; "The Cigar-Makers' Strike," *The World (N.Y)*, Nov. 27, 1877; "Cigar-Makers Still Determined," *New York Times*, Nov. 18, 1877; "The Wonderful Strike;" "The Cigar-Makers' Strike," *World* (N.Y.), Jan. 5, 1878; "Is the Cigar Strike Ended?" ibid., Jan. 1, 1878.

44 "The Cigar-Makers Strike," *World* (N.Y.), Nov. 16, 1877.

45 "The Cigar-Makers' Strike," *New York Daily Tribune*, Oct. 31, 1877; "Great Mass Meeting in Cooper's Institute," *CMOJ*, Jan. 15, 1878; "The Cigar-Makers' Strike," *New York World*, Nov. 9, 1877.

we had women in Cincinnati, such as you have in New York, all glory to them! They are genuine women, and as mothers, sisters, shopmates, we can work hand and heart with them, in killing oppression and elevating our trade."[46]

Rights could exist apart from the breadwinner's protective role. While Bohemian men resented the ways that employers curtailed the ability of their families to earn a living wage, single women working inside factories stood up for "natural rights." Strike activist Marie Hausler, who charged that the tenement system degraded women, expressed "the disappointment her countrymen had felt on discovering that the tyranny of the old country had been imitated in the new." But Gompers and his supporters linked rights with gender identity as they urged the Bohemians, to "strike for your rights like men and [the bosses] can no longer play the despot."[47]

Employers, though not a monolithic group, shared with Gompers this language of gender. Larger manufacturers, many of whom had tenements, dominated the forty-member NCMA. With the strike, this group had locked out employees and evicted tenants. It defended the tenement house system as beneficial, indeed preferred by workers, "as the cigarmaker claimed he could do the full amount of work and attend to household duties at the same time." Cigarmakers were "he," even if the rationale for their labor was "household duties," women's work. But soon the NCMA abandoned this stance for the right of employers to structure the production process as they saw fit.[48]

Meanwhile, small manufacturers condemned the NCMA, some sympathizing with the strikers, with whom they held a common notion of male respectability. D. Hirsch, the employer of Samuel Gompers, blamed the tenement house system for the strike and for the plight of the cigarmakers. "The cigar-makers, as a class, are very respectable and intelligent people, who would be contented with reasonable treatment from their employers," he told the New York Times, "but that they have been compelled to submit to repeated reductions until they have finally been reduced to a point almost of starvation." Even among small manufacturers, class solidarity predominated. Though many "opposed" the tenement system "because it ruins our trade," they could "not go against those manufacturers who have them." For in the struggle of capital against labor, they could "not go against bosses."[49]

[46] "As Determined As Ever," New York Sun, Nov. 1, 1877; "The Cigar-Makers' Strike," World (N.Y.), Oct. 31, 1877; "Correspondence," CMOJ, Nov. 1877.

[47] "Cigar Makers Locked Out," New York Sun, Oct. 21, 1877; "General Strike of Cigar Makers," New York Daily Tribune, Oct. 15, 1877.

[48] "Statement," Tobacco Leaf, Oct. 24, 1877; "The Cigar-Makers' Strike Extending"; "The Strikers Still Firm," New York Times, Oct. 24, 1877; "The Cigar-Makers' Strike," ibid., Nov. 12, 1877.

[49] "The Cigar-Makers' Strike," New York Times, Sept. 2, 1877; "Cigarmakers' Strike," New York Sun, Oct. 19, 1877; "The Cigarmakers' Strike," ibid., Nov. 2, 1877; "What the Tenement House Monopolists Say" and "Opinions of Manufacturers Opposed to Tenement House Factories," both in CMOJ, Mar. 10, 1879; "Tenement-House Cigars," World (N.Y.), Jan. 13, 1878.

By mid-December, the employers had all hands required and would not hire any union members. At the height of the strike only twenty shops with nine hundred workers agreed to union demands. Some employers had enough stock to wait out the strike; others began to manufacture cigars in Pennsylvania, Long Island, and New Jersey. But when the CMIU finally announced the defeat of the strike in February 1878, Strasser did so with fiery optimism. Cigarmakers across the nation had benefited from the drop in New York's production; they gained reduced hours of labor, increased employment, higher wages, and decreased exposure to the tenement house system and its unhealthy products. Continued agitation against the tenement house system over the next few years belied this prognosis.[50]

Employers were "glad to get their old hands back again without asking whether they are union members." While some dropped the tenement system, others aggressively searched for new markets for such cigars. The union would charge that manufacturers joined the anti-Chinese movement to protect tenement house production from lower cost-production. This anger at employers suggests that the CMIU might have sought to improve the conditions of Chinese labor instead of calling for its exclusion.[51]

By the end of the strike tenement house workers had become another tool by which manufacturers drove down the wages of those the union deemed the true cigarmakers, skilled northern European men.[52] The cause certainly had suffered because so many lacked homes separate from workplaces. The CMIU might have built on the desire of tenement workers to improve conditions instead of turning on them and refusing them membership in the union as long as they worked in the tenements. They might have squarely blamed the manufacturers, who after all had responded to the tenement workers' militancy with the trump card of eviction. Instead, the Great Strike taught the CMIU to be wary of the unorganized and unskilled, often female, immigrants because they could drag the more skilled, organized sector down with them. That this response was not unrealistic, given the power of capital and weakness of labor, did not make it inevitable. The Great Strike showed that homeworkers might be organized if they were seen as part of the working class and not dismissed as merely underminers of factory standards. Some members of the CMIU, who would secede to form the Cigar Makers' Progressive Union

[50] "The Strike of the Cigar-Makers," *New York Tribune*, Nov. 14, 1877; "The Cigar Manufacturers," *New York Times*, Dec. 16, 1877; "The Cigar Strike," *World* (N.Y.), Dec. 17, 1877; "Events of the Grand Strike," *CMOJ*, Dec. 24, 1877; "A Clique of Conspirators," *CMOJ*, Jan. 15, 1878; "Turbulent Cigarmakers," *New York Sun*, Jan. 6, 1878; "Ending the Cigar Strike," ibid., Feb. 4, 1878; "The Strike," *CMOJ*, Feb. 10, 1878; "Practical Results," ibid., July 10, 1878; but see, "State of the Trade," ibid., Aug. 10, 1879.

[51] "Ending the Cigar Strike;" "Items of Interest," *CMOJ*, Feb. 10, 1878; "The Situation in San Francisco," ibid., Jan. 10, 1879.

[52] "The Dangers That Surround Us," *CMOJ*, Aug. 10, 1879.

(CMPU), would offer an alternative by attempting to organize tenement and shop workers alike.[53]

To Albany: The pitfalls of legislation

After the Great Strike, the cigarmakers tried to win by legislation what they could not through contract. The state legislature in Albany became their new battle-ground; the union actively entered electoral politics and rallied its members to campaign against labor's foes.[54] A tenement house bill finally passed in 1883, with help from an unexpected supporter, the young representative from New York City's silk-stocking district, Theodore Roosevelt. The court of appeals declared it unconstitutional on a technicality. Soon afterward the legislature passed a more precisely drafted bill and the stage was set for judicial review on whether the police power of the state, the state's right to intervene to protect the health and welfare of its citizens, or right to contract would prevail.[55]

Debates in Albany exposed the class issues underlying the tenement house controversy. These became expressed in gendered terms and mixed with questions of ethnicity. One senator argued before the governor in 1883:"A factory was not a fit home; that the American people had a different view of the subject of home; that it meant privacy, decency and morality." Cigarmaking in homes was a "nuisance" to the public health,"highly injurious to the workman, and especially to the health of his wife and children," contended Edward Grosse, the first sponsor of the bill in 1880.[56]

Opponents of the bill rejected Grosse's evidence in favor of the authority of

[53] "Cigar-Making in Tenement-Houses," *New York Tribune*, Jan. 10, 1878, and "Home News," ibid., Jan. 11, 1878. It was possible for homeworkers to organize as the tenement workers of Sutro and Newmark did in 1880, see "New York Notes," *CMOJ*, May 10, 1880; In contrast, when 450 factory workers at Kerbs & Spiess struck, those in the tenement houses, about 120 families, remained working. "The Striking Cigarmakers," *New York Tribune*, Dec. 31, 1880.

[54] For text of the initial bill, *CMOJ*, Feb. 10, 1880; Gompers, *Seventy Years*, 1:186–97; for the history of this battle, "The Tenement House Bill," *CMOJ*, Apr. 10, 1880; "Dull Day in the Capitol," *New York Times*, Jan. 15, 1881; "Making Laws at Albany," ibid., May 18, 1881; "At the State Capital," ibid., May 1, 1884; "Closing Hours at Albany. Disgraceful Scenes of the Assembly's Last Day," ibid., June 3, 1882; for the union's political action, see the *CMOJ*, for example, "Legislative Notes," Jan. 15, 1883; "Condemned by the Legislature," Feb. 1883; "Vote on the Tenement-House Cigar Bill," Oct. 1883.

[55] The initial bill referred to only tenement houses in its title but its provisions also included dwelling houses which meant that it was mislabeled, enough for the court to rule against it. "Court of Appeals. In the Matter of the Application of David A. Paul," reprinted in *CMOJ*, Feb. 1884; "The Decision of the Court of Appeals," *CMOJ*, Feb. 1884.

[56] "Argument Before Governor Cleveland," *CMOJ*, Mar. 1882;"The Tenement House Bill in the Assembly," *CMOJ*, May 10, 1880. The CMIU thought the issue so important that it reprinted the first debate in 1880 over the course of six months; later debates merely present variations on themes raised in this one.

the Board of Health, dismissing the power of the legislature to declare a nuisance. Although one representative pointed out that government had removed a whole class of manufacturing – the slaughterhouses – from the tenements, and that it had the power to protect citizens, others claimed that such acts violated a man's "right to carry his business with him and with his family wherever he or that family resides," as Thomas Alvord from Onondaga County explained. Alvord provided the classic defense of the rights of men, rights that inhered in the realm of patriarchal power: "A man's dwelling house is his castle; he has a right to use that dwelling house, whether he uses it as a tenant or uses it as an owner, as long as it is not detrimental to public health and as long as it does not affect his neighbors in his immediate vicinity wrongfully, as he pleases." Bill supporters doubted such a doctrine applied to those whose only choice was unemployment or living and working in the same space.[57]

As a proponent of nineteenth-century liberalism, Alvord conceived of man as separate, as the individualist making his own way. Government would merely ensure that he did not hurt his fellows. Since Alvord rejected the idea that the bill was to protect the public health, it interfered with a man's freedom. But a man alone could not make cigars under this system; as one legislator reminded his colleagues, it took the whole family.[58] Yet both sides of this debate accepted the separation of public from private, one to reject state interference in the home, the other to distinguish proper from improper activities there. All discussed the impact of such homework mainly on the male household head.

Such analysis drew upon the gendered Republican notion of citizen (the citizen as free producer) in a struggle over what generated slavery: tenement-house manufacturing, which in forcing a man to work in his home as a condition of employment interfered "with the liberty of the working men," as Grosse claimed, or "communistic" unions which attempted to draw men into factories to fight the battle of labor against capital, a division that an upstate Republican like Alvord refused to recognize.[59] The CMIU men had accepted their status as wage earners; although often owning their own tools and possessing skill, cigarmakers were even less accurately described as independent proprietors than the butchers designated by Justice Field in his famous *Slaughter-House Cases* dissent, whose rhetoric Alvord echoed.[60] The question

57 "The Tenement House Bill in the Assembly," *CMOJ*, Oct. 10, 1880; ibid., July 10, 1880; Aug. 10, 1880.

58 "The Tenement-House Cigar Factories. In Assembly, Wednesday, March 4, 1881," ibid., Oct. 10, 1881.

59 "The Tenement House Bill in the Assembly," *CMOJ*, Aug. 10, 1880; "Tenement House Cigar Factories," ibid., Oct. 10, 1881. Employers, in contrast, compared unionization with slavery. Mr. Staiton quoted in "A Thousand Cigar-Makers Strike," *New York Tribune*, Feb. 19, 1884.

60 "Cigarmakers' Strike," *New York Herald*, Nov. 15, 1877; on slaughterhouses and the cases about them, see Forbath, "The Ambiguities of Free Labor."

became: What conditions made men free, instead of whether women who worked at home did so freely. This switch in gendered referent occurred despite employer assumptions that the system existed for women's benefit so they could execute their duties as mothers, wives, and housekeepers.

Theodore Roosevelt believed in freedom as a precondition for citizenship, but such an association led him to link protection of tenement workers with preservation of the American way which rested upon proper gender and age hierarchies within the family. Before the assembly in 1884 he explained how the dirt, disease, and child labor in the tenements led him to suspend his belief in laissez-faire. In terms that emphasized the menace of unassimilated children who failed "to learn our language, to acquire our notions of what the rights of citizenship demand," Roosevelt argued for ending tenement house cigarmaking not merely as a hygienic measure, or to facilitate enforcement of the child labor laws, but to maintain a notion of Republican citizenship, one that was gendered and racialist.[61]

Roosevelt's support broke the stalemate between conservative upstate representatives and downstate supporters of labor, including members of Tammany Hall. The 1884 bill made it a crime to manufacture cigars in tenements used for living purposes in all cities of fifty thousand population or over (New York and Brooklyn).[62] To safeguard small manufacturers, it exempted shops on the first floor of tenements which also sold cigars. While enforcement belonged to the city's sanitary inspectors, the bill permitted trade unions or any citizen to report violations, a measure no doubt reflecting the CMIU's distrust of the Board of Health.[63]

While the employers countered through the courts,[64] smaller manufacturers and some of the larger ones complied until the justices ruled on the law's

---

[61] "Bill. In Assembly, April 8, 1884," CMOJ, May 1884; Theodore Roosevelt, "A Judicial Experience," The Outlook 91 (Mar. 13, 1909), 563–4; Theodore Roosevelt, An Autobiography (New York: C. Scribner's Sons, 1913), 79–81; Howard L. Hurwitz, Theodore Roosevelt and Labor in New York State, 1880–1900 (New York: Columbia Univ. Press, 1943), 77–87.

[62] "The Tenement Cigar Law," New York Tribune, Oct. 9, 1884; decision reprinted in CMOJ, Oct. 1884.

[63] "On the Warpath," CMOJ, Apr. 15, 1883; "Laws of 1884, Chapter 272," Second Annual Report of the Bureau of Statistics of Labor for the Year 1884 (Albany, N.Y.: Weld, Parsons, and Co., 1885), 387–8; for union enforcement, "Defend the Tenement House Law. We Must Compel Its Execution!" Progress, Sept. 28, 1883; report in CMOJ, June 1884.

[64] "The Cigar Tenement-House Act," New York Times, Oct. 13, 1883; on In re Paul, "The Tenement House Cigar Bill. Before the Court of Appeals," CMOJ, Dec. 1883; on Jacobs, Court of Appeals, In the Matter of Application of Peter Jacobs for Writs of Habeas Corpus and Certiorari, etc., Case on Appeal (New York: Martin B. Brown, Printer, 1884), 9–15. Jacobs, an English immigrant, had seven rooms and lived in a tenement with only four apartments. Paul had an apartment that stretched the entire side of a floor, from back to front. The manufacturers got an opinion on the first act even before it went into effect: A lower judge declared the law valid because the legislature had the right to enact improvements for the public health. See "An Attempt to Obtain A Decision," CMOJ, Aug. 1883. For a discussion of this strategy, "Before the Courts," ibid., Oct. 1883; "A Test Case," New York Times, May 16, 1884.

constitutionality. The CMIU gloated over the impact of the acts, announcing that men in factories went on full-time after the 1883 law.[65] Large manufacturers who had abandoned the system heralded the bill; others who had retained the system foresaw hundreds of families unemployed or making less money in factories. Some threatened to relocate to Pennsylvania and New Jersey "where the farmers and their families can sit at home and make cigars." Many believed the law to be unconstitutional because "it will vitiate many contracts." Both the *New York Times* and the *New York Tribune* echoed manufacturers and their legislative supporters in editorials against the bill, claiming that its true purposes were to increase union control over the trade, prevent "women from making a living," and raise employer expenses.[66]

Briefs submitted in the two test cases sharpened the arguments heard in the legislature. When the case against David Paul went before the court of appeals in 1883, the lawyer for the defense portrayed the manufacturers as heroes for allowing "these poor people to substantially pursue their old industry at home." Wives and children became the proper helpmeets for free men. The law was unconstitutional because it interfered with private property and personal freedom, disenfranchised citizens or deprived them of rights without due process, and negated the newly minted right to contract under the U.S. Constitution. The lawyer for the union, in contrast, emphasized that regulating unwholesome trades fell under the proper use of the police power of the state; he relied on the majority decision in the *Slaughter-House Cases* rather than the dissent.[67]

This line of reasoning predominated in the brief prepared for *In re Jacobs* the next year. Defense lawyers responded by denying the force of the police power in this instance: "The State cannot under the pretence of prescribing a police regulation, encroach upon the just rights of the citizen, secured to him by the Constitution." That cigarmaking was allowed on the first floor negated the public health argument and revealed the act for what it really was, an attempt at coercion. The lawyers contended that cigarmakers were actually healthier than average.[68] The legislature could not interfere with "the natural right of every man to labor for the support of himself and his family." Conceiving of

---

[65] "The Tenement-House Cigar Law," *New York Tribune*, Oct. 2, 1883; "Complaints of Tenement House Manufacturers," *CMOJ*, Oct. 1883; for a negative report on the impact, "The Cigarmakers," *John Swinton's Paper*, Feb. 3, 1884.

[66] "Cigar-Making in Tenement-Houses," *New York Tribune*, Mar. 14, 1883; "Tenement-House Cigar-Making," *New York Times*, Mar. 14, 1883; "The Tenement-House Cigar Law," *New York Tribune*, Sept. 30, 1883; for newspaper editorials, *New York Tribune*, Oct. 15, 1883, and Jan. 30, 1884; *New York Times*, Oct. 2, 1883 and Dec. 7, 1883.

[67] "The Tenement House Cigar Bill. Before the Court of Appeals."

[68] The defense cited the death rate in the cigar tenements as only nine per thousand per annum, compared to thirty-one for the city as a whole. Such numbers are meaningless when uncontrolled for age structure. "Men's Right to Work at Home," *New York Times*, Feb. 9, 1884. Tenement house deaths were 56 percent of total mortality: "Monstrous Facts," *CMOJ*, Feb. 1884.

skill as property, the defense turned wage laborers into property holders, contending that the law "breaks up their property." Moreover, the tenement house law would substitute the "promiscuous association" of the factory for family industry, not only driving home laborers into the factory and ending economic competition but violating the family, regulating its domesticity, and exposing young girls to the physical and moral "mischiefs" of the shop floor.[69]

The *Jacobs* decision accepted all these arguments, especially the claim that the act was an arbitrary infringement of the police power on a person's right to property and not a justified protection of the public health. "Liberty. . . means the right, not only of freedom from actual servitude, imprisonment or restraint, but the right of one to use his faculties in all lawful ways to live and work where he will, to earn his livelihood in any lawful calling, and to pursue any lawful trade or avocation." This defense of the citizen appears gender neutral but actually referred to men. It assumed that the cigarmaker was the male household head, speaking of "supervision of his family and their help." Moreover, Justice Earl wrote this opinion in the context of legal traditions that elevated the husband as household head and limited the rights of citizenship of suffrageless women. *Jacobs* followed the gendered interpretation of freedom of occupation in *Bradwell v. Illinois* (1873) which denied women's right to practice law, and the restrictions on citizenship for women in *Minor v. Happersett* (1875).[70]

Manufacturer Louis Haas applauded: "I never anticipated any other result from the start. The law was clearly in violation of the spirit of American institutions." The *CMOJ* announced, "Slavery Declared to be Liberty," and President Strasser demanded that the court be impeached if possible; if the legislature failed to remedy the wrongs of workers, the only other option was "brute force."[71]

The concept of man's right to contract won out over the cigarmaker's belief in a man's responsibility to support his family with dignity and through his skills. This new understanding of masculinity reflected even as it shaped the class positions of men in the age of industrial capitalism. Right to contract, like male breadwinning, assumed the separation of home from marketplace central to the Victorian concept of women's place. The irony was that this

---

[69] "The Legal Argument," *CMOJ*, Jan. 1884; "Respondent's Points," "Supplemental Point," and "Appellant's Points," *In the Matter of the Application of Peter Jacobs*, 8–9, 14–17, 1–3.

[70] *In re Jacobs*, 98–9; 104–106 ff.; *Bradwell v. Illinois*, 83 U.S. (16 Wall) 130 (1873); *Minor v. Happersett*, 88 U.S. 162 (1875); Joan Hoff, *Law, Gender and Injustice: A Legal History of U.S. Women* (New York: New York Univ. Press, 1991), 164–81.

[71] *In re Jacobs*, 98 N.Y. 98 (1885); "Cigar-Making in Tenement-Houses. What Is Said of the Decision of the Court of Appeals," *New York Tribune*, Jan. 22, 1885; "Slavery Declared to be Liberty," *CMOJ*, Feb. 1885; "Cigars and Politics – Another Death-Dealing Decision," *John Swinton's Paper*, Oct. 19, 1884; "The Unclean Bench," ibid., Oct. 12, 1884; "Proceedings of the Sixteenth Session of the CMIU," *CMOJ*, Oct. 1885; "Retrospect and Prospect," *Progress*, Jan. 24, 1885.

doctrine developed out of a case that, by sanctioning wage earning within the home, exposed such dichotomies as "home" and "work," "private" and "public," as mere constructions. In these cases, even liberty to contract meant that women remained at home as part of a family labor system. Working-class opposition to the inequalities of contract doctrine maintained the home as separate from work. The ideal of the male breadwinner protected women by removing them from the marketplace.

The aftermath of *Jacobs*

Judicial defeat pushed Gompers and the AFL away from a direct reliance upon the state as an instrument for gaining trade union goals. Rather than build a workingmen's party, the CMIU chose to "accomplish through economic power what we had failed to achieve through legislation."[72] The campaign for tenement house legislation intensified faction fights among cigarmakers. Recent immigrant socialists split to form the CMPU which actively organized tenement workers and by 1884 consisted of nearly 67 percent of the city's cigarmakers.[73] This split further weakened workers in their contests against manufacturers, especially when the Knights of Labor took advantage of it to negotiate closed shop contracts. By September 1886, after the Knights failed to deliver on their promises to employers, a reunited CMIU stepped into the vacuum. For the next year and a half most large employers abandoned the tenement house system, fearing that it would destroy factory competition.[74]

Gompers and Strasser emerged out of these faction fights strengthened, as did the closed union structure that they had forged. But we must not regard Gompers and his allies as heroes in this initial fight against homework: The choice in the early 1880s was not to keep the current tenement house system or prohibit it. Organization promised a third way, and there was some basis for believing that the workers themselves would reject the conditions in the tenements. Although the 1884 legal contest occurred amid declining produc-

72   Gompers, *Seventy Years*, 1:183–97. For the state against workers, William E. Forbath, *Law and the Shaping of the American Labor Movement* (Cambridge, Mass.: Harvard Univ. Press, 1991). The AFL would forge an alliance with the Democratic party to maintain its own autonomy; Gwendolyn Mink, *Old Labor and New Immigrants in American Political Development* (Ithaca, N.Y.: Cornell Univ. Press, 1987), esp. 236–60.

73   "The Great Trade Unions," *John Swinton's Paper*, Oct. 21, 1883; "Hear Both Sides," ibid., Dec. 23, 1883; "A Local Conflict," *CMOJ*, April 1882; "Progressive Scabs," ibid., Aug. 1882; "Proceedings of the 15th Session of the CMIU," ibid., Supplement, Sept. 1883; Gompers, *Seventy Years*, 1:199–204.

74   State of New York, "Cigarmakers," *Fourth Annual Report of the Bureau of Statistics of Labor* (Albany, N.Y.: The Argus Co., 1887), 523–39; "The Culmination of the Rivalry between the CMIU and the Cigarmakers' Progressive Union of America," in Kaufman, ed., *The Samuel Gompers Papers*, 1:365–409; "Bolt of CPU from K of L into CMIU," *John Swinton's Paper*, Aug. 1, 1886. For the employers giving up the tenement system, "Tenement House Cigars," *New York Times*, Dec. 20, 1887.

tion and an oversupply of labor,[75] cigarmakers, including those in the tenements, continued to press their demands on the shop floor as well as in the
legislative halls.

Bohemian tenement house and shop workers kept meeting together. During an 1886 lock out, the mothers who worked in the tenements joined the
young single women who labored in the factories in rooms rented by CMPU
locals to discuss proposals set forth at other public meetings attended only by
men. The immediate interests of the two groups of women could conflict, but
the single women's expectations that they would soon marry and would
become tenement house workers upon motherhood provided a basis on which
to formulate a unified set of demands. Such actions suggested that these
workers were capable of trade unionism if they were educated instead of being
written off as the New York equivalent of "coolie" labor. Like Marie Hausler,
they demanded rights as workers. But disunity within the class – based on
politics, gender, skill, and ethnicity – hampered such efforts.[76]

The tenement house system persisted into the late 1880s and 1890s.[77] On
one hand, opponents of the system fought on the terrain of trade unionism:
organizing factories, contract negotiations, strikes, and the union label, which
became a major tool to educate the consuming public. The CMIU forbade
locals with any tenement house workers to maintain such workers in good
standing as long as they labored at home. Since employers eroded the craft
through tenement production, such a stand blocked union organizing of the
less skilled.[78] On the other hand, the trade unions appealed to "an enlightened
and humane public opinion," as the Working Women's Society of New York
City resolved, which would abolish the tenement menace. Composed of
middle-class reformers and working women, this society focused on "suffering

[75] While the numbers of cigarmakers rose during the first half of that year, from January until
June the number of cigars manufactured decreased by a quarter of a million. At a time when
about eight thousand people worked in the tenement houses, there were at least three
thousand surplus cigarmakers in the city. "The Cigar Trade," *CMOJ*, June 1884; "Cigar-
Making in Tenement-Houses," *New York Tribune*, Jan. 21, 1885; "Respondent's Points," *In the
Matter of the Application of Peter Jacobs*, 14.

[76] *John Swinton's Paper* most often reported these strikes: for example, "Strikes in this City,"
Dec. 9, 1883; "Live News of the Trades," Dec. 7, 1884; "The Cigarmakers," Sept. 20, 1885;
"Doings of the Workingmen," *New York Tribune*, Feb. 18, 1884; "Settled by the Girls: The
Congress of the Female Cigarmakers," *New York Times*, Jan. 24, 1886.

[77] "Tenement House Cigars," *New York Times*, Dec. 20, 1887; "Going Back to Their Old Plan,"
ibid., Dec. 21, 1887. Such manufacturing continued even during the period when the
Manufacturers' Association sought to restrain it. See listings by the Label Committee of
New York City, "Filthy Tenement-House Factories," *CMOJ*, Apr. 1887, which reports 26
houses with 546 families.

[78] "Their Labels Protected," *New York Times*, Mar. 9, 1888. By 1893, the *CMOJ* consistently
printed lists of tenement house factories; it also published warnings against specific cigar
brands whose tenement origins employers attempted to disguise. The 1891 union convention denied membership to Chinese and tenement house workers; "Proceedings of the
Nineteenth Session of the Cigar Makers' International Union," *CMOJ*, Oct. 1891 (suppl.).

women and children" in the tenements, with their health and morality in danger. Such a portrait of victimization was hardly new; middle-class reformers had painted a similar one of the garret seamstresses before the Civil War. By the late nineteenth century, as explored in the next chapters, their appeals generated public investigation, entrenching this image of the homeworker in the popular imagination.[79]

A more generalized sweatshop peril had replaced the cigar tenement houses by the time that the New York Bureau of Labor Statistics reported on the conditions of cigarmakers in 1895, ten years after *Jacobs*. All the themes of earlier exposés found ample confirmation. Home cigarmakers were exploited, they lived in cramped squalor, and, with all members of the household pressed into service, had a degraded family life. "Sad," "emaciated," "squalid," "barren" – such words described the inmates of tenement "prisons." Men failed as breadwinners and women, as housewives and mothers. Children could not claim their right to schooling and play.[80]

The Bureau of Labor rejected these factories in the tenements less for their working conditions and the threat of disease than because they were improper homes at a time when the home remained "the hope of the Republic." By definition, a tenement house, which lacked modern equipment, was "a demoralizing power. When these houses are converted into tenement factories the evils are multiplied," the Bureau argued. Manufacturing in the tenements perverted the function of the home to provide privacy and keep children away from "vulgar immodesty." It threatened the very "foundation of the state."[81]

Commenting on *Jacobs*, the Progressive Era feminist Rheta Childe Dorr later argued: "The tradition [of the innate sacredness of the home] is strongest in strong men. . . . It sways legislatures and the courts, which, being composed entirely of men . . . have no more than a theoretical knowledge of Home. *In this day the presence of manufacturing in a home turns that home into a factory.*"[82] Like Samuel Gompers thirty years before, Childe Dorr continued to separate public from private, work from home, the very discourse which buttressed many an argument against the women's suffrage she also supported. Like the New York Bureau of Labor in 1895, she would bring the state into the home to save the private from itself, asserting the right to interfere in a man's freedom by way of the police power of the state, not only as a health measure but also in the best interests of women and children.

[79] "Against Tenement House Cigar Factories," *CMOJ*, Feb. 1888; see Stansell, *City of Women*, 147–54.

[80] New York State, *Thirteenth Annual Report of the Bureau of Labor Statistics for the Year 1895* (Albany, N.Y.: Wynkeop Hallenbeck Crawford Co., 1896), 545–61.

[81] Ibid., 552.

[82] Rheta Childe Dorr, "The Child Who Toils at Home," *The Hampton Magazine* 28 (Apr. 1912), 183.

Jacobs had narrowed the meaning of the police power of the state by proclaiming *men's* rights over community protection. Men's freedom to contract justified women's necessity to labor at home. Its universalism obscured existing power relations between the genders, classes, and ethnic groups. Blocked by such an interpretation of the Fourteenth Amendment, labor standards legislation increasingly became restricted. Workingmen would negotiate contracts; women and children would be protected by the state. Despite its claim to voluntarism, the AFL would lobby the state in the interest of skilled male workers. It called for laws that reduced the labor supply, such as legislation to protect women and children and to restrict immigration. The union had become a man's castle. Men, no matter their class, agreed: Women's place was at home, whether or not that home served as a waged workplace. In promoting this sexual division of social space, unionized men stymied their own efforts to protect the factory from tenement labor by refusing to organize home-based workers.

In the 1890s, how best to preserve the home remained open to conflicting strategies: organization or regulation, mobilizing as workers or cross-class alliances. Though *Jacobs* limited outright prohibition of homework, it did not curtail regulation. Unionization was not necessarily incompatible with lobbying the state to limit in the interest of the whole what could not be won as a class. The tension between these strategies turned into an opposition when middle-class reformers discovered the "white slaves of the cities."

Figure 3: Jacob Riis, garment sweatshop, Ludlow Street, New York, ca. 1889.
Courtesy of the Library of Congress. Such "promiscuous" mingling of men and
women under the grimy conditions of sweated labor provided organized garment
workers and elite reformers alike a language of violated domesticity through which to
attack the tenement making of ready-made clothing.

2

"White slaves of the cities":
Campaigns
against sweated clothing

During the heat of July 1891, social gospel minister Louis Albert Banks exposed "the evils of the sweating system" before enthusiastic crowds of working people.[1] His initial sermon, "White Slaves of the Boston 'Sweaters,'" described desperate, hopeless seamstresses as poor, pathetic, and wretched as the chattel slaves portrayed by his abolitionist forefathers. Banks discounted the power of judges, the Fourteenth Amendment, or the Constitution as a whole "to unshackle all the slaves who, under the cruel whip of necessity, . . . sweated under the burdens imposed by avaricious taskmasters." His portrait of victimized women and children identified mothers with the home but also exposed the underside of the Republican party's own doctrines of free labor, economic choice, and the liberal market.[2] By describing immigrant homes as dark, diseased, and dirty, by presenting men as either unemployed, sick, or, "no good," Banks reinforced the dominant image of sweated labor and tenement homeworkers.[3] He revealed the class-based, gendered, and racialist assumptions behind the reform campaign against sweated labor.

Banks was no prophet howling in the wilderness. He belonged to a larger agitation initiated by clothing operatives that, like the cigarmakers', appealed to both self-interest and community well-being. Seized by Brahmin reformers and city ministers, this movement against sweated clothing led to the nation's first law regulating clothing manufacture in tenements. Massachusetts's 1891 "Act to Prevent the Manufacture and Sale of Clothing Made in Unhealthy

---

[1] "Plague of the Workshop," *Boston Herald*, July 6, 1891; F. K. F. [Frank Foster], "Visions and Visionaries," *Labor Leader* (Boston), July 18, 1891.

[2] Both apologists for and opponents of the South's antebellum labor system associated wage slavery with chattel slavery. Feminists also referred to women's condition in marriage as a form of slavery. The reality of African slavery differed considerably from the economic exploitation under a capitalistic free labor system because the obligations of master differ from those of employer and because of its roots in racial distinctions and hierarchies. See Marcus Cunliffe, *Chattel Slavery and Wage Slavery: The Anglo-American Context, 1830–1860* (Athens: University of Georgia Press, 1979); Amy Stanley, "Conjugal Bonds and Wage Labor: Rights of Contract in the Age of Emancipation," *JAH* 75 (Sept. 1988), 471–500.

[3] Rev. Louis Albert Banks, *White Slaves or The Oppression of The Worthy Poor* (Boston: Lee and Shepard Publishers, 1892).

Places" prohibited garmentmaking by unrelated persons in the home.[4] It sought to eliminate the home workshops that competed with factory tailors, but it maintained the home finishing of mothers whose plight symbolized the exploitation of the tenements in the first place. Male reformers joined union men in assaulting the sweatshop.

As with hours laws, factory inspection, and labor statistics, Massachusetts provided the model for many states, but not for Illinois.[5] Unlike the Bay State, Illinois had no factory inspectorate prior to its law curtailing tenement manufacturing; no bureaucracy existed to shape either the proposed law or its implementation. But state structures by themselves fail to account for different types of laws. Social and political movements in Illinois better explain why its law linked the abolition of long hours and low wages in the making of clothing with the curtailment of child labor and women's overwork. While the reform governorship of John Peter Altgeld encouraged bold initiatives, he was responding to protests by women activists, led by socialists Elizabeth Morgan and Florence Kelley. Women cloakmakers with women reformers shaped a law that addressed the status of women and children. Why women played a central role in Illinois and not in Massachusetts relates to the spaces for action open in the newer, less socially solidified city of Chicago and to the remarkable group of women who found their way there.[6]

The legacy of *Jacobs* haunted these laws. In *Ritchie v. People* (1895), a conservative Illinois Supreme Court invalidated the eight-hour limit on female labor. By applying "freedom of contract" doctrine to women, it denied a developing legal acceptance of gender distinctions in labor standards. It defeated an attempt to connect the home to the workplace.[7] Massachusetts had circumvented *Jacobs* by basing its law on public health without intruding upon the privacy of the family or threatening the cheapness of female labor. It faced no legal challenge. Economic arguments that empowered workers were less acceptable than those that called for their protection or focused on the concerns of the buying public. "Buyer beware" succumbed to the reformer's assault, but not "freedom of contract." In the process, the factory inspector's tag vied with the union label as the preferred means to curtail tenement house labor. Ten years after *Jacobs*, homework regulation would move from a trade

---

[4] Chap. 357, *Acts and Resolves*, May 1891, 197–8.

[5] William R. Brock, *Investigation and Responsibility: Public Responsibility in the United States, 1865–1900* (New York: Cambridge Univ. Press, 1984), 148–56; James Leiby, *Carroll Wright and Labor Reform: The Origin of Labor Statistics* (Cambridge, Mass.: Harvard Univ. Press, 1960).

[6] Sarah Deutsch, "Learning to Talk More Like a Man: Boston Women's Class–Bridging Organizations, 1870–1940," *AHR* 97 (Apr. 1992), 379–404; Eileen Boris, *Art and Labor: Ruskin, Morris, and the Craftsman Ideal in America* (Philadelphia, Pa.: Temple Univ. Press, 1986), 45–52, 92–8, 131–3, 180–3; Kathryn Kish Sklar, "Hull House in the 1890s: A Community of Women Reformers," *Signs* 10 (Summer 1985), 658–77.

[7] *Ritchie v. People*, 155 Ill. 98, 40 N.E. 454 (1895).

union plank to a key demand of a generation of women reformers who would play a central role in shaping the modern welfare state. The late nineteenth-century transformation of the garment industry provides the context for the politics of sweated clothing.

From tailoring to the task system: Sweating defined

The transformation of tailoring from an artisanal craft to a divided trade came not from the invention of the sewing machine or the arrival of less skilled immigrant labor but from the development of the "ready-made" market for men's clothing.[8] Where more than 75 percent of men's clothing was custom-made in 1865, fifteen years later, 40 percent was ready-made, which increased to over 60 percent by 1890. The Civil War initiated this shift as government relied on contractors to manufacture uniforms that led to further standardization of sizes. While shirtmaking and some forms of women's clothing – for example, skirt hoops – developed highly capitalized factories with a minute division of labor, women's garments continued to be made in smaller shops or by mothers for their own families. Coats would not move into factory production until the turn of the century.[9]

Manufacturers developed the contract system to protect themselves from the uncertain economy of the 1870s. In the "inside" shop of the merchant tailor, cloth first would be sponged, or flattened out and cleaned, then cut, and finally bundled into parcels to be distributed to numerous contractors. Clothing actually was assembled in the outside shop of the contractor, whom economist John R. Commons called in 1901, "an organizer and employer of immigrant labor." The contractor created shops that generally consisted of people from his community. A shared culture often led to a commonality of perspective between employer and employee, despite potentially divergent economic interests. Many contractors hardly made more than their lead operators.[10]

[8] Mabel Hurd Willett, "The Employment of Women in the Clothing Trades," *Columbia University Studies in the Social Sciences* (New York: Columbia University Press, 1902), 42; "Men's Ready-Made Clothing," *Report on Women and Children* 2 (1911), 413–512; Helen Sumner, "History of Women in Industry in the United States," *Report on Women and Children* 9 (1910), 115–55; David Montgomery, *The Fall of the House of Labor: The Workplace, the State, and American Labor Activism, 1865–1925* (New York: Cambridge Univ. Press, 1987), 116–23.

[9] *Report on Sweating,* iv–v; Sumner, "History of Women in Industry," 151–5; For the factory system after 1900, Thomas S. Adams and Helen L. Sumner, *Labor Problems: A Text Book,* 8th ed. (New York: The Macmillan Co., 1918), 139.

[10] "Better Prospects Ahead," *New York Times,* Aug. 18, 1885; John R. Commons, "Immigration and Its Economic Effects," Part 3, *Reports of the Industrial Commission on Immigration,* 15 (Washington, D.C.: GPO, 1901), 320–1; Rosara Lucy Passero, "Ethnicity in the Men's Ready Made Clothing Industry: The Italian Experience in Philadelphia, 1880–1950," (Ph.D. diss., Univ. of Pennsylvania, 1978).

Irregularity and seasonality came to characterize the entire industry, with rush seasons and fallow periods of up to three or four months a year. The contractor specialized in only one part of a suit. He relieved the wholesaler of labor recruitment and supervision, enabling the wholesaler to meet uncertain market demands and lower expenses for rent, lighting, heat, equipment, and wages. In 1892, the House Committee on Manufacturers estimated that about one-half of all goods were made up in the contractors' own inside shops and were subject to factory laws. But this first contractor subsequently subcontracted nearly half of his work. At least a quarter went to tenement workshops where living and manufacturing became "intimate," domestic life and wage earning flowed into each other as family and employees shared the same space. Another quarter came to "tenement home workers," individuals, sometimes aided by their immediate family, who sewed a considerable portion of children's clothes and various amounts of custom-made gear as well.[11]

Garmentmaking in the last third of the century varied among the major clothing centers in work organization and labor composition. Rochester and Cincinnati, with their greater number of factories and fewer tenement workshops, had more native-born and German workers. In New York, Jewish men predominated; women composed about 40 percent of the menswear workforce in 1900. In Illinois, there was a greater ethnic mix, with Poles and Scandinavians as machine operators. Women there made up slightly over 60 percent of all workers. In most cities, Italian women engaged in felling or finishing, the less skilled handwork performed most often at home. Since Jewish wives stayed home, the dominance of Jewish men among contractors led to ethnically mixed shops. Of the approximately one hundred thousand clothing and cloak workers in 1900, forty thousand of them concentrated in New York City, where another twenty thousand made undergarments and shirts.[12]

Men operated the machines in the tenement workshops that grew during the 1880s. The immigration to New York City of hundreds of thousands of Russian and Polish Jews encouraged a new organization of labor, the task system, that parceled the skills of tailoring to separate individuals each of whom had to complete an assigned number of coats a day to make a weekly wage. Since it took as little as fifty dollars to purchase machines, the number of contractors quickly increased. They began to underbid each other, pushing down the wholesale price per garment. While the weekly wage remained constant, the extent of the task had increased by 1900 from eight or ten coats

---

[11] "Men's Ready-Made Clothing," 413–23; *Report on Sweating*, vi–viii.

[12] Willett, "Women in the Clothing Trades," 217; Passero, "Ethnicity in the Men's Ready Made Clothing Industry"; William Franklin Willoughby, "Regulation of the Sweating System," *Monographs on American Social Economics*, ed. Herbert B. Adams (Boston: Wright & Potter, 1900), 6–7.

to twenty or more and workers commonly received wages for only four or five days' work. A lengthening workday, long a point of struggle between workers and employers, dropped wages. Speedup and "driving" resulted as "the most rapid worker spurs on his companions."[13]

The ferocious competition among contractors turned ready-made clothing into a "sweated" industry. One reformer articulated the emotions that undergirded much definitional discussion by calling it "the system of making clothing under filthy and inhuman conditions." Behind sweating lay competition, an oversupply of untrained labor, and the ability of small shops to produce more cheaply than larger ones in the labor-intensive clothing trades. The U.S. Department of Labor ignored location when defining sweating as "a condition under which a maximum amount of work in a given time is performed for a minimum wage, and in which the ordinary rules of health and comfort are disregarded."[14]

Conditions in the clothing industry grew not merely from the desires of employers or the availability of labor. Tenement workshops and homework built upon the preference among some Jewish immigrants to work at home and took advantage of social and cultural restraints on the labor of married women with dependents. Tenement homework developed in the context of both rising land values, population overcrowding, and a preexisting stock of buildings,[15] on the one hand, and an active, organizing working class, on the other.

Subject to more strikes than most other industries, the clothing trade underwent walk outs, lock outs, and other confrontations from the mid-eighties into the teens. Unions were unstable and took numerous forms prior to the formation of the United Garment Workers of America (UGWA) in 1891 and the International Ladies' Garment Workers of America (ILGWU) in 1900. Neither controlled anywhere near a plurality of workplaces. UGWA was particularly weak in the chaotic New York area, long subject to shifting allegiances between contractors, cutters, machine operators, and pressers.

---

13 "Men's Ready-Made Clothing," 423–4, 446–7; Willett, "Women in the Clothing Trades," 200–4; John Griffin, "Operations of the Law in Massachusetts Relating to the 'Sweating System,'" *Sixth Annual Convention of the IAFINA*, 1892 (Columbus, Ohio: The Electric Publishing Co., 1893), 91.

14 Joseph Lee, "The Sweating System," *Journal of Social Science* 30 (Aug. 15, 1892), 105–46, esp. 105; Henry White, "The Sweating System," in *Bulletin of Department of Labor* 4 (Washington, D.C.: GPO, 1896); "Sweat-Shops," *The New Encyclopedia of Social Reform*, ed. William D. P. Bliss and Rudolph M. Binder (New York: Funk & Wagnalls, 1910), 1178–81; George McKay, "The Sweating System," *Seventh Annual Report of the IAFINA*, 1893 (Cleveland, Ohio: Forest City Printing House, 1893), 102–8; State of Wisconsin, "Sweating in the Garment-Making Trades," *The Biennial Report of the Bureau of Labor and Industrial Statistics*, Part 3 1901–2 (Madison, Wis.: Democrat Printing Co., 1903), 177–218.

15 "Homes of the City's Poor," *New York Times*, Mar. 12, 1880; "Hell's Own Acres," *Labor Leader* (Boston) 17, Feb. 9, 1895; Roy Lubove, *The Progressives and the Slums* (Pittsburgh, Pa.: Univ. of Pittsburgh Press, 1962).

ILGWU could not organize a substantial portion of its industry until the teens.[16]

Alliances between shop and home workers proved difficult. In the 1870s, journeymen tailors attempted "to get this houseworker system done away with" by forming a cooperative to demand better prices from the bosses. "But I could not bring the men out," one of the leaders later recalled. "They remained at home; they [were] discouraged." While these German tailors came to believe that state action alone could end "house-work in all branches," the new immigrants, who were also new to the trade, were willing to strike at the start of each season. Many of the socialists among them distrusted state action.[17] Omaha's Journeyman Tailors' Union in 1889 continued to struggle against the homework of some tailors who relied upon "wives and daughters." Competing with American Federation of Labor (AFL) unions which sought to distinguish between the home and workplace, the Knights of Labor had no problem with merging the two realms; in Baltimore it established a shirt cooperative in the late eighties which "abolish[ed] the factory system and permit[ted] the girls to do the work at their homes."[18] Sometimes shop workers and homeworkers hung together, as during the 1885 New York strike. Although clothing workers denounced the sweating system and referred to each other as "fellow white slaves," perhaps the majority of Jewish immigrants among them gained their meager livelihood through it. In 1890 Jewish tailors demanded the end not of "outside contracting but *inside* contracting." By its very nature, the sweatshop drained efforts at organization, yet it provided common ground for a strength fed by ethnic and community bonds. In contrast, Irish and German cutters sought to abandon tenement shops.[19]

Competition led contractors to break agreements with workers. Illinois's first factory inspector Florence Kelley noted, "Any demand of the inside hands for increased wages or shorter hours is promptly met by transfer of work from the inside shop to a sweater; and the cutters alone remain secure from this competition." Some manufacturers responded to strikes in the early nineties by establishing larger inside shops in which the contractor was closer to a foreman than an independent entrepreneur. They added electric power and more machines and further divided the labor process, with the result that the factory began to dominate production of menswear. Outside finishing re-

---

[16] Montgomery, *The Fall of the House of Labor*, 119–23; Louis Levine (Lorwin), *The Women's Garment Workers: A History of the International Ladies' Garment Workers Union* (New York: B. W. Huebsch, 1924); Joel Seidman, *The Needle Trades* (New York: Farrar and Rinehart, 1942).

[17] Conrad Carl, *Report on Capital and Labor*, 417–19.

[18] On Omaha and Baltimore, see Ileen A. DeVault, "'Stalking Through the Workman's Door': Home and Union in the Late Nineteenth Century," 17, 10–11, paper presented at the Wisconsin Labor History Conference, Apr. 1992.

[19] "Cloakmakers on Strike," *New York Times*, Aug. 18, 1885; "Sweating System Denounced," ibid., Jan. 30, 1892; Montgomery, *The Fall of the House of Labor*, 119–23.

mained; the cheap labor of Italian homeworkers competed successfully with factory efficiency. Greater concentration led to more control over the labor process and the laborer. This shift in location inadvertently set the stage for the sweeping union drives that would give birth to the Amalgamated Clothing Workers of America in 1914.[20]

"Boston-made clothing is good enough for us"

The nation's first law regulating tenement-made clothing originated in the protests of trade unionists.[21] In 1886, during a period when Boston garment operatives joined that brief, but general, movement of working people into the Knights of Labor, cutters and trimmers began to notice a decline in employment. More and more work for local clothing wholesalers was being cut as well as made outside of the city. Certain classes of goods, usually of poorer quality, had long gone to homeworking women in Maine and rural Massachusetts, but the amounts of work New York City appeared to be receiving led even contractors to complain.[22] Boston once was the center of the wholesale clothing trade but now was in a battle with Rochester to retain even the New England market.[23]

There was tenement labor in Boston, but most garmentmaking took place in workshops.[24] In 1875, when 30,916 women in the state worked at home, about 30 percent engaged in the clothing trade. Ten years later, the total number of Massachusetts female homeworkers had decreased to 18,333, but clothing homework had increased to 46 percent of the total. In the spring of

[20] Florence Kelley, "The Sweating System," *Hull-House Maps and Papers* (New York: Thomas Y. Crowell, 1895), 28; Frieda Miller, "Industrial Home Work in the United States," *International Labour Review* 43 (Jan. 1941), 18–20.

[21] The subhead that precedes this section is a quote from Sidney Cushing, *Report on Sweating*, 45.

[22] For the strike of spring and summer 1885 in which three thousand garment workers, newly organized into the Knights, participated and lost, see "The Clothing Operatives: They Repudiate a Certain Label Now Being Issued," *Boston Herald*, Mar. 9, 1891; Jama Lazerow, "The Workingman's Hour: The Knights of Labor in 1886," *Labor History* 21 (Spring 1980), 200–20; William Barnes, Isaac King, Louis Asch, and Sidney Cushing, *Report on Sweating*, 101, 135, 156, 24–5.

[23] According to the 1890 Census of Manufacturing, Boston ranked sixth (after New York, Chicago, Cincinnati, Baltimore, and Philadelphia) among clothing centers, with 6,478 employees and $19,640,779 product value for men's ready-made and 1,073 employees with $1,506,212 product value for women's ready-made. Commons, "Immigration and Its Economic Effects," 318.

[24] Horace G. Wadlin, "The Sweating System," Report to the Governor, Mar, 12, 1891, published as House Document 255, in *Massachusetts Legislative Documents*, 2–11; Wadlin, "The Sweating System in Massachusetts," *Journal of Social Science* 30 (Aug. 15, 1892), 86–102; John Griffin, "The Sweating System of Massachusetts," in *Seventh Annual Report of the IAFINA*, 110.

1892, Boston home finishers stood at an estimated 5,000 women. Portuguese, Jewish, and Italian women predominated.[25]

By Labor Day 1889, a trade union campaign against sweated clothing appealed directly to the public. The Operative Tailors Union of Boston paraded with two open wagons, one "a Tailor Shop in active operation, men being engaged in cutting, sewing and pressing," with a sign proclaiming, "Away with filthy scab tenement house labor. We will investigate a few tenement houses for $20." Decorated as a tenement house interior, "with all its squalor and misery," the second wagon bore the motto, "Twenty coats a day's work." The tailors held other signs: "Long hours in New York, no hours in Boston," "Why don't the Boston board of health stop the New York goods?," "Why has the price of insect powder gone up?" These mottoes summarized the mounting campaign of Boston garment workers against sweated clothing which combined the languages of fairness and exploitation with the fear of disease.[26]

A delegation of trade unionists from the Boston Clothing Advisory Board – a group with perhaps 11,000 members that included tailors, cutters, trimmers, and contractors – investigated nearly one hundred of the tenements of Gotham. Where they "heard the machines rattling," they entered to find "dirt, overcrowding, and, in a number of cases, disease." Operative tailor Louis Asch reported that the smell was so bad in one place that his companion began to faint. The Boston workers expressed disgust in moral terms, using the gendered danger of unbarred female sexuality to condemn economic exploitation. That is, gendered expectations framed their arguments for class improvement. They pointed to men and women in the heat of summer in top floor apartments thrown together in a half-naked state, "degraded" by sleeping twelve to a room so "that no such thing as privacy or modesty on the part of men or women is possible," where "the girls were languid and listless. . . . All were bare-armed, some with their bosoms half bare and bathed in perspiration." Home and family no longer were private in these crowded rooms that jumbled sewing machines with cooking utensils, cotton batting with bedding. A cutter from the Clothing Trade Advisory Board objected to "turning the home into a workshop, and hiring outside people to come in to help."[27]

These skilled male workers used the language of violated domesticity to object to those who lessened operating costs by eliminating workshop rent. Yet it was a domesticity that distinguished between the respectable working class and the inhabitants of the tenements. The only sacred children were those who

---

[25] One firm, Myer & Andrews, contracted the making of knee breeches and finishing of men's suits to twenty-five hundred women in the city of Boston alone. "Prefer New York to Boston," *Boston Herald*, July 3, 1891; Wadlin, "The Sweating System in Massachusetts," 98; *Report on Sweating*, 237.

[26] "Labor's Great Army," *The Boston Herald*, Sept. 3, 1889.

[27] William Barnes, Louis Asch, and William Cogswell, *Report on Sweating*, 104–7, 156–7, 96–9.

would suffer from wearing clothes manufactured amidst scarlet fever and other zymotic diseases; tenement house children appeared as a form of vermin, seen as "lying about amongst the rags on the floor," described with horror as "SICK BABIES . . . LYING ON UNFINISHED GOODS." Child labor they condemned because it undercut the wages of grown men. Such children and their adult co-workers stood as victims rather than fellow workmen.[28]

To emphasize the gender ideology and self-interest behind such arguments does not negate the passion in which these men deplored economic exploitation. These more skilled workers, many of whom were English, Irish, or native-born, sought to distinguish themselves from the unskilled "hordes" whose entry into the United States they sought to restrict.[29] They condemned sweater Samuel Max for paying his men in clippings of cloth and reserved the term "white slavery, nothing more nor less" for Blumenthal who imported a fourteen-year-old from Germany to work only for board. They complained how the unionized workers' standard ten-hour day turned into fourteen hours and more, including work on Sundays.[30] They lamented how the pressmen's irons exacerbated the sweltering heat of the crowded tenements. The tenement house system injured those who worked under it, the consumers of its products, and the operative tailors who found their wages reduced in competition with it.[31]

In 1889 workers and contractors sought a cross-class alliance with employers. The Clothing Advisory Board appealed to an employer self-interest identified as similar to its own. While Boston manufacturing appeared more costly, it emphasized the hidden costs of New York: loss of business from consumers, made aware of New York conditions, who would reject clothing produced in diseased surroundings; loss of profit from New York contractors who cut additional clothes out of the remnants of fabric sent from Boston. The entire business community suffered from increased unemployment. While New Hampshire and Maine contractors had come to town for their goods and spent money in Boston, only a few New Yorkers became wealthy through the Boston trade. The Advisory Board recognized, "It is an injustice to deprive the New England mechanic of a chance to earn his living while expecting him to purchase the clothing made in New York tenements."[32]

[28] *Some Facts of Interest to Boston Clothing Merchants* (Boston: Clothing Trade Advisory Board, 1889), 9–18.

[29] *Report on Sweating*, 130, 100.

[30] Work on the Christian Sabbath was unacceptable in Boston where the Blue Laws still held sway; policing of violators discriminated against Jewish shops which took Saturday off as their religious day. See "Clothing Trade," *Labor Leader* (Boston), Aug. 17, 1889.

[31] "Working for Starvation Wages," *New York Times*, July 24, 1889; "Slavery in the Tenements," ibid., July 26, 1889; "Appeal to Boston Tailors," *Boston Herald*, Aug. 20, 1889.

[32] *Some Facts of Interest*, 5–7, 26–31; Alexander Keyssar, *Out of Work: The First Century of Unemployment in Massachusetts* (New York: Cambridge Univ. Press, 1986), 177–221, on garment unionists and unemployment.

The Advisory Board disclaimed sensationalism for the purpose of protecting community health, morality, and economic standards. *Some Facts of Interest to Boston Clothing Merchants* combined personal testimony, newspaper reports, and notarized statements. It evoked the subtext of the literature on tenement houses: the almost prurient interest in the physicality of the immigrant poor, whose body odors – indeed, whose very secretions of sweat, germs, excrement – mixed with the smell of garlic and the stink of rotting garbage and the dampness of faulty plumbing emitted by tenement living spaces to convey an anal horror, a fascination with the other who but for the protection of the wage could be the self. It revealed fear of and disgust with eastern and southern Europeans, seen as pauper laborers, dirty Jews and Italians who threatened the American workman's standard of living.[33]

Joining economic and justice arguments, the Advisory Board sought an equity based not on the market but on decency and a communal notion of self-sufficiency.[34] It proposed a voluntary policing of the industry by all sectors that included cooperation between employers and employees to stop sending goods to New York and to maintain fair prices. The goal of operative and contractor alike was to end the competition that had led wholesale manufacturers and merchant tailors to the cheaper labor of the tenements.

The garment unions understood that worker organization depended on ending tenement labor. But in a period of increasing labor supply and unrestrained competition, they were weak. The wholesale manufacturers ignored their call for cooperation; a few denied the existence of filth and low wages in tenement workshops, others expressed unconcern over where their goods were made as long as production costs remained low. Any alliance with contractors, their immediate employers, was inherently unstable.[35]

With interclass cooperation stymied, garment workers urged working-class consumers – the major purchasers of ready-made clothing – to buy union-made clothes. The union label represented a strategy prominent among those affiliated with the newly formed AFL, whose adherents by 1890 dominated Boston's Central Labor Union (CLU). Most effectively used by the Cigar Makers' International Union (CMIU) for high priced cigars, union label campaigns grew out of a sense of class solidarity. They were based on the power of producers as consumers that assumed an interdependency between those who supplied labor power and those who bought it. They also promoted a form of employer-employee cooperation, promising prosperity to employers who adhered to union demands. Such an assumption of the intertwined fate of workers and employers in a given industry was to hold for contractors and their

---

[33] *Some Facts of Interest*, passim.
[34] For this idea of justice, Alice Kessler-Harris, "The Just Price, the Free Market, and the Value of Women," *FS* 14 (Summer 1988), 233–50.
[35] "Appeal to Boston Tailors"; "Prefer New York to Boston"; "War on the 'Sweat Shops'," *Boston Herald*, July 8, 1891; Silas Loomis, *Report on Sweating*, 162.

employees. This form of cooperation replaced the worker-run and owned cooperative favored by the Knights, which had issued union labels. It involved the worker's wife as purchaser of family goods, while often denying her own position as either a waged or unwaged producer.[36] It also supplemented the even more difficult project of organizing the chaotic garment industry, where recent arrivals easily replaced those ready to protest the conditions of their toil.[37]

The campaign against sweated clothing intensified in 1890 and early 1891. Socialists argued for the end of wage slavery and class inequality as a prelude to any practical solution. *Labor Leader* editor Frank Foster, a spokesman for the CLU, insisted that higher wages would most improve the lives of clothing workers.[38] The union label would become a tool for organizing. The *Labor Leader* exhorted against the evils of the tenement system by admonishing readers to purchase labeled garments. It expressed the dualities shaping workingmen's protests against tenement labor: Self-interest interwoven with community interest, nativism with universalism, economic justice with moral outrage, fear of disease with fear of unfair competitors.[39] Yet only one firm adopted the union insignia from February 1889, when the AFL-affiliated Operative Tailors and Clothing Pressmen introduced their label, to March 1891, when the union pressed for state regulation.[40]

Merchants who advertised in the *Labor Leader* sought to distance themselves from tenement house clothing (and cigars). The Globe Clothing Store, which offered cheap ten-dollar Cheviot suits, reassured consumers that "none but pure and clean garments come into our stock." Plymouth Rock Co., later organized by the UGWA, constructed an advertisement out of its union label that not only associated union-made with microbe-free but asked, "So long as the union label is placed on our garments by union help, are we not clearly entitled to the patronage of union men?"[41]

36 Dana Frank, "Gender, Consumer Organizing, and the Seattle Labor Movement, 1919–1929," in *Work Engendered: Toward a New History of American Labor*, ed. Ava Baron (Ithaca, N.Y.: Cornell Univ. Press, 1991), 272–95. The Operators, Tailors and Pressmen's Protection Union ran a cooperative in Boston for a brief time. See "Three Shops," *Labor Leader* (Boston), Aug. 4, 1888.

37 Commons, "Immigration and Its Economic Effects," 312–13.

38 Edwin O'Donnell, "'Sweaters': The Root of the System Deep Down," *Labor Leader* (Boston), July 11, 1891; Frank Foster, "Anti-Tenement House League," ibid., Nov. 28, 1891.

39 "Going, Going, Gone!" *Labor Leader* (Boston), Nov. 22, 1890; John Crowley, "The Union Label," ibid., Mar. 7, 1891.

40 "Union Labels," *Labor Leader* (Boston), Feb. 2, 1889; "The Union Label: Its Adoption by the Continental Clothing House," ibid., Nov. 1, 1890; Crowley, "The Union Label."

41 "No Tenement House Clothing," advertisement for the Globe Clothing Store, *Labor Leader* (Boston), Apr. 11, 1891; advertisement, Plymouth Rock Clothing Co., ibid., Sept. 3, 1892. Plymouth Rock was among the few that operated on the factory system; its owner condemned sweating before the House Investigating Committee. See *Report on Sweating*, 170–3.

Certainly that was the position of John Crowley, secretary of the Clothing Operatives. Yet in his fight against the sweatshop from 1889 to 1891, he was never able to build a viable trade union. Membership in the Clothing Operatives National Union, a "national" union with two locals both in Boston, never reached above two hundred. This failure came in part from Crowley's personal animosities with other trade unionists[42] but also derived from his very conception of trade unionism. He would describe his union as chartered "exclusively" for the purpose of "exposing the workings of the Sweating System."[43] Such a definition confused trade unionism with social reform.

In March 1891 trade union opponents, who went on to form the UGWA, repudiated Crowley. They charged him with selling the label to clothing firms for personal profit and failing to issue it under trade union principles, that is, a "union scale of wages" and the democratic agreement of the workers. Crowley and his opponents would introduce successful anti-tenement house resolutions before state AFL conventions. While Crowley emphasized moral disgust, UGWA leaders stressed obstacles to organization.[44] In revoking the Clothing Operatives' charter in September 1891, AFL chief Gompers wrote Crowley that the UGWA promised greater success. Its head "assures me positively that no sweaters are or will be allowed in that organization." Strongly denouncing sweating, UGWA added its voice to the Massachusetts agitation by holding its first national convention in Boston.[45]

Even if opponents exaggerated charges against Crowley, he approached the problem of sweating from the perspective of class reconciliation rather than class consciousness. He applauded the birth of the Anti-Tenement House League in March, 1891 as creating a weapon to fight the sweatshop stronger

[42] Samuel Gompers to George Nisbit, Jan. 17, 1890, 414, reel 3, Gompers Papers, microfilm edition of Letterpress Books of Outgoing Correspondence; "Leaderettes," *Labor Leader* (Boston), July 18, 1891. The controversy over this union can be followed, although without details of the real issues involved, in Gompers's outgoing correspondence. For example, reel 4, to Crowley, Sept. 28, 1890, 122; to Crowley, Nov. 10, 1890, 233; to George Nisbit, Feb. 5, 1890, 436–7; to Crowley, Mar. 28, 1891, 654.

[43] *History and Report of the Work of the Anti-Tenement House League* (Boston: A. T. Bliss & Co., 1894), 6–7; for the Clothing Operatives National Union, see "AFL-CIO History of Organizations," typescript, Gompers Papers Project, University of Maryland, College Park. For another account of the Massachusetts campaign, see Arthur Mann, *Yankee Reformers in the Gilded Age* (Cambridge, Mass.: Harvard Univ. Press, 1954), 193–4.

[44] For example, "Massachusetts State AFL Convention," *Labor Leader* (Boston), Aug. 8, 1891; "AFL Convention," ibid., Aug. 12, 1893.

[45] "The Clothing Operatives. They Repudiate a Certain Label Now Being Issued," *Boston Herald*, Mar. 9, 1891; Gompers to Crowley, June 4, 1891, 915, reel 4; to Crowley, Aug. 3, 1891, 92, reel 5; to Crowley, Sept. 5, 1891, 197, reel 5; to Crowley, Sept. 19, 1891, 229, in reel 5; all in Gompers Papers; "To all persons whom it may concern," statement of UGWA against the sweating system, in *Sixth Annual Report of the New York Factory Inspectors* (Albany, N.Y.: The Argus Co., 1892), 44. UGWA opposition can be further traced in *The Garment Worker*.

than the trade union. The league consisted of gentlemen: concerned ministers and Brahmin reformers like Edward Everett Hale, lawyer Oliver Wendell Holmes, and Robert Treat Paine, Jr.; cooperators like former Knights of Labor leader George McNeill; and politicians like former governor J. Q. A. Brackett and senators George F. Hoar and Henry Cabot Lodge. Not that the league ignored labor standards; it stood "for the principle that the right to buy cheap is not a right to buy the lives of the working people for wages below the cost of production; that the right to sell dear is not a right to sell at price of honest goods, wearing apparel adulterated with dirt, disease and the degradation of the people." But it rejected strikes, which would "drive away every stitch of work to New York slums" for the light of exposure. As the league's first president, the Reverend O. P. Gifford, asserted, "There is moral power enough in the Christian conscience of America to destroy the tenement house and sweep away the Sweating System within a year if it were aroused." Crowley, who became the league's secretary, also counted on consumer rejection of "disease-bearing clothing at any price."[46] The league remained an organization for workers but not of them.

"Plague of 1893: The Terrible Scourge of the Tenement House And Reasons for State Control of the Clothing Trade" fully revealed Crowley's discourse of shock and moral outrage. Written in a Bellamyite manner as a future historian's account of how the government took over the manufacture of clothing, this tale recounted the brave but vain efforts of the half-starved clothing operatives to warn consumers of the tenement house peril. In this apologia for his own position on education, agitation, and legislation, Crowley blamed consumers of sweated goods, workers who had "no use for the golden rule" and clamored for only their own rights, a press that ignored the issue out of fear of losing advertising, and "the eye of law and order [that] winked" for the persistence of clothing made in the breeding grounds of plagues, even though Massachusetts legislated against the menace. His story turned the fears of New York factory inspectors[47] into a prophecy by having cholera break out in the tenement house district east of the Bowery and spread, from the infected clothing, throughout the country. Social disorder resulted:

> Frenzied mobs, black, frowning and terrible, whose eyes blazed like the enraged lion's, set fire to every clothing house and hunted down the owners, whom they slaughtered as a pack of wolves would their prey. Yet after all, these clothing dealers were only their [the people's] agents. Who shall attempt to describe these horrors: the desolation, waste, confusion, mortality, or the intense midsummer heat in which the air, poisoned by the stench of unburied corpses, quivered?

[46] *History and Report of the Anti-Tenement House League*, 79, 7–8, 90.

[47] *Fifth Annual Report of the New York State Factory Inspectors*, for 1890 (Albany, N.Y.: The Argus Company, 1891), 28; Frank Foster, "Look for the Label," *Labor Leader* (Boston), Mar. 7, 1891.

When the plague subsided, the people awoke and led by Massachusetts amended the Constitution to transfer the making and selling of clothing "from individuals and corporations into the hands of the government."[48]

Over the next few years, the Anti-Tenement House League agitated against sweatshops, convict-made shirts, and tenement-made postal uniforms. It also fought against tenement slums by incorporating the Peoples' Building Association to erect suburban low-cost housing for working people. It used the influence of prominent men to publicize the "evil" and introduce legislation more successfully than to convince clothing firms to drop the sweating system.[49] The league functioned, like the Massachusetts Society for Prevention of Cruelty to Children and other groups formed by elite reformers during these years, as a private agency that assumed public functions, sending its agents into the slums to report violations of laws and their own notions of family life.[50]

Agents, like Crowley, entered the houses of working people to condemn them as dirty, dark, and immoral. It was not enough to cite low wages or point out faulty plumbing, but the agents judged morality from whether women adhered to proper domestic values. A representative entry condemned a home finisher, off to return her work, who left "two children in a dirty room with the windows and doors locked. The youngest a mere baby had sore eyes, the oldest about three years made a number of faces at us which were astonishing in their variety." In spite of their intent, such terse reports suggest the determination of tenement dwellers to work despite meager piece rates. Agents became angry when homeworkers questioned their authority to investigate.[51]

The Anti-Tenement House League sought "to preserve and to protect the home." That goal did not keep it from sympathetically addressing the complexities of working-class women's lives. Trade unionists were interested in raising the standard of living for all families through a higher male wage rather than directly aiding female immigrants among the laboring poor. The league understood that such women needed to balance wage earning with dependent care. It proposed that employers build large buildings to accommodate finishing and place in the basement "accommodations and care-takers for the children of the mothers in their employ." In contrast, defenders of tenement labor deployed terms that would become a staple among manufacturers during the next century: Seamstresses did only certain processes at home, not because such labor was cheaper but because employers could not find sufficient numbers of workers "who can leave their homes at regular hours." Sympathetic contractors also opposed prohibition of tenement work because women

---

[48] This story was dated Boston, Jan. 5, 1998, though published in the May 1891 *Labor Leader*. See also Crowley, *Report on Sweating*, 108–16.

[49] *History and Report of the Anti-Tenement House League* for activities through late 1894; "Tenement-House Clothing," *New York Times*, Dec. 25, 1891.

[50] For such agencies, see Linda Gordon, *Heroes of Their Own Lives: The Politics and History of Family Violence* (New York: Viking, 1988), 27–58.

[51] *History and Report of the Anti-Tenement House League*, 52–3, 58–9.

dependent on such work ought to be able to "earn a livelihood in that way." Even government officials accepted the idea that homework aided poor women whose husbands were unable to support the family.[52] Woman's necessity, as opposed to man's freedom, justified home labor. Motherhood circumscribed their lives.

The league pushed for the Massachusetts law. "Plague of 1893" appeared while the state legislature was in the process of approving the first restriction on tenement manufacture. During the gubernatorial election of 1890, Crowley gained the promise of Democratic candidate William E. Russell to end "the shipment of manufactured clothing from New-York, provided the working-men should prove that the garments contained the germs of disease from the sweating houses where they were made."[53] Upon taking office in January 1891, Russell asked the head of the state sanitary police, who served as chief factory inspector, to send investigators to New York. A month later, Crowley himself toured the East Side with a New York deputy factory inspector and a local doctor.[54] Armed with evidence from these investigations, the chair of the state Senate's legislative committee requested Crowley to draw up a bill to prohibit the manufacturing of clothing in unsanitary surroundings, interdict menswear made outside the state under such conditions, and provide for tagging as "tenement-made." Though amended much to Crowley's chagrin, with "knowingly" added to qualify the responsibility of sellers, the bill became law in May 1891.[55]

Relying upon the power of consumers, this law derived from the clothing workers' campaign. It would eliminate competition from home workshops and New York-made goods. It distinguished between tenement shops where nonkin labored for wages and the home finishing by married women and widows. The former came under the factory law and required inspection by the district police who were to check for the presence of vermin and disease. But the latter remained untouched until the law was amended in 1892 to require licenses for families as a way to guard against contaminated clothing.[56] In essence, the clothing worker unions assessed the situation correctly – New York tailors were lowering their wages. The lot of home finishers, however miserable, engaged them less directly.

52 "Prefer New York to Boston"; John Crowley, Patsy J. Reilly, and appendix, *Report on Sweating*, 115, 134, 237.
53 The *Times* charged that Crowley delivered Russell fifteen thousand votes. "Horrors of Sweating," *New York Times*, Feb. 22, 1891.
54 "A Tour of 'Sweating Dens,'" *Boston Herald*, Feb. 22, 1891; Document 149, Governor's Message to the Legislature, Mar. 3, 1891, and "Report of District Police on Manufacture of Clothing in New York Tenement Houses," *Massachusetts Legislative Documents, House*, 1–274, 1891, especially 6–8.
55 *History and Report of the Anti-Tenement House League*, 10–16, 81; "The Sweat-Shop System," *Sixth Annual Report of the New York Factory Inspectors*, 38–40; "An Act to Prevent the Manufacture and Sale of Clothing Made in Unhealthy Places," Chap. 357, Massachusetts *Acts and Resolves*, May 1891, 197–8.
56 Griffin, "Operations of the Law in Massachusetts Relating to the 'Sweating System,'" 89–90.

By permitting homework by family members, the law proved flawed; finishing of men's and assembly of women's clothing continued in the tenements unabated. After a decade of agitation and legislation, in 1898 the newly formed Consumers' League of Massachusetts reported, "There are few sweat shops and garret workers, but there is also a lessening supply of work, and New England garment-workers are suffering because the manufacture of clothing is so largely carried on in New York and in other states, where factory laws are either more lenient or less respected."[57] In embracing the privacy of the family, organized workers and their reform allies in church and government had limited their power to interfere in the wage relation. Though the market entered what was considered the realm of the family, it was doubtful that the state could follow.

By 1900, twelve states had some form of tenement house regulation, modeled on the Massachusetts law. None prohibited work by family members in their own homes, though the 1892 New York law required licensing of family homework. It covered a wider range of goods than Massachusetts law.[58] The Bay state and New York amended their laws over the course of the decade to sharpen enforcement mechanisms. For New York, whose law became the most elaborate, amendments included licensing requirements and regulations on licenses; powers given to the health department and inspectors to tag or destroy garments exposed to infection; extension of the responsibility for illegal work to landlords and not just placed on the homeworkers – those with the least power and lowest in the chain of the sweating system. While the early New York law embraced dwellings as well as tenements and provided licensing for individual apartments, in 1904 it became restricted to the latter type of housing and licenses were given to entire buildings. This change responded to the problem of record keeping that developed with the constant movement of license-holding families, who had to be reinspected every time they moved into a new apartment. It also allowed agents to inspect halls, stairways, and water closets shared in common. Throughout this period the number of products covered by the law expanded.[59]

---

[57] The Consumers' League of Massachusetts, *Investigation of Hours and Other Conditions in the Mercantile Establishments of Boston, with a Report of the Work of the League from March to November, 1898* (no.2) (Boston: 1898), 13.

[58] Drawn up by the factory inspectors and introduced by Senator George Roesch in March 1892, the act (Laws of 1892, Chap. 655) amended Chap. 409 of the Laws of 1886, which regulated the employment of women and children in manufacturing and provided for the appointment of factory inspectors. "For the Toilers' Benefit," *New York World*, Mar. 6, 1892; "A Blow At Sweating Shops," ibid., Apr. 21, 1892; *Report on Sweating*, 261–4; *Sixth Annual Report of the New York Factory Inspectors*, 38–44; *Seventh Annual Report of the New York Factory Inspectors*, (Albany, N.Y.: James B. Lyon, 1893), 16–25.

[59] The states with tenement regulation were Massachusetts, New York, Illinois, New Jersey, Pennsylvania, Ohio, Maryland, Indiana, Missouri, Connecticut, Wisconsin, and Michigan. Willoughby, "Regulation of the Sweating System," 8–16; Miller, "Industrial Home Work," 15–18.

At best this early regulatory legislation improved "surface conditions" or pushed work into the surrounding countryside, as with Pennsylvania and Ohio, or out of the state, as with Massachusetts. Some acts, like New Jersey's of 1893 and Maryland's of 1896, were so general as to be meaningless or lacked enforcement mechanisms. Even with mandated inspection, enforcement proved difficult as employees were unable to read laws posted in English and inspectors could not prosecute the originators of the work. Reflecting on such early laws, New York's chief factory inspector Daniel O'Leary considered them "of no value. . . enforcement was practically abandoned after a couple of years of honest and earnest effort." Economic factors, rather than the law, accounted for any decline in the numbers of tenement workshops.[60]

State cooperation and the limits of the constitution

From the start, Boston workers and reformers doubted that individual state remedies were adequate to fight a national problem. The Anti-Tenement House League took its cause to Congress. Through the resulting hearings on the sweatshop problem, conducted by the U.S. House Committee on Manufactures in 1892, and the annual meetings in the 1890s of the International Association of Factory Inspectors of North America (IAFINA), the debate on the efficacy of state action faced the limits of the constitution. Freedom of contract doctrine blocked remedies against tenement-made clothing that creatively applied congressional power over interstate commerce or taxation, leaving homework regulation to the states until World War I. Men's right to contract left women to engage in sweated labor in their own homes.

In January 1892, after negotiations with leading Boston clothing firms to renounce tenement manufacturing broke down, the Anti-Tenement House League memorialized Congress for an investigation into the sweating system. Senator George Hoar (R.-Mass.), an honorary vice-president of the league, introduced its bill. Interstate sales of clothing would be forbidden if made in "improper" places, defined as any tenement house, any room in violation of factory laws, or any place with diseases or filth. The bill took the tagging principle to an extreme, with all places of production listed. Violators would be fined between fifty and a hundred dollars for each offense and the secretary of the treasury would appoint an inspector for each state.[61]

---

[60] Willoughby, "Regulation of the Sweating System," 7–16; William J. Milligan, "The Sweatshop," *Tenth Annual Convention of the IAFINA*, 1896 (Chicago, Ill.: Harman, Geng and Co., 1896), 54–5; State of New York, *Report and Testimony Taken Before the Special Committee of the Assembly Appointed to Investigate the Condition of Female Labor in the City of New York* (Reinhard Committee), Assembly Report, n. 97 (Albany, N.Y.: Wynkeop Hallenbeck Crawford Co., 1896), 1: 343, 349, 358; Daniel O'Leary, "Tenement House Manufacture," *Twenty-Third Annual Convention of the IAFINA*, 1909 (Ottawa, Canada: Esdale Press Printers, n.d.), 58–60.

[61] *History and Report of the Anti-Tenement House League*, 19–21; Mr. Hoar, *Congressional Record-Senate*, 52nd Cong., 1st Sess., v. 120 (1892), 139, 390.

The bill promptly went to the Committee on Education and Labor. Here too the Anti-Tenement House League initiated events, with Congressman Sherman Hoar (R.-Mass.) leading the fight for an inquiry. Budget-minded skeptics worried that Congress lacked jurisdiction; the Supreme Court had denied their ability to enact quarantine laws for the states. Admitting that the states controlled local health conditions, Sherman Hoar asserted that Congress too had its constitutionally sanctioned remedies in the power to tax or brand goods involved in interstate commerce. Moreover, Congress alone could touch one of the main "causes of the evil . . . our system of practically free immigration." Hoar joined other commentators on the sweating problem – from skilled workers and clothing merchants to factory investigators – who blamed sweating on immigration.[62]

Senator Hoar's bill generated favorable petitions from trade unionists in Ohio, Chicago, and Minnesota, concerned citizens in New York, and the Massachusetts legislature. The bill and the possibility of hearings also led clothing manufacturers to organize. They evoked the freedom of the market and the rights of the individual, seemingly gender neutral constructs that ignored the power relations under which freedom and rights were exercised. Boston clothiers authorized a committee to lobby Congress with the goal of killing the measure. Forty-nine Chicago firms denied that disease ever had come from clothing sold "by the regular dealers." Manufacturers complained that sanitary inspection belonged to the municipalities and not the national government; the proposed system would be expensive, cumbersome, and oppressive. Unscrupulous competitors could interfere with the tags of legitimate manufacturers. Such a law would infringe "upon the personal and property rights of American citizens."[63]

Unsuccessful in delaying House approval of an inquiry, the clothing manufacturers turned up in Washington to testify during the first session of hearings to discover that the Committee on Manufactures was interested only in evidence on the sweating system and not the Hoar bill. But congressmen did inquire into opinions about tagging and other remedies. The wholesale clothing trade of Boston accepted marking of contaminated goods but rejected indiscriminate tagging of all work for the expense of additional record keeping and potential misuse by competitors and labor organizers. Craft unionists joined this business opposition. Still hostile to the reformist style of the league, the

---

[62] *Congressional Record-House*, 52nd Cong., 1st Sess., v. 120 (1892), 202; 1116–20. For examples of blaming immigrants, see *Sixth Annual Report of the New York Factory Inspectors*, 40; George Gilbert, Louis Sheinwald, and appendix, *Report on Sweating*, 120, 140–1, 237.

[63] *History and Report of the Anti-Tenement House League*, 22–3; petition, Chicago Manufacturers; letter to Hon. John Sherman, U.S. Senate from A. B. Voorheis and M. E. Moch, Mar. 16, 1892; petition, Zanesville Trades and Labor Council, Mar. 21, 1892, Records of the U.S. Senate, Committee of Education and Labor, 52nd Cong., 1st Sess., RG46, NA; see *Congressional Record-Senate*, v. 122, 2180; v. 121, 1900, 1901; v. 122, 2032, 2299, 2300, 2680; v. 123, 3369, 3732.

UGWA claimed the union label as a more reliable guide to healthful conditions than a factory inspector's tag.[64]

The House Committee on Manufactures decided not to draft any legislation, preferring to watch the working of recent state and local laws. It looked favorably on some kind of tracing system. But federalism led the committee to recommend legislation with minimal "interference with the business of the citizen, and least exercise of Federal jurisdiction." A revised league bill, introduced in the next Congress, ran into additional roadblocks, including crippling opposition from southern senators who bottled the bill up in committee by questioning its constitutionality.[65]

Factory inspectors also debated the best methods to uproot sweating and end tenement house labor. Their annual meetings in the 1890s reflected a growing professional consciousness of those empowered to administer labor laws. Bureaus of labor statistics formed as a response to the economic and social upheavals of post–Civil War America. Factory inspectorates evolved under pressure from trade unionists and reformers who found that investigation alone could not mitigate "the labor problem." Despite chronic underfunding and often hampered by political appointees, the early factory inspectors established procedures. Often they were working-class women and men, close to trade unions. Through its annual meetings, the IAFINA spearheaded the growth of a national labor standards agenda.[66]

Although state officials, the factory inspectors searched for national solutions to tenement homework. Before local legislatures, they argued that labor laws would not drive manufacturing to other states because everywhere rules would limit permissible acts. But experience taught them otherwise. Despite regulatory laws, tenement clothing still was produced in New York, Massachusetts, and Illinois; enforcement of these acts actually facilitated the spread of homework to other states that lacked similar legislation.[67]

The 1894 convention asked association president John Franey of New York to prepare a paper on the best way to suppress the system. Franey, a trade

[64] Sidney Cushing, Max Silverman, John H. Prentiss, Edward Rose, Samuel Goldmann, Wolf Chuck, Silas W. Loomis, *Report on Sweating*, 33, 37–46, 55–6, 78–9, 82–4, 125, 145, 165–9; also see the appendix to this report, 236–42. For the UGWA, *Sixth Annual Report of the New York Factory Inspectors*, 44.

[65] *Report on Sweating*, xx–xxix; *History and Report of the Anti-Tenement House League*, 70–2.

[66] Jeremy P. Felt, *Hostages of Fortune: Child Labor Reform in New York State* (Syracuse, N.Y.: Syracuse Univ. Press, 1965), 17–37; Leiby, *Carroll Wright and Labor Reform*, 39–94; Brock, *Investigation and Responsibility*, 148–84; Kathryn Kish Sklar, "Why Did Women Factory Inspectors Wield More Power in the United States Than Elsewhere, 1890–1910?," unpublished paper, Conference on the History of Occupational Safety and Health, George Meany Center, 1991.

[67] John Franey, "The Factory Laws of New York and the Recent Amendments Thereto," *Sixth Annual Convention of the IAFINA*, 97; Franey, "A Plan to Abolish the Sweating System," *Eighth Annual Convention of the IAFINA*, 1894 (Cleveland, Ohio: Forest City Printing House, 1894), 101–2; Resolution of Mrs. Stevens, ibid., 96.

unionist from Buffalo, sought to relieve the "white slaves of the cities" by taxing
wholesale manufacturers, contractors, and subcontractors. Other remedies had
failed. Individual state laws improved sanitary conditions without raising wages
or preventing spread of the system. Union label campaigns suffered from trade
union weakness and public desire to buy cheap. Just as the state taxed tobacco
manufacturing and oleomargarine to regulate such industries, it could tax
clothing made in unclean places to "promote the health and welfare of the
people." Indirect legislation could accomplish what otherwise would be found
unconstitutional.[68]

Not all factory inspectors agreed that such a course was either constitutional
or necessary. Some wished to wait for the results of state legislation; others
believed in states' rights and felt that Franey's proposal interfered with individual rights as well, discriminating "against the home worker and in favor of
the corporations." It would "place a tax upon one feature, or branch of an
industry, and not upon the industry as a whole." Such objections put more
faith in private acts – the individual's refusal to purchase cheap clothing – than
in public laws.[69]

Nearly two-thirds of the factory inspectors endorsed the proposal. Florence
Kelley, who would play an increasingly central role in the fight against
homework over the next quarter century, expressed the dominant sentiment.
Despite an able corps of assistants and cooperation from many manufacturers,
her attempt to stop sweatshops had proved ineffectual. She needed "more
stringent laws." Congressman Sultzer from New York tried to give her one. He
introduced Franey's scheme as "a bill to raise additional revenue for the support
of the government." In early 1896 Franey toured the country to promote the
bill and reformers lobbied Congress, but it died in committee.[70]

Beliefs in freedom of contract and states' rights hampered congressional
action. Even Sherman Hoar felt that Congress was unable to interfere with the
labor contract. He explained to one tailor at the 1892 hearings: "All we can do
on earth is to simply regulate the interstate commerce in clothing. Now, there
is no need of taking up any theories outside of that possibility because you
might just as well undertake to have us change the time when the moon shines
as these matters." Yet the final report of the Committee on Manufactures also
approvingly cited Boston housing reformer Joseph Lee who argued, "the great
evil of the sweating system, then is not that it is a system of slavery, or that the

---

[68] John Franey, "A Plan to Abolish the Sweating System," 97–104; also reprinted as "The
Sweating Evil," *Labor Leader* (Boston), Dec. 29, 1894.

[69] *Ninth Annual Convention of the IAFINA*, 1895 (Cleveland, Ohio: Forest City Printing House,
1895), 68–75.

[70] Ibid., for the bill, Third Annual Report of the Factory Inspectors of Illinois for the Fiscal
Year Ending December 1895 (Springfield: Ed. F. Hartman, 1896), 62–3; *Congressional Record-
House*, 54th Cong., 1st sess., 513; flyer, "Abolish the Sweating System: Mass Meeting," "To
Abolish Sweat Shops," *Chicago Tribune*, Mar. 9, 1896, HH Scrapbooks, vol. 1, "Clippings –
1896," 68.

liberty of the workers is in any way interfered with, but that, on the contrary, too great liberty is allowed workers and employers as to conditions under which the work shall be carried on." Here the language of slavery and liberty conflated as the freedom of the market proved to be a greater peril than sweating itself. Whether liberty would take precedence over the police power depended on who defined the terms, a question not only of politics as usually understood but also of political economy.[71]

The factory inspectors also ran up against the emerging judicial interpretation of the Fourteenth Amendment. John Griffin of Massachusetts explained their dilemma: "If the State could limit the number of hours that men are employed, as it does the hours of women and minors, we might look for a speedy reform." But the courts had rejected interference with a man's freedom of contract. Though living in "the era of contracts," Franey argued for curtailing this power. Other state factory inspectors accepted that "the home of a man is sacred," but denied the applicability of this precept to "these miserable, persecuted foreigners [who] have no idea of home except as a shelter, and no thought of cleanliness." John Crowley already had exposed the contradictions in the freedom of contract doctrine when he declared: "A man's house was his castle, even though it breathed a plague."[72]

Hampered by the right to contract, state legislatures could regulate only in the name of public health. To justify the police power, Massachusetts relied upon the dominant ideological understanding of the home. Those who turned their homes into workshops, the state legislature declared, destroyed the privacy of the home, becoming subject to factory laws. Inspector Mary O'Reilley of Pennsylvania rationalized state invasion of the private: "If the community finds that its homes are being endangered because of this questionable liberty, then a sense of duty stronger than the consideration for one home, must impel the people to come to the rescue of all homes, and make the necessary division between home and workshop." If tenement sweatshops turned homes into factories, then government had the duty to rid the home of the workshop menace. Whether that duty would apply to home finishers as well as home workshops faced a stiffer legal challenge. For *Jacobs* stymied the state's ability to prohibit homework outright when engaged in by the family.[73] Shrouded in gender neutrality, policy discourse contained within notions of slavery, liberty, and contract a central paradox: Men's rights intensified women's wrongs.

[71] *Report on Sweating*, 152, xxviii.

[72] *History and Report of the Anti-Tenement House League*, 77, 86; Griffin, "The Sweating System of Massachusetts," 109–10; Franey, "A Plan to Abolish The Sweating System," 101; Milligan, "The Sweatshop," 55; Crowley, "Plague of 1893."

[73] John H. Plunkett, "The Sweating System," *Tenth Annual Convention of the IAFINA*, 67; Mary O'Reilley, "Sweat-Shop Life in Pennsylvania," *Ninth Annual Convention of the IAFINA*, 68; Reinhard Committee, 1:15.

The Chicago alliance:
The contest over "women's rights"

Organizing labor also initiated the agitation in Chicago against the sweat-shop, but here women trade unionists, socialists, and settlement workers played a key role in shaping, lobbying for, and administrating the resulting legislation. Only in Illinois was the prohibition of garmentmaking in un-clean places or tenement homes by unrelated people connected to other labor standards: the eight-hour day for women and the prohibition of child labor under fourteen. As muckraking reformer Henry Demarest Lloyd em-phasized, "The crucial point involved in the sweat shop law is the right of the state to control contracts made by women for the sale of their labor." Florence Kelley further hoped that enforcement of the law, by bringing larger numbers of laborers into the factory, would create conditions condu-cive to worker self-organization.[74]

Kelley and other Hull House women connected the general condition of women wage earners with the presence of tenement sweatshops and home finishing. They understood the problem of the sweatshops to be more than merely competition with inside or factory tailors, although Kelley was keenly aware of the "demoralization of a vast trade" brought about in its wake. Not beyond portraying home-made garments as carriers of dreaded diseases to the unsuspecting middle class, Kelley sought to unravel the system by linking public health to the end of exploitative labor and by providing better options for women workers through the eight-hour provision. Employers fought back in the courts. The resulting case – *Ritchie v. People*[75] – offered immigrant mothers and their children the right to contract even though economic inequality in-validated such a gift.[76]

Chicago stood as the nation's second major garment center, with some thirteen thousand employed in the trade. Its immigrant work force, even more diverse than New York's, was having a difficult time sustaining viable unions. As in Boston, wholesale houses bought cheap goods from the sweaters of Gotham, which further lowered the rates paid to local contractors. Like the Hub's CLU, skilled, native-born and northern European immigrants domi-nated the Chicago Trade and Labor Assembly (CTLA). Yet this group of worker organizations responded favorably to the request of striking Jewish cloakmakers under Abraham Bisno to investigate tenement sweatshops in August 1891,

---

[74] Florence Kelley, "The Sweating-System," 32, 34, 38; Henry D. Lloyd reported in "Talks to Toilers," Mar. 27, 1894, unidentified news clipping, in Morgan Scrapbook, "Reports of Woman's Alliance and Schools," Book 2.

[75] 155 Ill. 98, 40 N.E. 454 (1895).

[76] Meredith Tax, *The Rising of the Women: Feminist Solidarity and Class Conflict, 1880–1917* (New York: Monthly Review Press, 1980), 77–88; Sklar, "Hull House in the 1890s"; Mari Jo Buhle, *Women and American Socialism, 1870–1920* (Urbana: Univ. of Illinois Press, 1981), 71–3.

nearly half a year before Kelley arrived in Chicago.[77] Perhaps it feared a general lowering of wages; perhaps the strength of socialists within the organization led to labor solidarity. Certainly the presence of Elizabeth Morgan – housewife, trade unionist, trade assembly representative, and wife of socialist leader and CTLA founder Thomas Morgan – must be considered.

A child laborer in her native England, Morgan was part of a group of working-class women in the 1880s and early 1890s as remarkable in their own ways as the more privileged women that made Hull House the center of social reform during the next decade. They were socialists (or anarchists) and active trade unionists. Founders of the Ladies Federal Labor Union (charted by the AFL in 1888 as an occupationally diverse women's union), Morgan and her friends championed the woman and the child wage earner: receiving complaints, securing enforcement of local and state laws, and involving labor and women's organizations in the cause. In the fall of 1888, they responded to a series of *Chicago Times* articles on "City Slave Girls" by spearheading the creation of the Illinois Woman's Alliance. A cross-class umbrella of women's groups, the Alliance attacked child labor and the sweatshop as barriers to the unionization of women and detriments to health and welfare. Its goals included enforcement of existing laws and enactment of new ones.[78]

The Alliance was "a clear case of women helping women," leaders explained. In 1888 feminists as well as class-conscious workers brought a moralistic, social purity stance to that effort.[79] Poor sanitary conditions in the workplace destroyed "womanly purity," "dwarf[ed] the physique, starv[ed] the intellect, and weaken[ed] the morality of our children." The Alliance fought against the sweatshop in the context of women's overall position as workers, mothers of children, and free individuals. It simultaneously campaigned for compulsory education, lobbied for the appointment of women factory inspectors, and monitored the treatment of prostitutes and other women in the night courts. In doing so, it maintained dominant gender conventions by arguing for national strength through preservation of "manly and womanly virtues."[80]

In 1891 Morgan toured the sweatshops with other representatives from the

[77] In 1893 the male Cloak Makers only had 230 members and the Women's Cloak Makers' Union, between 30 and 50. CTLA, *The New Slavery: Investigation into the Sweating System as Applied to the Manufacture of Wearing Apparel* (Chicago: Detwiler Print, Rights of Labor Office, 1891), 8; Abraham Bisno also recounts the difficulty of organizing against Chicago employers in *Report and Findings of the Joint Committee to Investigate the "Sweat Shop" System, Together with a Transcript of the Testimony Taken by the Committee* (Springfield, Ill.: H. W. Bokker, State Printer and Binder, 1893), 242.

[78] Tax, *Rising of the Women*; "To Help the Slave Girls," *Chicago Times*, Aug. 18, 1888; "City Slave Girls," Ibid., Oct. 24, 1888, Morgan Scrapbook.

[79] Linda Gordon and Ellen DuBois, "Seeking Ecstasy on the Battlefield: Danger and Pleasure in Nineteenth-Century Feminist Sexual Thought," *FS* 9 (Spring 1983): 7–25.

[80] Tax, *Rising of the Women*; "Thanks 'The Times'," Aug. 20, 1888; "Women Make a Request," Apr. 1889; "AnotherVictory," Aug. 1889; "Women Factory Inspectors," Aug. 14, 1889; "The Women's [sic] Alliance," Dec. 8, 1889, unidentified clippings, Morgan Scrapbook.

CTLA, the city's attorney, a city health inspector, members of the Cloak Makers' Union, and the press. They visited thirty "sweating dens," of which nearly all were dwelling houses. *The New Slavery: Investigation into The Sweating System as Applied to the Manufacture of Wearing Apparel*, issued the next month, resembled reports from other cities. Its descriptions of overcrowded and filthy workshops contained those binary oppositions of natural and unnatural, pure and impure, light and darkness, clean and dirty, good and bad, and us and them that dominated discussions of sweated labor. To evoke working-class misery even further, the CTLA committee contrasted the sweaters' city with the White City being built for the World's Fair. The sweaters' victims deserved legal protection. But, in a racialist manner, Morgan and her fellow investigators blamed them for transporting an Old World system of exploitation to the New, destabilizing the labor market, and straining government resources.[81]

The Chicago labor movement appealed to "public opinion" to demand enforcement of municipal sanitary ordinances, establishment of a state Bureau of Sanitation, and fining of sweaters and their landlords for violations of such laws. Unlike the tone of the earlier exposé by Boston workers, an edge of class resentment pervaded their demands. Like many socialists of the day, Morgan held a belief in organized agitation for government action, especially in her case by women for women, with a class-conscious skepticism over its outcome. Her poem "The Sweater's Lament" expressed this tension:

> Abolish the sweat-shops;
>   Arise in your might,
> We women demand it
>   By all that is right.
> By all that is sacred,
>   By all that is just,
> We urge you go forward;
>   In you is our trust.
>
> And I and my sisters,
>   Poor, down-trodden slaves,
> Will praise you and bless
>   Aye! E'en from the graves
> To which we are driven
>   While earning our bread,
> Oh, would it were over!
> *There's rest with the dead.*

If the seamstress remains a "slave," Morgan has transformed her, even while relying on the conventions of sentimental poetry. If not an agent active for her own liberation, the sewing woman has become one who recognizes that she

[81] "Report of the Committee on Child's Labor," Nov. 1891, Morgan Scrapbook; *The New Slavery*.

has rights, one who demands justice, though dependent on others to pursue her struggle.[82]

Morgan carried on the struggle by aiding federal and state investigations, visiting nearly two hundred tenements from September 1891 through May 1892. She took members of the House of Representatives around Chicago during their hearings in the spring of 1892 and the following February she served as a special agent, with Florence Kelley, to a committee of the state legislature appointed to study the sweating problem and propose legislation. Building upon existent regulations, her recommendations included adherence by all manufacturing to sanitary and other state and federal laws, labeling of goods covered by these laws, monthly reporting of employee demographics and wages by manufacturers, licensing of manufacturers rather than contractors, and prohibition of child labor under fourteen. She would forbid all manufacturing in homes, but her proposal lacked an adequate enforcement mechanism or clear penalties. Perhaps skepticism about enforcement stymied creative thinking on the matter.[83]

The state investigation of 1893 responded to an agitation fanned by settlement house workers, their male allies in social reform and the churches, and the Cloak Makers' Union. By April 1892, Florence Kelley had thrown herself into the sweatshop campaign. Daughter of the radical Republican congressman from Pennsylvania William "Pig Iron" Kelley, Kelley belonged to that early generation of college-educated women who gained training in the social sciences. During postgraduate studies in Zurich, she became a socialist and married a comrade. She translated into English Friedrich Engels's *Condition of the Working Class in England in 1844*. By the time she reached Hull House, seeking a divorce from her husband and custody of their children, she was moving toward the gradualist Fabian variety of socialism and had already launched her career as an activist investigator of the conditions of women's and children's labor.[84]

"A fever heat of interest" surrounded the Chicago agitation. Kelley provided Engels with a close description of the campaign: of congressmen "travelling about the country looking into the dens at night and unattended," the CTLA "paying the expenses of weekly mass meetings," and the frustration

---

[82] *The New Slavery*, 18–20; "Committee on Child's Labor"; Mrs. T. J. Morgan, "The Sweater's Lament," Morgan Scrapbook.

[83] Mrs. T. J. Morgan, *Report on Sweating*, 71–4; *Report and Findings*, 10–12, 144–50; "Modern Slave Dens," Chicago *Inter-Ocean*, Feb. 12, 1893; "'Sweating' Must Go," [*Chicago News*], n.d.; "They Must Lie to Live," *Chicago Times*, Feb. 12, 1893, HH Scrapbooks, vol. 1, "Clippings 1893." For a more critical assessment of Morgan, see Kathryn Kish Sklar, *Florence Kelley and Women's Political Culture: Doing the Nation's Work* (New Haven, Conn.: Yale Univ. Press, 1994), vol. 1, chap. 9.

[84] Sklar, *Florence Kelley and Women's Political Culture*; *The Autobiography of Florence Kelley: Notes of Sixty Years*, ed. Kathryn Kish Sklar (Chicago: Charles H. Kerr, 1986); Josephine Goldmark, *Impatient Crusader: Florence Kelley's Life Story* (Urbana: University of Illinois Press, 1953).

of "sanitary authorities" with attempts at tenement inspection. "So we may expect some of the palliative measures pretty soon," Kelley predicted. The group behind this campaign consisted of Henry Demarest Lloyd, socialist physician Bayard Holmes, Kelley, and cofounder of Hull House Ellen Gates Starr, also a socialist – though Kelley, Lloyd, and the cloakmakers' leader Abraham Bisno "were in the heart of the movement" and were the ones who drew up the cloakmakers' bill submitted to the legislative committee the next year.[85]

Kelley proposed that the state Bureau of Labor Statistics study the system in Chicago and in May 1892 she became a special agent of the bureau, investigating nearly two thousand cases. Her report, "The Sweating System in Chicago," skillfully combined a powerful description of the facts, statistical tables, and moral outrage. Well versed in English and European precedents, she recommended legislation but argued, "The delinquent must be confronted not only with the law on the statute book but the law-officer at his door." That is, legislation required a well-funded factory inspectorate. She concluded with a powerful denunciation of those who defended the system as allowing "thrifty women to contribute to the support of their families, and widows to stay with their children while working for them." Kelley presented a class analysis of homework but understood class as a gendered experience. Throughout her career, she would support a living wage for men as an alternative to the economic and physical exploitation of mothers, holding this belief, like many women unionists, along with a defense of working women's rights. In less sympathetic hands, family wage ideology would justify a lower women's wage and a labor market segmented by sex. For Kelley, social welfare and decent labor standards provided an interconnected web that allowed working-class power and self-organization to flourish.[86]

Over the summer, Kelley continued the campaign, exposing sweatshop employers to their ministers and lecturing the department store magnate Marshall Field against sending out work. Field claimed to provide "worthy widows" a way to earn money while caring for their children. Kelley told Engels, "The only one I have yet found working for him, earned $9.37 in 13 weeks and we fed her children meanwhile!" Her report on the sweating system

[85] Dorothy Rose Blumberg, *Florence Kelley: The Making of a Social Pioneer* (New York: Augustus M. Kelley, 1966), 127–35, who reprints Kelley's letters to Engels; see also Abraham Bisno, *Abraham Bisno: Union Pioneer* (Madison: Univ. of Wisconsin Press, 1967), 122–3; Bisno, *Report and Findings*, 239; "Cloakmakers Frame a Labor Bill," 1893, HH Scrapbook.

[86] "The Sweating System in Chicago," *Seventh Biennial Report of Illinois Bureau of Labor Statistics*, (Springfield, Ill.: State Printer, 1892), Part 2: 357–443, especially 400–2; Martha May, "The Historical Problem of the Family Wage: The Ford Motor Company and the Five Dollar Day," *FS* 8 (Summer 1982): 399–424; Alice Kessler-Harris, *A Woman's Wage: Historical Meanings and Social Consequences* (Lexington: The Univ. Press of Kentucky, 1990), 6–56; Lawrence Glickman, "A Living Wage: Political Economy, Gender, and Consumerism in American Culture, 1880–1925 " (Ph.D. diss. Univ. of California, Berkeley, 1992).

confirmed that "the total insufficiency of the earnings of widows and dependent women . . . does not commend it as a boon even to them."[87]

Enough agitation on the question existed that the legislature, in January
1893, under the newly elected governor John Peter Altgeld, appointed a
special committee to survey Chicago's sweatshops. A commission created to
appease labor and provide rural legislators a "junket to Chicago" succumbed
to Hull House hospitality and the women's "personally conducted visits to
sweatshops."The committee emerged with "a report so compendious, so readable,
so surprising that they presented it with pride to the legislature," Kelley later
explained. The local newspapers promoted reform through sensationalized
stories; "no one was yet blasé."[88]

The reform coalition kept up public pressure during these hearings. A
February mass meeting at the Central Music Hall reflected a "united front"
among trade unionists, settlement workers, women's organizations, and reform clergy.[89] Chaired by bookbinder Mary Kenney, a working-class member
of the Hull House circle, arranged with CTLA representatives Elizabeth
Morgan and W. S. Timblin, the Central Hall meeting passed resolutions that
satisfied all interests in the reform coalition. Read by the well-respected Lloyd,
some of them derived from earlier statements by the Anti-Tenement House
League, especially those that attacked the system in graphic, moralistic terms.
Some decried the decentralization of the garment trade as being against the
technological advance of industry from foot power to electricity; others attacked
"our model merchants," requesting that Marshall Field and the rest end the
sweatshop. In a similar socialist vein, one called upon the people to take from
private hands the business of making clothing if such capitalists failed to act.
Others concentrated on the right of working people to trade unions and asked
for the formation of consumers' leagues. Led by the Illinois Woman's Alliance,
Chicago women "pledged" to purchase only "uncontaminated goods, made
under humane conditions" and those made "by union labor paid the full living
wages that are the due of every working member of the American commonwealth."[90]

Male speakers combined middle-class fears of contamination with a defense
of working women. Their class paternalism was gendered, embracing the
family wage and traditional morality. Reverend O. P. Gifford, then a clergy-

---

[87] Blumberg, *Florence Kelley*; Kelley, *Report and Findings*, 186–7; "The Sweating System in Chicago," 401.

[88] Florence Kelley, in *The Survey*, June 1, 1927, 273, quoted in Blumberg, 133.

[89] This phrase is from Tax, *Rising of the Women*, 89.

[90] Bisno, *Union Pioneer*, 148; "To Stop Sweating," *Chicago Inter-Ocean*, Feb. 20, 1893; "Down With Sweaters," *Chicago Herald*, Feb. 20, 1893; "Protest of Labor," *Chicago Tribune*, Feb. 20, 1893; "Like Priest and Levite," *Chicago Times*, Feb. 20, 1892; "Oppose Sweat-Shops," *Chicago News*, Feb. 20, 1893, HH Scrapbooks. Speakers included H. D. Lloyd, Florence Kelley, John Crowley, Thomas Morgan, and New York's *Daily Forward* editor Abraham Cahan.

man in Chicago, proclaimed, "The man should make the money and the woman remain at home to care for it. [A cry of 'Amen.'] Work should not be added to her burden of child bearing." He vigorously defended working-class women as women, which undoubtedly added to the crowd's favorable response to his speech: "The state should see that poor women shall not have to bear the burden of a mule. The state cannot afford to sink knee deep in evil for the sake of a fur cape on the shoulders of a society belle." Even middle-class male reformers could recognize that the economic realities of poor women's lives made labor a necessity. Though preferring the domestic ideal for all women, Gifford supported decent wages for those women who had to work. Working-class men like Abraham Bisno, in turn, combined proper gender roles with their own economic reasoning. Finishers, he inaccurately explained to the legislative committee, "compete with their husbands with their ability to work so cheap in the house themselves." Eliminate homework and husbands could support their families.[91]

Kelley revealed her socialist feminism. Praising the cloakmakers, she focused on the women among them. Unlike Bisno, she credited the antisweatshop bill to "the women cloakmakers [who] for years past have been watching the endeavors of their sisters in the Eastern States to get legislation and honest inspection." With the help of experts, like Kelley herself, they drafted a bill which their male counterparts and custom tailors accepted. While the enormity of the problem and intensity of capitalist opposition rendered the law inadequate, Kelley found the means for public education in its enactment and enforcement.[92]

The cloakmakers cast their 1893 bill broadly. It incorporated provisions for a factory inspector that Massachusetts and New York had prior to enacting sweatshop regulation. It sought to "prohibit the manufacture of clothing in any dwelling by any woman or child." Without this provision, Kelley testified to the state investigating committee, the whole bill would "fail of its object." This section distinguished their bill from acts in other states and from the final bill drawn up by the Illinois legislature. The Illinois law maintained the prohibition against manufacturing "coats, vests, trousers, knee-pants, overalls, cloaks, shirts, purses, feathers, artificial flowers or cigars" for wages in tenements and dwellings, "except by the immediate members of the family" (defined as husband, wife, and children). Even such goods made by families had to be free from vermin and made in clean places. It gave the Board of Health and factory inspector power to stop production in the face of infectious disease.

None of these specific provisions had appeared in the cloakmakers' original bill because it attempted to prohibit homework by women and children, not merely regulate it. Kelley later named "the home finisher, the most dangerous and wretched link in this chain" of subcontractors and sweatshops. With women

[91] "To Stop Sweating"; Bisno, *Report and Findings*, 241.
[92] "Like Priest and Levite"; "Protest of Labor."

allowed to work in their own homes, a significant portion of the system would remain unless employers – fearing the act's penalties – curtailed such employment. The additional eight-hour and child labor sections of the Illinois law, if enforced, offered some promise to curb even home finishing because another section of the act defined a workshop "for the purposes of inspection" as wherever manufacturing occurred with the intent to sell.[93]

Jane Addams and the other women of Hull House lobbied hard for passage of the Illinois law. They helped to create the Chicago Anti-Sweat Shop League, with Lloyd as president, to press for passage of the bill, visit sweatshops, and form a consumers' league. Addams recalled, "We insisted that well-known Chicago women should accompany this first little group of settlement folk who with trade-unionists moved upon the state capitol in behalf of factory legislation." At the time, employers mounted little significant opposition and the bill passed. Altgeld appointed Kelley the first factory inspector (after Lloyd turned him down), and Kelley chose socialist trade unionists Bisno and Alzina Stevens, as well as Mary Kenney, as her assistants. They fanatically inspected factories and workshops, examined children for working permits, educated workers in the provisions of the law, and brought court suits against employer violators. They went against the general feeling, as Bisno put it, that "labor legislation was . . . a joke," that it "was passed mainly as political fodder . . . [and was] not really to be enforced."[94]

But not all were so sanguine about the prospects of enforcement. After praising the noble intentions of the law, the *Chicago Post* editorialized: "No law can fix the hours of female labor or any other labor, excepting only the law of supply and demand, which was not passed by the legislature of Illinois." Against this classically liberal skepticism over whether the state could cure poverty by statute stood an equally harsh questioning of the outcome by radicals like labor journalist Lizzie M. Holmes. She was one of the organizers, with Elizabeth Morgan, of women's trade unions in the 1880s. Holmes mocked middle-class fears of contagion behind the resulting bill, which she viewed as at best an experiment that might lead to better remedies. Holmes predicted that the ethical aid of ladies, who pledged not to buy sweatshop goods, would throw poor workers onto the street without providing for them. Clothing manufacturing would become concentrated and "[t]he people will be burdened with several new offices." Questioning the impact of palliative mea-

[93] "Cloakmakers Frame a Labor Bill;" "Protest of Labor"; Kelley, *Report and Findings*, 135–40; "To Close 'Sweat-Shops,'" *Chicago News*, Mar. 1, 1893, HH Scrapbook; Kelley, "The Sweating System," *Tenth Annual Convention of the IAFINA*, 62; *Second Annual Report of the Factory Inspectors of Illinois* 1894 (Springfield: Ed. F. Hartman, 1895), 7–9.

[94] Jane Addams, *Twenty Years at Hull House* (New York: Macmillan Publishing Company, 1912), 201; Blumberg, *Florence Kelley*, 134–48; Goldmark, *Impatient Crusader*, 35–50; Bisno, *Abraham Bisno*, 148–9; "Crusade Against Sweat Shops Begun," *Chicago Mail*, Apr. 5, 1893, HH Scrapbooks.

sures, Holmes called for abolishing, rather than cleaning up, sweatshops by transferring wealth to its producers.[95]

In enforcing the act, Kelley and her associates faced an enormous task, made even more difficult by the smallpox epidemic of 1894 that hit the Polish and Bohemian districts of home workshops. The inspectors had to cover "between 950 and 1000 shops and about 25,000 other rooms." While the manufacturers denied the epidemic, Kelley and Hull House's Julia Lathrop, who would become the first head of the Children's Bureau, "risk[ed] their lives" by "fearlessly entering the rooms and tenements of the west side." In 1894, Kelley and her staff visited 1,437 sweatshops, employing 4,461 men, 5,921 women, and 721 children and found smallpox in 325 tenement houses from April to June.[96]

Kelley became convinced that homework could never be regulated; it had to be prohibited. She wrote in 1895: "Legislative restriction rests upon the theory of regulation by registration and such constant sanitary supervision of the shops as, it was believed, registration would make possible. The theory is disproved by two and a half years' faithful endeavor to apply it." The existing law was too narrow, leaving uncovered some types of clothing and foodstuffs. Indeed, Lizzie Holmes reported the condition of sewing women had degenerated, with factory workers forced by their low piece rates to "carry bundles home and work far into the night – the law to the contrary notwithstanding." Kelley confirmed in her last report (she was dismissed in 1897 after Altgeld lost re-election) that each year saw an increase in the number of tenement house shops.[97]

By then, the Illinois Supreme Court had nullified the eight-hour provision. Manufacturers had shown a callous disregard for the conditions under which garments were made, as long as the contractor accepted their price and returned the work in a satisfactory condition. But when it became apparent that the law would be enforced, they banded together as the Illinois Manufacturers' Association and raised five thousand dollars to carry a challenge to the state supreme court. They apparently neutralized the Woman's Alliance, which initially failed to support a union resolution condemning violation of the law. The manufacturers asked for equal time to present their side, to which the Alliance agreed. But when invited a few weeks later to a public debate on the eight-hour section, the employers failed to appear.[98]

[95] "The 'Sweat Shop' Bill," *The Chicago Post*, June 14, 1893, HH Scrapbooks; Tax, *Rising of the Women*, 49–54; Lizzie M. Holmes, "Sweatshop Clothes: Warning the Wearers, But How About the Makers!" *Labor Leader* (Boston), April 29, 1893.

[96] Blumberg, *Florence Kelley*, 142–5; Goldmark, *Impatient Crusader*, 44–6; Factory Inspectors of Illinois, *First Special Report, Smallpox Epidemic* (Springfield: Ed. F. Hartman, 1894); *Second Annual Report of the Factory Inspectors of Illinois*, 33–7.

[97] *Third Annual Report of the Factory Inspectors of Illinois*, 48; Lizzie M. Holmes, "The Hopeless Class," *Labor Leader* (Boston), Apr. 27, 1895; "Editorial," *Hull House Bulletin* 2 (Jan. 1, 1897).

[98] Joseph Beifeld to Burgland & Shead, May 4 [1896], IMA Papers, letterpress books, box 23, folder 12; Tax, *Rising of the Women*, 86–9.

That late March meeting regrouped the reform coalition. Speakers included Ellen Henrotin, a power in the Chicago Women's Club married to a prominent banker. For her, the eight-hour day was more humane and efficient. Without resorting to maternalistic language, she defended the rights of women workers. Lloyd, in contrast, portrayed women as weak, needing the state as "umpire" in their uneven game against the "strong man." Drawing upon the example of the English Factory Acts that prohibited women's work in the mines, he argued that the state already "controlled its men and women for their good and the general welfare" by regulating rail speeds and marriage. Lloyd attacked the doctrines of Herbert Spencer and the sacredness of the right to contract defended even by "preachers of Christ" who justified "the crucifixion of maternity."The other male speakers similarly relied upon biological difference to cast the woman worker as a mother. Reform rabbi Emile Hirsch exhorted, "The child's father must not be allowed to mortgage the strength of the child and the woman who bears the child must not be made to support it as well." Like Lloyd, he evoked a theme that would be increasingly heard during the next decade:The state had the right to interfere in family life to protect childhood from abusive parents, with abuse defined in economic as well as physical terms.[99]

The central ideological battle over labor legislation for women was joined in 1894 and 1895:Whether women's rights, women's necessity as a mother, or the right to contract would define the conditions under which women labored for wages. *Ritchie* interpreted women's rights in such a way that linked them to freedom of contract doctrines, relying heavily on *Jacobs* to reject any claim that the eight-hour section fell under the police power of the state as a public health measure.The Illinois justices dismissed the reasoning of their counterparts in Massachusetts who earlier had sustained the ten-hour day for women as a legitimate use of the police power. Not only did the act discriminate against one class of employers and employees, those involved in manufacturing, the court reasoned, but it discriminated against women. Defenders sought "to sustain the act . . . upon the alleged ground that it is designed to protect woman on account of her sex and physique." But since "it has been held that a woman is both a 'citizen' and a 'person' within the meaning of" the Fourteenth Amendment, "woman has the right to acquire and possess property of every kind . . . she has the right to claim the benefit of the constitutional provision that she shall not be deprived of life, liberty, or property without due process of law." And among those rights "is the right to make and enforce contracts."[100]

99 "Talks to Toilers." On Henrotin, Paul Boyer, "Henrotin, Ellen Martin," *Notable American Women, 1607–1950: A Biographical Dictionary* (Cambridge, Mass.: Harvard Univ. Press, 1971), 2: 181–3. She would become president of the General Federation of Women's Clubs in 1894.

100 "*Ritchie vs. People,*" reprinted as Appendix 2 in Florence Kelley, *Some Ethical Gains Through Legislation* (New York: The Macmillan Company, 1905), 259–79; see also her discussion of the case, 139–45.While Kelley adds "The" to the case's title; legal citation leaves that out.

Such was not the understanding of women's rights held by Ellen Henrotin or even those who also argued for protection on the basis of women's biological and economic weakness. As workers, women had the right to nonexploitative labor, to the eight-hour day, decent wages, and homes that were not factories. As women, workers had the right to a healthy womanhood and motherhood. Women, Kelley later would assert, had a right to leisure and children, "the right to childhood."[101] The Illinois interpretation of equality negated such rights. The court's equality substituted individualism and freedom for the actual unequal power relations and material resources between the genders, generations, and classes. The ways in which women's position in the workplace rested on their maternal role in the home became obscured as home and work remained separate spheres in law and public policy. *Ritchie* ignored female difference by proclaiming an equality that assumed that men and women were similarly situated in social life. With the eight-hour section voided, the reform coalition, now led by Hull House rather than the trade unions, turned its interest to national remedies;[102] in 1899 as the new secretary of the National Consumers' League Florence Kelley would carry the campaign for the prohibition of homework to the entire nation.

[101] Ibid., 3.
[102] For the shift in prominence in the reform coalition, see the list of dignitaries on the platform during an 1896 mass meeting: "To Abolish Sweat Shops," *Chicago Tribune*, Mar. 9, 1896, HH Scrapbooks.

3

"Women who work" and "women who spend": The family economy vs. the family wage

"Fashionable Ladies of Fifth Avenue Join Hands With Their Wretched Sisters of the Sweat Shops," announced the *American Magazine* on November 6, 1898. Featured in a line drawing was the beautiful Mrs. John Jacob Astor, "one of the queenliest leaders" of the wealthy Four Hundred. Next to her stood a Russian immigrant mother, child in tow, who stuffed under the grills of elegant brownstones circulars describing the plight of the locked-out ladies' tailors, the skilled, mostly male laborers who made the gowns worn by Mrs. Astor and her set. Six months into a strike for union recognition, the ladies' tailors and their families touched the conscience of society women, like Mrs. Astor, who pledged not to purchase dresses "wet with [the] tears" of exploitation. Upper-class women would join the Social Reform Club, the Consumers' League of New York (NYCL), and the Church Association for the Advancement of Labor to establish a cooperative shop for tailors. They not only supplied capital but "turn[ed] their parlours into fitting rooms."[1]

Maud Nathan, president of the NYCL, brought together women of her class with the striking workers. Married to a prosperous broker, this Sephardic Jewish socialite dedicated herself to social justice and women's rights. Society women were surprised that the actual makers of their clothes received only a fraction of what they paid the master tailor, who sent suits and gowns to be sewn in the tenements. To worker demands for fair wages and union recognition Nathan added a call for sanitary manufacturing in workshops that reflected upper-class fears of tenement disease. The cooperative shop derived from the converging needs of working men and society women.[2]

---

[1] "Fashionable Leaders of Fifth Avenue Join Hands with Their Wretched Sisters of the Sweat Shops," *American Magazine*, New York *Journal Advertiser*, Nov. 6, 1898; "'400' Women May Open Tailor Shop," *Morning Journal*, Oct. 27, 1898; "Women Study a Strike," *Journal*, Oct. 26, 1898; "Work of the Consumers' League," *New York Post*, Nathan Scrapbook 2. The available microfilm edition lacks pagination and often clippings are without source or date.

[2] Robert D. Cross, "Maud Nathan," *Notable American Women, 1607–1950: A Biographical Dictionary* (Cambridge, Mass.: Harvard Univ. Press, 1971), 608–9; Maud Nathan, *Story of an Epoch-Making Movement* (Garden City, N.Y.: Doubleday, Page and Co., 1926), 61–3; "Tailors Get Her Aid," *World*, Nov. 2, 1898; "Society Women to Help Strikers," *Herald*, Oct. 30, 1898, Nathan Scrapbook 2.

THE CONSUMERS' LEAGUE

OF

MASSACHUSETTS

4 Joy Street, Boston.

THIS LABEL

**Certifies that the goods which carry it have been
made in clean and safe factories under good conditions, and that the manufacturers who use the
label employ no children and give out no work to
be made up outside the factories.**

April, 1907

Figure 4. Cover, *The Consumers' League of Massachusetts*, pamphlet, April 1907.
Courtesy of the Schlesinger Library, Radcliffe College. The National Consumers'
League developed the Consumers' label to distinguish goods made "in clean and safe
factories under good conditions" from the products of child labor and tenement
homework. This strategy of the league played upon the fears of consumers in order to
improve the conditions of producers; as a class-bridging device, it connected the fates
of "women who work" to "women who spend."

The Ladies' Tailor Strike of 1898 marked a new direction in league activities, even as it revealed the class distinctions that separated "women who spend" from "women who work." The NYCL and the National Consumers' League (NCL) would spearhead the fight against homework until women trained in their battles entered the Department of Labor during the New Deal. Consumers' League leaders were suffragists who defended motherhood against the ravages of industrial exploitation. Although the league recruited prominent male members, it was essentially a women's organization. Organized in 1899 to end the sweatshop, the NCL attempted to raise the labor standards of all workers, particularly women and children. It drew upon the moral righteousness of more prosperous women and their power as the purchasers of household items to improve the lives of working women. Though dominated by upper-class women in its early years, and increasingly dependent upon the prestige and expertise of male academics and lawyers, the NCL blossomed under the leadership of Florence Kelley. It became known for social investigation and educational campaigns and then for legal briefs and legislative lobbying. It worked independently from, but in conjunction with, trade unions. Its inability to end homework through the goodwill of consumers led the league away from reliance on the consumer boycotts to the minimum wage, away from voluntary action to state mandates. What began as an extension of philanthropy and a redefinition of charity work pioneered modern social investigation and laid a cornerstone of the welfare state.[3]

The NCL was part of that ferment of reform that historians have labeled the Progressive Era. Bifurcated from the start, Progressivism combined ideals of social justice with concepts of efficiency in an attempt to alleviate the dislocations of capitalist development. It was a movement of the new white professional and managerial class, but one that responded to the self-activity of working people, sometimes to contain more radical solutions, at other times to push for labor's demands. It hoped for democracy and a return to community in an urban, ethnically diverse world. With roots in the social gospel and the language of religion, Progressivism appeared as a crusade against the forces of evil as much as a legislative agenda to promote labor standards and clean government, Americanize immigrants, and rationalize business. Women, in particular, pioneered in the use of the state to protect those who fell beneath the weight of unrestrained industrial competition. Progressivism did not fully embrace the state; it would combine private programs with public bureaucracies.[4]

[3] Allis Rosenberg Wolfe, "Women, Consumerism, and the National Consumers' League in the Progressive Era, 1900–1923," *Labor History* 16 (Summer 1975), 378–92; Kathryn Kish Sklar, *Florence Kelley and Women's Political Culture: Doing the Nation's Work* (New Haven, Conn.: Yale Univ. Press, 1994), vol. 1; William O'Neill, *Everyone Was Brave* (New York: Quadrangle Books, 1969).

[4] Daniel Rogers, "In Search of Progressivism," *Reviews in American History* 10 (Dec. 1982), 11–32; Alan Dawley, *Struggles for Justice: Social Responsibility and the Liberal State* (Cambridge, Mass.: Harvard Univ. Press, 1991).

The NCL also belonged to a larger woman's social justice network. In the first decades of the century, it worked closely with the mixed-sex National Child Labor Committee (NCLC) and the National Women's Trade Union League (WTUL), organizations that owed their existence to members of the NCL. Growing numbers of women passed between the leagues and the women's colleges as students or teachers and then entered state bureaucracies, especially labor departments and child welfare divisions. They often lived in the social settlement houses. These women reformers formed a network of activists who were responsible for shaping protective labor standards legislation for women and children. Their campaigns intensified the contested articulation of the home that earlier struggles over tenement labor expressed, but their efforts at maintaining the separation of home from work brought them an acute understanding of women's double burden.[5]

In the 1890s, a broad woman's movement had not yet adopted the term *feminism*. This movement had emerged out of women's shared exclusion from public life despite differences that race, class, and region made in the nature of that exclusion. Women could appear as a unified group, "woman," especially to those who were white and privileged and defined the movement's agendas. Women like Maud Nathan and Florence Kelley belonged to this movement. These suffragists and reformers sought equality with men but recognized women's difference from men. Their reform proposals took account of female experiences that stemmed from most women's becoming mothers. To the extent that they focused on mothers who earned, NCL leaders shared the maternalism of organized white womanhood which sought to improve the conditions under which women mothered. But Kelley was never simply a maternalist; she was first and foremost a socialist who sought to transform the economic and class relations of capitalist society. Commitment to working women distinguished NCL leaders from the majority of organized white women, in mass organizations like the General Federation of Women's Clubs or the National Congress of Mothers.[6]

When it came to industrial homework, the perceptions of the league and its supporters contrasted sharply with those of homeworkers. What privileged

[5] Sklar, *Florence Kelley*; Robyn Muncy, *Creating a Female Dominion in American Reform 1830–1935* (New York: Oxford Univ. Press, 1990); Elizabeth Anne Payne, *Reform, Labor and Feminism: Margaret Dreier Robins and the Women's Trade Union League* (Urbana: Univ. of Illinois Press, 1988); Nancy Shrom Dye, *As Equals and As Sisters: Feminism, the Labor Movement, and the Women's Trade Union League of New York* (Columbia: Univ. of Missouri Press, 1980); Walter I. Trattner, *Crusade for the Children: A History of the National Child Labor Committee and Child Labor Reform in America* (Chicago, Ill.: Quadrangle Books, 1970).

[6] Nancy Cott, *The Grounding of Modern Feminism* (New Haven, Conn.: Yale Univ. Press, 1987); Naomi Black, *Social Feminism* (Ithaca, N.Y.: Cornell Univ. Press, 1989), 12–29; for maternalism, Molly Ladd–Taylor, *Mother–Work: Women, Child Welfare, and the State, 1890–1930* (Urbana: Univ. of Illinois, 1994); Seth Koven and Sonya Michel, "Womanly Duties: Maternalist Politics and the Origins of Welfare States in France, Germany, Great Britain, and the United States, 1880–1920" *AHR*, 95 (Oct. 1990): 1076–1109.

and educated women viewed as "the wreck of the home,"[7] a threat to motherhood and childlife, provided the margin for maintaining the immigrant, working-class family. Reformers would substitute a family wage, given to the male breadwinner, for the mother's contribution through industrial homework. But because they recognized that not all women could rely on men for support, they would provide living wages through minimum wages for women. The meaning of homework shifted with the standpoint of the speaker. Artificial flower makers, feather plumers, embroiderers, and garment finishers interpreted their own lives in ways that differed significantly from the interpretations of both women reformers and male-dominated trade unions.

With the NCL, the politics of homework changed strategies. In place of state licensing laws that restricted who could manufacture specified items in tenements, the minimum wage became the tool that could best curtail homework. A floor on wages presumably would raise the cost of homework, seriously reduce profits, and so discourage employers. The minimum wage required court sanction. The NCL maneuvered around *Jacobs* and subsequent upholdings of freedom of contract by embracing sociological jurisprudence. But what one set of U.S. Supreme Court justices would permit in *Muller v. Oregon*, a decision that sustained maximum-hour laws for women, another group would take away in *Adkins v. Children's Hospital*, one that deployed freedom of contract to strike down the minimum wage. In 1923, homeworking women would be left with "a constitutional right . . . to starve."[8]

Regulation through consumption: The Consumers' label

The NYCL originated out of the attempts of working women to improve their own lot. The Working Women's Society of New York City organized in 1886. This group of wage-earning women later would provide the nucleus for the New York WTUL; it called upon prosperous women to boycott goods made by firms against which members were striking. A few years later, the society contacted the aristocratic Josephine Shaw Lowell of the Charity Organization Society who, outraged at the deplorable situation of department store clerks, helped to spark the formation of the NYCL in 1891.[9]

---

[7] Annie S. Daniel, "The Wreck of the Home: The Medical View," and [Florence Kelley], "The Wreck of the Home: Educational View," NCL, *Sixth Annual Report* (March 1905), NCL Papers, reel 3, frames 567–74.

[8] 208 U.S. 412 (1908); 261 U.S. 525 (1923). Florence Kelley, "The Minimum Wage – What Next?," *Survey* (May 15, 1923); Sybil Lipschultz, *Gender Politics: Creating Women's Labor Laws in America, 1890–1940* (New York: Oxford Univ. Press, forthcoming).

[9] Nathan, *Story of An Epoch-Making Movement*, 15–27; Robert H. Bremmer, "Josephine Shaw Lowell," *Notable American Women*, 2:437–9. Garment worker Leonora O'Reilly, a founder of the New York branch of the WTUL, was a leader; by late 1892, listed members included Florence Kelley (who may have joined a few years earlier), Shaw Lowell, and other women of their class. See Schrom Dye, *As Equals and As Sisters*; Dorothy Rose Blumberg, *Florence Kelley: The Making of a Social Pioneer* (New York: Augustus M. Kelley, 1966), 102–4.

Consumers' leagues organized initially to promote local "white lists" of shops worthy of patronage because they treated their employees justly. "A Fair House" provided equal pay for equal work, set a minimum wage of six dollars per week for a nine-and-a-quarter-hour working day, gave saleswomen seats, and generally engaged in "humane and considerate behaviour." By 1898, similar groups had organized in Illinois, Pennsylvania, Massachusetts, Minnesota, New Jersey, Wisconsin, and elsewhere in New York State; a year later, they formed the national league which focused on goods sold in stores. With the cooperation of sociologists and economists at major universities, the social science professional organizations, and the General Federation of Women's Clubs, the NCL began to study manufacturing conditions. Introduced in 1899, the Consumers' label covered fifty-seven manufacturers of women's whitewear by 1915. At that time, there existed eighty-nine leagues in nineteen states, of which thirty-four were in universities, colleges, and schools. Membership stood at thirty-three thousand in 1916. On the eve of World War I, consumers' leagues had grown in France, Germany, Belgium, and Switzerland, which sent representatives to international conferences in 1908 and 1913 – precursors to the postwar meetings that formed the modern International Labor Organization. Over the course of a decade and a half, the league would not only marshal the power of consumers but investigate labor conditions as a prelude toward securing legislation, which it then defended in courts.[10]

The Consumers' label first distinguished the organization. It offered a symbol around which organizing and education for securing labor standards could occur.[11] There existed an indigenous source for this strategy: the union label movement deployed, as we have already seen, by unionists to stop tenement manufacturing. As early as 1888, Florence Kelley, then on the East Coast, had advocated fighting child labor through a national alliance of women that would "furnish its label to all manufacturers of women's clothing as the Cigarmakers' Union does to union manufacturers who will comply with its conditions, and its members should pledge themselves to buy no clothing which is not properly labeled."[12]

Label campaigns further embodied the thought of economists and social thinkers who were reevaluating the role of consumption in modern, industrial

---

[10] Florence Kelley, *The National Consumers' League* (New York: NCL, June 1915), HSW Papers, box 3, folder 11; *The National Consumers' League* (New York: NCL, May 1937), Abbott Papers, box 67, folder 6; Florence Kelley, *Twenty-Five Years of the Consumers' League Movement*, from *The Survey*, Nov. 27, 1915, NCLVF; membership calculated by Kathryn Kish Sklar from annual reports, communication to author.

[11] "Consumers' League Label," *New York Times*, Nov. 18, 1899.

[12] The Illinois Woman's Alliance responded to Kelley by suggesting that a national alliance should give special attention to women's underwear since women predominated among makers of such goods. A decade later the league would adopt this approach. Such an exchange marks a network of trade union oriented women in the late 1880s and early 1890s. "Work for the Women," Nov. 1888, unidentified clipping, Morgan Scrapbook 2.

society. The popular Victorian sage John Ruskin had stressed the responsibility of consumers whose decisions influenced the style of objects, manufacturing processes, and ultimately the lives of their makers. Such a moralistic evaluation remained a key element in NCL appeals. As Columbia University economist E. R. A. Seligman put it before the meeting that ushered in the league, "Nothing is economically defensible which is not economically just." Economist George Gunton rejected the self-restraint preached by earlier generations in order to celebrate consumption and a higher standard of living for working people. Simon Patten, too, was beginning to elevate the significance of consumption for modern life.[13]

The Consumers' League gendered this emerging political economy of consumption. It interpreted the sexual division of labor through the evolutionist lens so much in vogue within the developing social science disciplines.[14] Such thought applauded how the work of the preindustrial woman had left the home for the factory with its greater division of labor and efficiencies of scale. Homework could only appear as a residue form of production, a system confirming the backwardness of the industries where it prevailed. In the sexual division of labor within modern economies, woman would buy what she once made. She would become the primary consumer. Charlotte Perkins Gilman and other "new" feminists celebrated a parallel movement of women with their work to the realm of paid labor outside the home. This transformation disturbed trade unionists and many social welfare workers who sought higher male wages to stem its course.[15]

When league women interpreted the meaning of consumption, the social construction of womanhood stood at the center of their analysis. The dominant gender system designated women as the caretakers of their sex and dependent persons – the young, aged, and ill. Privileged women had entered the public sphere through extending such duties to the less fortunate. The founders of the

---

[13] "The Consumers' League: Prof. E. R. A. Seligman of Columbia University Discusses the Movement at a Meeting," *New York Times*, May 18, 1898; "The Consumer's Influence on Production," State of Wisconsin, *The Biennial Report of the Bureau of Labor and Industrial Statistics, 1901–2*, 10 (Madison: Democrat Printing Co., 1902), 282–95; Eileen Boris, *Art and Labor: Ruskin, Morris, and the Craftsman Ideal in America* (Philadelphia, Pa.: Temple Univ. Press, 1986); Daniel Horowitz, *The Morality of Spending: Attitudes Toward the Consumer Society in America, 1875–1940* (Baltimore: Johns Hopkins Univ. Press, 1985), 30–49.

[14] Robert Bannister, *Social Darwinism in American Thought* (Philadelphia, Pa.: Temple Univ. Press, 1989); Mary Furner, *Advocacy and Objectivity: A Crisis in the Professionalization of American Social Science, 1865–1905* (Lexington: Univ. of Kentucky Press, 1975).

[15] Florence Kelley, "Aims and Principles of the Consumers' League," *The American Journal of Sociology* 5 (Nov. 1899), 298–9; Maud Nathan, "Women Who Work and Women Who Spend," *Annals of the American Academy of Political Science*, 27 (1906), 646–7; Charlotte Perkins Gilman, *Women and Economics* (1898, rpt. New York: Harper and Row, 1966); Martha May, "The 'Good Managers': Married Working-Class Women and Family Budget Studies, 1895–1915," *Labor History* 25 (Summer 1984), 351–72; May, "Bread Before Roses: American Workingmen, Labor Unions, and the Family Wage," in *Women, Work, and Protest: A Century of U.S. Women's Labor History*, ed. Ruth Milkman (New York: Routledge and Kegan Paul, 1985), 1–21.

NCL found it logical that a woman's organization should educate consumers. This is not to argue that male supporters failed to grasp the significance of the transference of woman's activities from the domestic realm into the market-place but rather to emphasize how reform-minded women stressed an extrafamilial maternalism. They had discovered a new realm for female altruism. That class and race privilege helped to shape their understanding of duty merely reflected the vantage point from which many in the NCL began.[16]

The early propaganda of the league stressed the connection between "women who work" and "women who spend." League thinkers developed an economics of shopping, a commentary on the class limitations of the sexual division of social life that had channeled the activities of privileged women into recreational shopping. Given women's position as purchaser, it became her responsibility to purchase wisely. The wise consumer would not only benefit her family but all of womanhood through indirect philanthropy. Nathan most graphically tied the ethical life of one group of women to the material conditions of the other: "If the crowds of well-dressed women who push and fight and struggle with each other to get to a bargain counter could realize that they are pushing and struggling to take the living away from helpless ones of their own sex, they would be ashamed to continue."[17] In such a portrait, the woman worker was victim, passive, subject to the active intervention of middle- and upper-class female consumers. But, as union label drives sometimes recognized, the woman wage earner also spent her wages. In dichotomizing *work* and *spend*, Nathan ignored the working-class consumer just as she neglected to name as work the unpaid labor of her own class.

Kelley, in contrast, grounded an ethical appeal to the consumer in the economics of garment production. She denied that sweating cheapened goods. Lower prices actually came from use of cheap materials, mechanical power, and improved industrial organization. Lack of schooling and destruction of child health increased the human cost of industry, jacking up the ultimate price of sweated goods. She argued that the moral "power of consumers" could aid the laws of economics and speed technological change.[18]

There was a harder edge to the political economy of consumption. As Seligman explained: "Wages are to a large extent determined by the productivity of labor. The more a man produces the more will he get and the greater

[16] Kelley, "Aims and Principles of the Consumers' League," 299; "Extracts from the Addresses Delivered at the Annual Meeting," *NYCL Report for the Year Ending December 1907* (March 1908), 48–9, NCL Papers, reel 112, frame 574; "New Era in the National Consumers' League," *Charities and the Commons* 21 (Mar. 13, 1909), 1208–9.

[17] Kelley, "Aims and Principles of the Consumers' League," 290; Nathan, "Women Who Work and Women Who Spend"; "The Consumers' League. Address by Mrs. Nathan Before the Yonkers Civic League"; Caroline Gray Lingle, "The Brutal Side of the 'Bargain,'" *Kate Field's Washington*, Nathan Scrapbook 2.

[18] Florence Kelley, "The National Federation of Consumers' Leagues," *The Independent* 51.2 (Dec. 14, 1899), 3355.

wages are paid him the more chance is there of good work on his part." Since competition "under conditions of inequality of opportunity" leads to "enslavement of the weaker," the community for its own good either through voluntary combinations like the Consumers' League or factory legislation should interfere so that all employers can compete "at a higher level." Such intervention in the market "in the interest of the less-favored producers" would generate higher wages, "better production, and therefore, in the long run, cheaper production."[19]

Self-protection joined reason, sentiment, and guilt to motivate the ethical shopper. Through a series of graphic stories of food and clothing custom-made in the presence of deadly disease – like the consumptive crone licking boxes for wedding cakes – Kelley revealed that rich as well as poor lacked the information necessary to make safe purchases. "Rights of Purchasers" included freedom from diseased and dirty products, Kelley reiterated in articles and books over the next ten years. This naming of perils to the consumer resembled the scare tactics of organized workers. Such a theme threatened to overwhelm the NCL's plea of justice for the worker precisely because it appealed to self-interest as the highest form of altruism. Individual solutions, as when clubwomen sent clothing to steam cleaners, could not overcome the risk of disease or end community befoulment. The program of the Consumer's League promised otherwise. It would protect the consumer against infected products by improving the labor standards of working women.[20]

When Kelley became NCL secretary in 1899, her first task was to establish the Consumers' label, with women's white muslin underwear chosen as a limited field to test the idea. The processes of production there had inhibited the spread of sweatshops and homework, making such goods a promising arena for success. To qualify for the label, manufacturers had to meet all state factory laws; produce goods in their own shops; employ no child under age sixteen; provide a ten-hour day and sixty-hour week; ban night work; and open their premises to league inspection at any time.[21] Absent from this list was the provision of a living wage, a major concern of Kelley's, but one that generated more controversy by challenging the heart of the employment contract.

Awarding the label was not an easy task. Because of the state's reliable factory

[19] "The Consumers' League: Prof. E. R. A. Seligman of Columbia University"; Frank L. McVey, "The Work and Problems of the Consumers' League," *American Journal of Sociology* 6 (May 1901), 767–9.

[20] Kelley, "Aims and Principles of the Consumers' League"; Florence Kelley, "Rights of Purchasers," *Charities* 14 (Sept. 30, 1905), 1112–18; Florence Kelley, *Some Ethical Gains Through Legislation* (New York: Macmillan Co., 1905); Florence Kelley, "The Problem of Sweating in America," *The Chautauquan* 60 (Nov. 1910), 414–21; "The Menace to the Home from Sweatshop and Tenement–Made Clothing," 1901, NCL Papers, reel 114, frames 124–30.

[21] Kelley, "The National Federation of Consumers' Leagues," 3354–5; "Report of Executive Committee [on] Public Meeting to Consumers' League," Feb. 3, 1898, NCL Papers, reel 16, frame 72.

inspectorate, Massachusetts firms dominated the initial list. Illinois had inadequate factory laws, but its league had granted the label to a Chicago manufacturer for whom Kelley had vouched. Department store magnate Marshall Field then wanted the label for garments that he produced. He also was willing to sell labeled goods. Despite "admirable" treatment of store employees, the league noted that "his conduct as a manufacturer has been quite the reverse." But by providing the label to one Chicago firm, the league had opened itself up to the charge of inconsistency. In May 1902 individual leagues voted for the National to give the label to Field. New York firms still could not receive the label because their factory inspectors were "incompetent."[22]

League members also faced problems stemming from the very division of labor within the trade for which their intervention promised a cure. A large number of factories and retailers advertised goods made on their premises, but actually sent out portions of the work, a practice Kelley named "shameless." Kelley's powers of persuasion sometimes prevailed. She convinced a reluctant manufacturer to put the label on his boxes when New York retailers refused to sell goods with labels sewn into them. The league faced "opposition, both open and secret" from these retailers who profited from the status quo. Such problems persisted: In 1913 the newly formed Consumers' League for the District of Columbia discovered managers and buyers cutting the label off goods.[23]

Convincing members to purchase labeled goods posed other problems. The first label, Kelley explained, went to a New England factory "which made very ugly, very substantial, and very high priced garments" that were poorly designed; the second to "one which made that exceedingly flimsy underwear of the kind which sheds its buttons the first time it is worn." These cheaper goods "appealed to the factory girls of New England mill towns, who knew all about labels and were staunch patrons of league goods." Wealthy league members, unable "to wear the product of either one," bought them to give to philanthropic "Old Clothes" rooms. Initial investigation taught that expensive goods were made under worse conditions than cheap and medium grade wear.[24]

This mismatch between class of goods and league members remained. Both locals and the National sent traveling exhibits of sample garments to schools, reform organizations, and women's clubs. The leagues addressed those classes in the community that would purchase labeled goods through working girls'

[22] Mass. Executive Board Minutes, Feb. 22, 1901, Mar. 24, 1902; May 9, 1902, Apr. 23, 1903; May 24, 1900, NCL Papers, reel 16, frames 45, 32–3, 31, 22, 50.

[23] Ibid., Apr. 23, 1903; May 24, 1900, frames 22, 50; *Summary Statement of the Work of the First Year of the NCL, May 1, 1899–May 1, 1900*, frames 469–72; "Report of the Committee on Label and Exhibits," *Consumers' League for the District of Columbia, First Report to March 1, 1913*, frame 463, both reel 112, NCL Papers.

[24] "Adventures of a Label," *Daily Tribune*, c. 1901, Nathan Scrapbook 2; *Summary Statement of the Work of the First Year*, 4.

clubs, mothers' meetings, Granger societies, and Catholic Church groups. The Massachusetts League set up booths at county fairs. The National also attempted to reach department store buyers, key figures who decided which goods would be displayed. Kelley spent much of her time on the road lecturing local groups, while Nathan spoke on the aims of the Consumers' League before Midwest and Pacific Coast audiences, often sponsored by women's clubs and Jewish organizations.[25]

Despite reliance on the idea of the union label, the league never held a monolithic attitude toward trade unions. The National under Kelley embraced them. The Illinois League supported striking custom tailors who demanded workrooms outside their homes. In contrast, the majority of New Yorkers preferred their own label not only to insure sanitation and fair wages but craftsmanship not necessarily guaranteed by the union label.[26] Massachusetts's executive board also rejected the union label. Unions had strong supporters, like Dennison House head resident Helena Dudley and Wellesley College economist Emily Greene Balch. But Massachusetts blocked a proposal at the NCL founding conference that would have adopted "the trade union standard of hours and wages" for NCL-endorsed shops; it rejected sole reliance on trade union labels or "sources of information." John Graham Brooks, the Cambridge writer and reformer who served as president of the NCL for its first sixteen years, noted these contradictory policies: "To work with trade unions is to antagonize much of present membership; to ignore them is to antagonize working people."[27]

As Brooks predicted, the league made trade unionists uneasy. In January 1904, the secretary of the Massachusetts Union Label League, Mary Kenney O'Sullivan (the former Illinois assistant factory inspector and first woman organizer for the American Federation of Labor [AFL], then a Dennison House resident) "violently opposed" the league label, which she charged was "stolen from the Unions." She questioned whether this label inhibited gar-

---

[25] Mass. Executive Board Minutes, "Report of Committee on Advertising," Jan. 27, 1904, "Annual Meeting," Feb. 19, 1903; May 28, 1903; NCL Papers, reel 16, frames 157–8, 162, 20–1. Kelley's activities are in yearly reports of the NCL, reel 4; Nathan's, in Nathan Scrapbook 2.

[26] Summary Statement of the Work of the First Year, reel 113, frames 469–72; "The Enemy of Sweatshops," Commercial Advertiser, Nov. 6, 1897, Nathan Scrapbook 2; McVey, "Work and Problems of Consumers' Leagues," 774–5.

[27] Mass. Executive Board Minutes, Mar. 1898, Apr. 2, 1898, May 24, 1898, Sept. 30, 1898, June 5, 1909, reel 16, frames 62–6, 42. The Boston-based group (organized in 1897) of settlement leaders, college professors, and Brahmin reformers included a number of educated and privileged women who would be active in organizing trade unions for women. Mary Morton Kehew, head of the Women's Educational and Industrial Union, represented the Federal Labor Union and later presided over the local WTUL. It appears to have had more – and more active – men than other cities, including Brooks, Robert A. Woods of South End House, and the wealthy reformers Robert Ely and John Gardiner, the last of whom acted as treasurer. Department store magnate Edward A. Filene supported its efforts.

ment trade organizing. The NCL claimed that it actually facilitated organizing; it had influenced garment union demands. In 1902 the United Garment Workers of America added that all work must be done on the premises of the employer as a condition for their decade-old label. Trade unions and the leagues were "natural allies," but their objectives differed because the interests of privileged-class consumers diverged from the self-betterment of working people. Most members probably agreed with Nathan "that we never sentimentally put the rights of the employee above the rights of the employer." Yet a strong minority[28] under Kelley tilted the organization toward a pro-labor program through vigorous championing of labor standards legislation.[29]

When trade unions provided some order to the chaotic garment industry, the Consumers' label lost its reason for being. The 1910 protocol agreement brought unionization to the women's garment industry in the wake of "the uprising of the 20,000." The NCL endorsed the International Ladies' Garment Workers Union (ILGWU) label and applauded the protocol for its prohibition of both homework and subcontracting and for its adoption of the nine-hour day. Three years later, the ILGWU and the Joint Board of Sanitary Control asked the NCL to help draw up a new label agreement. But during the strike-torn days of World War I, the garment unions again objected to the Consumers' label because manufacturers – engaged in a campaign to smash unions in both men's and women's clothing – were using it instead of their own. Kelley recommended the end of the label because its standards lagged behind those negotiated through collective bargaining. In a lapse of historical memory, twenty years later the NCL claimed to be "the forerunner of the union label."[30]

The Consumers' label was not the reason for the league; it was a means, not an end, part of a larger educational campaign against the exploitative conditions under which women and children labored. The label served as a tool to recruit members and provide them with ongoing work while investigations proceeded and legislation developed. Even though economic forces, including business rationalization, probably had more to do with changes in white muslin underwear than the label, it had given the locals a reason for being.[31]

---

[28] These included Dudley, Balch, Kehew, and Wellesley professor Katherine Coman in Boston, NCL staffers Pauline and Josephine Goldmark, and Frances Perkins in New York.

[29] Mass. Executive Board Minutes, Jan. 17, 1904, Mar. 9, 1904, Mar. 27, 1902, NCL Papers, reel 16, frames 165, 158, 35; Nathan, Story of an Epoch-Making Movement, 59.

[30] "Importance of Cloak Makers' Agreement," The NCL Report for Year Ending December 1910 (Mar. 1911), 13–14, NCL Papers, reel 112, frames 588–9; "The Fifteenth Annual Session of the Council, Dec. 11, 1914," NCL Papers, reel 4, frame 322; Eleventh Annual Report for the Year Ending March 1, 1910, ibid., frame 21; "Memorandum on the Label," ibid., frame 429; "Report of Sub–Committee on Proposed Change of Label Committee to Committee on Standards," RG107, box 10, folder 84 "NCL-NYC," 2; The National Consumers' League (May 1937), 2.

[31] Mass. Executive Board Minutes, Dec. 3, 1903, Sept. 30, 1898, NCL Papers, reel 16, frame 15, 61–2; Florence Kelley, "The Problem of Sweating in America," 414–17; "Evils of the Sweatshop," New York Times, Dec. 1, 1900, Nathan Scrapbook 2.

The league also fought for better state regulations. Locals sponsored bills to improve the workings of labor departments. In 1904 the NYCL transformed licensing procedures by sponsoring a law that targeted employers and tenement owners, rather than workers. The NCL viewed this law merely as a preliminary step, one which would reduce homework "toward zero" so that eventual abolition would affect fewer people. It believed that "the system cannot be retained and its evils abolished, because they are inherent in it and accompany it inevitably."[32] Like the Consumers' label, licensing belonged to a transitional program, with prohibition of homework the goal.

The home as a contested terrain

In the first decade of the twentieth century, the tenement homeworker dominated the problem of the married woman as wage earner. During a period when most wage-earning women were young and single, married immigrant women, over 90 percent of them Italian in New York City, composed the home labor force.[33] Discussion of homework became inextricably bound with social understandings of home, family, motherhood, and child welfare. Homework was an economic system, where foot power competed with the dynamo, where long hours and low wages undermined working conditions and threatened factory profitability with its higher overhead. But it implied a gender system, one viewed by reformers as subverting the home and the responsibility of men, women, and children within it.

When the NCL joined the New York fight against sweatshops in 1901, over 60,000 people were licensed to work at home, with countless thousands manufacturing without a license. By 1911, there were over 14,000 licensed tenements with between 3 and 30 homeworking families per dwelling, with each family having at least 2 and sometimes more than 5 homeworkers. At a minimum there existed 250,000 homeworkers in 1910, manufacturing at least a hundred items which represented a wide range of garments and related trades: from coats and knee pants to paper bags and umbrellas, feathers and artificial flowers, spaghetti and ice cream. By 1911 the licensing system included about forty-one items or processes, but a greater number required no license to be made in tenements. These included embroidery, baby bonnets, artificial jewelry, and tag stringing. At least 51,500 embroidery and 200,000 hand

[32] *Preventive Measures for Industrial Unrest: The Record of the NCL, 1900–1920* (New York: NCL, Dec. 1919), reel 113, frames 478–9; *The NCL: The First Quarter Century, 1899–1924*, reel 113, frames 559–60; "Tenement House Manufacture," *NCL Fifth Annual Report* (March 1904), reel 3, frames 532–6, all in NCL Papers.

[33] Lynn Y. Weiner, *From Working Girl to Working Mother: The Female Labor Force in the United States, 1820–1980* (Chapel Hill: Univ. of North Carolina Press, 1985), 83–8; "Men's Ready–Made Clothing," *Report on Women and Children* 2, (1911), 221–4, 369–70; Miriam J. Cohen, *Workshop to Office: Two Generations of Italian Women in New York City, 1900–1950* (Ithaca, N.Y.: Cornell Univ. Press, 1992).

crocheters labored at home in 1912. Handmade and fashion conscious goods cost more to make in factories with their expensive floor space because the work was highly irregular. Labor supply may have influenced spatial organization: The need of Italian women to stay at home meshed with the desire of employers to cheapen costs by sending work there.[34]

Tenement work involved children. In the early twentieth century, the campaign against homework joined the growing crusade against child labor. The plight of children in manufacturing spurred on the first laws regulating hours and working conditions. Following Massachusetts, nearly thirty states passed compulsory education laws after the Civil War to curb child labor. But in 1900, fifteen years after New York's factory act, the number of child laborers at best had remained constant at 4 percent of the factory work force. Garment production in New York, Philadelphia, and Chicago contributed as much to child labor as the southern textile industry or Pennsylvania and Ohio glass factories. Even with compulsory schooling, children worked well into the evening making rosebuds and pulling threads. There was no way to know how many children aided in homework and no way to keep them from working at night even with adequate enforcement of school laws.[35] At a time when Progressives were "rediscovering" the child, homework seemed an evil because it robbed children of their youth.[36]

The NCLC reflected the fractured interests of regional capital. Led by Florence Kelley, prominent settlement house leaders and liberal capitalists organized the New York Child Labor Committee (NYCLC) in 1902.[37] Two years later the New Yorkers joined with the crusading Alabama minister Edgar Gardner Murphy to form the NCLC. In this era of corporate mergers, rationalization of capital, and increase in industrial efficiency, northern finance capital sought to end child labor in southern mills; its representatives

[34] *The NCL: The First Quarter Century, 1899–1924*; Rheta Childe Dorr, "The Child Who Toils at Home," *Hampton Magazine* 28 (Apr. 1912), 184; Elizabeth C. Watson, "Home Work in the Tenements," *The Survey* 25 (Feb. 4, 1911), 3–4; Elizabeth Watson, "The Homework System in New York City," *Second Report of the FIC* (Albany, N.Y.: J. B. Lyon Co., Printers, 1913), 2:677; Cynthia R. Daniels, "Between Home and Factory: Homeworkers and the State," in *Homework: Historical and Contemporary Perspectives on Paid Labor at Home*, ed. Eileen Boris and Cynthia R. Daniels (Urbana: Univ. of Illinois Press, 1989), 13–32.

[35] Jeremy P. Felt, *Hostages of Fortune: Child Labor Reform in New York State* (Syracuse, N.Y.: Syracuse Univ. Press, 1965), 7, 35–7; *NCL Fourth Annual Report for the Year Ending March 4, 1903*, NCL Papers, reel 4, frames 489–93.

[36] Anthony M. Platt, *The Child Savers: The Invention of Delinquency* (Chicago: Univ. of Chicago Press, 1977); LeRoy Ashby, *Saving the Waifs: Reformers and Dependent Children, 1890–1917* (Philadelphia, Pa.: Temple Univ. Press, 1984). Investigators found that homework led to "retardation" in grade level. See "Men's Ready–Made Clothing," 231–5.

[37] This group included Lillian D. Wald of the Henry Street Nurses' Settlement, where Kelley lived, Mary K. Simkhovitch of Greenwich House, Pauline Goldmark of the NCL, Robert Hunter of University Settlement; Ethical Culture leader Felix Adler, corporation president and settlement founder James G. Phelps Stokes, Long Island Railway president William H. Baldwin, and bankers V. Everit Macy, Paul M. Warburg, and Jacob A. Schiff.

sat on the NCLC. Male ministers, including Owen R. Lovejoy who would become the secretary of the organization, and charity and social workers, like Homer Folks and Edward T. Devine, lobbied with women reformers for laws against child labor.[38]

Over the next decade, the NCL and the NCLC exposed the evils of homework and child labor through the survey, exposé, and exhibition. They provided middle-class viewers with a vicarious experience of tenement life. The language of reform, with its underlying messages, was as important as the facts to which the language gave meaning. Their exhibits pioneered the use of documentary photography and provided a forum for the developing genius of Lewis Hine, the NCLC special agent, whose images defined the homework system for the 1912 New York Factory Investigating Commission (FIC), as well as the larger community of concerned citizens.[39]

To educate the public, the NCL circulated pamphlets, printing the earliest, "The Menace to the Home from Sweatshop and Tenement House Clothing," in the thousands. It reprinted expert testimony to portray the threatening specter of disease, invisible but insulated in woolen fabric. It linked disease to lack of labor standards. Homework was "a curse" because "it invades all the privacies of life; it robs the child of its schooling, its parents, its very home." This metaphor of invasion, of the factory entering the home to destroy private life, pervaded reform discourse. So did the layering of fact, the reliance on evidence so central to the Progressive *mentalité*. The NCL developed exhibits that compared the products of the sweatshop and homework to labeled goods, with photographs of sweatshops and tenement homes that lacked light, were overcrowded, and mingled workers of all ages. Its display won the Grand Prix at the Paris Exposition of 1900 and found ready audiences at national and international expositions, tuberculosis exhibitions, and the Exhibit of Congestion of Population in New York City.[40]

In 1907 Chicago social welfare and labor organizations organized the most spectacular industrial exhibit to set forth the positive impact of trade unionism, legal protection, voluntary organizations, and "public spirited" employers. Like the artist who breaks through the "dead level of familiarity" so to gain

[38] Trattner, *Crusade for the Children*, 45–67; Martin J. Sklar, *The Corporate Reconstruction of American Capitalism, 1890–1916: The Market, the Law, and Politics* (New York: Cambridge Univ. Press, 1988).

[39] Maren Stange, *Symbols of Ideal Life: Social Documentary Photography in America, 1890–1950* (New York: Cambridge Univ. Press, 1989), 1–87. The NYCL, the NYWTUL, and other women's reform organizations had lobbied for the FIC in the wake of the Triangle Shirtwaist Fire. Its commissioners included labor Democrats Alfred E. Smith and Robert Wagner, Samuel Gompers, and Mary E. Dreier of the NYWTUL. See note 45.

[40] *NCL Fourth Annual Report*, NCL Papers, reel 4, frame 500; *Food Regulations: Every Woman Should Know*, ibid., reel 114, frames 725–7; *The Sweatshop Where Tuberculosis Breeds*, ibid., frames 405–7; *Preventive Measures for Industrial Unrest*, ibid., 2–3; *NCL Seventh Annual Report for the Year Ending March 1, 1906*, ibid., frame 615; *NCL Eighth Annual Report for the Year Ending March 5, 1907*, ibid., frame 683.

"the essence of life," Jane Addams argued, the exhibit was "designed to do something of the same sort for current industrial conditions, to reveal that hard and material side of life which goes on in factories and workshops, to epitomize the labor which clothes and feeds the modern world." Organizers promoted the union label and legislation on tenement homework, compulsory education, and industrial insurance. They drew attention to the need for a congressional investigation into the conditions of women and child wage earners. Living exhibits of modern industrial processes dramatized the ethics of consumption. Young women ran eyeleting and vamping machines for boots and shoes, made gloves, rolled cigars, wrapped candy, and threaded sewing machines. Members of a tenement family picked nuts in a replica of their home. There were lectures on "The Immigrant in Industry" and "Woman's Fitness for Industrial Life," tableaux and songs; graphic presentations, charts, and photographs.[41]

The Chicago Industrial Exhibit derived from a belief that facts would precipitate reform. The early twentieth century witnessed the rise of social science with its claims to objectivity and expertise in "the social problem." College-trained women who entered the ranks of reform drew upon new techniques, like the social survey and statistics, to create an activist social science. Under Sophonisba Breckinridge and Edith Abbott, social workers distinguished themselves from charity organizations by fact gathering. The subject of reform became the environment of poverty rather than the personality of the poor.[42]

Graphic representations, like photography, became a preferred means of awakening. The secretary of the Ohio Valley Child Labor Committee wrote NCLC secretary Owen Lovejoy: "This method of presenting the problem [through lantern slides] has been found to be much superior to a simple address, in awakening public opinion." Maud Nathan explained, "When we look at a photograph depicting a group of small children working by lamp light, in a small crowded tenement room, at tasks which would rasp the nerves and strain the muscles of grown-ups . . . we are moved to ask ourselves why child labor is tolerated and what we are doing to help abolish it." Lewis Hine told the 1909 meeting of the National Council of Charities and Corrections:

[41] Sponsors included the Chicago Consumers' League, the WTUL, social settlement houses, the University of Chicago, the Chicago Trades Union Label League, the Woman's International Union Label League, and private and public social welfare agencies. Jane Addams, "Interpretation of Exhibit," 20–3; "Program of Exhibits," 9–20; Mary E. McDowell, "National Investigation into Women's Work," 93–4; Edgar T. Davies, "Pending Labor Legislation," 102–12; all in *Handbook of the Chicago Industrial Exhibit*, March 11–17, 1907, WTUL Papers, reel 12.

[42] Ellen Fitzpatrick, *Endless Crusade: Women Social Scientists and Progressive Reform* (New York: Oxford Univ. Press, 1990); Thomas Haskell, *The Emergence of Professional Social Science* (Urbana: Univ. of Illinois Press, 1977); Martin Bulmer, Kevin Bales, and Kathryn Kish Sklar, *The Social Survey Movement in Historical Perspective* (New York: Cambridge Univ. Press, 1992).

"The photograph has an added realism of its own. . . . For this reason the average person believes implicitly that the photograph cannot falsify. Of course, you and I know that this unbounded faith in the integrity of the photograph is often rudely shaken, for, while photographs may not lie, liars may photograph."[43]

Hine's photographs illuminated truth. They showed dirt – revealing the hidden and confirming uncleanliness – but they also exposed the connection between producer, product, and consumer. The link was made – behind each flower was the dirty face of an unkempt child – behind the "dolly" was "disease" – the facts spoke. Yet the photographs were arrangements. Hine focused his lens to manipulate science and sentiment, drawing the onlooker into the crusade against the homework "evil." The photographs appeared in NCLC publications with Hine's field notes that further verified their authenticity, but these images were not random truths. Rather they were truths that presented the political position of the NCLC: its call for the abolition of child labor, work certification for fourteen- to sixteen-year-olds, compulsory education, the end of homework. Especially when assembled as poster montages, Hine's photographs reflected the philosophical assumptions behind the reform crusade. They demanded that middle-class notions of home and family be universal. Through his images, the fight for better working conditions became gendered, intimate, and personal. Still these photographs, which have taught succeeding generations how to see the tenements, suggested that beyond pathology lay another voice, that of the homeworker herself. Never merely victims, Hine's homeworkers retain dignity.[44]

Photographs functioned as evidence. The NCLC, NYCL, and Lillian Wald of the Henry Street social settlement submitted Hine's images to the FIC. Underfunding led the commission to ask the NCLC to conduct studies of tenement homework and child labor in canneries. The 1913 final report, which justified improving New York's homework legislation, printed Hine's photographs.[45] The tenement house photographs also appeared in the *Child Labor Bulletin*, the journal of the NCLC. They were mounted in wooden frames, assembled into poster montages, and exhibited around the country. The NCLC sent them out with press releases and stories as part of a systematic

---

[43] E. N. Clopper to Mr. Owen R. Lovejoy, Dec. 31, 1908, box 5, NCLC Papers; "Still Pictures That Move," *New York Times*, Feb. 25, 1913, Nathan Scrapbook 3; Lewis Hine, "Social Photography," *Classic Essays on Photography*, ed. Alan Trachtenberg (New Haven: Leete's Island Books, 1980), 111.

[44] "Dolly Dear," in "Child Labor Stories for Children," *Child Labor Bulletin* 2 (Aug. 1913), 28; "Contrasts: They Who Play with Dolls, They Who Help Make Them," in "Child Workers in New York Tenements," in *Child Labor Bulletin* 1 (Nov. 1912), 36–7; Alan Trachtenberg, *Reading American Photographs: Images as History* (New York: Hill and Wang, 1989), 190–209; Stange, *Symbols of the Ideal Life*.

[45] *Preliminary Report of the New York State FIC*, (Albany, N.Y.: J. B. Lyon Company, State Printers, 1912), App. 7, separately printed as *Home Work in the Tenement Houses of New York City; Second Report of the FIC*.

Figure 5. Lewis Hine, "Everybody works but _____," family of Dometrio Capilluto, Hudson Street, New York City, December 1911. Courtesy of the National Archives.

effort to plant articles on child labor in newspapers and magazines. Even when rejecting prepackaged stories, papers used the photographs, as the *New York Times* did on January 12, 1913, for a report on women strikers. Systematic and rationalized, the NCLC campaigns typified a new, scientific, and modern approach to reform. Photographs were propaganda as well as truth.[46]

The written sections of NCLC memoranda and reports to the FIC quanti-fied the conditions of homework, tabulating the numbers of child laborers

---

[46] Photographic analysis is based on lot 7481, Tenement Homework, a scrapbook of about 250 photographs with file drawer field notes, LC, Prints and Photographs Division. "A New Exhibit of Home Work," *The Survey* 28 (Apr. 6, 1912), 8–10; "The High Cost of Child Labor," Exhibit Handbook – NCLC, pamphlet no. 241 (Jan. 1915), 8; "Report of the General Secretary to the Trustees of the NCLC for the Eighth Fiscal Year ending Sept. 20, 1912," 3–6, 13, 19, 21, box 5, loose-leaf notebook; "Scrapbook – Press Releases," box 16, 39, 42, 57; "Home Work History in the Making," press release offered to *New York Times*, Jan. 9, 1913, "Returned Mss. Used 2 pictures," n.p.; "Gertrude Barnum Pleads Cause of Garment Strikers," *New York Times*, Jan. 12, 1913, NCLC Papers.

and the kinds of articles manufactured in tenements untouched by the current law. Photographs provided a human dimension to charts that listed the occupations of fathers in families that picked nuts and sewed doll's clothes, giving wage per week, rent per month, and number and ages of members of the family. Thus appeared the family of Dometrio Capilluto at 141 Hudson Street (see Figure 5). While the father sits off to the side rocking in his chair, the mother and girls busily crack nuts. Together they earned four dollars a week, with the oldest child at times working until nine at night. Hine jotted on his note card, in words transcribed into the report: "A common scene in the tenements. Father sits around. 'Sometime I make $9.00, sometimes $10.00 a week on the railroad; sometime nottin.'" Such an image contradicted the conclusion of NCLC investigator Elizabeth Watson that "the family budget . . . is small, *not* because the father is lazy, but because his daily wage is not sufficient to carry him through the dull season of his industry." Here the lesson framed by the camera – the lack of the work ethic – failed to consider the context in which the idleness of male wage earners occurred.[47]

The fathers in most homeworking families, overwhelmingly Italian by this time, held casual unskilled jobs. They earned anywhere from $12.90 to as little as $8.00 or $9.00 a week for factory work, not enough to support three to five children, the average family size. Generally, these men were not shirkers. Over 80 percent of the husbands of home finishers contributed to family support compared with about 66 per cent of those of other married women workers. Yet family income was lowest for homeworkers because their husbands worked fewer days. These out-of-work fathers often helped, despite the association of most of the home processes with women's work; they maintained their patriarchal position by not doing housework. In one poignant photograph, the unemployed father, who had been shelling nuts, removed himself from the camera, as if it would be unmanly to be recorded at such work, though his mirror reflection stands over the pyramid of his children (see Figure 6). Another small child watches the baby.[48]

Hine felt keenly the irony of celebrating the home while manufacturers turned homes into factories. "It is the best place for the family – therefore there is no better place for industry. – Q.E.D. Then, why be selfish and try to reserve the home for the family?" he asked. "It has other, broader uses." Like most settlement house leaders, Hine distinguished between home and workplace. As Greenwich House's Mary Simkhovitch declared in 1915, "We know very well these homes have the form but not the substance of home when the time has to be given entirely to this work." What the reform network added to

[47] Photograph no. 2689; Elizabeth C. Watson, "Report on Manufacturing in Tenements in New York City," *Second Report of the FIC*, 1:696–7.

[48] Watson, "Report on Manufacturing in Tenements in New York City," 696–7; Robert Chapin, *The Standard of Living Among Workingmen's Families in New York City* (New York, 1909); "Men's Ready-Made Clothing," 248, 300; no. 2698.

Figure 6. Lewis Hine, "A 'Reflection' on the Parent," Hudson Street, New York City, December 1911. Courtesy of the National Archives. Hine wrote in his field notes: "Reflection in looking glass shows the father who had been picking nuts but refused to be photographed. He is out of work. Tommy Mascela, 5 years, picks some, Minne, 7 years, Rosie 9, and Angeline 11. Make $3.00 to $4.00 a week."

this conventional notion was the state's responsibility to maintain homes as homes, saving them from the monetized social relations of the factory.[49]

Writing in middle-class magazines, journalists dramatized reform investigations, celebrating the home in a sentimental manner. Over time they would focus on the plight of children. Poet Edwin Markham described "The Sweat-Shop Inferno" in a 1907 issue of *Cosmopolitan*, exhorting: "'Home and mother!' These old syllables strike tender chords in the heart. Yet we have desert regions in our cities where there are children, but no home, no mother. 'Home and

[49] Lewis Hine, "Tasks in the Tenements," *The Child Labor Magazine* 3 (May 1914), 95–7; "Meeting of Committee on Industrial Relations. Constitutional Convention," June 9, 1915, 83–4, in series no. 640, New York Constitutional Convention, Working Files of Committees, box 14, NYSA.

mother!' Our grim system forces hundreds of thousands to lose the meanings of these sweet old words." *Harper's Weekly* had uncovered "The Slaves of the 'Sweaters'" during the early nineties. The new academic journals and the social reform *Charities* in the first years of the century had published the initial work of investigators like Mary Van Kleeck. By the 1910s *Good Housekeeping* was exposing "Children in Bondage." The emphasis over time had shifted from "white industrial slaves" to "the servitude" of children, who could not play or keep awake during school.[50] The NCL, the NCLC, their New York branches, and the College Settlements Association responded by investigating how to keep children from home labor.[51]

Certainly the image of the home as "factory annex" dominated the reports of NCLC agents; so did observations on homeworker lives. Watson lamented that about 63 percent of the fathers in homeworking families were in their prime wage-earning years, but she focused her attention on the burden that their failure to make a family wage placed on wives and mothers. Fifty-five percent of the adult women were between the ages of twenty-five and forty-five, "the best years of a woman's life, when if she is married her family cares are heaviest and she is most efficient and economically valuable." Homeworkers, though, ruined their own health, sacrificed their children, and neglected their housework for the constant grind of piecework. Watson judged dangers to the homeworking family more serious than those to the consumer. Working into the night made mothers "irritable and rough" with children. Receiving five or six hours sleep, women experienced a profound stretch-out of the working day, with waged and unwaged labor intermingling in the same place. An "American" embroiderer confessed: "I am very unhappy because I cannot take the children out. I am always tired and nervous. House going to the dogs."[52]

Hine's photo montages visualized the discourses of dirt, disease, and darkness, capsulizing the themes of the reform campaign. They appealed to the

[50] Edwin Markham, "The Sweat–Shop Inferno," *Cosmopolitan* 42 (Jan. 1907), 330–1; "Slaves of the 'Sweaters,'" *Harpers' Weekly* 34 (Apr. 26, 1890), 335; Nelle Mason Auten, "Some Phases of the Sweating System in the Garment Trades of Chicago," *American Journal of Sociology* 6 (Mar. 1901), 602–45; Lillian W. Betts, "Child Labor in Shops and Homes," *The Outlook* 73 (Apr. 18, 1903), 921–7; "A House of Paper Bags," *Charities* 14 (Apr. 29, 1905), 696–8; Mary Van Kleeck, "Child Labor in Home Industries," *The Annals of the American Academy of Political and Social Science* 35 (Mar. 1910), supplement: 145–9; Elizabeth Shepley Sergeant, "Toilers of the Tenements: Where the Beautiful Things of the Great Shops Are Made," *McClure's Magazine* 35 (July 1910), 2331–48; Mary Alden Hopkins, "Children in Bondage: Turning Children's Homes into Factories," *Good Housekeeping Magazine* 56 (June 1913), 743–52.

[51] Mary Van Kleeck, "Child Labor in New York City Tenements," *Charities and the Commons* 19 (Jan. 18, 1908), 1405–20. For notes on the progress of the investigation, NYCLC Papers, box 9, folders 39 and 45.

[52] George Hall, "Tenement–Home Child Labor," *Hygiene and the Child* 1 (Apr. 1911), 1, NYCLC Papers, box 9, folder 45; Watson, "The Homework System in New York City," 686, 691–3, 695–7; Edward Brown, "Embroidery Homeworkers in New York City," *Second Report of the FIC*, 1:745.

self-protection of consumers and to their sense of fair play. They embodied Progressive notions of childlife – the child as father to the man, childhood as a special time in the life cycle, and play as a valuable aspect of life. The montage "Child Life" quoted Charlotte Perkins Gilman:

> No Fledgling Feeds The Father Bird,
> No Chicken Feeds The Hen,
> No Kitten Mouses For the Cat,
> This Glory Is For Men.

Another montage, "Homework Destroys Family Life," presented the Basso family of Carmine Street making roses (see Figure 7). As with many pictures, we see a bottle prominently displayed, an object deliberately included in the camera's lens to suggest intemperance as a cause of poverty. The partially curtained window shows that homeworkers relied on natural light to cut down on fuel costs. Its caption declared, "Keeps the child from school," but Hine's own field notes prove otherwise. Homework, especially on flowers, was a before- and after-school activity. Although such labor did interfere with academic achievement, the discrepancy between the life of this family and the caption of this photograph suggests the mechanisms through which Hine manipulated his pictures. Similarly, viewers are invited to contrast in the lower half of the montage a comfortable household with its mother looking at her cuddled child and a tenement wreck with the mother sewing pants and her three children, one with pacifier in mouth, dirty and presumably neglected. Hine's report on Mrs. Guadina of Mulberry Street captured a more complex situation than the caption: "Would You Like Your Child to Grow Up Here or Here." Poverty-striken, with four days of work on her trunk (see Figure 8), "she was struggling along, (actually weak for want of food) trying to finish this batch of work so she could get the pay. There seemed to be no food in the house and she said the children had no milk all day. The father is out of work (sells fish) on account of rheumatism. Three small children and another expected soon."[53]

The images themselves offer mixed messages. That of Mrs. Annie De Dartius, nursing "a dirty baby" while picking nuts with a "sore throat," as Hine writes, reveals his disgust with the kinds of mothers found in the tenements (see Figure 9).[54] But this picture also powerfully presents the conditions of childcare that kept women from factory labor. It suggests how homeworking mothers cared for their children despite the circumstances of their lives. Looking at Hine's photographs from another angle, without their captions or as individual photographs apart from the montages – an angle from which

---

[53] Nos. 3589; 3750, 2811, 2821; Louise C. Odencrantz, *Italian Women in Industry: A Study of Conditions in New York City* (New York: Russell Sage Foundation, 1919), 257-9. Many four- to six-year-olds helped; those in school worked before and after until they qualified for working papers between the ages of fourteen and sixteen; many parents kept their school-aged children home to help. See "Men's Ready-Made Clothing," 383-4.

[54] No. 2703.

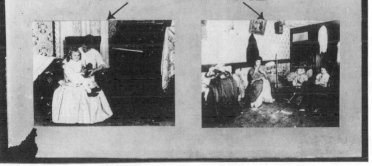

Figure 7. Lewis Hine, "Homework Destroys Family Life," poster montage for the National Child Labor Committee, Tenement House Exhibit, 1912. Courtesy of Library of Congress. Created to expose the problem of tenement labor, this multiimage display blames parents as well as employers. It embodies the major gendered argument of the reform campaign: Homework undermines both male breadwinning and female housekeeping, depriving children of education as well as proper mothering. Hine contrasts proper homelife marked by a piano with the degraded homelife of the "tenement wreck."

Figure 8. Lewis Hine, "A Tenement Wreck," Mrs. Guadina, Mulberry Street, New York City, December 1911. Courtesy of the National Archives.

individuals at the time could have viewed them because we are drawn into an image by its lines and masses as well as by its surroundings – the lives of homeworkers appear without reform moralizing. Homework may "degrade" family life, but homeworkers are not totally degraded. They made the best they could out of their poverty. They were resourceful contributors to the family economy, providing around a quarter of the total income, less than other married wage-earning women, but still a notable amount. Homeworking families, in fact, had perhaps the lowest per capita income, around two dollars a week.[55]

The tenement house photographs enter working-class life. Families pooled resources; the homeworking woman worked with other women, often her kin (see Figure 10). Children's contributions brought pride. One mother boasted of her seven-year-old daughter who was embroidering stems of flowers on ladies' waists: "See how smart she is. I show her how and right away she makes them." Neighbors would visit, conversing in the bedroom while the mother

[55] "Men's Ready-Made Clothing," 370–6.

Figure 9. Lewis Hine, "4:30 P.M.," Mrs. Annie De Dartius, Laight Street, New York City. Courtesy of the National Archives. Hine commented: "Nursing a dirty baby while she picks nuts. Was suffering with a sore throat. Rosie, 3 yrs old hanging around. Genevieve, 6 yrs. old, Tessie, [6 yrs. old,] picks too. Make $1.50 to $2 a week. Husband on railroad works sometimes."

sewed. What appeared to outsiders as "clannishness" one immigrant explained as "in Italy everybody helps everybody else." That could mean a neighbor would parcel out her homework bundle to needy compatriots or loan her tenement license. What reformers sometimes judged as ignorant behavior, like sewing pants while keeping company with the sick, women understood as providing community sympathy and solidarity. Watson described how neighbors warned a family on the top floor of her approach: An old woman delayed her by showing off new babies and pointing out cracks in the plaster while relaying a message in Italian (that Watson understood), "Fortunata, Fortunata, take the plumes into your godmother's. There comes a lady." While engaged in homework, women shared food preparation and childcare. Plumbing and cookstoves were primitive compared to those found in middle-class homes,

Figure 10. Lewis Hine, family of artificial flower makers, ca. 1911. Courtesy of the National Archives. Piece rates and overnight deadlines forced young children to labor along with mothers and older daughters.

but they were improvements on Old World conditions. Yet the women sacrificed fresh air and sunshine for the tenement towers of Gotham.[56]

Many Italian women were from Sicily where patriarchal conventions restricted their movements beyond the home. All claimed to prefer home to outside work. A young factory worker admitted choosing artificial flower manufacture: "It is the Italian's trade; and then I thought that when I get married I can still keep it up at home." Women reformers interpreted this devotion to home and family negatively because it was actualized through homework. For Italian women, homework

[56] Nos. 2703, 2691, 2805, 2876, 2704, 2881, Josephine Roche, "The Italian Girl," in Ruth S. True, *The Neglected Girl* (New York: Survey Associates, Inc., 1914), 101; Watson, "Home Work in the Tenements," 10-11; Betts, "Child Labor in Shops and Homes," 924; Donna Gabaccia, *From Sicily to Elizabeth Street: Housing and Social Change Among Italian Immigrants, 1880–1930* (Albany: State Univ. of New York Press, 1984), 89–90; Elizabeth Ewen, *Immigrant Women in the Land of Dollars: Life and Culture on the Lower East Side, 1890–1925* (New York: Monthly Review Press, 1985).

meant not the destruction of the home but the fulfillment of familial duties. A daughter in one New York City family, for example, brought artificial flowers home from the shop and worked at times until five in the morning to send her oldest brother to medical school. "'When he graduated,' she said, 'I cried all day and was as happy as though I had graduated myself. I often say to my mother that we treat my brother as if he were a king, – but I can't help it.'"[57]

Homeworking families suffered from some of the same periodic disruptions faced by other working-class families. Unemployment, seasonal work, and illness were common conditions in the early twentieth century. Why did these women turn to lower-paid, intermittent homework rather than enter the shop? After all, they earned considerably less. Nearly 70 percent received $3.49 or less per week, whereas over 75 percent of the comparable inside finishers earned more than that amount. Homeworkers had less education than shopworkers, but the location of their labor did not stem from their immigrant status or from their "inferior . . . progressiveness." Homeworking mothers chose to care for their own children to a larger extent than mothers who went out to work (see Table 1). Homeworkers had slightly larger families (4.5 to 3.8), but the age of their children was the key factor. About half had children under three and nearly 40 percent had children between three and five years old; less than 30 percent of other married wage-earning women had such young children (see Table 2). The turn to homework was not merely an Italian cultural preference for mothers to stay home with children and be ready to serve husbands. Jewish women also labored at home – until older children could assume childcare. Homeworkers made a practical decision because factories hiring women failed to accommodate to pregnancy and childrearing.[58]

Care of children interrupted homeworkers for, like other working-class mothers, few sent children to day nurseries. These mothers distrusted such institutions, often run by charities, for trying to control their children. Because immigration had broken many kinship networks, mothers or aunts were unavailable for childcare. Instead, reformers found "little mothers" and "little fathers," somewhat older children, minding siblings and performing housework for mothers who earned wages inside the home as well as in other locations.[59]

[57] Mary Van Kleeck, *Artificial Flower Makers* (New York: Survey Associates, 1913), 38, 86; Judith E. Smith, *Family Connections: A History of Italian and Jewish Immigrant Lives in Providence, Rhode Island, 1900–1940* (Albany: State Univ. of New York Press, 1985), esp. 50.

[58] "Men's Ready Made Clothing," 225–6, 247–9, 383–4, 239–40, 306, 301, 234; Mary Van Kleeck, "Women and Children Who Make Men's Clothes," *The Survey* 26 (Apr. 1, 1911), 68–9. The reasons homeworkers earned less than shop finishers were complex, including interruptions to their work due to housekeeping and children, less steady work given by employers, the nature of the work given out, time lost going to and from the shop, and their ages and other personal conditions.

[59] Sonya Michel, "The Limits of Maternalism: Policies Toward American Wage-Earning Mothers During the Progressive Era," in *Mothers of a New World: Maternalist Politics and the Origins of Welfare States*, ed. Sonya Michel and Seth Koven (New York: Routledge, 1993), 277–320; Betts, "Child Labor in Shops and Homes," 924; for the little mother, no. 2698.

Table 1. *Number of families of working married women with children and the caretakers of those children*

Relation to children of person taking care of them	Families of home finishers					Families of other than home finishers				
	Number having children of ages					Number having children of ages				
	Under 3	3–5	6–9	10–13	Totals[a]	Under 3	3–5	6–9	10–13	Totals[a]
Mother	127	110	124	98	243			2		2
Mother and other person	43	23	19	15	51					
Father	7	8	5	3	10	1	5	4	5	10
Father and other person	14	13	8	3	17	2	3	6	7	10
Brother or sister	12	10	13	11	18				1	1
Grandmother	18	13	9	4	20	7	6	5	4	15
Grandfather	1	1			1		1			1
Aunt	13	10	5	1	13	3		2	1	4
Other relative	3	2	1	1	3	1	3	2	3	5
Neighbor	37	35	19	9	54	1	5	3	1	7
Day nursery						2		1		2
No one							2	7	13	16
Not reported		1	1		1	1	1	1	1	2
Total	275	226	204	145	431	18	25	34	36	75

[a]In the details of this table each family appears as many times as it has children of the different age groups. Because of this duplication the totals are not comparable with the numbers in the several columns, the total being the actual number of families considered.

Source: From "Men's Ready-Made Clothing," *Report on Condition of Women and Child Wage Earners in the United States* (Washington, D.C.:GPO, 1911), v. 2, 283.

The homework that reformers condemned, parents saw as keeping children from dangerous streets. Parents presented complex reasons. Some felt "it is better for the children to learn something useful to do." One mother believed, "Costs too much to play outside; wears too much shoes." But she also regarded home labor as an avenue for mobility: "Carrie cuts embroidery to make money for her piano lessons. She might play in moving pictures when she gets big."[60] Some families turned work into play. One former homeworker recalled: "It was like a game. . . . Whoever did the most would get some extra snack or candy or fruit." A ten-year-old who crocheted bedroom slippers with three other girls exclaimed, "We have *such* good

[60] Nos. 2812 and 2829; Watson, "The Homework System in New York City," 696.

Table 2. *Number and percent of families of married homeworkers and of other working married women with children*

		Families having children									
		Under 3 years		3 to 5 years		6 to 9 years		10 to 13 years		14 and 15 years	
Families of	Total Families	Num-ber	Per-cent	Num-ber	Per-cent	Num-ber	Per-cent	Num-ber	Per-cent	Num-ber	Per-cent
Married home workers	590	285	48.3	229	38.8	215	36.6	192	32.5	103	17.4
Other married women at work	358	38	10.6	61	17.3	88	24.5	113	31.5	99	27.6
Total	948	323	34.1	290	30.6	303	32.0	305	32.2	202	21.3

Source: From "Men's Ready-Made Clothing," *Report on Condition of Women and Child Wage Earners in the United States* (Washington, D.C.: GPO, 1911), v. 2, 240.

times working together! Sometimes, we don't go to bed till eleven o'clock!"[61]

The work that reformers judged a demoralizing element of domestic life, immigrant families embraced as a strategy for household survival. They shared with reformers the assumption that mothers should stay at home with children. But, unable to live on the wages of their men, immigrant families at certain points of the life cycle eagerly sought homework – even while condemning its low piece rates. "Lace is too dam-cheap," a younger brother commented. One mother admitted, "I rather work for a factory," where she could earn more than $2.50 a week, but who would mind her children? Children themselves complained that they would rather be playing or even doing schoolwork. Boys, underage for working papers, resisted making flowers. Little children fought off exhaustion. Homeworkers accepted the necessity of their work. A Haverill, Massachusetts, tagmaker confessed: "Maybe I've been too hard on the kids. My husband and I have lots of fights about it. He wants them out playing – and the housework done. But there's the rent. . . . And shoes! What are we going to do about it? . . . Since Rosie died, I've thought maybe I did keep them at work too steady." As the family budgeter, she knew the difference that income from homework meant.[62]

[61] Smith, *Family Connections*, 54–6; Hopkins, "Children in Bondage," 748.

[62] No. 2719; Van Kleeck, "Child Labor in Home Industries," 145–6; Watson, "Manufacturing in Tenements," 105; Sergeant, "Toilers of the Tenements," 240; Hopkins, "Children in Bondage," 745.

Reformers viewed these working-class mothers as both victims and accomplices, for a chasm of class separated those who strove to relieve the burdens of working-class motherhood from the mothers of the tenements. Kelley implied that schools, with their hot lunches and medical staffs, could care for children better than such families. She promoted compulsory education laws and education scholarships (to replace income lost from child labor) as part of the campaign to abolish homework. Child labor investigator Mary Britton Miller viewed the Italian mother as having "a hungry eagerness" to turn her growing child into "a wage-earning home slave." One truant boy told her, "Our mothers makes us stay at home to work and licks us when we don't." Such mothers, she claimed, stunted children's minds, turning them into "slow, uncomprehending machines."[63]

Newspapers sensationalized the issue of homework by repeating testimony of child abuse. As far away as Wheeling, West Virginia, and Sioux Falls, Iowa, readers learned of "Where Babies Work" and how "the mothers are often forced to beat the children in order to keep them at work but it is that or starve." Some journalists faulted the environment of poverty. The *New York Evening Mail* editorialized: "Do the mothers of children force their babies to work at night because they wish to see them suffer? ... These mothers of the slum are not by nature less kind than others. They are themselves the victims of the system of toil which they force upon their children." Fathers were not free from blame in this portrait of child abuse. Abolition of homework might save "the bodies and the souls and the minds of thousands of children," Britton Miller argued. "And it might drive the fathers to work. ... They are shiftless and lazy and often drunkards." She would rely on the law "to attend to them [the fathers] in some way. And the children should be rescued at any cost."[64]

Homeworking mothers fought to protect themselves against reformers. They were "ingenious and resourceful in evading the school law and tricking the truant officers and the Judges." Britton Miller told of tenement mothers manipulating the judicial system by relying on their "wretched appearance," on their very poverty as evidence of how much they needed the help of their children, and winning over judges through the "sucking sound of drawn breath," their very hunger. Others reported how homeworkers knowingly

---

[63] "Forbid Home Work and End Child Labor," *New York Globe*, Dec. 7, 1912; "Home Work in the Tenements Makes Children Slaves. Mothers Who Were Merciless Taskmasters," *The Star*, Jan. 4, 1913, NCLC Scrapbook, "New York Factory Investigating Commission, 1912–1913," box 57, NCLC Papers.

[64] Reformers defined child abuse not only as physical violence but also as neglect and ill treatment, for which child labor provided evidence. Elizabeth Pleck, *Domestic Tyranny: The Making of American Social Policy Against Family Violence from Colonial Times to the Present* (New York: Oxford Univ. Press, 1987), 88–144. "Where Babies Work," Wheeling *News*, Jan. 7, 1913; "Child Labor Horrors," Sioux Falls *Argus-Leader*, Jan. 16, 1913; "The Cry of the Children for Protection," editorial, *Evening Mail* (New York), Dec. 7, 1912; Miller, "Home Work in Tenements," NCLC Scrapbook, NCLC Papers.

deceived inspectors and investigators by hiding evidence of child labor, feigning ignorance, tearing down scarlet fever signs, and ignoring other regulations. It took working-class women like the WTUL's Leonora O'Reilly to remind reformers, "Don't blame the mother . . . but come back on yourselves and say, 'This thing is injustice, and we will trace it to its very source, and do justice.'"[65]

"Mothers who must earn"

The attitude of women reformers toward tenement house mothers was a complex product of their feminism of difference. This perspective, when combined with a sympathy for the working class, tended to reject paid labor in the name of improving the lives of women strained to the "limit of human endurance" by "bearing, nursing and taking care of . . . children and at the very same time and place trying to earn a wage."[66] The poster of "The Sweated Mother," displayed at the Chicago Industrial Exhibit under the title "$acred Mother-hood," embodied this complexity. With a dollar sign replacing the S in "Sacred," this image of a tenement mother nursing her babe while running a foot-powered sewing machine mocked the sacredness of motherhood celebrated by the larger culture. The WTUL would adopt this image as its own, distributing it on postcards while fund-raising for garment strikers and against the sweatshop.[67]

Before the factory system, Sophonisba Breckinridge explained, women could "adjust their industrial activities to their maternal privileges and their social and family life." Because of the rigidity of factory life, "the problem is really one of controlling the factory system so as to benefit by its economies, allow women to share in the productive activity of society as they have always done, and at the same time save them and [keep] their children alive." To protect motherhood and childlife did not mean to remove women from worthwhile work and confine them to domestic duties alone. But the NCL questioned whether "your mother [could] have brought you up as she did" if she had labored excessive hours for pennies. Assuming that mothers would earn wages, it pledged to fight for the best conditions for both mother work, especially "the proper bringing up of children," and waged labor.[68]

[65] Miller, "Home Work in the Tenements"; Watson, "Home Work in the Tenements," 3–12; Leonora O'Reilly, "Extracts from the Address Delivered at the Annual Meeting," NYCL, *Report for the Year Ending December 1907,* 50–1.

[66] Edith Wyatt, "Garment Workers at Home," *Handbook of othe Chicago Industrial Exhibit,* 38.

[67] Payne, *Reform, Labor, and Feminism,* 118, 134. Univ. of Wisconsin students of John Commons (League member and later president) Irene Osgood (later co-director of the American Association for Labor Legislation with her husband John Andrews) and Helen Sumner (later noted investigator of women's work) sent such cards to clothing manufacturers right before Christmas 1908. I.O. to Mrs. Raymond Robins, Dec. 21, 1908, AALL Papers, reel 1.

[68] Sophonisba P. Breckinridge, "The Problem of Women in Industry," *Handbook of the Chicago Industrial Exhibit,* 54–5; NCL, *Your Mother &–,* NCL Papers, reel 114, frames 118–19.

The family wage could improve the lives of such mothers, but the NCL recognized that not all women could depend on men. It understood "so long as women's wages rest upon the assumption that every woman has a husband, father, brother or lover contributing to her support, so long these sinister incidents of women's industrial employment (tuberculosis, insanity, vice) are inevitable." The NCL was realistic enough about women's life situations to include "lover" in this list, a relation that perhaps underlined how all connections with men were relations of dependency. Staunch suffragist Maud Nathan declared it "immoral to teach girls that in order to live they must secure husbands who can support them." Championing equal pay for equal work and "training and organization" for women, she advocated the necessity of work not merely in terms of the family economy but because women's sphere extended "beyond the domestic circle" and women could contribute to the world's progress. But class determined whether one's working came from necessity or freedom.[69]

This need to work provided the strongest argument for minimum wage boards in those trades where women and children predominated. The minimum wage evolved into the major strategy of the Consumers' League to end sweated labor. This new departure derived from the wage boards established in Australia and which were then being set up in England. The British established wage boards for sweated industries, regardless of the sex of the worker. But in the United States, where courts struck down state interference in men's right to contract, such boards would address only the area of women's wages. They would peg the wages of women workers in female-dominated industries to a minimal but decent standard of living, also set in relation to what employers could afford to pay. The 1908 International Conference of Consumers' Leagues in Geneva asked national leagues to develop minimum wage legislation for their respective countries. Kelley at first seemed skeptical, thinking such boards would prolong the existence of homework. But during the meetings she became convinced and added the boards to her arsenal of weapons. The next year the NCL adopted the minimum wage as part of its ten-year program. By 1920, it would become its linchpin.[70]

---

[69] *Tenement House Workers – The Sweating System in 1910*, NCL Papers, reel 114, frames 337–9; NCL, *Eleventh Annual Report for the Year Ending March 1, 1910*, NCL Papers, reel 4, frame 15; Mrs. Frederick Nathan, "Position of Women as Wage-Earners," *New York Times*, Dec. 24, 1899, Nathan Scrapbook 2.

[70] *Eleventh Annual Report*, 22; "Extracts from the Addresses Delivered at the Annual Meeting: Mrs. Florence Kelley," *NYCL Report*, May 1909, NCL Papers, reel 112, frames 696–7; Florence Kelley, "Le Travail à Domicile Et La Ligue D'Acheteurs En Amerique," in *Première Conférence Internationale Des Ligues Sociales D'Acheteurs, Genève, les 24, 25 et 26 Sept. 1908* (Fribourg-Suisse: [no imprint], 1909), 454; Vivien Hart, *Bound by Our Constitution: Women, Workers, and Minimum Wage Laws in the United States and Great Britain* (Princeton, N.J.: Princeton Univ. Press, 1994); Clara M. Beyer, "Development of Minimum-Wage Laws in the United States, 1912–1927," *WBB*, n. 61 (Washington: GPO, 1928).

This turn to state action derived from the lesson of the white list: "Regulation of working conditions through organized persuasion was not enough." Licensing systems had failed; the NCL believed, "Regulation does not regulate and prohibition has become indispensable" even though the league by 1909 judged New York's labor department "honest" and "highly competent." Fifty inspectors could not inspect each tenement twice a year; in 1909, they looked at five thousand once, "leaving nineteen thousand required visits unmade." Given the vast and shifting population of the city, the provisions of the law were unenforceable and easily evaded, as when homeworkers claimed unrelated persons as family. By 1910 the league had shifted its focus from directly fighting tenement homework – though still calling for its abolition – to the gaining of protective legislation for women as a strategy to end sweated labor. By increasing employer costs, maximum hour and minimum wage laws would discourage homework.[71]

This new direction for the league did not mean that Kelley abandoned her "indictment against the present competitive organization of industry," which harmed the married woman wage earner. At the very time that the minimum wage for women became the center of the league's efforts, she called for "a minimum wage sufficient to enable fathers to support their families without help from wage-earning wives." Writing in 1910 on "Married Women in Industry," Kelley argued that the employment of such women not only led to fewer births but demoralized husbands and penalized children. Because these workers were unorganized, with irregular labor market participation, they lowered male wages. They had to neglect children by leaving them to roam the streets, locking them in rooms, or turning daughters into "little mothers." Homework, "the domain of married women," injured even employers whose reliance on its cheapness substituted for industrial modernization. Ultimately the community suffered from the "vice, crime and inefficiency" that came from the exploitation of wage-earning mothers.[72]

Kelley condemned women's suffering under "the twofold strain of home maker and wage earner." Philanthropic agencies exacerbated this "double burden" by establishing "day nurseries, charity kindergartens, charity sewing rooms, and doles of home sewing." Numerous studies had shown that charity and homework fed off each other, with employers providing less in wages because of charity and philanthropies giving smaller subsidies because of homework. The idea of a night nursery so women could "work at night after they have cared for their children by day" appeared "monstrous" since such arrangements encouraged overwork. Instead, Kelley praised European nations which, in accepting the inevitability of industrial work among mothers, initiated maternity leave, crèches within facto-

---

[71] *The National Consumers' League*, May 1937; Florence Kelley, "The Problem of Sweating in America," 414–21; Van Kleeck, *Artificial Flower Makers*, 142–3.

[72] Florence Kelley, "Married Women in Industry," *Proceedings of the Academy of Political Science* I (New York: Columbia Univ., 1910), 96, 90–2.

ries, and nursing breaks for mothers whose babies were dying under the bottle-feeding hands of neighbors and relatives. Kelley understood the horrible physical cost of industrial labor for mothers, so she promoted a "statutory provision for rest before and after confinement." Concern for women's welfare led her to call for a living ("minimum") wage for men; the language of weakness justified public support of motherhood.[73]

Kelley shared in the discourse of the trade union movement. The secretary of the Boston Central Labor Union explained the benefits of the minimum or living wage for men in 1913 in terms that hardly differed from Kelley's own. It would not only allow the working man to support his nonlaboring family but "it would mean the abolition of sweatshops and tenement-house work" as well as the end of child labor. Although he included "equal pay for equal work, whether done by men or women," among benefits, Kelley also struggled for minimum wages for women. Most working-class and middle-class thinkers associated the women's minimum wage with a subsistence wage, but Kelley intended that a woman also could maintain dependents on it.[74]

The grim realities of textile and garment labor led such reformers away from day care as a solution for poor families. In 1900, when homework appeared less entrenched, the Consumers' League approved of mothers moving with their work into factories, with day nurseries minding their babies. Still, views on this issue were hardly monolithic. In 1912 WTUL leader Mary Dreier called for more charity as a substitute for homework. Mary Britton Miller demanded nurseries and kindergartens so that mothers could go out to work, while Dr. Annie S. Daniels of the New York Infirmary for Women and Children explained that nurseries "always have room for children whenever they ask to go in."[75] But Kelley firmly held onto the predominant belief among trade unionists that it was men's duty to support their wives and children. (Daniels, it should be noted, also believed that ending homework "would result in making the husbands work in some cases.") Her feminist anger at husbands and fathers who refused to do their duty, shared with reformers like Lewis Hine and Mary Britton Miller, matched her condemnation of capitalist exploiters.[76]

With women's domestic and maternal responsibilities unquestioned, policy options became limited. Kelley condemned the lack of fact gathering on the real situation of working mothers. Legislation that made work more bearable

---

[73] Florence Kelley, "Married Women in Industry," 92–5.

[74] Statement of Henry Abrahams quoted in Lawrence Glickman, "A Living Wage: Political Economy, Gender, and Consumerism in American Culture, 1880–1925" (Ph.D. diss., Univ. of California, Berkeley, 1992), 337–8.

[75] "The Consumers' League," *The Silver Cross*, n. 25, Mar. 24, 1900, Nathan Scrapbook 2; "Women Hope to Get Law to Save Children," *New York Sun*, Dec. 8, 1912, and Miller, "Home Work in the Tenements," both in NCLC Scrapbook; Dr. Annie S. Daniels, "Manufacturing in Tenements," *Second Report of the FIC*, 1:113.

[76] Kelley, "Le Travail à Domicile Et La Ligue D'Acheteurs En Amerique," 455.

for all women had to be especially directed "to the urgent needs of married women." Yet she criticized current hours laws for doing nothing to curtail the labor of working mothers because speedup intensified their work and destroyed their health. She preferred another course: Eliminate the necessity of mothers' wage earning. If men could not support wives, then the state either had to force male support through laws against desertion, provide pensions for "orphans and widowed mothers of young children," or aid men in raising their wages. She would lengthen men's work lives – at a time when investigators found forty-five-year-olds superannuated – through "prevention of accidents and disease." The socialist in Kelley was willing to leap to the ultimate solution, the cooperative commonwealth, for only there could women "find just and beneficent conditions in which to carry on those industries which were theirs from the foundation of human life." Socialism would allow women to fulfill their work as mothers, but it was practically unthinkable to transform the gender system so that men also mothered. Unlike Charlotte Perkins Gilman, Kelley did not envision a different organization of domestic labor.[77]

A division by kinship position lay at the heart of this analysis. Testifying before the FIC in 1912, Kelley associated living wages not only with sexually defined roles, where men support families through wages and women through mothering, but also with economic independence for women without children (and presumably without men):

> Factory conditions which will give living wages to men will eliminate the necessity of the home work for women and children. I mean in the case of families where the father is able-bodied. I would provide a pension for widows just as Colorado has done. Then I would give the factory work to detached women. The deliberately idle men I would send to the workhouse for the week-end, as Judge Lindsey does, just to remind them of their obligations.[78]

Such a defense of the family wage, held with a belief in a man's obligation to support his wife and children, reflected the dominant gender system. Nonetheless, it also suggests the woman-centered analysis that these reformers brought to industrial life, how they based their programs on the real situation of women, not on abstract principles of equal rights. They strove not to keep women from the workplace but to end exploitation there and insure that mothers could perform nurturing work; so they connected the end of homework with mothers' pensions and child support laws.[79]

But states underfunded mothers' pensions, a welfare provision given to

---

[77] Kelley, "Married Women in Industry," 95–6; Charlotte Perkins Gilman, *The Home: Its Work and Influence* (1903; rpt Urbana: Univ. of Illinois Press, 1972).

[78] Kelley, "Forbid Home Work."

[79] Martha May, "The 'Problem of Duty': The Regulation of Male Breadwinning and Desertion in the Progressive Era," Institute for Legal Studies, *Working Papers*, 1:3 (Feb. 1986); Theda Skocpol, *Protecting Mothers and Soldiers: The Political Origins of Social Policy in the United States* (Cambridge, Mass.: Harvard Univ. Press, 1992), 424–79.

"deserving" widows with small children. Pensions provided no caretaker's grant, forcing women "worthy" enough to receive one also to work for wages. This inadequacy stemmed from larger political and structural forces over which women reformers exercised little control. More radical women, as those associated with Margaret Sanger's *The Woman Rebel*, criticized the pensions for restricting "the freedom of the mother," arguing that restrictions on "working outside the home" actually would "subsidize" sweated labor.[80]

Whether homework existed often depended on the structure of the labor market and the organization of specific industries, like artificial flowers where assembly went out to homes. Low rates forced mothers to deploy the labor of their children. Employers overcame hour laws by sending work home with factory employees.[81] Homework allowed them to save space in the process of circumventing a restricted labor supply. They took advantage of women's want of employment. One explained, "The quality does not suffer . . . the women know it must be done properly or it will be 'thrown at them' and they will have to do it over again." Another admitted: "The women do more at home – they work longer hours. No matter how quickly I want a lot of pants they get them to me, and I know they work unlimited hours." Employers justified self-interest, the savings of rent and wages, in terms of women's need to stay at home and the desires of their families. "The Italian men want their wives to keep on working, and at the same time cook the food and have plenty of children and care for them," complained an employer who would have preferred shop finishers. The sexual division of labor and dominant understandings of womanhood justified employer action but when it became more profitable to remove work from the home to the factory, employers were quick to do so. Massachusetts's more stringent homework licensing in 1913 led one major employer to substitute machine-made edging for handmade and reduce homework from a thousand to a hundred dozen items in a few months.[82]

To protect the children: Getting around *Jacobs*

By 1911, homework opponents clearly had linked saving the family with improved industrial standards. For years they had criticized child labor and women's hours laws for not covering the wage work of children or women at home, making a mockery of "protective" legislation. The rising tide of Progressivism had lifted into the New York State legislature politicians

[80] Joanne L. Goodwin, "An American Experiment in Paid Motherhood: The Implementation of Mothers' Pensions in Early Twentieth-Century Chicago," *Gender and History* 4 (Autumn 1992): 323–42; Benita Locke, "Mothers' Pensions: The Latest Capitalist Trap," *The Woman Rebel* 1 (Mar. 1914), 4–5.

[81] Van Kleeck, *Artificial Flower Makers*, 90–117.

[82] "Men's Ready-Made Clothing," 302–6; Susan M. Kingsbury and Mabelle Moses, "Licensed Workers in Industrial Home Work in Massachusetts," State Board of Labor and Industries, *Industrial Bulletin*, n. 4 (Boston: Wright & Potter Printing Co., 1915), 91–2.

supportive of consumer and labor legislation, while the disaster of the Triangle Shirtwaist fire increased public pressure for action. That year the NYCL, along with the Committee on Congestion of Population and the NYCLC, asked the legislature for a commission on tenement house manufacture. By collecting evidence on the need for restrictive state action, such a body could provide the facts necessary to sustain legislation and get around *Jacobs*.[83]

This case particularly irked Kelley who charged "the exclusively man made government of New York" with maintaining "the evils of child labor" through an "anti-social judicial decision." Work made illegal under the state child labor law could be sent into the homes; manufacturers could employ "[children] there while only the name of the mother, father or adult brother or sister appears upon the payroll." "The Abolition of Child Labor" was one result of "What Women Might Do With the Ballot." But even before suffrage, organized women pressured Albany. Although reformers failed to gain a separate commission, the FIC eventually covered tenement homework.[84]

Testimony before the FIC brought together the somewhat contradictory discourses that trade unionists and reformers had mounted against homework since the turn of the century. WTUL organizer Melinda Scott expressed the holistic approach of the social feminist agenda embraced by the WTUL and the NCL. She connected the end of tenement manufacture with paid pregnancy leave, a forty-eight hour work week for women, minimum wages for the sweated trades, more women factory inspectors, more inspectors for New York City, and laws protecting workers from fires. Homeworkers were mothers but they also were workers; the two activities shaped each other. NCLC reformers focused on the children of homeworkers and the impact of such labor on the larger community. For them, homeworkers were public charges, dependent on charity, who spread tuberculosis. They were undesirables who increased poverty by lowering the wages of factory laborers. Existing legislation failed to cover these home factories. Because regulation required almost as many inspectors as homeworkers (to check the tenements constantly), the NCLC considered prohibition "far simpler. . . . It is the *most* practicable solution of an intolerable problem."[85]

The NCLC called for child protection, but privacy arguments inhibited intervention in the family just as they had impeded labor legislation. So did "the tradition of parental ownership." Lovejoy argued: "The state is bound by the law of self-preservation to deny a father or mother the privilege of exacting from his own child what would be regarded as cruel or injurious if exacted

[83] NYCL, *Annual Report for the Year Ending December 1911* (March 1912), NCL Papers, reel 112, frame 612; Van Kleeck, "Child Labor in New York City Tenements," 1405–6.

[84] Florence Kelley, "The Abolition of Child Labor," *What Women Might Do With the Ballot* (New York: NAWSA, n.d.), NCL Papers, reel 100, frame 314.

[85] State of New York, *Preliminary Report of the FIC, 1912*, vols. 2, 3 (Albany, N.Y.: The Argus Co., Printers, 1912); for Scott, 3:1803–6; Membership Secretary, NCLC, to the editor of the *Sun*, Dec. 12, 1912, NCLC Papers, box 16.

from another's child. If the parent, either through poverty, vice or ignorance is unable to provide the care and protection needed, then the state is bound to enter and become the parent of that child." Kelley recognized the difficulty of such intervention: "Parental exploitation of young children within the home did not technically constitute cruelty in the judicial sense." The separation of home from work, private from public, protected "the selfishness of parents and employers."[86]

The rights of children, pitted against their parents, dominated reform discourse and offered a powerful plea for state intervention into the private sphere of the home. Commissioner Samuel Gompers urged the legislature, in terms hardly different from his words a quarter century before, "to pass these bills [recommended by the FIC] in the name of humanity and through patriotism and above all in the name of childhood and motherhood." In the name of "economy, efficiency, success, industrially, commercially, humanly," Gompers would "curb" the "evil" of tenement homework. Nearly every year since its birth, the AFL had passed a resolution against tenement house labor because it undermined the garment industry and other trades as well as "impair[ed] the home life of the people." What had changed was not only Gompers's status – from local labor radical, a political outsider, to the powerful and respectable chief of the AFL and a commissioner of a state body – but the willingness of a larger reform coalition to intervene in the wage contract in the name of protecting the weaker members of the working class. Some, like former state commissioner of labor P. Tecumseh Sherman, believed that unions alone could stop subcontracting into tenements, inspection being impossible. But most agreed with WTUL organizer Gertrude Barnum that legislation best could end the evils of homework, overwork, low pay, and child labor; it could codify the demands of striking workers.[87]

Reflecting a strategy that combined militant action with legislative lobbying, the WTUL hoped to insure the episodic victories on the picket line through state intervention. Laws for women and children provided an entering wedge for labor standards legislation in an era when the Supreme Court still upheld "right to contract" for men. Although its 1898 decision in *Holden v. Hardy* sustained an hour limit for miners, suggesting that state interference in the labor contract would be tolerated when a trade was dangerous and detrimental to the health of the worker, less than ten years later *Lochner v. New*

---

[86] Owen R. Lovejoy, "Some Unsettled Questions About Child Labor," *Annals of the American Academy of Political and Social Science* 33, supp. (Mar. 1909), 58; Kelley, *Some Ethical Gains*, 7; Wald, *Preliminary Report of the FIC*, 3:1742.

[87] *Hearing Before Joint Senate and Assembly Committee on Labor and Industry, New York, February 19, 1913 on Bills Recommended by the State FIC*, NCL Papers, reel 4, frames 254–5, 280, 287–8; *Proceedings of the 11th Annual Convention of the AFL* (1896), 49, quoted in Ileen A. DeVault, "'Stalking Through the Workman's Door': Home and Union in the Late Nineteenth Century," paper presented at the Wisconsin Labor History Conference, Apr. 1992; P. Tecumseh Sherman, *Preliminary Report of the FIC*, 2:561.

York, which negated a law limiting the hours of bakers, set an unreasonably high standard of proof when it came to male workers. When the subject was women and children, courts relied on their public and legal status as dependent and powerless and their presumed biological status as weaker to justify what came to be known as protective labor legislation.[88]

Protective labor legislation had an ambiguous impact on women workers; it never covered agriculture and domestic service where women of color were concentrated. Restrictive laws prohibited women from working at night, lifting heavy weights, or laboring in a given occupation. Regulatory laws sought to improve working conditions, increase wages, lower hours, or end health hazards. In raising the cost of hiring women, regulatory laws often restricted work opportunities, especially in mixed sex occupations in an era before antidiscrimination remedies. For those in female-dominated industrial jobs, though, such laws could improve working conditions. Homework was a female arena, but regulations here sought to remove women from such labor.[89] The discourse of restriction often highlighted the inappropriateness of women being out of the home (at night) or even working (in foundries). The one on homework switched negative referents. Work entering the home became improper; mothers belonged at home, but not laboring for wages there.

Protecting "the sex" culminated in the Supreme Court's 1908 decision *Muller v. Oregon*, which upheld maximum hours for women workers. This was the first major case for which the NCL submitted a brief. The "Brandeis brief," written by the NCL's Josephine Goldmark, exemplified sociological jurisprudence, for which Florence Kelley stood as a major formulator. The brief displayed a massive amount of evidence on health, work, and fatigue to argue that long hours injured wage-earning women and undermined their efficiency on the job and at home. Its portrayal of female difference projected an image of woman as weaker and more burdened by wage labor than man. Emphasizing biology more than the NCL had, the Court upheld the use of the police power to protect the welfare of women, seen as mothers or potential mothers, by collapsing the category "female worker" into the category "mother." It suggested a unity between family status and workplace, private and public, family economy and political economy. Such reasoning led the NCL to structure its campaign for the minimum wage around the state's interest in protecting women. Legal strategy, developed by male experts (like Felix Frankfurter) who lacked the NCL's commitment to women's

[88] 169 U.S. 366 (1898); 198 U.S. 45 (1905); Judith Baer, *The Chains of Protection: The Judicial Response to Women's Labor Legislation* (Westport, Conn.: Greenwood Press, 1978); Susan Lehrer, *Origins of Protective Labor Legislation for Women, 1905–1925* (Albany, N.Y.: SUNY Press, 1987).

[89] Alice Kessler-Harris, *Out to Work: A History of Wage-Earning Women in the United States* (New York: Oxford Univ. Press, 1982), 180–214. For questioning the distinction between restrictive and regulatory laws, see Lise Vogel, *Mothers on the Job: Maternity Policy in the U.S. Workplace* (New Brunswick, N.J.: Rutgers Univ. Press, 1993), 27–9.

advancement, reinforced the belief that female vulnerability necessitated state action.[90]

Women workers and their women allies faced a dilemma: They challenged the dominant discourse of womanhood but could not escape it. They demanded wage, hour, homework, and child labor laws in the name of motherhood but also as a working woman's right. The arguments of women reformers denied the simple dichotomy between public and private found in *Jacobs* but they tapped into the symbol favored by judges: woman as mother. The sameness of language hid different meanings. Judicial and legislative support of homework and other protective labor legislation relied upon dominant cultural conceptions of womanhood and the home. Women reformers justified state intervention into the private sphere on the basis of protecting motherhood. They meant a positively valued nurturing activity, as opposed to judges, politicians, and male trade unionists who reinforced dominant ideas of women's place. Nonetheless, the actions of both suggest that the private sphere never really existed for economically disadvantaged – often also considered racially, ethnically, or culturally inferior – families. The home would be saved from waged labor; women would find their place as mothers there.[91]

The FIC improved the existing law but did not prohibit homework, which it viewed as "deeply entrenched in our industrial life." To end it outright would disrupt industry and cause personal hardship. Instead, the commission sought "to make such work as 'unpopular' as it can, by abolishing the tenement manufacture of food products and children's clothes . . . and by strictly licensing the employer who gives out home work." It would establish a division of homework inspection and prohibit children under fourteen from such labor. Its recommendations became law in 1913.[92]

But would *Jacobs* nullify these new provisions, crafted to circumvent the earlier ban on cigarmaking?[93] In November 1913, Brooklyn factory owner Jacob

---

[90] Nancy S. Erickson, "*Muller v. Oregon* Reconsidered: The Origins of a Sex-Based Doctrine of Liberty of Contract," *Labor History* 30 (Spring 1989), 228–50; Sybil Lipschultz, "Social Feminism and Legal Discourse, 1908–1923," *Yale Journal of Law and Feminism* 2 (Fall 1989), 134–9; Joan Hoff, *Law, Gender and Injustice: A Legal History of U.S. Women* (New York: New York Univ. Press, 1991), 197–206; Joan G. Zimmerman, "The Jurisprudence of Equality: The Women's Minimum Wage, the First Equal Rights Amendment, and *Adkins v. Children's Hospital*, 1905–1925," *JAH* 78 (June 1991), 188–225; Vivien Hart, *Bound by Our Constitution*, chap. 4.

[91] Schrom Dye, *As Sisters and As Equals*, 140–61; on the problematics of motherist movements, Ann Snitow, "A Gender Diary," in *Conflicts in Feminism*, ed. Marianne Hirsch and Evelyn Fox-Keller (New York: Routledge, 1990), 9–43.

[92] *Second Report of the FIC*, 1:116–23; Abram I. Elkus, "Extract of Remarks," NYCL, *Report for the Year Ending December 1912* (March 1913), NCL Papers, reel 112, frame 656; State of New York, *Fourth Report of the Factory Investigating Commission* (Albany, N.Y.: J. B. Lyon Company, 1915), 1:377. A 1915 NYCL investigation of the impact of the new laws discovered children still making flowers in the Italian tenements of Greenwich Village. See *The Work of the Consumers' League of the City of New York, 1915* (March 1916), NCL Papers, reel 114, frames 102-3.

[93] The recommendations applied to all tenement houses used for living purposes and investigation provided evidence for their status as a health measure.

Balofsky gave a woman twenty children's coats to finish in her tenement home. The following April, the court of special sessions of Brooklyn convicted him under the amended labor law and the appellate division of the state supreme court upheld this verdict. In arguing for the constitutionality of the 1913 law, the FIC contended: "What was considered an undue interference with the individual, then, is to-day recognized as a proper regulation by the State. The strong individualistic tendencies of the period when the Jacobs case was rendered have given way to an appreciation of the rights of society as a whole and to the necessity for its protection and preservation." Such a statement not merely reflected the Progressives' positive attitude toward the use of the state but, in the context of who did homework and why, revealed the gender dynamics that lay behind the notion of "protection and preservation." For while this brief appended evidence of the health hazards posed by tenement manufacture, it cited women and children as the beneficiaries of such regulation because they were the homeworkers. When the court of appeals dismissed *Balofsky* in 1916 because the manufacturer failed to pursue the appeal, this line of reasoning left a legal legacy that corroded the power of *Jacobs*, but not the gender distinctions fundamental to it.[94] The state now held the responsibility to save the home from the factory, sustaining the private realm from invasion by the market but not from its own representatives or those from voluntary charity or child welfare organizations.

Women reformers continued the attempt to influence state action on tenement homework. At 1915 hearings to amend the state constitution, Mary Simkhovitch and Mary Van Kleeck advocated a constitutional amendment on tenement homework. The NCL worked closely with the committee in charge of industrial relations. Van Kleeck argued for giving the legislature "broad powers . . . to determine the need for extension of the police power for the protection of employes [sic]," a power recognized by recent court decisions that upheld legislative action based on "evidence" of need. But voters rejected the proposed constitution.[95]

Despite this defeat, the NCL and allied organizations persisted. They still preferred prohibition to licensing and continued to promote minimum wages. After the war, the Women's City Club spearheaded the agitation for the prohibition of tenement homework. Organized in 1915 when it appeared

---

[94] *Second Report of the FIC*, 1:121; Josephine Goldmark, *Tenement Home Work and the Courts*, reprinted from *The Survey*, Feb. 19, 1916 (New York: NCL, n.d.); "Brief on Law Prohibiting Certain Manufacture in Tenements," *Fourth Report of the FIC*, 371–85.

[95] "Meeting of Committee on Industrial Relations. Constitutional Convention," June 9, 1915; Mary Van Kleeck to Hon. Herbert Parsons, May 29, 1915, in Series no. 640, Constitutional Convention of 1915: Working Files of Committees, box 13; "Proposed Constitutional Amendment Regarding Tenement Homework," NYCLC Papers, box 9, folder 45; Josephine Goldmark, "The Constitutional Convention and Labor Laws," The Consumers' League of New York State, *Bulletin*, May 1915, NCL Papers, reel 113, frame 764; *Amendments Proposed to New York Constitution 1895–1937* (Albany: New York State Constitutional Convention Committee, 1938), 1190–1.

that New York women would gain suffrage (it took until 1918), the Women's City Club consisted of influential and wealthy women, some of whom had gained public prominence from their own efforts and others from marriage to powerful or famous men. In 1919 its Child Welfare Committee visited five hundred families throughout the city working on men's, women's, and children's clothing and miscellaneous household items. Although the club had legislation introduced over the next few years, its bills stayed in committee. The only result came ten years after the FIC, when the Child Welfare Commission included tenement labor among its investigations: a transference of responsibility for homework inspection to the Division of Women in Industry, then under City Club member and former NYCL lobbyist Frances Perkins.[96]

Women reformers defined the public meaning of wage labor in the home at a time when economic conditions left working-class women without many ways to maintain the family economy. They did not ask homeworkers for their solutions to low pay and long hours; nor did they try to organize homeworkers into trade unions or producer cooperatives. They encouraged bans on homework in union contracts. Rather than empowering homeworkers, they sought to end homework. Homework became a social as well as a labor problem, with the homeworker a victimized mother whose home had been invaded by the factory. Such terms framed a politics of regulation which sought to improve family life by setting boundaries to industrial production.

Reformers turned to the state to gain from the market what they could not through consumer label campaigns or unionization. This course of action privileged the law and legal reasoning, which led to maneuvering around constitutional roadblocks established by conservative interpretations of liberty and due process. The legal arena undoubtedly limited strategies. Yet when Florence Kelley spoke of the rights of consumers, children, working women, and mothers, she transformed human needs into rights. In the early twentieth century, such expansive rights talk constituted a radical act.[97]

[96] "National Consumers League – Report for the Years 1914–1915–1916," NCL Papers, reel 112, frames 529–30; Mary G. Schonberg, "Tenement Homework in New York City," *The American Child* 2 (Nov. 1920), 257–61; *Tenement Home Work and a New Bill Initiated by the Women's City Club and the City Club of New York* (Women's City Club, 1920); Elisabeth Israels Perry, "Women's Political Choices After Suffrage: The Women's City Club of New York, 1915–present," *New York History* 62 (Oct. 1990): 417–34.

[97] On rights and needs, Nancy Fraser, "Talking about Needs: Interpretive Contests as Political Conflicts in Welfare-State Societies," *Ethics* 99 (Jan. 1989): 291–313; Hendrik Hartog, "The Constitution of Aspiration and 'The Rights That Belong to Us All,'" *Journal of American History* 74 (Dec. 1987): 1013–34."

PART II

Visions and voices

Figure 11. (a) "Waiting Room for Operators." (b) "Receiving and Inspection Room –
Shirts and Bedsacks – Inspectors at Table on Right." Jeffersonville, Indiana, Army
Depot, ca.1917. Courtesy of the Library of Congress. Black and white homeworkers
wait for inspection. At the beginning of World War I, the army relied upon women
outworkers to sew its uniformas it had since the War of 1812. This division of the state
promoted homework while other departments sought to prohibit it.

4

"Soldiers of freedom," "garments . . . of slavery": Patriotic homework

"The war to end all wars" promised an opportunity to eliminate the homework that New York and other states could not. World War I was a turning point in industrial relations and homework control was central to that change. For the war opened the corridors of power to a generation of reformers who held an activist concept of the state. They would develop administrative structures and legal rules to regulate the economy and by extension society itself. With the establishment of the War Labor Board, the Women in Industry Service, and other agencies, proposals set forth by reformers and academics became public policy. Social feminists played a key role in this process but in the end, federal initiatives on homework failed to root out a system that during a period of national emergency wrapped exploitation in the flag of patriotism. World War I was a watershed in the history of state regulation of industry; the resulting policies were profoundly gendered.

Uncle Sam as contractor

Shaping both the extent and nature of labor, the war recast homework as "patriotic." The making of munitions, flags, and patriotic insignia offered new opportunities, even while restrictions on materials for "nonessential" industries dried up some of the traditional sources of homework during the last year of the war. In 1917 the war had shifted to the home production of items previously imported, like cheap beads. But other war-related factors decreased the amount of homework: shifts in employment away from industries like lace and jewelry to war production, new styles (for example, military laced instead of buttoned boots), and, perhaps most importantly, the rise in men's wages that lessened the need for additional earners. While some women with husbands and sons in the military turned to homework, others found more profitable jobs. Yet the rise in wartime wages and labor shortages offered marginal employers no alternative. A jewelry manufacturer admitted, "When I can get employees they are girls new from the munitions works, who insist on the munitions wages even when learning. I can't afford to give what they ask, so I get the work done outside."[1]

---

[1] U.S. DOL, Children's Bureau, *Industrial Home Work of Children: A Study Made in Providence, Pawtucket, and Central Falls, R.I.*, Bureau Publication no. 100, (Washington: GPO, 1922), 9–10, 67–8; "Memo, To: Miss Duke, From: Mr. Vitales," Apr. 16, 1919, file 20–20–8; "Mr. Maymon, Rhode Island Society for Prevention of Cruelty to Children," Mar. 27, 1919, file 20–20–12, both RG102.

Wars always have increased the significance of the federal government as a major purchaser of labor. Procurement policy could determine the extent of homework. At the start of World War I, the government manufactured army uniforms, shirts, and navy middies under outwork arrangements dating back to the 1870s. Expanded needs during the Spanish-American War had forced the army quartermaster to buy outside of the chief arsenal at Philadelphia, which had given out work since the War of 1812. The number of outside seamstresses there mushroomed from eleven hundred prior to the Spanish-American War to as many as five thousand. Hampered by shortages of specified fabrics, a condition that would plague the early months of World War I as well, much of this clothing fell below army standards. The secretary of war ordered manufacturing only in regular factories, but economic necessity overruled labor standards. New York's chief factory inspector discovered that tenement laborers received only about a third of the wages of inside workers. In addtion, increased homework generated charges that scarlet fever and measles in the camps came from the tenements where "Army Uniforms [served] As Sweat Shop Beds." The lack of written guarantee allowed contractors to ignore the requirement that work be done only on their own premises.[2]

In 1917, the navy also relied upon a homework system developed during the Spanish-American War. Homework had become a "customary" practice, given out to the wives of navy men or relatives of government workers, many of whom lived near its Brooklyn yard. Until June 1918, "pieceworkers" – women homeworkers, home shop owners, and small manufacturers who often relied on the other two groups – received from the depot "bundles" consisting of pieces of similar material to make a specified number of items: blue and white uniforms and dungaree clothing for machinists and gunners' mates, each with its characteristic style and decoration. Civil service rules governed selection. Sewers had to be citizens, at least eighteen years of age, and certified as healthy; they had to swear under oath that they were of good character and had to provide five references. Those who scored 70 percent became eligible for appointment; the highest rated received work first. The naval yard filed homeworker names and addresses with the New York Department of Labor for licensing. Rumors that uniforms were made in unclean one- and two-family dwellings, not covered by the law, led state inspectors to visit such housing in 1917.[3]

The Committee on Women in Industry of the Council of National Defense, a wartime voluntary agency composed of reformers and local elites, described

[2] Committee on Women in Industry of the Advisory Commission of the U.S. Council of National Defense, *The Manufacture of Army Shirts Under the Home Work System, Jeffersonville, Indiana* (July 1918); ibid., *Making the Uniforms for Our Navy* (Sept. 1918); Erna Risch, *Quartermaster Support of the Army, 1775–1939* (Washington: D.C.: Center of Military History, U.S. Army, 1989), 144–8, 520–7; "Evils of the Sweatshop," *New York Times*, Dec. 1, 1900; "Army Uniforms As Sweat Shop Beds," *New York Herald*, Mar. 4, 1899; "The Sweatshop System," *New York Times*, Mar. 9, 1899, newspaper clippings from Nathan Scrapbook.
[3] *Making the Uniforms for Our Navy*, 12–14, 17–18.

these home finishers as "a picked group of responsible, capable women workers who learn of the work through friends already employed." Pride in their status as government employees and interest in their labor made "for a high grade of workmanship and the prompt delivery of finished garments." Their feeling of "doing something for our country" eliminated "the stigma usually attached to home work." The paymaster allowed these women to sublet the operations of starring and taping of collars to workers not directly approved by the navy. They also could hire laborers to work for them in their own homes. Aspects of the homework system condemned in other circumstances, such as the sharing of work among kin and neighbors, here gained government sanction. In part, this shift of perspective – even by women investigators – came from the social composition of the work force. With fifty-six out of sixty-seven "bundle" women "Americans," from "families accustomed to a fairly high standard of living," homework turned into a genteel occupation – even though over a third of the women derived their only income from it. According to the Committee on Women, they resembled the "best women" sewing for the war effort and not the immigrant others of the tenements:

> The majority of the women would not think of taking ordinary finishing from a garment factory into their homes, or of going into a factory to work. The Navy work is considered a pleasant, superior kind of occupation. . . . The starring, since it is hand work, can be done in any part of the house, enabling the worker to entertain guests and embroider at the same time and therefore is very much in demand.

Most lived in "very attractive and well furnished" one- or two-family houses, sewed in the dining room or kitchen, and took pains to protect uniform pieces from dirt or mishaps.[4]

Yet these women suffered from the irregularity of the homework system; they too sandwiched homework between domestic duties. Prior to the war, the navy asked them to limit daily hours to eight; with the pressure of war production, homeworkers – like other workers – were requested to do as much as they could, labor standards aside. Women worked late into the evening to return blue uniforms the next morning. The navy encouraged those with home shops to expand into "summer kitchens, wash houses and basements." The paymaster actually "sent a letter to the women asking them to do more work and to get help on the work if they could," though foremen reportedly asked them to provide work only to licensed tenements and avoid child labor. One gave out work to about twenty-four others, paying them four dollars from the five dollars a bundle given to her by the navy yard. Payment rates were slightly higher than in most other forms of homework, yet only a third earned more than twelve dollars weekly.

[4] Ibid., 17–20; *The Manufacture of Army Shirts*, 20.

Homeworkers continued to absorb overhead costs, such as machine installa-
tion and subletting of eyelet and buttonhole making.[5]

By the second year of the war, the navy sought to sidestep the inefficiencies
of a homework system based on hand labor that took six to ten times longer
than machine work. Homeworkers insisted on handwork: "'The sailor boys
like them better by hand.' "Twenty-five large firms received contracts for lots
of twenty-five thousand garments or more, but their unfamiliarity with navy
specifications actually slowed production. In June 1918, 168 home pieceworkers continued to produce most uniforms. Because many of the new firms
lacked special equipment for stars and collars, the navy found itself expanding
homework. Higher efficiency never materialized, since collars often failed to
match the rest of the suit made inside the plant.[6]

Efficiency dropped further at the army's depot in Jeffersonville, Indiana,
where the organization of production hampered the effort to clothe a rapidly
expanding military force. There outwork caused a severe strain on transportation facilities. Approximately twenty-one thousand sewing women lived
scattered as far away as Frankfort and Pewee Valley, Kentucky, some between
twenty and fifty miles away from the distribution point. The Louisville
substation depended on one ferry boat for direct access to Jeffersonville. At
that station, forty-four inspectors stood at long tables to check the bundles of
about nine hundred women a day, each with a pass to take out shirts. Only a
third could sew two bundles of ten shirts each a week, while another third
finished more; still twenty shirts brought only $8.90 for sixty hours of work,
a rate dollars less than given in factories and not raised in over a decade despite
changes in style and war needs. Sewing machine agents set up sales booths,
while the depot itself sold bags at cost to carry the bundles. Although
government agents demonstrated proper shirtmaking, many home sewers
turned in unsatisfactory work. Unless readily corrected on machines available
in the building, repairs meant a trip home to fix mistakes. Regulations that
prohibited payment until acceptance of the entire bundle increased inefficiency. Receiving notice of homes with contagious disease, the Louisville
station called back sewing from quarantine places. Its initial inspectorate of
fifteen could hardly check all worker homes. So it fumigated returned shirts.[7]

The Frankfort substation called the sewing of army shirts "patriotic," but
women sewed for various reasons. The work enabled travel "to the city which
could not have been taken otherwise," a circumstance that often delayed return
of the shirts. Most women viewed the work "as an opportunity which should
be much appreciated, though it was not looked upon as easy," for many lacked
power machines that relieved the drudgery of working with heavy khaki. They

[5] *Making the Uniforms for Our Navy*, 20–2; Josie T. Nelligan to Daniel O'Leary, June 27, 1917,
and July 19, 1917, NCLC Papers, box 9, folder 49.
[6] *Making the Uniforms for Our Navy*, 26–7, 29–31, 35–6.
[7] *The Manufacture of Army Shirts*, 9–18.

complained about the limited amount of work and how "others with 'influence' " could get more, including those given the passes of "ladies" for whom they cleaned. Some, like a group of African Americans from Pewee Valley, combined sewing with farm work.[8]

Although the government employed homeworkers, homework on government contracts was illegal. Manufacturers attempted to use homeworkers anyway. Trumbull Waste Mfg. Co. of Philadelphia, for one, employed a hundred women at home. Claiming to be "very particular about the type of homes," not placing the work in the "foreign" district, this company also implied that war homework differed from the usual course of industrial homework. It appealed to patriotism while paying workers a half cent per piece. Consumers' League investigators questioned whether dirty waste material belonged in kitchen workshops, even though workers owned their dwellings and seemed beyond state laws. When informed that the company expected a second contract to make jute balls for the Chemical Warfare Branch, the Women in Industry Service (WIS) geared up to stop any such transaction as a violation of directives of the secretary of war and the quartermaster general against homework. Mary Van Kleeck, on leave from Russell Sage to head the WIS, relied upon contacts gained from her appointment to the Committee on Hazardous Occupations to end this abuse of labor standards. Not only did women reformers lobby for homework bans, as we shall see, but they monitored compliance.[9]

The WIS, the predecessor agency to the Women's Bureau, represented a triumph for women social reformers. Established in July 1918 as an advisory agency under the secretary of labor, it gathered information on wartime working conditions and developed appropriate labor standards for women wage earners. It was the last of a series of women's committees during the war which conducted numerous investigations. These studies brought earlier concerns to public notice – for example, the fear of disease from homemade goods and child neglect from the overwork of mothers. They reflected the emphasis on efficiency that pervaded wartime reform as much as the mobilization itself. The Committee on Women in Industry stressed less the plight of homeworking women than the inefficiency of the system. Here we see the influence of Frederick Winslow Taylor and his followers in the Taylor Society who promoted the rationalizing of production as a social good.[10]

---

[8] Ibid., 14–15, 20–1, 24.

[9] Agnes de Lima to Major Samuel J. Rosensohn, July 25, 1918; Rosensohn Memorandum for Miss Van Kleeck, July 30, 1918; Assistant Director [Mary Anderson] to Miss de Lima, Aug. 6, 1918; Van Kleeck to Rosensohn, Aug. 13, 1918; Van Kleeck to Captain H. G. Bradley, Aug. 18, 1918, RG1, box 32, entry 2.

[10] Judith Sealander, *As Minority Becomes Majority: Federal Reaction to the Phenomenon of Women in the Work Force, 1920–1963* (Westport, Conn.: Greenwood Press, 1983), 17–18; Maurine Weiner Greenwald, *Women, War, and Work: The Impact of World War I on Women Workers in the United States* (Westport, Conn.: Greenwood Press, 1980), 46–86.

News of other violations, gathered by Consumers' League locals (sometimes at the request of the Woman's Committee of the Council of Defense), poured into Van Kleeck's office. Alice Hunt of Rhode Island, chair for that state's Committee on Women in Industry, alerted the WIS that how the Metal Workers Corporation relied on homeworkers to assemble cartridge clips to meet a two-million-piece contract. The network of women reformers, now inside as well as outside the state apparatus, enforced regulations that they were central in formulating, with Van Kleeck contacting the War Department to authorize the women to investigate and report. Not all local investigations ended with action. The Committee on Manpower and Labor could withhold support. One woman factory inspector captured the general mood: "Even if I decide to make affidavits against [government contractors] in the local courts the chances are very great that they would be excused and probably given a medal for their patriotism."[11]

When it came to wartime homework, the public did not embrace reform. The *Providence Journal* proclaimed, "Eagle Park Women Speed War Work. Patriotic Immigrants Devote Leisure Moments in Their Homes to the Task of Assembling Cartridge Clips and Thus Assist Manufacturer of Munitions to Increase Production." Noting that the women had relatives in both the Italian army and the American Expeditionary Force, the story described their efforts as heroic. Beginning at 4:00 A.M., they "labor[ed] by lamplight until time to get breakfast and perform ordinary duties. Hustling through those, they return to the task of setting up cartridge clips, holding to it until time to prepare the noon meal. The afternoon is a repetition of the morning schedule." After dinner, they continued with the clips until they finished the day's task. One woman, with a drafted son, explained, "It may be that by my own hands I will help him when he most needs that help. It may be that the clips from which he slips the shells into his gun and brings down the enemy seeking to destroy him were of these I worked upon. Freely will I give of my time and services in such a cause."

The contractor for the clips – "Sergt. Alexander Carcieri of the Fifth Company" as the *Journal* described him in keeping with its theme of patriotism – would not think of "such sacrifice" from these hardworking housewives. So he paid them by the piece. The women earned between ten and twelve dollars a week for ceaseless activity, praised by Carcieri and by extension the reporter who offered his words to the public. (In comparison, he gained twenty-five dollars a week.) "Some of these have initiated the little children into the business," Carcieri said in admiration of his compatriots. The women worked outside, "on the door steps in the warm sunshine and where an

[11] Alice W. Hunt to Mary Van Kleeck, Sept. 23, 1918; Van Kleeck to Hunt, Sept. 26, 1918; Van Kleeck to Major F. N. Tully, Sept. 26, 1918, RG86, box 1, entry 1; H. Viteles, "Interview with Miss Alice Hunt, Secy. of Consumers' League," RG102, file 20–20–12; "Annual Meeting of the Consumers' League of Connecticut," Jan. 29, 1918, 3, CLC Papers, box 1, folder 3; Martha D. Gould to Grace Abbott, Aug. 5, 1918, RG102, box 1025.

eye can be kept on the bambinos . . . under pergolas covered not only with luxurious growths of grape vine, but by squash vines trained as only the Italian gardeners knew." Ethnicity turned into a positive attribute as Carcieri evoked joyful labor under the sun. The exotic qualities of homeworkers obviously appealed to the reporter, who described how "one of the women placing a cushion on her head, neatly balanced a big box on this, and trudged off with a load as though it weighed a few ounces only, instead of nearly 100 pounds." Conditions – the length of the working day, child labor, low piece rates, foreign ways – once condemned turned praiseworthy when motivation seemingly shifted from family to collective survival. The reporter failed to understand that the women worked not out of abstract patriotism, but for the money and to bring sons home alive.[12]

In Providence, Pawtucket, and Central Falls, Rhode Island, centers of cheap jewelry and lacemaking, teachers encouraged pupils to engage in wartime homework. The Children's Bureau uncovered such activity during a 1919 investigation of child labor that relied upon a canvass of public and parochial schools. Those responsible for enforcing the 1916 Keating–Owen Child Labor Act, struck down by the Supreme Court in 1918, had found "a considerable amount" of child labor in the home, leading to the bureau's study. A fifth grade teacher at the Federal Street School in an Italian neighborhood suggested that her class "earn their pledges" to the War Work Campaign through homework. The only negative effect came from a girl unable to study for a spelling test, but "usually all studying is done in school." She felt, "It keeps them employed, out of mischief and lets them earn spending money." A sixth grade teacher wrote the name and address of a neighborhood contractor on the blackboard. A manual training instructor gave out snaps to assemble in her special education class since wartime shortages had curtailed other materials for handwork; homework was "good practice." Reflecting long-held views that labor improved children, one elementary school principal thought "that this was a good method of raising the necessary funds [they earned $985.00], and that working in a well lighted room for 15 minutes was good for the children."[13]

Even principals who disliked homework felt compelled to introduce it in order to keep up with other schools. Principal Charles Holmes, the local chairman of Victory Boys and Girls, regarded homework as "poorly paid, tiresome and monotonous if overdone." He attributed most homework among children to "greed of parents and lack of Americanization" rather than economic need. Money for war pledges became "an excuse" for preexisting

[12] "Eagle Park Women Speed War Work," *Providence Journal*, Sept. 22, 1918.

[13] The Supreme Court struck down child labor regulation in *Hammer v. Dagenhart*, 247 U.S. 251 (1918). *Industrial Home Work of Children*; Interview Schedules, "Miss Mowry, Miss Beard, Miss Johnson, Federal St. School," Apr. 23, 1919; "Miss Tully, Teacher Special Class, Knight St. School," Apr. 24, 1919; "Miss Tully, Teacher of Old Beacon St. School," Apr. 24, 1919; "Mr. Fergerson and Miss Burns, Candace St. School," Apr. 7, 1919, RG102, file 20–20–12 (hereafter Interview Schedule).

homework. Still Holmes followed other principals and had classes string tags each day. "If I had it to do over again I would not consent to it. It was due to circumstances pure and simple."[14]

Hard-pressed to provide funds for various patriotic drives, parents apparently did not object to homework. Like teachers, mothers working in factories praised after-school homework for keeping children "off the street," though they considered it a substitute babysitter. But with fathers winning better pay and mothers finding industrial work open to them, fewer families wanted the dwindling supplies of homework. Jewelry firms removed foot presses from homes because they had no brass or gold. Lace was less prevalent. Daughters no longer helped through homework but by caring for younger children for mothers earning higher wages outside the home.[15]

Some Rhode Island school officials claimed ignorance. In a state where big employers wielded much political power, school officials were reluctant to "antagonize employers," despite young children carrying lace and tags between home and factory before their very eyes. Providence's truant officer phoned employers about any violation of child labor laws before informing the factory inspector and never issued employment certificates for homework. Pawtucket's officer refused to "interpret *Employment* to cover *home work* as we understand the term." Chief factory inspector J. Ellery Hudson "had not come across any cases of home work during 1918, because . . . 'It is none of my business, and we ain't looking for it.' " State labor laws did not cover homework and "he personally does not see any harm in light work such as carding snaps, pulling lace, etc." The executive secretary of the Child Welfare Department, a member of the local Woman's Committee of the Council of National Defense, confessed, "everything in this State, even the churches, is run by politics, and nothing can ever be done for Child Welfare until politics become less corrupt." The war made no difference.[16]

Social welfare and charity agencies handed out much wartime homework. Nearly a quarter of homeworking families appeared in the records of these agencies; the low piece rates of homework and charity continued to supplement each other. The District Nursing Service obtained homework on gun plugs from a government contractor. The American Red Cross provided garment homework to the pension cases of the Providence Society of Organized Charity. The Home Service Red Cross gave out adapter plugs but

[14] Interview Schedule: "Mr. Charles H. Holmes," Mar. 18, 1919.

[15] Interview Schedule: "Miss Mowry, Miss Beard, Miss Johnson"; "Miss Mary Hanley Principal, River Avenue Primary School," Jan. 7, 1919; "Rev. Father R.L. Sawistowski," Jan. 5, 1919; "J. Ellery Hudson," Jan. 14, 1919; "Dr. Helen Stone," Dec. 31, 1918; "Miss Mary C. Greene," n.d.

[16] Interview Schedule: "Dr. Isaac O. Winslow," Dec. 18, 1918; "Frank O. Draper," Dec. 14, 1918; "John A. Shea," Dec. 18, 1918; "James R. Cannon," Dec. 31, 1918; "William L. Leach," Dec. 14, 1918; "William L. Leach," Mar. 10, 1919; "J. Ellery Hudson," Jan. 14, 1919; "Mrs. Ira D. Hasbrouck," Dec. 26, 1918.

stopped after two weeks because of the trouble and cost of distribution, inadequate pay for the workers, and the greasiness of the work. Even social settlements distributed homework.[17]

Official recognition of homework by schools and public agencies helped to undermine the efforts of trade unionists to organize the Rhode Island jewelry industry. In 1917, the International Jewelry Workers Union (IJWU) linked "local unions, strong enough to abolish home-work," with ending child labor. Like other American Federation of Labor (AFL) craft unions, it contended that homework destroyed the craft and generated unemployment. The work of wives and children at home and older daughters in the shop displaced fathers. Organization and education could accomplish, it believed, what legislation could not.[18] The attempt of the IJWU to organize the Providence-Attleboro (Massachusetts) region would expose the difficulty of relying on trade union efforts alone to end homework even during a period of labor shortage.

The IJWU had no reason to believe that state action could aid them since manufacturers blatantly ignored existing protective laws, which left homeworkers uncovered. The child labor law prohibited children under fourteen from working in a manufacturing or business establishment; 86.2 percent of child homeworkers were under age fourteen. During the rush season, manufacturers sent factory "girls" home with work to get around the fifty-four hour law for working women. Jewelry manufacture brought presses, which could crush fingers, into the homes to undermine a state workmen's compensation law.[19]

The union's initial organizing drive occurred in the context of the war's disruption of the trade and increasing reliance on homework. Rhode Island manufactured cheap jewelry; its fierce competitive environment spawned new firms while bankrupting old ones. Contract homework had first intensified during the depression of the mid-1890s, when laid off workers engaged in self-exploitation as they gathered their families into cottage industries similar to garment subcontracting. In the first decades of the new century, growing consumer demand for mesh bags, pendants, and chains, machine-produced by larger firms but requiring hand assembly, intensified the amount of home-work. Homeworkers composed 75 percent of the Attleboro work force in 1914, yet they earned a mere 8.7 percent of total wages. Jewelry surpassed

[17] *Industrial Home Work of Children*, 12. Interview Schedule: "Mr. Richard D. Allen," n.d.; "Miss Helen Burr," Dec. 31, 1918; "Miss Flemming," Apr. 2, 1919; "Miss Moore," Dec. 28, 1918; "Miss Hanson and Mrs. Taylor," Mar. 11, 1919; "Mrs. Vernon," Mar. 21, 1919.

[18] "Home Work Done by Children in Rhode Island Jewelry Industry," *Jewelry Workers' Monthly Bulletin* 6 (Sept. 1922), 5–6; A. Greenstein, "Providence, R.I. and Attleboro, Mass.," ibid. 1 (June 1917), 10; "Our Second Annual Convention," ibid. 1 (Sept.–Oct., 1917), 32. International Jewelry Workers' Union, *Almanac* (New York: International Jewelry Workers' Union, 1923), 28; "Interview with Mr. A. Greenstein and Mr. Harry Schwartz," Apr. 29, 1919, RG102, file 20–20–12.

[19] *Industrial Home Work of Children*, 52–3.

other forms of homework in Providence, with at least ninety-one firms giving out work in 1918. By then, wartime shortages of materials, availability of alternative employment in war industries, and the jewelry manufacturers' refusal to raise wages, led to an exodus of workers from the trade.[20]

After successfully organizing the skilled New York sector, the IJWU turned to the low-priced Eastern region to which firms from organized cities were relocating. The next year it sustained an eleven-week strike at Otsby & Barton Company, but suffered defeat from a combination of employer power and union weakness. Increased use of homework to break the strike was only symptomatic of the control exerted by manufacturers. The Jewelry Manufacturers Association held an iron fist over hiring, with a central employment bureau supplemented by a blacklist and spy system. Strikebreakers came from the Rhode Island School of Design, founded and funded by manufacturers. As union officers explained, "The entire industrial and political control of the state is in the hands of the manufacturers."[21]

By January 1919, the Providence local had at most two hundred members out of the thousands employed in the industry, though it boasted four contracts, each of which prohibited homework. It had made no headway in organizing the Attleboros, where jewelry homework grew during the war years. It continued pushing for the abolition of homework to facilitate organization, offering resolutions at AFL conventions, refusing to allow members to work at home, and publicizing government reports and its own investigations. Unionization would not come to the Eastern jewelry region until the 1940s and homework persisted as an inhibiting factor. The IJWU never sought to incorporate homeworking women, who represented lower-skilled workers, into the union, although it set out to organize their female factory counterparts.[22]

[20] Philip Scranton, "Diversity in Diversity: Flexible Manufacturing and American Industrial Development, 1880–1930," 29–45, paper presented to the Woodrow Wilson Center, May 1990; Nina Shapiro-Perl, "Labor Process and Class Relations in the Costume Jewelry Industry," (Ph.D. diss., Univ. of Connecticut, 1983); Commonwealth of Massachusetts, *45th Annual Report on the Statistics of Labor* (Boston: State Printers, 1914), 100; *Industrial Home Work of Children*, 13–14; "Competition Poor Excuse," *Almanac*, 103–4.

[21] A. G., "The Wandering Jew-elry Manufacturer," *Jewelry Workers' Monthly Bulletin* 1 (May 1917), 9; John Schwartz, "Providence: The Black Hole of Calcutta," Ibid. 2 (Oct. 1918), 4; "Interview with Mr. A. Greenstein and Mr. Harry Schwartz"; on homework as a tactic of New York employers, "Keep This Circular for Reference," *Almanac*, 90–1.

[22] Shapiro-Perl believes homework was the major reason; Scranton presents a more complex analysis of the rise and decline of this industry. Interview Schedule: "Mr. Cushman," Jan. 6, 1919; "Mr. William Frost," n.d.; Viteles to Duke, May 2, 1919; "About the Situation in Attleboro," *Jewelry Workers' Monthly Bulletin* 2 (June–July 1918), 1–3; "Reports," ibid. 29; "To the Jewelry Manufacturers of Attleboro," ibid. 1 (May 1917), 1–2; A. Greenstein, "My Resignation," ibid. 8 (June 1924), 3–4; "Proc. G. Ex. B., July 1, 1922," *Almanac*, 29–30; "Home Work," ibid., 364–5; "Our Second Annual Convention," ibid., 31–4.

Federalizing the reform impulse

With homework hampering worker organization, unions needed to mobilize the state to end homework. World War I offered such an opportunity. It convinced Sidney Hillman, the leader of the Amalgamated Clothing Workers of America (ACWA), that the state could act in the interest of trade unions and not merely as an agent of capital. Hillman would become a major force behind New Deal policy and a founder of the Congress of Industrial Organizations. Samuel Gompers considered this industrial union a renegade for its break from the United Garment Workers of America, but Hillman and the ACWA gained the support of reformers who sought a partnership between labor, government, and business. Instead of organizing homeworkers, the ACWA embraced the campaign of the National Consumers' League (NCL) to eliminate them and raise the standards of women as well as men in factories.[23]

"The Government," announced Secretary of War Newton D. Baker on August 24, 1917, "cannot permit its work to be done under sweatshop conditions, and it cannot allow the evils widely complained of to go uncorrected." Equating fair conditions with industrial efficiency and patriotic duty with "prompt delivery for army needs," Baker launched the first federal regulation of tenement-made clothing. In so doing, he championed labor standards fought for by organized labor and promoted by social reformers.[24] The Board of Control of Labor Standards for Army Clothing brought one dream of the Progressives to fruition even as it foreshadowed government regulation of industrial homework – indeed, the industrial relations system – under the New Deal.[25]

Nearly a year before the establishment of the War Labor Policies Board, the Board of Control intervened in the economy to shape labor relations and so conduct the war more efficiently. Louis Kirstein, manager of Filene's Depart-

---

[23] Matthew Josephson, *Sidney Hillman: Statesman of American Labor* (Garden City: Doubleday & Company, Inc., 1952), 167; Steven Fraser, *Labor Will Rule: Sidney Hillman and the Rise of American Labor* (New York: Free Press, 1991); Fraser, "Sidney Hillman: Labor's Machiavelli," *Labor Leaders in America*, ed. Melvyn Dubofsky and Warren Van Tine (Urbana: Univ. of Illinois Press, 1987), 207–33; Fraser, "Dress Rehearsal for the New Deal: Shop-Floor Insurgents, Political Elites, and Industrial Democracy in the Amalgamated Clothing Workers," *Working-Class America: Essays on Labor, Community, and American Society*, ed. Michael H. Frisch and Daniel J. Walkowitz (Urbana: Univ. of Illinois Press, 1983), 212–55.

[24] NCL, *Saving Labor Power in Wartime: The Second Line of Defense* (New York: NCL, 1918), 3; "Baker Picks Labor Standards Board," *New York Tribune*, Aug. 25, 1917; "Uniforms from Sweatshops," *The Survey* 38 (Sept. 15, 1917), 519.

[25] Howell Harris, "The Snares of Liberalism? Politicians, Bureaucrats, and the Shaping of Federal Labour Relations Policy in the United States, Ca. 1915–47," *Shop Floor Bargaining and the State: Historical and Comparative Perspectives,* ed. Steven Tolliday and Jonathan Zeitlin (New York: Cambridge Univ. Press, 1985), 156–9; Melvyn Dubofsky, "Abortive Reform: The Wilson Administration and Organized Labor, 1913–1920," *Work, Community, and Power: The Experience of Labor in Europe and America, 1900–1925,* ed. James E. Cronin and Carmen Sirianni (Philadelphia, Pa.: Temple Univ. Press, 1983), 197–220.

ment Store of Boston and a noted proponent of labor-management cooperation, chaired the board, with Captain Walter Kreusi representing the quartermasters and Florence Kelley[26] as its other member. Within months, the Board
of Control forced the quartermaster to stop putting out contracts to those who
would have parts of army uniforms made in tenement homes.

Newton Baker, the former reform mayor of Cleveland, was not only the
secretary of war but the newly installed president of Kelley's NCL. Harvard law
professor Felix Frankfurter, one of his key assistants, had become legal advisor
to the league, after former advisor Louis Brandeis went to the Supreme Court.
Sidney Hillman, whose ACWA came under the board's command, was in some
sense a protégé of Kirstein and Kelley. Hillman still considered himself a
socialist; so did Kelley and former *New Republic* editor Walter Lippmann,
another one of Baker's wartime assistants and his intermediary on this issue.
Such a network of activists, committed for the most part to trade unionism and
industrial arbitration, not only had access to the secretary of war but offered a
solution to threatened industrial unrest that appealed to the sense of justice
and fair play of Wilsonian liberalism. They would manage key war industries
and, in the process, improve the lives of workers while protecting the health of
the larger community. Placed in strategic government positions, their ideas on
industrial relations and labor-management cooperation mattered.[27]

The Board of Control represented an early attempt at "industrial democracy," that elusive goal of labor-management cooperation heralded by Wilsonian
Progressives. A term with multiple meanings, *industrial democracy* analogized
worker and citizen. It implied that workers would have a say over management
of the workplace as citizens had over governance of the country. But the
content of that say became contested among those who adhered to the
concept. For radical proponents of "workers' control," democracy in the
workplace would usher in a new equalitarianism and dismantle the employer's
arbitrary authority and superior power. For the new profession of industrial
relations, it promised social harmony. In return for recognition, trade unions
would control shop-floor activism that disrupted the orderly procedures of
production negotiated with management. Technological and scientific advancement would bring abundance. Among unionists, the Women's Trade
Union League (WTUL) emphasized extending industrial democracy to working women who would find in trade unions "a new ideal of associated life."[28]

[26] Kelley opposed the war; she was a founder of the Women's International League for Peace
and Freedom. Yet she was willing to work with the war machine to advance the position of
women workers.

[27] Florence Kelley, *Twenty-Five Years of the Consumers' League Movement,* reprint from *The Survey,*
Nov. 27, 1915, NCLVF; Josephson, *Sidney Hillman,* 86–110; Ronald Steel, *Walter Lippmann
and the New Century* (New York: Vintage Books, 1980).

[28] Nelson Lichtenstein and Howell Harris, eds., *Industrial Democracy in America: The Ambiguous
Promise* (New York: Cambridge Univ. Press, 1993); Elizabeth Anne Payne, *Reform, Labor, and
Feminism: Margaret Dreier Robins and the Women's Trade Union League* (Urbana: Univ. of Illinois
Press, 1988), 81.

Most Progressive reformers hoped for social cohesion; they preferred to think of society as a whole rather than a collection of fragments in opposition to each other. With efficiency as their handmaiden, they would mitigate class conflict to generate social benevolence for the good of all. Lessening the human costs of industry would benefit both business and the people; labor standards were more efficient than poor working conditions. Like Newton Baker, they were committed to ending child labor and tenement homework not only to alleviate suffering but to rationalize capitalism. During the unprecedented strike activity of the war years, with the specter of revolt in the air, they embraced industrial democracy and the administrative state as means toward those ends.[29]

With Baker the president of the NCL as well as the secretary of war, the league saw it "no mere coincidence" that its program "should thus have become the program of the nation."[30] Kelley was midwife to Baker's directive and an active force in the early months of the board. The labor standards system that she helped to facilitate not only promised to curb labor militancy but derived from the pioneering efforts of white women's reform organizations. Understanding who worked in the tenements and why – and how they stood outside the constituency that was to exercise industrial democracy – forces a reevaluation of the Board of Control. Gendered constructions – of work, home, and politics – and the division of labor between the sexes encoded through such constructions ensured that the concept of industrial democracy would be partial, excluding homeworkers as not real workers, but rather mothers who took work away from the men and women who labored outside the home. Those were the true workers whose efforts would contribute to Allied victory.

On May 11, 1917, the NCL resolved that the secretary of labor "take all possible steps to minimize" tenement house labor on government contracts for uniforms and war supplies. In conveying this resolution to Secretary of Labor William B. Wilson, a former United Mine Workers official, Kelley added "a personal word to express my pleasure in doing this, knowing as I do that this is exactly in line with your own wish and intentions." Secretary Wilson asked the secretaries of war and the navy, whose departments dominated government purchases, to comply with the resolution. Though Josephus Daniels of the navy would gladly "carry out the resolution as far as may be practicable," his department took no action. It accepted the giving out of uniforms only to licensed workers as fulfilling Wilson's request. Nearly a year would pass before a policy of competitive bidding on large lots would replace the outwork system of the Brooklyn Navy Depot.[31]

29 Samuel Haber, *Efficiency and Uplift: Scientific Management in the Progressive Era, 1890–1920* (Chicago: Univ. of Chicago Press, 1964); David Montgomery, "New Tendencies in Union Struggles and Strategies in Europe and the U.S., 1916–22," in Cronin and Sirianni, eds., *Work, Community, and Power,* 88–116.
30 NCL, *Saving Labor Power in Wartime,* 1.
31 NCL, Resolution, May 11, 1917; Florence Kelley to William B. Wilson, May 12, 1917; Wilson to Kelley, May 15, 1917; Wilson to Hon. Newton D. Baker, May 15, 1917; Wilson to Hon. Josephus Daniels, May 15, 1917; Josephus Daniels to Wilson, May 21, 1917; Franklin D. Roosevelt to The Honorable Secretary of Labor, June 26, 1917, RG174, box 20, file 390.

Secretary of War Baker similarly asked Quartermaster General Henry G. Sharpe to survey the conditions under which the army manufactured clothing. In an antiunion reply, Sharpe argued "there is no law or regulation that prevents the Department from giving contracts to firms that do not employ Union labor." Except in times of emergency, the cheapest bids won contracts; costs continued to dominate purchasing operations during the war. The Quartermaster believed that he had insured production in factories through a 1916 directive that required contracts to state that manufacturing would occur "in the contractor's factory of which a careful sanitary inspection has been made." Sharpe denied tenement making of army uniforms even after documentation by the New York City Employment Bureau in August 1917. As factory inspectors realized, one visit hardly meant subsequent compliance; like state departments of labor, the depots lacked sufficient force to police outside contractors.[32]

By the summer of 1917, the garment industry was in crisis, despite the boost in production given by uniform orders. Men expecting to enter the armed services would not buy new suits; in a period of rising inflation, families could put off clothing purchases. New York City, with more than one-third of the industry, experienced layoffs as late as the winter of 1917–18. The women's trade, with at least ninety-nine thousand employees in the city, also suffered "a decided falling off" in 1917–18, losing some of its unemployed workers to uniform making. Such worker dislocation was emblematic of the chaotic, seasonal nature of the industry. But much of it was war specific. Woolen mills redirected their output to military uses, further fueling unemployment. Manufacturers actually started bidding on naval uniforms in order to fill plants with work. In July 1917 only half of the union's forty thousand members were working and almost none full-time. Seventy-five percent of the ladies' garment industry similarly suffered unemployment. Nonunion firms, with about 15 percent of the work force but – according to the ACWA – the bulk of government contracts, were able to hire from a huge pool of desperate workers. They could lower labor standards because people felt compelled to accept any terms.[33]

Hillman joined with the NCL and the National Child Labor Committee (NCLC) to document this deterioration. A Russian Jewish immigrant, a member of the socialist Bund, Sidney Hillman rose to leadership with the 1910

[32] Henry G. Sharpe, "Memorandum for the Secretary of War," May 24, 1917, in letter from Newton Baker to Hon. W. B. Wilson, June 4, 1917, RG174, box 20, folder 390; Risch, *Quartermaster Support of the Army*, 620–3; "Denies Sweatshop Charge," *New York Times*, Aug. 20, 1917.

[33] R. S. True, "Memorandum of the Needle Trades in America," Dec. 10, 1918, RG1, box 24, folder "needle trades"; *The Manufacture of Army Shirts*, 11 n.; *Making the Uniforms for Our Navy*, 29; Sidney Hillman, "Memorandum Submitted by the ACWA," to Walter Lippmann, July 5, 1917, 1–2, ACWA Papers, box 4, folder 7; "Blame War Office for Sweatshop Evil," *New York Times*, Aug. 20, 1917; Renee B. Stern, "Report on Needle Trades Investigation Chicago, June 6–July 1, 1917," WTUL Papers, reel 68, frames 194–203.

Hart, Schaffner and Marx strike in Chicago. He became part of the circle of immigrant working people around Hull House. There, ideas of class cooperation and labor rights mixed together to form a vision of "industrial democracy" that nicely meshed with Hillman's Jewish socialism. When he moved to New York in 1914, Chicago reformers sent introductions to their counterparts and Hillman began a friendship with Florence Kelley. There he served as chief labor clerk for the cloakmakers' "Protocols of Peace." Constructed by Louis Brandeis with the settlement of the industry's 1909–10 uprising, the protocols established orderly grievance procedures that weakened labor's right to strike. It was through such joint management of the unstable garment industry that Brandeis sought increased economic efficiency. Though Hillman left in less than a year to preside over the new ACWA, the protocols introduced him to the Progressives' version of industrial democracy. There he developed a friendship with Louis Kirstein. When the wartime crisis hit, Hillman was positioned to take advantage of contacts with Progressives who would help him pursue union goals as they sought to accomplish their own agenda. Reformers like Kelley, Pauline Goldmark of the NCL (a sister-in-law of Justice Brandeis), George Price of the cloakmakers' protocol board, and WTUL organizer Melinda Scott would feed him information.[34]

The *New Republic* best articulated the reformers' concept of industrial democracy in its July 7, 1917, editorial, "The Government and Organized Labor." It applauded Samuel Gompers, chairman of the Committee on Labor of the Advisory Commission of the Council of National Defense, because he not only brought the AFL into the war effort but also "gave equal representation on his committee to employers and trade unionists." Such representative parity provided "the foundation of a nation-wide industrial truce." Businessmen heading other committees earned the journal's wrath because they ignored the impact of their decisions on workers, nor did they "recognize the right of organized labor to be represented on the various special boards." For *New Republic* editors, the clothing industry was the model for collective agreements "in the interest of industrial peace and efficiency." The protocols established not only labor standards but mechanisms for both their modification during emergencies and "the adjustment of industrial disputes." With workers given a voice, along with management and the public, this arrangement promised to fulfill wartime needs for efficient and speedy production. But rather than promoting industrial democracy, the government undermined it by letting nearly all clothing contracts to the nonunion sector, when 85 percent of the industry in New York, Philadelphia, and Baltimore fell under protocol agreements.[35]

[34] Fraser, *Labor Will Rule*, 1–113; Josephson, *Sidney Hillman*, 86–110.

[35] "The Government and Organized Labor," *The New Republic* 11 (July 7, 1917), 263–5, partially reprinted in "The Manufacture of Army Clothing," *Documentary History of the ACWA, Proceedings of the Third Biennial Convention, Baltimore, Maryland, May 13–18, 1919*, 133–4.

Hillman attempted to communicate with the quartermaster prior to taking ACWA grievances to higher authorities. As early as May 18, he indicated the union's willingness to aid contractors to "promptly fulfill their contracts." Two categories of grievances stood out. Some manufacturers were cutting payrolls by replacing skilled cutters with unskilled young men. Others sent finishing home, "where these uniforms may become infested with disease breeding germs."[36] Organized workers continued to protest homework by linking maintenance of jobs with protection of community health.

The replacement of skilled workers by the unskilled, inside workers by outside, trade union members by married women homeworkers, "white help by colored" threatened the union. Women held nearly as many positions as men in New York's menswear industry; they predominated in the garment trades as a whole, though cutters were men and male tailors still formed a sizable presence. Men dominated union leadership, although contracts covered the women working beside them. Yet the ACWA made no demands for equal pay for equal work, as it would during the next world war. It was still a fragile institution, racked with ethnic loyalties and localistic shop-floor actions. Although an "industrial" union, it feared lower-priced unskilled workers (associated with "female" and "non-white") crowding out skilled (often Jewish and male) workers. Homeworkers would undermine union scales, especially for finishers who worked inside the shops.[37]

During June and July, Hillman "wore out the railroad ties between New York and Washington." Kelley arranged a meeting with Lippmann, who saw the war as a perfect opening for Progressive social engineering. Hillman also met Frankfurter, who would head up the War Labor Policies Board. Kelley already had seen Baker on the subject of army contracts; she had told Lippmann that "Mr. Hillman has the most accurate and wide reaching knowledge of the needle trades concerned that is in the possession of any man known to me at this time." During a second conference in early July, when Kirstein accompanied Hillman, the Amalgamated leader played upon the patriotic motives of his men, stressing the contradiction between a war "for democracy" and deteriorating labor conditions at home. Perhaps he let Lippmann know what he told his mentor, labor mediator John Williams of Hart, Schaffner and Marx: "A great number of our members who are of the conscriptive age claim that they will refuse to wear uniforms made by scabs." Reiterating this point, Kelley wrote Baker, "The question which six weeks ago was asked in anxious

[36] Major R. R. Stogodell, Q.M. Corps, to ACWA, May 21, 1917; Stogodell to Mr. J. P. Friedman, Clothing Cutters Union, June 16, 1917; Clothing Cutters Union to Provost Marshal-General, June 22, 1917, ACWA Papers, box 4, folder 7.

[37] Hillman, "Memorandum Submitted," 3; True, "Memorandum on the Needle Trades," 5, 8–9; Greenwald, *Women, War, and Work*, 13–45. African American women entered the trade in greater numbers; see Nelle Swartz, Mary E. Jackson, Eva Bowles, et al., *A New Deal for the Colored Woman Worker: A Study of Colored Women in Industry in New York City* (New York: Charles P. Young, Mar. 1, 1919).

whispers by friends, is now screamed in newspaper scareheads:'Are the drafted men to serve in scab uniforms?' "[38]

To argue his case, Hillman deployed the powerful language of industrial democracy. His union was "making our sacrifices as citizens of this country in upholding its laws and institutions." While some members already had joined the military,"all of them are doing useful work and contributing their share to the welfare of the country." Drawing upon the language of rights, as well as citizenship, Hillman argued,"It is the duty of the Government to guarantee to our members that their standards of living will not be lowered because of the present emergency in order to. enrich unscrupulous employers." The ACWA had asked its members "to refrain from striking on uniform work." Still he offered a veiled threat:"We shall be doing an injustice to our organization as well as to the country if we stand idly by and permit the enslavement of tens of thousands of people by union hating employers."The rhetoric of slavery and freedom, long a staple in talk of homework, appealed to a larger public swept up in the Wilsonian crusade. The *New York Tribune* explained, "In a war like this it is not fitting that the soldiers of freedom should go to the firing line clad in garments which are the product of one of the worst forms of modern slavery." If moral arguments failed, Hillman would evoke economic efficiency. Government could not afford to allow a labor shortage to demoralize uniform making, a shortage that was bound to develop when the industry readjusted and more attractive jobs opened.[39]

The ACWA marshaled an impressive case. In January 1917, the union had negotiated a standard week of forty-eight hours, but military shops ran from fifty to seventy hours. Hourly wages were considerably lower among those working on government contracts. Piecework and unskilled new workers dropped the general wage further. Men received wages of from $12.00 to $16.00 a week in the nonunion uniform shops; women, $5.00 to $12.00. But unionized tailor shops averaged $20.00 a week per employee. Union cutters received about $10.00 more than unorganized ones. People and materials crowded military shops with their unsanitary conditions and blocked passageways. Some large firms — like New York's Cohen & Goldman, B. B. Goldberg, and Mark Cowan – relied upon subcontractors, many of whom gave out cleaning, bottoming, ticket sewing, and putting in laces to Eastside tenement homeworkers at $2.50 per hundred.[40]

[38] Josephson, *Sidney Hillman*, 162–5; Kelley to "My dear Mr. Secretary," Aug. 13, 1917, Baker Papers, reel 2, frame 107; Lippmann to Baker, ibid., frames 154, 156, 174, 199, and 204. See also Western Union Telegram, Kelley to Hillman, June 26, 1917; Kelley to "My dear Mr. Price," June 27, 1917; Kelley to Lippmann, June 26, 1917, ACWA Papers, box 4, folder 15; Hillman to "My dear Mr. Williams," July 3, 1917, June 22, 1917, ibid., box 7, folder 17; Hillman to Lippmann, July 6, 1917, July 18, 1917, ibid., box 7, folder 4.

[39] Hillman, "Memorandum Submitted" and attachments; "No Sweatshop Uniforms," *New York Tribune*, Aug. 26, 1917, editorial.

[40] Hillman, "Memorandum Submitted."

ACWA organizers documented both work sent into homes and underage children employed in factories. *Advance*, the union's journal, proclaimed: "Society Devouring Its Own Children." An illustration of two children wheeling home a baby carriage full of military coats for finishing stood "as a burning indictment of our society . . . no more powerful indictment could be drawn against barbaric capitalism than that picture." Associating home finishing with child "slavery" and paternal unemployment, this editorial fanned the fears of disease long associated with tenement work. It envisioned a "germ ridden carriage . . .made to 'do its bit,' to infect the soldiers' uniforms while transporting them from the factory to the tenement and back again." Failing to pay adequate prices for contracts, despite heavy taxes, the government condoned such "brutish," "shameful," and uncivilized conditions of production. Government policy "endanger[ed] the lives of the American Army" and threatened the greatest "natural resource" of the people, its children. "The working class will protect its present and its future by saving from slavery the young generation, *Young America,*" *Advance* concluded with a flourish of rhetoric.[41]

The ACWA never spoke for all workers. Conspicuous among the unrepresented were the home finishers whose work the union sought to end. A portrait of those who toiled on uniforms in the tenements emerges in the detailed reports of child labor investigators. With initial help from New York's chief factory inspector, the New York Child Labor Committee (NYCLC) initiated investigations in late June 1917 to present Lippmann with "facts." It then provided material to the temporary "Committee to Investigate the Manufacture of Army Clothing," which Baker appointed in July as a result of the flurry of meetings between the NCL, the NYCLC, the ACWA, and Lippmann. Since the temporary committee lacked funds for investigators, Kelley called upon the NYCLC to follow leads on tenement house production just as it had conducted investigations for the underfunded Factory Investigating Commission. Expecting government "to take up the work," the NYCLC continued its investigation into September. Its results provided educational ammunition for an unsuccessful 1918 attempt to legislate prohibition of tenement homework. The problem was not so much unlicensed tenements (most homeworkers were in compliance with the state law), but homework in tenements itself. Arguing for stricter legislation, NYCLC secretary George A. Hall reiterated all the themes of the past decade of struggle against tenement homework, including graphic portraits of dirty babies and disgusting diseases.[42]

[41] "Society Devouring Its Own Children," *Advance* 1 (Aug. 24, 1917); with pictures reprinted in "The Manufacture of Army Clothing," 134–8.

[42] George A. Hall, "Memorandum Regarding Connection of Committee with Investigation of Finishing in Tenement Houses of U.S. Army Uniforms," Sept. 28, 1917; *Soldier Uniform Making in New York City Tenements Based Upon Investigation Conducted During August and September 1917;* "To the Editor" [*New York Tribune*], Aug. 28, 1917, NYCLC Papers, box 9, folder 49; *War-Time Needs of New York's Child Workers* (New York: NYCLC, 1918), 4–5, ibid., box 33, folder 17; "Child Labor Laws," *The Garment Worker*, Apr. 26, 1918; letter from Hall, Apr. 4, 1918, NYCLC Papers, box 9, folder 49.

Kelley believed that these reports helped convince Baker to create the permanent board. Though pursued to reveal the horrors of homework, the NYCLC investigations contained a subtext on homeworkers' lives within a tale of exploitative wages and communicative diseases. Those left out of the ACWA's definition of worker gained a voice through them.[43]

Somebody always seemed sick in homeworking families, whose poverty made the few dollars a week from finishing uniforms an economic necessity. During the summer of 1917, the availability of war jobs hardly shifted the social or demographic profile of homework. The women of these New York and Brooklyn tenements were resourceful survivors who joined each other to sew, sharing labor at the needle and childcare with kin and neighbors. They were predominantly Italian, with a minority of German and Yiddish-speaking Jews. A few Polish women, who had never sewed before, took up the work after being solicited by a "man in street with wagon load of uniforms to finish." A little more than a third, of nearly ninety cases, were either pregnant, nursing, or mothers of a child under two. Many others either had preschool children or large families.[44]

All married wage-earning women faced childcare and housework; homework was only one solution to the problem of combining waged with unwaged labor. It cannot be explained only in terms of the demands of some women. Homework in army uniforms existed because employers structured the garment industry to take advantage of a captive labor force. Manufacturers gave out subcontracts, as to the Italian contractor Strumolo who piled up finishing in his Brooklyn basement shop. Around Liberty and Atlantic avenues, a hawker "call[ed] upon all women to take the work." About a hundred came down from the tenements to accept his offer. Other contractors went door to door persuading "housewives to 'try their hand' at finishing the goods." The turnaround time demanded by the government on these war orders increased the use of subcontracting, intensified the pace of the work – and its irregularity.[45]

Although a few women earned ten or eleven dollars a week, more than on other finishing, "they had to 'work like the devil' " because they received only eleven cents a coat. Some labored from 4:00 A.M. to midnight. Most put in fewer hours, more typically earning five dollars a week even for coats worth seventeen cents each. The piece rate was somewhat arbitrary, with contractors providing different rates to different women for the same items or different contractors giving out the same kind of work for varying rates. One young girl reported that her mother "gave it up because it was too hard work to get the

<hr>

[43] The initial investigation, submitted as part of the ACWA case to Lippmann in July, appeared in "Memorandum Regarding Work in Tenement Houses in New York City on Government Contracts for the Manufacture of Army Clothing," NYCLC Papers, box 9, folder 49. Later reports in same folder remained typed notes.

[44] Hall, "Memorandum regarding Connection of Committee"; typed report of investigations, Aug. 20, 1917 to Sept. 20, 1917, NYCLC Papers, box 9, Folder 49.

[45] Ibid., Aug. 27, 1917; Sept. 6, 1917; Annie Cumano, Aug. 21, 1917, ibid.; "Against Sweatshop Work on Army Clothing," *New York Evening Post*, Aug. 30, 1917.

needle through the stiff clothing; said that her mother had a hard time to get paid for work on these coats, and that the 'boss' was ugly about paying her." Perhaps fearing retaliation from the contractor, the mother denied her daughter's story, saying "she only sewed on 'just men's' garments." Other women stopped uniform work because "it did not pay as well as finishing women's long coats." Did they have a choice? One woman reported, " 'Boss' says they can't get other work until soldier goods is finished."[46]

Women responded to work that, as Mrs. Benedette put it, "paid about the same as other work, only tired one more," by finding other home finishing if they could. Their understanding of home-based labor was not merely individualistic. These women thought in familial, communal terms; they sewed for the family economy and had developed work groups to share information as well as work. Sometimes these groups were creations of the subcontractor, perhaps a member of the group herself, who dropped off the goods at one woman's apartment for an entire floor. But these groups could function as centers of opinion creation and behavior control – and not just to reinforce the fatalism of the tenements, as one investigator learned shortly after the ban on uniform tenement work. Fifty Chrystie Street women had entered the shops, earning one cent more than the rate for home piecework. The boss blamed the investigator for the end of homework; "told them [other former homeworkers] that the woman that went around and talked to them about their work was the cause of their working being cut off, as if to incite them against the investigator and make it hot for her when she went back." Although some women refused to speak, in general "the women took it well." The investigator revealed the ways in which the homeworking group counseled its own when she described how those in one group of eight Italians argued with one who "felt a little aggrieved, in a sad way, not angry." Finally this woman agreed that "it was really best, that if somebody did not go around and see that the women were paid they would pull down the price of work, while on the other hand the price of food was going up all the time." Although "the woman thanked the investigator," the group reported how their boss had retaliated by denying them work: "Her investigation had made their children hungry."[47]

The sexual division of labor – within the industry and within the larger society – shaped both the homework system and the fight against it. Almost all the homeworkers were women, but the comments of male tailors seethed with anger over a system that idled men and put women to work at a

---

[46] Investigations: Mrs. Larosa, Josie Delesio, Aug. 20, 1917; Rebecca Feldman, Aug. 16, 1917; Annie Dumane, Aug. 21, 1917; Nicolette Mugarossa, Aug. 23, 1917, NYCLC Papers, box 9, folder 49.

[47] Investigations: Mrs. Benedette, Aug. 23, 1917; "General Information," Sept. 4, 1917; Pauline Deomiano, Aug. 21, 1917, ibid; for women as contractors, *Industrial Home Work of Children*, 33.

"starvation wage." A laid-off father and son team noted how the contractors "were getting customs tailor pay from the Government and letting the stuff out at sweat shop rates." The son "was indignant, but had to make the extra money during the dull season; hard as it went on his feeling of trade spirit – said the prices paid were not profitable, but taken only on extreme necessity of high cost of living." Another tailor, "who was afraid to give his name," worked a nine-hour day for only sixteen dollars a week on army shirts in an inside shop; "says many men there have large families and cannot properly support them at the wages they are paid on U.S. Army work," while the boss would earn a million dollars that year on army contracts. Men talked of a strike among uniform makers in the factories; "it is commonly said among the working people that it is among the poorest paid work now doing," the investigator stressed. They directed anger against employers, rather than homeworkers, who appeared as female victims of employer greed rather than as sisters in the larger class struggle.[48]

Baker not only had the report of the temporary committee under Kirstein but an additional plea from Kelley. In a memorandum of August 13, 1917, she urged, "There is no more time to be lost. . . . The rut of usage is deep and the Quartermasters are all in it. You alone can get them out. We outsiders are valueless in their eyes. To them we are civilians, theorists without experience." Kelley was furious: "No one of them seems to have imagination enough to recognize that deliveries depend upon conditions, – wages, hours, surroundings, methods of making labor bargains . . . the specifications are a disgrace to the Quartermasters, because they omit all safeguards for labor conditions. A workman is known by his tools. A quartermaster is known by the specifications he accepts." She demanded that Baker call for the eight-hour day, a wage scale agreed to by the unions, and investigation prior to awarding contracts into whether an employer had adequate facilities, machines, and workers to carry out the job on his premises. The actual report of the temporary committee substantiated her charges in terms of efficiency. It demanded contracts go only to manufacturers with some form of collective grievance procedure for labor disputes, who "comply with the local labor laws." The quartermaster's policy of placing cost above labor standards failed. "Offending contractors have held over the head of the Quartermaster curtailment of the all-important timely production." Cheap never translated into efficient.[49]

Baker easily linked the curtailment of industrial waste with the end of wasted lives. He believed in preserving the nation's human capital by eliminat-

48 Investigations Aug. 23, 1917, including Andrea Marina; Sept. 7, 1917, NYCLC Papers, box 9, folder 49.
49 "My dear Mr. Secretary"; "*In Re Army Uniforms*," Aug. 13, 1917, Baker Papers, reel 1, frames 107–8; Committee on Clothing Contracts, "Preliminary Report of Committee," Aug. 13, 1917, ibid., frames 400–1.

ing child labor and excessive work for women. Neither was he afraid of using the state for unleashing individual opportunity. He would tell the Consumers' League at its annual meeting the following November, "Let them [the soldiers] find that, as they were fighting at one end of the frontier and winning one corner of freedom's fields, we at home were enlarging the boundaries of industrial liberty."[50] Lippmann and Frankfurter similarly evoked industrial efficiency to contain labor unrest and control labor relations. Even Kelley had cited numerous disruptive strikes in greater New York City and New Jersey, one of which brought production to "a standstill" and employees to jail. These firms had large contracts, poor labor standards, and were fighting to keep the ACWA out. Months later when Lippmann claimed the newspapers regarded the Board of Control "as an obstructive body," he reminded Baker that it was an agency born of crisis, formed to avert a general strike and to maintain uniform production. Unwilling to wait for the board, Boston workers indeed struck on the day of its birth for restoration of the forty-eight-hour week and former wage scales.[51]

Frankfurter had approved of the Kirstein committee report on the need for the Board of Control. He firmly believed that the government had to "separate the constructive and responsible radicals" in the labor movement from the International Workers of the World and "in some way seek to utilize the leaders of such movements and not repress them or drive their following into methods of violence." He saw Hillman as one of the "experienced and responsible men who are trusted by the radicals, who are out of the A.F. of L. and yet thoroughly loyal to the Administration." Frankfurter recognized that Gompers failed to represent the entire labor movement and he would use mechanisms like the Board of Control to incorporate other labor leaders, like Hillman, into the war effort to curb the militancy that he found so disruptive.[52]

Hillman, however, criticized the Board of Control because it included no union member. To the press he explained that "no committee, such as was appointed by the Government, can be complete unless it included a representative of our organization. It is a committee on conditions and standards of LABOR. Who, then, is more vitally interested in the work of such a committee than the workingmen?" Government was the real employer, with the manufacturer only an agent; the union thus had a right to turn to government with its grievances. Although lack of union representation disap-

---

[50] "Industrial Liberty in Wartime: Address of the Hon. Newton D. Baker, Secretary of War," *Eighteenth Annual Meeting of the NCL*, Baltimore, Nov. 14, 1917, 7, in CLM Papers, box 31, scrapbook, vol. 5.

[51] "From Secretary of War Baker," *War-Time Needs of New York's Child Workers*; "My dear Mr. Secretary," Baker Papers, reel 2, frame 108; Lippmann to N. D. B., Dec. 16 [1917], ibid., frame 204; F. F., "Memorandum for the Secretary of War," Aug. 10, 1917, Baker Papers, reel 1, frame 399; "Boston Workers Act Despite Baker's Step," *New York Tribune*, Aug. 25, 1917.

[52] F. F., "Subject: Plan for dealing with so-called I.W.W. strikes and western labor troubles," Sept. 4, 1917, Baker Papers, reel 1, frames 401–3.

pointed Hillman, he was "glad" that the state responded to their protest and believed that the board "supplemented by the united power of the organized Clothing workers . . . will eradicate the evils which have crept into our industry through Army contracts."[53]

As the board worked out, Hillman had much to be pleased with: By November, private's uniforms no longer were put out to tenements, the friendly board consulted closely with the union, and both working conditions improved (with the forty-eight-hour week restored) and union membership soared. The union had become a recognized player in industrial policy. The following winter a single administrator, Dr. William Ripley of Harvard, replaced the three-person committee. A labor mediator friendly with Hillman, Ripley sought to standardize production and uplift morale in the clothing industry as a whole. He would create "a calling in which men may engage both with profit and with loyalty and enthusiasm." He invited Hillman to cooperate with the government by investigating "conditions. . . . If wages are unduly low, or if working conditions demand adjustment, we are here to be of such assistance as within our power lies." Ripley would ask Hillman to curb "restriction of output" among the cutters; Hillman, in turn, would manage the union's commitment to war production. That included suspending work rules and disciplining unauthorized strikers.[54]

Recalcitrant employers, in contrast, denounced the ACWA as disloyal and revolutionary, forcing Hillman to decry pacifism. They charged the ACWA with keeping thirty thousand unemployed cloakmakers from work by monopolizing uniform making, attempting to cause a rift with the International Ladies' Garment Workers Union. But Baker informed the public that lack of cloth was curtailing clothing production, not the ACWA. The liberal state helped to build Hillman's liberal union which greeted the 1920s with more organizational success than most craft unions. Embracing the state, the ACWA reaped the benefits of industrial democracy while still appearing militant.[55]

Wartime labor standards

"Democracy . . . cannot exist politically if there is industrial slavery," Hillman proclaimed in May 1918. "The sweatshop conditions in uniform factories

[53] "The Manufacture of Army Clothing," *Proceedings of the Third Biennial Convention*, 139–40. Gompers, in fact, blocked an ACWA representative to the board. Fraser, *Labor Will Rule*, 119.

[54] "Industrial Liberty in Wartime," 8, and letter from the War Department in "Minutes of the Meeting of the Department of Women and Children in Industry," Feb. 19, 1918, WTUL Papers, reel 13, frame 161; letter to Sidney Hillman from William Z. Ripley, Aug. 8, 1918, ACWA Papers, box 4, folder 47.

[55] Fraser, *Labor Will Rule*, 119–21; "The Manufacture of Army Clothing," *Proceedings of the Third Biennial Convention*, 148–50. For refutation of "unpatriotism," Hillman to Louis Kirstein, Jan. 7, 1918, ACWA Papers, box 7, folder 5.

were changed by our organization."[56] Yet Hillman's conception of democracy disenfranchised a group still without political rights, the mostly foreign-born homeworking mothers of the tenements. The labor standards issued by the secretary of war expressed the victory of women reformers and their male allies in defining who was a worker.

"General Orders, No. 13" of November 15, 1917, included all the categories thought impossible to obtain through legislation because of the court's interpretation of "freedom of contract" for men: daily hours, overtime, wage standards, health, and safety. The Woman's Committee of the Council of National Defense had been asking for such general standards and the WIS would adopt them. Section 4 called for direct negotiations between employers and employees. A special section on "Standards for Employment of Women" listed provisions for rest periods, seats, and lifting restrictions and a ban on tenement house work as a form of women's work. The Committee on Women in Industry also demanded women inspectors to protect the health and rights of women war workers.[57]

The women's war committees proceeded on the assumption that women were different from, as well as the same as, men. They asked that women caring for small children be exempted "from the call into industry" and receive leave "two months before and after child birth." Mothers of small children were to be freed from the burden of an additional job; this concept became embodied in the ideal labor standards adopted by war agencies and incorporated into the program of the Women's Bureau afterward. Regretting the presence of mothers in industry, Children's Bureau chief Julia Lathrop felt that legislation prohibiting nursing mothers from factory work "will not solve the difficulty." Not that homework was the solution. As the Council of National Defense resolved, "We deplore the breaking up of the home and recommend that everywhere special provisions be made to keep the mother and her young children together in the home, but this does not imply the indorsement of the homework system." Appeals to biology were strategic. Women reformers simultaneously drew upon social terms to argue for improved wages. They called for wage determination "on the basis of occupation and not on the basis of sex," that is, "equality with men's wages." The WIS actually justified its establishment of standards for women by citing "women's weaker position economically than men," rather than their potential motherhood. While reformers worked to improve the conditions of wage-earning mothers, war-

[56] "Hillman Raps Sweatshop Plan," *Evening Call*, May 14, 1918, in *Sidney Hillman: The Statesman of the New Industrial Order*, "Red Book, 1910–," no. 1, 251–2, ACWA Papers.

[57] "Labor Policy of the War Department," RG1, "War Labor Policies Board Papers, Correspondence of Chairman," box 32, entry 2, "War Department – November 1918"; U.S. DOL, WIS, "Standards Governing the Employment of Women in Industry," for release Dec. 12, 1918, RG86, "Women in Industry Service, Correspondence of Director," box 2. See also "Recommendations" in *The Manufacture of Army Shirts*, 7, and *Making the Uniforms for Our Navy*, 9–10.

time labor shortages led them to jettison the language of motherhood to attack homework in the name of efficiency, democracy, and equal rights in the workplace.[58]

The federal initiative of the war years was fleeting. Even the government had proved to be an unreliable opponent of homework. Increased war production took precedence over labor standards. "Patriotism" proved an ambiguous concept through which to fight the "slavery" of home labor. Still, the banning of industrial homework in army uniforms prefigured the regulation of homework under the National Recovery Administration. Such actions helped to develop a welfare state which shaped, even as it reflected, hierarchies within and between classes based on the place of work as well as the sex of the worker. Women reformers and labor law administrators were the initiators of such measures. Even before the winning of women's suffrage, voices new to the corridors of power offered a renewed vision for the polity, a vision that reflected the ways in which a gendered public policy opened opportunities for some women to translate the voices of other women without necessarily representing the vision of the other: the homeworking mothers producing for the war effort.

[58] "Standards of Industry for Government Contracts," Woman's Committee, Council of National Defense, Illinois Division, RG174, box 131, folder "Women's Bureau, 1913–18"; Julia Lathrop to Dr. B. Raymond Hoobler, July 13, 1918, RG102, file 6153; Lathrop to Miss Alde L. Armstrong, Oct. 2, 1918, ibid.; Minutes of the Child Welfare Committee, Philadelphia Council of National Defense, "Re: Employment of Mothers," Sept. 19, 1918, ibid.; Lathrop to Miss Gertrude Stone, Jan. 5, 1918, ibid.

Figure 12. Women's Bureau, "Where the Work Will Be Done During the Summer," Germantown, Pennsylvania, 1936. Courtesy of the National Archives. This photograph of the DeCroce sisters crocheting exemplifies the spread of auxiliary garment homework beyond the central immigrant districts that characterized the growth of industrial homework beginning in the 1920s.

5

"To study their own conditions":
States' rights to regulate

National reform ground to a halt during the 1920s, a decade that witnessed the renewal of the Ku Klux Klan, the Red Scare, the open shop, and immigration restriction. The stock market's climb to new heights seemed to symbolize the gap between business power and social justice. The Supreme Court proved unfriendly toward social legislation, striking down the second federal child labor law and the women's minimum wage. *Bailey v. Drexel Furniture Co.* rejected the use of the tax power to promote labor standards; *Adkins v. Children's Hospital* proclaimed that newly enfranchised women citizens were also free to contract. In this climate, a states' rights perspective dominated regulatory thought.[1]

But the fight against industrial homework reveals the persistence of reform on the local level. The women's movement did not die with the Nineteenth Amendment; neither did Progressivism end with the war. Although the Socialist Party collapsed and factionalism racked many trade unions, the Amalgamated Clothing Workers of America (ACWA) grew. To find reform we must move from the national level back to the states. We will not discover a story of vibrant success but rather one of dogged continuity. A states' rights approach limited effective response to national problems. Although homework remained concentrated in northeastern and midwestern cities, it had spread more deeply into rural and suburban areas. After World War I the federal government had ceased to regulate it, but the women of the Children's and Women's bureaus spurred state initiatives. Through the Association of Governmental Labor Officials (AGLO), the successor organization to the International Association of Factory Inspectors of North America, and their own personal networks, they were able to exchange information and generate proposals that awaited more propitious times. They maintained structures of reform that the crisis of the Great Depression would activate.

The persistence of homework

Homework remained uncountable; the location of the labor and its intermittent quality hampered the collection of official statistics.[2] In 1925, homework

---

[1] Alan Dawley, *Struggles for Justice: Social Responsibility and the Liberal State* (Cambridge, Mass.: Harvard Univ. Press, 1991).

[2] NYCL, "Tenement Manufacturing Prevalent in New York City," *Bulletin*, c. 1924, NYCLC Papers, box 40, folder 14.

appeared to be increasing in the Northeast. During the previous year, New York State had recorded the largest amount since record keeping began in the 1890s, with 16,050 licensed tenements housing 24,863 workers. Nearly half of this homework, which covered eighty items, was on men's clothing. Embroidery ranked second, with flowers and feathers a distant third. While more women would work in their homes in 1926–27, the shortness of seasons and fluctuation of styles demanded a constant learning of new processes.[3]

Piece rates had risen in the immediate postwar period, but strikes in the garment industry and New York City's housing crisis of the early 1920s led to deteriorating conditions. With an acute shortage of housing units, landlords and tenants engaged in a "rent war," in which landlords sought to have homework licenses for their buildings revoked (licenses were given out for buildings, not to individual households within them) unless tenants coughed up more rent or extra fees. Landlords and tenants struggled over sanitary conditions, the adequacy of which determined licensing. Owners reported illegal homework to remove uncooperative tenants. This went on until 1926, when pressures on the housing market seemed to ease. Such a struggle, which was not the first in the history of the tenement-licensing law, exposed inequalities inherent in the regulatory system.[4]

Slack times actually eliminated homework because its growth depended on the overall health of the garment trades. It increased only in the South as that region industrialized. But in 1925 one of the largest clothing firms in Baltimore went bankrupt, greatly reducing the numbers of homeworkers. The Danville Knitting Mills in rural Virginia put out no work to homes in May 1926 while "only running a part of our machines in the mill, because business is exceedingly poor." Wisconsin experienced a loss in clothing, knitting, and hosiery during a business recession in 1927. New York reported "a marked decline" for that year, with employers blaming general business conditions, labor conflict, women's refusal to work for such small earnings, immigration restriction, foreign competition, tariff laws, and stringent enforcement of labor standards. Low prices led "a great many" homeworkers "to work in the shop 'where the pay is better.'" These women used day nurseries or hired someone to care for their children at home, suggesting that by the 1920s even white ethnic women would leave the home if better alternatives existed. New Jersey saw a decline from over eleven thousand licenses in 1923–24 to under

3 Grace Abbott to Julia Lathrop, July 21, 1925, RG102, file 6–1–5–3; "The Outworkers," *The Survey* 55 (Jan. 15, 1926), 499; "Less Home Work," *The American Child* 10 (Feb. 1928), 4; "Miss Swartz, Director, Makes an Analysis of Some Figures on the Homework Situation," *The Industrial Bulletin* 4 (Jan. 1925), 96–7; Nelle Swartz, "Analysis of Homework Figures in the New York City District," ibid. 6 (July 1927), 298–9; Marie M. Elder, "The Trend of Homework in the New York City District," ibid. 8 (May 1929), 627–8.

4 New York DOL, *Annual Report of the Industrial Commissioner* (1921) (Albany, N.Y.: J. B. Lyon Company, 1922), 102–4; New York DOL, *Annual Report of the Industrial Commissioner* (1926) (Albany, N.Y.: J. B. Lyon Company, 1926), 323.

three thousand three years later. In North Carolina, mechanization for stringing and tagging bags eliminated homework, as did changes in the production process or fashion in other states and industries. Lamp shades, jewelry, hair goods, and trimmings increased in New York, while knit goods showed a marked decline.[5]

By the 1920s, the men's clothing industry consisted of a few elite firms and many small, marginal ones, a product of vertical mergers between retailers and manufacturers. By mid-decade, big New York firms, like Brooks Brothers, planned to forgo tenement homework and favored statewide abolition to solidify their own competitive advantage. But smaller manufacturers found any proposed change in the easily evaded homework law threatening. Production costs would soar which meant, as one maker of pajama loops explained, "a raising in the selling price."[6]

Provisions in clothing union contracts prohibited homework. In Cleveland, where homework practically disappeared after the war, large nonunion firms followed the practice of the unionized and stopped giving out work. Some small plants still sent inside workers home with garments. Although menswear continued to be the leading homework industry throughout the decade, the amount declined. The National Child Labor Committee (NCLC) attributed this drop not to labor-management cooperation but "to . . . the constant turmoil between the workers and their employers."[7]

Homework may have declined, but "a dual system of home and factory production" persisted in New York City, home to 35 percent of the men's clothing industry. In 1925 some five thousand people, 13 percent of the industry, still worked at home, the vast majority for contractors. About four out of five registered with the state. The amount of homework in this center of style and cheap clothes fluctuated only somewhat with the roller coaster business conditions of the first half of the decade. Inside shops employed more

[5] J. Knox Insley to Miss E. N. Matthews, Apr. 8, 1926; Maud Swett to Matthews, May 23, 1927; Swett to Matthews, Dec. 10, 1924; Charles H. Weeks to Ella Arvilla Merritt, July 12, 1927; L. B. Conway to Mrs. Mary L. Scrogham, May 24, 1926; E. F. Carter to Matthews, Dec. 17, 1926; M. F. Nicholson to Matthews, May 10, 1926; C. R. Ritter to Bureau of Labor & Industry, May 18, 1926; "Memorandum" with Matthews to Miss Louise E. Schutz, May 18, 1928, RG102, file 6–1–5–3; Nelle Swartz, "The Change in Styles As Reflected in Manufacturing Done in Tenements," The Industrial Bulletin 7 (June 1928), 277–8; New York DOL, Annual Report of the Industrial Commissioner (1924) (Albany, N.Y.: J. B. Lyon Company, 1927), 249–52; New York DOL, Annual Report of the Industrial Commissioner (1923) (Albany, N.Y.: J. P. Lyon Co., 1924), 60–1.
[6] Steven Fraser, "Combined and Uneven Development in the Men's Clothing Industry," Business History Review 57 (Winter 1983), 544–7; "Hearing on the Tenement Homework Law at City Hall, January 10, 1924," 5–6, NYCLC Papers, box 9, folder 44.
[7] New York DOL, "Homework in the Men's Clothing Industry in New York and Rochester," Special Bulletin, no. 147 (Albany, N.Y.: State Printers, Aug. 1926), n. 7; "Industrial Home Work in Cleveland," attached to Elizabeth S. Magee to E. N. Matthews, May 18, 1926, RG102, file 6–1–5–3; "Less Home Work," 4.

factory and home workers, but greater numbers of the latter; contractors increased their use of homeworkers slightly. Through rising and falling employment, homework remained available, though less certain than inside work. Investigators found "no uniformity"; some coat contractors employed more than 40 percent of their work force at home and some inside manufacturers, over 25 percent of theirs.[8]

Despite unionization, the New York industry remained unstable. More inside manufacturers existed in 1919 than in 1925, with coat contracting showing the greatest growth in homework since firms already were sending out vests and pants. A bitter lock out of the ACWA in late 1920 led to a decline in the amount of home finishing and a halving in prices. The strike ended in May 1921 with the dissolution of the employers' association but union acceptance of employer "production standards." For the next few years, collective bargaining ushered in Sidney Hillman's "new unionism" of labor-management cooperation that would rationalize production through industrial experts and transform labor and management into co-managers. Hillman recognized that the prosperity of his union depended on cutting costs to consumers. His alliance with scientific management provided resources for the Amalgamated to prosper as a social welfare institution. However, increased numbers of small establishments and the growth of branch factories as far away as Pennsylvania became new strategies for avoiding the union.[9]

In the small towns and suburbs around New York and Philadelphia, to which improved mail service and highways provided access, homework flourished in subsidiary occupations – like the production of garters, knitwear, beadwork, and neckties. Even in Chicago, 85 percent of the three thousand workers in embroidery, beading, and related industries remained in the home.[10] Throughout the previous century, outwork had existed as a crucial component of rural capitalist development. The homework and unorganized clothing factories that peppered the countryside in the early 1920s derived from a mature industrialization. Some employers responded to union organizing in cities; others sought lesser overhead costs as well as cheap labor. A Red Cross worker in southern Schuylkill County, Pennsylvania, was "struck with the alarming condition that many very young children are doing home work, such as taping shirts, underwear and the like," she told the Children's Bureau's Julia Lathrop. Small

[8] "Homework in the Men's Clothing Industry," 8, 14, 16–17, 19–20, 26, 33, 35.

[9] Ibid., 38–42; *Annual Report of the Industrial Commissioner* (1921), 104; New York DOL, *Annual Report of the Industrial Commissioner* (1922) (Albany, N.Y.: J. B. Lyon Co., 1923), 71; *Annual Report of the Industrial Commissioner* (1923), 61; Steven Fraser, *Labor Will Rule: Sidney Hillman and the Rise of American Labor* (New York: The Free Press, 1991), 146–97.

[10] Florence Kelley, "Current Mergers in Business and Social Fields," Consumers' League Luncheon, Nov. 1, 1929, CLM Papers, box 3, folder 41; "Says 'Sweating' Still Goes On," *Boston Globe*, Nov. 2, 1929; R. L. Forney to Miss E. N. Matthews, Apr. 24, 1926, RG102, file 6–1–5–3; *Annual Report of the Industrial Commissioner* (1927), 250; *Industrial Home Work and Child Labor*, Special Bulletin, no. 11 (Harrisburg: Commonwealth of Pennsylvania, 1926).

town migration of homework was not just an eastern phenomenon; in Streator, Illinois, near the ACWA's stronghold of Chicago, children made garters at home.[11]

Tenement house licensing laws restricted the number of urban homeworkers, but the potential work force in single-family dwellings and outside the large cities was nearly limitless. This possibility led employers to advertise. The Auto Knitter Hosiery Co. of Buffalo, New York, told "How They Make Money in Their Own Homes" in the March 1924 issue of *True Romances*. Mrs. Frank Unger confessed in the pseudointimate terms familiar to the readers of such a journal:

> My husband's wages were hardly enough to meet the household ac-
> counts, to say nothing of clothing. . . . I began wondering what I could
> do to help. To go out and work was impossible, because I had a four-
> months-old baby to care for. There was just one thing for me: I must find
> some sort of home work that would pay good wages. I began looking in
> the magazines and newspapers for some sort of paying home work, but
> no one seemed to have any work to offer me.

From the paper, Mrs. Unger learned of another woman in a similar situation who had made socks on a hand-knitting machine. She soon sent for machine, yarn, and instructions and, after a little practice, "started to work in real earnest, putting in every minute I could spare from my housework." She loved her work. In eleven months, she made $1,150, enough for a down payment on "a little cottage of our own."[12]

Other advertisers promised "pleasure" as well as "profit" from "dignified" labor. They attempted to appeal to women through the usefulness of the product (for example, "Victor Proctor" rubber menstrual protector), the opportunity to sell it on their own, and the high returns for little labor. Housewives turned into a category of worker who desired, as well as needed, to earn "extra money . . . in their spare time." Housewives could gain the means to be better consumers through homework. Government agencies suspected fraud and sought to investigate the claims of such advertisers, some of whom were attempting to sell craft materials rather than offer homework.[13]

Trade unions began to organize against rural homework. In 1920, feminist labor reporter Mary Heaton Vorse accompanied Amalgamated organiz-

---

[11] Pearl E. Ransom to Miss Julia C. Lathrop, July 30, 1921, RG102, file 6–1–5–3; "Little Children Employed in Garter Industry to Get Help from A.C.W.," *Advance*, 4 (Mar. 12, 1920), 2.

[12] "How They Make Money in Their Own Homes," *True Romances*, Mar. 1924, 77.

[13] Miss Fleming from ED [Emma Duke], May 21, 1919, with attached circular from the Artcraft Service; To Miss Emma Duke, From: Harry Viteles, Mar. 19, 1919, with attachments from Home Service Co., RG102, file 20–20–5; Mrs. Gersha V. Haney to Hon. Claire Bowman, May 17, 1927, RG102, file 6–1–5–3; *Annual Report of the Industrial Commissioner* (1925), 202.

ers to Schuylkill County, where nightly she witnessed "a boy coming out of
the shop bent under a terrific load of shirts. These are distributed up and
down the street. In some of those pleasant little houses with fruit trees
behind them women are working with the same awful unflagging haste of
tenement workers." Miners' wives needed extra money, but earned only
four cents a dozen for buttoning and finishing, a cent and a quarter for
labeling, and nine cents for fronts with button stays, so that at best a woman
gained ten cents an hour. The United Mine Workers, fathers of the factory
girls, supported the ACWA. But the girls feared their employers. This drive
was "the business of the workingmen of America," claimed Vorse. "The
mothers of little children are sitting up till midnight stitching in the nonunion labels of the shirts which they wear." Appeals to mother love were
no match for the persistent obstacles to organizing in depressed regions of
the country, especially those outside of cities.[14]

Contractual bans on homework did not necessarily end it. Employers continued to deploy homeworkers to hamper unionization. Despite agreement with
the major manufacturers of Rochester, the fourth largest center and seat of
higher-grade clothing, the ACWA in 1921 could not eradicate homework
among tenacious contractors. Cutthroat competition in the ladies' garment
industry also vitiated clauses outlawing homework. By the end of the decade,
a new generation of tenement workshops plagued the dress industry. During
the fall rush season in 1925, New York artificial flower factories broke a strike
through reliance on homeworkers.[15] When the United Neckwear Makers
Union signed its 1927 contract with 120 New York City firms, 4 of these
relocated (to Poughkeepsie, Glens Falls, and New Haven) rather than gradually end the use of homeworkers as called for by the agreement. These were
producers of high-grade slip neckties, a hand-sewn style that manufacturers
had promoted to counter knit ties during the depressed market of the early
twenties. This product reintroduced homework, which constituted a third of
the New York output. Strikes against recalcitrant employers spread from New
York to New Haven, where Yale students were arrested for handing out leaflets
in support of the right to organize.[16]

For some unions, opposition to homework shifted terrains: The language of

---

[14] Mary Heaton Vorse, "Sweatshops of Schuylkill City," *Advance* 3 (Jan. 30, 1920), 2.
[15] "Ridding All Rochester of Home Work," *Advance* 5 (June 24, 1921), 1–2; "Homework in the
Men's Clothing Industry," 45–58, 14–15; Julius Hochman, "Organizing the Dressmakers,"
American Federationist 36 (Dec. 1929), 1462–7; "The Outworkers," 499.
[16] Louis Waldman, *Labor Lawyer* (New York: E. P. Dutton, 1944), 164–74; "New Haven Gets
N.Y. Necktie Strike," *New York World*, Oct. 27, 1927; George Brooks, Frederick C. Hyde,
and J. B. Whitelaw, *Is This Fair Play: An Investigation of the Neckwear Makers' Strike in New
Haven* (New York: League for Industrial Democracy, 1927); Deborah Elkin, "Yale and the
United Neckwear Makers Union Strike 1927–28," unpublished paper, Popular Culture
Association, San Antonio, Mar. 1991.

economic rationality replaced that of disease. In keeping with its "new unionism," Amalgamated leaders attacked homework for inefficiency. So did Hillman's mentors among progressive Taylorites, like Morris Cooke whose 1921 study, "Waste in American Industries," labeled homework "inexcusable." The ACWA had not transcended dominant gendered understandings, but rather focused its rhetoric, as well as its actions, on restructuring the economy. In contrast, the American Federation of Labor (AFL) still emphasized a gendered danger. In 1928, the *American Federationist* asked "Shall Our Homes Be Factories?" under its section "Women In Industry." Homework "is really preventing the family from putting their affairs on a better footing," the article explained. "If it were not for the homework, the father would have to demand higher wages." This argument was hardly new; nor was the accompanying illustration of the mother working next to a sick child. But it considered the women themselves, about whom "we have very little real knowledge." The *Federationist* noted, "No one but the women themselves, who take the home-work, know why they take it, who helps them do it, or what their earnings do for them."[17]

Enter, the Women's Bureau

The perception of the AFL was not quite true. Social investigators, the majority of whom were women, had been studying the characteristics of tenement homeworkers since the turn of the century. After World War I, the U.S. Women's Bureau viewed the homeworker as one problematic "mother who must earn," a woman who appeared as both the object for social concern and subject of her own survival strategies in the bulletins that recorded her experiences. Former shoe worker Mary Anderson, a leader of the Women's Trade Union League, led the new agency from 1920 through 1944; this Swedish immigrant was a staunch trade unionist, suffragist, and protector of working-class women. Congress had responded to the perceived power of the women's movement and female enfranchisement by establishing the Women's Bureau as a fact-finding agency within the Department of Labor. It was to "formulate standards and policies which shall promote the welfare of wage-earning women, improve their working conditions, increase their efficiency, and advance their opportunities for profitable employment." It focused on what a later generation named "the double day," the problem faced by women who had to combine wage labor with childcare and housework. The bureau argued that without protective labor legislation, working women would be unable to fulfill their roles as childbearers and rearers. It served, with the

[17] "Ridding all Rochester of Home Work," 2; "Shall Our Homes Be Factories?" *American Federationist* 35 (Jan. 1928): 85–8.

Children's Bureau, as a rallying point for women reformers at both local and national levels.[18]

The bureau's bulletins, like earlier investigations by the National Consumers' League (NCL), were products of an emerging social science technique. But they were hardly neutral. They displayed the same contradictory attitudes toward wage-earning mothers held by the Consumers' League and trade unionists. The bureau called for family wages for men and the mother's responsibility for children, but it also called for improved labor standards for working-women. It defended the working-class mother as a vital contributor to the family economy even as it lamented the necessity that drove her from family labor into wage labor.[19]

Was the Women's Bureau feminist? Feminism, with its call for economic independence and sexual – as well as political – rights, developed in the teens as part of a diversification of the nineteenth-century woman's movement that marked the final years of the suffrage drive. The feminism of the teens then fragmented into an array of competing and conflicting organizations during the more conservative 1920s, changes that testified to its success in asserting women's individuality over any common womanhood. It lost its revolutionary thrust when the National Women's Party (NWP), under Alice Paul, captured the term and locked it into a legalistic conception of equal treatment that denied *woman* as a relevant category even as it relied upon gender consciousness to spur political activity. In formulating the Equal Rights Amendment (ERA), the NWP accepted a formalist jurisprudence that would deny special legal protection for women as a group. Equality under the ERA would negate women's labor laws because they provided women with "special" rather than "equal" treatment. The women of the Women's Bureau had spent years fighting for precisely such laws. The negative consequences of legal equality without economic and social justice led them to reject the term *feminist*.[20]

In the early 1920s, however, before the controversy over the ERA split the women's movement, the Women's Bureau spoke the language of feminism. It defended women's right to work for wages against those who cried "back to the home" during the recession following the war. It fought for public recogni-

[18] Mary Anderson, "Second Annual Report of the Director of the Women's Bureau, for the Fiscal Year Ended June 30, 1920," U.S. DOL, *Reports of the Department of Labor, 1920* (Washington, D.C.: GPO, 1921); Judith Sealander, *As Minority Becomes Majority: Federal Reaction to the Phenomenon of Women in the Work Force, 1920–1963* (Westport, Conn.: Greenwood Press, 1983); Eileen Boris and Michael Honey, "Gender, Race, and the Policies of the Labor Department," *Monthly Labor Review* 111 (Feb. 1988), 26–36; Edward T. James, "Mary Anderson," *Notable American Women: The Modern Period*, ed. Barbara Sicherman and Carol Hurd Green (Cambridge, Mass.: Harvard Univ. Press, 1980), 23–5.

[19] U.S. DOL, "The Share of Wage-Earning Women in Family Support," *WBB*, no. 30 (Washington, D.C.: GPO, 1923), 2, 21, 1.

[20] Nancy Cott, *The Grounding of Modern Feminism* (New Haven. Conn.: Yale Univ. Press, 1987); Sealander, *As Minority Becomes Majority*, 27–55; Sybil Lipschultz, "Social Feminism and Legal Discourse, 1908–1923," *Yale Journal of Law and Feminism* 2 (Fall 1989): 131–60.

tion of "women as providers for the home, as factors in industry." It rejected the dominant assumption, "women are the home makers and men the providers for the home," because it knew that this was not the case for large numbers of working-class women. Yet its feminism was a feminism of difference, valuing housework, mothering, and self-sacrifice even as it campaigned for equal pay, condemned double sexual as well as economic standards, and fought against occupational segmentation by sex.[21]

This tension between difference and equality typified the thought of women reformers in the bureau network, whose program to improve the lives of working people distinguished between daughters and mothers. The bureau upheld mother care of children, combining traditionalist solutions with a feminist valuation of women's unpaid, as well as paid, labor. It shared this perspective with local consumers' leagues and state departments of labor which would "improve working conditions so that [the mother] may not break down," but preferred "to keep the mother at home" over providing day nurseries. This position captured the lives of many women. Whether employed out of necessity, personal preference, or "a desire to be economically independent of their husbands," Nelle Swartz of New York's Bureau of Women in Industry explained, married women "in our industries can no longer be ignored or pushed aside because of prejudice or fear."[22]

From the start, the Women's Bureau argued that "home work should be abolished." Such a system of labor shifted the burdens of production from the employer to the employee. It defied adequate inspection for sanitary conditions or the presence of child labor. It was an inefficient business practice that relied upon unsupervised workers, one in which competitive pressures forced the more "conscientious" to adapt. In 1919, the bureau concluded "home work is a community question, and . . . it is closely tied up with the general wage rate paid in the community." The rate of male wages determined the availability of female homeworkers. Sensitive to the homeworkers themselves, it defined the problem as "how to avoid the privations which may be caused by removing even such undesirable work from this group of restricted and underpaid women." With localism and states' rights blocking national solutions, the bureau asserted that the issue "must be decided by the community."[23]

The Women's Bureau harbored a belief in the positive use of the state during a period when Republican administrations rejected such federal action. With the Children's Bureau, it called for state intervention to end the circumstances

[21] Agnes Peterson, "What the Wage-Earning Woman Contributes to Family Support," *WBB*, no. 75 (1929); "Family Status of Breadwinning Women in Four Selected Cities," ibid., no. 41 (1925).
[22] Helen G. Rotch, "Transcript 1921," CLM Papers, box 4, folder 49; Nelle Swartz, "Married Women in Industry," *The Industrial Bulletin* 7 (Nov. 1927), 45.
[23] U.S. DOL, "Home Work in Bridgeport, Connecticut, December 1919," *WBB*, no. 9 (Washington, D.C.: GPO, 1920), 5–7.

that pushed families to homework. Poverty encouraged homework; raising the minimum wage for women and the wage level for men would discourage it. So would sickness or disability benefits, unemployment insurance, maternity benefits, and mothers' pensions. The Women's Bureau requested short shifts for women unable to work a full factory day, equal pay for home and factory employees, employer payment of delivery and pick-up costs, home inspections by labor department and health officials, and greater intervention by private and public welfare agencies in families "where there is more need of social treatment than of home work." It wanted homework prohibited but would accept "strict regulation of wages and working conditions" as a means toward that goal.[24]

With British and European state intervention as a model, the bureau in its early years strove to be an activist agency. It insisted on trade-union input. It usually operated by investigating a subject after a state or another branch of the federal government requested a study. When it was still the Women in Industry Service, the agency not only analyzed what the increase of homework in Bridgeport, Connecticut, might mean for postwar reconstruction but attempted to facilitate community action. Since Connecticut had virtually no law that regulated or prohibited homework until the mid-1930s, only employer agreement – on their own or through union contract – could stop the sending out of work. So the bureau submitted its findings in advance of publication to employers, trade unionists, public officials, and social workers, who then met together in October 1919 to consider "the whole problem not only as a problem for the factories but as a social question" and to recommend actions.[25]

Each of these groups expressed attitudes common to their counterparts in other cities. Charity workers held a mixed opinion about homework, sometimes recommending it to clients. Employers justified the practice in terms of charity, labor supply, and worker choice. Although the employers submitted wage information to the bureau, they claimed ignorance of how many people earned a wage or how long it took. They insisted that none of their workers would relinquish homework; if law stood in the way, these newly enfranchised women would vote legal restrictions down. Women wanted to stay at home. The employers preferred a licensing system that would shift responsibility for determining homeworker eligibility to the state, which would serve as a de facto employment bureau.[26]

[24] Mary Skinner, "Child Labor in New Jersey, Part 2: Children Engaged in Industrial Home Work," *CBB*, no. 185 (Washington, D.C.: GPO, 1928), 55; "Home Work in Bridgeport Connecticut," 10, 21–6.

[25] "Home Work in Bridgeport, Connecticut," 5, 10, 17–20. "Conference Report: Home Work in Bridgeport, Connecticut," 1, typescript, RG86, box 3, file "Bulletin #9: Correspondence."

[26] "Conference Report: Home Work in Bridgeport, Connecticut," 13, 17–18, 21, 3–4, 7–9, 11, and attached list of wages, M. Hawie. For New York attitudes, "Hearing on the Tenement Homework Law at City Hall," 7.

No new regulations came from the Bridgeport conference. Ten years later the Women's Bureau was still arguing for "public regulation." Reasons for state interference — "irregular production" and shifting, unstable numbers of employers and tenement workers — "make the home-work industries preeminently difficult to regulate." In 1930 the bureau could only ask the states to investigate conditions in their locality and devise a way to bring the system under control. No other arena of action seemed possible.[27]

The ways of the states

In calling upon the states to investigate homework, the Women's Bureau confirmed the work of the AGLO. Led by E. Natalie Matthews, industrial division chief of the Children's Bureau, the AGLO spearheaded an attempt to have the states regulate homework. In 1925, the AGLO appointed a fact-finding committee — Matthews; Mary Anderson; the chief of Pennsylvania's Bureau of Women and Children, Charlotte Carr; New York's Swartz; New Jersey's deputy commissioner of labor, Charles Weeks; and Massachusetts's assistant commissioner, Ethel Johnson. Charged with finding out what the states knew about homework and what they were doing about it, the Matthews committee formulated minimum standards of regulation. Its findings suggest the extent to which the state regulatory regime remained underdeveloped even though homework existed everywhere except for predominantly agricultural or mining states. State responses ranged from acceptance of homework to schemes for its abolition. Separate laws based on licensing contrasted with the application of minimum wage or other state laws in regard to homework. These approaches reflected alternative philosophies toward homework regulation, both of which considered the homeworker but only the latter treated her like other wage-earning women.[28]

Many factors impeded regulation. Directors of state labor departments could stymie progress on issues, like homework, that heads of women and children divisions defined for national discussion and action. Directors were often political appointees, usually from the male-dominated crafts trades and AFL state councils. Budget cuts, an inadequate number of inspectors, and lack of legal backing hampered the states, even those that had homework laws. Fourteen had some regulation. Yet Connecticut and Ohio applied their laws only to nonfamily members in the home, Massachusetts only included gar-

[27] Emily C. Brown, "Industrial Home Work," *WBB*, no. 79 (Washington, D.C.: GPO, 1930), 1, 9–14.

[28] Ibid., 11–14; U.S. DOL, "Proceedings of the Fourteenth Annual Convention of the AGLO of the United States and Canada," *Bulletin of the Bureau of Labor Statistics*, no. 455 (Washington. D.C.: GPO, 1927), 83–96; Massachusetts Council on Women and Children in Industry, *News Letter on Women and Children in Industry*, no. 10, Sept. 1926, 6–9, NYCLC Papers, box 8, folder 38.

ments, and Maryland and Texas essentially regulated homework as a health measure.[29]

States could not even keep track of the problem. Meager appropriations provided the Texas Bureau of Labor Statistics with only six deputies. Budget cuts in 1923 led California to abort its attempt to draw up homework regulations. Lacking facilities to ascertain the extent of homework outside of Chicago, Illinois collected no data. Even Massachusetts, with its well-developed department of labor, had to rely on factory inspectors to note homework in unregulated industries. Though inspectors found none, minimum wage investigations uncovered homework in jewelry, stationary goods, and shoes. For garments, a decline in licenses (adjusted for changed procedures) suggested less homework than prior to the war.[30]

New Jersey particularly suffered from lack of staff. None of its twenty-two inspectors concentrated "full-time" on homework; they sought assistance from local boards of health. The state department had to contend with the diverse attitudes of these local officials that shaped enforcement of the law. One from West Orange admitted, "I try to delay as long as possible in granting these [licenses] as I think a good many of the mothers do better to devote more time to their children than doing this work for which they receive such a small revenue." Another from Somerville had no problem with old women and children, after school hours, pulling out lace. A third from Millburn, a town with a day nursery, considered it better for Italian husbands "to get out and hustle like a white man. There is altogether too much indulgence in the matter of allowing adolescents and housewives to support a father and husband, who might better be carrying his proper load." This enforcer of the law was equally unsympathetic to immigrant homeworkers and to employers who lied about giving out work.[31]

Some administrators were not convinced of the homework evil. Louisana's saw sewing as "relatively harmless"; it went "into homes of comparative refinement and cleanliness." Missouri's commissioner similarly evaluated the nature of homework in terms of worker characteristics: "Some finishing work has been done in homes on women's silk dresses, but I have found that this work was done under sanitary conditions and by respectable, clean persons,

---

[29] Brown, "Industrial Home Work," 11–12. Correspondence between women in the federal and state departments alludes to conflicts with directors.

[30] E. J. Crocker to Mr. E. N. Matthews [sic], May 4, 1926; Katherine Philips Edson to E. N. Matthews, May 17, 1925; R. L. Forney to E. N. Matthews, Apr. 24, 1926; Ethel Johnson to Matthews, June 4, 1926; Johnson to Miss Ella Arvilla Merritt, June 29, 1927; RG102, file 6–1–5–3; Ethel M. Johnson, "Industrial Home Work in Massachusetts," American Federationist 35 (Jan. 1928), 90–3.

[31] Charles H. Weeks to E. N. Matthews, Apr. 16, 1926, RG102, file 6–1–5–3; Charles H. Weeks, "Report to Andrew F. McBride: The Enforcement Of the Home Work and Sweat Shop Laws in the State of New Jersey, From June 1 to December 1, 1923," 23, 32, CLNJ Papers, box 5.

and that the amount of it was limited. It was handwork." "Clean" and "respectable" may have stood as code words for "white." Even California's Katherine Philips Edson, a leader in women's reform, was "not convinced that it should be prohibited entirely as I know a good many shut-ins who are not able to go into factory life are able to make a living."[32]

Many states placed homework regulation under divisions of women and children in industry, making explicit the association of this form of labor with the workers who dominated it. Massachusetts applied its child labor and women's hour laws to homework but acted only upon complaints outside of wearing apparel, which it investigated only for the purpose of licensing. California lodged its administration in the Industrial Welfare Commission which oversaw labor laws for women and children. As with Oregon, Washington, and Wisconsin, homework regulation came under minimum wage orders. New York mandated "continuous study and investigation" to its Bureau of Women and Children in Industry. Progressives under Governor Al Smith rejected the women-blaming recommendation of Daniel O'Leary, the somewhat inefficient, longtime chief factory inspector, "that the law have control over mothers who permit a child to work." Although labor investigators often expressed anger at the mothers of the tenements for forcing their children to work, women-centered departments promised to be more sympathetic to the plight of homeworkers and their families.[33]

Homework regulation belonged to the general category of women's labor standards. Given the legal difficulties of direct statutory regulation of homework, Colorado's deputy labor commissioner sought hours limitation for "*all* females engaged in gainful occupations regardless of where the work is performed." Oklahoma's agreed, claiming that "the woman's nine-hour-a-day and fifty-four-hour-a-week law and the child labor law are sufficient to discourage industrial home work." Section 11 of California's Manufacturing Order of May 1923 prohibited "any women from doing homework after factory hours." Yet Edson questioned whether states could apply such laws to homes. Not only was factory enforcement difficult, but "the sanitary, safety and working condition standards could not be made to apply to a home, which I believe in the language of the law, is a 'man's own castle.' "[34] Liberty

32 "Fourteenth Annual Convention of AGLO," 82, 85; Edson to Matthews, May 17, 1925.
33 "The Outworkers," 499; Madeline H. Appel to Jeanie V. Minor, Feb. 2, 1923, NYCLC Papers, box 8, folder 39; Brown, "Industrial Home Work;" Bernard L. Shientag, *Report on Manufacturing in Tenements Submitted to the Commission to Examine the Laws Relating to Child Welfare* (New York: DOL, Mar. 1924), 7–8; State of New York, *Third Annual Report of the New York State Commission to Examine Laws Relating to Child Welfare* (Albany, N.Y.: J. B. Lyon Company, 1924), 10–13, 33–80; Daniel O'Leary, testimony in "Hearing on the Tenement Homework Law at City Hall," 4; "Industrial Home Work of Children," *CBB*, no. 100 (Washington, D.C.: GPO, 1922).
34 Questionnaire filled out by M. H. Alexander, RG102, file 6–1–5–3; "Proceedings of the Fourteenth Annual Convention of AGLO," 91; Edson to Matthews, May 17, 1925.

of contract still defined employer-employee relations, continuing to shape homework discourse and limit state action.

Hour regulation in the home was nearly impossible; the main problem with homework remained its low wages, which mocked the number of hours spent on it. Children's Bureau chief Lathrop deployed a discourse of fairness to question, "How does such work fit into a fair scheme of industrial life? What excuse has an industry which loads upon the worker the cost of maintaining a work-place and makes up for the specious freedom from factory hours by a rate of pay which is admittedly not enough to support life?" Despite the difficulty of regulation, she called for "the standardization of pay for home work according to factory rates." New York's industrial commissioner agreed that a "living wage" for homework would eliminate it. But reformers understood that homeworkers would lose their jobs before employers would provide them with a living wage, perhaps forcing these women onto the resources of men rather than improving their earning abilities.[35]

On the question of wages, the progressive state of Wisconsin provided a model. To obtain a homework license an employer had to comply with factory labor laws and pay an adequate piece rate for homework. The Health Department inspected homes to insure that they complied with sanitary laws. "Personally, I believe that the evils of low wages, employment of children, etc., are a much greater evil than any danger which might come to the consumer from goods made in unsanitary places," confessed Maud Swett, that state's director of Women and Child Labor.[36] This focus on the earnings of the worker, rather than the perils to the consumer, marked a significant change in homework regulation. It represented a shift to the concept of "industrial equality," an argument for labor standards based on the rights of citizens and not only on the needs of distressed and overburdened mothers. It reflected the acceptance of the mother as a breadwinner, the reality that the Women's Bureau had been documenting. The minimum wage, promoted by the NCL for a decade, had become the chief mechanism to undermine homework.[37]

Wisconsin demanded that homeworker piece rates be set to yield the minimum wage. Prior to 1921, its law resembled earlier East Coast licensing measures "passed primarily for the protection of the consumer." That year, the state changed the basis of its law to protect the worker. "The fact that the home worker may be satisfied with the rate does not mean that it is adequate, as the worker is often not in a position to seek out other opportunities for home work and she considers a little work better than nothing," Swett explained. To implement the law, the Industrial Commission checked factory records to

[35] "Written Personally by Miss Lathrop at Request of Woman's Bureau," Dec. 11, 1919, RG102, file 6171; Shientag, *Report on Manufacturing in Tenements*, 8.
[36] Maud Swett to Miss E. N. Matthews, May 23, 1927, RG102, file 6-1-5-3.
[37] Sybil Lipschultz, "Hours and Wages: The Gendering of Labor Standards in America," unpublished paper, Social Science History Association, 1990, Minneapolis.

determine if the same rate was paid to inside and outside workers for the same kind of work. If operations differed, which they often did, then homeworkers came to the factory to be tested under government supervision to yield an hourly rate for an "efficient" homeworker. Where such a test was impossible to conduct, the commission relied upon the records of homeworkers, an extremely inadequate method because home conditions hardly matched those demanded by Taylorite rate-setting methods. The commission raised rates to meet the minimum wage, refusing permits for the lowest. Wisconsin claimed this approach to be effective, although Swett admitted that "the reduction in the number of home workers in the silk hosiery mills is not due so much to our law as to the change in styles."[38]

The Knitted Outer Wear Manufacturers Association, representing the industry that held the most homework permits in Milwaukee, attacked this interpretation of the minimum wage law. The law failed to apply to homeworkers "because they are casual laborers" and "they are not dependent upon the wage earned." Since other sources of income brought homeworkers above "reasonable comfort," they could not come under the minimum wage. But the chair of the Industrial Commission ruled in 1923 that the living wage concept covered homeworkers. He reasoned, "We think statistics show pretty conclusively that notwithstanding legislative interference, home service compared with the equivalent factory service is materially less remunerative, and that where a living wage requirement does not prevail, the wage of the home worker is not fixed with real regard for the value of the service." Although this ruling viewed homeworkers as women curtailed by domestic responsibilities, ignoring the similar constraints of wives and mothers who worked outside the home, still it recognized them as workers who contributed to the family maintenance and not dependents, as employers had argued. The law applied to all workers, "dependent" and "nondependent," home and factory, because "the language of the statute makes no distinction on the basis of the financial circumstances of the employe[e]." Paying less than a living wage violated the act.[39]

By emphasizing "value of the service" and not only a "living wage," the Wisconsin commission hoped to protect itself from the Supreme Court's recent decision in *Adkins*. This ruling argued against a woman's needs as a proper standard for her labor. The majority determined that "revolutionary . . . changes . . . in the contractual, political and civil status of women, culminating in the nineteenth amendment" superseded the reasoning of *Muller*. It rejected "restrictions upon liberty of contract which could not lawfully be imposed in the case of men under similar circumstances." But although the Court would consider biological difference as a factor for hour laws, this was not so for wage

[38] "Home Work in Wisconsin," RG102, file 6–1–5–3; "Minimum Wage for Home Workers"; Maud Swett to Matthews, May 14, 1926.

[39] F. M. Wilcox, "Minimum Wage for Home Workers," Dec. 6, 1923, "To Knitted Outer Wear Manufactures Association, Milwaukee"; "Home Work in Wisconsin," RG102, 6–1–5–3.

laws. These were "price-fixing laws" that the Court interpreted as interfering
with the right to contract and had nothing to do with the proper use of the police
power of the state.[40]

Did *Adkins* destroy the Wisconsin approach to homework regulation?
Wisconsin felt it irrelevant: "No extravagances can be indulged by the workers
receiving no higher wage than that provided for in the order. The hourly rate
fixed provides nothing beyond bare necessities economically obtained for the
woman who wishes to live in decently healthful and comfortable surroundings." The distinction here revolved around a fair as opposed to a living wage.
The Court had opened the door for fair wages to be determined not by what
a woman needed, but by the worth of her labor power, that is, her job
performance, hours of labor, and "surroundings of the employment." Wisconsin hoped that by covering both fair and living wages its minimum wage law
would stand. Florence Kelley thought otherwise. Local consumers' leagues
were disgusted "with all our past efforts to limit home work by regulation or
repression of any kind," she reported to Matthews. "The moral of our
experience is that since the Supreme Court has made it impossible for us to
have the only regulation that really regulates, – that is, minimum wage
commissions, we are wasting our energies and time in occasional turning of
the light on the hopelessness of the American substitute for the only possible
effective measure." Minimum wage legislation appeared as a necessity but the
Court, for the time being, had blocked the way.[41]

Few states actually applied their wage laws to homework; most continued the
licensing route that in some sense was more concerned with the conditions in
workers' homes than with the lives of workers. Both licensing and minimum wage
were gendered, although the first primarily defined the homeworker as a mother
in the home, whereas the second defined her as a type of woman worker. Licensing
focused on the needs of the community whereas the minimum wage promised to
turn a woman's need for a living wage into a right.[42]

Most states continued the older licensing method. In New Jersey, investiga-

---

[40] 261 U.S. 525 (1923).

[41] Wisconsin actually reacted to *Adkins* by reformulating its minimum wage law in 1925 in
terms of an "oppressive wage." Vivien Hart, *Bound by Our Constitution: Women, Workers,
and Minimum Wage Laws in the United States and Great Britain* (Princeton, N.J.: Princeton
Univ. Press, 1994), chap. 6. "Minimum Wage for Home Workers"; Maud Swett to
Matthews, May 14, 1926; Florence Kelley to Matthews, Apr. 6, 1926, RG102, file 6–1–
5–3; Vivien Hart, "No Englishman Can Understand: Fairness and Minimum Wage Laws
in Britain and America, 1923–1938," in *American Studies: Essays in Honour of Marcus
Cunliffe*, ed. Brian Holden-Reid and John White (London: Macmillan, 1991), 249–69.

[42] "Memorandum regarding report on migratory children" attached to E. N. Matthews to
Louise E. Schutz, May 18, 1928, RG102, 6–1–5–3; Vivien Hart, "Gendered in All But Name:
The Minimum Wage in Britain," unpublished paper, Social Science History Association,
1990, Minneapolis; Alice Kessler-Harris, *A Woman's Wage: Historical Meanings and Social Consequences* (Lexington: Univ. Press of Kentucky, 1990), points out how basing a woman's wage on
conceptions of needs rather than the amount of work vitiated even the minimum wage.

tions into homework sparked enforcement. In 1923, the NCLC and the Jersey City Bureau of Vocational Guidance exposed the extent of homework in that politically corrupt industrial city. A crackdown on contractors and increased licensing resulted. Parents and sweatshop owners faced charges of child abuse under the Child Welfare Act of 1915, which defined abuse "as the employing or allowing to be employed any child in an occupation injurious to health or dangerous to life." The first three "sweatshop bosses" received sentences of sixty days; homework conditions shocked the judge, who confessed, "It's the first time I ever had such cases . . . and I've got to do something. The jail sentence, instead of a fine, will stamp out the practice." But the county court suspended these sentences upon employer appeal and employers further used the courts to both end the prosecutions and question the applicability of the child welfare law to tenement homework.[43]

This investigation led to a statewide study of homework and temporary enforcement of New Jersey's weak tenement licensing law. The Department of Labor placed all of its inspectors (eighteen at the time) on the study. After an educational campaign aimed at both employers and workers, Deputy Commissioner Weeks claimed that both parties desired licensed homes. He prematurely announced that the department had "practically eliminated" "the objectionable features of sweatshops." Inspectors investigated a third of the fifteen thousand new applications for licenses, issuing over three thousasnd. Two years later, the Children's Bureau found ample evidence of the persistence of homework in New Jersey, though licenses increased to about a thousand.[44]

The clothing industry generated the most enforcement problems. Weeks explained, "A home will have work from probably three or four different concerns doing this class of work and as a rule it is conducted by foreign elements in undesirable buildings the work being discontinued and started again continually, thus producing a very difficult situation to follow up." The extent of the problem – magnified by work sent from New York and Philadelphia and too few investigators – curbed local efforts. With the state attorney general interpreting the law so that manufacturers or contractors could not be prosecuted for providing work to unlicensed homes, the department could only penalize employers for improper list keeping. Weeks called for revision, but there was a reluctance to amend the 1917 law unless the department could prove "marked abuse."[45]

43 Mary Skinner to My dear Miss Matthews, Mar. 5, 1925, RG102, file 20–91–1–5; "Jersey City Starts Intensive Drive to Eliminate Home Sweat Shops," The American Child 5 (July 1923), 1, 3; "Child Labor in Tenement Homes Arouses All New Jersey," ibid. (Aug. 1923), 1, 6.

44 "New Jersey Sweatshop Labor under State Control," The American Child 5 (Sept. 1923), 1; Charles H. Weeks to Miss Jeanie Minor, Aug. 16, 1923; "Report to Andrew F. McBride," 11, CLNJ Papers, box 5; Skinner, "Child Labor in New Jersey." The economic slump of mid-decade helped drop the number of homework licenses. The law, however, only covered tenements and could not regulate work originating out of state.

45 Weeks to Matthews, Apr. 16, 1926; Weeks to Matthews, Mar. 24, 1926; Weeks to Matthews, May 16, 1927, RG102, 6–1–5–3.

The International Ladies' Garment Workers Union had predicted such an outcome in 1923:"This sudden outburst of sympathy with the sweated women and children in the shops of New Jersey on the part of the authorities is likely to blow over as soon as the differences between the quarreling politicians are composed." Police and politicians gave protection to sweatshop owners while deporting union organizers from their towns. Embroidery accounted for the largest number of homework licenses issued in Jersey City, where no shop with extensive homework met health laws. Local 6 of the embroidery workers spent tens of thousands of dollars but could not overcome the collusion between city government and employers. Big manufacturers escaped prosecution.[46]

In New York, trade unionists complained that "corrective bills [are] all buried" but praised the efforts of the state department despite its chronic underfunding. The early 1920s witnessed yearly defeats in Albany of attempts to extend the homework law to one- and two-family dwellings. In 1926, the department finally received a work force adequate to make the two annual inspections of every licensed tenement required by law; "flying squadrons" visited unlicensed ones to see what else was going on. But such regulation proved unsatisfactory. Nelle Swartz confessed that she was "rather in a quandary as to know what is the best possible solution." New York City experienced a fluctuating homework market, with the type of work undergoing "constant change." Complicating matters, about 13 percent of homework firms, including 25 percent of embroidery employers and about 20 percent of women's clothing and neckwear, sent work outside the state, beyond department control.[47]

Swartz emphasized public education. In December 1925, she met with about twenty-five trade union leaders, who "were all much astonished to learn of the size of the homework problem," to enlist their aid in enforcing the law.[48] During the spring of 1929, the Bureau of Women and Children in Industry convened another conference, this one of fifteen welfare and charity organizations that gave out homework. Social agencies had considered homework as a form of handiwork, an attractive form of occupational therapy and an alternative to dependency. Yet only seven agencies distributed any work to the physically handicapped. Most continued to use it as relief for mothers with small children. Even those agencies that set piece rates high enough for a living wage lacked enough work actually to provide one for their clients. Although charity homework did not fall under the homework licensing law, the new head of the bureau, Frieda Miller, argued that "all agencies which give out

[46] "Child Slavery in Jersey Sweatshops," *Justice* 5 (July 13, 1923), 6; "Campaign Against Jersey Sweatshops Begins in Earnest," ibid. (July 20, 1923), 1; "Report to Andrew F. McBride," 18.
[47] Louis Stanley, "The Home–Work Evil Thrives Again in N.Y.," *New Leader*, Dec. 3, 1927, 1–3; Nelle Swartz to Miss E. N. Matthews, May 13, 1926; Swartz to Matthews, Mar. 17, 1926, with attached tables, RG102, file 6–1–5–3; "Does Tenement Home Work Still Exist?," *The American Child* 8 (Dec. 1926), 2.
[48] "Concerning Home Work in New York," *The American Child* 7 (July 1925), 6.

homework have a moral if not a legal responsibility . . . to comply with standards set for the protection of the consuming public." Despite attempts to consult with community groups and special research into the system, New York had to work with a law that remained inadequate to curtail homework. It only applied to tenements, although a Schenectady court ruled that the department could enforce in "private" homes the child labor provisions, which prohibited homework for children under fourteen.[49]

The Pennsylvania Bureau of Women and Children also sought to involve social service agencies, especially in Philadelphia, which contained more than half of the state's homework. It asked agencies to report violations witnessed during the course of their work as well as to furnish lists of homeworker clients. The bureau, in turn, would contact the employer of a violating client, not the client, thus maintaining agency privacy. The department pulled voluntary organizations, as well as other state agencies, into its orbit, compensating for inadequate staffing.[50]

Unlike New Jersey or New York, Pennsylvania would regulate by extending labor laws to the home. In 1925, it promulgated regulations that squarely placed the burden of compliance with the employer, making him responsible for worker conformity to the laws. Some employers appointed a supervisor of homework to check conditions in the homes; others required an employee to "sign a statement showing her knowledge of the regulations and her intention of observing them." Still others, who gave out products as diverse as screws and tobacco, organized distribution to curb abuse of night work, hours, and child labor laws. At first the new law discouraged many employers, but some applauded the greater efficiency and workmanship gained from stopping child labor in the home. The new law initially reduced the number of children under sixteen engaged in homework in licensed homes from 50 percent to 23 percent in a year. The bureau attributed this drop to employer cooperation, although economic competition and market conditions undoubtedly played a role. Those who praised the approach still wondered whether it could work in large cities like New York or Chicago, without an "intimate connection between labor and management."[51]

E. N. Matthews of the Children's Bureau felt all along that the difficulty of

[49] Frieda S. Miller, "The Use of Homework By Welfare Organizations," *The Industrial Bulletin* 9 (Sept. 1930), 356–7; Fredric G. Elton to Mr. George A. Hall, Nov. 2, 1923, NYCLC Papers, box 31, folder 36.

[50] Charlotte E. Carr, "Private Social Agencies and Industrial Home Work," *The American Child* 8 (Dec. 1926), 7.

[51] A. Estelle Lauder to Grace Abbott, Feb. 15, 1922; Abbott to Lauder, Feb. 20, 1922; Lauder to Abbott, Mar. 22, 1922; Ella Arvilla Merritt to Lauder, Mar. 25, 1922, RG 102, box 205–18; Charlotte E. Carr, "Pennsylvania's Regulation of Home Work," *American Federationist* 33 (May 1926), 585–7; Sara M. Soffel, "Industrial Home Work in Pennsylvania," ibid. 36 (Sept. 1929), 1062–4; "Home Work," *The Survey* 58 (Apr. 15, 1927), 94; B. A., "A New Handle for Home Work," ibid. 56 (Apr. 15, 1926), 97–9.

enforcing licensing regulations meant "that abolition of home work is probably necessary for the protection of the children who engage in it." But legal
doctrine blocked outright prohibition. So the Matthews commission issued
"minimum standards of regulation," which would serve as guidelines for the
states until the mid-1930s. Emphasizing health and safety protection, these
would prohibit "the [home] manufacture of certain kinds of articles" (foodstuffs, some clothing, explosives). They would apply labor standards to
homeworkers, going beyond those set up for women and minors to include
workmen's compensation and factory standards "for safety, sanitation, and
working conditions." They would place the burden of compliance, including
various record-keeping provisions, on "the manufacturer for whom the work
is done," no matter the contractor chain involved. Finally, they included
adequate inspection staff, a tag system, and involvement of health boards.[52]

These recommendations remained suggestions. The AGLO rejected the
idea "of a general inquiry into the efficacy of the various methods regulating
the home work problem to be made by some impartial outside agency." As
Matthews angrily wrote to Swartz, that idea "met with opposition from
certain of our States Rights friends, and to whom the idea of a 'national'
investigation was anathema, and so for an inquiry by a Foundation – that was
just as bad if not worse!" While the association called for the committee to "be
continued with the view of enlarging the scope of its investigation," Matthews
noted "it seems that all they want us to do is to continue to try to get the States
to study their own conditions."[53]

This states' rights orientation of labor law administrators, along with a
reluctance to authorize outside investigation of their professional turf, left
Matthews and her committee able only to suggest more discussions. The
committee recommended a future session featuring experienced homework
administrators as a way to explore regulatory options. But such a meeting did
not convene until the Great Depression: first under the NCL and then under
the new federal Division of Labor Standards. Homework was a national
problem, one that crossed state lines. It would take leadership from Washington
to overcome the states' rights impasse of the 1920s, to water the seeds of
cooperation planted by a national network of women reformers.

[52] Memorandum to Miss Abbott from E. N. Matthews, Feb. 17, 1922, RG102, box 205–18;
"Proceedings of the Fourteenth Annual Convention of AGLO," 74–7.
[53] Matthews to Swartz, July 6, 1926; Swartz to Matthews, July 28, 1926; Johnson to Matthews,
July 30, 1926; Louise E. Schutz to Matthews, Apr. 10, 1928; Schutz to Matthews, Feb. 18,
1928; "Report of Resolutions Committee"; Matthews to Schutz, May 18, 1928, RG102,
file 6–1–5–3.

6

"Homework is a community question": The worlds of the homeworker

"I have tow kids and my husband has oly 2 days work and we can hardly live from it. You can think whats 2 day pay . . . my kids are to[o] little to let home alone. Perhaps yous let me take work home from the factory so that I can earn a few dollars for my kid clothes and eats." Thus Mrs. Thomas D. Herb of Bechtelsville, Pennsylvania, pleaded to the federal government in 1934.[1] Though writing in the midst of the Great Depression, Mrs. Herb typified the average homeworker: a married mother of small children whose husband's intermittent labor and low wages compelled her to work for family necessities. Although most homeworkers still lived in urban areas, their numbers were growing in places like Bechtelsville. Mrs. Herb represented one community of homeworkers. But there were others – in Italian New Haven, Mexican San Antonio, Black Chicago, and Anglo Appalachia – separated by location, race, and ethnicity, even as they shared the dissolving boundaries between home, work, and community.

How do we understand the self-perceptions of homeworkers, their attitudes toward life and labor? How did homeworkers construct the relationship between home and work? To what extent did ethnic, geographical, or industrial differences matter? Uncounted by census takers, rejected by trade unionists, exploited by employers, homeworkers have been largely hidden from history. They have appeared as the objects, rather than the subjects, of a drama in which their voices were either dismissed or overwhelmed by the confrontation between women reformers, government agencies, social workers, trade unionists, contractors, and other manufacturers. Still they did not go unrecorded. In the published reports of the U.S. Women's and Children's bureaus and state divisions of Women and Children in Industry, and more directly in the original survey interviews of the Women's Bureau and the letters of homeworkers themselves, they interpret their own lives. Often mediated by the agendas of women reformers, whose class and race or ethnicity differed from the homeworkers', these materials nonetheless offer an entrée into communities of homework. We can uncover homeworkers in the matrix of the community and kinship relations that structured their lives.

[1] Mrs. Thomas D. Herb to N.R.A. Homework Committee, June 1934, HC Records, RG9, box 8383, folder "Correspondence."

Figure 13. "Mexican Industrial Home Worker Making Infants' Fine Garments," San Antonio, 1932. Mary Loretta Sullivan and Bertha Blair, "Women in Texas Industries," U.S. Department of Labor, Women's Bureau, Bulletin no. 126 (Washington, D.C.: GPO, 1936). Courtesy of the National Archives. Employers took advantage of the needlework skills of Mexican immigrant women when they offered them homework at increasingly lower piece rates in the 1930s. This image of a homeworking mother replicates the elements present in those framed earlier by Hine: With children by her side, she represents dignity amid extreme poverty.

Communities of homeworkers

In the 1920s and 1930s, the U.S. Women's and Children's bureaus responded to requests by women in related voluntary organizations to study homeworkers.[2]

[2] "Home Work in Bridgeport, Connecticut, December 1919," *WBB*, no. 9 (Washington, D.C.: GPO, 1920); "Industrial Home Work of Children: A Study Made in Providence, Pawtucket, and Central Falls, R.I.," *CBB*, no. 100 (Washington, D.C.: GPO, 1922); Mary Skinner, "Child Labor in New Jersey, Part 2: Children Engaged in Industrial Home Work," ibid., no. 185 (Washington, D.C.: GPO, 1928); Caroline Manning, "The Immigrant Woman and Her Job," *WBB*, no. 74 (Washington, D.C.: GPO, 1930); Caroline Manning and Harriet

In 1931, the Connecticut League of Women Voters and the Consumers' League of Connecticut urged the governor to invite a Women's Bureau investigation of the sewing trades because of the rise in sweatshops under depression conditions. Club women in San Antonio and the Texas State Federation of Women's Clubs requested a few months later a survey of women workers in their state, which included visits to homeworkers. In 1934, the bureau joined with other New Deal agencies to explore southern mountaineer home handicraft.[3]

These reports documented the exploitative nature of homework; they were briefs for its abolition and so presented the homeworker as a passive victim. Hundreds of surviving interview schedules provide a more detailed portrait of homeworker self-perceptions than the published reports. Though paraphrases of the interviewed person predominate over quoted remarks, interviewers expressed biases outright. They were judgmental when it came to evaluating the cleanliness of homes and children, a holdover from an earlier generation's focus on the meaning of homework for the consumer. Through these sources, we can understand more fully how the family economy intersected with the political economy, how women's responsibility for family labor shaped their choices of waged labor.[4]

The demographics of homework remained fairly constant from the turn of the century through the depression. The overwhelming majority of homeworkers were ethnic married women in their childbearing and childrearing years, with another cluster of women over age fifty. Following World War I, 71.3 percent of the fathers of homeworkers in Rhode Island were foreign-born, with about a third Italian. In New York during the mid-twenties, 68 percent of the homeworkers remained of foreign birth; New Jersey had an even larger proportion. By 1934, after a decade of immigrant restriction and the birth of a new generation of white ethnics in the United States, three out

A. Byrne, "The Employment of Women in the Sewing Trades of Connecticut," ibid., no. 109 (Washington, D.C.: GPO, 1935); Caroline Manning, "The Employment of Women in Puerto Rico," ibid., no. 118 (Washington, D.C.: GPO, 1934); Mary Loretta Sullivan and Bertha Blair, "Women in Texas Industries: Hours, Wages, Working Conditions, and Home Work," ibid., no. 126 (Washington, D.C.: GPO, 1936); Bertha M. Nienburg, "Potential Earning Power of Southern Mountaineer Handicraft," ibid., no. 128 (Washington, D.C.: GPO, 1935); Harriet A. Byrne and Bertha Blair, "Industrial Home Work in Rhode Island, With Special Reference to the Lace Industry," ibid., no. 131 (Washington, D.C.: GPO, 1935); "The Commercialization of the Home Through Industrial Home Work," ibid., no. 135 (Washington, D.C.: GPO, 1935).

3 Edith Valet Cook to Mary Anderson, May 6, 1931, RG86, box 8, folder "Bulletins: Conn. State Survey"; Alice S. Besseltien to Mary Anderson, Sept. 14, 1931, RG86, box 11, folder "Texas–1936"; Nienburg, "Potential Earning Power," 7–9.

4 Survey materials for *WBB* 74, *WBB* 126, *WBB* 128, *WBB* 131, and "Home Visit Schedules" for *WBB* 109, all in RG86. I have retained anonymity of interviewees by referring to last initials only. After taking account of interviewer bias, we can find the consciousness of homeworkers in these raw schedules.

of five homeworkers in Rhode Island were native-born, although 56 percent of the adults were foreign, primarily Portuguese, Italian, and French Canadian. Mexicans dominated in Texas; they often were older than their counterparts who labored in other kinds of workplaces. In Chicago the ethnicity of homeworkers nearly mirrored the 1930 census, with 48 percent foreign-born and 50 percent native-born white. At 2 percent, African Americans remained underrepresented. Windy City homeworkers came from twenty-four nationalities, with almost a third either Polish or Italian. Undoubtedly, a large proportion of the native-born urban homeworkers were children of immigrants. In California, the ethnicity of homeworkers reflected the diversity of that state. Among handkerchief hand sewers, a little over half were foreign-born, with Japanese predominating in the Los Angeles area; there were also Chinese, Korean, South and Central American, Mexican, and European immigrant workers.[5]

Family size was generally large. The average number of children in New York during the mid-twenties was 4.7, greater than for the state as a whole. The same was the case for Connecticut in the early 1930s. These families were "not small," with a third having four or five members and another third, six to twelve. Texas and Rhode Island homeworking families in the 1930s also had at least five members, with some up to thirteen. Homeworking women continued to have children under the age of six.[6]

Economic conditions, family composition, and skill levels determined whether daughters or mothers would engage in homework. Among rural whites in the South and Mexicans in Texas, older daughters joined mothers at such labor. About half of the women in the southern highlands were daughters. At least a third of the wives and mothers there had another family member to care for young children, who also did the housework while they tufted bedspreads or appliquéd quilts "sunup till sundown with time off for dinner." This profile contrasted with the one found in districts with southern and eastern European populations, where mothers were the primary homeworkers. Patriarchal restraints and incomplete kinship networks kept immigrant women at home; Appalachian women primarily lacked job opportunities.[7]

    [5] "Industrial Home Work of Children," 11; State of New York, *Third Annual Report of the New York State Commission to Examine Laws Relating to Child Welfare* (Albany, N.Y.: J. B. Lyon Co., 1924), 35; New York State DOL, "Some Social and Economic Aspects of Homework," *Special Bulletin*, no. 158 (Albany: J. B. Lyon Co., 1929) 6; Skinner, "Child Labor in New Jersey," 14–15; Sullivan and Blair, "Women in Texas Industries," 71; Byrne and Blair, "Industrial Home Work in Rhode Island," 10; Ruth White, "Industrial Home Work in Chicago," *Social Service Review* 10 (1936), 42–3; "The Hand Made Handkerchief Industry in Continental United States," 31–2, HC Records, box 8384, folder "Handkerchief, Hosiery, and Infant and Children's Wear."

    [6] "Some Social and Economic Aspects of Homework," 14; Manning and Byrne, "Women in the Sewing Trades of Connecticut," 32; Sullivan and Blair, "Women in Texas Industries," 73, 77; Byrne and Blair, "Industrial Home Work in Rhode Island," 22–3. For comparative purposes, see U.S. Bureau of the Census, *Fifteenth Census of the United States*, 1930, vol. 6, "Families," 228, 220, Tables 14, 5; vol. 4, "Occupations by States," 282, Tables 13, 14.

    [7] Nienburg, "Potential Earning Power," 29.

Immigrant families expected children to contribute to the family economy. Before the 1930s, children under sixteen, the legal age for working permits, aided more often than older children. Few in their late teens exclusively engaged in homework. The age of homeworking minors appears to have shifted upward with the Great Depression because the number of other jobs available to youths from age sixteen into their twenties declined. Child labor always varied with type of homework. While whole families would string tags, assemble flowers, or fasten garters, only the principal homeworker, the mother in most cases, would embroider, stitch neckties, or appliqué quilts. Family composition could determine choice of homework as much as proximity of employers. The nature of the homework and the availability of other employment options, then, determined if children would engage in home labor.[8]

But so did the sex of the child. "Boys don't string tags thats girls work," one eight-year-old boy argued. Girls more often helped their mothers; some, who learned from playmates or adult neighbors, even taught their mothers the work. One mother claimed, "You can't do anything with a boy, but just slap a girl and she'll do it." But girls equally could resist such labor. One confessed to a New York investigator in 1923: "She wished somebody would come and arrest her. She told her mother she was sick, but her mother would not believe her." When asked, " 'Wouldn't your mother let you go outside for an hour in the afternoon to play?' She said, 'No, because my mother knows I would not come back, and I wouldn't.' " Resistance usually took less direct forms. Children complained constantly. They became sleepy. "For spite" they went "slow." They begged not to work, even if it meant a whipping. A twelve-year-old boy spoke of having "the jitters," another strategy to reclaim time from homework.[9]

The vast majority obeyed. Four sisters, ranging from age ten to fifteen, "do not like it but they must to help" – their Polish mother was a widow. One older daughter explained, "Can I sit here and see my mother work hard [and] not help her? Of course they [the employers] think she can do it alone, but she can't." Some mothers enticed their children: "If she don't work, 'don't gets none,'" admitted one who bribed her six-year-old with a very large doll for Christmas. Often illegal, the actual amount of child labor consistently was underreported.[10]

[8] Elizabeth Ewen, *Immigrant Women in the Land of Dollars: Life and Culture on the Lower East Side, 1890–1925* (New York: Monthly Review Press, 1985); Byrne and Blair, "Industrial Home Work in Rhode Island," 9; survey material for no. 131: 4–1–1, 2–1–22; "Industrial Home Work of Children," 16.

[9] Commonwealth of Pennsylvania, "Industrial Home Work and Child Labor," 12, HC Records, box 8389, folder "States (N.C.–Wyoming)"; Survey materials for no. 74: 7–10–23, 7–10–27, 7–10–36, 7–10–57, 7–10–102 (daughters as teachers or chief homeworkers), 7–10–68, 7–10–108 (children's complaints); Skinner, "Child Labor in New Jersey," 18; *Third Annual Report . . . to Examine Laws Relating to Child Welfare*, 56; "Home Visit Schedules": Mrs. A., North Ave., Stratford.

[10] Survey material for no. 74: 7–10–68, 7–10–118; survey material for no. 131: 2–1–7; Jean Flexner and Mary Skinner, "A Study of Industrial Home Work in the Summer and Fall of 1934: A Preliminary Report to the National Recovery Administration," 24, HC Records, box 8387, folder "Reports."

Men engaged in homework as helpers and then usually under extreme economic distress. One disgruntled Rhode Island mill worker in 1934 was "most annoyed at having to sit and pull lace. He could arrange things better if he were President." But men were not always bitter or embarrassed. An Italian foundry laborer, working on short time in 1925, explained his tag stringing: "Best part me & the wife do. . . . Kids can't do much. I like keep my kids nice. Sama that my father keepa me nice." Whereas only 7 percent of New Jersey fathers aided in 1925, the more desperate circumstances of depression Rhode Island found about one-eighth of adult men pulling lace full-time and three-eighths, part-time. When family after family reported outside wage earners as unemployed from layoffs, plant closings, or business failures, nearly a quarter of men and boys did homework. Others helped by transporting materials between employers' premises and the homes of their kinswomen. During the winter, Mexican men joined the rest of their families in shelling pecans in San Antonio.[11]

Lace pulling was customarily woman's work; yet economic circumstances could break through the sexual division of labor, if not patriarchal power. Before the war, fathers were embarrassed at being caught at unmanly pursuits. The pressures of homework – speedup during the rush season, sudden drops in piece rates, new and more complicated patterns for the same rate – could suspend gendered work assignments within families. Recognizing the value of a highly skilled or proficient sewer's labor power, husbands and children relieved mothers of laundry, cleaning, and other household tasks during rush season.[12]

Feeling unable to leave the home, women worked there. "I have 4 small children" was the constant refrain of women when asked for reasons for homework. Those who returned home from factory labor displayed a complex set of motivations. A Romanian woman could not afford the five dollars a week for childcare in the mid-1920s. Christina P. of New Haven sent her four-year-old "baby" to a nursery so she could slip stitch neckties, but the "baby cried mornings when she had to get up. It broke my heart to see her. . . . My baby was too small to make get up when she wanted to sleep." So she "asked the boss would he please give me work at home. . . . I tell him my children need me." Working until midnight or one in the morning, she sacrificed her own sleep rather than make her child conform to the hours of factory life. Although some gave up homework shortly before confinement, more often pregnancy meant leaving the factory. If expectation of proper motherhood led to homework, reducing inadequate wages by a fourth, women had "to let

[11] Survey material for no. 131: 2-1-30; survey material for no. 74, 7-10-70; Skinner, "Child Labor in New Jersey," 16; Byrne and Blair, "Industrial Home Work in Rhode Island," 8; Sullivan and Blair, "Women in Texas Industries," 79.
[12] Byrne and Blair, "Industrial Home Work in Rhode Island," 8; Manning and Byrne, "Employment of Women in the Sewing Trades of Connecticut," 29.

housework go" and call upon sisters to meet deadlines. Depression conditions compelled homework, while the irregular demands of such labor – alternating periods of rush and slack – disrupted at least one component of family labor such women valued.[13]

At home, women could fulfill their duties as mothers. They could look after children, care for illnesses, and cook. They could protect virtue; as one Italian woman explained, "Had kept boarders before. Her oldest girl was growing up. Thought it better, on account of the girl, not to keep boarders any longer." Women spoke of their work in terms of female sacrifice and made claims to this work on the basis of their position within the family. Mrs. Aurora Vileti of New York City asked in 1934 for lace to trim "only for the baby." Violet Gannon from Long Island, "an honest working girl" as she described herself, would "worry all day over my baby. I want to be . . . home and help him grow up the way he should." When threatened with federal bans during the New Deal, most women would list motherhood as the reason why they wished to continue homework. Culturally acceptable, this explanation reflected the position from which they contributed to the family economy.[14]

Children also could mean interrupted labor, which led to a "stretch-out" of the workday well into night. A Mexican woman, who went to her mother-in-law's to sew on a machine, reported that she "works very brokenly when babies are awake" and also "complained she had no *leisure* for house work." This domestic stretch-out, where waged and unwaged labor merged into a continuous flow of activity, partially derived from women's belief that they had to stay home and care for their houses. Angelina B., a fifty-five-year-old mother of seven, felt that "women ought to keep children, clean, cook, and do housework." A necktie stitcher without help from other family members, she preferred homework because "if in factory have to work whether you feel like it or not—if at home, can do housework in a.m. + work on neckties late." Others viewed the demands of homework as incompatible with housework. One Rhode Island lacemaker explained in 1934, "Women who tell they can pull many bands a day don't tell truth. Those who pull many must let their hwk

---

[13] "Home Visit Schedules": Mrs. S., Pembroke St., Bridgeport; Christina P., Adaline St., New Haven; Mrs. A. C., Hallack Ave., New Haven; survey material for no. 74: 7–10–28, 7–10–44, 7–10–55, 7–10–56, 7–10–87, 7–10–88, 7–10–97, 7–10–99, 7–10–104, 7–10–106; 7–10–32 (prefers factory, but baby); 7–10–122 (day-care too costly); 7–10–40, 7–10–74 (quit with childbirth); 7–10–78 (stopped two weeks for babies); 7–10–103, 7–10–105, 7–10–107 (child old enough to do now).

[14] "Home Visit Schedule": Mary I., Olive St., New Haven; J. P., Hill St., New Haven; Mrs. B., Kent Ave., Bridgeport; survey material for no. 74: 7–10–1, 7–10–105. Of 161 letters written to the National Recovery Administration in 1934-35, 23 percent listed motherhood and another 23 percent family economy as reasons for homework. Mrs. Aurora Vileti to O. W. Rosenzweig, Mar. 15, 1934, HC Records, box 8385, folder "Correspondence;" Violet Gannon to General Hugh Johnson, Sept. 19, 1934, HC Records, box 8382, folder "Hmwk spindle."

[housework] go." With housework her first priority, she began "to pull after dinner – frequently works until late at nite."[15]

Most homeworkers accepted wage earning by married women; but preferred that men work. A group of Philadelphia knitters expressed the general attitude: "If regular wage earners were employed they would gladly give up homework as it brought so little income for the time spent and the home duties neglected. They would rather have their husband and grown children employed than eke out a sparse existence on homework."[16]

Although mothering dictated for these women where their labor would occur, the state of the family economy determined that they must earn wages of some kind. The practice had long been common, as we have already seen, among families whose men held unskilled or seasonal jobs. The husbands of Philadelphia's immigrant homeworking women were construction workers, railroad laborers, shoemakers, shoeshine stand operators, and other casual laborers. In 1927 half of New York homeworking families with five members earned less than the $30.00 a week considered necessary to meet a "minimum of decent subsistence." (Husbands' median weekly wages were $28.26.) Nearly half of Connecticut home sewers had husbands who were "irregularly employed," even though a mere 17 percent directly listed financial need as their reason for homework. Only a quarter had wage-earning husbands, some of whom had recently returned to work. By 1934, 35 percent of the fathers in one study of Chicago homeworkers were unemployed.[17]

Some older and disabled women lacked any other options besides homework. Fifty-five-year-old Stella Rock of Chicago explained, "I have no one to help me. I want to make my own way. I just can't get anything to do." Widows who turned to homework, with its meager returns, needed other sources of income. They depended on the earnings of older children, local charity, or, more rarely, mothers' pensions – the meagerness of which forced them to wage earning.[18]

Homework must be seen as a strategy to sustain the working-class family or to increase its standard of living, with the available work passed among kinswomen even if only one woman's name appeared on company records as the employee. Maine women, who obtained women's and children's knitwear through the mails, kept themselves with enough work by registering with more than one firm under several names. Some combined homework with

[15] Survey materials for no. 126: 36, 111, 103, 78, 75, 63, 61; "Home Visit Schedules": Mrs. Emma G., School St., So. Manchester; Jeannie F., Academy St., New Haven; Mrs. A., North Ave., Stratford; Angelina B., Greene St., New Haven; survey material for no. 131: 5–1–17.

[16] Women's Bureau, "Visits to Homeworkers in Philadelphia, 1934–35," May 29, 1935, RG86, box 1603, folder "Industrial Homework – Working Papers – ."

[17] "Some Social and Economic Aspects of Homework," 16–19; White, "Industrial Home Work in Chicago," 48–51. Connecticut figures calculated from surveys.

[18] Stella Rock to N.R.A. Homework Committee, June 18, 1934, HC Records, box 8385, folder "Correspondence"; survey materials for no. 74: 7–10–48; survey materials for no. 131: 5–3–12.

other paid labor: domestic service, laundry, factory sewing, store minding, and sales work, like selling magazines over the telephone or peddling soap through a home buyers club. Others mixed seasonal factory or agricultural labor with homework. One Texas woman canvassed potential customers for laundry bags while waiting in line for inspection of her homework.[19]

Most husbands of homeworkers were resigned to the labor of their wives. One thirty-two-year-old Italian admitted, "I shamed my wife works but what I going to do. Rent high. I don't always work full time." Another revealed that he "did not expect wife to work and she kept it from him for a long time." Yet "he was proud of her fine work & her Italian background." Fathers who adhered to traditional southern Italian concepts of honor approved of their daughters working at home, but refused to allow them to "go to a factory." Some men tolerated homework only because they were unemployed. Hidden from community gaze, homework allowed families to continue the appearance of male breadwinning.[20]

Other husbands objected. Mrs. Arthur L. did not work at night because "husband didn't like her to." Another husband reacted more violently: He "got disgusted at having the work around the house and at the poor pay she earned and at the trouble she had collecting her pay," his wife explained. "He threatened to put the dresses in the furnace one night & then [she] promised not to take the work again." Once when a Philadelphia hand embroiderer "worked hard all day," she "no make my beds up stairs even. Make 20 cents. When my husband come home at night he so mad he could kill me."[21] Homework affronted the breadwinning identity of these men; it underscored their inability to protect wives from exploitation. Labor expended on homework also meant that wives had less time to satisfy the needs of husbands and could not fulfill their duties as housewives. Women's labor in such circumstances benefited employers and not their men. Instead of reinforcing each other, employer interests and husband's needs conflicted when husbands found wage labor interfering with work for the family.[22]

Yet homeworkers performed a tremendous amount of family labor, in part because their households were large, in part because their economic circumstances were meager. The 1925 survey of Philadelphia immigrant women and

[19] Byrne and Blair, "Industrial Home Work in Rhode Island"; Mary Skinner, "Industrial Home Work Under the National Recovery Administration," *CBB*, no. 234 (Washington, D.C.: GPO, 1936), 32; survey materials for no. 74: 7–10–46; materials for no. 126: 44, 109, 43, 59, 70; materials for no. 131: 3–2–22.

[20] Survey material for no. 74: 7–10–7, 7–10–23; "Home Visit Schedule": Mary D. M., Fair St., New Haven; Mrs. Liboria L. C., Charles St., New Haven.

[21] Survey material for no. 74: 7–10–29; "Home Visit Schedule": Mrs. O. C. A., Quinnipiac Ave., Fairhaven; Mrs. Arthur L., Richards St., West Haven; Mrs. R. C. S., Anderson Ave., West Haven.

[22] Heidi Hartmann, "The Unhappy Marriage of Marxism and Feminism: Towards a More Progressive Union," *Women and Revolution: A Discussion of the Unhappy Marriage of Marxism and Feminism*, ed. Lydia Sargent (Boston: South End Press, 1981), 1–41.

their jobs, which interviewed 159 homeworkers, inquired about housework and dependent care. Caroline Manning of the Women's Bureau noted the typical day of pants finisher Mrs. Jeanie B., who baked her own bread and did all her own sewing, including suits for three little boys: "Rise at 5 to get [street laborer] husb. breakfast[,] then sews till 8 & gets child to school – then sews till noon. In p.m. works around house – goes to shop. Can't do all – & was apologetic about her house which was fairly neat & clean." Another woman explained, "I get a piece of cloth, a scissor here, a scissor there, a few stitches, I put it on the child and she walks out the door" – unless a peddler offered her a "cheap little dress." During the rush season, when sewing for money, other women neglected sewing for their families. But by the 1920s many immigrant homeworking women were buying bread and ready-made clothes for children and Sunday best. Others sent out wash, some regularly. Although a few husbands cleaned or cooked, and some daughters aided in the housework, homeworkers generally turned to commercial services.[23]

Homeworkers used earnings to participate in the growing consumer economy, not merely to eke out survival as reformer portraits of exploited victims suggested. Like other working-class Americans, homeworkers sought a more comfortable life. Although many labored to make ends meet and pay emergency bills, some during the 1920s worked to improve their standard of living, often to purchase a house or keep children in school. Their ambition was "to have a nice home," to rent, as did one recent Italian immigrant family of nine, eight rooms with a bathroom and avoid the overcrowding that typified tenement households. Even Mexicans who lived along San Antonio's unpaved streets in the early depression displayed radios, parlor sets, and other fine furnishings that indicated their quest for the good life. Depression conditions hardly ended this desire to improve one's condition. An older married Rhode Island woman claimed to pull lace "to have extra money for amusements." But the economic collapse made such a goal more elusive. As one of many single Mexican women in their early twenties, forced to home labor by lack of alternative employment, complained, "I can't even buy a dress with the money I earn." Another groused, "no clothes & no amusements in past 2 years."[24]

A few sought vacations. Embroidery cutter Mrs. Antoinette C., a forty-two-

---

[23] Survey material for no. 74: 7–10–1, 7–10–99; 7–10–4, 7–10–5, 7–10–27, 7–10–29, 7–10–31, 7–10–98 (bought bread and/or clothes and sent out wash); 7–10–2, 7–10–21, 7–10–53, 7–10–63 (sent out wash); 7–10–21 (gave up sewing); 7–10–9, 7–10–14, 7–10–27, 7–10–33, 7–10–102 (daughters as housekeepers).

[24] Lizabeth Cohen, "Encountering Mass Culture at the Grassroots: The Experience of Chicago Workers in the 1920s," *American Quarterly* 41 (Mar. 1989), 6–33; Susan Porter Benson, "Women, Work, and the Family Economy: Industrial Homework in Rhode Island in 1934," in *Homework: Historical and Contemporary Perspectives on Paid Labor at Home*, ed. Eileen Boris and Cynthia Rae Daniels (Urbana: Univ. of Illinois Press, 1989), 69; survey material for no. 74: 7–10–87; 7–10–33; 7–10–15, 7–10–44, 7–10–56 (for house); 7–10–20, 7–10–23, 7–10–58 (keep children in school, for the home); 7–10–38 (saving to buy a farm); 7–10–49 (save

year-old wife of a stonemason whose eldest two of four children already earned wages, longed for a bank account, but spent her extra money to take her whole family to Atlantic City for a week each summer. Her husband's job for the Reading Railroad cut down transportation costs to a dollar each. "At first they visited a relative, now they take rooms and she does the cooking and the stores are not near, so she doesn't find much rest." The family vacation did not stop family labor. She confided, "I believe in working and I believe in spending." She "used her money to furnish the home and always buys on the club plan, saysa that it only costs 3 cents more on each dollar." Her "well furnished" home contained a kitchen cabinet " – this she enjoys most of all." With the youngest children nine and eleven, Mrs. C. thought about earning even more money by going to work inside a new shop where she could "make terms" because " 'they are going to have a hard time getting experienced operators in this section.' " This was a woman who washed her heavy white bedspreads herself, although she would neglect housework and not bother to undress for the night during the rush season to make maximum money. Her ambition was to "keep the boys in school long as she can" and "to make a home for her family," though her husband drank and "never contributed his full wages." Proper furnishing and vacations belonged to that process. For such wage-earning mothers, consumption existed as a means to an end, not an end in itself.[25]

Though Antoinette C. thought her boys old enough to care for themselves, other homeworkers worried about childcare. Even in the early 1920s, European immigrant families were often incomplete, with the older generation still abroad. Women could not always find kin to aid them, in contrast to southern mountaineers and Mexicans who lived in multigenerational families. Only one Philadelphia woman reported using a grandmother (and one actually left her children in Germany). Another shared a house and childcare with her sister-in-law. But more left babies asleep or had a neighbor or a boarder look after them during trips to pick up or return work. Others could rely on night-working or unemployed husbands to be around during the day. Not all husbands were helpful. When Josephine B., whose neighbor minded her children, waited for hours to get more homework, her "husband scolded – did not want chi[ldren] left with anybody." She "did not take the work again." Women had to devise other networks of mutual assistance. Twenty-seven-year-old Louise P. exchanged work with her neighbor Mrs. C., who also carded safety pins. She scrubbed for the rheumatic Mrs. C. who, in turn, went with her for the hooks or pins and also sometimes picked up the work alone so Louise P. could stay home with her children.[26]

for sickness, buy extra), 7–10–53 (bring parents and children over, save for house); survey material for no. 126: 1, 75a, 90, 101.

[25] Survey material for no. 74: 7–10–24.

[26] Survey material for no. 74: 7–10–21, 7–10–108, 7–10–99, 7–10–7, 7–10–5, 7–10–35, 7–10–110, 7–10–46, 7–10–53, 7–10–100.

Reduced incomes during the depression apparently curtailed the movement of washing and other drudgery from the home. Only a small number
of Connecticut homeworkers had aid with domestic chores and these were
sewers or embroiderers, more skilled women whose labor time at homework
made a difference in earnings. When the husband of Mrs. Rose McS. was
out of work during the fall rush of 1931, he did most of the housework.
Mrs. P., a thirty-two-year-old embroiderer and mother of ten children, had
her own mother and "others" do much of the housework so she could sew.
Mrs. Mary K. put out her wash during the rush season for neckties while
her husband did the housework. When family members contributed little to
the maintenance of family life, they helped by aiding in the actual labor.[27]
Domestic work remained women's work, but the pressure to return homework on time, or risk receiving none in the future, broke through gender
and age barriers. Economic need fractured customary gender assignments
within the family.

Working conditions, worker consciousness

How did homeworkers feel about their work? Italian women held a fatalistic
work ethic: " 'We ask God to give us work & then we get so tired. More
curses go on to the cards than pins!' She laughed at the folly of it all. But still
it was something where otherwise there would be nothing & she felt she
couldn't give that something up." Mexican embroiderers in the early 1930s
displayed a similar resignation. Santos B., a thirty-six-year-old mother of
three separated from her husband, prayed "to God that she can keep this work,
tho it's low in pay – work is very scare – Glad to get any work – is from a
country where there is *no* work."[28]
Among Connecticut home sewers, a few preferred homework either because they were old or never had done any other kind of labor. Some found
more flexibility. Mrs. A "doesn't want to go to the factory – was here with
daughter. Has done home work in N.Y. likes to embroider – saw ad in paper
thought she'd embroider some instead of reading so much." Forty-five-year-
old Mrs. B., who assembled garters with her sister, explained: "At home we
can prepare warm meals. We work longer hrs. but don't have to hustle so. It
saves going out in the bad weather." Seventeen-year-old Julia D. turned to
beading, for which she earned twelve or thirteen dollars a week but worked at
least sixteen hours a day, because her pay of seven dollars at a shirt factory
disgusted her. But her case was unusual; other homeworkers criticized pay
rates and understood their labor as "sweated." A maker of women's dresses

---

[27] "Home Visit Schedule": Mrs. Rose McS., School St., Manchester; Mrs. P., 1st Ave., West
    Haven; Mrs. Mary K., School St., So. Manchester; Mrs. H., Huntington St., New Haven.
[28] Survey material for no. 74: 7–10–99; for no. 126: 28; also, 19, 119, 97, 88.

noted how dresses were "cheaper than ever but more work than ever before on them." Texas embroiderers agreed that employers required more work for less pay.[29]

Embroiderers felt pride in their skill which even poor pay and long hours could not dampen. Among Mexicans, such pride could grow within a familial context: "The work isn't easy. Very, very fine and close. It's not every family that can do the very fine work." Another explained, "never get our work returned to us, we'd be ashamed of that." Connecticut Italians took a more individualistic stance. One recent widow, who had suffered from the stock market disaster, claimed, "like to embroider and thought it would take my mind off of my trouble." Theresa P. relied on her Old World skills to earn extra money: "I was so proud of the luncheon set order. I did it perfect. I wanted to please her [the contractor], so she'd give me more work." Even though she had to withhold work to get paid by this contractor, Theresa P. continued to take embroidery from her because "she has lovely materials & the nicest work of any one in town." Another woman had found embroidery in America "so cheap," nothing like the work in her native Palermo, Italy; "Americans don't pay." Embroidery was also harder on the eyes because in Italy the work took place outdoors.[30]

Southern Appalachian women who tufted bedspreads for commercial firms experienced pleasure, if not in the making of the spreads, then in their aesthetics. Despite the difficulty of the labor and low pay, a forty-five-year-old mother of six who had tufted spreads for three years reported, "Likes handling the color – thinks this is one reason she can get along on the 30 color design so fast – would love to do the work & 'earn a little more, then it would be pleasant.' " In the same breath, such a woman could add, "but 'sitting so long makes my back hurt.' " Tufters complained of calloused fingers and aching limbs, but felt "spread work is the only thing women folks can get to do." Although some preferred housework or fieldwork to handicraft, many would rather avoid work in the sun; most wanted a better paying job, as in a factory, which only a small number actually had experienced before the depression left them unemployed.[31]

Social investigators at the time, as well as researchers following them, labeled homeworkers "unskilled" without questioning the categories by which we define skill. By considering sewing and similar abilities as part of the

[29] "Home Visits": Mrs. A., Sherman Ave., New Haven; Mrs. B., Goddard Ave., Bridgeport; Julia D., Dodge Ave., East Haven; Mrs. Liboria L. C., Charles St., New Haven; survey materials for no. 126: 117.

[30] Survey material for no. 126: 62, 76; also, 74, 113; "Home Visit Schedule": Mrs. M., Howe St., New Haven; Theresa P., Carlisle St., New Haven, attached notes; survey material for no. 74: 7–10–12.

[31] Survey material for no. 128: Handicraft Producers, Mrs. W., Ramhearst 29–c.b.; B. K. D., Tennga, Ga. 43, 44–c.b.; Mrs. S. C., Dalton, Ga. 153, 154–c.b.; Mrs. P., Chatsworth, Ga. 6–c.b.; Mrs. M. O., Chatsworth 3, 4–c.b..

generalized knowledge of womanhood, as a feature of women's culture, and by monetizing value in terms of a sex-segmented and male-dominated labor market, they further devalued the work of homeworkers. A South Manchester, Connecticut, woman made sure she told Caroline Manning that "she knew how to sew in Italy," so she did not have to spend two weeks in the factory as a learner. A slip stitcher relied on her knowledge of the labor process to point out that it took the same amount of labor to complete ties going for sixty-five cents a dozen as for those going for seventy-one cents. Even garter assemblers, like unskilled male workers, could find a sense of pride in their abilities; one boasted, "I'm a fast worker. I have timed myself."[32]

Employers relied upon the skill of these women even as they paid them low wages. One elderly West Haven embroiderer explained: "None of the work is stamped. Home workers have to make the dresses or collars look perfect – even correcting poor factory work." She noted, "They take advantage of homeworkers. You must use all your skill to make the designs very accurate no matter how difficult the pattern & without any stamping. All this takes time and you get nothing – practically nothing, for it – .03¾ cents per dress! They say home workers never count their time." They understood that competition from young, less skilled women, who "did not know about prices or what the work was worth," drove down the piece rate. As one woman put it, "It didn't do you any good to have worked long in a trade & gotten skill." These women knew that they were skilled but that the garment trade refused to reward them. Texas embroiderers also complained that their employers took advantage of their ability to do fine work; so did cloth menders and lace pullers in Rhode Island.[33]

A few women worked at home because there were no other jobs. Their perceptions reveal the social and economic forces – besides responsibility for home and family – that limited women's choices. Mrs. P. "went to several factories . . . I couldn't speak [E]nglish so they didn't want me." Racial stereotypes limited even those immigrant women who spoke English. A labor market divided by race and sex left Mexican women with the worst paying jobs, but only one homeworker expressed anger over how "prejudice" curtailed her possibilities, and she was among the few described as educated and living in an "americanized" bungalow. Some classified by the Women's Bureau as "American white" complained of reverse discrimination. "Don't get work ½ of the time – they give it to the Mexicans," one exclaimed. Overt sexism was another factor, especially against married women and mothers.[34]

[32] "Home Visit Schedule": Mrs. Mary K., School St., So. Manchester; Mrs. Ida S., Haynes St., So. Manchester; Mrs. S., Kent St., Bridgeport.

[33] "Home Visit Schedule": Mrs. M., Campbell Ave., West Haven; Mrs. E. L., Clinton Ave.; survey material for no. 126: 119; Porter Benson, "Women, Work, and the Family Economy," 57.

[34] "Home Visit Schedule": Mrs. P., Pembroke St., Bridgeport; Mrs. L., St. John St., New Haven; Mrs. B., Morse St., New Haven; survey materials for no. 126: 37, 49; Julia Kirk Blackwelder, Women of the Depression: Caste and Culture in San Antonio, 1929–1939 (College Station: Texas A & M Press, 1984).

In explaining, "I want a job that pays something. I'm fitted to hold a job," Mrs. B. suggested that homework was not real work, not a job that one left the home for, that brought dignity as well as wages. Homeworkers' use of phrases like "little," "extra," and "pick up work" indicated knowledge that such labor at best supplemented the wages of those employed outside the home. "Homework is good only for pin money – not to live on," one woman declared. Hidden from public view, homework faded into the domestic realm and appeared even to homeworkers not to be work.[35]

The majority had begun homework prior to the stock market crash of 1929. Half of Rhode Islanders interviewed in 1934 had undertaken homework for ten, and a third, for fifteen years. Yet more than a third of Chicago homeworkers in 1934 were at the work for less than a year. In some cases, the depression triggered the turn to homework, but crisis in the family economy for those living in a homework terrain, surrounded by employers who gave out work and neighbors who engaged in the practice, had led others in earlier decades to take in pants to sew, tags to string, or hooks to card. Indeed, they began because neighbors did such work, because neighbors taught them how to do it, or directed them to the factory. One woman admitted, "I stole my job, I watched other women – followed them."[36]

Many homeworkers grumbled over working conditions, including quality of the materials, work process, and timing of labor. In the 1920s, women would move from one contractor or factory to another, often changing a less desirable for a more promising form of homework. A Romanian woman left after four years making aprons at home because "man made me sick – pay bad – break so much needles – not give enough cotton thread." They distinguished between types of homework, trading off the bad points of one for the less burdensome conditions of another. "Tags do not pay any better than embroidery – in fact not so well, but they require less strict attention to work – thus easier," explained Antoinette C. Describing the hand sewing of ribbon ornaments, Mrs. H. revealed the combined toll of speed-up and manual labor: "Why when they have work they want it gotten out in a minute they keep you so nervous you can't work – calling for the work – then we'll have months with no work – busy fall & spring – sometimes we get so nervous we cry over the work you can't help it – you try so hard to get thru with it."[37]

Women resorted to homework when they were too weak to work in a factory, but they traded one set of health hazards for others. Homeworkers spoke of weak and strained eyes, shattered nerves, sore fingers, tight stomachs,

---

[35] "Home Visit Schedules": Mrs. B., Morse St., New Haven; Mrs. G., Huntington St., New Haven; Mrs. S., Ocean Ave., West Haven; Mrs. O. C. A., Quinnipiac Ave., Fairhaven.

[36] Byrne and Blair, "Industrial Home Work in Rhode Island," 10; White, "Industrial Home Work in Chicago," 46–7; survey material for no. 74: 7–10–1.

[37] Survey material for no. 74: 7–10–61, 7–10–64; "Home Visit Schedule": Mrs. B., Kent Ave., Bridgeport; Mrs. S., Pembroke St., Bridgeport; Mrs. H., Huntington St., New Haven.

and constipation. Mexican embroiderers particularly complained how hand labor hurt the eyes and put pressure on their backs. Carding snaps or pins could injure fingers. One woman put her hand in a bag of pins and pricked her right little finger, which festered. After going to an Italian doctor in the neighborhood, she felt unable to afford further treatment, but the finger got worse. She went to her employer, whose company nurse treated her and then brought her to a private physician who in turn sent her to another, both paid by the employer. The hospital where she finally ended up would not treat her unless the employer guaranteed payment which he would not because "she was not 'inside and therefore not insured.'" She eventually had her finger amputated at an Italian hospital, underwent another operation, and stayed hospitalized for a month. This woman, who with her older children helping only made $2 a week, had to pay the total bill of $160. With numerous children and arduous housework, the strain of homework was too much for some women.[38]

Although perceiving homework as flexible, most could not truly control their labor. The work was irregular, given to meet the employer's time, not the rhythms of family life. They rarely could get the right amount: either there was not enough work or there was too much. Women reported laboring from 4:00 P.M. to 5:00 A.M. to make special rushes and then waiting a month for another batch. They experienced arbitrary treatment. One assembler of snaps complained: "Have to climb 4 flights of stairs for work (50 steps). When you get to the top you are all out of breath. If they would put out a sign 'No Work Today' it would save your climbing, but they never do that." Those who bribed the distributing agent received materials. Some Mexican embroiderers regularly waited hours to have stitches checked before being given another batch, while others were quickly inspected. One woman confessed her impotence: "Examiners take their own pleasure. . . . The girls in the factory think they own the business. They make us lose a whole day waiting for work. I get mad but I know I've got to take the work when they give it to me." If the forelady was your friend, you had plenty of work; if the foreman could not speak your language, you would have trouble following directions. To return a batch undone risked losing future work.[39]

Such waiting gave "the boss your time." Homeworkers recognized how their labor brought wealth to employers. A thirty-year-old garter and lingerie sewer explained, "No one would work inside for what they pay." Her irregularly employed husband added, "They should not let work go out of factories – it pays too little & it deprives some one of work inside." One

[38] Survey material for no. 126: 94, 100, 106, 108, 109, 110, 113, 114, 117; for no. 74: 7–10–99, 7–10–86, 7–10–99, 7–10–86, 7–10–48, 7–10–52.

[39] Survey material for no. 74: 7–10–108, 7–10–98, 7–10–114, 7–10–110, 7–10–113, 7–10–114, 7–10–6, 7–10–98; for no. 126: 34, 76, 92, 93, 117; for no. 131: 1–1–7; "Home Visit Schedule": Mrs. G., Howard Ave., Bridgeport; Mrs. P., Pembroke St., Bridgeport; Mrs. A., Leete St., West Haven; Mrs. D. P., Pembroke St., Bridgeport.

Mexican sewer of infants' handmade dresses from San Antonio, resident in the United States for fifteen years, confessed to feeling "the injustice, they pay so little." She knew that her employers "make good profit. Co. Started 7 yr. ago. Mr. Randolph used to be a cutter. Now they've got a big factory, own big cars, have a beautiful home, & pay the workers very little. Their factories get bigger & bigger & they pay us less & less. We make very little & work so much. We work so hard & make no profits." Laredo embroiderers similarly expressed a class resentment toward their contractor, who paid them less than the rate received from the firm: "We are working for nothing and she is getting rich." The halving of the piece rate in the early 1930s may have fanned such discontent, but even in the mid-1920s a Philadelphia woman argued: "People like me make that factory prosper. If we wouldn't do the work they would have to pay more."[40]

Still many had no collective sense of being. The same Philadelphia woman admitted, "if she could do baby pins all the time might make $1 a day. 'I would feel rich.'" Her protest came in the form of rejecting the speedup, of refusing to work while eating: "I want to sit down to the table & eat like a lady." Another Philadelphia interviewee recalled the extent of strike breaking at a safety pin factory during the summer of 1924 where "a woman stood outside & had a knife & a woman w[ould] come (for homework) and she'd give her a scare (with the knife). But they wouldn't miss a cent because the women weren't all satisfied to have the strike. Some of the women would take the work if they paid 2 cents." Meanwhile the price per hundred cards of pins dropped from a World War I high of twenty-two cents to a dime.[41]

Homeworkers noted how conditions differed from those inside the plants, where workers received more and steadier work. Employers divided the labor process in the factory, but often expected homeworkers to perform many operations and the more time-consuming ones. "Girls inside couldn't make their day rate on turning coat hanger hook covers, so they gave the work to homeworkers," one Connecticut woman recognized. But factories could be stricter places to labor. A Mexican woman compared homework favorably to the factory when condemning her boss: "He's everything else but love, just a miser. Those who work inside are just miserable, no salaries – outside is best, can talk. If talk inside will lose job." But most did not link their working lives to factory workers even though they usually came from families where husbands or children were employed in or sought factory jobs. The nature of the interviews may limit our understanding. But this lack of connection might also reflect a labor market that segregated jobs not only by sex and race or ethnicity but also by kinship position so the unemployment of one's men or even daughters would not appear related to the availability of homework. In

[40] "Some Social and Economic Aspects of Homework," 31; "Home Visit Schedule": Mrs. M., Noble St., West Haven; survey material for no. 126: 88, 93, 4; for no. 74: 7–10–105.
[41] Survey material for no. 74: 7–10–105, 7–10–121.

the home, the site of mothering, homeworkers appeared not to be real workers.[42]

Factory and home labor actually were related, as seen in the six-month strike against the New Haven firm of Arthur Siegman that began in February 1931. One of the runaway New York necktie firms, Siegman employed at least 360 homeworkers. Aided by organizers from Boston, the necktie workers protested a wage reduction and demanded "union hours for union wages." Of the 300 inside workers who turned out, only 100 returned within the first few days when the firm promised not to implement its pay cut. Yet during the spring rush, homeworkers composed between 24 and 29 percent of the work force. Some homeworkers received no work after the rush season ended. One reported that work stopped because of the strike.[43]

Mrs. Gertrude S. learned the hard way that her employer saw homeworkers as an alternative to factory workers and relied upon their labor to check the militancy of those inside. When she tried to get more work from Siegman after having "to give it up because of carbuncles on her back" during the months of the strike, they "refused it—said she was a striker." At least one twenty-three-year-old mother discovered that factory workers saw a connection between her labor and theirs. She feared that the Women's Bureau interviewer "came from union. Says people from union have called on her. Strikers used abusive language to her when she went for work." Abusive language, much of it shouted in Italian, characterized the picket line throughout the strike. In contrast, Mrs. P., a fifty-year-old slip stitcher for "the other necktie place," Stern Merritt Co., lamented the apparent defeat of the strike. She thought that "they'll never get a union in New Haven. 'Would be better if they did – prices would be better—they get twice as much in N.Y. as here for the same work.' "[44]

Siegman practiced a benevolent paternalism. He gave out work "to families who have no other work" – one homeworker explained – while he crushed demands from inside workers who also needed to support families. Personalism dominated relations between employers and employees in the homework system: The same woman who told how the rush made her cry also called her contractor "a wonderful woman. She has fought for better pay for us." Comparing work as a private dressmaker with sewing at home for a company, an Anglo widow from San Antonio noted, "On sewing for a co. you get your

[42] "Home Visit Schedule": J. P., Hill St., New Haven; Mrs. R., Cedar St., Milford; Mrs. Rose M., School St., Manchester; survey material for no. 126: 8, 28.

[43] Manning and Byrne, "Women in the Sewing Trades of Connecticut," 38; "Home Visit Schedule": Mrs. Jane C., Foster St., New Haven; "Tie Strikers Ordered Back Within 5 Days," *New Haven Evening Register*, Feb. 10, 1931 (final edition); "Tie Strikers Deadlocked on Pay Agreement," ibid., Feb. 13, 1931 (city edition); Connecticut Federation of Labor, *Official Proceedings, Forty-Sixth Annual Convention, Sept. 8, 9, 10, 1931* (Bridgeport, Conn., 1931), 31, 43.

[44] "Home Visit Schedule:" Mrs. Gertrude S., Lamson, West Haven; Bertha W., Houston St., New Haven; Thelma V., Campbell Ave., West Haven; Rose G., Peck St., New Haven; Mrs. P., State St., New Haven. On picketing, "Women Fined After Battle in Greene St.," *New Haven Register*, Aug. 6, 1931 (final edition).

money each week, for private work – 'you get it when you can. In the end it's best to work for a co. Co does not pay each one so much, but payroll for home work is from [$]2500 to 3000 each week, that's a big help to San Antonio.'"[45]

Relations between contractors and homeworkers most fully reveal the complex interplay of gender, class, and self-interest within the homework system. Thirty-six of the New Haven interviewees worked at one time for the same contractor, a Mrs. B. As early as 1924 she kept back worker pay with excuses such as New York firms owed her money or sickness in her family made her short of cash. Women would embroider into the night to finish rush orders even though she owed them wages, from a few dollars to over two hundred dollars. They would travel two or more times a week on street cars to collect back wages, spending all they earned in the process, and still take more work. A few stopped after weeks, but many continued to work a year or two after she began cheating them.[46]

Depression conditions and beliefs in women's place may explain why women did homework but are inadequate for understanding why they continued working for such a woman. This contractor relied on the experiences she shared with her employees as a woman – their kin worked as well as directed responsibility for household maintenance – to keep her workers coming back even though she withheld earnings. She was their friend and they felt sorry for her. During her interview with Caroline Manning, Mrs. B. "appealed to sympathy of agent relating all her distressing family affairs." As one woman explained, "Mrs. B's husband doesn't work. Son is just home having been in a sanatorium – daughter married & divorced & re married. Mrs. B's mother died Christmas before last & son's baby died & had to be buried." She went on to assert, "Mrs. B. is a wonderful kind hearted woman, now if people will let her alone & let her pay them little by little they'll gain more than by pushing her." Still this former dressmaker for a "fashionable" firm, who once had known Mrs. B. as her customer, admitted, "her business has gone down & down. I loved her work & would like to take it, but I can't if she's not going to pay." Mrs. James C. reserved her anger for the husband of Mrs. B., whom she believed Mrs. B. had to support. Mrs. B. had told her that he "would be no good in her business because he would be too haughty with the women. 'I'd like to see him be insulting to me!,'" Mrs. C. declared. "He lives in grand style – and why shouldn't he? He's got half the women of New Haven supporting him, that's what he has!"[47]

45 "Home Visit Schedule": Mrs. C., Shelton St., Bridgeport; Florence S., New Haven; Mrs. H., Huntington, New Haven; survey material for no. 126: 60.

46 "Home Visit Schedule": attached note about Mrs. R., Huntington St.; i.e., Mrs. Joseph R., Collins St., New Haven.

47 "Home Visit Schedule": notes on Mrs. B., Distributor of Home Work; attached notes to Mrs. H., Howard Ave., New Haven; Mrs. M., Howe St., New Haven; Mrs. Edward B., First Ave., West Haven; Mrs. Martha T., Pond Lily Ave., Westville; Mrs. James C., Howard Ave., New Haven.

Mrs. B also relied on mutual understandings of gender and class respectability.
Mrs. Gertrude S. recounted how Mrs. B. convinced her daughter, who worked
inside the contractor's shop, not to become the contractor for a manufacturer
who had become dissatisfied with Mrs. B.: She told the daughter "terrible
things about Insler and the girls who worked for him and turned her away."
On another occasion, Mrs. B. drew upon her virtue to defend lack of payment,
saying "she could have or get money if she would accept the attentions, auto
rides, etc. of all the men who made such proposals, but she would not get
money that way." She taunted the father-in-law of one homeworker with
being an ex-saloonkeeper and said she "wouldn't speak to such as he." As if to
cover her unscrupulous and disorganized business methods in a cloak of
gentility, to Manning she "boasted of her blue blood, her preference for
American makers, not foreigners [and] said much of her artistic ability." She
also "refused names & addresses of workers" to avoid embarrassing them
because "many were fine Americans, not ordinary working women."[48]

Homeworker and contractor, then, each saw herself reflected in the other;
the only career ladder in this system for a woman was to become a contractor
and some women were or had been both. Mrs. B. deliberately drew upon this
knowledge, but so did some of her workers in fighting back. Mrs. S., advised
by a foreman friend at a dress company which subcontracted to Mrs. B.,
became very friendly with her, got more material, and then held back delivery
until payment. Others tried this strategy but few recovered the entire amount
owed; many just became sucked into Mrs. B.'s problems. Women were forced
to step outside of any shared work culture and draw upon husbands, fathers-
in-law, and the Legal Aid Society to try to collect wages. As one woman
explained, "My husband has been too, and she pays him more than she'll pay
me at the time." The husband of Angelina S. was not as lucky. She then stopped
working for Mrs. B.: "I had to have money for my work." It took Legal Aid
nearly six months to get her $22.36.[49]

Homeworkers needed their wages; ultimately they quit. Mrs. C. explained
that Mrs. B. "was good to me when I needed money. She was nice to talk to
but I am through with her." Though engaged in individual acts of coping,
these homeworkers were aware of each other. "She owes everybody" was the
refrain. Women said that they would not go to Legal Aid because too many
already were trying that route and they knew Mrs. B. would file for bank-
ruptcy. Despite knowledge that they were not alone, homeworkers never
attempted collective action, though they cooperated with Women's Bureau
agents by supplying names of co-workers.[50]

Homeworking was, after all, a woman's strategy to augment the family

[48] "Home Visit Schedule": attached notes to Mrs. Gertrude S., Lamson, West Haven; Mrs. S.,
Greenwood St., New Haven; interview notes on Mrs. B..

[49] "Home Visit Schedule": Mrs. S., Greenwood St., New Haven; Mrs. S., Sheffield St., New
Haven; Mrs. Angelina S., Carlisle St., New Haven.

[50] "Home Visit Schedule": Mrs. C., Richards St., West Haven; Mrs. H., Walton St., New Haven.

economy. In relation to employers, most were alone: They accepted piece rates on an individual basis, perhaps without precise knowledge of what the employer was giving others for the same work. Some, in fact, never had contact with the employer but instead received material from other family members who worked inside the shop. But they were not isolated. Rhode Island lacemakers who divided work with a partner shared the cost of delivery, an arrangement approved by employers. Makers of knitted women's wear similarly "clubbed together and hired a man to make deliveries for the group" to avoid numerous and lengthy trips to the factory. As Texas embroiderers stood in line waiting sometimes half a day to have their work inspected, they probably exchanged information with others. They knew which contractor paid the best rates or had more interesting work and they probably passed such information on to those closest to them.[51]

In their domestic work environment, homeworkers were rarely alone: Not only did husbands and children aid, but they shared their load with sisters, sisters-in-law, other kin, friends, and neighbors, even in the case of embroidery where each woman sewed her own piece. They lived near each other and often within walking distance of the supply of homework. This is not to speculate that all homeworkers stood in a supportive circle of family and ethnic community. There was the woman who used a suitcase to pick up and return work so that no one else on the streetcar would know.[52] But most provided information on contractors or factories, trained other women, and relied upon the labor power of friends and kin to meet rush jobs. They shared income, work for their family, and labor for their employers.

Black women and paid labor in the home

This exploration of the world of the homeworker has stressed similarities in experience. Italians in New Haven sound like Romanians in Philadelphia or Mexicans in San Antonio. But to what extent did region and race or ethnicity vary the world of the homeworker? No necessary link existed between ethnicity, region, and homework, although Latin immigrant cultures (Italian and Spanish heritage) taught women fine needlework. Certain industries concentrated in specific areas: lacemaking in New England; chair caning and coverlet weaving in the Southeast; buttonmaking in Iowa. Some industries seemed to develop in the vicinity of cheap skilled labor, as embroidery in San Antonio and Laredo, Texas; handkerchief making in the Chinatowns and little Tokyos of California; artificial flower making in New York City. These industrial

---

[51] "Home Visit Schedule": Mrs. A., Hollister Ave., Bridgeport; Mrs. G., Howard Ave., Bridgeport; Mrs. R., Nichols St., Bridgeport; Byrne and Blair, "Industrial Home Work in Rhode Island," 8; Skinner, "Industrial Home Work Under the NRA," 32; survey material for no. 74: 7–10–66; for no. 126: *passim*.

[52] Benson, "Women, Work, and the Family Economy," 63–4; "Home Visit Schedule": Betty C., Whaley Ave., New Haven.

concentrations produced some variations in the daily routine of homeworkers, but so did the economic health of the region, strength of unions and welfare agencies, concerns of organized women, and state capacity to enforce home-work regulations. Still racial divisions in a given labor market influenced which women predominated among homeworkers. "American white" Texas women competed with Mexican embroiderers who "set a speed for all of us," but Mexican women were homeworkers not only because they valued fine needlework and had learned the craft from their mothers and grandmothers, but because other work was closed to them.[53]

The case of African Americans in Chicago during the 1920s illuminates the way that race, and not just immigrant status or ethnicity, set the contours for homework. The cutting off of European immigration, along with the "Great Migration" of African Americans north, turned black women into an available labor force. But homework belonged to a larger tradition among African American women in the post-Emancipation period of using the home as a place for paid labor to remove themselves from the daily supervision of whites. The location of homework – a social space controlled by the black woman or her family – was its greatest attraction. Such home-based labor suggests a counter-theme in the history of African American women: a desire not to leave the home for wages but to be at home with their children despite a labor market that pushed them into white women's homes or into white men's fields. Home-based labor thus belonged to the African American women's quest for freedom but also related to the discrimination that they and their men faced in labor and housing markets.

During the late nineteenth century, northern-financed vocational schools in the South and special trade schools and the public schools in some of the northern states began providing African American women with the general-ized skills necessary for the garment industry. Met with racism in the garment shops from working women and their employers, some certainly tried to obtain home piecework. But, according to NAACP founder Mary White Ovington, "race prejudice has even gone so far as to prevent a colored woman from receiving home work when it entailed her waiting in the same sitting room with white women." Clothing manufacturers fanned racial tensions by hiring black women as strikebreakers during the major New York walkout of 1909–10. Although World War I provided African American women with an opportunity to enter the garment trades, they found themselves in the least skilled sections of the clothing industry; by the 1920s they seemed to have gained a permanent place as semiskilled operatives.[54]

[53] Survey material for no. 126: 107; Evelyn Nakano Glenn, "Racial Ethnic Women's Labor: The Intersection of Race, Gender and Class Oppression," *Review of Radical Political Economics* 17 (Fall 1985), 86–108.

[54] Mamie Garvin Fields with Karen Fields, *Lemon Swamp and Other Places: A Carolina Memoir* (New York: The Free Press, 1983), 33, 55, 62, 63, 87–90, 148–54; Mary White Ovington, *Half a Man: The Status of the Negro in New York* (1911; rpt. New York: Hill and Wang, 1969), 89;

African Americans experienced the economic necessity that brought other groups of women to homework. They also faced the high cost of segregated housing and limited job market of Chicago following World War I. Like immigrant homeworkers, they too were migrants; most came from the major states of the Great Migration during its early phase – Mississippi, Alabama, Georgia, and Arkansas. Like immigrants, many also were long-term homeworkers; about half labored at home for three years or more. Though homework was a short-term strategy for some, for many it was becoming an integral part of the family economy.[55]

The majority of homeworkers previously had worked in the garment trades but in less-skilled and unorganized sections, with over a third in factories or shops and nearly a half in home dressmaking. About one sixth had labored in lampshade factories. They found themselves without work because of discriminatory layoffs. One woman, a milliner, had spent six years at the same factory until layoffs of blacks forced her out. Three mail-order clerks could not retain their jobs after the war and so found themselves doing homework. A few former schoolteachers and a new normal school graduate took up artificial flower making and lampshade sewing. They could not find work in Chicago's schools because of their segregated system or because they lacked educational qualifications. But one preferred "the freedom and glamour of city life and industrial employment" to the more circumscribed life of the small town and rural South. Still others came from the farm, whose daily grind made making lampshades seem easy. "What did I do?" a woman from Pecan Point, Arkansas, answered, "Lawd, I chopped and picked cotton."[56]

Unlike Italian immigrant homeworkers, most of the African Americans lived in relatively high-cost, well-kept-up housing. Only two-thirds were married, and those who were had fewer children than other homeworkers despite being in the prime childbearing and rearing years, from twenty to thirty-five. In over half of the families there were no children. About 40 percent had children below working age. Such a profile suggests either decreased childbearing among the first migrants or that they had left their children with relatives in the South. There was little child labor among African American homeworkers. The reasoning of other homeworkers – to stay home with children – would only hold for a few mothers of small children, widows, and some female heads of households. By itself this

Meredith Tax, *The Rising of the Women: Feminist Solidarity and Class Conflict, 1880–1917* (New York: Monthly Review Press, 1980), 223–6; Nelle Swartz et al., *A New Deal for the Colored Woman Worker: A Study of Colored Women in Industry in New York City* (New York: Charles P. Young, 1919), 8, 14–17; "Negro Women in Industry," *WBB*, no. 20 (Washington, D.C.: GPO, 1922), 12–13, 24.

[55] Myra Hill Colson, "Home Work Among Negro Women in Chicago," unpublished master's thesis, University of Chicago, 1928, 54, 57, 60–4, 70; Allen Spear, *Black Chicago: The Making of a Negro Ghetto, 1890–1920* (Chicago: Univ. of Chicago Press, 1967).

[56] Colson, "Home Work Among Negro Women," 64–8, 84.

family responsibility inadequately explains homework among Chicago's African American women in the 1920s.[57]

An investigator telling of the wife of an ice and coal seller who desired to buy their house offered another explanation: "She wants to help him all she can." Hope for a higher standard of living, along with kin-based obligations, compelled women to homework. Some were sending money back to the South to support elderly parents. Mrs. Z. spoke of working "so they can have some savings" but also noted how "the piece work system and the loose organization of the lamp shade industry allow her to leave home after her little girl is off for school and to return when she is out of school in the afternoon, bringing a few shades with her." She found this flexibility attractive.[58]

These women, then, also took homework because they needed income. Many of their husbands lacked regular employment; they earned wages inadequate to maintain the family. Rents and train fares from the "black belt" further eroded a man's wage. But why did they choose homework rather than the better-paying labor of domestic service, including day work? Homeworking families may have had a larger male wage than average and could afford to keep wives out of domestic service, still the labor of two-thirds of the city's African American women. Twenty-five dollars a week was a common wage for black men in industry; an estimated two-thirds of husbands from homeworking families earned wages at this level or higher. These women may not have needed the wages of service badly enough to put up with its humiliations. They could take advantage of what appeared to be the greater flexibility of homework, when available, and still fall back upon day work for additional income.[59]

Unmarried homeworkers, living with parents or adult children, were not expected to fully support themselves. Others combined homework with taking in boarders, another home-based strategy to generate income common to married women in all racial and ethnic groups. A few others joined homework with factory or day work. The combination of day work and nighttime home needlecraft was not unusual. Still others with children relied on charity, parents, or other forms of labor to supplement their meager homework earnings of between $3.50 and $12.00 a week.[60]

A small number of single women preferred homework. Miss Lelia Smith, a thirty-two-year-old former schoolteacher from Mississippi, was making $13.00 a week, more than her former salary of $37.50 a month, and saving carfare and

[57] Ibid., 70, 90–1, 98, 110.

[58] Ibid., 96–7.

[59] Ibid., 91–2, 94, 95, 100–9; Spear, *Black Chicago*, 151, 155–7; Elizabeth Clark-Lewis, " 'This Work Had A' End': The Transition from Live-In to Day Work," *Working Paper*, no. 2 (Southern Women: The Intersection of Race, Class, and Gender, Center for Research on Women, Memphis State Univ., July 1985), 31.

[60] Elizabeth Clark-Lewis, *This Work Had A' End* (Washington, D.C.: Smithsonian Institution Press, forthcoming); Colson, "Home Work Among Negro Women," 104–8.

time. Mary Miller felt that she could work faster at home than in the factory, where inspectors and lack of materials delayed her. During the slack season, she tried working in a laundry factory but discovered the hours to be too long and the piece rate too low. She made only $2.00 a day for all that hard work, compared to $17.00 to $28.00 a week during the lampshade busy season. She " 'sure likes to make shades' and she expects to continue unless she finds something that fascinates her more." Another woman rejected laundry work for artificial flower making. Others did homework while they were studying to become teachers and one continued while she was waiting for an appointment to teach.[61]

African American women faced a homework system that hardly differed from the one that engaged Italians in Philadelphia, Connecticut, or Rhode Island. Rush seasons ruffled nerves; piece rates declined as the season wore on. As one beader of dresses put it, "You know they pay as little as they can." But unlike immigrant homeworkers, African Americans seemed to quit when prices dropped too low. "Only 3 or 4 foreign women would accept such work," a flower maker of five years noted. African American women had domestic service, a race- and sex-segmented occupation, that they could always fall back upon; they did not have to accept rate cuts that would lower their customary wage.[62]

Like other homeworkers, the African American women could move up the system by becoming contractors. The development of the lampshade industry in Chicago's black belt in the early twenties provided new opportunities. Manufacturers established "branch factories" under black workers who acted as contractors, training neighbors in the process of covering a parchelite shade with muslin or placing a lining in a silk shade, pleating, and sewing the entire product. The contractors would also give out work to homes. Some women who worked in factories by day took home additional shades at night. In this way, the number of workers increased so that by 1926 prices stood at about half of their former rate.[63]

Here too female contractor and female homeworker shared cultural values and social circumstances, but not without tensions. Mrs. A., a contractor, confessed, "It was very difficult to make colored girls understand that a colored woman could be fair to them." She claimed to act in the interest of workers against the company: timing the rate given to new shades to insure that the rate was fair and keeping a shade from being made "until the factory agreed to raise the rate even if it were no more than five or ten cents. She would tell the manufacturer, 'You'll have to send for these shades. I'll not be guilty of giving them to the girls.' "And when the manager would remind her that she received her commission (ten to thirty cents a shade) anyhow, she "would rejoin: 'I can't

[61] Colson, "Home Work Among Negro Women," 72–3, 74–84, 86–7.
[62] Ibid., 94, 86–7, 78.
[63] Ibid, 43–52.

be guilty of taking bread out of children's mouths.'" This woman listed shade rates on the wall for workers to consult, an unusual practice for any contractor, and claimed to pay the same as the factory. While she exhibited a sense of race and gender solidarity with her employees against the "outside" manufacturer, other contractors seemed more concerned "to get [their] own," especially as conditions in the industry deteriorated during the decade.[64]

Social workers questioned whether Southern blacks could adapt themselves to industrial, urban life. Myra Hill Colson, who investigated "Negro Homeworkers in Chicago" for her master of arts thesis, wondered whether homework could function as "a stepping stone to a more stable place in factory industries," which she judged – as did the Women's Bureau – superior to work in the home. A black YWCA secretary, Colson viewed African American homeworkers more positively than Women's Bureau agents looked at their immigrant counterparts. She noted that "the Negro woman home worker . . . is not a type such as the picture of the early 'sweater' recalls. She does not live in filth. Her surroundings are fairly comfortable. She does not work incessantly. She is conscious of a need of relaxation and rest. Home work for her is a means of aiding her to attain a slightly higher standard of living or a freeing her from the routine of factory work."[65] Although all homeworkers sought to raise family living standards, African American women presented a different profile from that of the immigrant. Racial discrimination more narrowly determined their place in the work force. In this larger social, cultural, and economic context, home-based labor appeared as the best of a set of bad options.

The impact of the Depression

The economic collapse of 1929 intensified the exploitation of homeworkers. Between 1929 and 1933, homework increased and earnings dropped lower. In Chicago, more than a third of those working forty to fifty hours received less than three dollars a week; a quarter earned less than 6 cents an hour, with nine cents the median. In late 1934, nearly 25 percent of homeworking families admitted to being on the relief rolls, about 10 percent more than the Cook County population in general. Most of this homework concentrated in auxiliary garment processes, like art needlework, women's neckwear, and embroidery. Carding bobby pins reflected another fashion trend. In contrast, New York experienced a decline in homework, as production slackened in the garment industry. Despite the decrease in the amount of homework, more people sought it. Some turned to homework after being laid off from factory or clerical employment; others to replace earnings lost through the unemployment of husbands and children. New York's Division of Home-

[64] Ibid., 44–6.
[65] Ibid., 118–19.

work Inspection claimed "fraudulent mail order houses" had cheated thousands by circulating brochures to "women all over the country, promising easy work and high pay on receipt of a deposit for materials which are never sent."[66]

Other states reported similar trends. Sixty percent of California handkerchief sewers had begun with the depression; over half of them could not find the factory jobs that they preferred. In 1931, two-fifths of Pennsylvania's homeworkers reported taking up the work since January 1930; in Philadelphia the number of unemployed wage earners was twice as high among homeworking families. Despite depressed business conditions, Pennsylvania reported during 1931 only a 7 percent decrease in homework, with intensified concentration in men's clothing. More firms sent knitting into the state. Meanwhile, depression conditions encouraged manufacturers to ignore labor standards, reducing enforcement since the State Department of Labor lacked adequate resources to confront such wholesale disregard of the law. Violations of the child labor law, which prohibited homework, nearly doubled to 18.8 percent of total investigations. Hourly earnings had plummeted 25 percent since 1928, while factory workers had seen their wages drop only 4.2 percent.[67]

Many homeworkers had been poor throughout the preceding decade. They felt the depression to be more of the same, perhaps worse. Unable to afford electricity, they curtailed work after dark or turned to kerosene. Certainly San Antonio and Laredo homeworkers suffered from their employers' drives to slash costs by lowering the wage bill. Embroidery that brought $8.00 dropped to $4.50 a dozen; dresses at $3.00 went down to $1.10. "When rates were better didn't have to work so hard – now work every minute trying to make a living," one thirty-five-year-old Mexican mother complained. But she was among the lucky ones. Blaming the depression, other women reported lack of work for the first time. One who sewed for Joseph Love Co., a New York firm whose San Antonio branch had four hundred homeworkers, thought that company favored inside employees. With work scarce, many women would embroider all day on the first floor of the plant, without factory supervision, "in order to get all that they can do." Economic pressure pushed companies to seek even cheaper labor. One who took out work from the Juvenile Manufacturing Co. explained, "Co. has a branch in Laredo, if women here refuse the work because it's too hard or pays too little, they send it to Laredo." One Laredo contractor smuggled the work

[66] White, "Industrial Home Work in Chicago," 24–6, 33–9, 42, 56; Frieda S. Miller, "Industrial Homework During Business Depression," *The Industrial Bulletin* 11 (Feb. 1932), 132–4; State of New York, *Annual Report of the Industrial Commissioner for the Twelve Months Ended December 31, 1930* (Albany, N.Y.: J. B. Lyon Co., 1931), 16.

[67] "The Hand-Made Handkerchief Industry in the Continental United States," 33; "Industrial Home Work in Pennsylvania in 1931," *Monthly Bulletin, [Pennsylvania] Department of Labor and Industry* (Nov. 1932), 3–6.

across the border, paying the women in Mexico 25 percent less. Caught twice and fined, she no longer handled work for San Antonio firms.[68]

In depression Rhode Island, workers who had steady jobs became causalized, turning to home lace pulling. A West Warwick lace puller had seen her husband's pay reduced by half; they had to cash in the children's insurance to buy fuel for the winter. Some lost personal possessions, including houses, along with jobs. The only income of one retired couple, whose investments had disappeared with the crash, came from lace. Longtime workers faced mill closings, while young people could not find factory employment. Elizabeth H. had mended fabric in a worsted mill for almost thirty years; she "never expected such a thing [as the mill closing down] could happen." No alternative factory work was available; many had to turn to the government for relief.[69]

Home mending allowed mills to transfer some of the burdens of their falling businesses onto workers by paying less for time-consuming labor. These mills took advantage of skilled, but slow workers, a factor that became more of a concern with the National Recovery Administration (NRA) codes that set minimum wages. With difficult work out of the factory, conditions inside improved, lessening the possibility of worker resistance. The depression emboldened bosses; mills demanded women become contractors as a precondition for work. Arbitrariness had little check since so many needed income.[70]

The New Deal tried to transform homeworkers' lives. Many benefited from various relief agencies like the Federal Emergency Relief Administration, Works Progress Administration, and the Civilian Conservation Corps. With a portrait of Franklin Delano Roosevelt on her kitchen wall, a rural Rhode Island mother of three "wish[ed] she could help Pres. 'Poor man is working so hard, people don't appreciate him.' " Yet many feared government regulations would further impoverish them. A lace puller from West Warwick complained that the minimum wage was too high for her sixteen-year-old daughter to find full-time work. Another woman saw New Deal regulations reducing her husband's hours, forcing her to take in lace to make up the difference.[71] These lace pullers experienced firsthand employer stratagems to negate codes of fair competition worked out under the NRA that promised to bring all workers minimum wages, maximum hours, and better working conditions. Many of the codes also promised to end or curtail homework. Whether the NRA would represent homeworkers, however, was problematic. Whose visions and voices would be heard with the gendered construction of the welfare state was no settled question.

[68] Survey material for no. 126: 62, 72, 49, 35, 26, 31, 60, 97, 104; Factory schedules for Joseph Love Inc., Juvenile Manufacturing Co., Texas Infants' Dress Co., and Randolph Kohlman Co., RG86, box 1287, folder "Texas Clothing – Children and Infants."
[69] Survey material for no. 131: 3–2–21, 5–1–8, 1–1–5, 1–1–12, 5–1–26, 5–3–15, 3–2–12, 3–2–6, 5–3–6, 5–3–5 (on relief); 2–1–12 (loss of home).
[70] Survey material for no. 131: 5–3–6; Benson, "Women, Work, and the Family Economy."
[71] Survey material for no. 131: 5–1–17, 4–1–13, 5–3–10, 1–1–14.

PART III

(En)gendering the New Deal

Figure 14. "Cracking Down," *Chicago Tribune*, Aug. 1, 1934, © copyright 1934, Chicago Tribune Company, all rights reserved, used with permission. Portraying Roosevelt's brain trust as ready to club a poor defenseless mother with NRA prohibitions against industrial homework, this cartoon sensationalized the case against Kathryn Budd, who defied the NRA ban. Its image of the state against motherhood dominated the employer defense of homework during the 1930s.

7

"To improve on business through law": Homework under the National Recovery Administration

In 1934 Kathryn Budd, a thirty-four-year-old deserted mother of two, sued the National Recovery Administration (NRA) for prohibiting her from making artificial flowers at home. Asking "What harm can it do anyone if I work in my room and make a few dollars a week to keep a home together for my children?" Budd challenged the right of the New Deal to ban industrial homework. Defended by the employer-created Homework Protective League and supported by much of the anti–New Deal press, Budd presented herself as the embodiment of wronged womanhood: "I earned that money working in a clean, sunny room in my own home, working about 5 hours a day and having plenty of time for my housework. If the blue eagle code provisions continue, I must go to work in some loft – if I can get a job – and my children, perhaps, to an orphanage."[1]

Budd and her defenders viewed the homework ban as an infringement on a woman's right both to work and to care for children, but social planners and women reformers thought the NRA codes a powerful tool to sweep away the evils of homework. In the eyes of most New Dealers, industrial homework curtailed factory employment, undercut wage and health standards, and lowered family purchasing power – impeding the recovery effort. Equally important for the Women's Bureau, such labor commercialized the home, undermining the "normal demands of home and children upon the housewife and mother." Restricting industrial homework through the NRA codes of fair competition would bolster factory employment and would ultimately aid the New Deal to put "the forgotten man" back to work. It would enable millions to earn the long-sought family wage. By making homework less profitable, regulation would prove a powerful first step toward abolition, now the clear goal of women reformers.[2]

The ban on homework in 101 of the 556 NRA codes (and its restriction in another 17) represented the federal government's first regulatory effort since

---

[1] *Washington Star*, May 14, 1934, 1. This article spells Mrs. Budd's name "Katherine"; for consistency I have used the spelling in the caption for Fig. 14.

[2] "The Commercialization of the Home Through Industrial Home Work," *WBB*, no. 135 (Washington. D.C.: GPO, 1935), 33.

World War I.[3] Under the National Industrial Recovery Act of 1933, tripartite governing boards, composed of representatives of business, labor, and government, developed codes of fair competition to regulate and encourage business activity. Only section 7(a) of the act – which mandated inclusion of labor standards for minimum wages and maximum hours and encouraged collective bargaining – dictated the content of the codes. The NRA provided a structure for competing interests – organized labor, small and big business, consumers, government administrators, and reformers – to stabilize production in a collective fashion. The homework bans were crucial in achieving that end.[4]

That homework prohibition became a standard labor provision reveals the power of "the New Deal network of women" and their coalition with labor leaders. Composed of social workers, Progressive reformers, women in the federal and state departments of labor, members of the National Consumers' League (NCL) and the Women's Trade Union League (WTUL), and Democratic party stalwarts, network women were a distinguished group. Many were college-educated and married or widowed, although some of the most important were single, living with other women. They defined themselves as pro-labor and opposed the Equal Rights Amendment as a threat to protective labor legislation for women. By the 1930s, some felt it possible to push for general labor standards while keeping protections for women when necessary. In short, they were the inheritors of Florence Kelley's vision. Those in state bureaucracies remained crusaders for the cause, for which they deployed expertise in labor economics and social investigation. Led by Eleanor Roosevelt, Secretary of Labor Frances Perkins, and Democratic National Committee Women's Division chief Mary (Molly) Dewson (former executive secretary of the Consumers' League of New York [NYCL] and drafter of the *Adkins* brief), the network played a key role in shaping New Deal social-welfare policy.[5]

In their search for industrial justice, the women's network targeted homework as an industrial practice most detrimental to labor standards. Some employers argued for the NRA as a means to raise production, end unemployment, and stabilize industry. However, the network claimed the abolition of homework and child labor its "two main propositions," with homework

[3] O. W. Rosenzweig, "NRA and Industrial Homework," Mar. 19, 1936, chap. 2, 2, typescript, HC Records, box 8387, folder "Reports."

[4] Ellis W. Hawley, *The New Deal and the Problem of Monopoly: A Study in Economic Ambivalence* (Princeton, N.J.: Princeton Univ. Press, 1966); Theda Skocpol, "Political Response to Capitalist Crisis: Neo-Marxist Theories of the State and the Case of the New Deal," *Politics and Society* 10 (1980), 155–201; Donald R. Brand, *Corporatism and the Rule of Law: A Study of the National Recovery Administration* (Ithaca, N.Y.: Cornell Univ. Press, 1988); Rhonda F. Levine, *Class Struggle and the New Deal: Industrial Labor, Industrial Capital, and the State* (Lawrence: Univ. Press of Kansas, 1988), 64–136.

[5] Susan Ware, *Beyond Suffrage: Women in the New Deal* (Cambridge, Mass.: Harvard Univ. Press, 1981); Susan Ware, *Partner and I: Molly Dewson, Feminism, and New Deal Politics* (New Haven, Conn.: Yale Univ. Press, 1987); Robyn Muncy, *Creating a Female Dominion in American Reform, 1890–1935* (New York: Oxford Univ. Press, 1991).

elimination perhaps the "more important." Such a difference of emphasis reflected not merely gendered perspectives; this group of reformers carried forward the social justice traditions of the Progressive Era to harness the power of the state for those thought to need the most protection, women and minors. Trade unionists sought to rationalize capitalism through collective bargaining but maintain the structures of social life. By bringing the state into the home, these New Deal women hoped to improve the conditions of working women, restoring the separation between home and workplace.[6]

During the 1930s, whether to regulate or to abolish homework generated a sharp debate over women's place within the political economy. Motherhood as symbol and reality continued to shape that debate. But a competing discourse of rights and fairness, grounded in economic rather than familial terms, came to the forefront. Fighting homework belonged to the larger quest for labor standards; gendered and ungendered at the same time, homework provided a major arena upon which to address questions of hours, wages, general working conditions, and unionization. Its regulation reflected the economic realities and political possibilities of the New Deal. The state served as a space of contention between contractors, manufacturers, trade unionists, reformers, and men and women within various government agencies; the gendered assumptions of these various groups, including homeworkers themselves, colored responses to the economic crisis.

The NRA experience illuminates the difficulty of regulating homework through the will of the state even when shifting economic circumstances contained the possibility of doing so. The ultimate failure of the NRA to end homework in many trades questions the effectiveness of detailed centralized planning when an industry lacks either an employer- or union-generated center. The extent of homework prohibition in the NRA codes testified to how strongly many employers felt about the potential of homework to undercut their profits. But homework employers were able to thwart regulation through stays of code provisions and inadequate administration. For unlike oligopolistic industries (like coal and automobiles) or ones with strong trade unions, garment-related trades were highly decentralized and on the periphery of economic life. In its need to define units for code making, the state created many of these "industries." It turned a number of disparate processes – machine and hand, factory based and home located – into a single entity whose component parts had conflicting interests. Industry definitions provided a loophole for unwilling employers; as we shall see, they also fueled the debate over whether craft or sweated labor dominated a trade. Meanwhile, homeworkers had less reason to applaud the NRA; compared to other workers

[6] Rose Schneiderman, "Infants' and Children's Wear Industry," Dec. 5, 1933, Night Session, 387, NRA TH, 217–105; Christopher Tomlins, *The State and the Unions: Labor Relations, Law, and the Organized Labor Movement in America, 1880–1960* (New York: Cambridge Univ. Press, 1985).

who found in it the promise of higher wages or unionization, they looked forward to losing their jobs.[7]

Although administered from Washington, the NRA built upon the trade association idea. It consisted of hundreds of particular regulations, organized by quite specific industries that were defined inconsistently by product, market, and process. The NRA Homework Committee and the women of the Department of Labor attempted to impose consistency upon the parochial interests of industry groups, but the NRA lacked a universal quality which made that more difficult. For the policy of homework regulators did not necessarily meet definitions of industry health put forth by associations of manufacturers, who were by the very design of the recovery act to have a dominant say in the construction of the codes. Yet what happened in one region or sector of industry often influenced the overall economy. This interlocking reality, despite the separate concerns of individual industries, was nowhere more apparent than in the political economy of homework in Puerto Rico. The NRA experience there illuminates the role of homework, sent out by mainland firms, in an international labor process – based on class, national, and sexual domination – that would intensify during the late twentieth century.

The need for labor standards

The U.S. Bureau of Labor Statistics reported the grim tale of the economic slump: Despite a 20.3 percent decrease in the cost of living between June 1929 and June 1932, manufacturing workers had their wages reduced on average by 49 percent. Sweatshop conditions proliferated in the clothing industry. In New York, women's clothing operatives saw their weekly wages reduced by $6.01; their counterparts in men's clothing lost $3.64, 20 cents more than the average reduction for all industries. Not only did "gypsy garment shops" move from location to location without ever making a payday, but work like infant's dresses, which had gone into the factory, returned to the home.[8]

Still no accurate count of homeworkers existed. The NRA Homework Committee calculated 154,000, allocating two homeworkers a family, on the basis of a U.S. Department of Labor estimate of at least 77,000 homes in 1930. Homework defenders claimed at least a million. Whether such estimates marked a decline in homework was difficult to determine. On the basis of its annual inspections of tenement houses in large cities, New York in 1932

---

[7] Stanley Vittoz, *New Deal Labor Policy and the American Industrial Economy* (Chapel Hill: Univ. of North Carolina Press, 1987).

[8] Bureau of Labor Statistics figures cited in *Bulletin*, CLNJ, Dec., 1932, 1, WTUL Papers, reel 70, frame 674; see also, WTUL, *Sweat-Shop News*, Jan. 1933, WTUL Papers, reel 70, frame 678; "Gypsy Sweatshops," editorial, Washington, D.C., *Daily News*, Nov. 15, 1932, WTUL Papers, reel 70, frame 659; "Material Prepared for Miss Miller for L.W.V. Meeting – Detroit, April 15, 1932," RG174, box 63, file "Minimum Wage – General, Feb. – July, 1933."

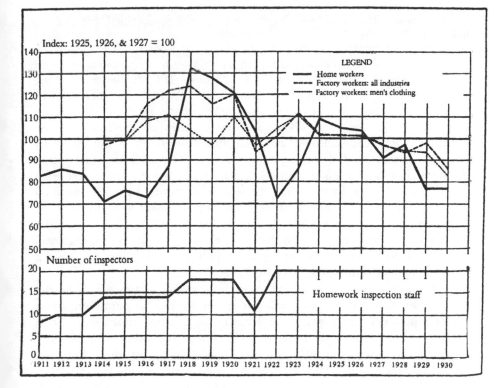

Figure 15. Trend of homework compared with factory work and relation to inspection staff, 1911–1930. *Source*: Frieda S. Miller, "Industrial Homework During Business Depression," *The Industrial Bulletin* 11 (Feb. 1932): 132.

recorded a drop in homework that followed "the downward trend of the curve of factory work, with a more precipitous decline in recent years." Because the number of inspectors had grown in the 1920s, the decline since 1911 was probably even greater (see Figure 15). Men's clothing, with more than a quarter of all workers, remained foremost in New York City, followed by novelties (including beads and flowers), with a fifth of the work force, and then embroideries. In the state, glovemaking was the second largest, with men's furnishings (especially neckwear), third. Because homeworkers on children's wear lived in upstate dwellings not covered by the law, they were uncounted. Official tabulations left out thousands until state law changed in 1935.[9]

The NCL took the lead in marshaling reform and labor forces to confront

[9] Rosenzweig, "NRA and Industrial Homework," 21–4; "Commercialization of the Home," 15; Anna Hochfelder to Donald Richberg, Oct. 1, 1934, HC Records, box 8384, folder "Homework Protective League"; Frieda S. Miller, "Industrial Homework During Business Depression," *The Industrial Bulletin* 11 (Feb. 1932), 132–4.

the breakdown of labor standards. Among labor leaders Amalgamated Clothing Workers of America (ACWA) president Hillman was nearly alone in promoting government interference in the labor contract. The American Federation of Labor (AFL) still clung to its philosophy of voluntarism, with the International Ladies' Garment Workers Union (ILGWU) embracing the idea of the WTUL for a new consumers' label. WTUL member Eleanor Roosevelt called for "better organization amongst the employers and better organization amongst the workers in order to keep up standards that are good." Nicholas Kelley, chair of the NCL Board of Directors and son of its recently deceased leader, justified reform action: "The leadership of business does not know what is good for itself. It is for the reformers . . . to impose on business through law the stabilizing elements that business has been unwilling to bring in for itself." Some saw the economic crisis as opening the way for enactment of the league program. Certainly Frances Perkins, then New York's industrial commissioner, believed that with the support of state officials and legislatures, reformers could convince the public that homework impeded community economic health and so gain legislation.[10]

In December 1932, the league called a national conference "On the Breakdown of Industrial Standards" attended by fifty organizations from twelve states, including members of departments of labor from Connecticut, New York, Massachusetts, Pennsylvania, and New Jersey, and the U.S. Women's Bureau. Also present were the National Child Labor Committee (NCLC), WTUL, ILGWU, labor and reform editors, church organizations, the League of Women Voters, National Council of Jewish Women, National Organization for Public Health Nursing, and representatives from various local consumers' leagues – groups belonging to a larger social welfare movement. Participants shared deteriorating conditions, problems with existing legislation, underfunded enforcement, and uncooperative courts. They deplored the undercutting of men by women. In the midst of public pressure to exclude married women from jobs, they proposed legislating higher wages rather than denying women jobs. Encouraged by trade unionists, reformers resolved to work for union labels in the needle trades and to pressure retail stores not to sell goods made under "sub-standard conditions" – the old strategy of the NCL. Throughout the decade, state labor law administrators reaffirmed the NCL program.[11]

---

[10] "Memorandum – December, 1932," ACWA Papers, 82/8; "Identification Label for Women's Clothes," *Life and Labor Bulletin*, home edition, WTUL Papers, reel 70, frames 721–4; "Mrs. Roosevelt Joins in Move Against Sweatshops for Women," *Union Leader* (Chicago, Ill.), May 6, 1933; NCL, *Conference on the Breakdown of Industrial Standards*, New York City, Dec. 12, 1932, 21, 12, 16, CLM Papers, box 15, folder 245.

[11] Molly Dewson also defended black workers from charges of undercutting wages made by southern delegates. NCL, *On the Breakdown of Industrial Standards*, 21–46, esp. 42, 36–7. See, in addition, "Recommendations of Second Interstate Eastern States Conference on Uniform Labor Laws, Jan. 27–28, 1933"; "President's Conference with Governors, March 6, 1933," both RG174, box 59, file "Labor Standards 1933–34."

The handling of homework laws in the midst of the general breakdown of labor standards was emblematic of the entire regulatory process. In the minds of reformers, homework inextricably connected to the general question of hours and wages even as it blighted the lives of women and children. The director of New Jersey's Bureau of Women and Children reported losing inspection duties to the Department of Health where "they will do it as it was done in the past – not at all." New York's Frieda Miller noted reasonable effectiveness in inspecting tenements, "still we have not come to the kernel of the situation" – the wage question. Florence Kelley had contended that equalizing rates paid in the home with those in the factory was the only way to solve the homework problem. Yet it was nearly impossible to check the number of hours worked.[12]

NCL endorsement of the eight-hour day and forty-four-hour week was hardly radical when Congress was considering an AFL-sponsored thirty-hour week bill and when much of American industry was running less than forty-eight hours a week. Depression conditions justified gender-inclusive and state-mandated labor standards; they provided a reason for extending minimum wage and maximum hours laws to men as part of the police power of the state. At its first conference on labor standards in 1934, the new Division of Labor Standards endorsed minimum wages for men as well as women, whenever possible. Still those who had built the case for labor standards in terms of women and minors were cautious. Dewson warned of the Supreme Court's reaction. Rose Schneiderman, president of the WTUL, and Mary Anderson urged if laboring men were unready to support legislation covering their sex – and the AFL had traditionally gone on record against such laws for men – "no committee should hold up legislation for women."[13]

Such laws no longer were necessary merely to protect the weak and dependent; raising wages and shortening hours could fight the economic crisis. Eleanor Roosevelt explained in *Scribner's Magazine*: "Limiting the number of working hours by law has a twofold result. It spreads employment, thereby giving more people work, and it protects the health of workers." Whereas some supporters of shorter hours for women and children argued in terms of "human rights above private profits," others spoke in economic terms. Alabama senator Hugo Black advocated a thirty-hour work week for men and women to "share the work" and counter those who merely asked for voluntary reductions by business. The Black bill, the one drawn up by the AFL, called for a six-hour day for five days a week. It passed the Senate in early April 1933.[14]

---

[12] NCL, *On the Breakdown of Industrial Standards*, 26–8.

[13] I have considered the shift to sex inclusive labor standards in "Quest for Labor Standards in the Era of Eleanor Roosevelt: The Case of Industrial Homework," *Wisconsin Women's Law Journal* 2 (Spring 1986), 53–74.

[14] Mrs. Franklin D. Roosevelt, "The State's Responsibility for Fair Working Conditions," *Scribner's Magazine* 93 (Mar. 1933); 140; "Governor John G. Winant of New Hampshire," RG174, box 81, file "Women General"; Benjamin Kline Hunnicutt, *Work Without End: Abandoning Shorter Hours for the Right to Work* (Philadelphia, Pa.: Temple Univ. Press, 1988), 147–58.

By then, the Roosevelt administration was focusing on wages as a remedy against the depression. The belief that underconsumption precipitated the depression would pervade New Deal thought. This proto-Keynesianism stressed spending and full employment: Although hours reduction certainly would have spread work, unless wages were enhanced, purchasing power would remain too low to jump start the economy. As the new secretary of labor, Frances Perkins submitted to Congress amendments to the Black bill that essentially represented this alternative strategy. She proposed a thirty-hour work week, with exceptions for industries needing flexibility, but also minimum wage boards under the department, relaxation of antitrust provisions, and supervision of "binding" trade agreements. These were the key elements of what soon would emerge as the NRA. Yet here also was Florence Kelley's adaptation of the British Trade Boards, the twenty-year campaign of women reformers for minimum wage federalized and gender-neutral.[15]

This entire quest for labor standards depended on the regulation and eventual abolition of industrial homework. Reformers long had argued that homework regulation would protect the health of women and children. In the 1930s, homework legislation became linked with the larger political economy. Allowing homework to exist, the NCLC argued, "would make the maintenance of maximum hour and minimum wage schedules and the prohibition of child labor practically impossible." Conferences of the Division of Labor Standards, which institutionalized the NCL agenda, called for the elimination of homework by whatever proved "most effective" – state regulatory legislation, interstate compacts, the NRA codes, or other federal legislation. Perkins explained that "the trick of manufacturers of sending work to be done in homes at low wages is breaking down our standards in some industries." In numerous meetings throughout the decade, the Labor Department included industrial homework among its issues; the restriction of homework became another device to improve overall working conditions.[16]

Although classifying homework regulation under the gender neutral category of labor standards, reformers well understood homework to be a form of women's work. Descriptions of the homework system explicitly recognized the gender of the homeworker, often conflating woman with mother. The 1936 Conference on Labor Legislation noted, "we issue a certificate to a home

---

[15] NCL, *On the Breakdown of Industrial Standards*, 20; Hunnicutt, *Work Without End*, 147–73; Vittoz, *New Deal Labor Policy*, 81–6. Commentators on NRA origins neglect the influence of women's labor law and the network of women reformers.

[16] "Second Interstate Eastern States Conference," 1–3; Courtney Dinwiddie to General Hugh S. Johnson, Aug. 16, 1933, with attached Memorandum, box 14, file "Child Labor 1933"; U.S. DOL, "Agenda: Labor Legislation Conference," Feb. 6, 1935, box 40, file "Conference-Washington"; DOL Division of Labor Standards, "Southern Regional Conference on State Labor Legislation," 1935, box 4, file "Conferences-Southern"; DOL, Press Release on Fourth Annual Labor Conference, Oct. 27, 1937, box 39, file "Conference-National," in RG174.

worker to do a certain piece of work *herself,*" but women have their children or neighbors help "regardless of the conditions on *her* certificate which make such assistance illegal" (emphasis added). This report concluded, "The woman – and it usually is a woman who works at home – is least able to bargain for the maintenance of her labor standards." The women of the Department of Labor used homeworker defenselessness to demand prohibition. Exploitation of mothers perverted the meaning of *home.* Such arguments became entangled in the fight for labor standards since the sexual division of labor and social construction of gender shaped concepts used to define *work* as well as the experience of working.[17]

Homework regulation occurred amid a renewed cultural emphasis on women as mothers and the home as the site of social life. The Great Depression strengthened traditional understandings of gender precisely because it disrupted men's ability to provide for their families. As if to compensate for the initial greater unemployment of men in a sex-segregated labor market, most Americans embraced notions of male breadwinning and female homemaking. They approved of government firings of married women to make room for men, assumed to be supporting dependents. Working people accepted the wage earning of women in need but rejected those who labored for extras. By mid-decade even the Communist party had abandoned images of the revolutionary girl for the proletarian mother, severing the connection between social and sexual revolutions that had developed since the 1910s. The labor movement as a whole envisioned women as victims or mothers, men as strong muscled workers. These were years when housework expanded into home manufacturing and, although many lost their homes, the private arena became the sphere for social life as families found recreation there. Homework fit into this pattern of "making do," but its merging of home and workplace was an unwanted reminder of larger insecurities.[18]

---

[17] No one study considers how gendered divisions and concepts shaped the meaning and experience of work, but see Sonya Rose, *Limited Livelihoods: Gender and Class in Nineteenth-Century England* (Berkeley: Univ. of California Press, 1992). "Proceedings of the Third National Conference on Labor Legislation," 1936, *Bulletin of the Division of Labor Standards,* no. 12 (Washington, D.C.: GPO, 1937), 39; "Suggestions for Possible Use at Hearing on Conflicts in the Homework Provisions," attached to Lucy Manning (Women's Bureau) to O. W. Rosenzweig, Nov. 19, 1934, HC Records, box 8386, file "Labor, U.S. Department of."

[18] Susan Ware, *Holding Their Own: American Women in the 1930s* (Boston: Twayne, 1982); Elizabeth Faue, *Community of Suffering and Struggle: Women, Men, and the Labor Movement in Minneapolis, 1915–1945* (Chapel Hill: Univ. of North Carolina Press, 1991); Paula Rabinowitz, *Labor and Desire: Women's Revolutionary Fiction in Depression America* (Chapel Hill: Univ. of North Carolina Press, 1991); Barbara Melosh, *Engendering Culture: Manhood and Womanhood in New Deal Public Art and Theater* (Washington, D.C.: Smithsonian Institution Press, 1991); Alice Kessler–Harris, *A Woman's Wage: Historical Meanings and Social Consequences* (Lexington: Univ. of Kentucky Press, 1991), 57–80.

"If the golden rule ever applied anywhere": NRA homework regulation

The NRA became law in late May 1933 and soon thereafter employers in the needle trades banded together to draft codes.[19] The dominant groups in these industries, major manufacturers associations, embraced the NRA as a means to stabilize their industry against price chiselers with lesser labor costs. Where unionized employers controlled the code-making process, they incorporated collective bargaining provisions. The Code for the Coat and Suit Industry (NRA Code No. 5), the first for the garment trades, immediately abolished homework with a clause that duplicated ILGWU language: "No homework shall be allowed and no work shall be done or permitted in tenement houses, basements or in any unsanitary buildings or buildings unsafe on account of fire risks." New York firms, who dominated code making as they did production, already had ended homework. In men's clothing, competing employer associations disagreed on trade unionism but agreed on ending homework. The resulting code abolished homework three months after its date of approval to give any remaining homework employers time to adjust production methods. Along with the coat and suit code, it provided a model for those that followed.[20]

Hillman called for a thirty-five-hour week and higher minimum wage, but nonunion employers predicted that higher prices would bring back homework. Troy, New York, shirt firms argued for a special allowance for homework for 125 collarmakers in terms that would permeate subsequent debates during the NRA years and beyond. One warned, "We will start, if we have to, tomorrow, to send no work home, but these elderly people will be deprived of work and we do not want to see that and I am sure you do not either." Cast as respectable ("of the very best families"), disabled by age or home responsibilities as housewives and mothers, Troy workers turned into artifacts, dying representatives of a venerated and old custom. Their employers then could appear as benevolent protectors, despite the economic reason for continuing home turning. Although machines had replaced most homeworkers, mechanization failed to pay for a few styles – out of poor sales or intricacy – and so hand turning persisted.[21]

[19] The quote in the subhead that precedes this section is from "Home-Work Status Detailed," *Knitted Outerwear Times*, July 27, 1934, in "Hearing on Regulations for Home Work System for the Code of Fair Competition for the Knitted Outerwear Industry," 26, NRA TH, 243–1–02.

[20] Vittoz, *New Deal Labor Policy*, 94–106; "Memorandum to the Labor Provision, Proposed Code for the Dress Manufacturing Industry," Dubinsky Papers, box 127, folder 3c; "Coat Front Manufacturing Industry," June 11, 1934, 74–5, NRA TH, 215–1–13; Miss Jean Flexner and Miss Skinner, "A Study of Industrial Home Work in the Summer and Fall of 1934," 57–8, mimeographed, HC Records, folder "Reports"; "Men's Ready-to-Wear Clothing Industry," July 26–7, 1933, 130, NRA TH, 216–1–06.

[21] "Cotton Garment and Shirt Industry," Aug. 3, 1933, 259–60, 245, NRA TH, 27–1–06; ibid., Aug. 2, 1933, 92–3, 123, 136, 126–7.

The Cotton Garment and Shirt Code permitted collar turning upon application for a homework exemption; it also allowed hand embroidery after pleas by wash dress manufacturers. Those from Los Angeles and Seattle had incorporated home embroidery into their businesses and had enough power within the International Association of Garment Manufacturers to maintain homework; the existence of Puerto Rican competition surely helped to sway NRA authorities. As with other codes that embraced both machine and hand sewing, only the former was banned from the home, while the latter – the source of homework in the first place – remained, in theory under code authority supervision. Since the cotton garment code was one of the early codes, employers fought any precedent that would eliminate homework altogether.[22]

Homework provisions in codes over the next months formed a patchwork of inconsistent regulations. Seventy-two of the 118 codes with provisions banned homework on the effective date of the code; 19 waited from one to six months before final prohibition, whereas 10 later codes incorporated the President's Executive Order of May 1934 which limited homework to the elderly, disabled and ill, or their caretakers. Altogether 86 percent of codes with provisions prohibited homework. Yet forty-four prohibitions were for industries without homework, while five homework industries lacked any regulation.[23]

Exceptions, stays, and official suspensions of provisions undermined the meaning of prohibition. The handkerchief code ended all homework except for the entirely handmade. Light sewing allowed homework for handwork on candlewick spreads and quilts. The knitted outerwear code condoned it for hand knitting, including hand crocheting and embroidering; the one for ladies' handbags exempted hand beading, crocheting, and embroidering from prohibition. Such codes reflected the economic reality that handwork could compete with machine production or foreign imports only when underpaying its makers. Employers regularly ignored provisions.[24]

One NRA official later reflected, "The specific homework provision written into a code was (like the entire code itself) a product of the special conditions in the industry and the bargaining powers of those who partici-

[22] Ibid., Aug. 2, 1933, 147; for the UGWA position on homework, testimony of Thomas A. Rickert, 482–3. For the final provisions of this code, "Commercialization of the Home," 42.

[23] Flexner and Skinner, "A Study of Industrial HomeWork," 58–9; "Commercialization of the Home," 39–48. Codes lacking homework provisions where homework continued were clothespin division, curled hair manufacturing and horsehair dressing, lace, pecan shelling, and punch board. Among those which only abolished or controlled some processes were art needlework, brush, candlewick bedspread, cotton garment, fishing tackle, freshwater pearl button, furniture, handkerchief, hosiery, infants' and children's wear, knitted outerwear, ladies' handbag, leather and woolen knit glove, needlework in Puerto Rico, novelty curtain, vegetable-ivory button, women's neckwear.

[24] "Commercialization of the Home"; Rosenzweig, "NRA and Industrial Homework," "Chapter II – Code Experience," 1–8; survey materials for WBB no. 131: 5–3–6, 1–1–12, RG86.

pated in the code negotiations," though labor fought for "the universal prohibition of homework." Codes for industries with extensive homework – lace, knitted outerwear, infant's and children's wear, leather and woolen knit gloves – kept the practice. The resulting code inconsistency perplexed home-workers. The same process – hand embroidery – prohibited under some codes, like dresses, flourished under infants' and children's wear and art needlework. Employers scrambled to be classified under a code more favorable to home-work than the one under which they originally fell.[25]

This emerging confusion prompted the NRA, with strong encouragement from the Department of Labor, to create a homework committee in March 1934. Members consisted of Clara Beyer and Mary Anderson from the Department of Labor, along with representatives from the NRA Consumers', Labor, and Industrial Advisory boards. The committee was charged with researching and monitoring the various codes and with resolving a dilemma that NRA administrators faced. As one of these men put it: "Provisions in codes summarily eliminating homework have caused severe hardships among those employed in such work. On the other hand, it is recognized that homework offers a vicious type of unfair competition in many industries." With Anderson's support, Beyer, then head of the Industrial Division of the Children's Bureau, offered what became the President's Executive Order.[26]

Clara Beyer – who felt about homework, it was said, "like the preacher ... towards sin" – stood at the center of the network of women who pushed for its abolition. This daughter of Danish immigrants had worked her way to a master of arts in economics from the University of California, Berkeley. While teaching at Bryn Mawr, she became involved with the NCL and the WTUL. She then worked with Felix Frankfurter on the War Labor Policies Board and went on to serve as the first director of the Washington, D.C., Minimum Wage Commission, soon invalidated by *Adkins*. After marriage, children, and part-time work in New York (for the NYCL), she returned to Washington in 1928 to the Children's Bureau. In 1934, she would become the assistant director of the Division of Labor Standards, where she ran the division's most important programs, but was not placed in charge out of fear that Labor was becoming a female fiefdom. More than any other network woman, Beyer saw that depression conditions made it possible to include men under labor standards.[27]

[25] Rosenzweig, "NRA and Industrial Homework," chap. 2, 1, 16–17; "Infants' and Children's Wear Industry," Dec. 5, 1933, 263–5.

[26] "Minutes of Meeting, NRA Homework Committee," Mar. 19, 1934, 2; "Report on Homework by O. W. Rosenzweig, Chairman, NRA Homework Committee," including office memorandum, Feb. 17, 1934, from Alva Brown, 2, HC Records, box 8383, folder "Committee, NRA Homework."

[27] U.S. DOL, WHD, "Hearing in the Matter of the Recommendation of Industry Committee No. 40 for the Gloves and Mittens Industry," Mar. 2, 1942, 42, typescript, DOL library; Ware, *Beyond Suffrage*, 145; "Conversation Between Clara Mortenson Beyer and Vivien Hart, Washington, D.C., Nov. 14, 1983," SL.

The Executive Order represented a political decision as well as "a humanitarian movement." Applying only to codes that totally prohibited homework, it exempted those workers thought discriminated against: people ill or with disabilities, those caring for them, and those too old to adjust to factory labor. Such a worker could obtain a homework permit upon presenting a doctor's certificate to her state department of labor. She was to be paid the same rate as a factory laborer and to adhere to all state labor standards. Over the next year states issued about twenty-six hundred permits, over half of them from New York, for all major types of homework. Beyer reported to ailing Children's Bureau chief Grace Abbott, "Through my insistence the Home Work Committee of the NRA has been given real power as far as home work policy is concerned. We now pass upon every home work proposal before it is approved by the Administrator."[28]

Who would fall under the Executive Order was hardly a foregone conclusion. NRA administrators, basically a male group, were open to the sentimental argument of including widows with preschoolers and even mothers with small children and unemployed husbands. However "pitiful and small the earnings," argued O. W. Pearson, homework was "an important part of the home economy, and one cannot ignore it, for to do so would be a grave injustice and would tend to add to the great want that already exists." Others emphasized the political consequences "of flatly denying homework certificates to nursing mothers, because of the manner in which this information could be used by anti-administration papers." But the women of the Labor Department saw excluding mothers from the ban as de facto nullifying prohibition. Not only were the majority of homeworkers mothers, making regulation impossible if mothers were included, but also mothers and their offspring were precisely the group that the women reformers would save from homework and restore to "normal" family life – that is, to the protection of a male breadwinner. Or, as Beyer explained, "in some instances where it might be possible for a woman to support (more or less) a family by homework, this would be too great a temptation for a husband who loved leisure more than honor to continue idle." In charge of labor standards, the women had the final say over the Executive Order.[29]

Despite a preference that mothers not work for wages, when it came to

---

[28] "Report on Homework by O. W. Rosenzweig," 13; "Number of Certificates Issued, Refused, Revoked, and Canceled to and including May 27, 1935, According to States Reporting," HC Records, box 8383, folder "Appendix"; Clara Beyer to Grace Abbott, July 27, 1934, Abbott Papers, box 35, folder 5. Disabled workers in codes allowing some homework could find themselves excluded from permits if employers had already fulfilled their factory-to-homework ratio. See O. W. Rosenzweig to Miss Elizabeth Christman, Oct. 26, 1934, HC Records, box 8382, Homework Spindle Correspondence.

[29] O. W. Pearson to Earl Dean Howard, Mar. 30, 1934, folder "Correspondence"; Rosenzweig to Beyer, Aug. 29, 1934, folder "Committee, NRA Homework," in HC Records, Box 8383; "Report on Homework by O. W. Rosenzweig," 15.

analyzing the actual situation of women workers, New Deal women – like their Progressive Era mentors in the NCL – continued to display a sensitivity to the power relations within families that led to an understanding of the double expropriation of women's labor power. Women's Bureau field investigators understood the economic hardships of women, how discriminatory firings of married and older women from office, shop, and factory forced them into "parasitic" homework. Opposition to industrial homework reflected a complex set of beliefs persistently held by the women's reform network: that mothers ought not to work and that homework most undermined motherhood because its low piece rates meant long hours, "jeopardizing their health and family life"; but working women belonged in the factory in order to benefit from minimum wages and better working conditions, to have a real chance at economic independence.[30]

This double perspective, continued from the 1920s, depended on family status. It led Schneiderman, a member of the NRA Labor Advisory Board, to fight for both the abolition of homework, resorted to by women whose husbands failed to earn a family wage, and the abolition of code wage differentials, thus gaining equal pay for equal work. Concerned with the homeworker as worker, Schneiderman reinforced the economic arguments of other homework opponents. Homework generated "chaos in the wage scale," stood as "the most extreme form of unscientific management," and was "the greatest enemy of artistic work." Other labor-oriented women, like the southern activist and new NCL executive secretary Lucy Randolph Mason, saw homework negating the idea of a living wage. Frieda Miller defined the state's interest not as "preventing them from working" but rather "their being paid if they did." Club women, more tenuously connected to the women reformers, emphasized the moral arguments of the past. Those in Texas insisted, "while the home is used as a workshop it can be no real home for the growing child." Class and race antagonism shaped their view of Mexican needleworkers.[31]

The Women's Bureau certainly was not beyond appealing to traditional constructions of family life, although it linked its portrait of proper behavior to a defense of labor standards. It joined economic to social arguments in

[30] "Industrial Home Work: Summary of the System and Its Problems," n.d., 11, HC Records, box 8384, folder "Industrial Homework General"; "Industrial Home Work," 1, 3, typescript [ca. 1939], RG86, box 1602, folder "Homework: Progress in Control, etc."; "Commercialization of the Home," 2.

[31] Rose Schneiderman, "Women in Industry Under the National Recovery Administration," c. 1935, WTUL Papers, reel 114, frames 463, 468; "Lace Manufacturing Industry," July 28, 1933, 112, NRA TH, 244–01; "Brief prepared by Women's Bureau for Miss Schneiderman's Use at Hearing," 5, HC Records, box 8384; Lucy Mason, "Hearing on Regulations for Home Work System for the Code of Fair Competition for the Knitted Outerwear Industry," Oct. 8, 1934, 227, NRA TH, 243–1–02; Frieda Miller in *Proceedings*, Conference of State Industrial Homework Law Administrators, 1937, 20, RG86, Women's Bureau Survey Materials, 1930–50, folder, "Homework"; "Rough Notes for the Dramatization of 'Women Workers and What They Do,'" RG86, box 11, folder "Texas State Survey – 1932."

viewing conditions of labor shaping home life. Writing to trade unionists, director Mary Anderson named homework "a powerful influence pulling down wage standards." Bulletins and pamphlets for a more general audience deployed the discourse of violated domesticity. "The Commercialization of the Home Through Industrial Home Work," a 1935 summary of existing data, argued for protecting factory labor, the community, and the home from substandard labor conditions. But its chief complaint was that homework demoralized the "home as the family shelter from the stress and strain of the outside world." *The Price of Industrial Home Work and Why It Should Be Regulated* (1936) presented a more nuanced analysis. It portrayed Mrs. Mary Brown as a heroic mother and breadwinner who relies on her mother-in-law for childcare while machine sewing children's dresses in a factory to supplement her husband's wages. Mrs. Brown loses her job when her employer no longer can compete with homeworking firms. Unable to find work, discriminated against at age forty, she turns to homework, gaining a mere four dollars for laboring into the night where she previously had earned fifteen to twenty dollars for a forty-four-hour week. The impact was devastating: "Recreation for the family became impossible. The children were neglected and sometimes kept out of school for lack of proper clothing." The lesson was clear: Homes turned into factories produced "bad working conditions and bad living conditions." But rather than blame moral flaws, the Women's Bureau considered unfair competition and low wages as the culprits destroying family life.[32]

Although bureau women supported mothers' pensions, they drew upon older charity discourses to portray homework as costing taxpayers. Here we see the interrelation between the regulatory and redistributive components of the welfare state. Two separate claims associated homework with relief. Opponents saw taxpayers as indirectly subsidizing employers by making up the difference between homework and a living wage. Low earnings forced homeworkers to turn to local and federal programs, as well as private charity. Defenders viewed homework as supplanting relief rather than intensifying its need. It provided dignity, allowing families their only cash income to spend on items that relief orders would not cover. It tided Georgia cotton farmers over until crops sold, keeping them from debt during famine times. In small one-industry towns, homework providers turned into country squires, acting in the best interest of the needy.[33]

---

[32] Mary Anderson to Mr. Adolph J. Fritz, Nov. 15, 1934, WTUL Papers, reel 68, frames 20-1; "The Commercialization of the Home," 33; U.S. DOL, *The Price of Industrial Home Work and Why It Should Be Regulated* (Washington, D.C., 1936), Miller Papers, box 4, folder 27.

[33] Mrs. Blodgett, Mrs. Florida M. Griffin, and Victor Lawrence, "The Lace Manufacturing Industry," Mar. 19, 1934, 55–7, 94–6 NRA TH, 244–01; Miss Edna M. Purtell in NCL, "Report: Third Annual Meeting of the Labor Standards Conference," Dec. 10, 1934, 6, CLM Papers, box 15, folder 245; Claud H. Hutcheson to General Hugh S. Johnson, Jan. 30, 1934, RG9, Box 2401, folder "Amendments and Modifications Labor A-D"; P. C. Martin to Code Authority, Furniture Division, Mar. 15, 1934; Swift Waugh to Code Authority, Mar. 14, 1934, RG9, box 2401, folder "Amendments and Modifications Labor E-O."

In ensuing debates, employers and NRA administrators alike viewed the women's network as speaking for homeworkers because homeworkers were unorganized and least able to protect themselves. Although generally true, such perceptions blinded officials from noticing grass roots attempts at organization. Puerto Rican contractors in New York City formed the Hand Drawn, Hand Embroidery, Hand Fagoting, Crochet Beaders and Appliqué Cutters Association to represent themselves and their workers. They called for equal pay with shop workers until the elimination of homework. Such representations were rare, especially when organizers came from outside an ethnic community. Local 66 of the AFL held a meeting of embroidery homeworkers in September 1934, but no more than sixty young women came out of an estimated pool of twenty to thirty thousand, mostly "Italian and Spanish." Manufacturers and unionists alike thought it impossible to organize home workers.[34]

Women reformers determined what was best for homeworkers. Committed to ending low wages, they would ban homework. Some, like Beyer, recognized the necessity of getting women into factory jobs, no matter domestic ideals. This represented a counter-discourse to the dominant position held by Women's Bureau chief Mary Anderson that stressed a home-based motherhood. Anderson argued, "The only thing to do about homework is to abolish it and to arrange for higher wages for the breadwinner in a family so that his wife and children do not have to supplement the family income by doing homework, or, if there is no regular breadwinner, to provide pensions or relief." A gendered welfare state would provide mothers' pensions rather than wages.[35]

Reformers considered the homeworker a mother, but this status was only one factor in their testimony at NRA hearings. However, motherhood provided the rationale for employers' descriptions of homeworkers as casual laborers, unavailable for the factory, despite previous social constructions of intermittent laborers as lower-class men. Responsibility for unpaid domestic labor somehow denied women the position of worker, justifying low wages and irregular work. As the Southern Furniture Manufacturers' Association reasoned: "A woman who does the work in her home can also do her housework

[34] Puerto Rican immigrant women had engaged in homework since their arrival in the 1920s. See Virginia Sanchez Korral, *From Colonia to Community: The History of Puerto Ricans in New York City, 1917–1948* (Westport, Conn.: Greenwood Press, 1983). Beatrice McConnell, Assistant Deputy Harned, "Hearings on Regulations for . . . Knitted Outerwear," Dec. 8, 1933, 332–3, 218–19; Pedro San Miguel and A. R. Hernandez, "The Pleating, Stitching and Bonnaz and Hand Embroidery Industry," Oct. 3, 1933, 256–76, esp. 273, NRA TH, 231-1-06; Herman W. Berger, "Hearings on Application for Exemption on Hours from the Code of Fair Competition for the Novelty Curtains, Draperies, Bedspreads and Novelty Pillow Industry," Sept. 20, 1934, 22–3, RG9, box 7123.

[35] [Mary Anderson], *Women at Work: The Autobiography of Mary Anderson as Told to Mary N. Winslow* (Minneapolis: Univ. of Minnesota Press, 1951), 244.

and avoid the necessity of employing a cook or servant to look after the children, get the meals, etc." These employers resented paying "female, aged, or disabled" workers equivalent or higher wages than those gained by "able-bodied men" in other codes, many of which contained a lower rate for women because they were women. Such an understanding – homeworkers were women helping their families and not real workers – justified the attempt by art needlework employers to exclude homeworkers from the term *employee* in their code, which in allowing homework for sample goods offered a loophole to have other products finished at home. This image of the homeworker as mother, not worker, held for employer opponents of homework as well. Like New Deal shapers of the welfare state, employers separated home from work, mother from worker.[36]

Women were consumers; employers argued that homemade goods could better satisfy their needs. Mother love would lead women to choose the flexible seams of a hand-assembled sweater, made "in some individual manner," over the stiff, machine-stitched one. The consumer also was a fashion setter if she was a woman of means, able to purchase handknitted sportswear. Homeworkers themselves were consumers, able to make installments on "radios, electric sweepers or washing machines, and similar semi-luxuries, which they otherwise would not have been able to enjoy." Such arguments, the flip side of the reform appeal to the woman shopper, undoubtedly reinforced the NCL, WTUL, and trade unionists in their consumer-directed label campaigns.[37]

Employers, then, mixed notions about motherhood with the language of the market, economics, and fair competition. Nearly in the same breath, homework defenders could contend "this work was being done by women who would not come to work" or who lived too far from the factory and that the labor put into the home was "a matter of style," "impractical to build up equipment for it." Some processes could not be adapted to the factory; they were too stressful to be performed continuously during a standard workday. "If handknitting is performed for a considerable length of time it becomes tedious and the knitter loses her speed and efficiency," claimed a Philadelphia sportswear manufacturer who associated knitting with women's leisure and artistic

[36] J. T. Ryan, Secretary, Southern Furniture Manufacturers' Association to Mr. C. R. Niklason, NRA, "Chair Seating Rates," May 11, 1934; "Excerpt from Bulletin No. 13, 15 May 1934, Minutes of the Furniture Code Authority Meeting held at Washington, D.C., 9–10 May 1934," 13–14; Green River Chair Co. to Mr. J. T. Ryan, May 2, 1934; see also Walter Estes to Senator Walter George, Senator R. B. Russell, Jr., Congressman E. M. Owens, May 14, 1934; Memo to double cane chair manufacturers from J. T. Ryan, May 11, 1934, RG9, box 2401, folder "Amendments and Modifications, Labor E–O"; "Art Needle Work Industry," Sept. 7, 1934, 5–9, NRA TH, 231–1–08.

[37] Mr. E. G. Lindemann, "Hearing on Code of Fair Competition for the Furniture Manufacturing Industry (In the Matter of Home Work)," Mar. 19, 1934, 26, NRA TH, 312–1–10; Mr. Peyser and Mr. Bohlen, "Knitted Outerwear Industry," Oct. 16, 1934, 127, 170, NRA TH, 243–1–02.

activities. Infants' and children's wear manufacturers argued that market power depended on the homework processes of "embroidery, hand work and other hand finishing." Taking homework away would destroy the industry for "[p]eople would again begin to put those hand touches on in their own homes." A furniture manufacturer graphically expressed the prevailing sentiment: "To win the privilege of home work at the prices suggested is about as useful to our industry as a trip thru an art gallery would be to a blind man."[38]

Factory production meant additional costs. A Chicago embroidery manufacturer claimed that Windy City businesses lacked equipment to compete with eastern firms. Others interpreted homework's lowering of costs quite differently. To shift overhead costs onto homeworkers and circumvent the minimum wage instigated ruthless competition. The National Association of Pleating, Stitching, and Hand Embroidery Manufacturers justified abolition "because we feel that home work, [despite] . . . sentimental or emotional reasons, is an unscientific and a non-economic way of producing."[39]

Homework opponents transformed the employer portrait of economic and physical dependence into one of victimization. ACWA vice-president Jacob Potofsky compared homework to slavery, relying on a metaphor long used by trade unionists to attack sweated labor as "a matter of principle." Hillman confronted manufacturers with the findings of Women's Bureau studies to prove that homeworkers were underpaid, rather than intermittent, laborers. Organized labor presented a vision of mothers suffering – though not from lack of homework. The WTUL fought for outright prohibition, along with the ILGWU, the ACWA, the United Hatters, Cap, and Millinery Workers Union, the Glove Makers Union, the Pocketbook Union, the Knitwear Union, and the Neckwear Union. But this victim could also be an exploiter. Schneiderman explained, "If a mother is hard-up and wants to earn a couple of pennies more, she will engage her little boy or her little girl, no matter how young, to help her." Such a portrait of desperate motherhood contrasted sharply with employer descriptions.[40]

Not only did employers argue that homeworkers were mothers who could or would not leave the home, but they asked homeworkers to make that claim

---

[38] Mr. Frampton "Art Needle Work Industry," Sept. 7, 1934, 182, 207; Mr. Mendlowitz, Mr. Bohlen, "Knitted Outerwear Industry," Oct. 16, 1933, 159, 167, 84; "Infants' and Children's Wear Industry," Dec. 5, 1933, 114, 263–5, NRA TH, 217–1–05; Walter Estes to Senator Walter George, May 14, 1934, RG9, box 2401, folder "Amendments and Modifications, Labor E-O."

[39] "Code of Fair Competition for the Schiffli, the Hand Machine Embroidery and the Embroidery Thread and Scallop Cutting Industries," Sept. 11, 1933, 22–1, 44–7, 63, NRA TH, 231–1–05; "Code of Fair Competition for the Pleating, Stitching and Bonnaz and Hand Embroidery Industry," Oct. 3, 1933, 51, NRA TH, 231–1–06.

[40] "Cotton Garment and Shirt Industry," Aug. 3, 1933, 259–60, NRA TH, 27–1–06; "Cotton Garment Industry," Aug. 2, 1933, 144–5, 148; "Lace Manufacturing Industry," July 28, 1933, 113; *Women's Wear Daily*, Mar. 19, 1934, 28.

if confronted by government investigators. Foremen warned against inspectors looking for information. Rhode Island and Connecticut lace mills and New York City artificial flower makers had workers sign petitions for the continuance of homework. A favored employee would go "around, house to house, threat[en]ing and forcing workers to sign a paper saying they wanted the work done at home – those who refused to sign were told they would lose their job." Handbag manufacturers had workers check off a form listing reasons for staying home: small children, distance and lack of transportation, sick parent, incapacitation, house duties. Sent to the NRA, these forms pledged women not to use child labor and declared the rate of twenty-five cents an hour "fair and acceptable." Employers also misinformed workers; a Los Angeles undergarment company had embroiderers protest NRA regulations – forbidding people under fifty from receiving homework and limiting homeworkers to only four dozen garments a week – that never existed. A New Jersey hand knitter admitted, "in one shop we were asked to write a letter stating we were glad to get the knitting so as the owner can show them to somebody in Washington." Other employers sent trusted workers to NRA hearings.[41]

Homework employers relied on *woman* as *mother* when they went on the offensive against the New Deal. In the wake of the President's Executive Order, they launched a series of vitriolic attacks in the press and a number of court suits on behalf of homeworking mothers. The anti-New Deal press fueled the controversy with sensationalist headlines. The *Carbondale* (Illinois) *Free Press* proclaimed, "Mother Denied Right to Work by President"; and the *New York Daily News* announced, "Two Mothers Draw Fire of NRA in 'Sweatshop War.' " Cartoons ridiculed the NRA; one in the *Chicago Tribune* of August 1, 1934, pictured New Dealers as "ogres, academic braintrusters, swinging a huge club at a small, helpless woman behind whose skirts children crouch in terror." Hiding behind the figure of the mother, however, was the Homework Protective League, an organ of the National Hand Embroidery and Novelty Manufacturers Association. (Lace manufacturers also organized their workers under a similar rubric.) A group of employers dependent on homeworkers, representing about one-seventh of the industry, the association objected to being included in the code for the Pleating, Stitching and Bonnaz and Hand Embroidery Industry, a code dominated by larger manufacturers who relied upon machine production. The Homework Protec-

[41] "Hearing on the Pleating, Stitching and Bonnaz and Hand Embroidery Industry," Nov. 20, 1934, 82, 112, NRA TH, 231–1–06; "Mother and Knitter," in *News-Letter*, CLNJ, vol. 3, No. 16, Apr. 1938, 2, CLNJ Papers, box 9; To Gentlemen, NRA, from Angelina Gustrazzochia, box 8384, folder "Art Flowers"; Signatures Attached to Administrator, Artificial Flower & Feather Industry, Apr. 12, 1934; Mrs. Ruffino to Mr. C. W. Rosenzereing [*sic*], Mar. 17, 1934, box 8385, Homework Spindle Correspondence; anon. to dear Sir, Mar. 28, 1934; Petition, Mrs. H. B. Maynard, Bell, Calif., and 40 others to The Honorable Franklin D. Roosevelt, Feb. 12, 1935; 58 signatures and letter from Frank Carano, attorney, Philadelphia to Hon. Franklin Delano Roosevelt, Jan. 23, 1935, box 8382, Homework Spindle Correspondence, all in HC Records.

tive League adopted three major tactics: It argued before the NRA that its members fell under the art needlework code; it lobbied for the inclusion of mothers in the Executive Order; and, after those tactics failed, it attempted to overturn the NRA decision through a series of court cases on behalf of mothers denied the right to work at home. In its opposition to any homework prohibition, the Homework Protective League represented only a fragment of the business-class, labor-intensive employers with the most to lose through prohibition, but its court cases generated much adverse publicity and deeply worried NRA officials.[42]

The case of Kathryn Budd brought notoriety to the Executive Order. This Italian-American mother was a skilled artificial flower maker who earned eighteen dollars per week, a substantial wage for a homeworker. Though Budd hardly typified the poor, desperate women in whose name the Homework Protective League spoke, as NRA officials were quick to point out, her situation nonetheless was a common one. She lived in her parents' mortgaged Brooklyn home with three unemployed brothers and two sisters working as stenographers. Her father was a bartender out of work due to ill health, and her mother, whose eyesight suffered from years of homework, was "too nervous" to care for the children. Like her mother, she long had worked for the Jacob de Jong firm, a supporter of the Protective League. Moreover, Budd held a personal grievance against the NRA, whose minimum wage rules she judged had cost her a job as a telephone operator. Those circumstances made Budd a willing litigant. Throughout the summer and autumn of 1934, through one legal maneuver after another, the Homework Protective League kept the Budd case before the public. In July the New York attorney general held that the rule prohibiting homework by mothers was unconstitutional; in October a lower court overturned the ban on the basis of state laws permitting homework under specified circumstances. Eventually, a higher court nullified those rulings, sustaining the state act which made the national codes applicable to intrastate business. Bolstered by their own legal rulings, NRA administrators acted as if state homework laws had no "binding force." In the meantime the Protective League effectively disrupted administration of homework codes in New York.[43]

[42] "Report on Homework by O. W. Rosenzweig," 35; *Chicago Tribune*, Aug. 1, 1934, 1; *Carbondale* [Ill.] *Free Press*, July 31, 1934; *New York Daily News*, Oct. 3, 1934, 36; Anna M. Rosenberg to Rosenzweig, Aug. 8, 1934; "Activities of Hochfelder-Zahn Group, Submitted by Herman W. Berger" to Rosenzweig, Aug. 7, 1934, 1–6; Ivar Axelson, "Report on the Subversive Activities of the National Hand Embroidery and Novelty Manufacturers Association, Inc., and Its Secretary, Mr. J. Zahn, from Code Authority for the Pleating, Stitching, and Bonnaz and Hand Embroidery Industry," n.d., 1–6; "Attached Wire – Homework" in M. D. Vincent to James Cope, Aug. 15, 1935; Anna W. Hochfelder to Donald R. Richberg, Oct. 1, 1934; Julius Hochfelder to Code Authority, Oct. 29, 1934, in HC Records, box 8384, folder "Homework Protective League"; Survey materials for no. 131: 2–3–2, RG86.

[43] "State of New York, County and City of New York, ss: Katherine [*sic*] S. Budd, Aug. 22, 1934, signed David H. Gottlieb, W. H. Schleichter, Notary Public, Bronx Co. Clerk, #89,

The Homework Protective League understood the depression era segmentation of the labor market in a manner not apparent in Roosevelt administration discussions; its arguments reflected the division of labor by sex, ethnicity, and life cycle. Because homeworkers were performing women's work, they were "*not* depriving men workers of jobs, because the men who are skilled in this kind of needlecraft are negligible in number." Moreover, the homeworkers did not "keep the rank and file of women in industry from jobs," because "the majority are of foreign birth and training, coming from countries where it was considered an art and incumbent upon every young girl to be taught to do fine crochet and embroidery work." In contrast, "Our American girls," one petition asserted, "become teachers, stenographers, bookkeepers, lawyers, reporters, instead."[44] That, too, was for the most part true, although the categorization of "American" jobs confused working-class with middle-class occupations. Native-born white women in fact dominated professional and white-collar work, though young, second-generation ethnic women had begun to enter the clerical field. In rural areas, such as upstate New York and New England, native-born white women worked at home as part of the customary organization of production in certain industries, like gloves in Fulton County, New York, or wood shoe heels in New Hampshire. The Protective League recognized homeworkers as a particular segment of the labor market and homework as a phase of the female life-work cycle. It put occupations dominated by single women in one labor market and claimed homework for the poor widow and mother with unemployed husband or without a male breadwinner.[45]

What was at stake, in the Protective League's mind, was the best interests of children. Although "some foes of homework have argued that the children should be sent to institutions and thus leave their mothers free to work in shops and factories," it contended, "any student of family welfare will admit that the child is best off under its mother's care." By "institutions," the Protective League meant childcare centers; such a designation drew on popular prejudices against separating children from their mothers and on the

H. L. Buck," affidavit; John L. Taylor, "Re: Mrs. Kitty Budd, 411 Caton Ave., Brooklyn, New York," Aug. 16, 1934; W. H. Schleichter, "Re: Mrs. Kitty Budd employee of Jacob de Jong, Inc., 19 West 36th St., New York City," Aug. 15, 1934, all in HC Records, box 8382, folder "Budd Case"; *Chicago Tribune*, May 15, 1934, 1; *Washington Herald*, July 20, 1934, 7; *New York Times*, July 24, 1934, 37; ibid., Oct. 3, 1934, 14; ibid., Oct. 4, 1934, 42; memorandum to John Swope from Senator Straus, Jr., July 10, 1934; Frieda Miller, "Memorandum to Commissioner," July 17, 1934, in NYDOL WHD files, folder "Legal Interpretation, 1930–37."

44 Anna Hochfelder, "Preliminary Memorandum of the Homeworkers' Council of the Homework Protective League of the United States," Mar. 3, 1934, 2–3, HC Records, box 8384, folder "Homework Protective League."

45 Folder "Leather and Woolen Knit Gloves," box 8385; folder "New Hampshire," box 8383, in HC Records; Alice Kessler-Harris, *Out to Work: A History of Wage-Earning Women in the United States* (New York: Oxford Univ. Press, 1982), 250–72.

reality that churches, welfare agencies, and charities ran most childcare facilities. "The foes of homework" also agreed that mothers ought to care for their children, but they understood that the pressures of homework increased the difficulty of doing so. Pennsylvania administrator Beatrice McConnell questioned the amount of care received from "a woman who has a family of children, for whom she must cook and bake and wash and iron . . . and then work ten or eleven hours a day." If earnings were necessary, "it is perfectly possible under ordinary circumstances for her to arrange for the care of her children in some other way." That homeworkers earned too little to pay for childcare meant that wages fell below New Deal standards. Mothers' pensions, as an alternative to homework, allowed time for children.[46]

Mother care of children was indeed a major reason why women accepted homework. Women who entered the factory after the NRA denied their applications for exemption from code prohibitions expressed anxiety over homes and children. Among a group of Troy, New York, neckwear sewers, the Women's Bureau cited Mrs. Z., who worried "about children having responsibility of locking the house before they go to school"; Mrs. M., who worried "about care of child during vacation"; and Mrs. D., who worried about an ill toddler kept by a neighbor. A local observer, opposed to mothers' working away from children, argued that "many of these homeworkers are not of the type who could complacently put their children [in day-care] where they would be exposed to the various hazards that are necessarily present in any heterogeneous group of children however carefully supervised. Is it right that they should be compelled to do so?" he asked the NRA.[47]

The arrangements of Troy factory workers reveal how the burden of childcare fell on individual mothers. Though the city had two sliding-scale day-care centers, one of which took infants, only two out of twenty interviewees placed children in them. The majority relied on the public schools without making any arrangements for the hours before and after school or during lunch. A few drew on grandmothers or husbands; others paid a neighbor to watch younger siblings. Such arrangements, including a reluctance to use institutional centers, resembled those reported to the sociologist Gwendolyn Hughes in the mid-1920s and hardly differed from what investigators discovered in the mid-1900s. Most women who entered the factory during the NRA period could make some kind of childcare arrangements. That childcare work added to their hours of labor went unrecognized by the same NRA officials

---

[46] Hochfelder, "Preliminary Memorandum," 2; "Suggestions for Possible Use at Hearing on Conflicts in the Homework Provisions," n.d., attached to Manning to Rosenzweig; "The Pleating, Stitching and Bonnaz and Hand Embroidery Industry," Nov. 20, 1934, 93–4, 96; Gretta Palmer, "Excepting of Mothers Held Weakening NRA," New York World Telegram, July 19, 1934, 12.

[47] Mary Skinner and Ruth Scandrett, "Report on the Investigation of Industrial Home Work in the Men's Neckwear Industry, Troy, New York," 1934, 14–15; Crawford R. Green to O. W. Rosenzweig, Dec. 19, 1934, HC Records, box 8385, folder "Men's Neckwear Industry."

who called evenings spent getting lunches ready for children to take to school or to day-care "free" (as opposed to taken up by homework). The privatization of childcare, an outcome of a general attitude that mothering was not work, reinforced the set of beliefs that judged waged labor for mothers socially undesirable even if necessary for some families. Yet the opposition of the mothers themselves to institutional childcare provided a barrier that New Deal reformers (including the women's network) never attempted to breach.[48]

The Homework Protective League petitioned in the name of motherhood through the rhetoric of feminism. One favorable lower court decision, according to the Tammany Hall politician and Protective League lawyer Julius Hochfelder, settled for all times "the question that women are also people." Its president Anna Hochfelder, his wife and former assistant corporation counsel for Tammany Hall, mixed the old concept of "republican motherhood," which stressed female difference, with the concept of equality when she reminded NRA chairman Donald Richberg, "discrimination against one group of women – the mothers of our future citizens – is un-American, and not in keeping with the equality of opportunity guaranteed by the Constitution." The codes were undemocratic; homeworkers "had no voice in the making" and they discriminated "between the industrial homeworkers who are not unionized and cannot go into the factories to work, and the workers who are unionized, and who work in factories." Yet the other arguments of the Protective League – that the provisions in the homework codes violated the "constitutional" right to work and the general rights of employers; that the work process of the home crafts was incompatible with factory production; that cheap foreign imports would ruin them if forced to a factory – exposed it as the voice of certain marginal capitalists.[49] That the press and the administration took Protective League arguments so seriously suggests the powerful appeal that could be made in the name of motherhood.

Tammany Hall connections shaped the Protective League's opposition to regulation. Ideology may have been less important than New York politics. That state's Democratic machine stood in an ambivalent relation to the New

[48] Rosenzweig to Green, Nov. 28, 1934, HC Records, box 8382, folder "Request for Information and Materials"; Gwendolyn Hughes Berry, "Mothers in Industry," *American Academy of Political and Social Science* 143 (May 1929), 319–21; Ware, *Beyond Suffrage*, 87–115; Lois Scharf, *To Work and to Wed: Female Employment, Feminism, and the Great Depression* (Westport, Conn.: Greenwood Press, 1980), 110–38.

[49] *New York Daily News*, Oct. 3, 1934, 36; Anna W. Hochfelder to Donald R. Richberg, Oct. 1, 1934; Rosenberg to Rosenzweig, Aug. 8, 1934, both in HC Records, box 8384, folder "Homework Protective League"; Hochfelder, "Preliminary Memorandum," 1–8; Anna W. Hochfelder, "Regulated or Bootlegged Homework: Which?" 5, 8, attached to Anna W. Hochfelder to Owen R. Lovejoy, Aug. 17, 1934, NYCLC Papers, box 1, folder 2; *New York Daily News Record*, Feb. 12, 1934, HC Records, box 8383. Pro-homework groups had diverse politics. Newark contractor Gladys Mayhew of the Home Workers' Protective Association of New Jersey served as president of a Republican party woman's auxiliary. "Women in Politics," Newark *Evening News*, Jan. 17, 1936, CLNJ Papers, box 9.

Deal. Supporting Fusion candidate Fiorello La Guardia, Roosevelt had campaigned against the bosses. But despite a mutual hostility, Tammany attempted to use New Deal work and relief programs to maintain patronage-based influence. With Italian immigrants and small ethnic entrepreneurs as part of its political base, Tammany's defense of homework made political sense.[50]

The impact of the NRA: The perils of compliance

The general difficulties of the NRA – reliance on employer voluntarism, the dominance of stronger sectors of capital over others, unclear and conflicting bureaucratic rules – plagued homework regulation. This certainly occurred with the National Hand Embroidery and Novelty Manufacturers Association (known as the Zahn group after its head, Joseph Zahn), whose battle Julius Hochfelder took up. This group consisted of about a hundred members, as opposed to the nearly seven hundred shops of the associations supporting the code (the National Association of Bonnaz and Embroidery Manufacturers and the National Association of Pleating, Stitching, and Embroidery Manufacturers). All of these groups employed homeworkers, although the Zahn group nearly exclusively so; the larger associations sent out 75 percent of all homework to as many as twenty thousand women in the New York City area. Greater reliance on machinery and concern for industry stabilization made ban proposers willing to reorganize and bring homeworkers inside.[51]

Having failed to exempt homework from the hand embroidery code, the Zahn group began to disrupt the workings of the code authority, which was not difficult. For here was an artificial industry, a collection of "crafts or processes performed on [a] multiplicity of articles." The prohibition of homework, while the practice continued in related industries, not only created a confusing situation but also led to the "bootlegging" of garments to more permissive codes. The failed Prohibition experiment provided the metaphor for government regulation gone awry. Employers claimed to lose qualified workers to those industries that let workers labor at home. Certainly the Zahn group added to the chaos. Although the administration set up a transition period prior to the June 1, 1934, date of the homework ban, the Zahn group continued to appeal to higher authorities. Hochfelder approached the Darrow Commission, an independent review board set up to evaluate the NRA. At a hearing in early May, the Darrow Commission

---

[50] Steven Erie, *Rainbow's End* (Philadelphia. Pa.: Temple Univ. Press, 1990).

[51] Memo to O. W. Rosenzweig from Ivar Axelson, Executive Director, Code Authority for the Pleating, Stitching and Bonnaz and Hand Embroidery Industry, Aug. 7, 1934, HC Records, box 8384, folder "Homeworker Protective League"; "Hearing on the Pleating, Stitching and Bonnaz and Hand Embroidery Industry: Proposed Interpretation," Nov. 20, 1934, 6–8, 11, 15, NRA TH, 231–1–06.

dismissed charges against the code authority; the demise of the commission stymied a second hearing.[52]

Meanwhile, Zahn instructed his membership "not to recognize our code." That meant refusing to register homeworkers, sign a compliance certificate, pay an assessment, or send for a labor provisions poster. When cited for minimum wage violations, these employers would pay only thirty-five cents per hour for specific violations but not any general restitution. Zahn would "cooperate with this Code Authority *when the Government grants his group homework.*" His disruptive tactics persisted with a suit in the name of two Italian mothers who had their homework permits revoked by New York State, a case with a denouement similar to that of Kathryn Budd's.[53]

Organizations of recalcitrant employers, though a minority in an industry, plagued the functioning of other codes. The code for the furniture industry applied its thirty cents an hour minimum wage rate to home as well as factory workers. Represented by the Southern Furniture Manufacturers Association of High Point, North Carolina, about twenty double-bottom cane chair manufacturers – employers of nearly six hundred factory workers and three thousand part-time home "contract" workers – gained a stay of the labor provisions in relation to homework. Their protest against higher rates belonged to the larger regional lobbying for lower wage differentials for predominantly Southern industries that sought to pay low wages to African Americans. The manufacturers battled NRA administrators over the highest hourly rate they could pay and not have their market succumb to competition from machine-made chairs, with the NRA claiming twenty-two cents and the chair makers insisting on sixteen. Some turned out extra stock before the code went into effect; in the fall of 1934 others began appealing to various NRA boards and to the courts, which sustained the NRA. But compliance was weak.[54]

These small-town firms viewed themselves as embattled, fighting for both a customary way of doing business and "the right of these contract seaters to earn needed incomes rather than to be thrown upon public charity." They saw NRA decisions as favoring the one large urban manufacturer in their field (who hired black women) and as forcing them to lose out to the wood seat bow-back chair or to homemade seating "*which is not subject to any code of fair competition.*" According

[52] Brand, *Corporatism and the Rule of Law*, 159–62; Ivar Axelson, "Report on the Subversive Activities of the National Hand Embroidery and Novelty Manufacturers," 1–5; Axelson to Rosenzweig, Aug. 7, 1934, 1–4.

[53] "The Pleating, Stitching and Bonnaz and Hand Embroidery Industry," Oct. 3, 1933, 54, 57, 60; "Women Lose Fight on Homework Ban," *New York Times*, Jan. 1, 1935, 45.

[54] John M. Hunter, "Homework in the Furniture Manufacturing Industry," July 2, 1935, especially 6, 1, 10, Exhibit "M" to final report of the Furniture Code, box 27, Records of the Review Division Code Histories for Industries; "Brief of Manufacturers of Double Cane Seat Chairs Concerning the Matter of Home Work"; Memorandum from O. W. Rosenzweig to C. R. Niklason, May 15, 1934; both box 2401, folder "Amendments and Modifications, Labor (P–Z)," RG9.

ing to a vocal protester from Rex, Georgia, the administration's proposal must have come "from some theorist or 'brain truster,' if you will, with no practical knowledge of the subject with which he or she is attempting to deal." While professing belief in the president and viewing their homework as compatible with the promotion of home industry by the Subsistence Homesteads Program, these southern businessmen presented the raise in their piece rates as a trampling of individual freedom by malevolent and ignorant bureaucrats. They threw the language of the NRA back at administrators, arguing that the proposed piece rate undermined *"present productive capacity of industries,"* would *"promote monopolies,"* and *"eliminate or oppress* small enterprises," all contrary to the program's goals.[55]

To defend themselves, employers cited the characteristics of their work force. One from Darlington, South Carolina, not only presented the usual claim that home duties interfered with full-time work but deployed the racist ideology that justified low wages by arguing that his predominantly black employees were incapable of other labor. More often, employers – and the politicians who defended them – listed motherhood, widowhood, old age, and disability as disqualifying workers for other labor. They cited an Eleanor Roosevelt article, "Too Old for the Job," to defend homework for older women, although only "15 percent were as old as 50." Real handicap or age, the Women's Bureau pointed out, could gain a certificate under the Executive Order. Despite employer claims that a mere 17 percent of the workers could enter the factory, the Women's Bureau found that 40 percent could, and at least one worker could in almost 60 percent of the families. Rather than gaining independence through homework, 40 percent of the workers had been on relief part of the year, contrary to the claims of congressmen and other local elites. The low weekly wage – four to nine dollars – actually was a family wage. Believing that the NRA was going to take away whatever work remained, intimidated workers signed petitions. Meanwhile employers benefited from reduced overhead and family labor.[56]

How effective, then, were the NRA codes in ending the exploitative conditions of homework? Many were clearly inadequate; impact depended on the industry and its locality. Strong trade unions and interested women's organizations enhanced enforcement. Prohibition appeared more effective than

[55] E. G. Lindemann, "The Furniture Manufacturing Industry (In the Matter of Home Work)," 21–2; "Brief of Manufacturers of Double Cane Seat Chairs," 2, 4, 19; Congressman E. M. Owen to Deputy Administrator Nicklason, May 17, 1934; Walter Estes to Senator Walter George, Congressman E. M. Owens, May 4, 1934; Walter Estes to Mr. J. T. Ryan, May 2, 1934; Green River Chair Company to Mr. J. T. Ryan, May 2, 1934; "A Letter Against Prohibiting Home Work in the Double Cane Seat Chair Industry Filed by the Livermore [Kentucky] Chamber of Commerce," RG9, box 1401, file "Amendments and Modifications Labor (E-O)."

[56] Hon. J. Walter Lambeth (N.C.), Hon. John W. Boehne (Indiana), Hon. Glover H. Cary (Kentucky), "The Furniture Manufacturing Industry," 43–62, which includes letters from constituents asking for continuation of homework; "Brief of Manufacturers of Double Cane Seat Chairs," 19; "Points Made at Hearing on Chair Caning Before Industrial Appeals Board by Representatives of Women's Bureau, Sept. 25, 1934," WTUL Papers, reel 68, frames 22–3.

regulation. General code provisions could increase homework despite the goal of raising labor standards. To keep infants' wear manufacturers in their code, Knitted Outerwear permitted homework. Its certification system encouraged noncompliance. Despite efforts to pay homeworkers a rate to yield them thirteen dollars for a forty-hour week, the lacemaking industry fell far short, with not even 20 percent of chief homeworkers making thirty cents an hour and 71 percent earning less than twenty-five cents an hour. False reporting by both homeworkers and their employers marred any attempt by the code authority to regulate hours. The thirteen-dollar minimum wage for freshwater pearl buttons, an industry that regulated rather than prohibited homework, pushed more work into Iowa homes. In California, handkerchief manufacturers ignored their own piece rates; some switched to higher-priced items to continue homework. Mandated minimum wage rates increased the number of Pennsylvania embroidery homeworkers about 10 percent; but, overall, the number of registered homeworkers halved. As one prominent employer recollected, "the minute the NRA was abolished . . . homework continued as freely as before. . . . Whatever we did . . . during the time that had contemplated the end of homework was forgotten."[57]

Tag stringing responded to homework prohibition through mechanization, except for a few varieties with little demand. So did some sections of the New York City button industry. Beseiged with competition, many contractors still were "for homework because it means a livelihood." As long as the flower and feather code authority allowed homework, it was rampant. But after prohibition in May 1934, only 3 percent of interviewed families made flowers at home. Code contradictions sent work to industries with the cheapest labor, from those prohibiting homework to those allowing it. Long-term market or stylistic changes – in infants' wear, shoe heels, and cheap jewelry – could account for a decrease in homework.[58]

[57] Mary Skinner, "Industrial HomeWork under the National Recovery Administration," CBB no. 234 (Washington, D.C.: GPO, 1936), 24–30; Flexner and Skinner, "A Study of Industrial Home Work," 37–9; "Child Labor in 1935–1936: Report of the National Child Labor Committee," 9, Abbott Papers, box 65, folder 4; E. W. Brand to O. W. Rosenzweig, "Homework in the Fresh Water Pearl Button Industry," July 29, 1934, 3, HC Records, box 8384, folder "Industries"; "Homework in the Button Industry in New York City," Feb. 2, 1937, 10–12, NYDOL Library, vertical files; "The Hand-Made Handkerchief Industry in Continental United States," 3–4, 9, HC Records, box 8384, folder "Industries"; "Hearing on the Pleating, Stitching and Bonnaz and Hand Embroidery Industry: Proposed Interpretation," Nov. 20, 1934, 90, 107, 162, NRA TH, 231–1–06; Abraham Friedensohn, "Conference and Executive Session of Industry Committee No. 15 for the Embroidery Industry," Sept. 4, 1940, 84, RG155, box 62.

[58] Secretary [GAH] to Miss Elizabeth C. Watson, May 14, 1935, NYCLC Papers, box 8, folder 52; C. M. Kendrick to Mr. Sherman Trowbridge, Assistant Deputy Administrator Textile Division, Feb. 8, 1935, and R. C. Crawford to Mr. O. W. Rosenzweig, July 16, 1935, HC Records, box 8386, folder "Industries"; "Homework in the Button Industry in New York City," 10–12; Mary Skinner, "Prohibition of Industrial Home Work in Selected Industries Under the National Recovery Administration," CBB, no. 244 (Washington, D.C.: GPO, 1938), 14–15; on shoe heels, Carrie Graves to My dear Miss Skinner, Aug. 31, 1935, RG102, 20–163 5.

A committed union, like the Amalgamated, improved enforcement by reporting violations. Ninety-four percent of the homework in men's clothing ended. Manufacturers with space took former homeworkers into their plants. Outside finishing shops developed in urban neighborhoods formerly dominated by home finishing. These operated like contract shops, specializing in one component of the production process. The end of homework did not necessarily mean the full reemployment of homeworkers because "operators in plants average longer hours at work and are probably more productive."[59]

Organizing drives could eliminate homework. A successful ILGWU strike in Cleveland organized 100 percent of embroidery factories, ending homework in 1934. Neckwear manufacturers, confronted by attempts at unionization, set up stitch shops in factories, though they returned to homework in the post-NRA period. But not all industries had a strong union to watch over the code process. In Gloversville, New York, "the factory workers are walking the streets and home workers are working day and night" despite union agreements that included homeworkers. To take advantage of local unemployment, a unionized woman's garment factory in Decatur, Illinois, dismissed its regular workers and began giving out homework and hiring "learners" to get around the code which it had signed.[60] Willingness of employers to abide by the codes, a function of the state of unionization and market conditions, accounted for the effectiveness of codes, not any formal code enforcement mechanisms. These reflected the general lack of schematic regulations and uneven coordination between Washington and the states.[61]

Employers and workers alike abused licensing procedures. Desiring certification under the Executive Order, women falsely claimed disability. About 30 percent of the special certificates in Pennsylvania went to men's neckwear workers, although only 2 percent had before the NRA. Certified workers in New York's artificial flower industry circumvented the code by acting as contractors. Faced with agents about to seize illegal homework, some women became violent and chased the agents away. "A chiselling manufacturer," a business opponent explained, "can meet any requirements of a licensing board. Once he knows he can get home work – I won't go so far as to say he will rent

[59] Grace Overmayer, "4 Cents an Hour," *Today*, Aug. 25, 1934, 10–11; NRA, Men's Clothing Industry, "Hearing on Proposed Amendments to the Code of Fair Competition," Feb. 2, 1935, 303–15, 244–5; "The Home Work Problem," Aug. 13, 1934, HC Records, box 8384, folder "Industries."

[60] Elizabeth Magee, "Third Annual Meeting of the Labor Standards Conference," 7; Frances Perkins to Hugh Johnson, July 2, 1934, HC Records, box 8386, folder "Labor, U.S. Department of"; Elizabeth Bunn to M. D. Vincent, Jan. 28, 1935, HC Records, box 8384, folder "Gloves,"; Mary Anderson to David Dubinsky, Sept. 31, 1933, with attached letter, Mrs. Rose Lewis Kuhner to Frances Perkins, Sept. 6, 1933, and Mary Ann Walker et al. to Hon. Frances Perkins, Sept. 11, 1933, Dubinsky Papers, box 78–2.

[61] Ruth Shallcross, a disgruntled former homework inspector, recounted the confusion in the field from constantly changing NRA rules in *Industrial Homework: An Analysis of Homework Regulation Here and Abroad* (New York: Industrial Affairs, 1939), 61.

crippled mothers – but it can be done. More evasions can be thought of in an hour than safeguards can be established in a month." One flower manufacturer used a building a few blocks from his factory for distribution, with the finished goods placed in subway station parcel lockers.[62]

Despite such loopholes, the Children's and Women's bureaus studied the impact of code regulation with the goal of "furnish[ing] effective arguments for the abolition of homework." As long as their facts showed loss of work "much less serious" than predicted, they could undermine "the sentimental appeal of the argument that the homeworker would suffer unduly if deprived of the work." With this goal, it is not surprising that the Children's Bureau found that 85 percent of homeworkers were able to enter the factory, most could make adequate childcare arrangements, and the loss of homework did not increase relief rolls. The published report omitted the observation of investigator Mary Skinner that women labored part-time but "often stayed at the factory the regular hours to take the work whenever it became available" – a kind of irregularity long associated with operations previously put into homes. And the experiences of those transferred to the factory probably "represented a rather picked group, since the less able workers were probably weeded out at a very early stage," according to an internal critique that then dismissed this fundamental criticism of the sample as a "minor point" that did not really need to be noted.[63]

The Women's and Children's bureaus claimed that most homeworkers had overcome unwillingness to leave the home. One manufacturer declared, "They have tasted better now; they will never go back to home work." There was certainly truth here. An Italian neckwear worker found "that my home is clean, that I have taken my oldest daughter into the factory with me, and between us now we earn $35.00, where formerly, working at home, we all earned $15.00, and I have time to go to the movies." Even those who believed "that a mother's place is in the home" admitted that factory wages were better. Yet 15 percent of the new factory-working mothers found their childcare arrangement "so difficult" that they longed for homework.[64]

Homeworkers did not enter the debate over government regulation with one voice; they presented an array of attitudes toward the abolition of their system of labor. Like trade union leaders, some compared homework to slavery. "A Sweatworker" from the Greek community of Haverhill, Massachu-

[62] Clara Beyer, Ralph K. Ginzburg, "Third Annual Meeting of the Labor Standards Conference," 8, 10; Shallcross, *Industrial Homework*, 198–9, Skinner, "Prohibition of Industrial Home Work," 12–13.

[63] Skinner, "Prohibition of Industrial Home Work," 18–25; "Proposed Study of Industrial Homework by Children's Bureau in Cooperation with Women's Bureau"; Skinner to Miss McConnell, Feb. 5, 1936; Mr. Myers to Miss McConnell, June 14, 1938; RG102, 20–163–2.

[64] Skinner, "Prohibition of Industrial Home Work," 18–25; Frieda Miller, "Pleating, Stitching, and Bonnaz and Hand Embroidery Industry," Nov. 20, 1934, 106.

setts, complained that the fathers "went to the coffee houses and beer joints and enjoyed themselves, on their children's sweat money. While their wives and children slaved themselves." Reflecting a sense of justice that condemned taking work away from others by laboring too long into the night or by having other income, a glove homeworker thought, "if homework is stopped it would be the best thing ever happened. Then let the mfr. hire the poor home workers and fire the factory workers that don't need work but want it." An upstate New York woman asked: "Why should our women . . . be obliged to work at such wages? Is there any way of making things different and women as well as men get living wages?"[65]

Homework defenders divided into two groups: those with philosophical objections to prohibition and those desperate for work. Some company lawyers kept raising the issue of including mothers with young children in the Executive Order. Ministers complained that the NRA was taking away people's livelihoods. Contractors called for freedom, applauding the self-reliance that kept homeworkers from relief, a condition that code provisions would end. Like other ordinary Americans, homeworkers personalized their relationship with the Roosevelts. A woman from rural Pennsylvania expressed a common disappointment in the NRA that it was not providing more work. A Maine knitter of infants' wear inquired whether Mrs. Roosevelt could find her homework because she read in the papers "what wonderful things you are doing for the needy." An upstate New York woman told the President that the NRA "does more harm than good." Referring to the Arthurdale subsistence homestead project, she protested: "Why can't we have the benefit of the work in the same way as your wife has been doing. They tell me she has been supplying people with work in the Virginia mountains."[66]

Homeworkers pleaded for an opportunity to earn wages, to maintain their standard of living, and to fulfill their duties as breadgivers. Many told tales of ill health or unemployment; most spoke of their need to act as caretakers, of children and sometimes the elderly, ill, or disabled. Whether or not these

---

[65] "A Sweatworker" to the NRA Labor Dept., Mar. 4, 1934, attached to Max Berkowitz, Code Director to Code Authority, Apr. 16, 1934, box 8385, folder "Ladies Handbag"; Mrs. Blendinghurst, Gloversville, N.Y. to Dear Sir, Mar. 8, 1934, box 8382, folder "Correspondence"; Mrs. O. H. Brinkerhoff to Franklin Delano Roosevelt, Feb. 16, 1935, box 8385, folder "Industries," all in HC Records.

[66] HC Records, Homework Spindles in box 8382, 8383, 8385, and letters in folder "artificial flower," box 8384. Feldman and Barrett to the NRA, May 17, 1934, box 8382; Clyde H. Johnson to Hon. Hugh S. Johnson, Mar. 24, 1934, box 8382; Lillian J. Levesque to The Hon. President Franklin D. Roosevelt, June 25, 1934, box 8383; Mrs. C. E. Beierminski to United States Senator Royal S. Copeland, Mar. 4, 1935, box 8382; Mrs. Josephine Cichon to O. W. Rosenzweig, Mar. 15, 1934, box 8385; Mrs. Effie Edwards, Oxford Maine, to Mrs. Roosevelt, Nov. 9, 1934; Mrs. Ada Richmond, Cropseyville, N.Y. to President Roosevelt, May 30, 1934, both in box 8382, folder "Homework Exemptions and Requests."

stories were exaggerated, or merely narratives constructed to gain certificates for homework, they reinforced the portrait of homeworker as victim of the economy, the state, and the gender division of social life.

Bringing the NRA to Puerto Rico

Puerto Rico offers a significant contrast to conditions on the mainland. Home needlework was central to its economy and could not be prohibited without severe dislocations. Over 75 percent of needleworkers labored at home compared to an estimated one-fourth of 1 percent in the United States. Their numbers grew during the early depression, while those in the United States fell. Factory employees worked a 47 hour week, seven hours longer than stipulated by NRA codes, yet made nine cents an hour when even those in the U.S. South earned thirty-one cents an hour. Federal and insular labor department officials, with the aid of trade unionists and U.S. manufacturers, attempted to regulate homework under an islandwide NRA code. They proposed workshop centers in rural regions. Some rank and file unionists sought to organize and defend the rights of homeworkers to living wages. This approach differed from garment unionists in the United States who almost universally classified homeworkers as unorganizable and strove to ban homework. Puerto Rico stands out as an exception: Shopworkers, nearly all of whom had worked at home, sought to organize homeworkers. Home and factory workers shared culture, class, gender, and community. Still even here political divisions among socialists and male dominance in trade union leadership hampered the effort. Few homeworkers actually became unionized.[67]

U.S. occupation of Puerto Rico in 1898 diverted whatever tendency had existed toward noncolonial capitalist development in the waning years of Spanish rule. What emerged from U.S. domination was a "monocultural colony" based on sugar, where absentee ownership drained profits back to the mainland. Export production removed land from food cultivation so that by the early thirties, the urban poor faced higher prices for necessary items than their counterparts in New York City, who received wages four to ten times higher. As families became dependent on wage labor, and male employment suffered from the seasonal nature of sugar and the declining

[67] Walter M. Barrow, "Report on Homework Conditions in the Island of Puerto Rico: Part One: Conditions Prior to Codification," NRA, San Juan, Puerto Rico Office, July 12, 1935, 9, 13–14, RG9, box 63; "Rise in Imports of Puerto Rican Cotton Wear Cited," *Daily News Record*, Mar. 20, 1934. See also Maria del Carmen Baerga, "Social Hierarchies and Expressions of Resistance: Gender, Class, and Age Among the Needleworkers in Puerto Rico in the 1930s," paper at the History of Latina Women Workers, George Meany Memorial Archives, Feb. 1993; Blanca Silvestrini, "Puerto Rican Workers and the Socialist Party, 1932 to 1940," (Ph.D. diss., SUNY at Albany), 1973, 48–51, 71–3.

production of coffee and tobacco, women increasingly became incorporated into the paid labor work force, into a sex-segmented labor market.[68]

During the early 1930s, seventy thousand needleworkers embroidered, sewed, and finished women's garments at home or served as sub-contractors. They lived in cramped and drafty shacks in outlying mountain regions, on sugar and tobacco plantations, and along the swampy outskirts of cities. They worked for piece rates as low as one or two cents an hour. Unlike most homeworking women in northeast and midwestern cities, less than 40 percent were mothers; they resembled those in the Appalachian South where lack of alternative employment also pushed daughters to home labor. Unlike the classic image of the homeworker bent over for fifteen-hour days, those in Puerto Rico rarely had enough work to labor long hours. Homework existed not so much because women preferred it but because employers structured work that way, because the island was underdeveloped, lacking roads and alternative employment, and garment firms could exploit this situation.[69]

Needlework ranked by 1930 as Puerto Rico's second largest industry, worth between ten and fifteen million dollars a year. Its origins lay in the crisis of World War I which stopped exports from northern France, Belgium, Madeira, and Ireland. Searching for an alternative source of cheap, but fine embroidery, manufacturers turned to the U.S. colonies of the Philippines and Puerto Rico. Since the days of Spanish rule, some urban women had learned fine lace and drawn work as proper activities that could occur in the shelter of the home. Beginning in 1918, the public schools of Mayagüez offered needlework instruction. U.S. department stores, however, felt that few could produce fine work in the amount and at the prices needed, so they hastily trained workers to embroider "stamped designs . . . [of] wreaths and sprays of leaves, petals and flowers" in large quantities, geared to the developing chain store trade.[70]

U.S. firms supplied garments for contractors to distribute to home sewers and embroiderers. Some contractors ran inside shops and a few mainland firms set up Puerto Rico operations. Mayagüez, with its thirty to forty contractors of "recognized standing," became the center of the industry, with Ponce and

[68] James L. Dietz, *Economic History of Puerto Rico: Institutional Change and Capitalist Development* (Princeton, N.J.: Princeton Univ. Press, 1986), 79–133; Victor S. Clark, et al., *Puerto Rico and Its Problems* (Washington, D.C.: The Brookings Institution, 1930); Maria del Carmen Baerga, "Wages, Consumption, and Survival: Working-Class Households in Puerto Rico in the 1930s," in Joan Smith and Immanuel Wallerstein, eds., *Households and the World Economy* (Beverly Hills, Calif.: Sage, 1984), 233–51.

[69] Barrow, "Report on Homework Conditions," 16; Caroline Manning, "The Employment of Women in Puerto Rico," *CBB*, no. 118 (Washington, D.C.: GPO, 1934), 2.

[70] "Memorandum on Homework in Puerto Rico," 23–4, HC Records, box 8389, folder "Puerto Rico"; J. R. McKey, Special Report no. 14, "The Needlework Industry of Porto Rico," Oct. 29, 1929, 1–3, ACWA Papers, box 97, folder 8; J. A. E. Rodriguez and "Brief of Mr. Jose C. Benet" in "Hearing on Code of Fair Practice and Competition for Puerto Rico presented by Needlework Industry Code," [Puerto Rico Hearings] Feb. 28, 1934 and Mar. 1, 1934, 172–80, 256–7, RG9, box 7117.

San Juan other distributional points. Because many of the homeworkers lived in isolated rural regions, the contractor often would hire subcontractors to actually bring and collect garments. There was no standard arrangement between homeworkers and contractors, some of whom kept from 12.5 to 33.5 percent of the price given by the mainland firm. At an extreme, agents withheld pay or reimbursed workers with food or other goods, sometimes forcing home- workers to buy items at a "company store."[71]

In the early years of the depression, needlework prices further declined because manufacturers could get work made in rural Pennsylvania for two cents an hour and be rid of the freight charges, delays, and cumbersome contractor system of the island. In August 1933, the needlewomen of Mayagüez, both inside and outside workers, struck for higher pay. Police, called to protect employer property, killed and wounded strikers who had stoned the workshop of Representative Maria Luisa Arcelay, the only female member of the Puerto Rican legislature and a contractor who would represent Puerto Rican business at the NRA code hearings the following year. Union organization mushroomed in response; more than three-quarters of the factory and shop workers organized in 1933 and about three thousand homeworkers formed nine of their own unions within a year. Workers received an increase of 15 to 25 percent when the commissioner of labor mediated the strike. However, most agents broke the agreement, keeping the raise for themselves and never informing the homeworkers of the increase.[72]

In this context, the NRA opened hearings for a special needlework code for the island in March 1934. It had provided exemptions from the thirteen-dollar minimum wage for Texas manufacturers of infants' and children's wear who claimed to be suffering from Puerto Rican competition. But the island was a different case since factories undertook more than one line of production, depending on the season, and it seemed more efficient to have one code authority for all garment-related industries except the separate area of men's clothing (with its own code and problems with homework). Mainland manufacturers who did not send work to Puerto Rico feared the labor differentials proposed for the needlework code. Those who used island homeworkers usually accepted the existing organization of labor and opposed any code that would match mainland standards. Businessmen assumed that Puerto Rican goods lacked the market power – especially since they were of inferior workmanship or made from cheap materials – to command higher prices. "We want all the workers to be contented and happy," one declared, "We want you to do

---

[71] Manning, "The Employment of Women in Puerto Rico," 7–12; "The Needlework Industry of Porto Rico," 4–7, 9–10; Manning, Puerto Rico Hearings, 128–9; Barrow, "Report on Homework Conditions," 17–18.

[72] Blanca Silvestrini, "Women as Workers: The Experience of the Puerto Rican Woman in the 1930s," in The Puerto Rican Woman: Perspectives on Culture, History and Society, ed. Edna Acosta-Belen, 2d ed. (New York: Praeger, 1986), 66–9; Manning, "The Employment of Women," 11–12, 14–15; Dietz, Economic History, 175.

your work happily, improve your efficiency." Despite this paternalistic language of class consolidation, he and others were not going to pay more than such labor was worth. Raise the minimum weekly wage to eight dollars and they would go to China and cheaper labor markets. Only with homework could Puerto Rico compete in world trade.[73]

The Puerto Rican Needlework Association – mostly a subcontractor group controlled by a few employers with direct ties to mainland firms – assumed that homework would continue. Their proposed code attempted to safeguard the worker from the worst abuses of the system by including the subcontractor as a "member of the industry" and making her liable for paying the minimum wage. These business people preferred protective tariffs, which could be evoked under NRA procedures, to raise wages for homeworkers, rather than the use of code minimums that would apply to all workers, regardless of where they labored.[74]

Insular officials and employers alike appealed to a sense of Puerto Rican nationalism to chide organizing labor. They appropriated the language of justice. The assistant commissioner of agriculture and commerce contended that elimination of homework would bring even greater hardship and misery. The Mayagüez Chamber of Commerce asserted that homework was "essential and indispensable for the welfare of the community." Its spokesmen championed the "inalienable right" of homeworkers to their work and argued that its end would "lower the standard of living of a considerable part of the Puerto Rican proletariate." One male contractor reinforced this point when claiming homework bans in other codes had ruined handicraft businesses and thrown millions of women onto relief rather than protecting such workers.[75]

Homework defenders gendered their economic arguments. Moving work into factories would force rural people into cities, bringing economic ruin to industry and moral ruin to women. Factory girls and homeworking mothers equally benefited from the homework system. Where once girls could only become servants, now they could work in factories, becoming more intelligent, alert, and able from this "larger social and business intercourse." Removing homework would jeopardize factory jobs because U.S. firms would go elsewhere. As for the worker who wished to remain at home, she "enjoys more liberty and better health in the rural districts." Abolition of homework was a scheme on the part of the labor unions to "dominat[e] . . . the masses." By associating tyranny with trade unions and freedom (and even women's libera-

---

[73] "Infants' and Children's Wear Industry," May 22, 1934, 32–3, NRA TH, 217–1–05; Puerto Rico Hearings, 269, 13, 254, 267–8, 76, 245, 183–4, 211–12; H. O. Stansbury Co. to Beatrice McConnell, Aug. 20, 1934, HC Records, box 8389, folder "Puerto Rico."

[74] Puerto Rico Hearings, 6, 41, 187–8, 220–2. The Needlework Association had 3,115 members, of which 3,000 were subcontractors. See Memo to NIRB thru Boaz Long from the Puerto Rican Needlework Authority, May 17, 1935, RG9, box 47, folder "Needlework Amend."

[75] Puerto Rico Hearings, 44–5, 238–9, 234–7, 41, 46–9, 194–6.

tion from drudgery and backwardness) with homework, defenders obscured actual power relations.[76]

Shop workers recognized that their fate interconnected with that of homeworkers. They called for regulation, rather than elimination, asserting an identity of interests with homeworking women, a position that many once had assumed. (About a quarter of homeworkers at one time had worked in a factory.) Gloria Rivera, treasurer of Union #2 of San Juan, defended the homeworker: "What we want is that they earn the same amount of money as we do. A woman who works at home does as good a job as the woman who works in the shop on the same kind of work, so I do not see why she is getting less money on it." Other local union officials, from Mayagüez and Cabo Rojo, similarly connected notions of justice – for workers and human beings – with concepts of care – one woman to another, the homeworker, who but for the force of circumstance could and has been the self. One exclaimed, "A worker should be well fed and our children also [well fed], because we are human beings, we need food and demand a decent living and at the same time some recreation." This speaker combined such universalist justice arguments with that of a mother's duty to educate, clothe, feed, and raise her children. Denying the charge that they were all socialists, these working-class women rejected business arguments that higher wages would destroy the industry. This group of homeworkers affirmed homework to be "a sacrifice," rather than "a help," as the employers considered it. "The value of such work is so small that we have to work the whole week, day and night disregarding our housekeeping obligations, in order to earn 50 cents or 60 cents a week." Recognizing that "our services are used in order to make competition among contractors," these workers pleaded that the codes bring about a better world. They would rather see the work disappear than the employers pay them less.[77]

The needleworkers' unions strove to raise the pay of all workers, with homeworkers part of their constituency. The Insular Council of Needleworkers called for an across-the-board minimum wage of eight dollars and demanded the gradual abolition of homework. So did Rose Schneiderman of the NRA Labor Advisory Board, who maternalistally viewed herself as "labor adviser for these girls" and felt "a great responsibility" not "to chase the industry out of Puerto Rico." While some trade unionists called for intensive organizing to end homework, Insular Council President Teresa Angleró promoted the community workshop plan proposed by the Women's Bureau and embraced by the NRA. This plan would establish branch factories in the rural districts where women would work from two to six hours a day. Workers could be more efficient than at home,

---

[76] Puerto Rico Hearings, 256–66.

[77] Puerto Rico Hearings, 197–9, 199–202, 203–4, 204–6, 219, 213–17; Manning, "Employment of Women," 3; for a female consciousness derived from the domestic economy, Temma Kaplan, "Female Consciousness and Collective Action: The Case of Barcelona, 1910–1918," *Signs* 7 (Spring 1982): 545–66.

become more proficient, and be surrounded by cleaner conditions which would be healthier for both the worker and the consumer of hand embroidered goods. Eleanor Roosevelt herself traveled to Puerto Rico to warn mainland women "to boil" Puerto Rican embroideries "before putting them on or using them," the old strategy of the NCL.[78]

Drawing upon the often used discourse of freedom and slavery, Angleró labeled homeworkers who defended the system "slaves"; they needed "to be set free by those at liberty to clamor for human freedom." But homeworkers regarded their labors in a different light, defending the only "honest means" by which they could provide children with bread. They relied upon the same image, the mother as breadgiver, that local trade union women evoked to demand higher minimum wages for all women. From Camuy, women wrote officials not to end homework "from which Puerto Rican mothers earn a living working in their independent homes, during spare hours in a useful occupation." Contractors organized the sending of telegrams, but this fact hardly negates the language in which women argued. While economic discourse dominated the code hearings (with only the commissioner of labor condemning homework for undermining the home), homeworkers emphasized their role as mothers which included providing for children and helping husbands. Yet homeworkers also claimed the mantle of justice. "It would be inhuman that a large part of the district of Mayagüez, a fifty percent of which has contributed so that we can come here to defend them, should be left without work, merely because they can not go to the factories. This would not be human, and I think the Department of Labor is just," another homeworker declared. A rural woman contended that branch factories would be impossible to establish; without homework they would starve. "The country women need it and there must be justice for all."[79]

The resulting code was a compromise. Employers won on wages, with factory workers given a minimum of five dollars a week, and homeworkers a differential of three dollars less. The code banned from the home many processes, such as stamping, cutting, and washing; those employed at machine sewing in the previous year could continue if registered with the code authority. Contractors, subcontractors, and homeworkers had to register themselves and their sewing machines. Finally, commissions would work out piece rates and investigate the feasibility of the Community Work Room plan.[80]

The NRA existed in Puerto Rico for less than a year. Effective July 19, 1934, the code became operational about a month later, after a commission established piece rates for the myriad needlework processes. The Mayagüez union published a public notice in local newspapers "to help us enforce the law." It

[78] Puerto Rico Hearings, 82–9, 66, 227–33, 223–6, 151–2, 145, 166–70, 159; Manning, "The Employment of Women," 14; Eleanor Roosevelt, *This I Remember* (New York: Harper, 1949), 138–40.

[79] Puerto Rico Hearings, 85, 154, 253, 270–2, 147–50.

[80] NRA, "Code of Fair Competition for the Needlework Industry in Puerto Rico," June 28, 1934 (Washington, D.C.: GPO, 1934).

informed homeworkers of the increase, asking "all the organized workers in the island" to teach the homeworkers to stop work until their piece rate increased. Inside workers took the lead, educating homeworking kin and neighbors.[81]

Work became scarce when economic conditions on the island further deteriorated; mainland manufacturers held back orders, waiting to see if rates would remain stable. Contractors sent work home rather than pay more expensive factory labor. Seeing their work and rates reduced, subcontractors kept back increases from homeworkers who, the NRA surmised, permitted this cheating "because there was no work and they needed to work even if for only one or two cents an hour." These conditions led Schneiderman to burst out at another NRA hearing, "the Puerto Rican Code is the worst Code we have." ILGWU officials Rose Pessota and Charles Zimmerman went down to the island to lobby for higher minimum wages. But deputy NRA administrator Boaz Long felt that raising wages would drive away any remaining work. If homework ended, urban migration would grow and the policy of rural resettlement fail. Labor standards could conflict with fulfillment of other state policies.[82]

In January 1935, the code authority actually revised piece rates downward to halt the bleeding of business. Its application for tariff revision to stop the importation of even cheaper Chinese handkerchiefs stalled over the extent of Puerto Rican imports to the mainland. Like other authorities, it lacked compliance officers; with workers not complaining, employers violated code provisions. Workers registered only seven thousand sewing machines, although officials estimated at least a hundred thousand home machines. The NRA failed to appoint a homework commission; the Puerto Rican Emergency Relief Association studied community workrooms, but never shared its findings with the NRA. A May 1935 attempt to include subcontractors as "members of the industry" may have improved the operation of the code, but it came too late.[83]

[81] Manuel Serra, Jr., "Report on Homework Conditions in the Island of Puerto Rico: Part Two: Conditions During and After Codification," July 12, 1935, 37–66; "Ningun Traba Lador Ni Del Taller Ni De La Casa," translated as "No Worker in the Shop nor in the Home," clipping, RG9, box 48, folder "Corres. #2."

[82] Serra, "Report on Homework Conditions: Part Two," 46–7; Pedro Ronda Rivera to National President of the United States of America, Oct. 18, 1934, HC Records, box 8389, folder "Puerto Rico"; Schneiderman, "Hearing on the Novelty Curtains, Draperies, Bedspreads and Novelty Pillows Industry," Nov. 2, 1934, 130, NRA TH, 226–1–06; Boaz Long to Blanton Winship, Oct. 2, 1934, RG9, box 48, folder "Needlework – Chinese Competition."

[83] Walter Franklin to Victor Domenech, Aug. 21, 1934, with attached table, folder "Correspondence #2 May 1, 1934–July 31"; H. D. Gresham to Victor Domenech, May 2, 1935, folder "Needlework – Chinese Competition," both in box 48; William D. Lopez to Linton Collins, Dec. 2, 1934, box 57, folder "Piece Work-Piece Rates Commission"; Victor Domenech to William A. McLaren, Feb. 15, 1935; "Registration of Sewing Machines in the Home Conference," Oct. 27, 1934, both in box 59, folder "Sewing Machines Reg."; Maria Luisa Arcelay to Boaz Long, Oct. 29, 1934, folder "Piecerate Com. #1 July–Dec. 34," box 47, folder "Needlework-amend."; radiogram July 23, 1935, box 48, folder "Community Workrooms," all in RG9.

Needlewomen themselves felt positively about the NRA. Interviewed six months after the demise of the recovery program, when piece rates were at a starvation level, most agreed that prices had been better under the NRA, although there was less work.[84] Subcontractors, who were somewhat better off, agreed. An Aquadilla woman, who distributed for Mayagüez contractors, revealed a rare sense of collective consciousness: "If the s.c.'s in P.R. were organized in a society during the codes," she told the interviewer, "these would have been very beneficial to all." One homeworker expressed a similar belief that needlewomen should organize. Although most homeworkers, like their contractors, failed to entertain unionization, they nevertheless clung to a sense of a just wage; husbands and sons often were involved in labor activism. Still others evoked the concept of justice itself, sometimes embodying it in the U.S. government: calling for investigations and the return of the NRA. As a young married English-speaking woman put it, "Draft a code that will meet Supreme Court's approval and place it in force."[85]

Homeworkers believed that their labor should be regulated rather than transferred to the factory; "every worker should be given a fixed quantity weekly for a fixed salary," one from Peñueles explained. Very few desired to move to community workrooms and none wanted the work transferred to factories.[86] Homework was part of the family economy; women desired to remain with their families but they also wanted a living wage. The tenacity with which homeworkers held onto the home as workplace suggests that their consciousness hardly derived from employer threats alone. The solidarity of local trade union women with their homeworking counterparts reveals that the division between home and factory was permeable among working-class women in Puerto Rico – where ethnicity united, rather than divided, laborers.

Market conditions and the short life of the NRA impeded effective enforcement. When the U.S. Women's Bureau surveyed the island in 1935, gloves and women's linen suits appeared as new homework industries. Competition with the Philippines, Japan, Mexico, and the southern United States decreased the amount of cheap cotton underclothes and children's dresses embroidered in Puerto Rico. Embroidery on women's dresses had gone out of style. Still, in 1940, home needlework would account for more than 44 percent of all manufacturing, with homeworkers exempt from the island's minimum wage law. After passage of the Fair Labor Standards Act (FLSA) of 1938, politicians continued to sacrifice needlewomen. The U.S. Congress amended FLSA in 1940 to allow

[84] Survey interviews: A. Corcore, B–7–2; J. Colon, B–7–3; O. Alvarado, B–7–4; M. Colon, B–7–5; E. I. Galarza, C–13, RG9, box 67.

[85] Survey interviews: M. Rodriquez, B–7–1; E. Rodriquez, B–9–1; A. Santiago, B–2–3; E. I. Galarza, C–13; de Jesus, B–2–1; V. M. Burgoes, B–7–3; M. de Colon, B–7–3, RG9, boxes 66 and 67. On connections between homeworkers and union activism among other family members, Baerga, "Wages, Consumption, and Survival," 247–8.

[86] NRA, San Juan, P.R., Reverse Needlework Survey, Case B–2 Ponce, RG9, box 67; interview with Hijinia C.; Test Survey, table 27, RG9, box 67.

lower minimums for Puerto Rico; by 1949, homeworkers – still predominant on the island – gained only fifteen cents an hour, which hardly kept up with the cost of living. During the next decade, they remained among the lowest paid, earning no more than one-third the median wage of other industrial women. But with the insular government pushing fair wages to meet the island's high cost of living, needlework manufacturers relocated to lower-wage countries. From 31 percent of all women workers in 1940, less than 1 percent of women sewed and embroidered at home in 1979. Economic transformation, guided by state policy and union watchfulness, would end most homework.[87]

Homework as craftswork

No one judged the bulk of Puerto Rican needlecraft "artistic." Such was not the case in the southern mountain regions from Knoxville and Nashville through Dalton, Georgia, and North Carolina, where families peddled handicrafts at roadside stands. Yet ILGWU vice-president Charles Zimmerman found significant parallels between this "Bedspread Belt" and the homework whitegoods industry of Puerto Rico. He claimed in 1937 that firms "who learned the tricks in Puerto Rico" had established the production process in the South. "Every step . . . is followed exactly and the net results here are the same: poverty, destitution, exploitation; child labor, ignorance and hunger, an endless chain of human misery which has as its end the same link." In response, the Textile Workers Organizing Committee (TWOC) began organizing bedspread makers in Georgia and Tennessee. But when they managed to sign a contract with one Dalton factory, which sent spreads out to homeworkers, the firm relocated to another town which promised "full protection of all city officials against unions." Mass organization eluded the TWOC here as it would among the cotton textile mills, whose decade long slowdown had pushed many to homework in the first place.[88]

Mountain homework had roots in traditional crafts. "We are going to have a terrible job distinguishing between industrial home work and handicraft," a Tulane University professor told the Southern Regional Conference on Labor Standards and Economic Security in 1934. Many Americans were unable to understand the difference between industrial homework and the New Deal promotion of the crafts. Reacting to NRA prohibitions, distraught and outraged homeworkers wrote to the president to exempt them. Some, who hoped to establish crafts shops or sell their own work, wondered whether their activity fell under the codes. The NRA told sixty-seven-year-old Sarah B. of Minne-

[87] Mary Anderson to Frances Perkins, Jan. 29, 1936, RG174, box 81, file "Women's Bureau"; Dietz, *Economic History*, 224–6.
[88] John S. Martin, "Not All in the Hills Is Mountain Music," *Justice* 19 (Sept. 15, 1937), 14; Jacqueline Dowd Hall et al., *Like a Family* (Chapel Hill: Univ. of North Carolina Press, 1988).

apolis that the codes "are not intended to, and will not, prevent you from buying materials and making an article in your own home and selling it whenever you can find a buyer." Mrs. W. G. B. of Hobart, Indiana, was "planning to open a gift show [sic] in our city – merchandise for sale consisting of hand embroidered articles, paintings, etc." She would purchase "some of the handwork from local women who have been doing this work for a living." But the NRA textiles division ruled that her show would "automatically come under the provisions of the Pleating, Stitching, and Bonnaz and Hand Embroidery Code which prohibits homework," though artwork, like painting, could be done at home.[89]

"None of us want arts and crafts eliminated," Lucy Mason of the NCL claimed. But the women's reform network wanted to stop the bedspreads, quilting, and appliqué coming from New York into Kentucky and other southern states, for which women earned at best a dollar a week. They would stop illegal contracts that held a weaver in thrall to one company whether or not it supplied her with work. They would raise the awareness of southerners "that exploitation is equally bad for the South as for the North," as explained by a representative of the Full Fashioned Hosiery Workers Union who was fighting the fancy clocking of socks in North Carolina homes. Mason distinguished between "industrial exploitation of labor" which took place "when contractual merchants and manufacturers send work into the homes for processing" and handiwork cooperatives where the maker received profits.[90]

The Division of Self-Help Cooperatives of the Federal Emergency Relief Administration (FERA) recommended that "if handicraft is to be developed, it should be done in cooperative shops rather than as a home industry in order that satisfactory supervision can be exercised to prevent sweated industry." Machine competition and foreign competition, "the crying need for cash" among rural handicrafters, and the home location of such industries all encouraged a low return to crafts workers. FERA and other New Deal agencies discovered that their desire to use handicraft "for its social and therapeutic value," to encourage the work ethic and provide creative and useful leisure activity, conflicted with its use "as a method of cash income" because if "sufficiently regulated and supervised," handicraft priced itself beyond a ready market. If sold cheaply, sweated labor resulted.[91]

[89] U.S. DOL, Division of Labor Standards, "Proceedings of Southern Regional Conference on Labor Standards and Economic Security," Jan. 20–21, 1935, 23, RG174, box 40, folder "Conf.: Southern Regional on State Labor Legislation"; Sarah B. to NRA, Aug. 3, 1934, O. W. Rosenzweig to Miss B., Aug. 10, 1934, folder "Correspondence"; Mrs. W. G. B. to Mr. Jack Lazerwitz, n.d., and Dean G. Edwards to Mr. Edward Hollander, Oct. 17, 1934, folder "Homework Spindle, Oct. 4, 1934, to Nov. 26, 1934," HC Records, box 8382.

[90] "Proceedings of Southern Regional Conference," 22–4.

[91] Nathaniel K. Fairbank, "Handicraft: An Investigation of the Present and Potential Market for Non-competitive Handcraft in the United States," June 1, 1934, 1–4, RG86, box 12, folder "Handicraft 1934: Catalogues and Plans"; for an extended discussion of these issues,

These different aims found graphic form in the conflicts between the Women's Bureau and the Tennessee Valley Authority (TVA) over the promotion of handicraft in the Southern Highlands. TVA was one of the New Deal's experiments in regional planning that would not only bring electricity and economic growth to that neglected rural area but encourage social and cultural development. In the spring of 1934, the Tennessee Valley Associated Cooperatives postponed work on handicraft until the Women's Bureau could make an economic study. The bureau desired "to formulate policies which will put existing handicraft on a sound economic basis, prevent sweated industries, and serve to guide further Federal activities for handicraft development among peoples living at below subsistence levels." They would "prevent exploitation of these women, through developing opportunities for them to work under controllable conditions which will bring fair wages for their skilled labor." Improving the economic position of women in the Appalachian region was their central concern, with development of the crafts as a means to this end.[92]

With the backing of Secretary of Labor Perkins and Eleanor Roosevelt, the Women's Bureau studied the "Potential Earning Power of Southern Mountaineer Handicraft" because of "the efforts being made to abolish homework" under the NRA codes. Substituting central production centers for home-based labor was as important as devising marketing strategies. They found home handicraft to be hard work; "the people now doing it are doing it with the same speed that they would do it in a factory because it is so irregular that they take all they can get at the time and work just as hard as they can." But the TVA felt it unnecessary "to try to change or recommend changed methods of production." It argued: "Take them as they are. If they want to manufacture in homes, let them. If in little groups, let them. In other words we . . . will cater to whatever they like to do best." This difference of opinion derived, in part, from divergent focuses: TVA, thinking of the handicraft worker as the male woodcarver, wanted "to supplement their ordinary vocation" of agriculture, but the Women's Bureau was "looking at the girl for whom the work would be a vocation because she has not now anything to do." TVA believed "her vocation is taking care of a home" but the Women's Bureau refused to confine daughters to the domestic ideal, believing that they were not needed for housework. Whereas the Women's Bureau strove to end the home as a workplace, TVA chairman Arthur Morgan promoted home labor as a means to

see Jane Becker, "Selling Tradition: The Domestication of Southern Appalachian Culture in 1930s America," (Ph.D. diss., Boston Univ., 1993).

[92] Mary Anderson to the Secretary of Labor, "Re: Economic and Social Study of Handicraft, April 30, 1934," RG86, box 12, folder "Handicraft 1934 Catalogues and Plans"; Anderson to the Secretary of Labor, "Re: Formation of Advisory Committee on Economic Development of Handicraft in the Southern Appalachian Mountains, May 17, 1934," RG174, box 82, folder "Women's Bureau General"; U.S. DOL, Women's Bureau, "Meager Earnings of Women Making Candlewick Bedspreads Investigated By Women's Bureau," press release, Feb. 18, 1935, 1, vertical file "Employment-industrial homework," SL.

teach children that work was "a normal expression of personality and . . . an enjoyable part of a well-balanced life."[93]

The Women's Bureau survey indeed showed that 95 percent of the home-workers were women, with nearly half of them daughters. A third of the wives and mothers were free to work at centralized workshops because they had another family member (usually their own mother) to care for young children. Nearly all were white; as the ILGWU noted, such industry "gave 'money work' to the 'white trash,' and thus took the burden of relief [off the] taxpayer's back." Some of them gave spreads for a fee to their African American neighbors, which led other mountain whites to complain that blacks drove down prices.[94]

Candlewick bedspread making was a sweated industry, employing about ten thousand factory to thirty thousand home workers. With little capital neces-sary to enter, "members of the industry," as the NRA code termed such companies, "produce only upon order and accumulate little stock"; they solicited orders "from department stores, mail-order houses, and coverlet jobbers." While the firms gathered the raw material – cotton sheeting of various weights and yarn – and stamped patterns, they relied on a system of "haulers" and "subhaulers" to hire workers, distribute and collect work, and supervise quality of production. As in Puerto Rico, haulers took a commission so that homeworkers never received the full worth of their labor. Having a family member (often a husband or son) as a hauler provided a woman first choice of patterns, important since larger ones usually paid better and smaller ones took more time and required more unpaid labor. The NRA code initially reserved the category "employee" for the haulers alone, which had no impact on piece rates. An amended code in November 1934 made industry members responsible for the wage rates of homeworkers. Plagued by inaccurate measur-ing, rates ranged around ten cents an hour.[95]

In 1935, TVA implemented a handicraft cooperative to buy materials and sell craftswork. With cooperation from the Southern Highland Handicraft Guild, it established the Southern Highlanders, Inc., with a crafts shop at Norris Dam, Tennessee. By 1937, this cooperative had added salesrooms at the Patten Hotel, Chattanooga, Chickamauga Dam, Tennessee, and Rockefeller Center, New York City. It apparently never pushed for the production centers that the Women's Bureau hoped would end homework. The Women's Bureau encouraged such potential customers as the National Young Women's Christian Association, which sought candlewick bedspreads

[93] U. S. DOL, Women's Bureau, "Minutes of the Conference on Southern Appalachian Crafts," Aug. 1, 1934, 1–2, 4–9, RG 86, box 12, folder "Correspondence"; Morgan quoted in Becker, "Selling Tradition," 344.

[94] Bertha M. Nienburg, "Potential Earning Power of Southern Mountaineer Handicraft," WBB, no. 128 (Washington, D.C.: GPO, 1935), 14–16, 28; Martin, "Not All in the Hills," 14; a few black workers are scattered in survey materials for no. 128, RG86.

[95] Nienburg, "Potential Earning Power," 42–51; Nienburg to Rose Schneiderman, "Concern-ing: Provisions Essential for the Protection of Home Workers in a Revised Code for the Candlewick Bedspread Industry," RG86, box 12, folder "Correspondence."

but desired not to place its order with companies guilty of the "anti-social practice" of paying women two cents an hour. Without the power to establish cooperatives, the bureau could support this alternative to the homework system; it could encourage new marketing strategies and more "modern" designs. More significantly, its relentless definition of the crafts as labor forced the Southern Highlands Handicraft Guild to distinguish arts and crafts from sweated industry.[96]

The NRA experience strengthened the conviction within the women's network that homework could not be regulated and had to be prohibited. As Beyer exclaimed, "How can you ever know that these laws are being lived up to, particularly in the home which is a man's own domain?" NRA authorities certainly ran into numerous roadblocks. Frequent changes in the labor process and different jobs for homeworkers flawed the attempt to set piece rates. That only a few exceptional homeworkers could earn hourly rates "led to a great deal of false reporting," with workers admitting to field investigators that employers premarked their record-keeping cards with the number of hours necessary to add up to the minimum wage. Employers were responsible for hindrance, by subverting the codes through use of subcontractors, "buy back" schemes (whereby they sold the material to the homeworker and then bought the product back), or sheer coercion of factory employees forced to take work home. When states with vigilant labor departments, like New York and Pennsylvania, attempted to enforce their own and NRA regulations, manufacturers sent work across state lines to New Jersey and as far away as Texas and Puerto Rico.[97]

The proliferation of homework from regulated to unregulated areas illuminates a flaw in the NRA itself. A national program, the NRA was particularized. It organized around industries which often concentrated in regional markets. Many of the homework-prone trades centered around New York and a few other eastern cities. The politics of achieving universal provisions across codes meant that the NRA had to trade off differentials based on sex, region, or subgroup within an industry. The patchwork quality of homework provisions derived from the very nature of the program; the NRA suffered from its own balkanization. With its nullification in May 1935, the states again offered the major arena for the women's network to stop homework. But the gendered assumptions behind the NRA that separated home from workplace and distinguished mother from worker would persist.

[96] Allen Eaton, *Handicrafts of the Southern Highlands* (New York, rpt.: Dover, 1973), 251–2; "Recommendations as changed for submittal to Dr. Morgan, Chairman, T.V.A., by Secretary Perkins, Aug. 21, 1934"; Mary Anderson to Mr. Sherman W. Dean, Apr. 12, 1935, RG86, box 12, folder "Correspondence." See also Becker, "Selling Tradition," chap. 6.

[97] "Third Annual Meeting of the Labor Standards Conference," 14, 9–16; Flexner and Skinner, "Study of Industrial Home Work," 44–5; U.S. DOL, Division of Labor Standards, "Proceedings, Conference of State Industrial Homework Law Administrators," June 16, 1937, RG86, box 1602, folder "Homework – Progress in Control, etc."; Beyer to Rosenzweig, Sept. 24, 1934, HC Records, box 8386, folder "Labor, U.S. Department of"

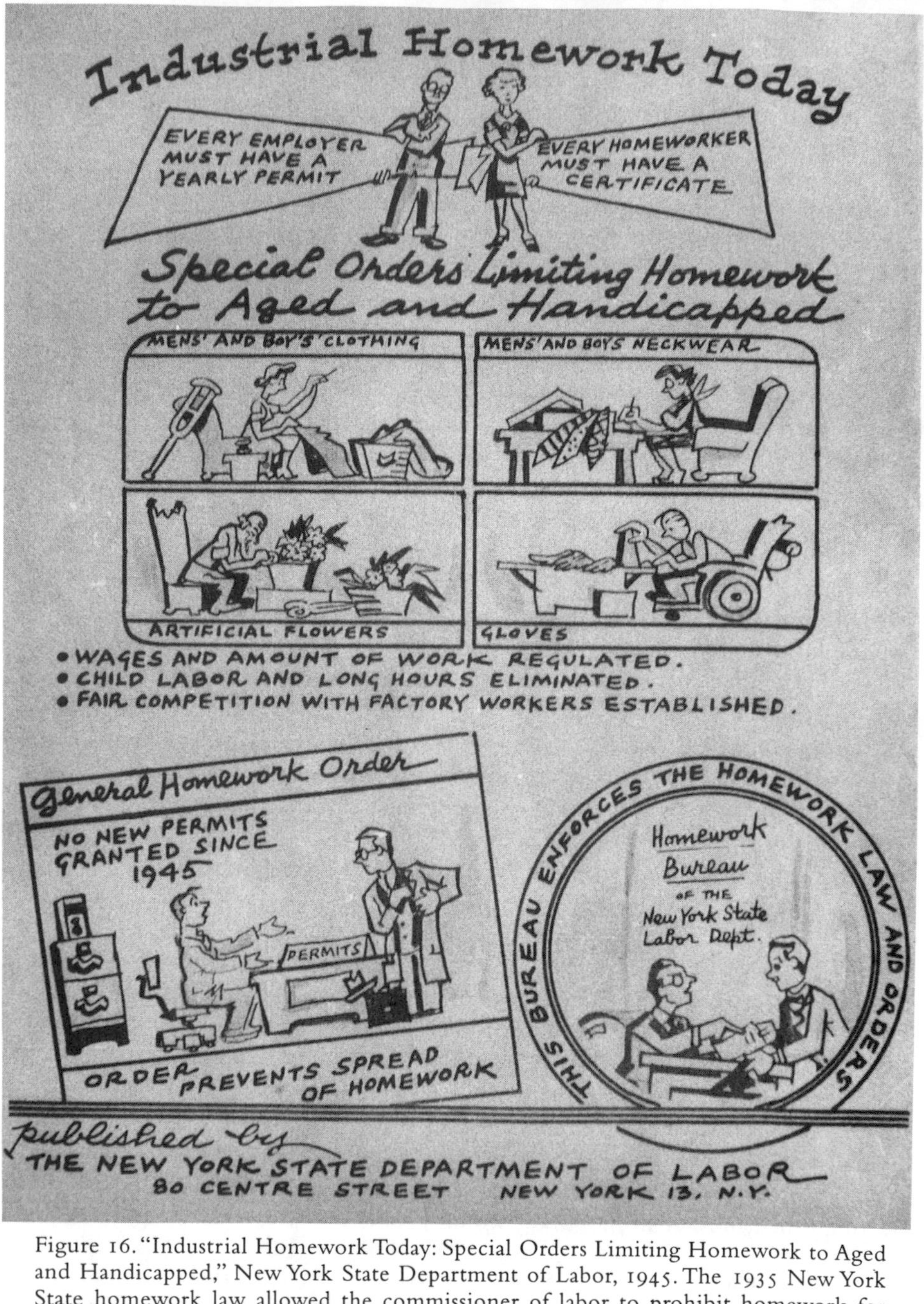

Figure 16. "Industrial Homework Today: Special Orders Limiting Homework to Aged and Handicapped," New York State Department of Labor, 1945. The 1935 New York State homework law allowed the commissioner of labor to prohibit homework for industries where it undermined labor standards of factory workers and hurt the health and welfare of women and children. These orders restricted homework licenses to the aged and disabled. Notice how the drawing genders the employer and inspectors as male and homeworkers as female or disabled male.

8

"Strike . . . while the iron is hot":
The politics of enactment,
the perils of enforcement

"There are constitutional difficulties in the way of home work prohibition by the states which do not apply in the case of the N.R.A.," noted Clara Beyer in 1934. "Therefore State legislation will probably have to be limited to strict regulation which will take the profits out of home work and thereby prevent its development." Within six months, the National Recovery Administration (NRA) was dead, killed by the same legal reasoning that had hindered homework regulation on the federal level since the 1890s: the national government's inability to interfere in intrastate business where the "right to contract" held sway. Homework opponents returned to state action after *United States v. Schechter Poultry Co.* ended the NRA, curbing what the court considered an excessive delegation of legislative powers to the executive branch.[1]

Ever since *Jacobs*, state governments had relied upon a broad interpretation of the police power to regulate homework as a public health issue. There seemed no authority to abolish the practice directly. By overruling the state minimum wage, *Adkins* had hampered efforts to make homework unprofitable for manufacturers. But, despite the setback of *Schechter*, the legal and political climate of the 1930s changed. Emboldened by depression conditions, the political support of the New Deal, and the rise of the Congress of International Organizations (CIO), the women's reform network and its trade union allies pushed for new state laws that relied upon the minimum wage, taxation, licensing, certification systems, and administrative authority to end homework where it adversely affected workers or the general public.[2]

The New Deal success at the federal level developed in a symbiotic manner with state initiatives; when Washington aided local campaigns, administrative makers of policy often relied upon their counterparts in the states and among voluntary organizations to draw up legislation and provide working models. State government, however, did not always embrace national programs. The New Deal had to confront the particular political configurations and eco-

---

[1] 295 U.S. 495 (1935); Clara Beyer to Elinore Herick, Nov. 2, 1934, HC Records, box 8387, folder "Memoranda – Consumers' League"; NCL, "Report of Third Annual Meeting of the Labor Standards Conference," 9–16, B–24, box 15, folder 245, SL.

[2] Eileen Boris, "The Quest for Labor Standards in the Era of Eleanor Roosevelt," *Wisconsin Women's Law Journal* 2 (Spring 1986): 53–74.

nomic contours of individual states. This uneven transfer of political goals and specific programs becomes apparent in tracing the history of homework regulation after the NRA. Where political conditions favored new legislation, as in New York, state officials quickly responded to the demise of the codes with new initiatives. But where factionalism split the Democratic party, as in Massachusetts and New Jersey (where the Republicans also suffered from a debilitating division), labor standards legislation failed to overcome conservative opposition. Labor standards constituted an arena where state capacities had developed since the Progressive Era in part from the efforts of the women's network and yet, even with a favorable national administration and a supportive labor movement, the policy process proved to be fraught with difficulties.

This road to reform was slow despite the efforts of women reformers.[3] Beyer offered technical counsel, moral support, and political advice to those on the local level who had to steer the labor standards agenda through the shoals of state particularisms. Here we witness the process of reform: the difficulties that women lobbyists faced in male-dominated state legislatures in an era after suffrage but before many women sought elective office themselves. The gender of political actors influenced their roles in the policy process, whether seen in the initiation and lobbying of the consumers' leagues or the location of women in federal or state agencies. With homework associated with women and children, trade unions expected the Consumers' League to take the lead in securing and monitoring homework laws. The lacunae in the reform agenda – seen through women whose voices were lost, not consulted, or ignored, whose perceptions this book has attempted to recover – illuminates much about the limits of the network's efforts.

The political culture of white women reformers persisted into the 1930s. Without a mass movement behind it, the women's reform network depended on access to the state, a precarious position since the agencies dominated by its members were underfunded and removed from the center of power. When it came to the labor of mothers, its discursive framework combined pragmatism and economism with traditional gender constructs. Gendered understandings of homeworkers and the home remained constitutive elements in the implementation of state law, most starkly revealed in the administration of New York's model regulations. The economic crisis gave the defense of motherhood a new urgency.

The 1935 New York State Homework Law

In New York State, the women's network lobbied for stricter legislation in order to indirectly bring about the abolition of homework. The unions con-

---

[3] These included Frieda Miller and Kate Papert of New York's Division of Women in Industry; Mary Dewson, Lucy Randolph Mason, Emily Sims Marconnier, and Mary Dublin [Keyserling] of the NCL; Mary Anderson of the Women's Bureau; and Rose Schneiderman of the WTUL. Some of these women, like Beyer, had their start in the Progressive Era, but did not come into power until the 1920s and 1930s. Keyserling would be head of the Women's Bureau under Lyndon Johnson.

cerned with this issue also turned to the state and played a significant role in gaining implementation. In 1934 the industrial commissioner proposed a bill to supplement the assault against homework through the NRA codes which the New York Department of Labor coordinated on the state level. Not only would an employer – redefined as an "owner or operator of a factory" – pay a twenty-five-dollar fee for a license, an innovation to finance increased administration, but certificates would be issued to individual homeworkers rather than to tenement houses. The law extended coverage to "all residences in New York State except one- and two-family houses in communities having fewer than 200,000 inhabitants" – a limit, imposed in the legislative fight over the bill by representatives of rural sections, which curtailed full effectiveness. By the early thirties not only did homework increasingly happen in dwellings, but there existed "a gradual but steady movement" of homeworkers from Manhattan to other boroughs and throughout the state, including "tiny villages and hamlets." This locational change was particularly noticeable for children's wear, a shift which led the commissioner to prohibit homework in that industry.[4]

A 1935 act amended this law in significant ways; it provided the model for the "Proposed State Law to Regulate and Tax Industrial Home Work," the "model Bill" drafted by the Home Work Committee of the International Association of Governmental Labor Officials. It finally applied to all homes throughout the state. The act also geared cost of employer permit fee to number of homeworkers, charging a hundred dollars to those with more than five hundred certified homeworkers. Most importantly, section 351 empowered the commissioner to "determine within what industries conditions may permit of industrial homework . . . without unduly jeopardizing the factory workers . . . as to both wages and working conditions and without unduly injuring the health and welfare of the industrial homeworker." This meant that the commissioner could issue industrywide rules for permits, restrict the extent of homework in any industry, or prohibit the practice. It presumed prohibition unless otherwise specified by the commissioner.[5]

The "Legislative purpose and definitions" of the bill reflected the particular concern of the Division of Women in Industry, then directed by Frieda Miller. "The employment of women and minors in industry," the bill declared, "under conditions resulting in wages unreasonably low and conditions injurious to

---

[4] New York, Acts of 1934, c. 825; Ruth Shallcross, *Industrial Homework: An Analysis of Homework Regulation Here and Abroad* (New York: Industrial Affairs, 1939), 62; George A. Hall, "Interview with Miss Miller, April 27, 1934," NYCLC Papers, box 1, folder 21; State of New York, *Annual Report of the Industrial Commissioner for the Twelve Months Ended December 31, 1932* (Albany, N.Y.: J. B. Lyon Co., Printers, 1933): 33–4; for complaints of children's wear manufacturers, "Bill Jacket 1935 Homework Law," NYSA.

[5] Frieda S. Miller, "Industrial Home Work in the United States," *International Labor Review* 43 (Jan. 1941): 32–6; U.S. DOL, Division of Labor Standards, "Interstate Shipment of Industrial Homework," mimeographed report, Nov. 5, 1936, DOL library; Shallcross, *Industrial Homework*, 63–5, 213–17.

their health and general welfare is a matter of grave and vital public concern."
"Uncontrolled" homework undermined "sound public policy" because "wages
are notoriously lower and working conditions endanger the health of the
worker; the protection of factory industries, which must operate in competition therewith and of the women and minors employed therein and of the
public interest of the community at large in their health and well-being."[6]
Appeals to gender difference and women's biological weakness persisted at a
time when the courts had not yet sustained minimum wages for women or
general labor standards legislation. Gendered reasoning, however, mixed with
nongendered economic arguments.

Miller was firmly rooted in the women's network. A leader of the Women's
Trade Union League (WTUL) in Philadelphia, a founder of the Bryn Mawr
Summer School for Women Workers, and a former factory inspector for the
Joint Board of Sanitary Control of the Ladies' Garment Industry, she had
assumed her state position when Frances Perkins led the New York department.[7] More than a hundred civic, social, religious, and trade organizations
urged passage of the homework bills for which she would be the chief imple-
menter. In 1934 so did that sector of the clothing industry which formally
adhered to the NRA codes and which deplored the "unfair competition" of
homework. The New York Times reported in 1935, "no opposition was expressed
at the hearing."[8]

The New York Women's Trade Union League (NYWTUL) campaigned
for this act. The National League would call for "effective home work
legislation with a view to its final abolishment in all the states of the
union." Although less directly involved in union organization than it had
been twenty-five years before, the NYWTUL in the fall of 1934 initiated
the Labor Conference for the Abolition of Industrial Homework as a response to employer attacks on NRA codes, particularly the Homework
Protective League's assaults on the President's Executive Order.[9] With the
strong financial and political support of the International Ladies' Garment
Workers Union (ILGWU), under Executive Secretary Frederick Umhey who
became chairman of the Labor Conference, the NYWTUL brought together representatives from twenty-three international and local garment-

[6] Shallcross, Industrial Homework, 213–14.

[7] Dee Ann Montgomery, "Frieda Segelke Miller," Notable American Women: The Modern Period,
    ed. Barbara Sicherman and Carol Hurd Green (Cambridge: Harvard Univ. Press, 1980),
    478–9; "Miss Miller Becomes Commissioner," The Industrial Bulletin 17 (Aug. 1938): 354.

[8] "Homework Bill Gets Pledges of Support," New York Times, Apr. 16, 1934, 2:6; "Albany To
    Speed Six Labor Bills," ibid., Jan. 18, 1935, 8:5.

[9] WTUL Resolution, in testimony of Elisabeth Christman, 4, WTUL Papers, reel 68, frames
    33–47; Press Release, NYWTUL, n.d., and letter from Elsie Gluck to Fred Umhey, Oct. 15,
    1934, with attached resolutions, in Umhey Papers, 53–5; for an earlier coalition against
    sweatshops, WTUL, Press Release at Once, n.d., and "Press Release – Monday, April 17,
    1933," in Dubinsky Papers, 172–20.

related labor bodies. Together these unions represented over three hundred thousand women workers in the industries with the most homework, though men dominated their leadership.[10]

Although the NRA codes apparently curtailed the practice in men's clothing, trade unionists reported in early 1935 "that homework is becoming an increasing menace" even in industries, like dresses, with code prohibitions. Despite a depression era drop, homeworkers – estimated at thirty thousand in 1935 – still represented a reserve army of labor. With industry picking up, the Labor Conference felt "unless organized labor takes measures on every possible front – in the code authorities, through publicity, through state legislation and through interstate legislative pacts – it is obvious that employers will increasingly resort to this method in certain industries to defeat unions which are strong among the factory workers."[11]

The Labor Conference mounted a publicity campaign and sent members to lobby in Albany and testify at code hearings in New York City. It also worked with homeworkers. Elsie Gluck, secretary of the Labor Conference, reported, "Quite a number of homeworkers had come into the office [of the NYWTUL] to register complaints on hours and wages." State enforcement of NRA codes undoubtedly spurred them on; Miller claimed, "Home workers have cooperated with the department . . . and they are now looking to the State to provide effective regulation and protection for them." In early 1935 Gluck suggested that the WTUL "form these women into some sort of group . . . in order to get information on a first hand basis, to be able to show that the League spoke for homeworkers, and to educate these women to the necessity of abolishing homework." The Labor Conference agreed to this strategy since it "would take some time" and would be a project of the WTUL, despite Umhey's questioning "as to whether organization of homeworkers would not be contradictory to going on record for their abolition."[12]

[10] Other active unions included Embroidery Workers' Union Local 66, the Joint Board of the ACWU, the United Hatters, Cap and Millinery Workers' Union, the Men's Neckwear Union, and the Glove Makers' Union. Fred Umhey, Chairman of the Conference, and Elsie Gluck, Secretary, letter "Dear Sirs and Brothers," Aug. 15, 1935, with attached minutes, "Meeting of the Labor Conference on Homework under the auspices of the NYWTUL," [Jan. 14, 1935], Umhey Papers, 53–5. On male domination within the garment unions, Alice Kessler-Harris, "Problems of Coalition-building: Women and Trade Unions in the 1920s," in Women, Work and Protest: A Century of U.S. Women's Labor History, ed. Ruth Milkman (New York: Routledge and Kegan Paul, 1985), 110–38.

[11] State of New York, Annual Report of the Industrial Commissioner (Albany, N.Y.: J. B. Lyon Co., Printers), 1930–37, especially 1933, 32–4; "State's New Social Program Covers an Extensive Field," New York Times, Jan. 6, 1935, sec. 8, 3:6–8; Umhey and Gluck, "Dear Sirs and Brothers"; Edmund Gottesman, Abraham Miller, F. Umhey, Elsie Gluck to the Secretary or Manager of the Unions Participating in the Homework Conference, Dec. 10, 1934; Umhey to Gluck, December 19, 1934; all Umhey Papers, 53–5.

[12] "Meeting of the Labor Conference on Homework," Jan. 14, 1935; Miller in "Albany to Speed Six Labor Bills"; "The Homework Bill," Weekly News, New York League of Women Voters, 14 (Jan. 25, 1935); Gluck to Umhey, Nov. 15, 1934, Umhey Papers, 53–5.

Indeed, Umhey was correct, insofar as trade unionists and women's reform groups from the 1880s had juxtaposed organization and abolition as oppositions, choosing the end of homework over the empowerment of homeworkers, accepting the goal of the family wage over a cross-class alliance of women working at home and in the factories. The only time that the ILGWU attempted to organize homeworkers along with inside workers was in 1937 during a strike among Mexicans in the San Antonio dress industry where a shared ethnic community facilitated their effort.[13]

Whether the NYWTUL actually ever tried to organize homeworkers is questionable. Women reformers apparently saw women homeworkers as a resource for the abolitionist cause instead of viewing themselves as a resource for homeworkers to develop their own agenda or express their own concerns. Gluck reported to Umhey a few weeks later: "The possibility of getting material from stories of homeworkers seems very good just now. We have made some valuable contacts with groups of workers in Harlem and in the Lower East Side." However, she thought "that before any groups of homeworkers are approached, the whole problem of union attitude toward such activity ought to be the subject of another conference." Women reformers obviously felt that male trade unionists were not truly convinced of this course of action and they were dependent on the unions for financing the Labor Conference. Although dedicated to improving the lives of working women as a group, the WTUL also committed itself to working with trade unionists and would not jeopardize that relation, especially in a case when their legislative program nicely meshed with that of the union leadership. The proposed conference seems never to have taken place.[14]

However, the Labor Conference – by then firmly dominated by its constituent unions – organized to insure full implementation of the new homework law. Joseph Tuvim, manager of the Ladies' Neckwear Workers Union-142 (later president of the Artificial Flower and Feather Makers Union), stressed how the WTUL would organize such a conference only if "the important organizations in this state [meaning the bigger clothing unions] are ready to begin such [a] campaign."[15] A committee of the Labor Conference (Edmund Gottesman of the Men's Neckware Union, Abraham Miller of the Amalgamated Clothing Workers of America [ACWA], and Umhey) drew up guidelines for union

---

[13] Pecan shellers in that city had attempted in 1934 to gain the cooperation of homeworkers while calling for the end of the practice. See Julia Kirk Blackwelder, *Women of the Depression: Caste and Culture in San Antonio, 1929–1939* (College Station: Texas A & M Press, 1984), 94, 139.

[14] Gluck to Umhey, Feb. 7, 1935, Umhey Papers, 53–5.

[15] Joseph Tuvim to Frederick Umhey, June 20, 1935, Umhey Papers. "Flowers on Hats Subject of Rally," *New York Times*, Mar. 20, 1938, sec. 6, 5:2. By then, Gluck was no longer secretary; where the WTUL dominated early meetings with leaders like the ILGWU's Pauline Newman and Rose Schneiderman present, union men seemed to have taken over, perhaps the original plan of the WTUL.

locals to lobby the Commissioner for restriction in their industries. Sent to over fifty locals and regional boards, mostly of the ACWA and the ILGWU, these guidelines urged each union to "write at once to the Industrial Commissioner, asking for a hearing with a view to discussing such prohibition in its industry and giving the reasons on which the request is based; (2) begin immediately to gather specific information [that is, homeworker affidavits, wages, hours, and extent of homework in union shops before, during, and after NRA codes] to be presented in a brief to the Industrial Commissioner."[16]

Union representatives discussed ways to maneuver around the hesitation of the Department of Labor to act. They offered suggestions to the industrial commissioner on how to use a common piece rate to determine wages and how to counter homework sent out of state by controlling employer permits. But the department proceeded slowly, stymied by inadequate budget appropriations, which led an angry Miller to inform the commissioner: "I have no hesitation about asking hard work of my staff but I refuse to ask it in the cause of preventing exploitation while at the same time I help disgracefully to exploit that staff." Commitment to the cause of adequate labor standards for women workers made her predominantly female staff willing to work long hours at low wages. Delay in fully funding the new Bureau of Homework and establishing a supervisory level position impeded Miller's efforts.[17]

Miller responded by asking the unions to pressure her department to enforce the new homework law so she could secure funds for implementation. In October 1935, she told readers of the ILGWU's paper *Justice*, "The law cannot be self-administered, for it would be impossible for the State to allow the tremendous sum of money necessary to police the entire State thoroughly." It depended upon trade unions to report "trouble spots." The rank and file regarded state regulation with pessimism; leaders accepted it since collective bargaining alone was not rooting out homework.[18]

The state opened up the administrative process to union demands. The Department of Labor began the process of restricting homework with the Men's and Boy's Outer Clothing Industry, which continued to top all industries in the number of homework permits.[19] However, Sidney Hillman, by then a major architect of labor corporatism, claimed that the NRA had nearly eliminated homework but felt "it very important that the Department

---

[16] Edmund Gottesman, Abraham Miller, Fred Umhey, Anaya F. Smith to the Unions Participating in the Homework Conference, Aug. 8, 1935. Copies of this letter are in the collections of the ILGWU, the ACWA, and the WTUL.

[17] Memo to the Honorable Elmer F. Andrews, Industrial Commissioner, unsigned, [Labor Conference Executive Committee], c. Aug. 1935, Umhey Papers, 53–5; "Memorandum to Mr. Andrews," Sept. 13, 1935, from Frieda S. Miller, 7 pp., Miller Papers, box 2, file 16.

[18] Edith Kine, "Standout Women on the American Labor Scene: Frieda Miller," *Justice*, Oct. 15, 1935, 14.

[19] Custom tailoring and the traditional practice of hand finishing accounted for homework. See *Annual Reports of the Industrial Commissioner, passim*.

of Labor exercises its authority in not permitting home work to return to the clothing industry." After hearings the following January, the commissioner virtually banned homework in men's clothing under Homework Order No. 1.[20]

The other homework orders also met trade union concerns. No. 2 for men's and boy's neckwear, initiated by another major union in the Labor Conference, followed in 1937. The next year saw No. 3 for artificial flowers and feathers, again prompted by union demands. In this case, a private conference between union representatives and the Division of Women hammered out many of the specifics, including the definition of the industry, the date of the hearing, and the list of manufacturers to be invited to a conference with the industrial commissioner. The unionists went over a proposed draft of the homework order, but they also confessed, "At the hearing the union will officially stand for complete prohibition, actually it will be content with a regulation somewhat like that in union agreements today, which permits a manufacturer to give out homework only when he operates a shop of not less than 6 workers." Stringent rules accounting for amount of work and piece rates applied to such homework. In 1941, the glove industry joined the severely restricted industries and, in 1945, a general homework ban set out to abolish the system. This order restricted permits to both employers and employees already holding them and further limited employer permits only to those who had a factory with at least one inside worker. Employers also could not increase their numbers of homeworkers.[21]

Women's networks and the enactment of legislation

Labor and women reformers together formed a key component of the Democratic party in New York; with the popular and powerful Governor Herbert Lehman behind their efforts, they easily secured a more effective homework law in the mid-thirties. Legislative enactment in other states proved more complex, reflecting the character of the legislative process and the strength or weakness of the New Deal coalition on the state level. The Consumers' League, while hardly a mass organization in the 1930s, continued to prove itself central to the fight against homework.

The "female dominion" in Illinois – with its roots in Hull House and the School of Social Service Administration at the University of Chicago and with its ties to the U.S. Children's Bureau through former heads Julia Lathrop and

---

[20] Frieda Miller to Sidney Hillman, July 16, 1935, file 21; Hillman to Miller, July 20, 1935, file 23; Andrews to Hillman, Jan. 20, 1936, file 21; all in ACWA Papers, box 76.

[21] Miller to Hillman, May 11, 1936, ACWA Papers, box 76, file 21; Miller, "Industrial Home Work in the United States," 36–8; "General Background, 1/19/51," typescript, in folder "Homework: Direct Mail, Reports re Industry"; "Conference Re Abolition of Homework in the Artificial Flower Industry," Sept. 27, 1937, folder "Artificial Flowers," both in NYDOL files; "Industry Homework Curb Up to State After Hearing," clipping, Beyer Papers, box 10, folder 153.

Grace Abbott – mobilized to pass a homework law in 1935 based on the Department of Labor's model bill. The retired Grace Abbott, then editor of the University of Chicago's *Social Service Review*, coordinated the effort, with the state Department of Labor and support from women's organizations, the Illinois State Federation of Labor, and the Illinois Child Labor Committee. Two years later a simplified version without tax provisions passed, Illinois's first general licensing law.[22]

Massachusetts, a leader in such regulatory legislation, also took two years to pass the model bill; New Jersey did not have a version until 1941, after the Fair Labor Standards Act (FLSA) already was curbing homework in interstate commerce. Rural interests proved stronger in New Jersey where both political parties suffered from factionalism and the New Deal lacked strength. With its proximity to New York City, New Jersey proved a more important place for "bootleg" homework after New York's law, a place where homework employers fought harder. In Massachusetts, opposition came from self-interested sectors of the garment industry who obscured the dimensions of industrial homework by confusing an employee relationship with crafts work or independent contractor status. The Democratic party badly split between those who supported the colorful but corrupt James Michael Curley and those who supported Al Smith, who did not trust Roosevelt and his policies of federal intervention. Although ethnic politics dominated the party, and the Catholic church was fighting the Child Labor Amendment as state invasion of the family, the unpopular anti-New Deal governor Charles F. Hurley did not block the homework bill – perhaps succumbing to pressure from organized labor. Divisions in the Democratic party did not prove fatal in Massachusetts, as they would in New Jersey.[23]

The case study of Massachusetts illustrates the close tabs Clara Beyer kept on her model homework bill as it worked itself through state legislatures. With bills in five other legislatures, Beyer urged "Massachusetts to strike . . . while the iron is hot. This is the time if there ever was one to put on the statute books restrictive legislation on home work. No one knows what next year will

---

22 Abbott Papers, box 56, folder 2, especially, Grace Abbott to My dear Mr. Durkin, Apr. 15, 1935; G. Abbott to Elizabeth B. Oakes, Apr. 24, 1936; Clara Beyer to G. Abbott, Jan. 14, 1935; G. Abbott to Beyer, Jan. 21, 1935; Ralph Wilson to G. Abbott, Aug. 18, 1936; G. Abbott to Wilson, Oct. 13, 1936; G. Abbott to Mr. Olander, Jan. 15, 1935; see also correspondence with Katharine Lenroot on Ruth White's research on homework in Chicago, box 56, folder 1; Robyn Muncy, *Creating a Female Dominion in American Reform, 1890–1935* (New York: Oxford Univ. Press, 1991).

23 Felice D. Gordon, *After Winning: The Legacy of the New Jersey Suffragists, 1920–1947* (New Brunswick, N.J.: Rutgers Univ. Press, 1986), suffers from looking at what women did without a full analysis of the overall politics of the state. But no adequate history of New Jersey politics in the 1930s exists, nor is there a study of women in Massachusetts for this period. Charles Trout, *Boston, the Great Depression, and the New Deal* (New York: Oxford Univ. Press, 1977); Robert K. Massey Jr., "The State Politics of Massachusetts Democracy, 1928–1938," (Ph.D. diss., Duke Univ., 1968).

bring." But the iron proved much less searing than Beyer had hoped in 1935, the year of the NRA's invalidation. Rampant homework continued to disrupt the industrial landscape, with only New York and Connecticut passing major legislation against the practice that year.[24]

But in October, the Second National Conference on Labor Legislation put the heads of state departments of labor on record for legislation to apply existing labor laws to homework and to "ultimately abolish" it. These confer- ences of state officials took over from earlier meetings convened by the National Consumers' League (NCL) before the establishment of the Division of Labor Standards. They reveal the interconnection between the women's labor stan- dards networks inside and outside of government in the mid-1930s. Beyer worked with Columbia University law professor Walter Gellhorn and a committee of male and female state labor law administrators to draft the model law that drew heavily from New York's recently revised act. Adopted by the International Association of Governmental Labor Officials at their 1936 meeting, as well as the Third National Conference on Labor Standards, the model bill became the basis for lobbying efforts by local consumers' leagues, whose membership included the state officials who initially drafted or endorsed the bill.[25]

Margaret Wiesman, the executive secretary of the Massachusetts League, tried to introduce the model bill in 1936. A graduate of Bryn Mawr college, Wiesman was a thirty-two-year-old social worker when she assumed the task in 1930 "to rebuild the League gradually to a position of constructive critic of the Labor Department." The league had suffered from loss of members..ip and leadership in the unpropitious times of the 1920s when its original members aged or moved. The "reappearance" of the sweatshop greeted her. Her investigations provided the American Federation of Labor (AFL) with ammu- nition to secure a legislative inquiry into the administration of the state's pioneering minimum wage law, resulting in the appointment of a more favorable commissioner of labor. She gained funding for an Anti-Sweatshop Committee to educate, agitate, and investigate. Returning to the tactic of the early NCL, this committee issued a list of "honor retailers" who pledged not to sell the products of sweatshops. Wiesman blamed homework on chiseling employers and lack of industrial rights which stemmed from "the difficulty of enforcing the labor law in homework." She understood the economic impact of homework on different groups of women, arguing in such terms, not on the basis of "the sanctity of the home" or the disarray of homeworkers' lives.[26]

The 1936 attempt to pass the model homework bill proved a fiasco. Revealing

---

[24] Clara Beyer to Margaret Wiesman, Feb. 1, 1935, CLM Papers, box 29, folder 492; U.S. DOL, Division of Labor Standards, *Industrial Home-Work Legislation and Its Administration*, bulletin no. 26 (Washington, D.C.: GPO, 1939), 4.

[25] *Industrial Home-Work Legislation and Its Administration*, 7–10; Miller, "Industrial Home Work," 34–5; Shallcross, *Industrial Homework*, 63–5; "Third Annual Meeting of the Labor Standards Conference," which focused on industrial homework.

[26] "Margaret Wiesman," obituary, Boston *Daily Globe*, Monday, Aug. 10, 1953, 19:2; "Con- sumers' League – Past and Present: Organization and Early Years," 1932 typescript, box 1,

her astute knowledge of the political process, Wiesman planned to find a good bill for the next session and "persuade" the commissioner to make it his own. "I hope to see that it carefully excludes the handicraft people and hope to have them agree on the bill before we introduce it," she told Mary Anderson. "The effect of the department bill last year was to alienate almost permanently all the arts and crafts people [who misunderstood the provisions as applying to them] and they have a tremendous lobby." From Beyer she received a shorter version of the standard bill. Wiesman also turned to the old tactic of investigation, using students from the Simmons School of Social Work to gather data. Months before the new session, she initiated meetings to come up with "a unanimous program."[27]

Wiesman was able to convince the commissioner to present Beyer's bill rather than one drawn up within the state Department of Labor. Confessing that they all feared "that out-of-state employers may still be able to mail goods into Massachusetts," she asked Beyer for any suggestions on how to protect against "such invasion." Beyer responded with customary encouragement – "Good for you!" – but could offer no comfort until federal legislation stopped the interstate passage of homework, although she had a draft bill on that matter ready for Congress. By March, Wiesman was reporting good progress to Frieda Miller; by early May, Beyer was praising her, saying she "must have handled negotiations with gloves in order to have reached the present stage of success." Beyer continued to keep close tabs on the Massachusetts bill, pointing out where it departed from the model and instructing on tactics.[28]

In June 1937, Wiesman reported success to Beyer. "There has never been such a day as last Thursday." She described "the new way of lobbying" where there was "not one word of opposition in the open hearing before Labor and Industries." All seemed "serene progress" with no changes in the bill until Wiesman "called the Chairman of the Committee who has been exceedingly cooperative," but who under their operating procedures had delegated the bill to a subcommittee "where apparently, dirty work went on." For she then learned that the commissioner of labor agreed to omit the homework ban on children's garments. With the commissioner away, a

folder 5; Mary Heaton Vorse, *The Watchdog: A Memorial to Margaret Wiesman*, unpublished manuscript outline, chap. 6, 6, 11–19, box 32, both in CLM Papers. For Wiesman's mode of analysis, *Sweatshop . . . Home Model: A Study of Industrial Homework* (Boston: CLM, 1937), 2–7.

[27] Wiesman to Anderson, Nov. 18, 1936, folder 493; Wiesman to Beyer, Nov. 18, 1936, folder 492, both box 29; John P. Meade to Rosamond Lamb, Dec. 28, 1936, box 26, folder 430; Wiesman to Ralph, Jan. 28, 1937, box 6, folder 87, all in CLM Papers. These papers contain other letters depicting the network in action. Mary Anderson sent Weisman "The Commercialization of the Home Through Industrial Home Work" at the request of Lucy Randolph Mason of the NCL. Anderson to Wiesman, Oct. 8, 1935, CLM Papers, box 29, folder 493.

[28] Wiesman to Beyer, Jan. 13, 1937; Beyer to Wiesman, Jan. 15, 1937; Beyer to Wiesman, May 4, 1937; Beyer to Wiesman, May 29, 1937, box 29, folder 492; Miller to Wiesman, Mar. 27, 1937, box 26, folder 446, CLM Papers.

distraught Wiesman had to go lobbying alone. She convinced the chair of the labor committee to try to delete the offensive section.[29]

Days later she became "aware of the real under-cover work against the bill." She learned that "the argument which almost threw the whole bill out was one first advanced in the Executive Committee of Ways and Means by a Senator whose girl friend makes 'little' cookies at home. That story and others about dear little women in the homes who make jellies [to preserve their self-respect, it was said] spread like wild fire and every one was all for pushing this wicked bill right out the window where it belonged."

Opponents of regulation were using one prohibition to attack the entire bill, not expecting Wiesman to be, in Frances Perkins's words, "a half-loaf girl," one who would make concessions to get her bill passed. But Wiesman was determined to concede whatever was necessary to win the bill: "So to each one after they announced the bill ought to be killed, and this included one labor Senator, I said no, that we would omit those prohibitions and next year fight them quite apart from the bill and this is the only thing that saved the darned thing."[30]

Wiesman revealed the political acumen that a generation of women reformers forged in the maelstrom of state politics when she told Beyer: "Logic amounted to nothing. There was no intelligent help from the Labor Department and the old propaganda mill was working at its best. . . . If you had been here, I think you would have agreed that we did awfully well to salvage what we did, . . . it was lucky the Consumers' League was interested."[31] Aware of how the legislature worked, Wiesman understood what she was doing as a lobbyist. She explained, "I had to compromise right and left on it but finally got a darned good framework enacted." After a few years of haphazard administration, Wiesman would join the chorus calling for homework prohibition.[32]

New Jersey provides a more complex story, but one that also shows the power of women's networks, the mutual reliance between state departments of labor and the Consumers' League, and the skill of women reformers in the legislative process. It reminds us that state politics could cripple the New Deal. The Democrats suffered under the Jersey City machine of Mayor Frank Hague, "a master of ethnic politics" with close ties to local AFL leaders. The state party only halfheartedly embraced the New Deal, especially those measures that would set labor standards as advocated by the CIO. Hague

---

[29] Wiesman to Beyer, June 1, 1937, CLM Papers, box 29, folder 492.

[30] Wiesman to Beyer, June 1, 1937; George Martin, *Madam Secretary: Frances Perkins* (Boston: Little Brown, 1976), 98.

[31] Wiesman to Beyer, June 1, 1937.

[32] Wiesman to Ethel [Johnson], July 23, 1937, box 10, folder 152; Wiesman to Louise Stitt, box 29, folder 493; Beyer to Wiesman, June 3, 1937, box 29, folder 492; Annual Meeting, Secretary's Report, Mar. 15, 1939, box 2, folder 24, CLM Papers.

claimed that there were "no sweated industries" in Jersey City, a notorious homework center. He did not directly oppose industrial homework bills; instead he allowed them through the assembly fully knowing they would fail in the state senate where rural legislators held disproportionate power. The Republicans divided into two factions: one under the "very reactionary" governor Harold Hoffman, who apparently had allied with Hague, and the Clean Government group, a "remnant" of Republican Progressivism that combined fiscal austerity with support of some New Deal programs, including labor standards. In short, the Consumers' League could not count on the ability of pro-labor leaders from either party to carry others with them.[33]

In February 1934, Helena Simmons, president and then executive secretary of the state Consumers' League, began pushing Commissioner of Labor John Toohey, Jr., to introduce a Women's Bureau draft bill regulating industrial homework. Simmons, a fifty-eight-year-old Elizabethan matron with grown children at the time, had gone from the suffrage campaign to the League of Women Voters (LWV), the Consumers' League, and the Democratic party. A transitional figure, Simmons moved between the partisan and social welfare politics of the women's network.[34]

With the LWV, the State Federation of Women's Clubs, and other members of its Labor Standards Committee, including the State Federation of Labor, the Consumers' League introduced the model bill in 1935. Sponsored by Clean Government Republican Assemblywoman Olive (Mrs. Frederick H.) Sanford, a former president of the LWV, the bill floundered from a combination of political infighting and organized business opposition. Despite backing from the state Department of Labor and the New Jersey Federation of Labor, and lurid stories by the *Newark Ledger* (personally placed on each senator's desk by Simmons), senators raised objections at the last minute. "Charging that 'social workers are running us to the ground,' " one from rural Salem County insisted that the bill would keep distressed women from earning their living from dressmaking, even when told that "what we are hitting are the contractor-employe[e] relation shops," not the self-employed. Such arguments clouded the economic and ideological reasons why many rejected the bill: Many believed that homework was growing in the state, especially in rural areas, and that homeworkers were not real workers, but rather old women with idle time on their hands or mothers making some extra money for their families. One of

---

[33] Helena Simmons to Louise Stitt, Apr. 22, 1937; Simmons to Isetta J. Miller, Sept. 26, 1935, both in CLNJ Papers, box 9; *The Governors of New Jersey*, eds. Paul A. Stellhorn and Michael J. Birkner (Trenton: New Jersey Historical Commission, 1982), 12–13, 197–201, 205–9, 212–13; *Biographical Directory of the Governors of the United States, 1789–1978*, ed. Robert Sobel and John Raimo (Westport, Conn.: Meckler Books, 1978), 1038–41; Ronald Grele, "Structural Development of Urban Liberalism," (Ph.D. diss., Rutgers Univ., 1971); Susanna P. Zwerner, "History of Consumers' League of New Jersey (1900–1950)," 14, Ac.1811, Alexander Library, Rutgers University.

[34] Simmons to Toohey, Feb. 19, 1934, CLNJ, box 9; Gordon, *After Winning*, 124–6.

the two senate supporters of the measure, the majority leader, also felt he did "not want to deprive [a great many fine women who have been forced to do homework] of the chance to earn some money," but as a pro-labor Republican he accepted the arguments of the women's groups which in this case included the local chapters of the Business and Professional Women's Federation (BPWF). A staunch advocate for the Equal Rights Amendment, the BPWF rejected protective labor laws for women, but opposed homework for its "coolie wages," diseased environment, and burden to the taxpayer.[35]

The disarray of the state legislature and rising opposition from both employers and the rural homeworkers whom they mobilized bottled up the bill for the next six years in a hostile committee.[36] But Helena Simmons would not be put off easily. She suggested planks for both party platforms and skillfully used the local newspapers to publicize her efforts. Like Wiesman, Simmons pleaded in the language of labor standards, emphasizing the rise in homework since the "demise" of the NRA, New Jersey's role as "a dumping ground" for New York manufacturers, and the economic cost to the community. Homework licenses had jumped from about three hundred in 1934 to twenty-two hundred during the six-month period following the end of the NRA codes. (By 1939, fewer than four thousand people had received licenses, but an estimated twenty thousand homeworkers took material from New York and Pennsylvania contractors.)[37]

Assisted by the labor commissioner, Simmons got the Democrats to go along; for the Republicans, she had additional help from the New Jersey Laundryowners Association, a business group that supported the women's minimum wage order for their industry. Rather than incorporating her gender-neutral approach, the Democrats included homework under their plank on "Women and Children," maintaining the framework of protection set by women's labor laws. The league grilled candidates. Armed with information supplied by Beyer and other labor law administrators, Simmons began an intensive educational campaign before women's groups. Into the state came outside leaders like New York's Miller and National Secretary Lucy Randolph Mason.

[35] "Women Press Bill Curbing Work Evil," *Newark Ledger*, June 10, 1935; Rita Wagner, "Society Women Support War on Home Sweatshops," ibid., June 11, 1935; "Sweatshop Fight to Win; Barbour to Support Bill," ibid., June 25, 1935; Jacob Mogelever, "Sweatshop Bill Defeated; Leap Opens Attack," ibid., June 26, 1935; "It Was Slaughtered!," unidentified clipping; all in scrapbooks, CLNJ.

[36] *Votes and Proceedings of the General Assembly of New Jersey* (Trenton: Macadish and Quigley Co., 1935–1942); *Journal of the Senate of the State of New Jersey* (Trenton: Macadish and Quigley Co., 1935–42); Simmons to John Toohey, June 2, 1937; Simmons to Mrs. Frances W. Hopkins, Apr. 13, 1938, and May 31, 1938, CLNJ Papers, box 9; Simmons to Marconnier, May 29, 1936, frame 73; Simmons to Marconnier, June 8, 1937, frames 147–8; Simmons to Mason, Apr. 22, 1937, frame 154; Simmons to Mary Dublin, May 23, 1939, frame 223, all in NCL Papers, reel 18.

[37] Simmons to Carl Holderman, Sept. 26, 1935; Simmons to Toohey, Sept. 19, 1935; "Resolution for Party Platforms"; Ethel Mosher to Member of the Consumers' League, n.d.; on amount of homework, "Article for Mrs. Reagan's Clip Sheet, Sent 11/4/1935"; letter from President [Mrs. Allen P. Zwerner] to Elmer F. Andrews, Sept. 18, 1939, CLNJ Papers, box 9.

Before club women, the league continued to use the old victimization metaphors, speaking in terms of exploited women and children.[38]

The homework exhibit, long a tactic of the league, became the central tool for public education. The league closely worked with the state Department of Labor, particularly Mary McGowan of the Division of Women and Children in Industry. Over the years McGowan fed Simmons data (numbers of licenses and who worked for which contractors) and provided confiscated samples of homework. She also shared copies of model bills. The two women, one inside and the other outside of the formal agencies of the state, discussed policy. In 1936 McGowan questioned whether New York would succeed in returning work to factories "if the work can come here legally and be done at such low rates." She confided to Simmons, "It is doing the unemployment situation in both States no good whatsoever, and you can figure for yourself the strike breaking possibilities, each group being unaware, practically, of the existence of the other."[39]

The model homework bill finally gained passage in 1941 under Governor Charles Edison, a strong supporter of the New Deal. By then, the state was regulating homework through minimum wage orders for apparels and light manufacturing, a strategy adopted after the league won funding of minimum wage enforcement in the mid-thirties. It came after passage of the federal FLSA and an equivalent state wage and hour law. Still rural legislators attempted to exempt their communities. Simmons argued for the necessity of the homework law because out-of-state suppliers were becoming intrastate businesses and no other law regulated child labor in the home. Politics proved crucial, with enough Republicans committing themselves after a bitter 1940 primary fight between Hoffman and the Clean Government candidate.[40]

This long-drawn-out battle illuminates the means, ends, and perceptions of

---

[38] Copy, telegram Bertran Mott from Harold C. Buckelew, Sept. 27, 1935; Ethel D. Mosher to Mr. Morris, Oct. 21, 1935; Frank Durand to Mrs. Mosher, Oct. 28, 1935; Lewis Ballantyne to Mrs. Mosher, Oct. 25, 1935; Mary P. Ames to Mr. Williams, Oct. 27, 1939; Simmons to Mrs. Herman Cohn, Oct. 21, 1935; Simmons to Ruth Kimberlin, Oct. 16, 1935; Frances K. Chalmers to Simmons, May 8, CLNJ Papers, box 9; Simmons to Lucy Mason, Nov. 7, 1935, NCL Papers, reel 18, frame 102; Mildred Jesslund, "Consumers' League," unidentified clipping, Oct. 4, 1935; "League in Fight on Home Work," Elizabethan Daily Journal, Sept. 30, 1935; "War on Sweatshops Intensified in New Jersey," Newark Ledger, May 12, 1936, all in scrapbook, CLNJ Papers.

[39] Mildred A. Jesslund, "Sweatshop Products to Tour New Jersey," Newark Ledger, Nov. 8, 1935, 15; Simmons to McGowan, Nov. 14, 1935; McGowan to Simmons, Nov. 19, 1935, Dec. 28, 1935; Simmons to McGowan, May 8, 1936; McGowan to Simmons, May 7, 1936, Oct. 28, 1936, Jan. 7, 1938; Simmons to Toohey, Oct. 11, 1935; Toohey to Simmons, Oct. 21, 1935, all in CLNJ Papers, box 9.

[40] The homework law curbed the amount of licensed homework: There were only 134 employer certificates and only 1,025 homework permits from Oct. 1941 to Feb. 1942. McGowan to Simmons, Feb. 21, 1942; Simmons to Mrs. Robert Levinson, May 26, 1941; Simmons to Mary McGowan, Feb. 20, 1939; Simmons to Cornelia B. Schwartz, Apr. 24, 1939; Mary L. Dyckman to Governor Edison, July 26, 1941, all in CLNJ Papers, box 9; Simmons to Mary Dublin, Apr. 29, 1940, NCL Papers, reel 18, frame 217.

women reformers. Simmons evaluated the maneuvers of the legislature in political terms rather than the moral terms that the prewar movement had often employed. Representing a nonpartisan group, she engaged in a political division of labor with the Democratic commissioner of labor. She had to appeal to the fiscal conservatism of the majority of legislators by dropping the processing tax of the model bill. License fees would have to finance enforcement, though she appealed to club women: "You cannot pass Labor Laws and give no money for research and enforcement."[41]

Lobbying required constant attendance at the state house "even if it is well nigh impossible to get to the persons one desires to see. Any real interviews with legislators in the interests of bills must be carried on in their own offices or homes and preferably by their own constituents." Simmons chided the league's inactive membership: "We shall never get our bills passed without great difficulty until our members take a personal interest and responsibility for working for them with their own representatives." She continued to contact leaders from the Federation of Women's Clubs and other women's organizations to enlist their aid. Yet the elitism of her coalition partners could prove trying. She described "a wonderful garden party given for the Y.W.C.A. in Summit," where she "packed and unpacked the exhibit and made my best speech" and netted only "*two dollars.*" To a New York League official she complained: "You see how good I *really* am – I don't mind speaking for nothing but after all that fuss and that exhibition of wealth. They asked me last fall – I ask you – Doubtless you know the feeling."[42]

Not all organized women could be counted upon to oppose homework. The inability of Ida E. Brown, president of the New Jersey State Federation of Colored Women's Clubs (a member of the league's Labor Standards Committee), "to get women signers of the bill" suggests that the debate over homework was outside the central concerns of African American women. The racial division of women's work meant that most African Americans did not labor in homework industries. Many black women had to leave the home to earn wages, no matter their preferences or childcare arrangements. Brown reported that some "favor[ed] the retention of home work" so women with children unable to leave the home "would be able to earn something at home."[43]

[41] Simmons to Marconnier, May 29, 1936, NCL Papers, reel 18, frame 73; Simmons to Robert Pascoe, Apr. 5, 1937; Simmons to Frieda Miller, Oct. 10, 1935; Simmons to Kate Papert, Mar. 6, 1941, all in CLNJ Papers, box 9.

[42] *Annual Report of the Executive Secretary, April 1937,* NCL Papers, reel 18, frame 151; Simmons to Mrs. Chester E. Reagan, Apr. 3, 1939, CLNJ Papers, box 9; Simmons to Marconnier, June 8, 1937, NCL Papers, reel 18, frame 148.

[43] To Simmons from Ida E. Brown, May 6, 1939; from Simmons to Brown, May 11, 1939, CLNJ Papers, box 9. Brown's letter suggests the class differences among black and white organized women. Having to travel by bus to their executive meeting, the members of the federation left at 7:00 A.M., picking up members along the way. Bus travel being what it was, they reached their destination at 1:30 P.M. instead of 10:00 A.M. and had only a little more than two hours to cram in their business. "It was almost more than I could stand," wrote Brown.

Those who sought freedom for homeworking continued to speak in the name of homeworkers. In response, the league claimed itself the true guardian of the family, children, and mothers. Simmons rejected amendments to exempt rural women because homework produced little economic gain for working-class mothers while harming their families: "Mothers have to work so hard for a pittance that the home and family are neglected." She relied upon the language of wronged motherhood and childhood to express the economic argument that exempting farm women would be for naught since federal wage and hour law required a higher wage than the proposed amendments. Rather than separate discourses, family and economy merged into a single powerful argument against a labor system that itself blurred home and work.[44]

Margaret Wiesman once confessed, "I have never felt it wise for the Consumers' League to bring in bills if we could get a stronger group such as the Federation or now the Department of Labor to do it in our place. We have been much more effective behind the scenes, endorsing, getting the material in order, lobbying."[45] What does this pattern suggest about the role of the women's reform network during the 1930s in the enactment of legislation and the broader issue of their relation to the policy process? Inheritors of the Progressive Era social welfare impulse, the network carried over many of the techniques and forms – as well as the goals – of the earlier political generation. What differed by the 1930s was that some of them had obtained positions in the administrative apparatus that earlier lobbying had created on the federal as well as on the state level. Still they worked "behind the scenes" and not in the limelight; reformers worked out of conviction more than for personal glory.

Yet Wiesman's confession testifies to the weakness of the women reformers as well as their strength. Others in the labor standards coalition, like labor leaders, progressive state administrators, and reform-minded legislators, valued their work, indeed, relied upon their efforts. But those in voluntary organizations lacked formal power and had to move indirectly. The world of reform replicated the larger sexual division of labor. These white women gained acceptance through specializing in protective labor laws. Their defense of motherhood and the family against the exploitation of industrial capitalism gave them the credibility to tackle the general issue of labor standards, to speak in terms of economics during the 1930s even though the measures they focused on – minimum wages for women, night work prohibitions, child labor, and homework – affected those already recognized as part of their political sphere.

Network women outside the state bureaucracy could provide valuable services for those inside. But, as volunteers or executive secretaries with few resources, they relied upon these other women for information and aid. On

---

[44] Simmons to Mildred Preen, Mar. 23, 1942; see also telegrams sent Mar. 16, 1942, CLNJ Papers, box 9.

[45] Margaret Wiesman to Mrs. Marconnier, Feb. 5, 1936, NCL Papers, reel 16, frame 207.

the federal level, their power bases – the Women's and Children's bureaus – proved to be marginal, with major New Deal labor legislation they helped draft, like Social Security and the FLSA, going to other agencies. On the state level, there often was only one woman in the department of labor who enforced the legislation for which they had fought. Though they had a place within the councils of the Democratic party, after 1938 they had little real power to shape the overall agenda of the Roosevelt administration which had turned to foreign policy.[46] Nonetheless, their role in the enactment of home-work legislation not only exemplifies the political skills of the postsuffrage generation of white women reformers but reveals the close ties among women in the national and local consumers' leagues, documented not only in the content of their letters, but in the letters themselves, the material embodiment of friendship and trust.

The perils of implementation: Can men legally do homework when women cannot?

How effective were the state homework laws? Implementation of New York's 1935 law reveals gender ideology to be central to the policy process. Assumptions about women and men influenced the administration, as well as the enactment, of labor standards. Language mattered, guiding state officials and providing a rationale for defenders of homework. The 1935 law relied upon arguments that had justified protective legislation for women since the turn of the century when it crafted its rationale out of the duty to protect women and minors from "wages unreasonably low and conditions injurious to their health and general welfare."[47] But an employer who wanted to maintain homework could strike out on a new road: He could hire men. That was the strategy of First American Natural Ferns, a Long Island City artificial flower manufac-turer.[48]

Order No. 3, severely restricting homework in the artificial flower and feather industry, referred to the homeworker as a woman or a "she" when originally promulgated in March 1938. The few men in the industry cut and prepared materials inside the shops and did not labor at home. After suspend-ing the order during an employer challenge to its validity before state boards and the courts, Miller – by then industrial commissioner – reissued the order in late October 1939, but with different wording. "Persons" replaced "women" in the order, an action First American claimed "prohibited Industrial Home-

---

[46] Ware, *Beyond Suffrage*; Judith Sealander, *As Minority Becomes Majority: Federal Reaction to the Phenomenon of Women in the Work Force, 1920–1963* (Westport, Conn.: Greenwood Press, 1983); Eileen Boris and Michael Honey, "Gender, Race, and the Policies of the Labor Department," *Monthly Labor Review* 111 (Feb. 1988): 26–37.

[47] Article 13, Section 351 Labor Law, State of New York.

[48] Unless otherwise noted, all materials on First American Ferns and the New York orders are on file at the NYDOL.

work in the Artificial Flower Industry to Males" and interfered with their employment practices. Such a revision was "invalid, arbitrary, unreasonable and unconstitutional" because the legislature never mentioned "males" in the intent and purpose clause of the act. The industrial commissioner, it argued, encroached upon legislative power. Drawing upon the distinction between men's rights and women's needs that prior court decisions had affirmed, company attorneys rehashed before the state supreme court the argument that the Fourteenth Amendment precluded applying the homework law to "males." That is, it deprived men of their property, which included their ability to labor, without proper due process.[49]

The first two homework orders had also embodied assumptions about the gender of homeworkers. Order No. 1 assumed that the aged or disabled homeworker exempted from its ban would likely be a male tailor. Not only was the male pronoun used, but it was used where the artificial flower order had a female one. Those running the Homework Bureau of the Labor Department recognized that this order was "for male homeworkers almost exclusively." Order No. 1 also was without a clause that had been central to the exceptions allowed under the NRA codes and would be placed in the next two orders: "is unable to leave home because the worker's presence is required to care for an invalid in the home." Though gender neutral, this rule referred to behavior, dependent care, performed overwhelmingly by women. Women were the subjects of the next two orders. They were the slip stitchers in the neckwear industry covered by Order No. 2. Employers did not challenge these initial orders: Unions were strong enough to police both men's clothing and neckwear, less homework existed, and small operators could easily ignore the law.[50]

First American had a long history of violating labor standards. In June 1934 it lost the NRA's Blue Eagle for not paying overtime wages and employing more homeworkers and apprentices than specified by the code for artificial flowers. From the start, it opposed Order No. 3, calling the 1937 public hearing on artificial flower making unfair because it was not notified in time to submit a rebuttal to the Labor Department's investigation of the industry. First American contended that the order would interfere with its ability to meet existing contracts. Removal of its forty homeworkers, who actually

49 NYDOL, *Homework in the Artificial Flower and Feather Industry in New York State*, Special Bulletin no. 199 (1938), 25–6; Supreme Court of the State of New York County of Albany, "*First American Natural Ferns Company, Inc., vs. William J. Picard and Frieda Miller*," Brief filed by its attorneys, Berger & Levison, July 11, 1940; State of NYDOL, Board of Standards and Appeals, "In the Matter of the Petition of Max Kaplan and Jacob Kaplan," Case no. 1681–39, Legal Brief Submitted on Behalf of the Industrial Commissioner and *Decision and Resolution*, June 28, 1940.

50 Shallcross, *Industrial Homework*, 217–23; "Memo to Miss Papert; Subject: *Coverage of Men under the Homework Law*," c. 1939, file "legal"; Mary Skinner and Ruth Scandrett, "Report on the Investigation of Industrial Home Work in the Men's Neckwear Industry, Troy, New York," 1934, HC Records, box 8385, folder "Men's Neckwear Industry."

assembled cheaper grades of flowers, would create bottlenecks that would lead to laying off two hundred factory workers.[51]

First American resembled the majority of flower manufacturers. A seasonal, labor-intensive handwork industry, threatened by low-priced foreign imports and dependent on style, artificial flower making lent itself to the homework system – even among larger firms. Employers defended the practice by drawing upon industry characteristics. They cited structural considerations even while painting the familiar portrait of the homeworker as homemaker, choosing to do flowers for merely a few hours each day to make ends meet while fulfilling family responsibilities.[52]

From this firm's first citation in March 1938 through a January 1942 hearing to revoke its homework license, general counsel Samuel Berger offered excuse after excuse to the Homework Bureau for not meeting legal requirements. He claimed no control over the homes of employees who shared work with non-certified and unrecorded helpers, arguing that the state should revoke the certificates of such violators.[53] Nor did he accept responsibility for the actions of his contractors, some of whom were giving out illegal homework in order to increase their income beyond the meager sums gained from his jobs. He constantly excused inaccurate entries in record books with "I did not know that we were supposed to keep production record books" or blamed foreman Angelo for "getting careless." Berger even went to the trouble of setting up a subsidiary company "to defeat the provisions of the Wage and Hour Law." When cited for "excessive distribution of homework," or providing more work to those outside than those inside the factory, he responded: "I don't consider this a serious violation. My spring season is now at a finish. In the fall, I will try to do away with homework entirely." That was in May 1939; two and a half years later he still was excusing such noncompliance.[54]

First American's lawyers also tried numerous arguments against the law. Along with questioning the constitutionality of the order itself and its coverage of "men," their petition to the Board of Standards and Appeals urged that mothers with infants be allowed to work at home – an argument rejected by federal officials

---

[51] "Blue Eagle Lost for Labor Abuses," *New York Times*, June 2, 1934, 34:2; Samuel S. Berger, "Artificial Flower and Feather Industry. Hearings August 29, 1933," HC Records, box 8384, folder "artificial flowers"; NYDOL, Division of Women in Industry and Minimum Wage, "Public Hearing in the Matter of Proposed Order No. 3 Prohibiting Industrial Homework in the Artificial Flower and Feather Industry," Dec. 16, 1937, 13–14, 36–7, NYDOL, file "Industrial Homework Order No. 3 Hearings, Minutes, 1937."

[52] For employers' descriptions of their industry, see, for example, "Hearing of Manufacturers in Flower and Feather Industry – December 1, 1937," in file "Artificial Flower Order."

[53] The Court of Special Sessions on June 25, 1940, upheld this contention when deciding that the DOL could not prove employer prior knowledge of a certified homeworker distributing work to others.

[54] "Summary of Contacts with First American Natural Ferns Co. Inc.," Dec. 10, 1941; "In the Matter of First American Natural Ferns Co. Inc.," Jan. 6, 1942, New York City, typed transcript, 45–8.

during the NRA years. Federal enactment of FLSA, they contended, superseded the state law. The board of Standards and Appeals rejected both arguments, contending that state and federal laws complemented each other. As for exempting mothers from regulation, a variation clause permitted modification in individual cases. The Board emphatically championed "the welfare of the industry and of the workers as a whole rather than the wishes of particular individuals who may feel that their liberties are being unduly fettered."[55]

In this context, the employment of male workers became another subterfuge. In February 1939, Berger had canceled his homework permit, citing difficulty in complying with the bookkeeping – an outcome formulators of the act hoped for. But within a week he asked for renewal because many "homeworkers had come to them to complain of their plight." By June, he was signaling "the intention of the firm to distribute no more homework to women . . .," announcing other plans "by which they intend to handle the problem arising from the Homework Order." By October, the department was citing First American for employing noncertified men.[56]

The company's record books listed the names of men like Dominick Cicero as homeworkers, but these men actually obtained artificial flowers for their kinswomen to make. Since the late nineteenth century, Italian women with their children rolled stems, pulled out buds, and assembled the various parts of flowers. While husbands occasionally would aid, flower making was considered women's work, a craft fitting for the "nimble" fingers of females and the "small" fingers of children. In 1936, 40 percent of women in the flower industry were homeworkers; a year later during the Easter rush season, 67 percent of women worked at home, more than before the NRA period.[57]

Inspectors presented the case of Mrs. Domenica Cinquemani, found on October 9, 1940, assembling yellow and orange chrysanthemum pieces with her eighteen-year-old daughter, her sister-in-law, and an elderly Italian woman and her thirty-year-old daughter. This mother and daughter were in the apartment, they said, just for "a social visit" – which included making some flowers while they chatted. But it was husband Angelo, an unemployed house painter and disabled veteran, who received and returned the flowers and had been on the payroll of First American as the employee since July. He did not know how to make flowers. Asked by inspectors whether anyone "in the firm . . . [knew] that she, [Mrs. Cinquemani], instead of her husband, was doing the homework on the artificial flowers, she would not answer."[58]

[55] Board of Standards and Appeals, *Decision and Resolution*, 4–7.

[56] "Summary of Contacts," 1–5.

[57] Mary Van Kleeck, *Artificial Flower Makers* (New York: Survey Associates, 1913); "Homework in the Artificial Flower & Feather Industry," Apr. 15, 1937, file "Industrial Homework Order No. 3 – Procedure, Enforcement."

[58] Memorandum on Domenica Cinquemani, H. Molbert & M.H. Sorkin, inspectors, Oct. 9, 1940; "Re: Mrs. Domenica Cinquemani, 347 E. 105th Street, New York City. *Review of Department's Contacts With Above Homeworker.*"

Mrs. Cinquemani functioned as a subcontractor, the only mobility for home-workers within the system. She paid sixty cents a gross, the same price received from the firm. Her sharing of work expressed the continued mutuality of the tenements; as we have seen, homeworkers were not the isolated victims portrayed by social reformers. At the time of the inspection she had fifteen gross, which it would take about sixty hours to complete, and these had to be brought back within two or three days. Given the amount of time needed, the company probably assumed that more than one person was working – even though it feigned ignorance.[59]

Mrs. Cinquemani had worked for First American or one of its contractors since September 1938 when the state initially inspected her for a certificate. She eventually received one in August 1939 on the basis of her own physical disability, although she had tried to qualify as a caretaker of her husband, who suffered from acute eye trouble. In May 1940 the inspector found First American paying her twenty cents per hour, instead of her claim of thirty cents, and cited Mrs. Cinquemani and the firm in violation of various provisions. A month later, the inspector came to pick up her employee handbook because the firm no longer had a distributor's permit. First Ameri-can had voluntarily relinquished its permit and would not ask for restoration until the Superior Court judged men to come within the scope of the 1935 homework law.[60]

The Department of Labor attorney assured the Homework Bureau "that the men have been covered by the Homework Law from the beginning; in fact, the old law was written in such a way that there was no question as to whether the person doing the work was a man or woman." But the department was worried. Previous illegal homework cases involving men brought convictions "only because the employers pleaded guilty." Labor officials recognized that by "stressing the economic and general welfare of women and minors," the new law opened the question "whether or not men were intended to be covered by the law."[61]

The public hearings on the artificial flower order, held to present evidence in support of restriction, emphasized the gendered nature of the labor force. As with the NRA hearings, all agreed that homeworkers were women, mostly mothers and housewives. Gender justified their homework, explained it away, or provided the reason to condemn it. Women's organizations, like the Women's City Club, the LWV, and the WTUL, substituted their understanding of "woman" for the homeworker's own, viewing her as a victim needing pro-tection. Homeworkers thought not in terms of labor standards, but in terms of family economy: how homework allowed them to meet familial obligations. This was true even among those who testified to low wages. Their understand-

59 Ibid.
60 Ibid.
61 "Memo to Miss Papert; Subject: *Coverage of Men Under the Homework Law*."

ing of role and responsibility – where underaged siblings who helped got not "a reward for working," but "a living" of food and clothing – stood apart from that of unionists and reformers who, like Joseph Tuvim, called for living wages for factory-employed fathers and older daughters and play for children. A common perception framed reformer remarks; encoded within the homework law was an expectation that it would benefit women, that gender neutrality would generate a gendered result.[62]

On November 9, 1940, the Supreme Court of Albany County affirmed the gender neutrality and the scope of the law. Although the special sessions had acquitted First American for distributing homework to a noncertified man, a decision that undoubtedly encouraged continued distribution, the superior court agreed with the industrial commissioner. "The purpose of the law is not the protection of 'women and minors' in industrial homework but the 'strict control and gradual elimination of industrial homework,' " the legal brief for the commissioner argued. Reading the statute in its entirety, the state claimed, would make it clear that men came under its purview. " 'Industrial homeworker' " was defined as "*any person* who manufactures in a *home*" (emphasis in the brief). The generic use of the male for person provided evidence that the statute referred to both sexes. If anything, the brief implied, the initial Order No. 3 incorrectly used "woman" and "she." Agreeing with this reasoning, the judges concluded, "The legislation is aimed directly at the eradication of a social and economic evil, and with the idealistic motive of promoting the general welfare."[63]

Prior to issuing homework Order No. 3, labor investigators noted that only women with children under six or without family childcare preferred homework. "Many of these women had worked in flower factories and would do so again." Despite ideological rationales, employers structured the industry in a way that heavily contributed to women's position as homeworkers. For with the implementation of Order No. 3, nearly a thousand more women entered the factory during the peak season of 1939 than were working inside the year before. Employers had reorganized production, offering factory jobs where they once only provided homework.[64]

---

[62] "Public hearing on Proposed Order # 3," 18–20, 31, 51–2, 67–76, 80–2, 90, 87–9, 92–4, 44–5.

[63] "First American Natural Ferns Co., Inc. v. Picard," 175 Misc. 280, Nov. 5, 1940, Supreme Court, Special Term, Albany County; "Legal Brief Submitted on Behalf of the Industrial Commissioner," 7–11.

[64] "Homework in the Artificial Flower & Feather Industry," Apr. 16, 1937, 6. Division of Women in Industry and Minimum Wage, "Report to the Industrial Commissioner on a Review of the Operation of Homework Order No. 3 and Recommendations for the Continued Regulation of Homework in the Artificial Flower and Feather Industry," Oct. 16, 1939, in file, "Order No. 3 – Reports." Former homework firms increased their factory operatives more than other firms (71 percent to 43 percent), suggesting the effectiveness of the order. Homework permits dropped from 2,543 to 198 (with 351 homeworkers discovered on payrolls, indicating the persistence of illegal homework). Most employers adjusted successfully, helped by unsettled European conditions that hampered import of cheaper, but more artistic, goods.

Gender continued to shape interpretations of the New York law. A 1957 case illuminates how men working at home became independent contractors because enforcers of the act assumed that men were not homeworkers who were, by definition, mothers laboring intermittently at home. Frank Pacifico sewed slip covers and draperies on order for furniture stores. The supervisor of the industrial division thought it unnecessary to grant him a homework permit because he "is a businessman, not a homeworker, except for the statutory construction flowing from the fact he operates from his house." Pacifico did not consider himself a homeworker; he was "engaged in building up a business." Classifying him as an independent contractor met "the spirit of the Homework Law." Male self-employment generated choices; homeworkers were women who were not really breadwinners.[65]

But the question remained, what was a home? During the NRA period, Clara Beyer extended the definition of home or living quarters to include "the entire apartment or dwelling constituting the worker's place of residence or any part thereof," which would have eliminated places "entirely disconnected from a place where the employee lives." State laws varied, with Pennsylvania excluding tailors who employed others and Maryland determining status by "the exits and entrances to the street." The 1935 New York law limited the meaning of home "to buildings where one or more persons regularly sleep" and cook. Fulton County glove employers and their homeworkers sought to circumvent the order for their industry in the early 1940s by shifting the physical location of labor from inside the domestic dwelling to garages, sheds, and other outbuildings, ranging from converted horse stalls and chicken coops to children's playhouses.[66]

Homework on gloves had existed in this region of New York as the customary organization of production for nearly a century. In 1941, glove firms employed 15,183 workers in factories, more than two-thirds of whom were women performing essentially the same labor as 5,422 homeworkers. Used by only a small number of firms, homeworkers concentrated in the Republican stronghold of Fulton County, a place which prided itself on independence and "fighting off the industrial revolution." Half of them earned under $330 a year, while half of the factory women earned under $630. Whereas factory workers were on short time, homeworkers toiled overtime. In

---

[65] John Bila to Esther Bennin, Jan. 22, 1957; Emily Sims Marconnier to Isador Lubin, Feb. 28, 1957; Lubin to Jack Stanislaw, Feb. 15, 1957; Bila to Bennin, Feb. 15, 1957; Stanislaw to Lubin, Mar. 11, 1957, all in NYDOL, file "1950s."

[66] Clara Beyer to Mr. Merle Vincent, Dec. 4, 1934, HC Records, box 8385, folder "Industries (Merchants and Custom Tailoring)"; "Memorandum in Support of Amendment to the Definition of 'House' in Reference to Industrial Homework," Jan. 8, 1945; Kate Papert to Mr. Edward Corsi, Jan. 25, 1944; "Attempts to Circumvent the Homework Law by Claiming That Barns, Garages, and Other Out Buildings Are Not 'Homes' But Factories," all in NYDOL folder "Proposed Amendment to the Homework Law – Proposed Definition of 'Home.'"

social composition, though, the two groups of women workers resembled each other: older married women with few children under eighteen, with "similar domestic responsibilities." Although the 1941 homework order would bring some individual hardship, Miller insisted that restriction would benefit the industry as a whole. As with other orders, the old, disabled, and their caretakers could obtain exemptions; in this case, industry had six months to adjust itself to the new rules which restricted permits after May 1942 to only those who came under these categories and only in numbers equivalent to those employed by a firm prior to the order.[67]

When employers responded by advising workers to establish work spaces in outbuildings, the Department of Labor interpreted the law to include such buildings. Meanwhile, the ILGWU and the State Federation of Labor introduced an amendment to the law to change the definition of home. What was homework and what legitimately constituted a branch factory not only involved perceptions but also affected implementation, the bureaucratic routines of the department. If a factory, an outbuilding would be inspected by the Division of Factory Inspection, which would post a notice listing factory regulations. If defined as homework, the Homework Bureau had jurisdiction. If understood to be a factory, the homework regulations would not apply and such labor on the premises of the home could boldly continue. Apparently the Division of Factory Inspection prematurely – in the minds of the homework regulators – posted notices on some of these outbuildings which the Homework Bureau considered mere extensions of the home, set up to evade the homework order, compounding the difficulty of enforcement.[68]

To solve this confusion, the Homework Bureau relied upon notions of family. "The pre-requisite for factory" became that "there be two or more persons, one of whom shall be a non-resident." Assistant director George Ostrow explained: "It may be asked why two members of one family may not work but could do so if there is a non-resident person. The reason for introducing a non-resident is dependent upon the thought that where a husband and wife or any two members of a family are employed, there actually exists a homework situation with the exception of some minor alterations in the structure of the home." Lack of kinship, then, would "indicate the intention of setting up a bona fide factory." This meant that a manufacturer

[67] Miller to Miss Papert, June 25, 1941, in NYDOL folder "General file: Glove Industry"; John Lear, "The Temperamental Wizards of Fulton County," *The Saturday Evening Post* (May 17, 1947), 32, 145–6, 148, 150; "N.Y. Curbs Homework in Glove Industry," *The Advance*, Aug. 1941, NYDOL.

[68] Kate Papert to Mr. Edward Corsi, Jan. 25, 1944; Mr. Ostrow to Miss Papert, "Work in Out-Buildings," Aug. 16, 1943; Mr. Ostrow to Mrs. Marconnier, Mar. 5, 1947; Mr. Gagnon to Miss Papert, "Exceptions to definition of 'home' – Industrial Homework Law," Nov. 24, 1942; Arthur H. Gagnon to Miss Papert, Nov. 13, 1942; Mr. Gagnon to Miss Papert, "Amendment to the Definition of 'Home' – Industrial Homework Law," Feb. 2, 1943, in NYDOL folder "Barns and Garages."

could not use his wife as a machine operator at home unless "his wife was a partner and owned the materials," that is, unless his wife was an independent contractor or a manufacturer. To which, one such maker of leather gloves replied, "that she is his wife and doesn't have to be listed as a partner of firm." Such a ruling also meant that companies could not establish "branch shops" in "private homes," another device that employers seized upon by the late 1940s to evade homework rules. "Foreladies," whose living quarters became the branch, hired friends and relatives. Employers had to have written leases to call such arrangements factories and all workers had to be in the employment of the lessee; that is, the building could not function as a workshop for outworkers to gather. Yet the problem persisted throughout the decade, suggesting that the possibility of penalties from getting caught offered no deterrence.[69]

After the NRA, the Division of Labor Standards served as a "clearing house" for information on homework, especially for its passage across state lines. By 1945, nineteen states, the District of Columbia, and Puerto Rico had enacted laws that prohibited either the making of specified items or the employment of nonfamily members in the home. California, Puerto Rico, Pennsylvania, and West Virginia, like Massachusetts and New Jersey, followed New York's lead in providing the power to prohibit homework in industries that injured the health and welfare of homeworkers or the labor standards of factory employees. Most state laws required record keeping systems; many incorporated factory labor standards. Connecticut's 1935 law and Rhode Island's of 1936, states with major concentrations of homework, allowed the standard exemptions for the ill, the elderly, and their caretakers; the commissioner could also permit homework to remain in industries where hand processes were customary if neither business nor labor would suffer. Both were among the states that restricted homework through minimum wage orders, with Connecticut fixing minimums for thread drawing in the lace industry and Rhode Island prohibiting homework in jewelry and wearing apparel. Wage orders in California banned homework in manufacturing and nut cracking without a permit. An Oregon wage order prohibited the practice in needlework. Massachusetts already had determined that all minimum wage rates set after November 1937 would include homeworkers. The retail trade order in Colorado and Utah prohibited "giving out work that can be done on the premises to be done elsewhere." Certainly the 1937 Supreme Court decision upholding the women's minimum wage, *West Coast Hotel v. Parrish*, facilitated this approach.

[69] "Proposed Application of Factory and Homework Laws to the Definition of 'Home' "; Mr. Ostrow to Miss Papert, "Comments on Proposed Regulations Governing Exceptions that are to apply to the Special Homework Orders," Nov. 13, 1942, in folder "Barns and Garages"; Inspector's Report on Jos. Perrone, 12–2–44, in folder "Proposed Revision of Glove Order,"; J. D. Wolf to George Ostrow, "Factories located in homes," June 1, 1948, in folder "Proposed Amendment to the Homework Law," all in NYDOL.

Yet enforcement of state orders met with varying success, depending on the capacity of departments of labor, the extent of the problem, and the power of both trade unions and organized white middle-class women. The problem of interstate activity remained, with homework employers moving their operations from areas with better enforcement to those with less restrictions.[70]

State regulation proved as flawed during the economic crisis of the depression as it had during the preceding decade. But during the mid-thirties the federal government became the site of regulation. Congress passed in 1936 the Walsh–Healey Public Contracts Act, interpreted to prohibit homework; two years later came FLSA, the Wage and Hour Act. Gender neutral, FLSA would not be subject to the same ambiguities that plagued enforcement of New York's model law. It specified minimum wages, maximum hours, and child labor limits, first through wage committees and then through statutory decrees.

State laws had originated in women's labor law, legislation forged to protect women and minors. In the economic crisis of the 1930s, this gendered legacy determined who led the battle for homework regulation. But the language of reform reflected the depression context. The depression made it politically possible to gain labor standards for most workers, no matter their sex. The language of economics dominated the discourse of women reformers. Still homework remained the work of mothers, providing the regulatory debate with a gendered subtext.

[70] 300 U.S. 379; U.S. DOL, Division of Labor Standards, "Interstate Shipment of Industrial Homework," Nov. 5, 1936, ILGWU Library; Russell Lindquist and Donald K. Smith, "Industrial Home Work," *Minnesota Law Review* 29 (Apr. 1945): 295, 303–8; "Coverage of Industrial Homework in Minimum Wage Orders," Jan. 1939, RG86, box 1602, folder "Homework: Progress in Control, Laws, etc.";"Industrial Homework in the United States," 55–6, NYDOL, folder "Summary and Reviews."

Figure 17. "Industrial Homework Makes a Home a Factory," 1945, cover, *Labor Laws in New York State: Homework* (Albany: New York State Department of Labor). By bringing waged labor into the site of family life, industrial homework explodes the division of home and work. It was precisely this separation that the architects of the Fair Labor Standards Act maintained by distinguishing between "a real home" and a home that had "become a factory."

9

"Unknown to the common law": The Fair Labor Standards Act

The Fair Labor Standards Act (FLSA) stood as the culmination of a fifty-year struggle to regulate homework. It represented a new strategy for an old crusade: the ending of sweated labor, which it defined as state provision of "the minimum standard of living necessary for health, efficiency, and general well-being of workers."[1] This gender neutral language derived from its constitutional grounding in the commerce clause that gave the federal government authority to regulate interstate activities. Such justification, which emphasized the state's right to protect commerce from unfair competition, provided an escape from the "gender trap" that had associated labor standards with the protection of women and children – a line of reasoning undermined by the majority opinion in *Adkins v. Children's Hospital* as well as by the fierce debate over the Equal Rights Amendment during the preceding decade.[2]

The women's reform network had understood the intertwined nature of social welfare and labor standards. But FLSA – and by extension the entire postwar labor standards regime for which it stood as the linchpin – addressed labor standards only at the workplace. FLSA failed to account for the divisions of labor by sex, race, ethnicity, age, and kinship within homes and other workplaces. The labor liberals who crafted FLSA, including Clara Beyer and Frances Perkins, assumed that home should be a separate realm from the workplace, that the private world of the family needed protection from intrusion by the all too public market.[3] FLSA would prove to be a limited solution to the homework problem. It banned homework only in specified industries where reformers and unions exerted political pressure, promising regulation for all others. It forecast a gradual disappearance of the system but neglected adequate monitoring of wages, hours, or child labor. This strategy overlooked the underlying reasons for homework, failing to confront why women were homeworkers in the first place.

[1] *Fair Labor Standards Act, Statutes at Large,* 52, sec. 2 (a), 1060.
[2] Vivien Hart, "Minimum-Wage Policy and Constitutional Inequality: The Paradox of the Fair Labor Standards Act of 1938," *Journal of Policy History* 1 (1989): 319–43.
[3] Frances E. Olson, "The Family and the Market: A Study of Ideology and Legal Reform," *Harvard Law Review* 96 (1983): 1496–578.

In and out of the Fair Labor Standards Act

FLSA developed out of the political compromise that characterized Roosevelt's second term. Pushed by "the Keynesian left," those economists and industrialists who would attack underconsumption through higher wages and more efficient business methods, FLSA was designed to aid the newly formed Congress of Industrial Organizations to organize the South. Sidney Hillman was one of its chief architects. However, the "Roosevelt recession" of 1937 impeded both this unionization drive and the progress of FLSA in Congress. Newly emboldened conservatives, especially southern and western Democrats, kept the bill "hostage" until the act contained hampering restrictions, exclusions that limited its coverage and severely stymied Hillman's efforts to end competition from low-waged southern textiles.[4]

FLSA's initial rate of twenty-five cents an hour stood lower than the hourly wage in most union contracts; white men in basic industry made a higher wage. Of the twelve million workers first under FLSA, only three hundred thousand received a raise. Intrastate jobs – in hotels, laundries, hospitals, state and local government, schools, domestic service, retail, agriculture and even within the garment industry – could not benefit from FLSA's standards. Its limited coverage defined out of the act large numbers of both white women and people of color, upon whose low wages southern capital depended. The intransigence of regional capital had generated compromises that offset higher wages by omitting agriculture and service industries from coverage.[5]

The legislative history of FLSA was tortuous, with Senate and House versions that differed significantly in their basic mechanisms, as well as numerous amendments over a two-year period. The original 1937 Black-Connery Bill provided for a maximum work week of forty hours, a minimum wage of forty cents an hour, exclusion of children under sixteen from industry, and prohibition from interstate commerce of goods manufactured in violation of these provisions. Prohibition of industrial homework went in and out as a specified element of the act, but was finally eliminated in conference committee before passage in 1938.[6]

The International Ladies' Garment Workers Union (ILGWU) had advised co-sponsor Senator Hugo Black (D-Alabama) that "there should be an 'Industrial Homework' definition and a provision that Industrial Homework

---

[4] Steven Fraser, *Labor Will Rule: Sidney Hillman and the Rise of American Labor* (New York: Free Press, 1991), 392–4, 399–412.

[5] Vivien Hart, "The Right to a Fair Wage: American Experience and the European Social Charter," in *Writing a National Identity: Political, Economic, and Cultural Perspectives on the Written Constitution*, ed. Vivien Hart and Shannon C. Stimson (Manchester: Manchester Univ. Press, 1993), 106–24; Phyllis Palmer, "Outside the Law: Agricultural and Domestic Workers Under the Fair Labor Standards Act," unpublished paper, OAH, Reno, Nev., 1988.

[6] Brief for Petitioners, *Gemsco v. Walling*, Supreme Court of the United States, October Term, 1944, 10–19; Brief for Respondent, ibid., 33–52; *Gemsco v. Walling*, 324 U.S. 244 (1945), 12–17.

shall be prohibited on findings of oppressive labor practices." Secretary of Labor Frances Perkins firmly supported such an addition. During 1937 joint hearings she proposed giving a wage board the right to prohibit or regulate homework "to prevent circumvention of the Act." Longtime homework opponents in the National Child Labor Committee (NCLC) and the National Consumers' League (NCL) joined Perkins in requesting "more definite provision for control . . . if this system of unfair competition is to be eliminated." Courtenay Dinwiddie of the NCLC claimed, "long consideration of this evil has convinced all who know the facts that the only solution is to abolish home work" which would stop the employment of whole families and the abuse of children for "starvation pay." State labor law administrators also favored "eliminating the products of child labor and industrial home work from interstate commerce."[7]

Most homework opponents argued in economic or administrative terms; although they agreed that homework was a social "evil," they pressed for inclusion under FLSA because of its negative impact on the carrying out of the act. Such language reduced the exploitation of women workers and their families to an inefficient system of production and an administrative nightmare. Such a discourse was hardly new in the late 1930s, but by overshadowing "sacred motherhood" and consumer contamination, this argument set the perimeters for legal battles over interpretation of the act.

Whether homeworkers, who were generally understood to be "women and minors," could be classified as "employees," and subject to the bill, troubled some within the administration. Independent contractors did not come under the act's definition of employee as one who was "suffered or permitted to work." The Social Security Board had judged "independent contractor" to be "the legal status of most 'homeworkers.' " Because FLSA proposed "to restrict or prohibit 'home-work' as an evasion," lawyers advised the Roosevelt administration that "unless 'home-workers' are expressly included, you may have omitted from the coverage of the Act large groups of workers, particularly in the needle trades." In 1937, Social Security, the Bureau of Internal Revenue, and state unemployment compensation boards determined that homeworkers fell within the employer-employee relationship. But until the Supreme Court ruled on the matter, such decisions rested on "some 'natural' justice," explained administration counsels, rather than legal precedent. Attorney General Robert H. Jackson distinguished between independent craftsmen and homeworkers: "The factory which sends out and makes use of people in their homes are [sic] not exempted just because they are using premises they do not pay any rent for."[8]

[7] Merle D. Vincent to the Honorable Hugo L. Black, May 29, 1937, sent to David Dubinsky, Dubinsky Papers, 81–7b; FLSA *Joint Hearings*, Part 1, June 2–5, 1937, 190–1; Part 2, June 7–15, 1937, 408, 402; DOL, press release, Oct. 27, 1937, RG174, box 39, file "Conference: National Conference on Labor Legislation, October 25–27, 1937."

[8] John M. Gallagher to Mr. Thomas G. Corcoran, Aug. 9, 1937, in Corcoran Papers, box 255, Special Files, "New Deal Era, FLSA, 1938," folder 1; FLSA *Joint Hearings*, Part 1, 77.

Women dominated this shadow status; yet because there was strong pressure to prohibit interference with the objectives of FLSA, their work site, the home, would be covered – though not specified – in the final version of the act to avoid cumbersome illustrations. The act included both fixed statutory wages and an administrative board to review those industries selected to receive the mandated minimum wage more rapidly than the statute proposed – a board that would be used to save the factory from the home by restricting homework.[9]

Attempts at regulation

Control of homework was high on the agenda of the new Wage and Hour Division of the Department of Labor. An early "Progress Story" on FLSA asserted, "Knottiest of the problems confronting administrators . . . is Industrial Homework in the so-called 'sweated trades' where exploitation, particularly of women and children, has been most prevalent. On this rock, the act itself might be wrecked." Certainly Clara Beyer and other labor officials had prohibition in mind when they established regulatory mechanisms to control homework under FLSA. They recognized that if employers had to pay minimum wage, the economic advantage of homework would be gone, which would force some employers to turn to factory labor. They understood "the ease of evasion in homework tends to make it an avenue of escape from effective enforcement in factories."[10]

The first interpretative bulletin of the Wage and Hour Division declared that "since the Act contains no prescription as to the place where the employees must work," otherwise eligible employees laboring at home came under the act. After January 1939 hearings on the need for special or additional records for homework, the administrator announced new regulations. These required the employer "who distributes work directly or indirectly" to record the name, home address, and date of birth (if under nineteen) of each homeworker and the name and address of each agent or contractor used in his business. Employer records had to show the hour and date on which work went out and was subsequently returned, the amount and type of work (including type of article and operations performed), hours worked, piece rates, wages paid, deductions for Social Security, and date of payment. Many of these items, as well as overtime pay, had to be specified by work week. Employers had to keep a separate

---

[9] Briefs for Petitioners and Respondents, *Gemsco v. Walling*, esp. Brief for Respondents, 49; "Women in Industry: A Report to the Annual Meeting," IAGLO, Sept. 8–10, 1938, Charleston, South Carolina, in RG174, box 82, "Women – General"; Hart, "Minimum Wage-Policy."

[10] "Putting the Wage and Hours Act to Work," *Wage and Hour Legislation in Action*, New York City, Dec. 9, 1938, NCL Papers, reel 54, frame 589–92; U.S. DOL, Wage and Hour Division, "Progress Report on Homework Under the Fair Labor Standards Act," Oct. 1940, NYDOL Library, vertical files, "Home Labor – United States."

handbook for each homeworker in which the distributor of the homework would record the required information. Homeworkers were to retain such handbooks. Taylor-like methods provided tools to rid the home of its factorylike production.[11]

Before the special record keeping hearings, representatives of industrial associations clung to the gendered arguments of the past. They justified homework because it was performed by women, often rural and sometimes disabled, in the home. "It is a form of supplemental income," claimed the executive director of the National Knitted Outerwear Association. Women working only a few hours in their spare time accounted for the average earnings of only a few dollars a week. Fitting in the work "between taking care of the baby or cooking the meals at home," they hardly could record "every five minutes they spent knitting." The National Association of Leather Glove Manufacturers viewed homework as a logical component of a woman's life cycle, coming after marriage: "If she is a very good operator naturally the factory dislikes to lose her, so some arrangements are made whereby she can continue to work for the factory and at the same time run her home." Other women, desiring "supplemental income," informed the factory of their readiness to accept homework. In contrast to business apologists, male trade unionists and women New Dealers argued that such work by mothers was necessary rather than supplemental.[12]

Clara Beyer asserted that the home location of labor posed a danger to FLSA because you could not control hours or even the number of people engaged in the work. "It is quite the custom to bring in the neighbors and members of the family [when] one person is on the payroll," she testified at the record keeping hearing. What trade unionists saw as "little neighborly groups who come in and sit around together and work and chat," making it impossible to calculate an adequate minimum wage, industry representatives interpreted as part of the leisurely routine of small town life where a woman "might start at eleven o'clock and after lunch she would begin about two in the afternoon. The women from the church come over there and sit around and talk until five o'clock at night."[13]

Over the years, investigators reported deliberate falsification of record keeping books. In some cases homeworkers used books filled in advance by

---

[11] "Hearings Start Jan. 4 on Homeworker Rules Under Wages Act," *Daily News Record*, Dec. 24, 1938, Red Books, v. 7, 1938–9, 178, ACWA Papers; U.S. DOL, Wage and Hour Division, "Industrial Homework Records Regulation Announced," press release, Feb. 18, 1939, DOL Library; "In the Matter of: Hearing on Proposed Amendments to Part 516 of Regulations with Respect to the Keeping of Special or Additional Records by Employers of Industrial Homeworkers, in the United States and Puerto Rico," Washington, D.C., Jan. 6, 1939 (Ward & Paul Official Reporters), in files, Office of Special Minimum Wages, Division of Labor Standards, DOL.

[12] Harold R. Lhove, 15; James H. Casey, Jr., 232–3; James Kennedy, 385–7; Bertha Nienberg, 458–61, all in "Hearing on … the Keeping of Special or Additional Records."

[13] Clara Beyer, 489; Kennedy, 386; Casey, 441, all in ibid.

employers that would make piece rates come out exactly to a forty-hour week at minimum wage. Homeworkers agreed with labor department officials that constant interruptions from family obligations deterred the keeping of accurate hours. Such regulations proved their "nuisance value" when some employers gave up homework.[14]

Home and work were being linked, not because administrators desired such an association, but because they expected to find it impossible for employers and homeworkers to keep accurate records. The idea was to use the handbooks as evidence to prove that homework by definition violated FLSA hour and wage mandates. As one inspector later testified, "without exception, *every* firm was in violation in regard to home-work production, either directly or through their home-work contractors." Although she could check the rates of inside employees, who knew of the law and often were union members, homeworkers were difficult to find and reluctant to provide information. Homeworkers, often on relief and non–English speaking, feared losing their work. A Children's Bureau agent investigating New York City and Brooklyn exclaimed, "They don't know what handbooks are in these places." One studying the candlewick bedspread industry in rural Georgia reported: "The whole town is scared to death of us and watch the movement of our car with eagle eyes. Violation is rampant. Sometimes I almost wish we were the enforcement division. . . . They lie to us so terribly."[15]

During the first two years of the act, homework violations composed a little over 1 percent of 4,513 litigated actions. Still homeworkers, 13 percent of all workers receiving restitution, received nearly a quarter of the total amount of back pay and damages. On average they gained $46.01, to only $25.52 for others. Such figures suggested "the extent to which homeworkers are exploited in comparison with other employees." From 1939 until mid-1942, Wage and Hour and the Children's Bureau discovered 895 children illegally at homework, 12 percent of the total number of children found in violation of the act. By bringing actions against all violating employers in an industry, the Wage and Hour Division would "stabilize" industrial conditions.[16]

Needlework firms violated the act and owed at least fifty thousand homeworkers back wages. The Wage and Hour administrator first concentrated on the needlework industry in Puerto Rico and on the garment trade. Other early cases came from New York, Pennsylvania, Illinois, and New England – where most homework activity historically resided and state de-

---

[14] "Progress Report on Homework," 10–11, 15; conversation, Eileen Boris with Clara Beyer, Dec. 1986.

[15] U.S. DOL, Division of Labor Standards, "Industrial Home Work Under the Fair Labor Standards Act in the Jewelry Industry," 1, mimeoed statement by Mrs. Rebecca L. Landow, Jan. 21, 1941, in ILGWU Library; Caroline Legg to Mrs. Warburton, Nov. 29, 1939; Amber Warburton to Elizabeth S. Jonson, Oct. 10, 1939, both in RG102, file 20–194–5.

[16] "Progress Report on Homework," 4–13; Golda Stander, "Child Labor in Industrial Home Work Under the Fair Labor Standards Act," *The Child*, Jan. 1943, 100.

partments of labor attempted to enforce laws. The American Textile Company and nine other Rhode Island lacemaking firms paid back wages of sixty thousand dollars to three hundred homeworkers. Major judgments also went against producers of novelties and flowers, crochet shade pulls, dolls, hairpins, and punch boards. Assessing the impact of these early actions, the administrator recounted the story of what a women, "who had struggled for years to provide the bare necessities of life for herself and her children," did with her "sizable" back paycheck: "She looked at the check a long time and then asked: 'Mister, how do you go about it to get a permanent wave? I've heard about them things and the first thing I am going to do is get me one of them.'" That the universe of homeworkers remained unknown and the effectiveness of enforcement open to question, as major investigations in garment-related trades would prove during the next few years, could not distract from the moral of such stories: FLSA worked; the New Deal continued to improve the lives of forgotten Americans.[17]

Defining the employment relationship

Employers attempted to circumvent FLSA by classifying employees "independent contractors," but courts stymied their efforts. The Hand Knitcraft Institute case of November, 1939, which netted a quarter of a million dollars in back pay for ten thousand workers from Maine to Tennessee, foiled the most spectacular of these early evasions. Local 155 of the Knitwear Workers' Union filed the initial charges against eleven outerwear firms that had formed the Institute with the express purpose "to avoid the employer-employee relationship." Institute members arranged with yarn companies to sell directly to their workers, whom they called independent contractors. But "the yarn companies were actually nothing more than distributing agents for the manufacturers" who guaranteed the accounts of homeworkers or paid the companies directly. Workers finished the yarn according to the same samples and directions that had guided them prior to the special homework regulations in April 1939. They then sold the finished work at prices high enough to include the cost of the yarn. Their returns stayed the same, eight to ten cents an hour when the minimum wage was twenty-five cents. In this scheme, contractors became "selling agents" for both yarn companies and workers.[18]

[17] "Progress Report on Homework," 4–13; "In the Matter of a Hearing on the Minimum Wage Recommendation of Industrial Committee No. 15 for the Embroideries Industry," Oct. 1, 1940, 284–90, 246, RG155, box 63.

[18] Mary Dublin, "Abolish Industrial Home Work System," letter, New York Times, Dec. 8, 1939, NCL Papers, reel 54, frame 539; "$250,000 Back–Pay To Homeworkers on Knit Union Charge," Justice 21 (Dec. 1, 1939), 1–2; Louis Nelson to David Dubinsky, President, ILGWU, May 18, 1939, Dubinsky Papers, 304–4a. In another example, a Dallas firm asked the local employment service "for 200 'customers' to buy whole pecans and resell them shelled to the company." See "Progress Report on Homework," 7–10.

In *Jacobs v. Hand Knitcraft Institute* (1939), the U.S. District Court, Southern District of New York, defined homeworker as "any person producing goods for or on behalf of the defendants in or about a home," no matter where materials came from.[19] "Homeworkers Are Not 'Merchants,' " the ILGWU rejoiced. "A labor law, no matter how simple and drastic, is not much help unless it is backed up by union policing." Such had been the lesson of National Recovery Administration (NRA) compliance. An eager and dedicated state agency, like New York's Division of Women and Children in Industry, lacked the inspectors necessary to ferret out homework violations even in industries covered by homework orders.[20]

Although some courts clung to freedom of contract doctrines and ruled that homeworkers were independent contractors,[21] higher courts began to redefine the employment relationship and its consequences. *Walling v. American Needlecrafts* (1943) subverted common law understandings of the master-servant relationship that homework defied by removing the worker from the premise of the employer. It relied on the legislative history of FLSA to interpret the meaning of employee.[22]

American Needlecrafts was a New York corporation that hired about five hundred rural Kentucky women to appliqué, quilt, and perform other skilled needlework. It depended on the crafts skills of wives, widows, and daughters of farmers, instructing them in its studio workshops. The sexual division of labor in such rural areas provided the lower court with evidence for independent contracting. The U.S. Western District Court of Kentucky had held that since the homeworker "perform[ed] the duties which are usually performed by the women workers and members of a farmer's family, such as cooking the meals, taking care of the house and children, milking, churning, canning, raising chickens and sewing for the members of the family," her needlecraft was "done at odd times when the farm duties permit" and she could not be an employee.[23]

---

[19] 2 Lab. Cas. (CCH) 144, 145 (S.D.N.Y. 1939).

[20] Ibid.; "Editorial Notes," *Justice* 21 (Dec. 15, 1939).

[21] In *Walling v. Todd*, the U.S. Middle District Court of Pennsylvania upheld the contract between rag workers and employer that classified them as independent contractors because "the home worker was not subject to discharge, the defendant being obligated to accept the finished product at any time delivery was made." 52 F.Supp., 62, 64 (M.D. Penn. 1943).

[22] 139 F. 2d 60 (6th Cir. 1943). See also *Fleming v. De Vera*, 1 Wage & Hour Cas. (BNA) 367 (D.P.R. 1940).

[23] For examples of lower court rulings, see *Walling v. American Needlecrafts*, 46 F.Supp. 16, 19–20 (W.D.Ky. 1943) and *Walling v. Todd*, 52 F.Supp. 62 (M.D. Penn. 1943). Other courts noted the "remarkable feature," as one northern Illinois District judge put it, that the homeworkers were married women with children, "of high intelligence," whose men belonged to the "low income class" and "were seeking to help out, seeking to supplement the family income" – a feature that did not necessarily affect the contest at law (*Walling v. Buettner*), 2 Wage & Hour Cas. (BNA) 351, 354 (N.E. Ill. 1942). Indeed, the court in *Fleming v. De Vera* rejected the defendant's argument that her status as a married woman vitiated the suit because under the laws of Puerto Rico her husband, "as manager of the conjugal partnership," must join her as a defendant *Fleming v. De Vera*, 1 Wage & Hour Cas. (BNA) at 369.

The court of appeals rejected such gendered reasoning. Although no direct supervision occurred, women "strictly" complied with patterns and specifications. The finished product, as with other forms of homework, stood as proof of satisfactory labor. Other aspects of the work arrangement also stepped outside the terms of the traditional master–servant relationship: the home-worker suffered no discrimination if she refused work; she set the pace of her labor limited "only by the date set for completion and return"; and she provided the necessary equipment, could share the work with others and could work for other companies, even competitors. Yet the judges viewed the law as belonging to "a class of regulatory statutes designed to implement a public social, or economic policy through remedies not only unknown to the common law but often in derogation of it." They drew upon the section of the act that covered homeworkers in Puerto Rico and the Virgin Islands to argue for the act's relevance to all homeworkers, but they found final authority in congressional debates: "The purpose of the Congress was not to open the door to the return of the sweatshop system of unpleasant memory." *American Needlecrafts* helped to establish what legal scholars have called "an expansive 'economic reality' test for determining employee status" that cut across all the major New Deal labor legislation. Courts turned to the purpose of FLSA which was, as *United States v. Darby* (1941) explained, "to exclude from interstate commerce goods produced . . . under conditions detrimental to the maintenance of the minimum standards of living necessary for health and general well-being," as well as to insure that such commerce "should not be made the instrument of competition . . . of goods produced under substandard labor conditions."[24]

Courts recognized, "Drawing the line between employees and independent contractors cannot be done mechanically."[25] In 1948 the Edward S. Wagner Co. received knitted infants' wear from thousands of homeworkers, although most "sold" only a few items to the firm. *McComb v. Wagner* (1950) defined the status of such knitters. It embraced the Wage and Hour Division's criteria for independent contractor status: Were "contractor" activities "an integral part of the employer's business?" How much did they invest in plant and equipment? How permanent was the relationship? How much control did the employer exercise over them? Did they have opportunity to profit or lose "as the result of sound management or risk undertaken?" Finally, "what amount of initiative, judgment and energy" did they need for success?[26]

The court returned to the intent of Congress. Although no written contract

---

[24] *Walling v. American Needlecrafts*, 139 F.2d 60, 62, 63, 64 (6th Cir. 1943); *United States v. Darby*, 312 U.S. 100, 109, 115 (1941); Hether Clash Macfarlane, "Dropped Stitches: Federal Regulation of Industrial Homework in the 1980s," *Albany Law Review* 50 (Fall 1985), 118; Herman A. Wecht, *Wage-Hour Law Coverage* (Philadelphia, Pa.: Joseph M. Mitchell Publisher, 1951), 91–104, 111–23.

[25] *Walling v. Twyffort, Inc.*, 158 F.2d 944, 947–8 (2d Cir. 1947).

[26] 9 Wage & Hour Cas. (BNA) 286, 288 (E.D.N.Y. 1950).

existed, the pattern of the employer's behavior – letting home knitters know what kinds of work were acceptable at what rates – "was tantamount to the issuance of specific instructions."The National Knitted Outerwear Association called this decision "extreme" and warned its members carefully to investigate any deals in handmade goods.[27]

Employers further tried to undermine the act by transforming businesses into "cooperatives," a form of organization outside the reach of FLSA. But this was a difficult maneuver even if the articles of incorporation met all legalities. Santiago R. Palmer reorganized his Caribbean Embroidery Company into the Caribbean Embroidery Cooperative, Inc. as part of "necessary steps to continue our business after the minimum wage law goes into effect." The U.S. Circuit Court of Appeals for the First Circuit found that Palmer and not the workers controlled this "cooperative" which conducted its business much as it had prior to the reorganization. The homeworkers had no representative among the incorporators or initially among the board of directors, although one existed for contractors.[28]

Neither did the U.S. Circuit Court of Appeals in Richmond accept the Homeworkers' Handicraft Cooperative as anything but a front for the Millhiser Bag. Co. in a 1949 case concerning homeworkers who inserted strings in tobacco bags. Since the beginning of the decade, Virginia employers of tobacco bag stringers had responded to Wage and Hour investigations by encouraging their employees to organize a union to "police" wages and hours under FLSA. Whether or not this was a "company union," it suggested an alternative means to control homework abuses. So did the few cooperatives that actually were associations of individuals formed to market their wares. After the Hand Knitcraft Institute fiasco, a Maine priest created the St. John Valley Handcraft Cooperative with sixteen hundred members in twenty-five localities. Southern highland crafts entrepreneurs attempted to form cooperatives. In the early 1960s, the NCL and the National Council of Negro Women organized rural black North Carolinians into a cooperative to maintain employment when FLSA enforcement threatened to end homework.[29]

[27] This case was reversed on the grounds that language defining homeworker was unclear; after the administrator corrected the language, the courts upheld a second case against Wagner. *Tobin v. Wagner Co.*, 187 F.2d 977 (2d Cir. 1951), *remanded, sub. nom.; Durkin v. Wagner Co.*, 115 F.Supp. 118 (E.D.N.Y. 1953), *aff'd sub nom.; Mitchell v. Wagner Co.*, 217 F.2d 303 (2d Cir. 1954). Sidney Korzenik, "New Court Blow to Homework Analyzed as Labor Law Landmark," *Knitted Outerwear Times*, Feb. 13, 1950, 3, 25, 28. "Part 617 – Knitted Outerwear Industry, Minimum Wage Order, Home Workers: Definition of Certain Terms," [April 20, 1951], quoted in Brief for the Petitioner, *Mitchell v. Whitaker House Coop.*, 64–7.

[28] *Fleming v. Palmer*, 1 Wage & Hour Cas. (BNA) 382 (1st Cir. 1941).

[29] *McComb v. Homeworkers Handicraft Coop.*, 176 F.2d 633, (4th Cir.), *cert. denied*, 338 U.S. 900 (1949); DOL, Office of the Solicitor, Case Analyses No. 101, Jan. 10, 1950 (DOL files, Solicitor Office); "Progress Report on Homework," 19–20; Jane Becker, "Selling Tradition: The Domestication of Southern Appalachian Culture in 1930s America," (Ph.D. diss., Boston Univ., 1993), 357–9; Ruth Jordan in D.C. Hearings, Feb. 18, 1981, 240.

The Supreme Court would judge the members of a cooperative to be employees in *Goldberg v. Whitaker House Coop.* (1961), which considered a cooperative subject to homework regulations.[30] This case revealed the interlocking network of homework distributors and manufacturers in the knitted outerwear industry, exposing how some women continued to find mobility within the homework system as contractors providing low piece rates to other women. In the early 1930s, (Mrs.) Evelyn Whitaker, who lived in Troy, Maine, began purchasing handmade infants' knitted outerwear for various out-of-state businesses, including Edward Wagner Company. She handled goods from one hundred women. About the time of the 1942 federal prohibition against homework in the industry (see below), she transferred her yarn business to another Troy woman, (Mrs.) Pearl L. Nutter. Nutter also was convicted of violating the homework provisions of FLSA in 1958, as was (Mrs.) Doris Law of Carroll County, Tennessee, to whom Mrs. Whitaker sold some of her goods. Law became a special agent for the cooperative (with Law's former homeworkers becoming cooperative members). All three of these married women were homework employers and distributors for New York firms. In September 1954, Whitaker resumed her business, no longer supplying the yarn, but determining piece rates, providing samples, and instructing on designs and colors. After a Wage and Hour investigation in January 1957 determined that the home knitters were employees under FLSA, Whitaker and her attorney, perhaps on advice from the investigator, organized the cooperative.[31]

Rural women desperately clung to homework and rejected the interventions of Wage and Hour on their behalf. Testifying before the district court, cooperative homeworkers defended their right to work. A thirty-nine-year-old mother of two, whose husband was a teacher, "joined because she felt her rights to make things in her own home had been challenged." A sixty-six-year-old housewife, who also owned her own home but whose husband had retired, "felt that I had a right to do this kind of work in my own home and to sell it where I pleased and to get the most out of it as I could, and I thought the Cooperative was the best way to do that, to get a wider market and more money." Yet she admitted that the women "talked it over as to how – what arrangements could be made so that you would not come under the Wage and Hour Law." These women hardly resembled the desperate immigrants of the Lower East Side, but they too sought to improve their standard of living and found few other ways to combine wage earning and home duties. They saw their work as " 'pick up,' or spare-time work." Nearly two hundred eagerly responded to the call for a cooperative that would permit them "to continue to

---

[30] 366 U.S. 28 (1961).
[31] *Mitchell v. Whitaker House Coop.*, 170 F.Supp. 743, 746 (D. Me. 1959); Brief for the Petitioner, *Mitchell v. Whitaker House Coop.*, in the Supreme Court of the United States, October Term, 1960, 4–5, passim; *Mitchell v. Nutter*, 161 F.Supp. 799 (D. Me. 1956); *Mitchell v. Law*, 161 F.Supp. 796, (W. D. Tenn. 1957).

make products in your home" and "enable them to comply with the Federal Laws concerning wage and hour regulations" – by slipping under them.[32]

The Whitaker House Cooperative met state incorporation procedures and appeared to be a bona fide cooperative. Both the U.S. District Court and a divided U.S. First Circuit Court of Appeals ruled that homeworking producer members did not fall within the employee classification of FLSA. These courts dismissed evidence that revealed the cooperative to function identically to Mrs. Whitaker's prior business and ignored the ways that Whitaker, her lawyer, family, and a few trusted employees controlled the firm. But the Supreme Court majority led by Justice William O. Douglas agreed with the dissenting opinion of Circuit Judge Aldrich who presented both an economic reality argument and an ideological assault on "freedom of contract." Not only was the competition of these "ladies" with others who abided by the act unfair, but, Aldrich claimed, "I see no more basis for a court's saying that as the members 'suffer or permit' themselves to work they do not require the protection of the Act, than there is for so determining as to any other worker who 'voluntarily' chooses to work."[33]

Employment status determined whether the social wage extended to homeworkers. When courts and government bureaus defined homeworkers as independent contractors, then employers could not be held liable for social security or state unemployment taxes, although such workers could be considered employees under FLSA. Although the Bureau of Internal Revenue had ruled in 1937 that homeworkers were employees, the Commissioner revoked that order in 1944 after the case of *Glenn v. Beard*,[34] which held that such workers were not employees for federal employment tax purposes. Secretary Perkins protested this reversal and the solicitor of labor looked for a case to overturn it. As in the past, Clara Beyer attempted to activate the larger labor standards network to protest the narrow interpretation of employee for Social Security and other tax purposes. She drafted a letter in January 1945, a few months after the change, for American Federation of Labor president William Green to send to the secretary of the treasury, with copies to the Social Security Board and the secretary of labor, "ask[ing] their assistance in bringing about this change in the regulations." But the network was unable to overturn what appeared to be "an added incentive" to homework. A 1948

---

[32] U.S. District Court, District of Maine, Division (Northern), *Mitchell v. Whitaker House Coop.*, before Honorable Edward T. Gignoux, Sept. 23, and 24, 1958, vol. 1, 70–3; vol. 2, 183–4, 205–6, 213–14, in box 274. Correspondence and transcript, USCC Oct. 1960, papers relating to *Goldberg v. Whitaker House Coop.* 366 U.S. 28 (1961), Judicial Branch, NA; see also *Mitchell v. Nutter* 161 F. Supp. 799; *Mitchell v. Law*, 161 F. Supp. 796.

[33] *Mitchell v. Whitaker House Coop.*, 170 F. Supp. 743; *Mitchell v. Whitaker House Coop.*, 275 F.2d 362, 367 (1st Cir. 1960); *Goldberg v. Whitaker House Coop.*, 366 U.S. 28 at 32.

[34] 141 F.2d 376 (6th Cir. 1944). Eleanor Beard established her appliqué and quilting studio in Hardinsburg, Kentucky, around 1931; by 1933, she employed seventeen women in her studio and fifty at home. See Becker, "Selling Tradition," 273–4.

amendment to the Social Security Act sealed Beyer's defeat by holding to the common-law test of employee, rather than the broader standard of FLSA.[35]

New York State, however, maintained that homeworkers were employees for unemployment purposes. Piecework, by itself, failed to "determine" status. Nor did the lack of continuous supervision because "the very nature of the work does not permit constant supervision." Supervision came from the employer's right "to hire and discharge" as well as from his instructions on how the work should be done. To clarify the law, New York amended its homework act in 1942 to call homeworkers "employees."[36]

But under what circumstances could homeworkers receive unemployment? Could unemployment be given to those who refused to enter the factory because of care of small children but who had become ineligible for homework because administrative orders restricted such labor to the old, ill, disabled, and their caretakers? New York State agencies faced this problem in 1942, after the May deadline for special homework certificates in the glove industry. Many women, who had contributed to the unemployment insurance fund and failed to qualify for special permits, refused to accept factory employment and were denied benefits. The local unemployment office denied a permit to Beatrice M. Wilmer, a married mother of a five-year-old. Male bureaucrats in the Unemployment Insurance Referee Section relied on the same construction of motherhood that Wilmer embraced: "Here the claimant must remain a homeworker until her child no longer requires her attention. Her unemployment is due to her inability to obtain such work. Surely, it was contemplated that this type of applicant would receive the protection of the statute."[37]

[35] Mrs. Amber Warburton to Miss Caroline E. Legg, Nov. 23, 1939, RG102, file 20 194 5; *Kentucky Cottage Industries v. Glen,* 39 F.Supp. 642 (1941); *Walling v. Hastings,* 6 Wage & Hour Cas. (BNA) 554 (S.D. Ind. 1946); Social Security Act, 42 U.S.C.A. par. 410 (K) (2) and 26 U.S.C.A. par. 1426 (d), as cited in *Mitchell v. Northwestern Kite Co.,* 12 Wage & Hour Cas. (BNA) 495, 496 (D. Minn. 1955); Virginia Weston to Mrs. Beyer on "Employment Tax Status of Homeworkers – Beard Case," Nov. 13, 1944, folder 152; Frances Perkins to The Honorable Secretary of the Treasury, Nov. 11, 1944; Joseph J. O'Connell, Jr., to My dear Madam Secretary, Dec. 6, 1944; Douglas B. Maggs to Clara Beyer on "Home-Work Litigation," Nov. 24, 1944; A. J. Altmeyer to Hon. Joseph D. Nunan, Jr., Dec. 20, 1944, all in folder 153; Clara Beyer to Florence Thorne, Jan. 14, 1945, with attached draft of letter, in folder 151, all in Beyer Papers, box 10.

[36] *Andrews v. Commodore Knitting Mills, Inc.* 257 A.D.2d 515 (3d Dept. 1939) (outside pieceworkers as within Social Security or Unemployment Compensation Act); Kate Papert to Clara Beyer, Jan. 10, 1946, Beyer Papers, box 10, folder 148. The same 1942 amendments also limited the status of contractor to "a person who does *not* supply any additional material of substantial value to the article or material delivered to him by another person for processing." Otherwise, such a person was an employer under the act. Mr. Gagnon, July 17, 1942, in NYDOL, file "Legal Interpretation New York 38–48."

[37] Memorandum from Mr. Ostrow to Miss Papert, Feb. 4, 1942; Kate Papert to Milton O. Loysen, July 23, 1942; Case No. 34–50–41R, Unemployment Insurance Referee Section; Case No. 532–630–41R; Case No. 6757–42 34–20–41R; Case No. 7153–42 4–34–41R, all in NYDOL, "Legal Interpretations: Unemployment Insurance."

Industrial Commissioner Miller responded by having the Division of Placement and Unemployment Insurance issue an administrative interpretation in November 1942 denying benefits to claimants without a homework permit "and who are not ready, willing or able to accept any employment outside their homes." Although the Appeals Board would consult the homework orders in evaluating applicants, it defied the wishes of the Department of Labor by "also consider[ing] a further standard, namely a homeworker with small children living at home," a standard that undermined homework regulations. Labor Department officials charged that such former glove homeworkers "would not come to the factory because they were intent on collecting their Unemployment Insurance benefits first and that after they had collected these benefits, they came into the factory."[38]

Mothers would not receive special dispensation for collecting unemployment after the restricting of homework. This ruling may have discriminated against those women without childcare. But in the midst of World War II, such mothers would be treated as workers and not as a special category of person, the mother. As in World War I, the Women's Bureau would monitor women's pay and working conditions; the rhetoric of "sacred motherhood" belonged more to the defenders of homework than to the agency for women workers.

Amending the act

Attempts to bypass homework rules differed from proposals to amend FLSA to exclude homeworkers or to stymie enforcement. At least six times between 1939 and 1957, various congressional amendments suggested the exemption of rural homeworkers from FLSA, a provision proposed (but then dropped under a flood of negative public comments) by Secretary of Labor Raymond Donovan during the renewed debate of the 1980s. Always coupled with the concern to safeguard employment, these rural exemptions neglected the national extent of the homework system. They also discriminated on the basis of residence. As Kate Papert of the New York Division of Women in Industry and Minimum Wage in 1939 informed Georgia congressman Robert Ramspeck, a key member of the House Committee on Labor: "The needs of farm women are as great as those of their city sisters. Their labor has the same intrinsic value as that of other workers in the productive process."[39]

[38] Frieda Miller to Herman A. Gray, July 18, 1942; "Minutes of Meeting: Re: Homeworkers," Sept. 28, 1942; Milton O. Loysen to Commissioner Miller, Oct. 5, 1942; Division of Placement and Unemployment Insurance, "Administrative Interpretation No. 7," Nov. 16, 1942; Mr. Gagnon to Miss Papert, "Homeworkers-Claimants-D.P.U.I.-Homework Bureau Problem," Dec. 23, 1942; Gagnon to Papert, Dec. 28, 1942, all in NYDOL, "Legal Interpretations: Unemployment."

[39] Brief for the Petitioner, *Mitchell v. Whitaker House Coop.*, U.S. Supreme Court, October Term, 1960, (n.274), 20–45; Brief for Appellees, Brief for Appellants, *ILGWU v. Donovan,*

Yet in 1949, Congressman John Cooper (D.-Tenn.) introduced an amendment to meet the needs of women in his district who crocheted baby bonnets at home. He was trying to counter a 1949 ruling that directly curtailed the business of a constituent who gave out homework. The Wage and Hour Administration had informed her that she could only employ the disabled. His amendment would have permitted homework on the part of a rural person "not subject to any supervision or control by any person whomsoever, and who buys raw material and makes and completes any articles and sells the same to any person, even though it is made according to specifications and the requirements of some single purchaser." Because Cooper accepted such home labor as natural among his constituents, he did not have to specify its gendered nature.[40]

A powerful coalition of reformers, trade unionists, and labor administrators defeated such amendments. Those proposed in 1939 particularly demonstrate the confusion over the status of homework under FLSA. Homework remained a volatile political issue, fueled by cultural understandings of women's place – held even by defenders of labor standards. Leading the fight for FLSA was House Labor Committee chair Mary Norton (D.-New Jersey). Norton was not a suffragist, but a product of New Jersey machine politics, contemptuous of Consumers' League "moral prodders." A New Dealer who defended trade unions, she failed to judge amendments in terms of their impact on women.[41] The women's network considered her proposals lethal despite Norton's intention to improve FLSA enforcement. She was hampered in an increasingly conservative and hostile Congress by southern legislators and other opponents who saw any opportunity to amend FLSA a signal to cripple it. [42]

Norton introduced amendments that allowed lower-waged homework in rural areas but empowered the Wage and Hour administrator to make regulations for homework, including special piece rates and restrictions. She apparently was responding to the desire of Administrator Elmer Andrews for more direct

U.S. Court of Appeals for the District of Columbia Circuit (no.82–2133); House of Representatives, 76th Cong., 1st sess., Report no. 522, "Amendments to the Fair Labor Standards Act of 1938," Apr. 27, 1939; Kate Papert to Robert Ramspeck, June 12, 1939, 4 in vertical files, NYDOL Library. All of the following also were defeated: H.R. 4661, 82d Cong., 1st sess., June 29, 1951; H.R. 237, 83d Cong., 1st sess., Jan. 3, 1953; S.1950, 83d Cong., 1st sess., May 20, 1953; H.R. 84, 84th Cong., 1st sess., Jan. 5, 1955; S. 2963, 84th Cong., 2d sess., Jan. 18, 1956; H.R. 2812, 85th Cong., 1st sess., Jan. 14, 1957; S. 1160, 85th Cong., 1st sess., Feb. 11, 1957. The Southern Highlands Handicraft Guild attempted to gain special rules for crafts production. See Becker, "Selling Tradition," 356–69.

[40] Brief for the Petitioner, *Mitchell v. Whitaker House Coop.*, 40–3.

[41] Felice D. Gordon, *After Winning: The Legacy of the New Jersey Suffragists, 1920–1947* (New Brunswick, N.J.: Rutgers Univ. Press, 1986), 88–90.

[42] No adequate history of this struggle yet exists; the pages of the *New York Times* are a beginning point. See, for example, "Andrews Attacks Foes of Wages Act," Aug. 1, 1939, 3; "House Curbs Move to Rush Wage Bill," June 6, 1939, 8.

authority over homework. Believing that the act covered – rather than prohibited – homework, he sought better enforcement mechanisms.[43]

Such amendments provoked the Consumers' League into a major lobbying
effort. Within days, Clara Beyer alerted Mary Dublin, NCL general secretary,
to the danger posed by such amendments. The provision for fixing piece rates,
Beyer noted, "was urged by the knitgoods employers with the desire to put the
stamp of approval of the Government upon the piece rates set by them." There
were at least eighteen hundred processes in that industry alone and, given the
disaster of the NRA experience with rate setting, Beyer argued that such a
provision "would have the same general effect as the one on rural workers,
taking the home workers out from under any practical application of the Act."
She urged not only action by the league, but a steady stream of letters from constituents of Congresswoman Norton. Dublin essentially carried out her suggestions, contacting Labor's Non-Partisan League and joining with the International Association of Governmental Labor Officials to lobby the House.[44]

The network chose to work behind the scenes. New Jersey Consumers'
League counsel Herman Marx argued that the piece-rate provision, which
based wages on amount of production, would disrupt New Jersey's regulations, which were based on flat hourly wages. In a letter to Congressman
Ramspeck, he further articulated the shared objections of reformers. The rural
homework exemption "confers no economic or social benefits upon
homeworkers themselves . . . but establishes criteria whereby an employer is
legally authorized to sweat his employees." Not only would a new class of
employee be created, but employers would be encouraged to send homework
to rural areas. Reflecting the moral indignation of the NCL, he contended, "It
is truly shocking that national legislation should, in such cold-blooded
fashion, select our rural population as victims of sweatshop practices." Rural
communities would suffer from child labor, encouraged by the premium put
on production through piece rates, and from increased relief brought about by
the low wages earned by homeworkers. Finally, such amendments would lead
employers to pressure states "to reduce their standards to the bases contemplated by the amendments." Already New Jersey suffered, in Marx's analysis,
from nearly fifteen thousand homeworkers whose numbers were growing from
work "bootlegged" from New York.[45]

---

[43] "Includes Home Workers," *New York Times*, Apr. 14, 1939, 16.

[44] Clara Beyer to Mary Dublin, May 4, 1939, with Beyer to Morgan Mooney, May 4, 1939;
General Secretary (Dublin) to Beyer, May 7, 1939; Beyer to Dublin, May 9, 1939; Dublin to
Beyer, May 10, 1939; NCL, "Minutes," May 9, 1939, 1–2; Mooney to Dublin, May 10, 1939;
Dublin to Mary T. Norton, May 11, 1939; Dublin to Herman Marx, May 10, 1939; Dublin
to Alice Liveright, May 22, 1939; Dublin to Gardner Jackson, May 22, 1939, all in NCL
Papers, reel 55, frames 571–630.

[45] He also chaired the state minimum wage board for the wearing apparel industry. Herman
Marx to Hon. Mary T. Norton, May 11, 1939; Marx to Hon. John J. Toohey, Jr., May 11,
1939; Toohey to Marx, May 16, 1939; Toohey to Hon. Elmer H. Andrews, May 16, 1939;
Toohey to Morgan Mooney, May 15, 1939; Marx to Hon. Robert Ramspeck, May 19, 1939,
all in NCL Papers, reel 55.

Norton admitted that she "did not realize" the consequences of her amendments; "you know that I would not want to sponsor anything that would in any way be of benefit to the homework employers." But to bring the bill back to committee would invite "emasculation." When the bill failed under the complex rules of the House, Norton introduced a new bill without the section empowering the administrator to set piece rates for homeworkers.[46]

But the new bill continued to exempt rural homeworkers, which led the NCL to continue its lobbying. Dublin enlisted the aid of Lucy Randolph Mason, then with the Textile Workers Organizing Committee, and the industrial secretaries of the Young Women's Christian Organization and their rural contacts to generate southern and rural pressure on the Labor Committee. Southern congressmen thought many constituents relied upon homework. Norton herself justified regional differentials as helping "the poor farmer to supplement his family income." Women and children, as in North Carolina, had engaged in ancillary home labor throughout the decade, but such work was disappearing; bedspreads already were becoming a factory industry. Either congressional supporters of rural exemptions failed to recognize changing circumstances or were willing to use the emotional aspects of the issue to undermine FLSA. Again restrictive House rules blocked Norton's amendments, not because congressmen objected to the homework exemption but because they wished to extend agricultural ones, which the rules of debate prohibited. Norton's attempts to allow limited homework exposed the lingering opposition to the women's network's goal of abolition.[47]

Framing the administrative bans

World War II encouraged the restriction of homework. As the Wage and Hour administrator explained, "The need for efficient utilization of labor in time of war makes it especially advisable that the wasteful methods of industrial home work be eliminated." Although the War Manpower Commission (WMC) encouraged "relaxation of laws which impeded the recruitment and utilization of manpower," it rejected any easing of homework regulations. Its official policy was to maintain labor standards for women and minors. Instead of deploying homeworkers, it encouraged part-time work, community workshops, day nurseries, and shopping services to draw unavailable women into the work force. With increased production its goal, WMC

---

[46] Mary T. Norton to Mrs. H. N. Simmons, May 16, 1929, frame 600; Norton to Miss Mary Dublin, May 16, 1939, frame 603; Dublin to Mr. Herman Marx, May 22, 1939, frame 587; Charles H. Leavy to Dublin, May 16, 1939, frame 603, all NCL Papers, reel 55.

[47] Dublin to Lucy Randolph Mason, June 1, 1939; Dublin to Miss A. Louise Murphy, June 1, 1939; A. Louise Murphy to Dublin, June 3, 1939; Mary T. Norton to Miss Jeanette Studley, June 2, 1939, all NCL Papers, reel 54, frames 579–80, 576, 577; "House Curbs Move to Rush Wage Bill." For one example of southern homework, Dolores Janiewski, *Sisterhood Denied: Race, Gender, and Class in a New South Community* (Philadelphia, Pa.: Temple Univ. Press, 1985), 133–4.

rejected homework not only for the good of workers but for the efficiency of the war machine.[48]

The Wage and Hour administrator had the power to determine minimum wages, acting upon recommendations of industry committees, until the statutory level of forty cents an hour came into effect in 1945. Between 1941 and 1944, he prohibited industrial homework out of the belief that otherwise FLSA could not be sustained for seven industries: jewelry, gloves and mittens, knitted outerwear, button and buckle, women's apparel, handkerchiefs, and embroideries.[49] These industries shared key structural conditions that encouraged homework: seasonal cycles, undercapitalized firms and low initial capital requirements, fierce competition, unstable markets, hand or simple machine processes. Unions had organized the larger employers in each and this partial organization on the part of both unions and associations of firms with union contracts provided the political pressure for homework restriction. The ILGWU argued that "homework must go . . . like a badly infected tooth, [it] can best be cured by removal"; it threatened decent American standards by exploiting women and children. The New York State Federation of Labor passed resolutions for further state regulation. Employer misuse of existing state and federal handbook systems offered the justification for union allies in the Department of Labor to gain tighter controls over homework.[50]

Unable to calculate the wages and hours of homeworkers, the administrator restricted homework in these industries "except by persons who have obtained home work certificates." The elderly and disabled or their caretakers could gain a certificate, which was similar to the NRA process, but here they had to have been engaged in homework in an industry prior to the date of restriction.

[48] U.S. DOL, Wage and Hour Division, "The Recommendation of Industry Committee No. 45 for a Minimum Wage Rate in the Embroideries Industry and Industrial Home Work in the Embroideries Industry: Findings and Opinion of the Administrator," Aug. 21, 1943, 89, Beyer Papers, folder 363; Lawrence A. Appley to Paul V. McNutt, "The Use of Industrial Home Work," July 20, 1943, NYDOL Library, file "General"; Stander, "Child Labor in Industrial Home Work Under the Fair Labor Standards Act"; State of New York, DOL, Division of Women, Child Labor, and Minimum Wage, "Trends in Homework Industries in New York State," Aug. 1944, NYDOL Library; U.S. DOL, "Reconversion and Fair Labor Standards," *Annual Report: Wage and Hour and Public Contracts Divisions* (Washington, D.C.: GPO, 1947), 5.

[49] The dates of these bans were: jewelry, Nov. 3, 1941; gloves and mittens, Sept. 21, 1942; knitted outerwear, Dec. 1, 1942; button and buckle, Dec. 1, 1942; women's apparel, Dec. 1, 1942; handkerchiefs, April 26, 1942; and embroideries, July 26, 1944 (originally dated Nov. 15, 1943).

[50] Eileen Boris, "Homework in the Past, Its Meaning for the Future," *The New Era of Home-Based Work: Directions and Policies*, ed. Kathleen E. Christensen (Boulder, Colo.: Westview Press, 1988), 15–18; "Editorial Notes," *Justice* 23 (Oct. 15, 1941), 16; "ILGWU Urges Wage and Hour Division to Ban Homework," ibid. (Oct. 1, 1943), 1; press release, "Knitgoods Union Calls on Wage and Hour Administrator to Abolish Homework," 11/13/41; Phil Heller to Frieda Miller, Nov. 29, 1941, with copy of resolution, both in NYDOL, folder "Knitted Outerwear."

Employers still had to keep homework handbooks. By the end of 1945, the Wage and Hour and Public Contracts Division estimated that "the number of home workers to whom certificates have been issued in these industries had dropped to approximately 15 percent of the estimated number of home workers prior to the restrictions."[51]

As during World War I, homework supporters sought to wrap themselves in the flag while offering mother love. Children's needs provided their justification. Glove sewer (Mrs.) Emma Nellis, president of a "Homeworkers Federation" in Fulton County, New York, typically declared in 1942 testimony before the Wage and Hour Division:

> I'd overthrow that ban again
> For there is stamps and bonds to buy [sic]
> I say, we'll lift that ban once more
> Give those homeworkers a try.

With minor variations, such words had characterized employer discourse during the NRA period. (Mrs.) Nellis, though, was not an employer. Claiming authority from experience as a homeworker for over twenty years, Nellis – who also had worked in a factory – explained, "As the [homework] order considers invalids, we consider mothers with tiny children in the same class. Yet no consideration is given to the children. We are told to put them in day nurseries, children's homes, or institutions. What kind of a country would we have if we were all brought up without the benefit of our own homes? . . . Could it be possible that you think the head of an institution and the institution itself can take the place of a mother and a home of your own?" In a similar vein, an attorney for embroidery manufacturers predicted that the order for that industry would herd "the children of these poor home workers in common nurseries."[52]

Nellis recounted the stories of women met during house to house canvassing for the Federation, which numbered 1,119 members and boasted that it represented thousands more. Women, with five and eight children each, begged for the continuance of homework; they lived beyond bus lines, could not find competent girls to baby-sit, and feared they would be unable to provide necessities or higher education for their children. Forced into factories by New York State administrative orders, these women were, according to Nellis, "frantic" and "nervous" as their children roamed the streets. Nellis's comment about one such mother summarized a whole worldview: "This

---

[51] U.S. DOL, Wage and Hour and Public Contracts Division, "Industrial Home Work and the Fair Labor Standards Act," mimeoed bulletin, G–436, revised 12/47, 3–6, DOL Library.

[52] Organized in June 1941 in Fulton County, New York, the Homeworker Federation may have been started by employers, as had been the Homeworker Protective League of 1934. Mrs. Emma Nellis, U.S. DOL, Wage and Hour Division, "In the Matter of the Minimum Wage Recommendation of Industry Committee No. 40 for the Gloves and Mittens Industry," Apr. 20, 1942, 40–5, esp. 42, 44; ibid., Mar. 2, 1942, 187–202, transcripts in DOL Library; Elias Lieberman to David Dubinsky, Nov. 5, 1942, in Dubinsky Papers, 83–2.

woman doesn't want or ask relief; all she wants is her Homework and we think she certainly needs to be in her own home."[53]

Clara Beyer rejected such a discourse for one built through economic arguments. She reiterated how homework was inefficient, connected to child labor and exploitative working conditions. It undermined the minimum wage and wasted resources during wartime. Numerous investigations, she argued, proved "that the presence of children in the home does not prevent women from doing factory work." Studies tracing the impact of homework curtailment in New York State concurred. Ruth Crawford of the Wage and Hour Division found in women's war work evidence against the "sentimental" argument for homework. "Society has an obligation to provide for the care of children when the mother must work, rather than to condone a method of employment which works to the detriment of both mother and child."[54]

In the midst of World War II when mothers were taking defense jobs and childcare became a public need,[55] women reformers dropped their rhetorical disapproval of maternal wage earning. They understood that, given economic incentives, mothers would leave the home for the factory even without adequate childcare. They judged homework more damaging to social life than even maternal employment.[56] Some of their male colleagues in the Department of Labor (DOL) also argued for more daycare provisions for children so that factory work could replace inefficient home labor. But men in the Wage and Hour Administration had more trouble seeing beyond the homeworker as "the married woman with small children that she can't leave and she can't afford to have anybody take care of" who desperately needed homework. Even trade union allies, who recognized that "a woman will come into the factory," distinguished between "the woman who has the time and isn't bound by children" with the type of woman who worked at home, a mother who by her circumstances had to put up with less than a decent wage.[57] DOL women

[53] Nellis testimony, Mar. 2, 1942, 188–90.

[54] Beyer testified at most hearings for the Division of Labor Standards. She was right; consider the various bulletins of the Women's Bureau from 1920, as well as studies such as Katherine Anthony, *Mothers Who Must Earn* (New York: Russell Sage Foundation, 1915). Beyer testimony on Mar. 2, 1942, 48–66, esp. 60; Kate Papert testimony, ibid., 93; Crawford, "Development and Control of Industrial Homework," pamphlet reprinted from the *Monthly Labor Review* (June 1944), 12.

[55] Susan M. Hartmann, *American Women in the 1940s: The Home Front and Beyond* (Boston: Twayne, 1982); Karen Anderson, *Wartime Women: Sex Roles, Family Relations, and the Status of Women During World War II* (Westport, Conn.: Greenwood Press, 1981).

[56] The contradictions between the goals that women reformers had for working-class women and their own lives can be traced through their personal biographies. Beyer was among the few who was both married and a mother. Susan Ware, *Beyond Suffrage: Women in the New Deal* (Cambridge, Mass.: Harvard Univ. Press, 1981).

[57] A. F. Hinrichs, in U.S. DOL, Wage and Hour Division, "The Recommendation of Industry Committee No. 45 . . . Findings and Opinion of the Administrator," Aug. 21, 1943, 87; Examiner Campbell testimony, "Minimum Wage Recommendation of Industry Committee No. 40," Mar. 2, 1942, 134; for a trade union perspective, Abraham Plotkin, in U.S. DOL, Wage and Hour Division, "Conference and Executive Session of Industry Committee No. 15 for the Embroideries Industry," Sept. 4, 1940, 97, all in RG155, box 62.

overcame men's sympathetic reactions; their arguments tapped into government concerns over "manpower" and industrial capacity.

Yet the war provided justification for defenders of homework as well. Homework increased where shortages of skilled labor or supplies developed. European refugees "salvag[ed] zippers from second-hand garments"; North Carolina hosiery manufacturers sent work into the homes of former employees who wanted only part-time labor. "Luxury industries," like lace, also found a home work force. Import restrictions led to more homework on beaded bags and the substitution of homemade rayon hair nets for Chinese nets of "real" hair. The demand for gold-bullion-threaded emblems for officers' military uniforms skyrocketed. Wartime styles further generated homework, aided by an Office of Price Administration regulation that increased profits in relation to amount of trimming on a garment. New York State officials noted a 150 percent jump in the number of certificates requested for embroidery between November 1942 and May 1945, while the number of overall certificates merely doubled to 30,546.[58]

As with Emma Nellis, "patriotism" joined "motherhood" to justify homework. In Connecticut, the Governor's War Council in 1943 considered "the revival of homework as a means of employing young Mothers." Buttressed by arguments that homework solved labor shortages without placing additional burdens on transportation or housing facilities, the state's commissioner of labor permitted open violation of the homework law. He stopped an investigation in Westport, where Vivien Kellems had begun to give out grips for weaving for the war effort. Kellems claimed permission from the governor who "said that he intended to ask wartime emergency powers to enable him to cope with just such situations," although he apparently never did. But Kellems went ahead "under the exceptions provided in the law."[59]

Featured in the June 1943 issue of *Better Homes and Gardens* under the "glamorous" title "Yankee Kitchens Go on the Production Line," Kellems hoped to hire a thousand nearby women to meet new contracts – even though, as the Consumers' League noted, such work was illegal under Walsh–

---

[58] Increases justified New York's 1945 General Homework Order to restrict the practice in all industries and provide for postwar stability in factory employment. However, some embroidery manufacturers argued that War Production Board restrictions curbed their labor force and limited their ability to function without homework. See "The Recommendation of Industry Committee No. 45 ... Findings and Opinion of the Administrator," 83; Crawford, "Development and Control of Industrial Homework," 7; Forrest H. Shuford to Mrs. Clara M. Beyer, Aug. 1, 1945, Beyer Papers, box 10, folder 151; Caroline E. Legg to Miss Elizabeth Johnson, Oct. 31, 1939, RG102, 20–194–5; "In the Matter of a Hearing . . . Industry Committee No. 15," Oct. 1, 1940, 219; Mr. Ostrow to Miss Papert, Sept. 12, 1945; New York State DOL, "General Order Restricting Homework for all Industries," May 4, 1945, both in NYDOL, folder "Not Covered – NY Law."

[59] Jeanette Studley to Mrs. Edith Valet Cook, June 8, 1943; Studley to Mrs. Chase Going Woodhouse, June 10, 1943; Studley to Woodhouse, June 11, 1943, all in CLC Papers, box 24, folder 388; "Vivien Kellems Sees Labor Solution in 'Home Work,'" *Hartford Times*, June 3, 1943, 6.

Healey. She would give preference to those tied to the home, like Clara Keller, who said, "I wanted to get into war work and make money . . . but I couldn't go off to a factory and leave my children, and certainly I couldn't leave my [150] chickens." Before the New York Kiwanis Club, Kellems posed the advantages of her solution to the "manpower" shortage in terms of its primary benefits for the family: "Isn't it thrilling that a mother rivets the wings of an airplane on which her son may fly to victory, but isn't it tragic that while mothers are riveting airplanes our juvenile delinquency has assumed alarming proportions?" Mother care of children could continue with homework instead of forcing working women to rely on that "poor substitute," day nurseries. Moreover, at a time when war plant work was said to increase the numbers of abortions, homeworking women could combine biological reproduction with production for wages. Kellems cited a case of an expectant mother who worked nearly up to the moment of her baby's birth and was able to take up the work again soon thereafter. Homework, which she viewed as a wartime emergency measure, also promised to ease postwar reconversion because "the woman has never left her home, therefore she does not have to return to it. She has never taken some man's job who naturally wants it back when he returns from the war. If after the war, there is no more homework . . . there just isn't, and nothing can be done about it."[60] Wartime homework emphasized that women were mothers first. During a period when women's public work challenged traditional notions of womanhood, such rhetoric was comforting.

Celebrated by the *Hartford Times* and *Bridgeport Post*, mentioned in the *Congressional Record*, the Kellems case became "too hot to handle" for the "non-partisan" League of Women Voters, which judged the incident as "merely a political argument." Beyer sought to activate labor and women's groups to counter this story with its so familiar narrative line: "The marvelous opportunities for mothers to earn a living, to cooperate in the war effort, how they love their work, and how happy the children are because Mother is occupied. . . . Read it and weep." Beyer urged local leaders to construct an alternative story about the low wages, long hours, and exploitative child labor inherent in homework. But, as the secretary of the state Consumers' League informed the industrial division of the Children's Bureau, "It is amazing how 'patriotism' is interpreted in cases like this." The war blunted the impact of the women's network when local officials refused to heed existing laws.[61]

[60] Webb Waldron, "Yankee Kitchens Go on the Production Line," *Better Homes and Gardens* 83 (June 1943), 17, 64–6; "Vivien Kellems Sees Labor Solution." She also recommended providing disabled veterans with the right to do homework rather than turning them into objects of charity. For abortion, Gretta Palmer, "Your Baby or Your Job," *The Woman's Home Companion* 70 (Oct. 1943), 4.

[61] Even the press found the league's counterstory "too hot" and never ran it. Jeanette Studley to Joseph M. Tone, June 11, 1943; Studley to Beyer, June 10, 1943; Beyer to Studley, June 4, 1943; Studley to Mrs. Elizabeth B. Coleman, June 10, 1943; Chase G. Woodhouse to Studley, June 15, 1943, all in CLC Papers, box 24, folder 388; "Home Work to the Rescue: Extension of Remarks of Hon. Joseph E. Talbot," Thurs., May 27, 1943, in 78th Cong., 1st sess., *Congressional Record*, v. 89, Jan. 6, 1943, to June 9, 1943 (Parts 9–10), Appendix 10, A2655, reel 244.

Homework opponents joined defenders in justifying their position as patriotic. The Knitgoods Workers' Union demanded immediate prohibition because the country was at war and had to conserve "materials and manpower." At a time when manufacturers could only obtain 40 percent of needed wool, homework employers were deemed selfish and unpatriotic, with inefficient and backward production methods that would "circumvent our national needs." The National Association of Leather Glove Manufacturers, in contrast, attempted to have New York's restrictive order for gloves "temporarily" suspended, citing the difficulty of simultaneously producing for the military and "liquidating their leather inventories." Not surprisingly, Commissioner Miller accepted union arguments because "the need of the hour is for the greatest possible efficiency, maximum output and the recruiting and training of skilled workers."[62]

The disingenuousness of glove manufacturers became apparent when administrators considered the small percentage of government contracts actually awarded to Fulton County, only 27 percent of the total given to the glove industry. Despite reports of expected curtailment in the glove factories, employers were clamoring for homeworkers. As Louis Fuchs of the Glove Workers' Union of Greater New York put it, the employers "have suddenly become patriotic." Fulton County manufacturers apparently were more interested in civilian production than on bidding on government contracts; only when they realized that the former would be curtailed did they rush to join midwest firms in supplying the war effort.[63]

The war could generate hardship. New York issued "temporary" certificates to the wives of service men. Such gendered variations rested on assumptions about hardship created by sexual divisions in the employment market. But men also suffered from the homework orders. In the air force at the time of the 1945 general restriction, Lewis F. Valachovic was not in business, thus he was ineligible to receive an employer's certificate. Demanding his rights as "an ex-service man," he complained that he lost "my rights to start a small business for myself" and claimed that the law bound the service man to big manufacturing concerns. Valachovic belonged to that category of employer whom the Labor Department hoped to keep from homework production. Following the war, some employers attempted to undermine homework bans by amending the law to permit "special certificates for veterans and their wives." To those who

[62] "Statement Submitted by the Knitgoods Workers' Union, Local 155; Re: Abolition of Industrial Homework in 'Knitted Outerwear for Human Use.' "; Memo from Mr. Gagnon to Miss Papert on Triangle Knitwear Mills, Feb. 18, 1944, both in NYDOL, file "Homework Not Covered NYS – Knitted Outerwear", James H. Casey to The Honorable Herbert H. Lehman, Apr. 17, 1942; Frieda Miller to James H. Casey, Apr. 28, 1942, both in NYDOL, file "Gloves General."

[63] Kate Papert to Frieda Miller, May 6, 1942; "Comments on a Letter of Mr. James J. Casey, Secretary of the National Manufacturers' Association, to Governor Lehman, Dated Apr. 17, 1942," Apr. 27, 1942, both in file "Gloves-Inter-office Memos"; Louis Fuchs to Miller, Apr. 23, 1942; Nat. M. Keene to Miller, Apr. 25, 1942, both in file "Gloves – Against Changes in the Order," all in NYDOL.

saw no other solution for the disabled veteran than homework, the Consumers' League of New York answered, "Why – in Heaven's name – should men who have fought so gallantly for the economic and social institutions of our democracy be condemned to sweat shop slavery in their homes?" As in the previous world war, patriotism provided a powerful discourse through which to fight – and defend – government regulation.[64]

In 1945, the Supreme Court sustained federal homework bans in *Gemsco v. Walling*,[65] a challenge by embroidery manufacturers to the authority of the administrator to issue such restrictions. A grouping of a number of needlework processes – including Schiffli and Swiss hand-machines, bias binding, passementerie, lace cutting, crochet beading, and hand embroidery – this industry relied on homeworkers, as many as fifteen thousand who composed 40 percent of the work force. Investigations exposed nearly universal failure to keep records or pay homeworkers the minimum wage. Given its structural relation to the clothing industry, embroidery could undercut minimum wages in the rest of the apparel trade. Striking a balanced wage rate within the garment industries promised to be a delicate task for industry committees. Abolishing, rather than registering, homework appeared an appropriate means toward that end.[66]

The Pleaters, Stitchers and Embroiderers Association of New York challenged the homework bans. These employers resorted to homework to offset the high cost of plant overhead. Claiming exemption from FLSA, they argued that "services do not constitute commerce . . . [or] production . . . [or] the manufacture of goods." Rather than produce anything, they embellished items produced and owned by others. Embroidery was "a wholly intrastate activity." For such reasons, these employers refused to recognize the constitutionality of FLSA or its administrative orders.[67]

[64] Memo from Mr. Ostrow to Miss Papert on Variations, June 26, 1945, in file "Procedure for Promulgation of Order #4"; Lewis F. Valachovic to Governor Thomas E. Dewey, Jan. 21, 1946; Lois B. Hunter to Lewis Valachovic, Jan. 31, 1946, both in file "Gloves, Permits, Applications Denials," all in NYDOL; William Green to David Dubinsky, May 9, 1945, Dubinsky Papers, 304–4a; "To the Nation," Elinor Herrick, NYCL Papers, box 99, folder 23.

[65] 324 U.S. 244.

[66] U.S. DOL, Wage and Hour and Public Contracts Divisions, press release May 29, 1945, in NYDOL, folder "Legal"; U.S. DOL, Wage and Hour Division, "Conference and Executive Session of Industry Committee No. 15 for the Embroideries Industry," Sept. 4, 1940, 8, 47, 54–5, 73–80, 85, 87, RG155, box 62; "Excerpts from proceedings before the Wage and Hour Division," in Supreme Court of the United States, October Term, 1944, no. 368, *Gemsco v. Walling*, on Writs of Certiorari to the United States Circuit Court of Appeals for the Second Circuit (Washington, D.C.: Judd & Detweiler Printers, Oct. 24, 1944), 80, 102; U.S. DOL, Wage and Hour and Public Contracts Divisions, "The Current Status of Home Work in the Embroideries Industry," Oct. 1942, 36. For the 40 percent figure, *Gemsco v. Walling*, 324 U.S. at 271 (Roberts, J., dissenting).

[67] "Brief in Opposition to Report and Recommendation of Industry Committee #15," Submitted on behalf of Pleaters, Stitchers & Embroiderers Ass'n., Inc. of New York City and Abraham Friedensohn, individually, and as proprietor of Public Art Embroidery of New York City, 3–4, 7–8, 14, RG155, box 63.

Other embroidery employers asked the state to "protect us against home industry." They feared competition from those who relied upon homeworkers. As unionized firms, they supported demands for homework restriction, although their contracts recognized the reality of the existing market and contained no homework clause. Despite complaining about chiselers, these employers adhered to cultural norms where male camaraderie existed side by side with cutthroat competition: "The fact is that nobody will squeal." Government regulation would absolve them of individual action.[68]

Administration legal arguments considered the social and familial context of homework only as evidence for the impossibility of adequately regulating wages and hours. What was at stake in the administrator's order was not "the question whether home work is desirable or undesirable from a social point of view or as a form of economic organization" – the questions foremost in the minds of women reformers – but "whether the home work system . . . furnishes a means of circumventing or evading a wage order putting into effect the minimum wage recommendation of Industry Committee No. 45."[69]

The regulatory discourse turned on the narrow question of whether the administrator had overstepped his authority. This question the Supreme Court answered by agreeing that homework was not a separate industry but "conducted largely by the same employers who maintain factory establishments or by 'contractors' who are in competition with such employers." The Court discounted fears of undue unemployment; employers would transfer work into factories. The gender of homeworkers – their need for protection because they were women and minors, as earlier labor standards statutes had argued, or the reluctance many of these caretakers of dependents felt about leaving home for the factory – played no role in this opinion. Although the plaintiffs had argued the rulings to be "experimental social legislation" rather than a "method of enforcement," beyond the coverage of the statute, the Court accepted the narrower perimeters of the administrator. It agreed that Congress did not intend that the rules of the administrator should end when the statutory wage took over in 1945.[70]

Wage and Hour sought injunctions soon after *Gemsco* to show its seriousness about cracking down on illegal homework. In 1946, the Women's Bureau

---

[68] "Official Report of Proceedings before the Wage and Hour Division in the Matter of Hearing to Consider the Recommendations of Industry Committee No. 2 for the Apparel Industry," Dec. 6, 1939, 2033, DOL Library; "In the Matter Of a Hearing on the Minimum Wage Recommendation of Industry Committee No. 15 for the Embroideries Industry," Sept. 30, 1940, 171, RG155, box 63; "Conference and Executive Session of Industry Committee No. 15 for the Embroideries Industry," 30, 99–100, 107, 113.

[69] Embroideries had two committees under FLSA. The first, in 1940, set the wage at 37.5 cents; the second in 1943, set it at 40 cents and restricted homework. Many of the arguments during the first set of hearings appeared again during the second. "Excerpts from Proceedings before Wage and Hour Division," 75; "Conference and Executive Session of Industry Committee No. 15 for the Embroideries Industry," 99–100.

[70] *Gemsco v. Walling*, 342 U.S. at 256–8.

reported that about a fourth of homework employers in the restricted industries had organized community workshops and day nurseries to facilitate bringing homeworkers into the factory. But such actions did not end homework. Federal restriction of embroideries pushed homeworkers to the handbag and millinery industries rather than into the embroidery shops. Employer associations and unions asked New York, which issued far more permits for embroidery than did the federal government, to consider a separate state embroidery order since the federal rule excluded manufacturers "who perform incidental embroidery." New York offered no order, perhaps because the extent of the problem (only eleven hundred embroidery homeworkers in other industries) failed to warrant the resources needed for enforcement, perhaps because the commissioner thought the general homework order – recently issued as a "post-war stabilizing factor" – eventually would solve the problem.[71]

In 1949 Congress provided explicit language on homework regulation. It incorporated existing homework restrictions as section 11 (d) of FLSA which authorized the administrator "to make such regulations and orders regulating, restricting, or prohibiting industrial homework as are necessary or appropriate to prevent the circumvention or evasion of, and to safeguard the minimum wage rate prescribed in this Act." Despite other amendments to FLSA, none in relation to homework passed over the years; nor did the administrator make any additional rulings of note until the Reagan-era challenge to 11(d) itself.[72]

FLSA as dichotomy

Whether homework was part of the language of FLSA was less important than interpretations of the act. The debate during the late 1930s and 1940s turned on technical issues: the intent of Congress, the powers of the administrator,

[71] The general order only provided for the minimum wage, whereas factory workers earned more. It did not cover all industries that used embroidery or distributors who operated from their homes, nor did it prohibit certified homeworkers from working in other homework fields. U.S. DOL, Wage and Hour and Public Contracts Divisions, press release, July 11, 1935; U.S. DOL, Women's Bureau, "Industrial Homework in the United States," Jan. 1946, 5, Beyer Papers, box 10, folder 148; Memo from George Ostrow to Emily Sims Marconnier, Feb. 14, 1949; Mr. Ostrow to Miss Papert, Sept. 21, 1945; K. Papert to Mrs. Lois B. Hunter, May 15, 1947; Mr. Ostrow to Mrs. Marconnier, Nov. 14, 1946; Ostrow to Hunter, Nov. 3, 1947 with attached chronology, all in NYDOL, file "Embroidery."

[72] Wage and Hour and Public Contracts Divisions, Division of Regulation and Research, Branch of Research and Statistics, "Employment of Homeworkers under the Fair Labor Standards Act," July 1959, mimeoed report, 20–1, DOL Library. In 1948 the administrator changed the jewelry order to permit Native Americans to make handcrafted items on reservations as a means to increase employment opportunities. When it came to homework on reservations, the policy of Wage and Hour was to investigate only on complaint. See U.S. DOL, *Annual Report of the Wage and Hour and Public Contracts Divisions, 1948* (Washington, D.C.: GPO, 1948), 51; Daniel A. Daly to George Ostrow, Apr. 6, 1955, on "Enforcement of Homework Law, Frontier Feathers"; George Ostrow to Emily Sims Marconnier, Apr. 18, 1955; Marconnier to Ostrow, Apr. 20, 1955, file "1950s," NYDOL.

the application of directives from industrial committees to statutory wages. Not considered to be social legislation, homework restrictions in fact were interventions on the part of the state in the political economy. They represented social preferences for manufacturing in factories rather than homes. Home and work interconnected in the lives of homeworkers, but it was this reality to which Wage and Hour objected. Administrator Metcalfe Walling explained in 1943 that

> the very factors which make home work seem attractive to the home workers, namely, the absence of factory discipline, the fact that the work can be done on the worker's own time, and in a casual way, and that she is enabled to attend at the same time to her household responsibilities while supplementing the family income, preclude any possibility of reasonable assurance that even home workers who, on the basis of the piece rates paid, seem to be earning the minimum wages prescribed by the Act are in any given case actually receiving the minimum.[73]

FLSA promised to provide a mechanism to restrict a labor system that undermined the separation of home from work. Behind the technical features of FLSA, then, lay not only the agenda of safeguarding labor standards but also the one of maintaining gender norms and cultural conceptions of motherhood, childhood, work, and home.

The Bureau of Labor Standards continued to bring together state and federal administrators to share information and maintain "a common approach to the control of industrial homework." In 1953 Beyer noted that employers "widely approved" the federal restrictions; "few complaints are received by the administrators on their operation." Still most of the New England and Middle Atlantic region, where homework historically concentrated, reported illegal homework. Jewelry violations persisted throughout the decade not only in Rhode Island but also in the watch repair and engraving industry of Rochester, New York. Among industries uncovered by federal restrictions, the system grew in shoes, dolls' clothing, and toys. New York State continued to investigate knitwear and art needlework firms, which tried to circumvent the law by designating their homeworkers independent contractors. Homeworkers ignored state and federal laws as they made "sanitary goods" in California; rolled rag balls in Scranton, Pennsylvania; assembled clothespins in Waterbury, Vermont; folded, banded, pasted, and sewed tickets and cards in Muncie, Indiana; put together toy kites in Minneapolis, Minnesota; bent, gauged, looped, and trimmed metal springs in Illinois; wound guides on fishing rods in Royal Oak, Michigan. Advertisements for knitting machines directed toward housewives continued to appear, and such firms could fall between the cracks of federal and state enforcement. With each raise in the minimum wage, state

---

[73] "The Recommendation of Industry Committee No. 45 . . . Findings and Opinion of the Administrator," 60.

homework supervisors and the Wage and Hour Division worried that violations would increase.[74]

How effective was enforcement of homework? Sources before the controversy of the 1980s are thinner than during the 1930s and early 1940s,
indicating that governments had turned to other issues. New York measured a
drop from 1,407 employers' permits and 30,031 homeworkers' certificates on
July 1, 1945, to 665 employers' permits and 4,907 homeworkers' certificates by
June 30, 1958, a change in the legal number of industrial homeworkers.[75] In
1958, the Wage and Hour and Public Contracts divisions investigated the issue
of FLSA effectiveness with a survey that underestimated the extent of employer
violation "because of the difficulty of determining the number of hours
worked by homeworkers and whether or not children participated in the
work." The survey, which included 2,635 establishments with 22,580 homeworkers, failed to cover the universe of homeworkers – the division identified
others within months of completing it. Nonetheless, Wage and Hour concluded that violations of FLSA in restricted industries occurred at about the
same frequency as in nonrestricted ones (nine-tenths of the sample), adding up
to about one out of six employers, with minimum wage violations the most
common. More violations existed among contractors and within handwork
industries. Homeworkers remained overwhelmingly urban, with four-fifths
residing in communities of twenty-five hundred or more, except for North
Carolina where three-quarters were rural. In restricted industries, the majority of
homeworkers were in women's apparel, embroideries, and gloves and mittens; in
nonrestricted, 31 percent were in business services. As early as 1953 the states had
reported increased amounts of clerical homework; in 1956 the chief of the Wage
and Hour Division noted the spread of homework in direct mail advertising.[76]
These industries were highly competitive and required relatively little capital.

[74] U.S. DOL, Bureau of Labor Statistics, "Industrial Homework Conference," New York City,
Dec. 1, 1953; Albert Gilman to Emily Sims Marconnier, Jan. 25, 1956, on "the tremendous
problem of illegal homework in the custom jewelry and button industries." Marconnier, a
former NYCL official, was one of the last of the second generation of women reformers to
move from voluntary organizations to the state bureaucracy. On watches, see untitled
mimeo report. On knitwear and art needlework violations, Ostrow to Marconnier, July 1,
1955; George H. Schwartz to Jack Wolf, Mar. 7, 1955; Esther T. Bennin to Ostrow, Mar. 15,
1955; J. D. Wolf to Esther T. Bennin, Mar. 7, 1955; Frank X. Michel to Marconnier, June 24,
1955; M. P. Catherwood to Florence G. Clifton, July 1, 1964; George Ostrow to Frank J.
Muench, Mar. 20, 1956; Muench to Ostrow, June 18, 1956, all in NYDOL, file "1950s." For
various local violations, *Walling v. Freidin*, 6 Wage & Hour Cas. (BNA) 166 (M.D.Penn.
1946); *Fleming v. Demeritt*, 56 F.Supp. 376 (D.Vt. 1944); *Walling v. Muncie Novelty, Co.*, 6 Wage
& Hour Cas. (BNA) 557 (S.D.Ind. 1946); *Walling v. Hastings*, 6 Wage & Hour Cas. (BNA) 554
(S.D.Ind. 1946); *Mitchell v. Northwestern Kite Co.*, 12 Wage & Hour Cas. (BNA) 495 (D.Minn.
1955); *Figura v. Cummins*, 4 Ill.2d 44 (1954). On fishing rods, William S. Singley to James S.
Thorburn, Nov. 4, 1953, in NYDOL, file "Legal." For the rise in minimum wage in 1956,
U.S. DOL, Bureau of Labor Standards, "Industrial Homework Conference," Mar. 7, 1956,
in Beyer Papers, box 10, folder 150.

[75] George Ostrow to Gilbert E. Donahue, Aug. 27, 1958, NYDOL, file "1950s."

[76] "Employment of Homeworkers Under the Fair Labor Standards Act," 2–5, 7–8, 20–1;

Homeworkers continued to be mothers of small children. Only 22 percent of homeworkers said they could adjust to factory labor, while 50 percent claimed the "need to stay home to care for young children" as their reason for remaining home. This was particularly true in the nonrestricted industries because permits for the restricted ones were limited to the elderly, the disabled, or their caretakers. No breakdown was made by gender or age because Wage and Hour was interested in the nature of homework violations, not the characteristics of homeworkers, still assumed to be women. But the fact that 69 percent of those in nonmanufacturing industries listed childcare and that seven thousand of the homeworkers were typists suggests that the changing political economy of white-collar work in the postwar years also affected the shape of industrial homework without breaking its association with the mother who must earn.[77]

By the early postwar years, labor standards appeared assured. Debates over technicalities and problems with administration would characterize discussions of FLSA, but state intervention in the labor market seemed settled. The sweatshop apparently belonged to an industrial dark age vanquished by the New Deal. Wages, hours, child labor – the moral issues of the past – had become routinized, with their own bureaucracies. Under new leadership, the Women's Bureau focused on gaining equal pay and upgrading women's occupations. With collective bargaining governing labor-management relations, liberals turned away from the labor question to concentrate on civil rights and the Cold War. Homework subsided as a burning social issue. But it never disappeared; it festered behind the doors of new immigrant districts and along the edges of middle-class suburbs. With the sweated mother of the tenements gone, a new icon emerged: the woman typing at home, a baby by her side.

"Industrial Homework Conference," 1953, 2; "Industrial Homework Conference," 1956, 1.
[77] "Employment of Homeworkers Under the Fair Labor Standards Act," 2–5,7–8.

PART IV

Home/work redux

ACROSS THE BOARD

The Conference Board Magazine   Vol. XXIV No. 4   **APRIL 1987**

■ LESS TAXING IRS FORMS ■
■ WORK IN THE ELECTRONIC COTTAGE ■
■ UNFETTERING TRADE IN SERVICES ■

A Hard Day At The Office

Figure 18. "A Hard Day at the Office," cover, *Across the Board*, 1987. Reprinted, with permission, from the April 1987 issue of *Across the Board*, published by the Conference Board. Champions of telecommuting projected the homeworker as middle class, even elegant, able to care for her infant while working on a keyboard. Defenders of white-collar home-based labor promoted it as a solution to the work and family dilemma of the late twentieth century.

10

"With a keyboard in one hand": White collars in the home

"Goodbye, Rat Race," the *Washington Post* declared in April 1991. "Establishing a Home Office Means a New Way of Working . . . And Living."[1] Promising to generate an "electronic cottage," new technologies in the 1970s and 1980s projected an image of freedom and creativity, a release from a nine to five schedule and the commuter's daily battle with traffic. They suggested a reintegration of home and workplace and a solution to the work and family dilemma that became a national preoccupation in the 1980s as nearly half of all mothers entered the labor market. The image of the telecommuter was more fantasy than reality, however. It confused the freedom of the skilled computer professional, usually a man, with the necessities that made home-based labor attractive to female clerical workers in a society without adequate dependent care. Gender and class divided the world of homework in the late twentieth century into multiple realities, offering some men and fewer women a liberating form of work, but circumscribing the employment conditions of the female majority. Still, home-based labor in the 1980s and 1990s envisioned relief from social problems, a change from the beginning of the postwar era when attempts to regulate clerical homework reflected national anxiety over the Cold War.

Cold War politics and the rise of clerical homework

Homework regulation developed in response to abuses in garment and related trades, but government officials wondered whether clerical work could be regulated under an industrial homework law. Could typing ever be labeled industrial labor? During the 1950s and 1960s, various district courts ruled that "persons who address envelopes and labels in their homes" were employees under the Fair Labor Standards Act (FLSA) and that advertising agencies, addressing services, and insurance companies were not the kinds of retail or service industries exempted from the wage and hour law. Though they

---

[1] Cover headline, "Goodbye, Rat Race," *Washington Home, Washington Post*, Apr. 25, 1991; see story, Terri Shaw, "The Perils and Pleasures of Home Offices," 10–13, 28. Significantly the cover cartoon portrays a man in comfortable clothes. See also, for its photographic portrayal of telecommuting fathers, "Work and Family: Companies Are Starting to Respond to Workers' Needs – And Gain From It," *Business Week*, June 28, 1993, 480–8.

provided business services, they engaged in interstate commerce and produced a product, typed and stuffed letters to mail.[2]

Clerical homeworkers were married women, often former office workers. Their status as mothers and the conditions under which they labored provided the terrain for the political struggle over homework in the direct mail industry. In 1948 Local 16 of the United Office and Professional Workers of America (UOPWA), which had organized 10 percent of its industry, asked the New York Department of Labor to investigate home typing. This was one of the CIO's left-led unions, with Communists and fellow travelers prominent members; it organized insurance, clerical, and social workers, blacks as well as whites, women as well as the men who dominated both the insurance industry and the union's leadership.[3] After a series of public hearings and private meetings, the commissioner of labor issued "Order No. 5" in July 1950 under the state's industrial homework law with the intent to restrict home typing. The United Addressers Association, some forty employers, appealed to the state Board of Standards and Appeals, staying enforcement of the order. But before the board ever decided on the case, the state legislature in April 1953 excluded typists, bookkeepers, and stenographers from the 1935 law.[4] By then, direct mail had 114 employer permits and 7,337 homeworker certificates, as opposed to 579 permits and 5,586 certificates for all other industries – an indication of the extent of home clerical work.[5]

During the early Cold War, the working mother remained a su! 'ect of political discourse. Business proponents of homework continued to associate motherhood with patriotism and protection of the American way. But rather than simply a defense of traditional gender roles, the homeworking mother offered an updated version of domesticity, one that celebrated a "work ethic for women"[6] even if that work stayed confined to the home. Women's freedom to choose homework reflected the free market. In contrast, opponents offered

[2] *Goldberg v. Roberts*, 15 Wage & Hour Cas. (BNA) 412 (S.D.Cal. 1962); *Mitchell v. American Republic Ins. Co.*, 13 Wage & Hour Cas. (BNA) 210 (S.D.Iowa 1957); *Durkin v. Allied Agencies*, 11 Wage & Hour Cas. (BNA) 439 (E.D.Tenn. 1953); *Walling v. Sieving*, 5 Wage & Hour Cas. (BNA) 1009 (N.D.Ill. 1946). These cases also document the extent of clerical homework, covering Tennessee, Illinois, California, and Iowa.

[3] UOPWA Papers are merged with those of its successor union, District 65. Steve Rosswurm, ed., *The CIO's Left-Led Unions* (New Brunswick, N.J.: Rutgers Univ. Press, 1992), 1–17.

[4] This section draws on my article "Mothers Are Not Workers: Homework Regulation and the Construction of Motherhood," in *Mothering: Ideology, Experience, Agency*, ed. Evelyn Nakano Glenn, Grace Chang, and Linda Rennie Forcey (New York: Routledge, 1993). Analysis of this event is based on files still in the New York State DOL, Brooklyn office. Unless otherwise noted, all documents come from the NYDOL. State of New York, DOL, "Order No. 5," box 8, folder 3, NYCL Papers; "To: New York State Board of Standards and Appeals," 1–4, folder "Direct Mail: Briefs and Statements"; "To: Supervisors, From: George Ostrow, Re: Direct Mail Order, Date: Aug. 17, 1953," file "Homework: Direct Mail."

[5] J. D. Wolf to George Ostrow, "Review of Direct Mail Industry Legislation," Apr. 6, 1966, folder "Homework: Rulings and Interpretations, 1960 to date."

[6] Joanne Myerowitz, "Beyond the Feminine Mystique: A Reassessment of Postwar Mass Culture, 1946–1958," *JAH* 79 (March 1993), 1461.

a version of motherhood freed from economic exploitation but continued to focus on the homeworker as victim or victimizer. "Mother" and "worker" became oppositions in spite of the women from Queens and Brooklyn who typed envelopes while caring for their children, despite the working mother becoming subject and object of both unions and management.

The debate over clerical homework occurred during a period of rapid demobilization, when Rosie the Riveter lost her well-paying industrial job and found herself back in the pink-collar ghetto of women's work. Trade unions were militant, including those in female dominated service industries that were organizing department stores, hotels, restaurants, and telephone exchanges. Women reformers promoted equal pay for equal work. The turbulence of the late 1940s, when many feared a renewed economic collapse and others anticipated expanding opportunities, generated public concern with domestic life. In the aftermath of depression and war, most Americans desired to form families, have children, and move away from cities.[7]

Growth in clerical work was part of that new world. In 1947 it composed the largest occupation for women, consisting of over four million, one out of four women workers. Although nearly half of married women workers were classified as clerical or operatives, clerical workers were younger than other working women. Of all clerical workers, 37 percent were single, 23 percent married, and 19 percent widowed or divorced in the late 1940s.[8]

The married woman worker remained a social problem; sympathetic experts wondered whether such women were "neglecting, or discharging inefficiently, responsibilities that are theirs by virtue of their marital and parental status" and, if not, were they hurting themselves through lack of leisure? In 1946, the Bureau of the Census reported that when children were small, women tended to leave the labor force. Most married women who earned wages worked to support themselves and others. Yet such women did not fully control their choices. Hiring and dismissal practices discriminated against married and older women in office work. Despite the high turnover rate among clericals – who, without financial or professional incentives, left to marry and have children – employers judged the married and older worker less desirable and spoke of a labor shortage.[9]

7　William Chafe, *Unfinished Journey* (New York: Oxford Univ. Press, 1986); George Lipschultz, *Class and Culture in Cold War America: "A Rainbow at Midnight"* (Holyoke, Mass.: Bergen, 1982); Dorothy Sue Cobble, "Reassessing the 'Doldrum Years': Working Class Feminism in the 1940s," Eighth Berkshire Conference on the History of Women, June 1990; Cynthia Harrison, *On Account of Sex: The Politics of Women's Issues, 1945–1968* (Berkeley: Univ. of California Press, 1988).

8　"Changes in Women's Occupations, 1940–1950," *WBB* no. 253 (Washington, D.C.: GPO, 1954), 2–9.

9　Hazel Kyrk, "Family Responsibilities of Earning Women," in "The American Woman – Her Changing Role as Worker, Homemaker, Citizen," *WBB*, no. 224 (Washington, D.C.: GPO, 1948), 63; "Handbook of Facts on Women Workers," ibid., no. 225 (Washington, D.C.: GPO, 1948), 1–12, 32–3; Janet M. Hooks, "Women's Occupations Through Seven Decades," ibid., no. 218 (Washington, D.C.: GPO, 1951), 77; " 'Older' Women as Office Workers," ibid., no. 248 (Washington, D.C.: GPO, 1953), 57.

The feminization and transformation of clerical work under the growth of the modern corporation had precluded the rise of substantial homework. Prior to the invention of typewriters in the 1880s, "deserving" widows had received copy work to do at home, especially from government agencies. Into the twentieth century, some married women performed home clerical work for former employers, who gave such work on an ad hoc basis and out of their own sense of largess. After all, the overall function of typing, filing, and other office work was to centralize and dispatch information efficiently and aid managers on a daily basis. When demands for female labor led to a shortage of typists during World War II, clerical homework emerged as a problem in the rapidly expanding direct mail industry: the most factorylike, lower-paying, proletarianized form of office work.[10]

Consisting of letter shops, which reproduced letters by hand or machine prior to addressing and mailing them, and "list houses," which compiled and sold or rented mailing lists, the direct mail industry was a key business service. Frequently housed in lofts, direct mail houses resembled printing factories more than offices; the work was, even the contractors admitted, "dull, repetitive and not too stimulating," especially for the typists who had to produce three- and four-line addresses. Rush orders and overnight deadlines contributed to an irregular work flow; a production bottleneck developed at the typing stage, especially for smaller shops that lacked sufficient personnel. Though companies tried overtime and additional shifts, many turned to homework or homework contractors for flexibility to meet the varying volume of business. They complained of a shortage of typists, but in the late forties, wages and working conditions well below those in offices made recruitment difficult.[11]

The industry had employed some homeworkers since the 1920s, but most firms preferred inside workers to get out production rapidly and efficiently. The forties witnessed the growth of the "homework contractor" who, located in residential areas of Queens and Brooklyn, drew upon neighborhood housewives for a labor force. A hundred firms operating shops used these contractors, while another twenty-two with their own homeworkers also

[10] Joan Wallach Scott, "The Mechanization of Women's Work," *Scientific American* 41 (Sept. 1982), 166–7; Margery Davies, *Women's Place Is at the Typewriter* (Philadelphia, Pa.: Temple Univ. Press, 1982); U.S. DOL, Bureau of Labor Statistics, "Proceedings of the Fourteenth Annual Convention of the Association of Governmental Labor Officials of the United States and Canada," *Bulletin*, no. 455 (Washington, D.C.: GPO, 1927), 90; "Homework on Direct Mail Operations, New York State," State of New York DOL, unpublished typescript, c. 1949.

[11] "General Background, 1/19/51," typescript, 13–15, folder, "Homework: Direct Mail, Reports Re: Industry"; "Homework on Direct Mail Operations," 7–18; "To Control Homework in Direct Mail Industry," *NEWS*, July 18, 1950, NYCL Papers, box 8, folder 3; "Memorandum for the Industrial Commissioner, Re: Application of Labor Law, Article 13, to 'Homeworkers' in the Direct Mail Industry," Aug. 1, 1949, file "Legal"; George Ostrow to J. D. Wolf, July 2, 1952, 2–4, file "Homework, Direct Mail, Reports Re: Industry."

employed them. Contracting intensified competition, and in a scenario common to the garment trades, led to price cutting and ultimately lower piece rates for homeworkers and layoffs or lower rates for inside workers, mostly time workers who received premium pay and bonuses.[12]

UOPWA protested such undercutting of its members. At James True in New York City, a union grievance form noted in 1945, "Home workers get all good jobs. Mr. Aronson, dept. head, gives the 3 girls in the dept. the harder lists, and sneaks other work to homeworkers." This firm proved particularly recalcitrant, sending out typing rather than hiring additional workers through the union. Three years later organizers reported layoffs in the typing department "while homework continues at greater pace." The union relied on the collective bargaining process to rally members. Yet this employer continued to assert his right to reorganize production through mechanization and homework. He supposedly threatened, "I'M an American – I'M gonna use the Taft–Hartley law and do as I please!" One union flyer exclaimed, "Our bosses are beginning to get bright ideas about how they can use the new weapon *their* Congress gave them – and next week TRUE may be talking about jailing us under the Mundt Bill." The anti-Communist offensive would weaken the ability of Local 16 to resolve the grievances of members. Even after UOPWA entered District 65, the Distributive, Processing and Office Workers of America (DPOWA), as Local 14, it could not stem the opposition of True, who eventually fled the city for lower-waged Long Island.[13]

DPOWA was born in October 1950 as a safe haven for a number of left-wing groups cast out of the CIO for their failure to adhere to the anti-Communist provisions of Taft–Hartley and for their independence from the national CIO leadership. The direct mail union continued under this umbrella, but had an uphill fight, further hampered by Korean War caps on wages. Not surprisingly the members heard in July 1951 that "homework still remains" because of "our failure to organize unorganized shops."[14]

At the time when UOPWA first proposed the homework rule (between May and October 1948), the number of homeworkers actually increased by 30

[12] "Homework on Direct Mail Operations," 23–7.
[13] Grievance Report, James True, 3/1/45; Grievance Report on Homework, Mar. 25, 1948; Grievance report for Typing Dept., 7/8; memo to Bob [Ingersoll], with Bob's comments, 2/2/48; memo to Jack [Greenspan], 2/10/48; memo, Mar. 25, 1948; memo, Mar. 26, 1948; memo, Oct. 21, 1948; memo to Max Feder from Jack Greenspan, Aug. 2, 1948; flyer, "Help James True Workers; Keep Taft-Hartley Slave Law Out of Our Industry"; Jack Greenspan to True-Sullivan-Neibart, Feb. 8, 1949, box 138, folder 2; "Agreement at Meeting on October 27, 1949"; True-Sullivan-Neibart, status as of 10/1/50; Samuel Sacker to True-Sullivan & Neibart Associates, Inc., May 23, 1951, both in box 138, folder 1; "Report to Direct Mail Membership Meeting-Feb. 26, 1951"; Minutes of Emergency Meeting of Direct Mail Executive Committee, June 14, 1951, both in box 16, folder 71, District 65 Papers.
[14] Leon Fink and Brian Greenberg, *Upheaval in the Quiet Zone: A History of Hospital Workers Union, Local 1199* (Urbana: Univ. of Illinois Press, 1989), 25–6; Membership Meeting, July 9, 1951, District 65 Papers, box 16, file 71.

percent. The number of shop typists (who were mostly women) declined 2 percent, though printerlike operations performed by men experienced about a 17 percent growth. Homeworkers earned on the average sixty-eight cents an hour without accounting for the added cost of typewriters, repairs, and utilities for the home workplace. The comparable earnings of homeworkers averaged nearly a third less than the $1,755 gained by shopworkers employed more than thirty-nine weeks a year. High turnover, intermittent use by employers, and the relatively recent entrance of individual women into the trade kept wages low.[15]

The meagerness of annual earnings and hours highlights how homeworking was neither the only nor the major activity of such women. They were housewives and mothers. Like other homeworkers, they were supplementing the earnings of husbands while caring for children. Only 13 percent claimed that they could leave home for shop work; most reported that they had to remain at home to care for children, the elderly, or the disabled. But, compared to other homeworkers, typists had fewer children (one or two, with the youngest between two and six in half the families).[16] They were native-born[17] and had more education, usually having finished high school – a characteristic typical of clerical workers. Most had been clerical workers prior to marriage. Yet at thirty-six, they were older than the average office worker, whose median age was less than thirty. Office clericals were younger, often more skilled, considered more attractive, and certainly more mobile. Social conditions that shaped choice separated the two groups of clericals. Clerical workers preferred the office to the factory; even those laboring at home did not have to put up with conditions in the direct mail lofts.[18]

Most husbands of homeworkers were employed. These men were nonmanagerial white-collar workers, craftsmen and operatives, transportation and utility workers, policemen, and firemen – working-class occupations that by themselves usually were inadequate to maintain higher living standards in the

[15] "Homework on Direct Mail Operations," 31–51. Direct mail earnings were down from many other average hourly and weekly earnings among typists in New York City in the late 1940s. The lowest that class B typists earned an hour in early 1948 was .95 (women) and $1.02 (men). U.S. DOL, Bureau of Labor Statistics, "Salaries of Office Workers in Selected Large Cities," *Bulletin*, no. 943 (Washington, D.C.: GPO, 1948), Table I, 29.

[16] This figure did not necessarily capture the extent of completed families or the beginning of the baby boom. Given the age range of the women, it is possible that many had not yet completed their families.

[17] Many may have been second- or third-generation Italian or Jewish, suggesting how the daughters and granddaughters of industrial homeworkers merely switched work process, not site of labor. Ethnicity was not recorded in the Labor Department's survey, and the original survey interviews have not survived.

[18] Four percent at home were fifty-five or older; in the direct mail shops, 13 percent were fifty or older. The average age in the direct mail shops was thirty-seven. "Changes in Women's Occupations, 1940–1950," 5; "Homework on Direct Mail Operations," 28–31, 18; D. Maier and E. Kadish to Mrs. Marconnier, "Data on Supply of Typists Available for Letter Shop Work," Aug. 29, 1949, 3–4, in "Homework: Direct Mail. Surveys and Complaints."

inflation-prone late forties. One in twelve was a professional or proprietor. About one in five families had income from additional adults in their households and a few others, from pensions and rents. Most lived outside of Manhattan – in Flushing, Brooklyn, or Long Island. Their place of residence reflected urban expansion and population diffusion, the movement of second and third generation white ethnics from the inner city.[19]

Like previous generations of homeworkers, typists worked "because they needed the money," with a mere 7 percent claiming "to keep busy or to save money for luxury items." State investigators presented the case of Mrs. K., "a secretary for 10 years before her marriage," as typical. With young sons, eleven and five and a half, and a husband whose job as a maintenance mechanic provided sixty dollars a week, "she had been doing addressing homework for a year before the interview. She reported, 'Last year I wanted to get bicycles for Christmas for my boys. Now the money goes for food and clothing.' " Spiraling costs of basic items pushed such mothers into the labor market.[20]

By itself, economic need never accounted for why some women did homework and others went to the shop or factory. About a quarter of mail order shops instituted one shift, from 1 to 5 or 2 to 6 P.M., staffed by housewives, presumably women who could travel into Manhattan and had childcare arrangements. Homeworkers not only stated their preference for the location of their labor but were offered such work by contractors who organized businesses around the availability of such a labor force.[21] Some small direct mail shops, which relied upon homeworkers, were family businesses, with wives and children listed as officers of the corporation.[22]

The debate over homework regulation in the direct mail industry overlapped with U.S. entry into Korea. Because the UOPWA was "communist influenced," opponents of restrictions linked patriotism, motherhood, and freedom to work at home. Trade unionists and reformers continued to portray homework as undermining domesticity. Even those who defended homeworking women as workers relied upon domestic virtue to attack those who would exploit them. But in the renewed consumer culture of these years, the homeworker also became a selfish woman who took work and decent wages away from the deserving in order to satisfy unnecessary longings. To justify reliance on homework, contractors in turn drew their own portrait of mothers as not serious about jobs and tied down by children. But homework employers presented a contradictory picture. Although they would agree that pitiful need

---

[19] Earnings for husbands averaged $65.52 a week, with 13 percent gaining less than $50, and 6 percent, at least $90. "Homework on Direct Mail Operations," 28–9.

[20] Ibid., 29.

[21] Ibid., 17.

[22] Ben Marlowe to George Ostrow, "Variation Request – Rita Carol, Inc.," Sept. 8, 1950; M. H. Sorkin to Ostrow, "Variation Request – Allee Business Service Inc.," Sept. 29, 1950, both in folder "Homework: Direct Mail Variations, 1950–53."

pushed some to homework, their interest lay in emphasizing the worthiness of their work force.

Henry Hoke, editor of the industry's trade journal *The Reporter of Direct Mail Advertising*, and John J. Patafio of Ambassador Letter Service Co., one of the leaders of the United Addressers Association, organized a letter-writing campaign through which employers and their workers complained to the governor and the Department of Labor.[23] Similarity of rhetoric and charges both attested to this origin and created a distinct discourse. One correspondent graphically expressed ideas promoted by Hoke in claiming, "While our neighborhood boys are fighting Communism in far away Korea, we at home are being Sovietized by the Reds in our midst." The commissioner of labor threatened "to violate the privacy of American homes to tell us what we may or may not do." Another letter writer explained, "The general feeling is . . . this definitely breaks the ice for Sovietizing the American home under a Commisar." The order, in short, was "most un-American." A Brooklyn homeworker expressed this individualism in a manner that emphasized her role as mother (just as some men stressed their parental role): "True my two little girls are not dependent on my working for their daily bread, but that is of no concern of theirs [the state]. Just as it would be no concern of theirs if my children were destitute."[24]

This interpretation of domesticity called not for a retreat into an isolated suburban ranch house – a predominant theme during the early Cold War years. It was rather a paean to the self-sacrificing, hard-working mother and represented a postwar discourse that shunned the idle bridge player and lauded she who combined some labor or service work with motherhood.[25] As one small businessman protested to the industrial commissioner, "This Order No. 5 is unfair, not only to small businesses employing less than five workers, but unfair to women with small children who, in these troubled times when their husbands are in military service, must supplement their income." A "wife helping out" combined such arguments from women's necessity with those that promoted man's freedom, the motif of "a man's home is his castle" that defenders of homework had relied upon since the 1880s. She questioned Governor Dewey: "Why should the State of New York suddenly try to regulate

[23] Henry Hoke, "A Report on a Mess," reprint from *The Reporter of Direct Mail Advertising*, Aug. 1950, in NYDOL files; copy of memo from John J. Patafio, June 17, 1949; John Patafio to Hon. Lee B. Mailler, Aug. 24, 1950; E. C. Walker to Emily Sims Marconnier, Oct. 12, 1950, explains that the letters "were originated by the Reporter of Direct Mail Advertising who published the original information that reached the smaller people out in the sticks, like ourselves." Emily Sims Marconnier to Hon. Samuel Faile, Oct. 4, 1950, all in "Correspondence 50–5."

[24] John D. Brerton to Hon. Thomas E. Dewey, Aug. 28, 1950; Christian Weyand to Hon. Charles E. Dewey [sic], Oct. 2, 1950; Gregory Greubel to His Excellency Thomas E. Dewey, Aug. 29, 1950; Mrs. Agnes Lyons to dear Sir, Sept. 1, 1950, all in "Correspondence: 50–8."

[25] Elaine Tyler May, *Homeward Bound: American Families in the Cold War Era* (New York: Basic Books, 1988); Myerowitz, "Beyond the Feminine Mystique," 1455–82.

our home life – or what we do with our own time in our own houses?" Countering a theme of homework opponents, she argued, "This homework is not 'slave labor.'" Another homeworker connected breadgiving with breadwinning, roles that women social investigators had emphasized since the turn of the century. "We work to supplement the small incomes of our husbands so that we can give our children the necessities of life. Some, unfortunately have no husbands and depend on what they earn to support their families."[26]

Mothers worked for their children and their families – this characterization had justified homework in the past and had made the homework contractor into a savior who kept women from welfare. Women continued to prefer work to the public dole. Such situations were all too real. A deserted mother, a secretary by day, explained that she worked because state laws could not return a husband who had deserted her to live in California "with the other woman," taking the new car with him. "I haven't received a cent, although I have a separation action pending," she complained. "It seems very easy for the State to enforce a law forbidding you to earn a few extra dollars but the District Attorney or the Judge of a Court can't make a husband take care of his legal family properly but allow him to remain out of the State absolutely free to come and go and not pay a cent to us." Women resented a state that allowed a man who failed in his obligations to children and wife "to do as he pleases," as another divorced homeworking mother complained to the governor. It was not just basic survival items that these postwar mothers defined as needs in a renewed consumer culture. Homework provided one child "with the little things a boy desires plus building his education." A contractor argued that women worked "to buy little necessities like a television," which they watched while at work. They would not fulfill such needs "if they did not do typing."[27]

Consumer goods continued to lure women to homework. As during the 1920s, the line shifted between what a family needed to survive and what a woman desired for her family, depending on larger economic factors. A self-described "liberal" manufacturer of household hardware products in 1950 remembered this transformation:

> On my first visit to our Homeworkers in lower Brooklyn I was astonished to find that all our people lived in comfortable homes and were clearly middle class . . . the men had prospered. They no longer needed the money but it gave the women something to do while they were bringing up the

[26] R. De Pace, Manager, Elliott Addressing Machine Company to His Excellency, Thomas E. Dewey, Aug. 21, 1950; Henry Benisch to Hon. Anthony R. Saverese, Jr., Dec. 28, 1950; Robert R. Updegraff to Mr. Edward Corsi, Sept. 21, 1950; (Miss) Frances Micalizzi to Hon. Thomas E. Dewey, Sept. 11, 1950; to Honorable Governor Thomas E. Dewey with copies to Senator MacNeal Mitchell, Assemblywoman Maude Ten Eyck, and Commissioner Edward Corsi, no name, n.d., "Correspondence 50–8."

[27] (Mrs.) Robert B. Boothby to Governor Thomas E. Dewey, Sept. 8, 1950; (Mrs.) Louisa Bidanset to Gov. Thos. B. Dewey, Sept. 7, 1950, "Correspondence 50–8"; Jack Aronoff in "Of Public Hearing on Industrial Homework in the Letter Shop Industry," May 24, 1949, 42, unpublished typescript, file "Home Labor – Letter Shop Industry."

children. I was greeted with wine and brandy and all sorts of home baking. I noted that the children were part of the process, illegally of course. Clearly I was not exploiting them as I had expected.[28]

In letters to government officials, homeworkers appeared "self-reliant," "skilled," "not . . . under pressure," working "at their convenience."[29] They were needy, but hard workers who put home, children, and husbands first. Proponents of the homework ban, in contrast, portrayed such women as victims of exploitation, as workers for pin money, or both. The *New York Post* labor columnist condemned the low wages that Manhattan firms offered young Queens housewives; employers were exploiting the domesticity venerated by the larger culture. At the public hearing on direct mail homework in May 1949, a representative from the U.S. Women's Bureau repeated its long-standing claim "that homeworkers are exploited," while the executive secretary of the New York Women's Trade Union League classified these clerical homeworkers as industrial workers, envisioning the same kinds of "sanitary, health and child labor" abuses that accompanied homework elsewhere. She argued that homeworkers depressed wages without any accompanying social benefit.[30]

According to male trade unionists, home typists engaged in antisocial behavior. Like other homeworkers, they involved children, who carried boxes of envelopes and sometimes helped with the typing. Jack Greenspan, the chief organizer of Local 16, embraced the myth of the male breadwinner. Since most homeworkers were housewives "with children, whose husbands *work*," they took jobs away from those "who urgently need jobs, in order to merely supplement their own income." A male typist and UOPWA member exclaimed, "To hear some people speak about homeworkers needing money – they do not need it worse than typists do . . . so far as the cruelty of depriving homeworkers of needed work, I say we need work as much as they do." In this representation, the homeworking mother became a designing woman, who through carelessness or selfishness forced real workers, those who derived their full maintenance from wages, to seek unemployment insurance or welfare.[31]

---

[28] Kyrle Elkin to Eileen Boris, Apr. 6, 1985.

[29] Clarence M. Roach to My dear Governor, Aug. 29, 1950; P. O. Johnson to the Honorable Irving Iyes, Aug. 28, 1950, in "Correspondence: 50–8."

[30] Oliver Pilat, "Department of Labor," *New York Post Home News*, Apr. 19, 1949, 38; May 2, 1949, 34, in file "Homework, Direct Mail: Publicity"; and Pilat, "Department of Labor," May 25, 1949, in file "Homework: Direct Mail, Procedure and Inter-Office Memo"; Miss Angus and Miss Kaye in "Public Hearing on Industrial Homework in the Letter Shop Industry," May 24, 1949, 28, 25.

[31] Mr. Fixler, Mr. Greenspan, and Mr. Sobel in "Public Hearing on Industrial Homework in the Letter Shop Industry," May 24, 1949, 15, 10, 20–1; "Statement on Typing Homework, Submitted by Local 16, United Office and Professional Workers of America, C.I.O.," 2, file "Home Labor – Letter Shop Industry."

In denying that they ran sweatshops, homework employers reinforced this image. They claimed, "Homeworkers are very largely home owners, working in comfortable, airy, healthful, sanitary homes, under pleasant working conditions, of assured privacy, and with freedom to work in such spare time as is available." "Their little stand in the dining room" or living room hardly took up space; they shunned child labor, the work required too much skill. But their characterization of homeworkers was contradictory, embracing "wives, sisters, mothers of fighting men in Korea," caretakers of the old, disabled, ill, and young; wives helping to pay bills; "pregnant women who urgently need money," the retired who need more than social security; the ill or disabled; "older women, ex-office workers, striving to help their children or grandchildren." Protesting the loss of earnings that regulation would bring, contractors also portrayed the homeworker as victim, a worthy but poor woman trying to keep hunger from the door. This portrait hardly matched the one researchers discovered of "relatively young married women with small children who cannot or do not wish to travel to offices to work." Homeworkers were neither desperate nor well-off, a change in condition that reflected improvement in white ethnic working-class living standards from the early twentieth century.[32]

Only the Congress of American Women, an organization in the Communist party orbit, accurately recognized the relation between women who worked at home and those in the shops. It opposed "any attempt to pit the housewives income needs against the wage standards of the working women." It skillfully deployed the language of domesticity and motherhood. Defining its objective as "improving the lot of women as workers, mothers, and citizens," spokeswoman Halois Moorehead argued for a guaranteed right to work for all women, made meaningful through regulated wage and working standards and "proper nursery school facilities." The Congress of American Women supported the restrictive order "because we consider homework to be inimical to the interests of women as wage-earner[s] and as mothers." Like pro-labor women reformers, Moorehead drew upon the image of the home turned into a sweatshop to attack economic exploitation of women workers. For her, mothers were workers. The symbol of the heroic proletarian mother, which had developed during the Communist party's Popular Front period, continued to shape constructions of womanhood.[33]

Contractors, however, defined homeworkers as housewives and mothers

[32] George Ostrow, "Re: Brief of Petitioners Before the New York State Board of Standards and Appeals," July 2, 1952, 9–10, "Homework: Direct Mail: Reports re Industry." Comment on typing stand by Mr. De Groodt in "Minutes of Public Hearing on Industrial Homework in the Direct Mail Industry," Oct. 5, 1949, 19–20.

[33] Halois Moorehead in "Public Hearing on Industrial Homework in the Letter Shop Industry," May 24, 1949, 26–7. She claimed the organization to have three hundred thousand members. For the Communist party's conceptions of womanhood, Paula Rabinowitz, *Labor and Desire: Women's Revolutionary Fiction in Depression America* (Chapel Hill: Univ. of North Carolina Press, 1991).

whom they happened to employ, rather than workers. Contrary to union claims, they would not flock to offices. Neither would they drag children on the subway to obtain work in Manhattan. Instead, "they push a baby buggy with one kid in the back and the other kid on the side and they pick up a thousand envelopes and dump it into the carriage and wheel it home." These women were neither steady nor dependable. If space and typists were available, inside workers were actually preferable because when an "order has to be finished in a week, the typing has to be finished in three days and the homeworker may not be feeling well or going to a movie or visiting relatives, she holds it back." Homeworkers typed during their "odd moments or half hours" because their priorities were children and housework. Yet small employers preferred inefficiency to increasing overhead costs.[34]

Homeworkers were also "girls," no matter their age. Despite praise of mothers who contributed to the family economy, contractors held deeply misogynist views. Not only did they refuse to view homeworkers as serious and trustworthy workers, they heaped scorn on typists who came from offices to the direct mail firms: "They work for half an hour and say 'this is too hard' "; "they will talk in the shop and you can't run the business on that basis." The image of the "average typist," "slated for 40 hours a week," who "puts in three and the rest of the time she spends out in the wash room" justified the use of homeworkers. This picture also defined what employers meant by labor shortage: a lack of women willing to work under the terms offered. Contractors seemed to share the attitude of one man who protested the homework order out of fear that it would interfere with "the prerogative" of "business men, and professional men . . . of having typing done at home by women who cannot work full time in an office."[35]

This identification of homeworker with housewife provided the basis to mystify employment status. The director of the American School of Business Administration complained to the industrial commissioner:

> Any regulation that would arbitrarily give these outside addressers the status of employee – subject to unemployment insurance and other employee benefits – would create an incongruous situation. These individuals – whose primary occupation is that of housewife – certainly cannot be considered as being unemployed when they are not doing addressing work for us. They may be performing such services for other organizations, or they may choose to be *idle*. (emphasis added)

[34] A. J. Howard, Harry Stein, Mr. Gilman and Mr. De Groodt, "Minutes of Public Hearing on Industrial Homework in the Direct Mail Industry," Oct. 5, 1949, 17, 33, 12–13, 4; Harry Ochshorn in "Of Public Hearing on Industrial Homework in the Letter Shop Industry," May 24, 1949, 13.

[35] Mr. Stein in "Public Hearing on Industrial Homework in the Letter Shop Industry," 32–4; Mr. De Groodt in "Minutes of Public Hearing on Industrial Homework in the Direct Mail Industry," Oct. 5, 1949, 5; Wendell F. Adams to The Honorable Thomas E. Dewey, Nov. 24, 1950, 3, "Correspondence, 50–8."

Because family obligations led addressers not to accept as much work as this employer was willing to offer, they had to be classified as "independent contractors," or workers not subject to FLSA, Social Security, or other state protections. Others found in the rhythms of the work, done without immediate supervision and presumably at the worker's own pace in her own time, justification for that designation. Yet these rhythms derived from the position of housewife and mother, the very factors behind both women's availability for homework and attractiveness to employers. Lawyers for the giant interstate R. H. Donnelley Corporation concluded a brief against providing homeworkers, defined as "former stenographers or typists whose principal occupation has changed to that of housewife," with unemployment insurance by claiming, "It is because these people cannot accept definite working hours that they rent or purchase typewriters and set themselves up as home typists in which capacity they can work solely at their own convenience free from direction, supervision or control." Just as some contractors attempted to argue that home clerical work could not be regarded as industrial homework because "the type of work is easy and genteel," others drew upon the task-oriented and less-routinized world of housework to obscure the employer-employee relation.[36]

In 1952, the Unemployment Insurance Appeal Board reversed an earlier decision and defined homeworkers as employees, not independent contractors. It cited how the employer checked the typewriter, demanded work be redone, gave further directions by phone, and could discharge a worker. It noted that supervision existed, especially over the manner and acceptability of work, and that piece-rate payment failed to determine status.[37]

Whether or not addressing envelopes was manufacturing, the Department of Labor claimed direct mail as factory work. Prior to promulgating the regulation, it argued that "the Legislature sought to avoid the restrictive meaning given by the courts to the word 'manufacturing' " by defining it in the homework statute as "preparation, alteration, repair or finishing, in whole or in part, or handling in any way." Typing came under the law since "prior to the placement of the address on the envelope, one has simply a plain paper envelope"; the typist altered or finished the envelope. Moreover, the law had wide social significance: If home typing was injurious to "the health and general welfare" of typists, it could be regulated.[38]

[36] Paul Kline to Mr. Edward Corsi, May 31, 1949, 2, in file "1950–55: Briefs and Statements"; Brief for Appellant, "In the Matter of the Claim for Benefits Under Article 18 of the Labor Law made by Josephine F. Riley, Claimant," Appeal No. 18,687–49, 13; "Minutes of Public Hearing," 8.

[37] State of New York, DOL, Unemployment Insurance Appeal Board, "Decision," Case No. 29,904–51, May 9, 1952, esp. 7–8; see also, Supreme Court, Appellate Division, Third Judicial Department, Appeal Board Case No. 29,904–51, decision handed down March 11, 1953, file "Legal."

[38] Abraham H. Goodman to Hon. Edward Corsi, May 11, 1949, 2, 4, 7; William G. DeLamater to Hon. Abraham H. Goodman, Aug. 22, 1949, file "Legal."

Mothers, after all, could be workers. But the state legislature soon would affirm the contractor's position that clerical homeworkers could not be regulated under the industrial homework law. At stake was also the status of clerical workers inside the direct mail houses. Even the big unionized employers feared the consequences of defining the industry as industrial for homework regulation: Typists would come under hours, wage, and other women's labor laws which up to that time applied only to industrial – not clerical – workers.[39]

Further attempts at regulation

Mothers continued to type at home in increasing numbers during the 1950s. Some fell prey to mail order homework "rackets"; others turned to part-time home typing. Massachusetts, which noted homework in mail order and direct mail as early as 1946, responded to this growth with a minimum wage order for clerical, technical, and similar occupations that contained a two cents an hour premium for homeworkers who had to provide their own overhead. An investigation the previous year had discovered that clerical homeworkers earned "well above the state minimum wage of 75 cents an hour." As long as their labor remained hidden in the home and appeared not to violate labor standards, even opponents of the evils of homework accepted clerical work. Milton Derber, a noted professor of industrial relations and opponent of homework exploitation, concluded his 1958 survey of homework with a defense of the "useful social function" behind legitimate (that is, "properly supervised") homework: It provided work for both the disabled and "the housewife and mother who is generally preoccupied with the concerns of her family but who may wish to supplement the family income." The 1963 *Report* of the President's Commission on the Status of Women – a harbinger of the new feminism of that decade – strongly supported continuation of homework prohibition, even calling for more effective enforcement. But it too recognized that "many women who withdraw from the labor force to raise families have clerical skills . . . [which] lend themselves to part-time work . . . ; their use is subject to exploitation and should be monitored, but it should not be made impossible by legal inflexibility."[40]

---

[39] Daniel Arvan, "Public Hearing on Industrial Homework in the Letter Shop Industry," 23; Albert Gilman, "Do You Want Homework Eliminated?", Dec. 8, 1949, in file "Homework: Direct Mail: Briefs and Statements."

[40] "Fraudulent Homework Schemes Prey on P[eople]," *The Machinist*, May 5, 1955, 1,6; Simmons School of Social Work, "State Labor Laws and Their Relationship to Social Work," Nov. 13, 1946, 2–3, box 1, folder 6; Speech by Hattie Smith, May 23, 1956; Everett G. Martin, "Unions, State Seek Homework Curb," *Christian Science Monitor*, Apr. 5, 1955, both box 4, folder 24, Smith Papers; Milton Derber, "Industrial Homework: An Old Problem Lingers On," Lecture Series No. 17 (Institute of Labor and Industrial Relations, Univ. of Illinois, Champaign, 1958), 10; *American Women: Report of the President's Commission on the Status of Women* (Washington, D.C.: GPO, 1963), 38.

Gender functionalism dominated postwar thinking and justified nonindustrial home-based labor. In the conservative political climate of the 1950s, when 95 percent of all women married, Parsonian sociology designated the family as the site of women's work. Employers continued to discriminate against women in hiring and pay; state funding for childcare had ended in 1948 and the legal system gave preference to men. New standards increased time spent on housework, and household appliances brought some tasks, like clothes washing, back to the home, but technology generally provided more time for the venerated work of mothering. Moreover, suburbanization in these years took white housewives away from the centers of employment. Nonetheless, women increasingly entered the paid labor force: One-third of white women and one-half of black women worked for wages during their childbearing years. From the 1950s into the late 1960s, many white women worked before marriage, left the labor force with the birth of their first child, and returned to nondomestic paid labor after their last child started school. Homework fitted into such a life pattern.[41]

This ideological and demographic context accounted for a shift in thinking in Massachusetts about whether mothers should be exempted from homework prohibitions. In the postwar period, homework persisted in the making of knitted goods, brushes, jewelry, dolls' clothes, and baseballs. In 1955, a special legislative committee to study and review homework laws responded to demands of the Massachusetts Federation of Labor – supported by Assistant Commissioner of Labor Hattie H. Smith – to curtail competition from an estimated four thousand homeworkers. A failed strike in late 1954 by the International Ladies' Garment Workers Union (ILGWU) precipitated this action. The Totsy Manufacturing Company of Springfield, a maker of dolls' clothes, bypassed ILGWU picket lines by "farming out" its work to nearby women, many the wives of CIO and American Federation of Labor (AFL) members who were suffering from the unemployment that plagued the area. With a homework permit, this company – one of two hundred similar firms that had left New York to escape homework restriction – claimed to be breaking no laws.[42]

Declaring that a "law intended to benefit handicapped people [was] abused by industrial misuse," the AFL filed two bills: The first "would automatically revoke the industrial permits of employers who become involved in labor disputes," while the second promised to "restate unequivocally the original

---

[41] Rochelle Gatlin, *American Women Since 1945* (Jackson: Univ. of Mississippi Press, 1987), 3–73; Ethel Klein, *Gender Politics: From Consciousness to Mass Politics* (Cambridge, Mass.: Harvard Univ. Press, 1984), 32–46.

[42] The strike was under Sol Chaikin, later president of the ILGWU. "Unions, State Seek Homework Curb"; "Industrial 'Homework' Hit By Chaikin; Asks State Bill," [Springfield] *Daily News*, Dec. 7, 1954; "Totsy Said Abiding by Law on 'Homework,' Has Permit," ibid., Dec. 8, 1954; "AFL to War on Home Work As Practiced by Totsy Firm," ibid., Dec. 9, 1954; "Kelley, Chaikin Hit Industrial Homework Plan," n.d.; "State House Briefs," *Springfield Union*, Aug. 12, 1955, Smith Papers, box 4, folder 24.

intent of the Legislature, which was to provide industrial home work only for persons who are both physically handicapped and housebound." Yet the housebound here included not only the disabled, elderly, and their caretakers but "persons . . . with children under seven years of age," those – as the special commission noted – "whose services are essential in the home to care for children." Hattie Smith, a generation apart from the women's network, accepted the inclusion of mothers under the proposed homework exceptions, perhaps to facilitate passage. This new language never entered the revised laws because no general prohibition passed. Other changes lobbied for by the AFL and proposed by the special commission did become law: homework prohibition during labor disputes, a ban on contractors, and an increase in employer permit fees. Home typing remained uncovered.[43]

New York State amended its homework law again in 1966; this time new understandings of civil rights and the political power of labor overcame any sympathy for homeworking women. District 65 and the unionized employers of the Direct Mail Master Contract Association (DMMCA) won a victory after having gained the support of the lieutenant governor and approval of the commissioner of labor. The legislature quickly passed without debate an act to exclude inserting, collating, labeling, nesting, sorting, stamping, and similar work from the clerical exemption of the law. An industrial homeworker, then, was not only one who returned manufactured articles to an employer but also one who "delivered, mailed or shipped" such goods "to others." The amendment clarified the 1953 removal of clerical work, although the Division of Budget noted that some confusion might develop "as whether a secretary who types a letter in her home and puts it into an envelope might by that action fall under the Labor Law."[44]

[43] In 1953 Beatrice McConnell, then with the Division of Labor Standards, also accepted such language; either the remnants of the women's network had succumbed to the dominant gender ideology or they felt homework so little a threat to factory standards that regulations could accommodate mother care of children. The Commonwealth of Massachusetts, Division of Labor and Industries, *Report of the Minimum Wage Commission for the Year Ending June 30, 1956*, 3, box 1, folder 9; Beatrice McConnell to Mrs. Hattie H. Smith, Dec. 23, 1953; McConnell to Smith, Oct. 8, 1954; Smith to Senator G. Henry Glovsky, Aug. 18, 1955; Smith to Mr. John D. White, Sept. 10, 1955; "To Eliminate the Middleman," *Daily News*, Aug. 29, 1955; all in box 4, folder 24, Smith Papers; The Commonwealth of Massachusetts, *Report of the Commission Established to Study and Revise the Laws Relating to Industrial Homework*, Aug. 15, 1955 (Boston: Wright & Potter Printing Co., 1955), House Document No. 3118; Smith speech May 23, 1956; Commonwealth of Massachusetts, Department of Labor and Industries, "Containing the Laws Relative to the Control of Industrial Homework and Revised Rules and Regulations Concerning Homework," *Industrial Bulletin*, no. 20 (Boston: Wright & Potter, 1960).

[44] Bill jacket, State of New York, Print 5644, [Senate 4602], in Senate, March 31, 1966, with attachments: Office of the Industrial Commissioner, May 19, 1966, Approval Report; Budget Report on Bills, Division of the Budget, May 26, 1966; Daniel Arvan to Robert Douglas, May 17, 1966; David Livingston to Robert Douglas, May 13, 1966; New York State AFL-CIO, "We Endorse This Bill;" Department of Audit and Control, Report to the

"Administrative difficulties" had led the Department of Labor in 1953 to "withhold enforcement of that part [the mailing operations] pending further examination of the whole situation." It informed employers that "in the event that a subsequent ruling makes it necessary to obtain a permit you will be advised accordingly" and then took no action for thirteen years. But collating homework grew only after 1953, with sporadic complaints over the next decade. In early 1961, the Long Island firm of Mailman, Inc. asked for a permit. Subsequent investigation revealed that it had distributed collating and other "secondary" operations to nearly 40 homeworkers since 1956; "information" visits to other Long Island firms confirmed extensive use of homeworkers. One typical firm employed only 25 in the factory out of a total work force of 135. Although it paid homeworkers workmen's compensation, it considered such laborers ineligible for unemployment, disability, and withholding. After providing Mailman a one-year permit, the department returned to its earlier decision "not to pursue enforcement of the secondary operations."[45]

In 1964 the DMMCA, joined by District 65, called attention to this homework. District 65 organized support for curtailment, enlisting the state AFL-CIO in the fight to abolish all homework in direct mail and related industries. DMMCA would cooperate with the union, although it would go off the record when it came to informing on its own members. To determine the significance of collating homework, the Division of Labor Standards asked for a list of homework firms. With a legal opinion that considered the department on "shaky ground" if it tried to enforce the homework law on secondary operations, the director did nothing because no list of offending firms came from the union. In the midst of this activity, the industrial commissioner revoked the old, moot Order No. 5.[46]

The Labor Department had issued no permits under the General Homework Order from 1950 to August 1964 for collating and similar occupations. That winter union vice-president Al Bernknopf and the DMMCA's Daniel Arvan requested support for legislation; labor standards officials advised the industrial commissioner to provide "whatever encouragement we can (treating [the amendment] in the same manner as we have the hours bill for women over

Governor on Legislation, May 12, 1966; To Counsel to the Governor, Louis J. Lefkowitz, May 12, 1966, NYSA. *Legislature Record Index Book*, 1966, 433, NYSL; State of New York, DOL, "Public Hearing on Proposed Homework Order Governing Insertion, Collation and Similar Work in the Direct Mail Industry," Oct. 13, 1966, 5, 3, in file "Record of Homework Order Governing Insertion, Collation, Labeling, and Similar Work."

45 Wolf to Ostrow, "Review of Direct Mail Industry Legislation," 2–3; "Investigation Report: Armstrong & Steward, Inc.," 2–2–62, file "Direct Mail Investigations."

46 "Home Work in Direct Mail Hit at State AFL-CIO Convention," *The 65er* 5 (Oct., 1965); George Ostrow, "Direct Mail Meeting-August 20, 1964," Aug. 20, 1964; Ostrow to Jerome Lefkowitz, "Application of Article 13 to Certain Direct Mail Homework Operations," July 15, 1964; Lefkowitz to Ostrow, "Application of Article 13 to Certain Direct Mail Homework Operations," Aug. 12, 1964; Ostrow to Administrative File, "Direct Mail," Jan. 11, 1965; "Order of Repeal," in file "Homework-Direct Mail."

18)." Meanwhile, during the summer and fall of 1965, the Division of Labor Standards investigated more Long Island firms employing from one to hundreds of homeworkers. About half performed both the exempted "primary" job of typing and the secondary one of collating.[47]

In these discussions, Arvan argued that the 1945 General Homework Order made such work illegal. But the draft order allowed for gradual elimination so as not to disrupt existing businesses, concerns without prior permits that the General Order was supposed to bar from homework. The draft gave relatively new firms a monopoly which, Arvan protested, "would mean potential raids on the customers and firms of our Association." District 65 equally was "shocked, enraged and disappointed."[48] The commissioner of labor refused to end collating homework outright, but the final order incorporated changes proposed by Arvan to eliminate homework competition from businesses who previously had done work "in-house."[49]

District 65 represented about three thousand workers in seventy-five printing and lettershops, of which sixty belonged to the DMMCA. After the 1953 amendment, homework had eliminated about five hundred typing jobs; its spread to mailing operations by 1966 had cost about a thousand additional factory jobs. Though confined mostly to hand operations, homework could disrupt plants since other aspects of the business would shift to homework firms. Its opponents feared that some competitors would use the legality of home typing as a loophole through which home inserting and collating would slip unless the administrative order was highly prohibitive. Homework proponents admitted that women often handwrote and nested "at the same time," questioning the logic of "bring[ing] back two-thirds or three-quarters of the operation from the women . . . into our plant to complete it." According to Arvan, proponents deliberately confused shortages of typists with a lack of labor for collating, which was plentiful even outside New York City.[50]

Most clerical homeworkers lived on Long Island; they were white ethnics with Italian or Jewish last names. Most inside mailing workers were Spanish-

---

[47] Ostrow, "Direct Mail," Feb. 24, 1966; Wolf to Ostrow, "Review of Direct Mail Industry Legislation," 3–5; Jerome Lefkowitz to Commissioner M. P. Catherwood, "Direct Mail-Homework Orders," Apr. 26, 1966, in file "Homework-Direct Mail."

[48] "Public Hearing on Proposed Homework Order," Oct. 23, 1966, 13–19, 39.

[49] Employers were to have at least five full-time employees working at the same kind of labor for at least thirty-five hours a week to qualify for a homework permit, ibid., 19–38; George Salvatore, "Report to the Industrial Commissioner on Proposed Homework Order Governing Inserting, Collating, Labelling, and Similar Work," Nov. 25, 1966; M. P. Catherwood, Industrial Commissioner, "Homework Order Governing Inserting, Collating, Labelling, and Similar Work," Nov. 30, 1966, Part 166 of Labor Law, Article 13, as amended by Chapter 505 of the Laws of 1966.

[50] "Public Hearing on Proposed Homework Order," 7, 39, 41; "We Endorse This Bill"; State of New York, DOL, "Public Hearing on Proposed Homework Order Governing Insertion, Collation and Similar Work in the Direct Mail Industry," Nov. 21, 1966, 140, 110, 99, 113, file "Record of Homework Order."

speaking and African American, located in and around New York City. Not only were the homeworkers suburban women, but Bernknopf pictured them – as Greenspan before him had – as not really needing the money. They "were not handicapped," whose need to work at home the union conceded. They "drove beautiful cars, many of them 1965 and 1966 models." In displacing the $2.17 an hour factory laborer or the $2.52 inserter machine operator, these $1.25 an hour homeworkers forced minority women out of factory jobs onto welfare, an observation confirmed by antipoverty workers. Union officials reminded government officials that by allowing homework to "steal" the "decent salaries under Union contracts and Union rates," they increased poverty.[51]

Ending homework, then, would contribute to both the War on Poverty and the civil rights crusade. This division of labor by race and sex did not merely pit urban women of color against suburban white women and breadwinners (female now as well as male) against female supplementers. For the union, pin money earners undermined female heads of households; in-plant hardship cases, those with "husbands or fathers in Vietnam," were just as needy as homeworkers who sought to supplement military pay.[52]

The employment profile of the industry reflected employer decisions but also a trade union that fought against discrimination. Union culture derived from the commitment to equality in the Communist party milieu. The union long had celebrated "Negro History Week," struggled for its African American and Puerto Rican members as well as its white ethnic ones, and had encouraged female leadership. Trade union dignity and racial pride merged; as Morris Doswell of the New York Chapter of A. Philip Randolph's Negro American Labor Congress explained, "This operation must be taken out of the slave market type operation that it is today ... so that the employees can enjoy dignity and self-respect." District 65 brought minority workers better wages and trade union benefits: sick leave, holiday pay, medical coverage, pensions. The proposed order would provide "an opportunity to get jobs in decent surroundings, where regulations are made, where Union standards and good pay and health conditions are established."[53]

Homework employers and their employees rejected union arguments. Those who relied on homeworkers during peak periods found the order too restrictive. Others pleaded for time to implement the order but questioned whether the Department of Labor had calculated its impact on employment. An employer of a hundred home inserters raised the specter of thousands of bankruptcies among one-person operations (which, if self-employed, actually would not come under

[51] Lists attached to "Investigation Report-Narration: Mailmen Inc.," 2/7/61, file "Direct Mail Variations"; "Public Hearing on Proposed Homework Order," 40–3, 10–11, 55, 69, 71–2; Livingston to Douglas.

[52] "Public Hearing on Proposed Homework Order," Nov. 21, 1966, 112, 114, 96.

[53] "Public Hearing on Proposed Homework Order," Oct. 13, 1966, 75; Fink and Greenberg, Upheaval in the Quiet Zone, passim; Frank Patten, "Negro History Report," Direct Mail Membership Meeting, box 25, folder 1, District 65 Papers.

the law) and the loss of business from New York to the lower-priced Chicago area. R. H. Loyer, manager of mail circulation sales for McGraw-Hill Publications, supported the administrative order, but undercut its reach by calling for "due attention . . . to demonstrated hardship cases" – businesses as well as homeworkers themselves, especially caretakers of dependent children and the elderly who could not come to the plants. Differing rules on typing and collating would generate an absurdity: The homeworker who typed a letter and then folded and inserted it into an envelope would, under the order, "only type the address and fill in the name unless she has a certificate." (State exemption of clerical work had encouraged use of home typists.) Unemployment came not from homework but from seasonality, competition from other advertising media, or individual loss of clients. Neglecting the unified structure of the industry, Loyer claimed that suburban homework never led to the loss of shop jobs.[54]

Employers assumed that women would not come into the plants. They argued, as did one from Long Island who polled his workers after the collating amendment, that few "even *thought* that they would be able to come into the plant and work for a couple of hours per day. The great majority turned us down flat." Women would not move inside for part-time labor similar to homework; perhaps better jobs would have encouraged them. These Long Island women were mothers of small children and caretakers of elderly relatives. Like a previous generation of homeworkers, they defended the site of their labor in familial terms. They were contributing to the family economy. With the specter of "narcotics" and juvenile delinquency haunting the nation, some justified homework as a solution to "unsupervised" children, even as trade unionists charged that home inserting led to illegal child labor. The health of the nation remained invested in its overburdened mothers who could "seek employment in order to maintain their homes" but not at the cost of children.[55] This midcentury formulation differed from earlier conceptions only in that the universe of women needing to work had expanded to include "the middle class" and not merely the beleaguered mothers of urban immigrant districts.

A work-at-home revolution?
Toward the electronic cottage

Two decades later, futurologists envisioned a work-at-home revolution. In the best-selling *The Third Wave* (1980), Alvin Toffler predicted "a return to cottage industry on a new, higher, electronic basis, and with it a new emphasis on the home as the center of society." The religious right supported home-work as part of its "family values" campaign, while the *New York Times* joined other media in heralding a trend: "Liberated by their computers and eager to

---

[54] Eustace W. Stewart to Judge George Salvatore, Oct. 18, 1966; Statement of Direct Mail of Suffolk, Patrick J. Doyle, manager; R. H. Loyer to Judge George Salvatore, Oct. 19, 1966, in file "Record of Homework Order."

[55] "Direct Mail of Suffolk"; Mrs. Catherine Ambrose to Whom It May Concern, Nov. 16, 1966;

increase the time they spend with their families, millions of Americans are finding that the most satisfying and productive work place is home." Telecommuting would mitigate the energy crisis by eliminating traffic jams and air pollution. It would move clerical work away from central cities, with their increasingly minority and undereducated but union-conscious population, to suburbs, with their better-educated and less-organizable labor force. It offered an electronic fix for the overwhelming numbers of mothers with small children in the paid labor force and alienated fathers who sought more time for their families.[56]

By 1988, more than 35 percent of homeworking households had a personal computer, twice the rate for the nation. Most telecommuters were managers and programmers who divided their time between home and office during a few well-publicized corporate experiments. Others appeared to be self-employed entrepreneurs or independent contractors. Sex and occupation shaped the meaning of home-based white-collar labor in the 1980s. Professionals, predominantly male, could gain a quiet place for creativity; for most clericals, overwhelmingly female, home-based labor meant reduced wages and increased stress.[57]

Homework, whether in its traditional industrial form or newer white-collar varieties, belonged to the structural shift to a contingent work force. As part of a corporate search for flexibility, downsizing, and general cost cutting,

Mrs. Anna Montalto to Dear Sir, Nov. 18, 1966; Mrs. Shirley Solomon to Judge Salvatore, Nov. 17, 1966; Mrs. H. Natalie to Dear Sir, Nov. 17, 1966; Mrs. Edna DeRosa to Dear Sir, Nov. 18, 1966; Mrs. M. Mohr to Dear Sirs, Nov. 17, 1966; Mrs. Deanna Corozzeli to Dear Sir, Nov. 17, 1966; Mrs. Barbara Ingrassia to Dear Sirs, Nov. 17, 1966; Mrs. Josephine Natale to Dear Sir, Nov. 17, 1966; William Sinnreich to Judge George Salvatore, Oct. 18, 1966; "Public Hearing on Proposed Homework Order," Nov. 21, 1966, 138, 146, 96, all in "Record of Homework Order"; James Gilbert, *A Cycle of Outrage* (New York: Oxford Univ. Press, 1988).

[56] Jack Niles of USC is said to have coined the term *telecommuting* during the 1970s energy crisis. Alvin Toffler, *The Third Wave* (New York: William Morrow and Company, 1980), 210; Tim LaHaye, *The Battle for the Family* (Old Tappan, N.J.: Fleming H. Revell Co., 1982), 240; Jonathan Friendly, "The Electronic Change: House Becomes Office," *New York Times*, May 15, 1986, C1; Cynthia Crossen, "No Place Like Home," *Wall Street Journal*, June 4, 1990, R6–10; "How Computers Create Paying Jobs at Home," *Computer Digest*, May/June 1983, 6; Erik Sandberg-Diment, "Bringing Home the Business," *Investment Vision: The Magazine for Fidelity's Investors*, Sept./Oct. 1989, 27–8, 47; Ellen Goodman, "America: Land of Moving Offices, Not to Mention Talking Buildings," *Daily Progress* (Charlottesville, Va.), Aug. 1, 1991, A4; Richard Perez-Pena, "For Traffic-Weary Workers, an Office That's a Long Way from the Office," *New York Times*, Jan. 7, 1992, A12; Barbara Baran, "The Technological Transformation of White-Collar Work: A Case Study of the Insurance Industry," in Heidi Hartmann, ed., *Computer Chips and Paper Clips: Technology and Women's Employment*, vol. 2 (Washington, D.C.: National Academy Press, 1987), 25–62.

[57] Kathleen Christensen, "Home-Based Clerical Work: No Simple Truth, No Single Reality," in *Homework: Historical and Contemporary Perspectives on Paid Labor at Home*, ed. Eileen Boris and Cynthia R. Daniels (Urbana: Univ. of Illinois Press, 1989), 185; Kathleen Christensen, ed., *The New Era of Home-Based Work: Directions and Policies* (Boulder, Colo.: Westview Press, 1988); Margrethe H. Olson, "Organizational Barriers to Professional Telework," in Boris and Daniels, eds, *Homework*, 213–30; Margaret Ambry, "At Home in the Office," *American Demographics* 10 (Dec. 1988), 61. For a study that mixes professional and clerical samples, Beverly Lozano, *The Invisible Workforce: Transforming American Business with Outside and Home-Based Workers* (New York: Free Press, 1989).

employers began to replace full-time "regular" employees with involuntary part-time, home, and contracted-out or temporary workers. Business services was the fastest growing sector for contingent work. Between 1980 and 1986, years of both concession bargaining and renewed debate over homework and its regulation, the number of contingent workers doubled to 17 percent of the labor force, Including voluntary part-timers, that percentage rose to a quarter of U.S. workers. Also growing was self-employment, particularly among women; 59 percent of all homeworkers considered themselves self-employed in 1979. With the number of unionized white-collar workers having jumped to 38.5 percent by 1985, homework appeared as a strategy to neutralize labor organization. Moreover, telecommuting promised increased productivity, with firms like New York Telephone offering seminars on the profitability of "Work at Home."[58]

The popular press rediscovered home labor as a solution to women's conflicting demands of family and career. *Redbook* advised its readers how to "Stay at Home and Work" and warned about "Work-at-Home Con Games – How to Spot a Shady Business," those envelope-stuffing schemes that promised quick returns on a small initial investment. The author of *Entrepreneurial Mothers* explained in 1984, "Women want control over their own lives. . . . They're frustrated and fed up with the inflexibility of 9-to-5 jobs and the conflicting needs of their families. We are not rejecting our work lives. We are simply redefining them on our terms." Just as independent contractor and employee status became confused, so the press conflated the home-based businesswoman with the homeworker in celebrating exemplary women who had "made it" at home. Articles mixed discussions of professional men and clerical women; both were "home-based."[59]

But like independent contractor status, self-employment in a period of unemployment could indicate precarious economic health as much as entre-

58 William Serrin, "Part-Time Work New Labor Trend," *New York Times*, July 9, 1986, A1, 14; Michael A. Pollack and Aaron Bernstein, "The Disposable Employee Is Becoming a Fact of Corporate Life," *Business Week*, Dec. 15, 1986, 52–4; Virginia duRivage and David Jacobs, "Home-Based Work: Labor's Choices," 260–1, and Hilary Silver, "The Demand for Homework: Evidence from the U.S. Census," 106–7, both in Boris and Daniels, eds., *Homework*; Peter A. Susser, "Modern Office Technology and Employee Relations," *Employment Relations Today* 15 (Spring 1988): 16–17; Eileen Appelbaum, "Restructuring Work: Temporary, Part-Time, and At-Home Employment," in Hartmann, ed., *Computer Chips and Paper Clips*, 268–310; Leslie Stackel, "The Flexible Work Place," *Employment Relations Today* 14 (Summer 1987), 189–97; Andrew Pollack, "Rising Trend of Computer Age: Employees Who Work at Home," *New York Times*, Mar. 12, 1981, A1, 32; "How to Increase Employee Productivity Through Work at Home," advertisement, ibid., Oct. 9, 1983, F23; Joani Nelson-Horchler, "Sending Employees Home to Work," *Industry Week* 219 (Oct. 17, 1983), 80; Marcia M. Kelly, "The Work-at-Home Revolution," *The Futurist* 22 (Nov.–Dec. 1988): 30.
59 Barbara Lovenheim, "Stay at Home and Work," *Redbook* 162 (Mar. 1984), 75, 77, 150; Patricia O'Toole, "Work-at-Home Con Games – How to Spot a Shady Business," ibid, 162 (Feb, 1984), 14; Sarah Ban Breathnach, "Trends: Mothers and Others of Invention," *Washington Post*, July 16, 1984, B5; "Home for Work," *Executive Female* 10 (Sept./Oct. 1987), 56; David E. Gumpert, "Doing a Little Business on the Side," *Working Woman* 11 (Oct. 1986), 41–5; Tamara H. Wolfgram, "Working at Home: The Growth of Cottage Industry," *The Futurist* 18 (June 1984), 31–4; Joel Schwarz, "Terminal Loneliness," *American Way*, Dec. 24,

preneurial adventuresomeness. As one expert put it, "Women have always had these kinds of jobs." Coralee Smith Kern established the National Association for the Cottage Industry; she preached, "working at home is a real movement that is as significant as the civil-rights, women's, and disabled movements." Paul and Sarah Edwards wrote a *Complete Start-Up Kit for a Home Business with Your Computer* as part of a new generation of advice books and founded the Association of Electronic Cottagers. The National Alliance of Homebased Businesswomen grew to fourteen hundred members representing a wide – and at times inventive – range of services and products, whose founder promoted homework for fostering "economic and social independence" and "a close family structure" not available under "conventional work modes." Yet women also had the least resources. During a recession when many middle managers were laid off, women-owned businesses were the least capitalized and the most without additional employees. At the same time that middle-class mothers were finding it difficult to secure adequate employment, conservatives proposed turning welfare mothers into home businesswomen to provide them lessons in independence and economics while taking them off the dole.[60]

Determining the precise number of such workers, as in the past, proved difficult. By 1988, about 350 companies had adopted some telecommuting, defined as "working at home or at a satellite office and communicating with the home office or plant by phone, usually with a computer or terminal." These were "information-intensive" or "information processing" firms, in banking, insurance, financial services, market research, data analysis, and telemarketing. Among the largest corporations were IBM, Mountain Bell, J C Penney, Travelers Insurance Company, Control Data, Continental Illinois National Bank, American Express, Manufacturers Hanover Trust, and Blue Cross and Blue Shield. Washington State, Los Angeles County, Wisconsin, California, and the federal government also began allowing some employees to work at home. Few programs went beyond a hundred workers, many had only a handful.[61]

Of the largest companies with homework options, U.S. West involved 300 to 600 nonunionized and managerial workers and Pacific Bell encompassed

1985, 41–5; Janet Rohan, "Options: Expanding the Office and Staying at Home," *Washington Post*, Feb. 26, 1991, B5; Cynthia R. Daniels, "There's No Place Like Home: The Politics of Home-Based Work," *Dollars and Sense*, Dec. 1986, 16–17.

60 Serrin, "Part-Time Work New Labor Trend," A14; Schwarz, "Terminal Loneliness," 41–2; "AEC: The Association of Electronic Cottagers," pamphlet in author's possession; Breathnach, "Trends: Mothers and Others of Invention"; testimony of Marion R. Behr, in "Pros and Cons of Home-Based Clerical Work," *Hearing Before a Subcommittee of the Committee on Government Operations,* House of Repesentatives, 99th Cong., 2nd sess., Feb. 26, 1986 (Washington, D.C.: GPO, 1986), 10–18, esp. 11; Silver, "The Demand for Homework," 109.

61 Jonathan N. Goodrich, "Telecommuting in America," *Business Horizons* 33 (July–Aug. 1990), 31–2; ILO, "Telework," *Conditions of Work Digest* 9, 1/1990, 49–97; Mike Causey, "The Federal Diary: Homework Redefined," *Washington Post*, Dec. 22, 1990 F2.

between 500 to 1,000 managers at remote work sites; most of the women were unmarried professionals. Only 4 percent of the participants in the state of California's pilot project (230 workers) were clerical or secretarial. Reducing commuting time was a major goal of this program, as was the one initiated by Los Angeles County. Nonetheless, an evaluative team described the program as "very useful for retaining the services of mothers during maternity leave, as well as keeping or attracting employees with scarce expertise or talents." Travelers Insurance, which also was among those companies sending work "off-shore" to Ireland and the Caribbean, employed 200 home data processors – equally divided by sex. A number of programs aided the disabled, most notably American Express's Project Homebound, established in part to overcome the cost of office space in New York City. The University of Wisconsin's Hospital and Clinics entered into a collective bargaining agreement with American Federation of State, County, and Municipal Employees Local 2412 in 1984 to allow a small number of medical transcriptionists to work from home, with the employer supplying equipment and providing the same pay. Like many other small programs, it sought to tap a labor force of homebound women as well as utilize specialized skills. IBM instituted homework arrangements as part of its extended leave program "to help its employees balance the pressures of work and home life." But of the 2,500, mostly female, employees on leave, only a small number took advantage of the homework option in 1988.[62]

Some corporate pilot studies developed to retain skilled employees. Besides improving productivity and increasing staffing flexibility and cost control, these hoped to improve employee retention and save office space. Managerial style was crucial to success, but not all businessmen advocated homework. A "Guest Opinion" in *Office Administration and Automation* contended, "A company can't teach its values through a computer terminal . . . teamwork, commitment to quality, and creativity are best transmitted through a personal link between management and employees." The nature of the work determined whether managers felt comfortable with remote employees. Along with insurance examiners and other clerical work, one manager proclaimed, "The task of auditing and managing . . . is simplified by having all their work instantly accessible in the home office via the computer system." Such electronic monitoring could lead to the electronic sweatshop. Other business writers claimed that workers needed to be brought periodi-

---

[62] *Office Workstations in the Home* (Washington, D.C.: National Academy Press, 1985); Robin Leidner, "Home Work: A Study in the Interaction of Work and Family Organization," *Research in the Sociology of Work* 4 (New York: JAI Press, 1988), 69–94; ILO, "Telework," 51, 64, 57–9, 52–7, 62, 11–12, 118–21, 95–7, 126–7; Frank Swoboda, "IBM Sets Flexible Work Rules to Ease Home, Office Strains," *Washington Post*, Oct. 19, 1988, A1,17; duRivage and Jacobs, "Home-based Work: Labor's Choices," 266–7; Office of Technology Assessment, *Automation of America's Offices* (Washington, D.C.: GPO, Dec. 1985), 211–30.

cally to the office for lessons in corporate culture, socializing, training, and group work.[63]

The extent of homework remained unknown, as surveys continued to differ in design and definition. Studies commissioned by companies with products or services to sell the homebound tended to count anyone, no matter their employment status, who worked any amount of time at home. A 1982 AT&T marketing survey came up with twenty-three million undertaking some paid employment at home. Others tried to delineate their sample in a more precise manner. Estimates from the 1980 census, based on the journey-to-work question, revealed a drop in the percentage of nonfarm, civilian labor force working at home for a primary employer from 3.2 percent in 1960 to 1.6 percent in 1980. During that decade, nonfarm homework rose slightly, but overall numbers "held steady." In 1991, one estimate put the actual number of telecommuters at five million. A Current Population Survey (CPS) that May concluded that 18.3 percent of the labor force performed some work for their primary employer at home, but only a fraction of employees received pay for such home labor. By 1992, one estimate counted some 6.6 million telecommuters, a 20 percent increase from the previous year.[64]

Race, gender, and kinship continued to shape the homework system within the structures of economic life. In 1991 women tended to perform all their wage labor at home twice as often as men; they composed more than half of all employees. Although men predominated among self-employed homeworkers, women still possessed a higher "work-at-home" rate (59 percent to 44 percent). A decade before, "primary" homeworkers, both the self-employed and employees, tended to be female, part-time, older, more rural, and "to have a work-limiting or transportation-limiting disability." Having access to another income also increased the odds of working at home. Where once husbands of homeworkers were casual laborers, in recent times they have held more conventional employment that brought the family health care and other

[63] Kelly, "The Work-at-Home-Revolution," 28–31; David Redmong, "Guest Opinion," *Office Administration and Automation* 45 (June 1984), 108; Patricia Mortenson, "Telecommuting: The Company Perspective," *Best's Review Property-Casualty Edition* (Nov. 1983), 114; William Atkinson, "Home/Work," *Personnel Journal* 64 (Nov. 1985), 105–9. On computer monitoring, Susser, "Modern Office Technology and Employee Relations," 9–14.

[64] Robert E. Kraut, "Telecommuting: The Trade-Offs of Home Work," *Journal of Communication* 39 (Summer 1989): 20–3; Kathleen E. Christensen, "Introduction: White-Collar Home-Based Work – The Changing U.S. Economy and Family," in Christensen, ed., *The New Era*, 5–6; Hilary Silver, "The Demand for Homework: Evidence from the U.S. Census," 109–10; Ambry, "At Home in the Office," 31–3, 61; Goodman, "America: Land of Moving Offices"; U.S.DOL, "Employed Persons Who Work at Home," press release, Oct. 8, 1992, table 3. Reflecting the overall problem with data, this study asked different questions and used other definitions than Francis W. Horvath, "Work at Home: New Findings from the Current Population Survey," *Monthly Labor Review* 109 (Nov. 1986), 34, which found 16 percent of the labor force working at home for a primary employer in 1985; Robert E. Calem, "Working at Home, for Better or Worse," *New York Times*, Apr. 18, 1993, sec. 3, p. 1.

benefits. Marriage increased the probability of homework for "nonblack" women but decreased it for black women whose men generally earned less; living with children also increased the probability of such labor, but only if the woman was married. Homeworkers were conscious of such demographic perimeters; as one put it, "If you were single or a single parent working at home, no benefits and not having a dependable paycheck would be hard."[65]

In the mid-1980s, three times as many women than men with preschool children performed paid labor at home for at least thirty-five hours a week. Their labor occurred in a context in which 50 percent of women with preschool children were in the labor force. Women still seemed to come to homework because of their responsibility for dependent care and domestic labor. As with industrial homework, cost-saving employers sought the "homebound," those with few employment options.[66]

Insurance companies took advantage of the lack of affordable childcare to retain employees without raising the total wage package or contributing to providing caretaking services. A North Carolina insurance firm countered employee demands for in-house childcare with a work-at-home program; managers at this and other companies believed that homework could effectively "substitute" for day-care. In 1985, New York Life Insurance Company contracted with about twenty former programmers who had left to have children. Declared one of these women: "I want to spend as much time as possible with my child, and not having to commute gives me extra time. . . . If the baby is sick . . . I can easily change my schedule, and that's something that is important to me." But, unlike home clerical workers who would try simultaneously to care for children and fill out claims, she turned on her computer "when the sitter arrives or when my husband is at home, on Saturdays."[67]

As most academic studies concluded by the end of the decade, although homework could make it easier to combine paid labor and family obligations, it was no substitute for childcare. In contrast to the enhanced feelings of autonomy and integration reported by both homeworking women and men "without primary child care responsibilities," mothers experienced more stress

[65] U.S. DOL, "Employed Persons Who Work at Home," 1–2; Kraut, "Telecommuting: The Trade-Offs of Home Work," 23–31; Robert E. Kraut, "Homework: What Is It and Who Does It?," in Christensen, ed., *New Era*, 30–48; R. E. Kraut and Patricia Grambsch, "Home-Based, White-Collar Work: Lessons from the 1980 Census," *Social Forces* 66 (1988), 410–26; Kathleen Christensen, "Impacts of Computer-Mediated Home-Based Work on Women and Their Families," Center for Human Developments, The Graduate School and University Center of the City University of New York, June 1985, 25.

[66] Horvath, "Work at Home," 34; "Labor Force and Employment Experience of Women with Young Children, 1960 and 1986," in Sara E. Rix, ed., *The American Woman, 1988–89: A Status Report* (New York: Norton, 1988), fig. 11, 375; Robin Leidner, "Home Work," 77–9.

[67] Kathleen Christensen, *Women and Home-based Work: The Unspoken Contract* (New York: Henry Holt and Co., 1987), 165; Katya Goncharoff, "Telecommuters Say There's No Workplace Like Home," *New York Times*, Mar. 24, 1985, sec. 12, pp. 35–6.

when they tried to combine paid work and child minding. Travelers Insurance, for one, rejected "telework to be ... a substitute for child care." A Wisconsin mother reported her coping strategy: "When I get the claims at night, I try to put in an hour while the kids are watching t.v. Then I get up at 4:30 A.M. to work before the kids get up. It all depends on what the kids are doing. . . . During the day, I turn on the t.v. and tell my preschooler to watch. . . . Then, when she takes a nap, I can work." A Massachusetts claims processor, who worked on her dining room table, complained, "It didn't take long before things began to unravel: The children were at her elbow every minute demanding a tissue or a cookie or fighting with each other." Gil Gordon, management consultant and editor of the *Telecommuting Review*, explained, "The great myth is that someone can sit there with a keyboard in one hand and the baby in the other."[68]

Yet some advocates of clerical homework projected that image. The Lanier Company advertised its "telestaffing" system by picturing a baby in a playpen overlooking its mother at her terminal; the cover of the October 1984 issue of the libertarian monthly *reason* featured a woman at a computer and her toddler nearby, with the headline, "Electronic Sweatshop? The Strange Opposition to Telecommuting," as if such a portrait of mother and child could be confused with a sweatshop. So did *Across the Board*, the journal of the Conference Board, in April 1987. Certainly this image attracted many self-selected home clericals. These viewed themselves as mothers first; three out of four in one major survey undertook nearly all of the housework as well. These women accepted conventional definitions of womanhood but often found that economic circumstances – the inadequate earnings of spouses – necessitated a shift, though some were angry. One Italian American woman explained: "Just being a housewife is not supposed to be enough, you know? We're expected to take care of the family, run the house, and hold a job." Yet she accepted "low pay, boring work, no opportunities for advancement, and no benefits," because "I get to stay home with my daughter" and somehow working at home seemed easier than having to return to cook dinner after a full day at the office.[69]

Others were more sanguine. "When I found out I was pregnant, I wanted

[68] ILO, "Telework," 62; Cynthia B. Costello, "The Clerical Homework Program at the Wisconsin Physicians Services Insurance Corporation," in Boris and Daniels, eds., *Homework*, 205; Marjorie Howard, "Home Work: Escape from Office Means Stress Can Hit You Where You Live," *Boston Herald*, Jan. 29, 1989, A24; Alex Kotlowitz, "Working at Home While Caring for a Child Sounds Fine – in Theory," *Wall Street Journal*, Mar. 30, 1987, sec. 2, p. 21; for academic studies, Margrethe H. Olson and Sophia B. Primps, "Working at Home with Computers: Work and Nonwork Issues," *Journal of Social Issues* 40, no. 3, 108–9; Margrethe Olson, "The Potential of Remote Work for Professionals," 129–30; Judith Gregory, "Clerical Workers and New Office Technologies," 113–14, both in *Office Workstations in the Home*.

[69] Lanier advertisement described in Gregory, "Clerical Workers and New Office Technologies," 113; cover, *reason*, Oct. 1984; cover, *Across the Board*, 24, Apr. 1987; Christensen, *Women and Home-based Work*, 7–38.

the job as a 'cottage coder' because I wanted to raise my kids myself and be home with them," admitted Cindy Coombs, one of fourteen women married to in-plant employees, who keyed insurance forms at home for Blue Cross and Blue Shield of South Carolina. "When my son David took his first steps, I didn't want to hear about it from someone else." Her manager claimed that "day-care expenses 'put a hole in your pocketbook . . . it's a definite benefit to work at home.' " But was it? Consider the routine of Ann Blackwell, who after waking at 6 A.M., turned on the terminal in her den to transmit yesterday's work to a computer in Blue Cross's office. "A few hours later, having seen her children [aged 7 and 13] off to school and cleared the breakfast dishes, she returns to the terminal. . . . With breaks for household chores and lunch, she remains at the keyboard until it is time to prepare dinner." Averaging a fifty-hour week, working at night when behind her quota, she finished about two thousand claims a week to net only a hundred dollars after deductions. Her "work is boring and lonely, but she likes not having to get dressed up and drive to an office." It provided flexibility, but she admitted, "You've got to discipline yourself."[70]

Cottage Keyers, as Blue Cross called homeworkers like Ann Blackwell, sweated themselves. They had to lease a machine from the company for twenty-five hundred dollars a year, pay for paper, and become a part-time employee, that is, ineligible for health benefits. After subtracting benefits that went to in-office employees and the leasing fee, they reportedly earned more per year than in-office counterparts. Productivity jacked up earnings in a piece-rate payment system that required a minimum of fifteen hundred claims processed per week.[71]

Although not as poorly paid as garment homeworkers, home clericals still engaged in a self-monitored speedup and found themselves subsidizing the employer's overhead cost. "At home, you are always under pressure," one New York City home typist explained, "There is always a time limit to the work, plus if you don't type, you are just not paid for it. There is absolutely no pay for the time you have to collate, staple, count, put together all your work you have typed, or for the time you spend making your tally sheets or inventory forms." According to one labor educator, "Telecommuting . . . could leave the drudgery of work intact, but remove all that was pleasurable about work – seeing other people."[72]

[70] David Rubins, "Telecommuting: Will the Plug Be Pulled?" *reason*, Oct. 1984, 26; Kotlowitz, "Working at Home While Caring for a Child"; Greg Geisler, "Blue Cross/Blue Shield of South Carolina: Program for Clerical Workers," in *Office Workstations in the Home*, 20; Philip Mattera, "High-Tech Cottage Industry: Home Computer Sweatshops," *The Nation* 236 (Apr. 2, 1983), 390.

[71] Geisler, "Blue Cross/Blue Shield of South Carolina," 21–2.

[72] "Statement of Mary Dworjan," "Pros and Cons of Home-Based Clerical Work," 38; Richard Moore and Elizabeth Marsis, "Telecommuting: Sweatshop at Home Sweet Home?," *In These Times* (Apr. 18–24, 1984), 13.

Independent contractor arrangements offered possibilities for abuse. In 1981, California Western States Life Insurance Company presented claims processors with the option to work at home; such workers could gain flexibility, spend more time with their children, and avoid commuting, clothing, and childcare expenses. Cal Western planned to save on hourly wages and fringe benefits, which could amount to up to 40 percent of the pay package. One manager explained, "The average at-home claims examiner represents more than $1,000 in reduced costs to the company each month." Nearly four years later, about a third of the women (eight in all) quit, taking the company to court for $250,000 in back benefits and at least $1 million in punitive damages. They charged fraud, arguing that the independent contractor contract was merely a "subterfuge" to maneuver around benefits. Needing to work as much as fifteen hours a day to meet company quotas, with mainframe overload causing delays, and additional procedures adding to workloads, the women explained, "You had less freedom when you went home." One "said her daughter would stand outside her workroom and ask, 'Mommy, are you going to be done tonight before I go to bed?' " Although earning more than office employees (between $15,000 and $20,000 compared to $14,000 to $16,000 a year) on a piece rate of 90 cents per claim, they worked without paid vacation, sick leave, health insurance, and contribution to Social Security. They leased terminals from the company. These women really were not independent contractors; as their attorney asserted, "The company imposed so many stipulations on the women. . . . They had no time to work for anyone else and were constantly being issued commands for changes in procedures and could only work when the company computer was in operation." This constant supervision undermined the independent contractor designation; so did the company's right to discharge the worker at will. In January 1988, Cal Western terminated its telework program and settled out of court the following May.[73]

Independent contractor status served as a rubric to circumvent FLSA from the start. The 1985 *Donovan v. DialAmerica Marketing Inc.*, a case against a telemarketing firm, reinforced previous broad interpretations of employee. The district court had found for the defendants on the basis that the firm "exercised little control" over its home researchers who combed telephone directories for phone numbers. But this court also shaped its decision on the basis of a gendered negation of a woman's right to earn, no matter her family status. It misinterpreted worker dependence on continued employment as economic dependency. As the U.S. Court of Appeals for the Third Circuit

73 Christensen, "A Hard Day's Work in the Electronic Cottage," *Across the Board* 24 (Apr. 1987), 20; Andrew Pollack, "Home-Based Work Stirs Suit," *New York Times*, May 26, 1986, A27–8; "Statement of Roderick MacKenzie, Attorney, Sacramento, Ca., Representing Home-Based Clerical Workers," in "Pros and Cons of Home-Based Clerical Work," 68–82; Mortenson, "Telecommuting," 114; ILO, "Telework," 23.

summarized the district court's argument: "The court found that the home researchers were not economically dependent on DialAmerica because, for
most of them, the money they earned from DialAmerica was not the primary
source of family income, but merely 'pocket money.' " The company asserted
control of its researchers based on their gender and status as mothers by
demanding that they not wear shorts to the office while picking up or
delivering index cards and by scheduling appointments for such transactions
to reduce the numbers of children (who accompanied mothers) on company
premises. Such reasoning reflected the continued devaluation of homeworking
mothers.[74]

But not all home-based programs differentiated between home and office
workers. To meet fluctuating sales orders, J.C. Penney instituted a telemarketing
program in 1981. It employed homeworkers in Atlanta, Milwaukee, and Columbus, Ohio, where the company then had its telephone sales centers. Receiving
the same pay and benefits as office staff, homeworkers were eligible for
promotion. The company paid for terminals and telephone costs; it checked to
insure that the worker had "an appropriate work space – about 35 square feet,
off the beaten path of home traffic." The homework program benefited Penney
in numerous ways: It made available a new pool of workers, saved on building
new phone centers, and may have promoted long-term consumer confidence.
"The associates 'feel more of a one-to-one relationship with the customer than
they would feel in a phone center. . . . They feel a little more emotionally
responsible because they are alone and not surrounded by 200 or 300 people
and all the noise they would have if they were in a phone center,' " one
manager revealed. Such "emotion" work could add to employee stress. Yet the
"associates," who numbered over two hundred by 1990 and belonged to half of
the company's marketing centers, "love it because they have more time with
their families," management claimed.[75]

But women understood the disadvantages of clerical homework. Before a
government subcommittee, one testified: "You never see anyone except for
family." People failed "to take you seriously," thinking that you really were not
working. The hours were longer: "You just cannot leave 'it at the office.' You
are in your office, even though it is separated from the rest of your home."
Physical injury ("back, neck and shoulder problems") plagued them. "There is
no time at all to slow down or 'goof off.' " Missing the culture of the office, as
well as its benefits, she concluded, "There is no comparison to any outside
job." For most home clericals, though, the choice was not between outside
work and homework; the choice was between home or no work. In that
context, homework appeared better than no income at all. As one researcher
concluded, such "women represent a vulnerable labor pool; they are hungry to

---

[74] *Donovan v. DialAmerica Marketing, Inc.*, 757 F2d 1376, 1363 (3d cir. 1985).
[75] Kathleen Christensen, "A Hard Day's Work in the Electronic Cottage," 23; ILO, "Telework," 82; "At J. C. Penney, It's Home Sweet Home Work," *Management Review* 73 (Nov.
1984), 20–1.

work, and they are apt to take well below market rates for the opportunity to earn a little extra cash and feel productive."[76]

Part-time homeworkers could threaten office counterparts. The Wisconsin Physicians Services Insurance Corporation (WPS) of Madison hired homeworkers to type, code, and adjust claims. The program began in 1980, a year after the company signed – under threat of a strike – a contract with Local 1444 of the United Food and Commercial Workers that established a union shop for the full-time clerical staff. The homeworkers were part-timers, not under the contract. One former manager admitted that they strove to eliminate union "staff without having to go through all the hassles with the union. . . . One of the things you face in a union setting is the possibility of a strike or a work stoppage . . . you run into problems if people are picketing. . . . [The company] did have a plan in mind if that ever did happen and the homeworkers were part of that plan." A homeworker explained, "They are getting homeworkers to do the work that they have to pay union workers more money for and they are getting cheap labor." By 1985, there were 150 homeworkers; most earned $4 an hour, with pay dependent upon productivity; yearly income averaged $2,380. Although workers could choose their own hours, they had to be home for the company distribution truck between 4 and 7 P.M.[77]

In this college town, WPS deliberately hired middle-class,[78] educated women with small children to "provide meaningful, gainful employment for the homebound." Managers felt, "Married women didn't need the benefits. Mostly women were looking for a second income or something to do; they were bored. . . . They did not need the money." Although most entered the WPS program to stay home with children, many became disillusioned with homework. These reported the attempt to combine mothering with claims processing as stressful. They resented having to wait around for the company truck. The work was often frustrating, with supervisors unavailable and procedural changes inadequately explained. Even at its best, "once you get it . . . it is like a factory or assembly line," one woman declared. Although homeworkers created informal work networks (many knew each other and others met during initial in-office training), they could use networks to support and aid each other but not to influence the company. Individual acts

---

[76] Dworjan, "Pros and Cons of Home-Based Clerical Work," 42–3; Christensen, "Impacts of Computer-Mediated Home-Based Work on Women and Their Families," 13, 35.

[77] Costello, "The Clerical Homework Program at the Wisconsin Physicians Services Insurance Corporation," 198–200, 208; duRivage and Jacobs, "Home-Based Work: Labor's Choices," 262; Cynthia B. Costello, "Clerical Home-Based Work: A Case Study of Work and Family," in Christensen, ed., *The New Era of Home-Based Work*, 135–45; Cythia B. Costello, "The Office Homework Program at the Wisconsin Physicians Service Insurance Company," Appendix, "Pros and Cons of Home-Based Clerical Work," 121–2.

[78] Mean family income ranged from $12,000 to $50,000, with the average at $29,600. Costello, "The Office Homework Program at the Wisconsin Physicians Service Insurance Company," 126.

of resistance prevailed. Some disobeyed company mandates and took other part-time jobs. Others rejected the irregular flow of work by making their own hours, determining how many claims to process daily, and shortening procedures. Still others quit. Management did everything it could to block the union from contacting homeworkers. Physical isolation and employee turn-over further impeded union efforts.[79]

The promise of white-collar home-based labor generated congressional activity. In 1983, Republican Newt Gingrich (Ga.), then a New Right upstart, introduced the Family Opportunity Act to provide tax credits to families that purchased home computers for business or educational purposes. It would "allow working mothers with pre-school children to earn a living while staying at home." The *Wall Street Journal* responded to fears of increased child labor with the claim: "Working on computers at home surely is not going to produce a generation of dullards; more likely, it will spawn a generation of whiz kids and would-be millionaires."[80]

Three years later, the Employment and Housing Subcommittee of the House of Representatives Committee on Government Operations, under the liberal Democrat Barney Frank (Mass.), investigated "the pros and cons of home-base clerical work." Citing inadequate wages and benefits, health and safety problems, and inappropriate use as childcare, Jackie Ruff of District 925, the Clerical Division of the Service Employees International Union, argued "for an early ban on clerical homework." With Conservative Howard Nielson (R.-Utah) charging that such a ban would "deprive" mothers of "a chance to combine motherhood and . . . outside income," this hearing encompassed both the political polarities and the definitional confusion over employee status besetting discussions of white-collar home-based labor. Liberals seemed inclined to find a middle ground. Frank's committee called for insuring that the cover of "protective legislation" fell on "those who choose or are compelled to give priority attention to family obligations by working at home." The committee recommended amending the law "to remove the financial incentive for employers to treat their off-site workers as contractors."[81] This discussion over the merits of white-collar homework occurred in the midst of a regulatory maelstrom: a challenge to those prohibitions against industrial homework incorporated into FLSA forty years before that was both an assault on the New Deal order and a pre- ventive strike against any restriction on telecommuting.

[79] Costello, "The Clerical Homework Program at the Wisconsin Physicians Services Insurance Corporation," 206–13.

[80] Gingrich in Mattera, "High-Tech Cottage Industry," 392; "No Workplace Like Home," *Wall Street Journal*, Feb. 23, 1984, sect. 1, 28.

[81] "The Pros and Cons of Home-Based Clerical Work," 87–96, 102; "Home-Based Clerical Workers: Are They Victims of Exploitation?" *Thirty-Ninth Report by the Committee on Government Operations Together with Additional Views* (Washington, D.C.: GPO, 1986).

11

Deregulating
"the rights of women"

Picture Mrs. Audrey Pudvah as the *New York Times* described her in March 1981, "working at her knitting machine in a quiet room looking out on snow covered fields, tall trees, and craggy hills." While earning nearly four dollars an hour, more than the minimum wage, she also "can keep an eye on her two young children and keep the woodburning stove stoked and the house spotless." Mrs. Pudvah's knitting, however, was illegal. It violated the 1942 Fair Labor Standards Act (FLSA) ruling that banned industrial homework in knitted outerwear. Yet she claimed not to "feel the least bit exploited . . . she thinks that her job knitting ski hats in her own pleasant log home at her own pace is a pretty good deal."[1]

In the early 1980s, the plight of Audrey Pudvah and other New England knitters became a cause célèbre among free market conservatives who argued for lifting the homework ban because it deprived workers of their constitutional "right to work." For the administration of Ronald Reagan, ending the ban fitted nicely into plans to deregulate the economy.[2] But Audrey Pudvah offered herself another set of reasons for homework: "All the time the Government says to be more family-oriented and spend time with your children and to save energy," she explained. "That's what I am doing. I don't have money for an extra vehicle, extra clothes, or for baby sitters that I would need to go out to work."[3] Given her responsibilities for children and household, given the low wages available to women in the workplace, homework made sense.

Whereas the media portrayed the Vermont knitters as mothers challenging the Goliath of Big Government, these homeworkers projected themselves as craftswomen, "worksteaders," and pioneers of "the American cottage industry" who also cared for children and tended wood furnances. Though they saw themselves as independent producers, they actually were employees. Their fight to knit ski caps and sweaters at home began in the partisan preelection atmosphere of 1980 as a routine Labor Department suit against homework wage and hour violations. With the shift to a Republican administration,

[1] Philip Shabecoff, "Dispute Rises on Working at Home for Pay," *New York Times*, March 10, 1981, A1.
[2] Zillah Eisenstein, *Feminism and Sexual Equality: Crisis in Liberal America* (New York: Monthly Review Press, 1984).
[3] Shabecoff, "Dispute Rises on Working at Home for Pay," A1.

Figure 19. Jeff Danziger, "Throw Out Your Knitting Needles," cartoon, ca. 1980, used with permission of the artist. The 1980 Wage and Hour case against home knitters in Vermont generated intense public controversy. This cartoon captures what appeared, in the context of the times, to be governmental overreaction.

hearings on the issue expanded to consider the continued necessity for homework regulation. Initially Secretary of Labor Raymond Donovan attempted to end all seven bans in May 1981, but after a four-year battle with the International Ladies' Garment Workers Union (ILGWU), the Department of Labor (DOL) rescinded only the rule prohibiting industrial homework in knitted outerwear.[4]

---

[4] DOL instituted an employer certification program for knitted outerwear in Dec. 1984 to comply with FLSA. This analysis is based on an extensive reading of the public record, including written comments and unpublished testimony, housed in the Division of Labor Standards, Office of Special Minimum Wage, DOL, Washington, D.C. *Daily Labor Report*, Feb. 18, 1981, A11–13, and July 4, 1981, F21; Brief for the Appellees, *International Ladies' Garment Workers Union et al. v. Raymond J. Donovan et al.*, in the U.S. Court of Appeals for the District of Columbia Circuit (no. 82–2133), 3–21; Brief for Appellants, ibid., 4–33; *Daily Labor Report*, Nov. 30, 1983, A1, 9–10, and D1 ff.; "Court Reinstates Federal Rules Affecting 'Industrial' Home Work," *New York Times*, Nov. 30, 1983, A25; U.S. DOL, Employment Standards Administration, Wage and Hour Division, 29 CFR Part 530, "Employment of Homeworkers in Certain Industries: Final Rule," *Federal Register* 49, n. 215, pt. 2, Monday, Nov. 5, 1984, 44262–72.

During the mid-1980s, political opposition delayed the DOL from eliminating other prohibitions; it proposed to keep the ban on only hazardous processes in jewelry and women's apparel – an industry with the most homework (nearly a quarter of its work force)[5] and strongest union. Joined by the Amalgamated Clothing and Textile Workers, Service Employees International Union, the states of New York and Illinois, and some employer associations, the ILGWU continued to challenge the government in court. In December 1989, the U.S. District Court of the District of Columbia sustained the government. According to the Administrative Procedure Act, the DOL had made a "reasoned decision, based on the record, that a certification system would be superior to a total homework ban in enforcing" FLSA.[6]

Washington insiders had expected DOL to lift the remaining bans, but the defeat of George Bush in the 1992 election stopped the Reaganite war against labor standards. Although deregulation had emerged as a major strategy to fight the recession of the early nineties, homework was no longer front page news. In a period of heightened economic crisis, it became a "life style" choice; its regulation had returned to the administrative state and the union contract.[7]

This 1980s debate questioned the exploitative nature of home labor and the "fairness" of labor standards legislation toward women – both assumptions underlying homework prohibition. From the perspective of the knitters, the regulatory state seemed to ignore women's dual role as family nurturers and wage earners in its attempt to protect workers from homework. Whether seen as a potential welfare recipient, a harried half of a dual earner couple, an isolated farmwife, or a victimized immigrant, mothers remained both the subjects of this debate and the objects of policy-making. The deregulation campaign reflected national tension over the issue of mothers and paid labor as well as ideological disagreements over the role of the state in the economy, the relationship between family and wage earning, and the feminist challenge to the sex segmentation of social life. Deregulators emphasized the lack of freedom under homework rules; for defenders of the bans, homeworkers became victims of the marketplace rather than the state.

The debate over industrial homework appeared to have only two sides: rescind the 1940s prohibitions against homework in the garment-related

---

[5] "Testimony of Jay Mazur," Hearings on Industrial Homework in the Women's Apparel Industry, New York City, Mar. 29, 1989, from the ILGWU.

[6] "ILGWU Sues to Prevent DOL from Lifting Homework Ban," "Text: Complaint Filed in ILGWU v. McLaughlin," *Daily Labor Report*, Jan. 6, 1989, A1, 8–9, E1–7; "DOL's Homework Action Survives Legal Scrutiny," ibid., Dec. 12, 1989, 1–2, A12–13, F1–6; "Industrial Homework Chronology," xerox from the ILGWU.

[7] In early 1992 *Business Week* predicted, "The last vestige of Depression-era rules regulating the cottage industry in apparel is about to be abandoned." Such a denouement measured "the waning clout of unions." *Business Week* failed to account for the changing politics of the election campaign. Conversations with interested parties in DOL, Dec. 1989; "Capital Wrap-up: Homework," *Business Week*, Feb. 17, 1992, 49.

industries or maintain them. Despite the "prohibitions," homework in most
industries remained legal as long as employers complied with the wage, hour,
child labor, and record-keeping provisions of FLSA. Homework opponents
questioned the effectiveness of regulation since the Wage and Hour Administration lacked the funds needed to enforce certification and record-keeping
systems of employers. It had always been impossible to monitor whether
homeworkers received fair piece rates. No one questioned the strategy of the
1930s – require employers to pay homeworkers minimum wages and undermine the cost-cutting advantage of the system – even though unionists admitted that "the ban was enforced sporadically . . . usually against employers who
hired immigrants to do piecework for menial pay." Until the late 1970s the
bans seemed to work only because unions reported infractions to federal and
state regulators.[8] But what would happen under a hostile state that refused to
accommodate union concerns?

A shifting political economy

During the quarter century following World War II, the extent of industrial
homework subsided as a consensus apparently developed on its regulation.
Measured in terms of certificates issued, knitted outerwear, for example,
dwindled from about 7,000, 28 percent of the industry before the ban (down
from a National Recovery Administration high of over 20,000), to about
1,000 by 1981, about 6.3 percent of the industry. In 1963–64, California
issued only 1,710 certificates and New York, only 3,239. No one counted
illegal homework.[9]

---

[8] Kenneth Noble, "U.S. Weighs End to Ban on Factory Homework," *New York Times*, Aug. 20,
  1986, A8; "Earn! In Your Own Home!," ibid., July 30, 1986, A22, which claimed that
  "Government stopped enforcing the rules unless there were union complaints."

[9] U.S. DOL, Wage and Hour Division, Research and Statistics Branch, "Current Status of
  Home Work in the Knitted Outerwear Industry," Nov. 1941, 4–33, and Findings and
  Opinion of the Administrator, "In the Matter of: The Recommendation of Industry
  Committee No. 32 for a Minimum Wage Rate in the Knitted Outerwear Industry and
  Industrial Home Work in the Knitted Outerwear Industry," Mar. 30, 1942, 13–20 ff., both
  in the DOL Library; State of New York, "Report to the Governor and the Legislature on the
  Garment Manufacturing Industry and Industrial Homework, February 1982," unpublished
  report, Division of Labor Standards, NY DOL, Albany; "Statement of International Ladies'
  Garment Workers Union in Opposition to the Removal of Restrictions on Industrial
  Homework," July 1, 1981, before the U.S. DOL, Employment Standards Administration,
  Wage and Hour Division, 42–3, in DOL files. The figures for the others are: women's
  apparel from an estimated 9,000 in Dec. 1941 to 933 (639 certified) in 1959; embroideries
  from 8,500 to 12,000 from Apr. 1, 1939 through July 15, 1942, dropped to 752, with 611
  certified; handkerchief, 398 in Sept. 1942 down to 14 in 1959; in button and buckle, 900
  homeworkers in period March 1939–40 down to 40 in 1959, from *The Growth of Labor Law
  in the United States* (Washington, D.C.: Dept. of Labor, 1967), 265–72, cited in Carla Lipsig-
  Mumme, "The Renaissance of Homeworking in Developed Economies," *Relations Industrieles*
  38 (1983), 547.

But in the unstable economy of the 1970s, homework began a resurgence not only in old industries, like knitted outerwear, but in new ones as well, like microcomputer assembly and word processing. The 1982 Census of Manufacturing listed 17,224 firms with homework for the seven restricted industries, an estimated 75,000 workers, excluding women's apparel. Such numbers, the DOL admitted, were "very soft." As the garment unions weakened and economic and political refugees from the Americas and Asia entered the work force in increasing numbers, garment manufacturers and their contractors began to pay less for homework, taken by the new immigrants. Two other factors encouraged the spread of homework. First, women increasingly entered the labor market, putting strains on family life. Second, enforcement funds dried up in the budget-cutting climate of the Reagan years. Losing two-thirds of its enforcement officers in the early eighties, even a liberal state like New York could not check on whether violations ended after employers paid fines. In October 1985, it funded a special sweatshop enforcement unit – consisting of only six investigators when there were between 25,000 and 50,000 women's apparel homeworkers in New York City alone.[10]

Even when inspectors caught violators, legal deterrence proved inadequate. Under federal law, a first-time offender was to pay up to two years worth of back wages and stop future violations. But only after being caught more than twice could the offender be ordered by the courts to repay wages. In 1988 the General Accounting Office concluded that "little effort is made to track repayment of back wages." Most offenders closed business merely to reopen under another name. By the early 1990s, however, both California and New York began to hold manufacturers responsible for the violations of their contractors. In prosecuting garment firms, California drew upon a neglected provision of FLSA that prohibited interstate shipping of goods made in violation of the act, a provision first suggested in the 1890s. But the numbers of federal enforcement officials continued to drop, from twelve hundred in 1980 to about nine hundred in 1991.[11]

Cutting down on enforcement officers belonged to a larger ideological assault against government. Sectors of capital faced with growing competition promoted the deregulation of industry and joined supporters of "free enter-

[10] Naomi Katz and David Kemnitzer, "Fast Forward: The Internationalization of Silicon Valley," in *Women, Men, and the International Division of Labor*, ed. June Nash and Patricia Fernandez Kelly (Albany: SUNY Press, 1983), 332–45; Hardy Green and Elizabeth Weiner, "Bringing It All Back Home," *In These Times*, Mar. 11–17, 1981, 8–9; State Senator Franz S. Leichter, "The Return of the Sweatshop: A Call for State Action," Oct. 1979, pt. 2, Feb. 26, 1982, typescript, NYDOL; census numbers from the DOL, Wage and Hour Division, Apr. 1989; Marilyn Webb, "Sweatshops for One: The Rise in Industrial Homework," *Village Voice*, Feb. 10–16, 1982, 27; Alexander Reid, "Thriving Sweatshops Feed on Immigrants' Desire for Work," *New York Times*, Mar. 25, 1986, B2; interview with Hugh McDaid, head of the New York State Sweatshop Investigation Unit, Apr. 1989.

[11] Monica Rhor, "Dust, Sweat, and Tears," *Sun-Sentinel* (Miami), Sept. 1, 1991, A14; Rhor, "Enforcing Laws Ends Violations," ibid., Sept. 3, 1991, A8.

prise" and "the right to work" to dismantle homework regulations. The desire to make American industry more competitive by cutting labor costs and ending government protection of organized labor informed Senator Orrin Hatch's (R.-Utah) pro-homework Freedom of the Workplace Act as much as the desire to appeal to women who wished to work at home. U.S. competitiveness would increase through the creation of low-waged jobs for women.[12]

The crisis in garment manufacturing had begun in the mid-1960s when the New Deal order still dominated political thought. Since the 1950s, Japan and Hong Kong had sent clothing into the United States, but imports accounted for only one out of twenty-five garments. This trickle, mostly luxury European goods, swelled during the sixties and seventies and shifted to lower-priced wares. Although New York City continued to house 40 percent of the industry, unionized firms and high rents increased the costs of production. Faced with import competition from Korea, Taiwan, the Dominican Republic, and elsewhere in the third world, manufacturers started to both move production out of the city and seek other ways to reduce costs. They "brought back" the sweatshop with its long hours, subminimum wages, and health and safety violations. By 1981, when the percentage of New York–made garments had dropped to 15 percent, imports composed more than 20 percent of the wholesale clothing market and 41 percent of women's and children's goods. They continued to expand throughout the next decade; whereas a U.S. garment worker cost employers more than seven dollars an hour, including benefits, workers abroad earned as little as twenty cents an hour in China and only a dollar an hour in Hong Kong. From two hundred sweatshops in the early seventies, New York City had at least three thousand ten years later.[13]

With sweatshops came a rise in homework. In 1982, New York had over fifty thousand underground garment workers; northern New Jersey, at least five thousand. The "legitimate" work force only amounted to two hundred thousand, with merely half organized. Admitted Hugh McDaid, New York's chief sweatshop investigator: "I expected homework would be so surreptitious that we'd have to ferret it out. . . . But all you have to do is stand on a corner in the South Bronx and watch women walking to and from the shops with bags full of the stuff. It's an opportunity full of riches for an investigator, but full of sadness for the workers." Formerly concentrated in Chinatown, homework spread all over the city, from the South Bronx and northern Manhattan to Flushing, Astoria, and Corona in Queens, Brooklyn, and Union City –

---

[12] "To amend the Fair Labor Standards Act of 1938 to facilitate industrial homework, including sewing, knitting, and craftmaking, and for other purposes," 98th Cong., 1st sess., 1984, S.2145; and *Daily Labor Report*, Mar. 28, 1984, A6–7, D1–11, and Nov. 6, 1984, A6; telephone interview with aide in Senator Hatch's office, Dec. 1984.

[13] Green and Weiner, "Bringing It All Back Home," 8–9; Barbara Koeppel, "The New Sweatshops," *The Progressive*, Nov. 1978, 22–6; William Serrin, "After Years of Decline, Sweatshops Are Back," *New York Times*, Oct. 12, 1983, B4; "Sweatshop Renaissance: The Third World Comes Home," *Dollars and Sense*, Apr. 1984, 6–8.

places where immigrants had settled during the seventies. ILGWU staff also found homework in Boston, San Francisco, Los Angeles, Chicago, Miami, New Hampshire, and upstate New York. With wages hovering at the then minimum of $3.35 an hour, many found themselves taking additional sewing home after work, sometimes forced by employers, always driven by necessity.[14]

Not all employers were undercapitalized and obscure. Adolfo, designer of ensembles for First Lady Nancy Reagan, contracted out work in the early eighties to the Queens shop of Ping Y. Hsu who sent material to homeworkers. In 1987 the New York State Department of Labor fined fashion designer Norma Kamali, subject of an unsuccessful ILGWU organizing drive, for repeatedly violating the state's ban on industrial homework. Kamali claimed that she desired more control over her creations, marketed under OMO – "On My Own". – than possible when contracted to a unionized shop. This fitting ideological match between high fashion and homework came together in Kamali's antiunionism: "As an American," she declared, "I want the right to choose."[15]

With such shifts in production locale, unions lost members and political power. In the 1950s, perhaps 80 percent of the industry was unionized. In 1983, it appeared that only a quarter of the garment work force belonged to unions, with between 50 and 65 percent in New York and New Jersey. In the preceding decade, the ILGWU lost 40 percent of its membership, declining to 280,000 members. The ILGWU reacted by abandoning its long-term policy of not organizing the undocumented; by 1975 it was attempting to organize all workers, no matter their immigrant status. At the same time, it called for stricter immigration laws coupled with amnesty for undocumented workers currently residing in the U.S.[16]

Immigration reform in the 1960s, which liberalized quotas from Asia and the Americas, increased migration to the United States. Census figures put legal migrants at around 191,000 annually from 1924 to 1965. After changes in the law, this number jumped to 435,000 per year in 1981, with 76 percent

---

[14] Webb, "Sweatshops for One," 24, 27; Frederick Siems, " 'Homework' Defies Law,"Tarboro, N.C. *Southerner*, Sept. 12, 1979, clipping file, ILGWU library; John Marcotte, "Homework: Legal Sweatshop," *News and Letters* 31 (Oct. 1986), 3, reports on a corrupt unionized buckle and button assembly shop where foremen and other privileged workers were given work to subcontract to others; "Statement of Delia Gonzalez, Homeworker in Chicago, Illinois," ILGWU prepared testimony, 1986, available from ILGWU.

[15] Allen F. Richardson, "Contractor Under Fire for Homework," *Daily News Record*, Mar. 26, 1983, from ILGWU handout; Joseph Perkins, "Garment Work: Home Is Not a Sweatshop," *Wall Street Journal*, Mar. 6, 1987, sec. 1, p. 30; Irene Daria, "Kamali Versus the ILGWU," *Women's Wear Daily*, Dec. 12, 1986, 1, 12–13; Kevin Haynes, "The Union Response," ibid.; Maria Laurino, "Are Exploited Workers Turning Norma's Rags to Riches," *Village Voice*, Feb. 13, 1987, 12; Richard J. Polsinello to Norma Kamali, Feb. 20, 1987, "Order Under Article 13 of the New York State Labor Law," NYDOL.

[16] Serrin, "After Years of Decline, Sweatshops Are Back," B4; Lisa Schlein, "New Sweatshops in California," *In These Times*, Feb. 22–8, 1978, 5.

coming from Latin America, Asia, and the Caribbean. "Illegal" immigration further mushroomed during the 1980s. Between 1980 and 1986, undocumented workers grew from 2,000,000 to 4,600,000. The newly arrived comprised nearly half of all garment workers. One employer explained, "If there were no immigrants, the needle trades would be out of New York." With native-born white-workers moving into white-collar jobs and discrimination barring native-born blacks, immigrants provided a willing labor force for the poorly paid garment industry. They were recruited through kin and community networks, like Cambodian bowmakers in Brooklyn, and through advertisements in the *China Post* and *El Diario-La Prensa*. Even in Utah, Southeast Asians provided the cheap home labor behind "Native American" crafts sold to the booming tourist industry; in California's Silicon Valley, Mexican, Korean, Filipino, and Vietnamese women brought dangerous chemicals into their homes to make computer chips. The 1986 Immigration Law, which legalized the status of immigrants who arrived prior to 1982, pushed more recent arrivals deeper underground, making homework an attractive option.[17]

Like New York, Miami and Los Angeles saw increased homework. The Miami area witnessed a doubling of labor law violations each year from 1988 to 1991; federal homework violations in 1990 numbered eighty-five, about twelve times greater than Los Angeles. But illegal operations in both cities went undetected, limited by underfunded enforcement. Small, mostly unregulated, shops characterized each city. Los Angeles, whose garment industry had mushroomed in the postwar years, emphasized casual wear; Miami harbored a seasonal trade stemming from transplanted New York Jewish manufacturers. "Hundreds of the factories in Dade are little more than shells with a desk and a skeleton staff," reported the *Sun-Sentinel* in late 1991. Cuban immigrants provided the labor force; there were male contractors and female factory operators and homeworkers. The particular conditions of this ethnic enclave

[17] In the 1950s, Puerto Rican migrants continued to engage in garment homework in New York City. See Altagracia Ortiz, "Puerto Rican Workers in the Garment Industry of New York City, 1920–1960," in *Labor Divided: Race and Ethnicity in United States Labor Struggles, 1835–1960*, ed. Robert Asher and Charles Stephenson (Albany: SUNY Press, 1990), 105–25; U.S. General Accounting Office, *"Sweatshops" in the U.S.: Opinions on Their Extent and Possible Enforcement Options* (Washington, D.C.: GAO, Aug. 1988), 34; David Reimers, *Still the Open Door: The Third World Comes to America* (New York: Columbia Univ. Press, 1985); statement by John C. Brooks to the Subcommittee on Labor Standards, Oversight Hearing on Lifting the Ban on Industrial Homework, Sept. 23, 1986, 2, from ILGWU packet 1986, available from ILGWU; Roger Waldinger, "Minorities and Immigrants – Struggle in the Job Market," *Dissent* Fall 1987, 519–20; "Illegal Homework Advertised Blatantly in Newspapers," ILGWU packet 1986; Colman McCarthy, "Bringing the Third World Home," *Washington Post*, Oct. 18, 1986, A23; Roger Waldinger, *Through the Eye of the Needle: Immigrants and Enterprise in New York's Garment Trades* (New York: NYU Press, 1986); Leah Melnick to Eileen Boris, Aug. 13, 1987; Christine Gringeri to Eileen Boris, Feb. 25, 1992; Rebecca Morales, "Cold Solder on a Hot Stove," in *The Technological Woman: Interfacing with Tomorrow*, ed. Jan Zimmerman (New York: Praeger, 1983), 169–80; Linda Golodner, "Comments in Response to Proposed Rulemaking," Mar. 8, 1989, in author's possession.

Figure 20. Sweated motherhood, 1980s-style. Photograph by Bob Gumpert. Courtesy of the ILGWU. With the arrival of new immigrants from the Americas and Asia, homework appeared to be on the increase in New York City, Miami, and other garment districts. This picture is of Mexican immigrants in Los Angeles.

encouraged even Cuban women of the middle class to earn wages at home to help husbands' business ventures. Only a third of homeworkers were undocumented. By the early 1990s, Nicaraguan political and Dominican economic refugees also sewed fashion garments at home.[18]

Mexican women predominated among garment operators and homeworkers in Los Angeles (see Figure 20); more of them faced proletarianization as wage-

[18] M. Patricia Fernandez-Kelly and Anna M. Garcia, "Hispanic Women and Homework: Women in the Informal Economy of Miami and Los Angeles," in *Homework: Historical and Contemporary Perspectives on Paid Labor at Home*, ed. Eileen Boris and Cynthia R. Daniels (Urbana: Univ. of Illinois Press, 1989), 165–79; Rhor, "Dust, Sweat and Tears," A1, A14; "Firms Sew Up Profits at Workers' Expense," *Sun-Sentinel* (Miami), Sept. 2, 1991, A1, A12; "Industry Thrives in Homes," ibid., Sept. 3, 1991, A1, A8. Dominican women in New York seemed to be replicating the pattern of Cubans in Miami by turning from shop to homework as their family's economic status improved. See Patricia R. Pessar, "Confronting Essentialism in Writings on Working-Class Women: Dominican Women in New York's Apparel Industry," paper presented at the History of Latina Women Workers, George Meany Archives, Feb. 1993.

earning heads of households than did their Cuban counterparts. For recent immigrants, one explained, "The problem was the language.... So I ended up sewing." She became pregnant. "I didn't want to live with relatives then, so I had to work at home. Fortunately, the old man [her employer] gives me enough so that I don't have to go to the shop." Undocumented workers feared immigration authorities. Others worked at home because the factory paid too little to afford a babysitter, an explanation that hardly differed from the motivations of other home-based workers.[19]

Rural homeworkers faced their own poverty, desire to care for children, lack of transportation, and limited supply of jobs. This was true not only in Vermont, but in North Carolina, upstate New York, and the Midwest, particularly the depressed farm belt of Iowa. Homeworkers in "remote, mountainous Wilkes County," North Carolina, stitched gloves. They wanted such part-time work "to preserve a way of life" that included gardening and tending black Angus cattle.[20] In the mid-1980s, homeworkers in central New York assembled and finished products for multinational firms, including IBM, Ford, Magnavox, Kodak, and Squibb. They produced "subcomponents for electrical devices (transformers, coils, circuit boards), electrical distribution units, automobile dashboard plates, dental floss, and fishing line." They painted and placed decals on a wide variety of products, tested electrical instruments, and assembled craft objects. Between 1969 and 1981, when New York began cracking down on electronics homework, hundreds of these native-born "working- and middle-class women" of childrearing age built transformers. As with other homeworkers, this labor kept their families "above poverty." One woman admitted: "Most people . . . don't even have enough money to take their kids to the movies. They have no savings, nothing to fall back on in an emergency. We're all just living from week to week."[21]

Other rural mothers also faced the problem of finding additional income while laboring on family farms, hit by severe economic downturns in the 1970s and 1980s. About sixty farm families drove to Guthrie Center, Iowa, to pick up a "kit" of fifty-four hundred pieces for assembling front-end suspension components for ITW-Shakeproof, a General Motors subcontractor. Attracted to Iowa and Wisconsin by generous economic development programs, created to ease unemployment and generate part-time work for farmer's wives, this company took advantage of the distress in America's "heartland" to bypass the

[19] Fernandez-Kelly and Garcia, "Hispanic Women and Homework," esp. 172; Merle Linda Wolin, "Homework: The Alien's Secret Support System," *Los Angeles Herald Examiner*, Jan. 18, 1981, A1, 12.

[20] Allen Norwood, "Caught in Threads of Bureaucracy," *Charlotte Observer*, March 2, 1986, C1, 4. The plight of these North Carolina homeworkers became a second conservative cause célèbre. "Statement of Virginia Deal," *Work in America: Implications for Families*, Hearing before the Select Committee on Children, Youth, and Families, House of Representatives, 99th Cong., 2nd sess., Apr. 17, 1986 (Washington, D.C.: GPO, 1986), 169–76.

[21] Jamie Faricellia Dangler, "Electronic Subassemblers in Central New York: Nontraditional Homeworkers in a Nontraditional Homework Industry," in Boris and Daniels, eds. *Homework*, 147–64, esp. 151, 156.

higher wage scales of Detroit. Although classified as "independent contractors," members of these families were employees, taking instructions from the company. The piece rate meant that more than one person would work on the kit; it took up to fifty hours to earn the $250 that each kit could bring.[22] Similarly, the Bordeaux Co. of Clarinda, Iowa, provided between 100 and 150 women with intricate appliqué for home sewing of sweat suits. Founded in 1980 by two former teachers and a decorator, the company underpaid its workers, demanded numerous trips in town for rush work, and generally exploited employees (again called independent contractors) through chiseling on materials or rejection of finished goods. The U.S. District Court for the Southern District of Iowa found it owed nearly $730,000 in back pay. Former employees reported relying upon husbands and children to complete the work. They suffered from a rash of occupational hazards: chemicals in fabrics, fur dust, "sewer's neck," and other repetitive motion disabilities. Still one woman emphasized, "My husband and I are farmers, and these days it's hard to make a living off the land." Relying on traditional gender divisions within rural communities, homework employers found a ready labor supply during hard times.[23]

In these same years, women from all classes rapidly joined the paid labor force on terms that easily provided a rationale for deregulating homework. The labor force grew from the entrance of more than a million women workers a year during the 1970s and early 1980s. The participation of married women with children under six increased from 19 percent in 1960 to 54 percent in 1985. Half of all women with babies under a year worked for wages in 1987. By 1988, the traditional family of male breadwinner and nonemployed wife had dropped to about a fifth of all families, while the number of female-headed families had doubled since 1965.[24]

Wages brought unequal remuneration for women. Although dual earner couples had higher median incomes and were less likely to fall below the poverty

[22] Osha Gray Davidson, *Broken Heartland: The Rise of America's Rural Ghetto* (New York: The Free Press, 1990), 145–8; Davidson, "Rural Sweatshops: Doing Home Work Down on the Farm," *The Nation*, 249, July 17, 1989, 87–90; Christine Gringeri, "Homework in the Heartland," (Ph.D. diss., Univ. of Wisconsin, 1990).

[23] Davidson, *Broken Heartland*, 144, 148; "A Sweatshop – Or a Good Job?" *Newsweek*, Nov. 3, 1986, 53; "Statement of Connie Jorgensen, Homeworker for Bordeaux, Inc. in Clarinda, Iowa"; "Statement of Barbara Mackey"; "Statement of Barbara J. Winkler"; "Statement of Lois Slaten"; "Statement of Jo Carmack"; "Statement of Rita Daniels"; Press Release, "DOL Delays Suit Charging Homework Manufacturer with Massive Minimum Wage Violations," ILGWU, n.d., all available from the ILGWU; *McLaughlin v. Bordeaux*, Judgment, filed Dec. 30, 1988, U.S. District Court for the Southern District of Iowa, Western Division, Civil Action File no. 86–104–W; Steven P. Galante, "Cottage Businesses Help Ease Farm-Belt Economy Burdens," *Wall Street Journal*, June 2, 1986, sec. 2, 19; Denise Goodman, "Home Knitting – a Boom Business," *Boston Globe*, Aug. 21, 1983, 65–6; Leda Hartman, "Working at Home," *ruralamerica*, Nov.-Dec. 1983, 11–13.

[24] Jack Golodner and Judith Gregory, "Unions and the Working Family," from *Work and the Family: BNA Special Report* (Washington, D.C.: BNA, 1986), 2; Francine D. Blau, *Work in America*, 77; Tamar Lewin, "Day Care Becomes a Growing Burden," *New York Times*, June 5, 1988, A11, 22; Howard V. Hayghe, "Family Members in the Work Force," *Monthly Labor Review* 133 (Mar. 1990), 16.

line than single earner households, two-thirds of those earning minimum
wage were women. Sex segmentation of the labor market, still crowding
women into fewer occupations, meant that full-time female workers received
only sixty-four cents to every dollar earned by equivalent male workers.[25] Lack
of a national family policy curbed women's choices. In the mid-1980s, only 23
percent of children attended preschool or day-care centers, with another 37
percent in family day care. Most family care was unlicensed; the quality and
cost of centers varied considerably, with low wages for childcare workers
leading to rampant turnover. Though President Bush signed a limited childcare bill in 1990, only after his defeat did a weak family and medical leave bill
become law in 1993. This dearth of social supports led some to propose a
"mommy track," in which women professionals would trade maternity leave
and shorter hours for wage and work stagnation. Others saw homework as the
solution to the work and family dilemma which led to the overwork of the
wage-earning mother. Homework would, the *Wall Street Journal* explained,
"help welfare mothers free themselves from dependency on the state, and . . .
help working mothers devote more of their attention to their families."[26]

Homework and motherhood in the 1980s

The 1980s controversy marked a profound shift in the decades-old debate
surrounding homework analyzed in this book. Although homework defenders always have cited its advantages for mothers, advocates for the Vermont
knitters, self-identified as political conservatives, added a critique of protective
legislation that echoed feminist demands for equal rights: they claimed laws
that ostensibly "protect" women from poor wages and long hours actually
intensify employer discrimination by making women as expensive to hire as
men, limiting women's opportunities in the labor market.[27] In a period when
liberal feminism was influencing public discourse, they began to defend
homework in the name of women's rights – to choose the domestic realm for
waged labor. The dominant feminist discourse defined equality as women's

---

[25] Blau, *Work in America*, 77; Peter T. Kilborn, "Rise in Minimum Wage Offers Minimum Joy,"
New York Times, Mar. 29, 1990, B8; table, "Men's and Women's Earnings," *Monthly Labor
Review* 111 (Feb. 1988), 34.

[26] Lewin, "Day Care"; Rebecca Blank, "Women's Paid Work, Household Income, and
Household Well-being," *The American Woman, 1988–89: A Status Report*, ed. Sara E. Rix
(New York: Norton, 1988), 123–61; Fern Marx and Michelle Seligson, "Child Care in the
United States," *The American Woman, 1990–91: A Status Report*, ed. Sara Rix (New York:
Norton, 1990), 132–69; Felice N. Schwartz, "Management Women and the New Facts of
Life," *Harvard Business Review* 89 (Jan.–Feb. 1989), 65–76; "Kitchen Mittens," *Wall Street
Journal*, May 26, 1981, sec. 1, p. 32; Flora Davies, *Moving the Mountain: The Woman's Movement
in America Since 1960* (New York: Simon & Schuster, 1991), 448–50.

[27] Judith Baer, *The Chains of Protection: The Judicial Response to Women's Labor Legislation*
(Westport, Conn.: Greenwood Press, 1978). Title VII of the 1964 Civil Rights Act actually
negated much of this legislation.

right to leave the home for the labor force. This association of homework with rights reflected a gendered shift. Whereas *Jacobs* had struck down restrictions on the basis of a man's right to contract, women's rights took center stage during the 1980s debate. The expropriation of the language of liberation by homework defenders mocked the women's movement, given the cultural, economic, and political factors on which the homework system continued to rest.

Women's rights and the right to work each originated in classical liberalism. The residue of patriarchial thinking within liberalism itself, that regarded women as dependents, kept these terms apart. Because liberalism divided social life into private and public, family and state, women and men, because its generic individual was the man, who was associated with the market and the polity, its concepts of choice, opportunity, and rights applied to only one sex. Connected to nature rather than culture, women were controlled by biology and belonged to the private realm of the family, represented in the world by men.[28]

With women thought of as "wards of the state," the law justified protective labor legislation in terms of women's biological function as mothers or potential mothers. Except for *Ritchie* and *Adkins*, such "false paternalism" dominated legal discourse, rather than the "false equality" of the right to contract. Title VII of the 1964 Civil Rights Act, which prohibited discrimination on the basis of sex, led state courts to invalidate women's labor laws, the legacy of the women's reform network and their feminism of difference. The new feminist push for the Equal Rights Amendment (ERA) in the 1970s and early 1980s enshrined a concept of rights that too often defined equality in terms of the standard life experiences of men.[29]

The arguments of homework advocates relied on the major tenets of classical liberalism: equal rights, equal opportunity, separation of private from public, and the right to work. Using the rhetoric of sex equity, defenders of homework labeled the bans discriminatory, undermining due process: They barred women from sewing or knitting at home while permitting men to work at carpentry or other home-based labor. Gender classification in the homework restrictions, according to Ruth Yudenfriend of the Center on Labor Policy, failed to meet the Supreme Court's test of serving "important government objectives."[30] They "discriminate[d] against women by eliminating their rights to raise their children and earn a living at the same time." "Prohibitions

---

[28] Frances Olson, "The Family and the Market: A Study of Ideology and Legal Reform," *Harvard Law Review* 96 (May 1983), 1497–578; Carole Pateman, *The Sexual Contract* (Stanford: Stanford Univ. Press, 1988).

[29] Frances Olson, "From False Paternalism to False Equality: Judicial Assaults on Feminist Community, Illinois, 1869–1895," *Michigan Law Review* 84 (May 1986), 1518–41; Joan Hoff, *Law, Gender and Injustice: A Legal History of U.S. Women* (New York: New York Univ. Press, 1991), 192–206, 233–5.

[30] By the early 1980s, gender discrimination was subject to an intermediate form of scrutiny beyond this notion of "important government objectives" but still fell short of the strict scrutiny that the Supreme Court had held for race discrimination; both of these standards faced erosion with the increasingly conservative Court under Reagan and Bush.

against industrial homework disenfranchise women from the workplace," reiterated Mark A. de Bernardo of the U.S. Chamber of Commerce. "It is therefore a women's issue."[31]

Feminist rhetoric struck a particularly strange chord in the voice of New Right conservatives like Senator Hatch who equated "right to work" with "rights of women . . . the right to be able to support your family . . . in the privacy of your home." The regulations were "an artificial control that works to the detriment of women's rights."[32] Social and moral terms meshed with economic ones when such defenders spoke of unshackling business from federal regulation in the same breath as they bemoaned the increased number of women on welfare. For homework regulation, historically supported by trade unions, restricted the "right to work," long associated with business's defense of the open shop. A pro-homework stance complemented the conservative assault on government regulation of industry, union power, and the welfare state. "Right to work" became a woman's right to earn wages at home without challenging the sexual division of labor within the family or economy.

Homework opponents also shifted their arguments away from those who had advocated mother care of children and had prophesied the downfall of domestic life if work for pay "invaded" the home. These labor liberals contended that homework undermines labor standards, encourages inaccurate reporting to the Internal Revenue Service, tramples the rights of undocumented workers, and condones competition unfair to law-abiding businesses and unions. They called for childcare in the workplace so that mothers can work "in decent places" instead of being forced to take work into their homes. Opponents continued to present the homeworker as a victim of unscrupulous employers, who lacked the economic, political, and legal resources needed to defend herself. ILGWU president Jay Mazur argued, "To license industrial homework is to license exploitation." Only toward the end of the eighties did he and other homework opponents truly address the social and cultural conditions affecting all women that made homework a solution to some women's double day. By maintaining home and work as separate spheres, antihomework liberals sought homes free from homework but not from the unwaged labor that remained the cornerstone of power inequities between the sexes.[33]

[31] Ruth Yudenfriend, Burlington Hearings, Jan. 1, 1981, 26–33; Mark A. de Bernardo, "Statement on the Freedom of the Workplace Act (S. 2145) before the Subcommittee on Labor of the Senate Labor and Human Resources Committee for the Chamber of Commerce of the United States," Hatch Hearings, Feb. 9, 1984, 127.

[32] Hatch remarks on "It's Your Business: Industrial Homework: Why Not?" transcript of program no. 231, air dates: Feb. 4–5, 1984, 11, available from U.S. Chamber of Commerce, Washington, D.C.; Kenneth B. Noble, "Farewell to Ban on Work at Home?" New York Times, July 10, 1986, B6.

[33] George Miller, Manny Eagle, Eugene Steinberg, Yale Garber, Samuel Butler, Jermone B. Kauff, Joseph Moore, Sol C. Chaikin, Ray Denison, Joseph Montoya, all in "The Reemergence of Sweatshops"; Frederick Simms, N.Y. Hearing, Apr. 2, 1981, 97; Jay Mazur, "Back to the Sweatshop," New York Times, Sept. 6, 1986, A27.

Defenders still associated homeworkers with motherhood. Before hearings in 1981 to rescind the outerwear prohibition, Vermont knitting entrepreneur C. B. Vaughan urged that "we work together to enable the mothers of small children to stay at home to care for their children and at the same time have the opportunity to earn income." In a resolution supporting homework in 1984, the Iowa senate argued that "no rational legislative objective is served by effectively forcing mothers out of the home and into the factory." Vermonters, the state's secretary of labor Joel Cherington asserted, prefer mother care to day-care because they value "the family as a building block in our society, and because of the costs associated with child care."[34] As the Center on National Labor Policy (counsel for many of the Vermont knitters) argued, "The children know their mother is home with them and she can teach them the skills and values which would otherwise go untaught." The knitters themselves constantly attacked day-care out of the belief that "it is important that preschool children be with their mothers," although a few bemoaned lack of available services in their rural regions. Others recognized that the cost of childcare would consume most of their wages so that it would not be worth working outside the home.[35]

In the debate over the Vermont knitters, the most diehard supporters of motherhood as woman's noblest profession, like Senator Jeremiah Denton (R.-Alabama), recognized the economic necessity for two earner families and viewed homework as the perfect compromise between economic reality and cultural preferences. Acknowledging the entrance of married women with small children into the official labor force, the conservative Heritage Foundation favored abolition of homework restrictions. According to the Center on National Labor Policy, homework offered society a huge "non-monetary advantage." Its flexible hours gave women more time than a factory or office job for unpaid labor, such as volunteer work, nurturing, and other traditional tasks.[36]

In the rhetoric of deregulators, welfare and dependence stood in opposition to homework and independence. The Heritage Foundation argued that prohibiting homework "would be a serious blow to thousands of women seeking financial independence." Hatch introduced the Freedom of the Workplace Act in 1983 as part of "a comprehensive initiative aimed at removing the barriers

[34] C. B. Vaughan, D.C. Hearings, Feb. 17, 1981, 440; Senate Concurrent Resolution no. 105 (Iowa 1984 Bills) (see also 1984 sess. House Joint Resolution, no. 49, Virginia Bills); Joel Cherington, D.C. Hearings, Feb. 18, 1981, 66–7, DOL files.

[35] Michael Avakian and Edward F. Hughes, "Statement of the Center on National Labor Policy, Inc., in support of Proposed Rulemaking to Rescind Restriction on Homework in the Knitted Outerwear Industry," May 11, 1984, 5, 9–10; Debra Waugh to William M. Otter, May 11, 1984; Beth Fitzammson, Newtown, Conn., to Otter, Apr. 23, 1984; a Mother Grandmother and Great Grandmother to Otter, Apr. 10, 1984; Pamela Morris, Akron, Ohio, to Otter, May 6, 1984, DOL files.

[36] Jeremiah Denton, Hatch Hearings, 76–7; Peter Germanis, "Why Not Let Americans Work at Home," *Heritage Foundation Backgrounder*, no. 325 (Jan. 30, 1984), 6–7, 9; Avakian and Hughes, "Statement."

[that] prevent families and women in transition [female heads of households] from reaching their potential and achieving economic self-sufficiency." Appropriating the phrase "feminization of poverty," previously deployed by the feminist left, Hatch perceived homework to be one tool – along with various workfare schemes and private sector training programs – that would take women off welfare and make poor women "independent." Moreover, it would allow them to care for small children in the process.[37]

Homeworkers also associated their work with autonomy, self-sufficiency, and independence, factors which were otherwise difficult to achieve in the rural New England economy. No precise statistical data on the social status of the knitters and other New England homeworkers are possible, but their letters and comments indicate a range of situations, including divorced heads of household on welfare, retired couples on social security, and college-educated, home-owning dual earner families. Like other rural homeworkers in the past, the Vermont knitters were primarily female, white, native-born, either mothers with young children or older women. Whether working class or middle class, all faced a labor market in which jobs for women consisted of part-time work or low-paying service, retail, and nondurable manufacturing. Years of education failed to translate into better pay. Economic pressure in the stagnated economy of the late 1970s encouraged them to earn wages; at a time when women earned three-fifths of a male wage, homework appeared a viable alternative to pink-collar jobs that included the hidden costs of childcare, transportation, and wardrobe.[38]

As Violet Jones of Hardwick, Vermont, a divorced mother of two preteen boys, wrote to the Wage and Hour administrator, home knitting "gives me the opportunity to become self supportive and get off of state aid." A Maine woman commented on the proposed deregulation of homework: "It just doesn't make sense to ban homeknitting when it is helping people to help themselves and helping the economy at the same time." A Massachusetts woman poignantly combined feelings about traditional mothering, distaste for dependence on the state, and need for "productive" labor when she confessed: "My husband is under medical care for a pre-ulcer condition and because I can knit at home I can relieve him of some of the burden of our financial support. There are many women like me. We want to be productive not just reproductive. Many of us do not want to be on welfare and foodstamps and medicaid.

[37] Germanis, "Why Not Let Americans Work at Home"; Orrin Hatch, "Women's Initiative," *Congressional Record – Senate*, 98th Cong., 1st sess., Nov. 18, 1983, S–16981–2; Diana Pearce, "The Feminization of Poverty: Women, Work, and Welfare," *Urban and Social Change Review* 11 (Feb. 1978): 28–36; Barbara Ehrenreich and Karen Stallard, *Poverty in the American Dream* (Boston: South End Press, 1983).

[38] Gloria Gill, Burlington Hearings, Jan. 14, 1981, 189; National Institute of Education, "Women in the Rural Economy: Employment and Self-Employment," Draft Report, DOL files.

Some of us don't want full time careers and 'latch-key' children. We need our 'at home' jobs."[39]

Many women have internalized a criterion of worth that undervalues bearing children and the tasks related to nurturing them. At the same time, many of the same women criticize the organization of wage labor that interferes with their ability to care for dependents. A Norridgewock, Maine, woman protested that working in a factory was not worth the sacrifice: "I know what working seven to three is like; getting to work when the sun is just rising in the morning, getting home just as it is going down, not seeing the sunshine for five days a week. I know mothers and fathers who only see their babies when they are asleep in their cribs. Believe me, 'minimum wage' doesn't begin to cover it." The labor standards that emerged from the New Deal regulated, but hardly transformed, the deadening experience of most factory work. During public hearings, the ILGWU constantly linked homework with sweatshops. However, the knitters imagined the home as a place of rest and became offended that anyone could call their well-maintained houses "sweatshops." They felt that "working at home has dignity," which was missing from factory labor.[40]

Homework, the knitters believed, fostered independence. Not only did they earn money but they controlled their own labor. Lacking direct supervision, having no card to punch or bell to obey, these homeworkers reported a relative autonomy over their labor. They thought of themselves as artisans, skilled workers making arts and crafts rather than mass-produced products. The Vermont women knitted between ten and thirty hours a week and chose how much work to accept over a two-week period or whether to knit at all during a particular week.[41]

But their control varied considerably, depending in large part on whether they designed the hats or sweaters they knitted. Although most owned knitting machines (which were hand-operated shuttle types with a row of little teeth

[39] Violet Jones, Box 322, Hardwick, Vt., to Otter, n.d., and attached untitled paper; Mary Berard, R.F.D. 1, Box 890, Oxland, Maine, to Otter, Apr. 11, 1984; Mrs. Ellen Z. Lampner, 48 Orchard St., Randolph, Mass., to Otter, May 3, 1984, 4–5, DOL files.

[40] Linda Clutterbuck, R.F.D. 1, Box 1540, Norridgewock, Maine, to Otter, Apr. 18, 1984; Audrey Pudvah and Peggy York, Burlington Hearings, Jan. 14, 1981, 232–68; exchange between Lazare Teper and a number of the Vermont women in D.C. Hearings, Feb. 17, 1981, 460–76.

[41] References to homeworkers as craftsworkers exist throughout the Burlington and Hatch Hearings. Audrey Pudvah, Nancy Smith, Emma Pudvah, Christine Brown, Bonnie Merhier, and Virginia Gray, Burlington Hearings, Jan. 14, 1981, 232–66; Robin Frost, Anson, Maine, to "Dear Sir," n.d.; Linda Thomas, Wapella, Ill., to "Dear Sir," Apr. 21, 1984; Kathleen Berube, Starks, Maine, to Otter, Apr. 21, 1984; Nancy A. Baillie, Boothwyn, Penn., to Raymond Donovan, May 1984; Mrs. Jan Kuhn, Johnson, Vermont, to Mr. Henry T. White, Jr., Jan. 2, 1981, in "Exhibits, Public Hearing to Commence Labor Dept. Review of 'Homeworker Rules,' " DOL files.

resembling knitting needle tips along the top), many had purchased them and had lessons from the "manufacturer" who became their major source of orders. If a knitter bought goods, especially yarn, from this person and the finished product went back to that same person for marketing, then FLSA considered the knitter an employee, even if the "employer" did not instruct on colors and design. Working without supervision remained insufficient for independent contractor status. The law had remained constant.[42]

Most of the knitters followed patterns determined by manufacturers; they were also subject to the rhythms of their machines. The Stowe Woolens receipt and order sheet for Gene Gray revealed handwritten notes: "The little border just before and after the reindeers is the only navy in those sweaters. The flakes and the reindeers itself is white. Thank you. Please do these sweaters last." Certainly descriptions provided by knitters suggest a predetermined quality to the work, albeit of a skilled kind. After setting up the machine by pushing out the amount of needles, the knitter simply moved the shuttle back and forth except when finishing or beginning an item. Reliance on punch cards eliminated the need to manually change needle lengths per row. For some machines, the design came on computer-programmed cards that further diminished the need for skill or creativity.[43]

Whether discontinuous labor created worker control or merely stretched women's paid and unpaid labor into one constant stream depends on the boundaries between paid labor and the rest of life. The home knitters offered a different model than factory employment, one with potential for increased control but also fraught with the abuse that comes from piece-rate work. The possibility of abuse increased when companies gave homeworkers daily or weekly production quotas, a practice that further stretched out the working day.

Some of the most outspoken homeworkers defended their labor in terms of women's rights. Mary Clement of Ripon, Wisconsin, proclaimed, "I am tired of the antiquated idea that women must be taken care of." Many knitters rejected the concept of government "protection" with the bitter comment that such protection was depriving them of their work. This rejection of "protective legislation" echoed the sentiments of ERA supporters in the 1920s, who were backed by the National Manufacturers Association, but also parodied the rejection of protection on the part of feminists of their own day. The homeworkers held a less positive stand toward work outside the home than did the professional and independent women of either the National Women's Party in the past or the National Organization of Women (NOW). But they hardly rejected women's paid labor. Vocal Audrey Pudvah suggested times had changed, women were more aware of their rights, and if opportunity and

---

[42] Roberta Orticerio, D.C. Hearings, Feb. 18, 1981, 121–9; Nancy Smith, Burlington Hearings, Jan. 14, 1981, 265–6.

[43] Stowe Woolens Receipt and Order Sheet for Gene Gray, exhibit no. 21, Burlington Hearings, DOL files; Peggy York, Burlington Hearings, Jan. 14, 1981, 268–71.

inclination existed, "they can go out to work . . . whereas in 1946, I feel as though maybe the woman's place was in the home, behind closed doors, taking care of your family." Most homeworkers confessed to having turned to machine knitting to avoid leaving their families. Embracing motherhood and the home, they accepted notions of female difference, that women's experiences varied from men's, even as they rejected the protection that reformers historically had evoked in the name of "difference."[44]

Few homeworkers identified themselves as feminists, even when drawing on an ideology of rights. Writing to the Department of Labor, Mary Louise Norman from Denver attacked organized feminism (and the ERA campaign):

> Not every woman is inclined to march for equal rights. Many of us prefer to stay at home with husband and children and *work* for equal rights. We believe in FREEDOM OF CHOICE. I can knit, be at home when my two teenagers need me, bake a chocolate cake, collect my neighbors UPS packages and deliveries, keep an eye on the neighborhood for vandals . . . *and* provide city & state with taxes all at the same time. This makes me something of a Wonder Woman compared to my "sister" marchers.

Evidence suggests that knitters drew on existing kinship and women's friendship networks (for example, Audrey Pudvah and her sister knitted for the same firm); they belonged to a woman-centered, but rarely feminist, culture. Yet one woman who sold knitting machines and had hired homeworkers in the past declared that the practice allowed women to feel "some independence from their husbands."[45] Although the meagerness of homework wages never led to complete economic independence from spouses, homework income supplemented men's earnings and provided a check on men's absolute power.

Kathy Hobart, one of the most combative of the Vermont women, identified herself as a feminist. At a public hearing, she declared: "I don't believe that a woman should be home, that she needs to be home with her children. The only reason that I choose to be home is because it keeps me from getting an ulcer." But she also felt that her children "benefit[ted] most by my staying at home. I think I have a right and my children have a right to have me home with them." Hobart's stance in favor of both women's responsibility as mothers and women's right to work and be economically independent reflected the new complexity of women's dual role in the late twentieth century: "I look at this as a women's issue because I just think women have been forced to choose at this point in our society to being full-time mothers or workers finding work in the workplace, and I think for those of us who have found an alternative measure to both and can get them to work together, we

---

[44] Audrey Pudvah, Burlington Hearings, Jan. 14, 1981, 232 ff.
[45] Mary Louise Norman, Denver, Colo., to Otter, Apr. 21, 1984; Martha A. Hall, Yarmouth, Maine, to Otter, Apr. 15, 1984; Wendie Ballinger, Oreana, Ill., to Otter, Apr. 21, 1984, DOL files; William Fern, Division of Special Minimum Wage, DOL, interview with author, Washington, D.C., June 10, 1985.

should be encouraged rather than discouraged."[46] Though 1920s feminists promoted motherhood and wage labor for themselves, the women's network assumed that conditions of working-class life made it nearly impossible for women of the laboring poor to be successful at both.[47] Hobart, in contrast, drew upon the ideology of liberalism to undermine its basic dichotomy. Rather than accept the work or motherhood split assumed by traditional liberals, Hobart proposed a third way: paid work and motherhood.

Whether homework offered a third way in the late twentieth century depended on the conditions under which earning and mothering both occurred. What appeared a reasonable alternative for Hobart and others living in single-family dwellings with employed husbands opened the way for the continued exploitation of poorer, more desperate women, with or without wage-earning men. For whether homework encourages self-sufficiency, whether it could reorganize social life rested not on best-case scenarios. Indeed, homework proved an illusionary solution to finding more time for the family in the 1980s as it had sixty years before. A national survey in *Family Circle* discovered that half of white-collar homeworking women relied upon childcare. Researcher Kathleen Christensen concluded: "The notion that a woman can hold a baby in one hand and handle a computer terminal with the other is a fallacy. It is also an insult to the seriousness with which women approach both their child care and their work."[48]

At 1982 House hearings, Senator Daniel Patrick Moynihan (D.-N.Y.) defended the historical argument for protective legislation by portraying homework as a system for exploiting the defenseless woman "locked up in a house with a month's supply of gloves ... to sew at 20 cents an hour." He too deployed the language of rights, evoking the success of the New Deal's Frances Perkins who "got those women out of those sweatshops. She got them their rights."[49] Whereas homework defenders referred to women's right to work, Moynihan suggested a different notion of rights: women's right to worker's rights, to be protected under the law from unfair labor practices.

Moynihan and other homework opponents, like ILGWU's retired presi-

[46] Kathy Hobart, Burlington Hearings, Jan. 14, 1981, 314; Hobart, D.C. Hearings, Feb. 17, 1981, 490–1; Hobart questioning of Gerald Coleman and Alice Ruotolo, D.C. Hearings, Feb. 18, 1981, 30–1, 53.

[47] Nancy Cott, *The Grounding of Modern Feminism* (New Haven, Conn.:Yale Univ. Press, 1987), esp. 117–42.

[48] Gerri Hirshey, "How Women Feel About Working at Home," *Family Circle*, Nov. 5, 1985, 70, 72, 74; Kathleen E. Christensen, "The New Era of Home-Based Work," *Chicago Tribune*, Aug. 20, 1986, 1:19.

[49] Jill Pollack, "Stamping Out New Sweatshops," *News, North Jersey*, Sept. 8, 1981; Frederick Siems, "Sweatshop Close-up: Filth, Crowding, and Child Labor Are the Norm," *Herald Journal* (Indiana), Sept. 21, 1979, ILGWU clippings file; Alice Ruotolo, D.C. Hearings, Feb. 18, 1981, 39–40; "Proceedings of The Thirty-Seventh Convention of the International Ladies' Garment Workers Union, Oct. 4, 1980," 1–3, Exhibit 54, D.C. Hearings, DOL files; "Statement of Hon. Daniel Patrick Moynihan," in "The Reemergence of Sweatshops," 38–45.

dent Sol Chaikin, argued the portrayal of homeworkers as middle-class women handcrafting while toddlers play by the fire distorted "the real world." Class, race, and citizenship stratified homeworkers not only by material condition but also in terms of their ability to see themselves as part of a single economic system. A Vermont woman expressed her resentment of "a regulation that the manufacturers and the union people feel that we need to protect the illegal alien," as if FLSA applied only to immigrants.[50]

Homework opponents continued to argue for justice and moral right through a discourse of disease and degradation that reemphasized concerns for health and family welfare. One state AFL-CIO official noted, "How industrial homework . . . fosters a nurturing, loving home environment is beyond our belief." Rather than address the actual conditions of the Vermont knitters, such opponents saw only the exploited tenement mother. Another opponent relied on equal rights feminism to state that "the laws have to apply to everyone, no matter where I live or what kind of a family I have." Although homework benefited women with dependent children, permitting it "would discriminate against those with older or no children."[51]

Advocates for women rejected the portrait of the homeworker as victim even when they generally opposed homework. Grace Lyu-Volckhausen of the New York City Commission on the Status of Women, a consultant to Local 23–25, ILGWU, emphasized that homeworkers are skilled seamstresses whose self-image suffers from the lack of recognition given to their labor. Representing the National Consumers' League and the Coalition of Labor Union Women, Ruth Jordan couched testimony in the rhetoric of sisterhood. She advocated a public policy based on women's values, the same female difference that her predecessors at the league had drawn upon and that the Vermont knitters themselves associated with women: "I stress the caring part, because I think as women workers, we should be concerned with all aspects of nurturing. And part of the aspect is what is happening to our other sisters, whether they work in rural settings or in urban slums." She rejected any proposal that threatened to undermine national standards as pitting one group of "sisters" against another or that inhibited the ability of workers to organize, as homework apparently did. Homework became a women's rights issue: "It is more of a women's issue than anything else. Women already earn less than 59 percent of what men earn, and as in the knitwear case it is the women who are workers. They are denied the ability to upgrade their skills and economic well-being."[52]

---

[50] Moynihan and "Statement of Sol C. Chaikin," in "The Reemergence of Sweatshops," 66–73; Corinne Lunt, D.C. Hearings, Feb. 17, 1981, 481.

[51] "Prepared Statement of Amado H. Gallardo, California Labor Federation, AFL–CIO," in "Reemergence of Sweatshops," 200; Billie Ann Pilling, D.C. Hearings, Feb. 18, 1981, 99–100.

[52] Grace Lyu-Volckhausen, New York Hearing, 106–14; Ruth Jordan, D.C. Hearings, Feb. 18, 1981, 230–44, esp. 233–6; "Statement of Ruth Jordan, Member, Board of Directors, National Consumers' League," in "Reemergence of Sweatshops," 148.

Jordan hardly presented new arguments when she stressed the exploitative nature of homework, how it enmeshed women and children in relations of dependency. New York State labor commissioner Lillian Roberts, a former organizer of fellow and sister African-American hospital workers, expressed the conflicting notions of rights found in the homework debate throughout the century. She explained at a 1986 House hearing: "The legalization of industrial homework is not a highminded attempt to extend women's rights. The removal of these restrictions would perpetuate the role of women as second class citizens," denying them "the right to union wages" and keeping them "in a situation where home duties and work requirements are in conflict."[53]

Discourses of homework

In announcing the deregulation of industrial homework in five industries in November 1988, then secretary of labor Ann McLaughlin explained how "changing workforce demographics demand that we provide employment opportunities that allow workers the freedom to choose flexible alternatives including the ability to work in one's own home." The *Wall Street Journal* editorialized that "the recision of the federal ban on homework represents a victory for American families." Despite such talk, despite a discourse where "women" became subsumed under "families" and men desired to stay home and parent, men's greater earning power would more likely predict which parent would earn at home even if gender socialization did not. Speaking of "families" was part of a disingenuous appeal to the dual earner couple that allowed them to project their situation onto the less prosperous, often single mother, and suggest homework for her as a choice made out of freedom rather than from necessity. Policymakers conflated the traditional garment industries where immigrant women of color toil with the new clerical homework where white women predominate; the small business entrepreneur and independent contractor became one with the employee. Forgotten in the extolling of homework as relief for women's double day was how it all too often stretched out the working day. The language of gender masked unequal class relations, even as some mothers found needed earnings through homework.[54]

In the media and before government committees, discussion of homework contributed to the larger conversation about home, family, and women's status. The working mother overshadowed economic factors, like labor standards. While the ILGWU continued to speak of low wages, deregulators successfully focused on white, seemingly middle-class women, providing categories that

---

[53] Statement on Indsutrial Homework, New York State Labor Commissioner Lillian Roberts before the House Education and Labor Committee, Subcommittee on Labor Standards, Washington, D. C., Sept. 2, 1986, 3, xerox, from ILGWU.

[54] DOL Office of Information, "New Industrial Homework Rules to Take Effect," News, for release Nov. 10, 1988; "Help for Homeworkers," *Wall Street Journal*, Nov. 14, 1988, editorial.

others had to counter. By "using feminist rhetoric for 'choices' and 'opportunities in the workplace,' " an advocate of Wages for Housework charged, deregulators "claim to be responding to women's demands for flexible hours and child care. In fact, just the opposite is the case. Industrial homework imposes on women two jobs for way below the price of one." Even if that wage topped the minimum, homeworkers still would find themselves subject to a continuous workday, where "the phone rings, someone comes to the door, the baby cries, the pot boils over, you forget to record your time."[55] Such a description hardly differed from those given by employer representatives in the late thirties. Yet it was precisely such home interference with labor standards that FLSA sought to eliminate.

The courts provided a narrower discourse. They restricted their opinions to the scope of FLSA or administrative procedures. In rescinding five regulations in 1986, the Labor Department had argued that "prohibition . . . did not prevent homework from being done . . . [it] merely prevented homeworkers from reporting wage violations because reporting such violations would result in the loss of homework employment opportunity." It claimed that certification would encourage reporting. In *ILGWU v. Dole*, Judge Gerhard Gesell ruled for the U.S. District Court for the District of Columbia that the department had engaged in reasoned decision making and that the certification program would improve enforcement, even though homework with all its evils persisted. The ILGWU could not win on such narrow legal grounds, even though it documented through use of the Department of Labor's own files (released under the Freedom of Information Act) that nearly every certified employer in knitted outerwear had violated the law. Indeed, only fifty-five employers asked for certification and Labor had investigated only thirty-five of them.[56]

Whereas the Department of Labor spoke in terms of "protection" through certification, the ILGWU clung to the language of victimization. It talked in terms of "a green light to exploit some of the most vulnerable workers in America," those alien immigrant women who long have appeared as a threat to organized labor. The *New York Times* "saw opportunities for job–family flexibility," but charged that the AFL-CIO "denounced the change as inviting a

[55] "Testimony by Jay Mazur," Hearings on Industrial Homework in the Women's Apparel Industry, New York City, Mar. 29, 1989, available from the ILGWU; Henry Weinstein, "Witnesses Describe the Misery of Home-Based Garment Work," *Los Angeles Times*, Mar. 24, 1989, 1, 4; Marjorie Howard, "Home Work," *Boston Herald*, Jan. 29, 1989, A24.

[56] 29 CFR Part 530, "Employment of Homeworkers in Certain Industries; Notice of Proposed Rulemaking," *Federal Register* 51, Aug. 21, 1986, 30037; *ILGWU v. Dole*, 729 F.Supp. 877 (D.D.C. 1989); "DOL's Homework Action Survives Legal Scrutiny," *Daily Labor Report*, 27, Dec. 12, 1989, 1–2, A12–13; Before the U.S. DOL, "Comments of the International Ladies' Garment Workers Union," in reference to 29 C.F.R., Part 530, May 5, 1989, 38ff., available from Shea & Gardner, Washington, D.C.; Laura McClure, "Homework's Horrors," *Guardian*, Nov. 5, 1986, 8. A confidential report made for the DOL concluded that the certification program had failed.

'return to sweatshops.' "[57] Meanwhile, deregulators made emotional gendered arguments for homework as an employment option.

The ILGWU initially failed to capture the public imagination and gave the impression that it, and by extension the labor movement, was insensitive to working parents. Labor was addressing this issue; as early as 1981, one labor paper charged that homework was "just an excuse for demanding double duty" and that "daycare should be provided." But this theme lay buried in the labor press, a subtheme in homework discourse until the late 1980s. The ILGWU had formed a coalition against homework in 1986 with women's as well as civil rights groups, including the Children's Defense Fund, Child Care Action Campaign, and the Women's Equity Action League. The union began arguing for the feminist work and family agenda: "decent jobs with equal pay, benefits, opportunities for promotion," parental leave, "quality, affordable child care," and care for the elderly and infirm. Vice-president and legislative director Evelyn Dubrow wrote in the *National NOW Times*, "Homework traps women and children into jobs which offer poverty wages and invite child neglect." President Jay Mazur persisted with the image of victimization; only when the ILGWU began to use as its spokesperson Susan Cowell, who became a vice-president during the course of the homework campaign, did it effectively counter administration rhetoric. Facing the nation on the "McNeil-Lehrer News Hour" in December 1988, she plainly explained that homework was no solution to the problem of childcare, undermining the strongest appeal of its defenders without insulting the women who believed homework to be a viable wage-earning option. Subsequently in 1990 the ILGWU launched "Campaign for Justice" to facilitate labor organizing, end sweatshops, support undocumented workers, and expand adequate dependent care.[58]

Still it appeared that homework defenders had captured the high ground with their talk of "rights." They certainly had set the terms of the debate. Reflecting the ideological climate of the period, homework became "cottage industry," a boon for the working mother. Even the meaning of exploitation changed from underpay and overwork to regulators denying opportunity. Rather than the friend of workers, trade unions turned into an enemy, putting their interests above those of working people who found employment at home. Unshackled by interference, homework promised freedom.[59] North

---

[57] Kenneth Noble, "Q & A: Bill Brock: A Rosy View of the State of Labor," *New York Times*, Sept. 1, 1986, A24; Frank Swoboda, "Agency Lifting Ban on Work at Home," *Washington Post*, Dec. 30, 1988, A4; "How Labor Could Lead," *New York Times*, Sept. 1, 1986, A22; editorials, "Get Serious About Work at Home," ibid., Nov. 14, 1984, A4; "Earn! In Your Own Home!," ibid, July 30, 1986, A22.

[58] "Homework Laws Vital, Members Say," *Labor Unity*, Mar. 1981, 5; Jay Mazur to Eileen Boris, Jan. 12, 1987; ILGWU, "Questions and Answers on Industrial Homework," 4, available from ILGWU, c. 1988; Evelyn Dubrow, "Analysis: The Case Against Industrial Homework," *National NOW Times* 20, Apr. 1987, 4–5; "McNeil-Lehrer News Hour," PBS, Dec. 20, 1988; ILGWU, *Campaign for Justice*, pamphlet, 1990, available from ILGWU.

[59] "Capital Wrap-up," 49; David R. Henderson, "Free the Women," *Policy Report*, Nov. 1981,

Carolina's commissioner of labor John Brooks captured the contradictions central to this defense when he questioned how advocates of a constitutional right to homework would react to safety and health inspections: "Are they then going to cry 'foul' because they then claim that these homes aren't businesses at all, but are 'homes' the privacy of which are protected under the U.S. and most state constitutions?"[60] If rights depended on the separation of public from private, the merging of the two realms certainly challenged existing definitions of justice. Deregulation or prohibition were not the only options, although they appeared as such after reformers turned to state regulation rather than pursuing homeworkers' own desires for a better life through unionization or cooperative enterprises. Could we move beyond the dichotomous thought on which labor standards as well as the rest of social life rested?

The international challenge

Regulation, with the goal of prohibition, became the predominant policy in the United States. It never exhausted possible strategies that could have both ended the exploitation of homework and improved the lives of homeworkers. That becomes apparent when U.S. policies stand next to those of other countries. While the Reagan administration was attempting to curtail government oversight, an international movement developed to protect and aid homeworkers. Encouraged by the International Labor Organization (ILO), especially its Employment and Development Department, women in India spearheaded homeworker organization and placed on the ILO agenda a call for an international convention to provide homeworkers with labor standards. The European Community, the International Confederation of Free Trade Unions (ICFTU), and other interested groups began to take the problems of homeworking women seriously.[61]

The economic changes that generated greater homework in the United States belonged to a larger international trend: the growth of the informal sector, temporary contracts, and part-time work. An international gender

reprint ILGWU library; Sheldon L. Richman, "Labor Sees Devil in Movement for Cottage Industry," n.d., ILGWU library; Marion R. Behr and Omri M. Behr, "Working at Home Is a Blow for Freedom," Letters, *New York Times*, Dec. 10, 1984; reply by Robert D. Parmet, Dec. 11, 1984, both in letter Robert D. Parmet to Eileen Boris, June 5, 1985; James Grant, "In Praise of Sweatshops: Everyone Should Have the Right to Work," *Barron's*, Mar. 16, 1981, ILGWU library.

60 "Statement by John C. Brooks," 5. Ironically, the worst factory disaster since the Triangle Shirtwaist Fire took place under his watch in Hamlet, N.C., in 1992.

61 I have observed and participated in the unfolding of these events first at the Conference on Home-Based Labor, Ahmedabad, India, Apr. 1989, and at the meeting of the Association for the Study of Women in Development, Washington, D.C., Nov. 1991. See Elisabeth Prügl, "Globalizing the Cottage: Homeworkers' Challenge to the International Labor Regime" (Ph.D. diss., American University, 1992); Prügl, "Tracing the International Debate on Homework," paper submitted to the International Labor Organization, Oct. 9, 1990.

division of labor made global the production of a wide range of goods and services, from data entry to garments. The decline of mass production for many consumer goods ushered a "post-Fordist era"; "flexibility in fashion and design" promoted small-batch production and variable labor needs provided by homework. Decentralized production encouraged local subcontractors, whether in Manila, Mexico City, or London. Subcontractors in the United States competed with those from Asian and Latin American countries who relied mostly on homeworkers.[62]

In European nations as well as developing countries, homeworkers proved their willingness to be organized. Regulation in Great Britain took a different course than in the United States. The Trades Board Act of 1909, as we have seen, included homeworkers, providing a living wage for all workers in "sweated" industries. The 1961 Factory Act asked employers to register homeworkers. Under the Thatcher regime, this system atrophied, with the boards ended in 1993. Meanwhile, in the 1970s, private and public agencies funded local Low Pay Units to research homework and publicize the conditions of homeworkers. The resulting findings encouraged the Trade Union Congress (TUC), along with a number of individual unions, to place homeworker needs on their agenda and led to proposed government action in the area of health and safety. In 1979, the unions supported an unsuccessful Homeworkers Bill that would have extended to homeworkers the same protections as factory laborers.[63]

The 1980s witnessed a number of locally based campaigns to organize and improve the conditions of homeworkers. Supported by the TUC, campaigns emanated from the larger left and women's communities, but they trained homeworkers to carry out organizing. The TUC saw these local organizations as a prerequisite for trade union initiative; only when faced with already unionized in-plant workers who moved into homework did the unions initiate homeworker organization. The campaigns reflected "community development principles which aimed to empower oppressed groups . . . so that *they* can bring about the changes needed in their lives," one organizer emphasized at an international meeting in the Netherlands. They printed outreach newsletters in multiple languages, particularly those of the Indian subcontinent. They organized social activities to end the isolation of homeworkers, set up Christmas stalls to publicize the extent of homework, facilitated skill training, aided women to establish independent businesses and cooperatives, and helped

---

[62] Saskia Sassen-Koob, "Notes on the Incorporation of Third World Women into Wage Labor Through Immigration and Offshore Production," *International Migration Review* 18 (1984), 1144–67; Swasti Mitter, "Women Organizing in the Informal Sector: A Global Overview," in *Dignity and Daily Bread: New Forms of Economic Organizing Among Poor Women in the Third World and the First*, ed. Swasti Mitter and Sheila Rowbotham (London: Routledge, forthcoming).

[63] Prügl, "Tracing the International Debate on Homework."

with legal agitation against employers who defaulted on wages, redundancy pay, and other mandated worker benefits.[64]

In 1984, these local efforts combined to issue the "Homeworkers' Charter" at the first National Conference on Homeworking. Demands included free and adequate dependent care for homeworkers, resources for homeworkers to meet together for mutual support, the legal status of employee (as opposed to independent contractor), the end to racist and sexist practices, adoption of a national minimum wage, amendment of relevant health and safety regulations to protect homeworkers and their families, and comprehensive training and educational opportunities for homeworkers. Such demands attempted to improve conditions of homeworkers as workers as well as increase their opportunies to choose other labor. Although unions have stood in a different relation to the state in Great Britain and have been stronger, such an approach recognized homeworkers as workers with specific needs and problems, and not as competitors or victims. Under unsympathetic Tory governments, such demands went unrealized, but locally based efforts persisted among the native-born and within Asian immigrant communities.[65] Whereas a shared culture had encouraged organization in Puerto Rico, ethnic diversity complicated organizing in Great Britain. With socialist influences stronger within the women's movement, British feminists in the 1980s regarded the homeworker as a working mother more directly than did their U.S. counterparts. They began to revive the old strategy of the consumer boycott, which in an era of instant communication could be more effective than in the days of the consumer leagues.

The Indian Self-Employed Women's Organization (SEWA) of Gujarat offers another model for homeworker organizing. Started by members of the women's wing of the Textile Labour Association (TLA) in 1971, this union of the home-based left the TLA a decade later and has fought for governmental union status ever since. Its nearly two hundred thousand members (1990) included industrial homeworkers (especially garment, cigarette rolling, incense stick making), vendors, and agricultural laborers. As a cross-class and cross-caste organization, SEWA has striven to empower homeworkers. It has lobbied for and defended the rights of homeworkers, trained them as paralegals, provided credit through its women's bank, created cooperatives, and given decision-making powers within the organization to homeworkers themselves. SEWA also has worked for legal protections from the state and the international community. Its push for an international convention derives

64 "'Not A Proper Job': Report on the International Conference on Homeworking," *News From IRENE* (International Restructuring Education Network Europe) 12 (Sept. 1990), 24; Yorkshire Homeworking Group, *Outworkers News* 7 (Jan. 1992).

65 Shelley Pennington and Belinda Westover, *A Hidden Workforce: Homeworkers in England, 1850–1985* (London: Macmillan Education, 1989), 102–25, 152–70; Sheila Allen and Carol Wolkowitz, *Homeworking: Myths and Realities* (London: Macmillan Education, 1987), 153–8, 190–200; ILO, "Homework," *Conditions of Work Digest* 8 (2/1989), 204–7, 235–9.

from an attempt to gain legislation in India where the government tends to follow the international labor code.[66]

SEWA developed its strategies for an economy where home labor represented a major form of production. But even in Western economies, like Australia, garment trade unions joined the state to protect the rights of homeworkers as workers. Urged on by SEWA, the ICFTU asked member unions to direct special programs to mobilize homeworkers in 1988. The historically hostile International Textile, Garment and Leather Workers' Federation responded to members from countries with home-based economies by softening its demand for the eventual elimination of homework: "Where the practice of homework is firmly rooted and the prospects for its eradication remote, all affiliates meanwhile should put pressure on their respective governments to secure homeworkers the same wages, working conditions and benefits as factory workers." This position resembled that adopted in the United States by reformers and trade unionists alike when they called for minimum wages and other labor standards applied to homeworkers in the hope of ending the advantages that employers found in homework. In Toronto, the ILGWU began a campaign in late 1991 "to win fair wages and working conditions for homeworkers" through a community-based approach that resembled British organizing.[67]

The ILO had included homework in its minimum wage and maternity leave conventions. In the mid-1940s, the United States asked the agency to investigate homework but no action derived from its survey of existing laws and practices. Representatives of concerned industries – clothing, textile, leather, and footwear – debated the issue in their tripartite technical meetings over the next years. Typically, that for the clothing industry resolved to ban homework in 1964. Such a decision reflected the influence of Western industrialized nations; only France and Switzerland, nations committed to the enforcement of homework laws, posed regulation as a viable alternative. By the Second Tripartite Technical Meeting in 1980, the division between industrialized and industrializing nations became apparent: Where it appeared that homework had declined in the first group, it was central to the economy of the second and could not be eliminated without grave dislocations. The governing body of the ILO decided to study the issue and continued to do so throughout the 1980s in the context of improved working conditions, equal treatment of women and

---

[66] My analysis of SEWA is based upon visiting the organization in Apr. 1989. ILO, "Homework," 227–8; ILO, "Meeting of Experts on the Social Protection of Homeworkers (Geneva, 1–5 Oct. 1990), Draft Report," 27; Renana Jhabvala, "Self-Employed Women's Association: Organizing Women by Struggle and Development," in Mitter and Rowbotham, *Dignity and Daily Bread*.

[67] ILO, Meeting of Experts on the Social Protection of Homeworkers, *Technical Background Document* (Geneva: ILO, 1990), 54–5; Prügl, "Tracing the International Debate on Homework," 4; Alexandra Dagg et al., "Dear sisters and brothers," Sept. 7, 1991, in author's possession.

men, and promotion of rural employment. The Employment and Development Department made homework a priority in its work on women in the informal sector. It aided SEWA and, funded by the Danish government, tried to establish a similar organization in Southeast Asia. In 1984, an interdepartmental task force set about exploring the possibility of a labor standard on homework. These efforts led the Conditions of Work and Welfare Facilities Branch of the ILO to conduct research and gather materials for the Meeting of Experts on the Social Protection of Homeworkers in October 1990. Although some sentiment existed for an international convention, homework was not the top priority of enough nations to become the subject of one in the early 1990s. However, worker organizations led by SEWA kept on pushing governments, donor agencies, and international groups to keep homework before the ILO.[68]

The international campaign to protect homeworkers remained unresolved in the early 1990s. But the international coalition of homeworker organizers had established a North-South dialogue that undermined the assumptions behind Reaganite policy in the United States. Asking "how we value and define work, particularly women's work, both paid and unpaid," they questioned assertions that homeworkers could not be organized and immigrants not learn their rights. Equally important, they recognized the international connection between production, distribution, and consumption. A world economy demanded international organization. Not only did women need to be "organized around their paid work," but homeworker campaigns illuminated "the division of resources in all our societies and ways in which women can be empowered."[69] Whether empowerment came from their rights to homework or their rights as workers depended on whether homeworkers emerged from their identities as mothers and became visible as wage earners who happened to mother.

Family and state, home and work, private and public are false dichotomies that sustain hierarchy. Work in the family, as well as power relations among family members, not only becomes a crucial factor – along with class and race – in shaping positions in the labor market but is itself contingent on public policies, from taxation and immigration to welfare. Homework and its regulation illustrates this process. A deregulation policy that would undermine labor standards hardly serves the needs of working women who might discover in home-based labor a way to ease their double day, but who might also find that shifting the location of labor comes with a price. By sustaining the association of women with the home, policymakers place a barrier in the way of reorganizing social life to recognize the earning and nurturing obligations of us all.

[68] Prügl, "Tracing the International Debate on Homework;" C. Dumont to Mrs. Bhatt, Oct. 7, 1991, in author's possession; discussions at Association for Women in Development Forum, Nov. 22–3, 1991.

[69] Jane Tate, "Working with Homeworkers in West Yorkshire, Britain," 15–16, paper presented at the AWID Forum, Nov. 21, 1991.

Index of cases

Index